Baedeker

South Africa

Hints for using the Guide

Following the tradition established by Karl Baedeker in 1844, buildings and works of art, places of natural beauty and sights of
particular interest, as well as hotels and restaurants of especially high
quality, are distinguished by one ★ or two ★★ stars.

To make it easier to locate the various places listed in the "A to Z"
section of the Guide, their co-ordinates are shown in red at the head of
each entry: e.g., Durban M 7.

Coloured lines down the right-hand side of the page are an aid to finding
the main heading in the Guide: blue stands for the Introduction (Nature,
Culture, History, etc.), red for the "A to Z" section, and yellow indicates
Practical Information.

Only a selection of hotels, restaurants and shops can be given; no reflec-
tion is implied therefore on establishments not included.

In a time of rapid change it is difficult to ensure that all the information
given is entirely accurate and up-to-date, and the possibility of error can
never be entirely eliminated.

Although the publishers can accept no responsibility for inaccuracies and
omissions, they are constantly endeavouring to improve the quality of their
Guides and are therefore always grateful for criticisms, corrections and
suggestions for improvement.

Preface

This guide to South Africa is one of the new generation of Baedeker guides.

These guides, illustrated throughout in colour, are designed to meet the needs of the modern traveller. They are quick and easy to consult, with the principal places of interest described in alphabetical order, and the information is presented in a format that is both attractive and easy to follow.

This guide covers the Republic of South Africa and the two independent kingdoms of Lesotho and Swaziland. It is in three parts. The first part gives a general account of the country, its topography, climate,

flora and fauna, political structure, population, economy, history, famous people, art and culture. A number of suggested routes for visitors provide a lead-in to the second part, in which the principal sights – towns, regions, mountains and lakes, coastal areas, nature parks – are described; and the third part contains a variety of practical information designed to help visitors to find their way about South Africa and make the most of their stay. Both the sights and the practical information are listed in alphabetical order.

South Africa, a paradise for nature-lovers: Berlin Falls and Golden Gate Highlands National Park

The new Baedeker guides are noted for their concentration on essentials and their convenience of use. They contain numerous specially drawn plans and colour illustrations; and at the end of the book is a large map making it easy to locate the various places described in the "A to Z" section of the guide with the help of the co-ordinates given at the head of each entry.

Contents

Nature, Culture, History
Pages 10–125

Sights from A to Z
Pages 128–395

Practical Information from A to Z
Pages 398–474

A World in

"A world in one country": this is the promise held out to visitors by South Africa. A slogan to attract tourists, no doubt, but a claim that has a great deal of truth; for since the peaceful end of apartheid, the "miracle on the Cape" South Africa is indeed one of the world's finest holiday destinations. Though it is a ten- or twelve-hour flight from Europe, the country offers visitors from the northern hemisphere a welcome change of climate in the less agreeable seasons of their year – South Africa has sunshine on something like 250 days in the year – magnificent scenery, fascinating wild life and a great range of leisure activities.

South Africa is a land of striking contrasts. Visitors arriving in the country will be struck at once by the juxtaposition of modernity and tradition and the mingling of people of different origins and race – black, white, coloured, Indian – who meet visitors with openness, ready interest and friendliness.

Everywhere in South Africa visitors will come upon evidence of the country's long history – a history as old as mankind itself. Here, it is now believed, are to be sought the origins of man. The rock drawings of the Bushmen bear witness to its oldest known inhabitants, but there is evidence too of the life of the black peoples of South Africa and of the white people who first settled on the Cape in 1652 and thereafter, for more than 300 years, controlled the destinies of the country.

Although since the abolition of apartheid relations between the races are

Table Mountain
seen from Bloubergstrand

Drakensberg
the Alps of South Africa

One Country

much more relaxed its after-effects can still be felt. Poverty, lack of education, homelessness and a high unemployment rate mainly affect the black population, leading sometimes to violence and crime. But these problems do not usually impinge on the ordinary visitor. As a rule the person sees almost exclusively the inviting aspects of the country: the lively cities – rich in tradition, like Cape Town, the "mother city" of South Africa, or ultra-modern, like Johannesburg, the country's economic capital – and idyllic little towns like Stellenbosch, Graaff-Reinet or Paarl. South Africa's

real wealth, however, lies in its magnificent scenery, still largely unspoiled by mass tourism: rugged rocky coasts, broad sandy beaches, mountains, rolling plateaux, lakes, rivers, fertile arable land, arid desert-like regions and luxuriant subtropical forests. In seventeen National Parks, including the famous Kruger Park, and hundreds of private game reserves visitors can observe South Africa's unique flora and fauna. Here they can see the world's largest terrestrial mammal (the elephant), the tallest (the giraffe) and the smallest (the pygmy shrew). The list of superlatives could be continued: South Africa also has the second largest mammal (the rhinoceros) as well as the fastest (the cheetah) and the world's largest bird (the ostrich).

Big game

to be found in South Africa's game reserves in large numbers

Once you have discovered South Africa – its variety, its ready hospitality, its beauty – you will want to come again.

Protea

South Africa's national flower

etoria

country's green administrative re

Nature, Culture History

Facts and Figures

General

Situation

The Republic of South Africa occupies the southern tip of Africa, lying between latitude 22° and 35° south and between longitude 17° and 33° east.

The country lies between two oceans, the Atlantic to the south-west and the Indian Ocean to the south-east and south. Its coastline of almost 3000km/1865 miles is flanked by two currents: on the west the cold Benguela Current, flowing northward from the Atlantic as far as Angola, and on the east the warm Agulhas Current, flowing south from the equatorial region.

South Africa has common frontiers with Namibia, Botswana and Zimbabwe in the north and with Mozambique and Swaziland in the north-east. For much of the way these frontiers run along the rivers Orange (opposite Namibia), Molopo and Limpopo (opposite Botswana and Zimbabwe). The most southerly point in South Africa (and in the whole of Africa) is Cape Agulhas, less well-known than the Cape of Good Hope to the west of it.

Within South Africa is the mountainous enclave of Lesotho, a small independent kingdom.

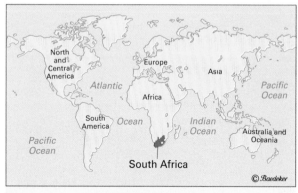

South Africa

Area: 1,223,000sq.km/472,000sq. miles

Population: 40,285,000 (1994)

Languages: eleven official languages, including Afrikaans and English

Capitals: Cape Town (parliamentary capital)
                 Pretoria (seat of government and administration)
                 Bloemfontein (judicial capital)

◀ The magnificent canyon carved out by the Blyde River
in the Northern Drakensberg

Other enclaves were reincorporated in the Republic of South Africa in 1994: the TBVC states (Transkei, Bophuthatswana, Venda and Ciskei), which under the system of apartheid had from 1976 onwards been declared independent (though without international recognition) as "homelands" of the Bantu people. At the same time the exclave of Walvis Bay, on the coast of the Namib Desert, was ceded to Namibia.

Following the changes introduced in 1994 South Africa has an area of 1,223,000 sq.km (472,000 sq. miles). Its greatest extent from west to east (between Oranjemund on the frontier with Namibia and Richard's Bay on the Indian Ocean) is about 1500km/930 miles and from north to south (from the Limpopo to the coast of the Indian Ocean) about 1100km/685 miles.

Extent

Topography

Regions

The heartland of South Africa is a large and gently undulating plateau lying between 1200m/3900ft and 1500m/4900ft, the highveld, which falls away to the Kalahari basin in the north and north-west and the Limpopo depression in the north-east. It drops steeply down to the coast in the Great Escarpment, with only narrow coastal plains on the Atlantic and the Indian Ocean. A number of major regions can be distinguished.

The interior plateau (northern Cape Province, Orange Free State and southern Transvaal) is part of a very ancient and stable mass in the

Central plateau

View from the Drakensberg in the Eastern Transvaal

11

Topography

earth's crust, consisting of magmatic rocks of the Palaeozoic era and younger Mesozoic sedimentary rocks. As a result of continuing erosionary processes in the course of geological history the surface forms have been levelled down, leaving rump areas in the form of individual tabular formations and long ridges of hills (e.g. the Witwatersrand), through which rivers (Vaal, Orange) have carved a passage. In the Palaeozoic rocks of the highveld are the rich deposits of precious metals, non-ferrous metals and coal which have made South Africa one of the world's leading mining countries. The diamond fields (e.g. round Kimberley) are the result of Mesozoic intrusions.

In some parts of the country intensive mining operations have led to great man-made alterations in the landscape. The best known example is Kimberley's Big Hole (a diamond mine). On the Witwatersrand, near Johannesburg, great areas have been completely transformed by opencast mining and spoil heaps.

To the north the central plateau slopes gradually down into the arid Kalahari basin, with the characteristic features of a sandy desert, which continues into Botswana. To the north-east, towards Zimbabwe and Mozambique, the plateau falls away to the middleveld (alt. 600–1200m/2000–4000ft) and the wetter lowveld along the Limpopo, here also known as the bushveld.

Great Escarpment   The central plateau is bounded by the sharp drop of the Great Escarpment. It is particularly marked to the east and south-east (Eastern Transvaal and KwaZulu/Transvaal), in the form of the Drakensberg mountains, an imposing range of quartzite, dolomite, diabase, basalt and granite hills rising to over 2300m/7500ft in the Transvaal, over 3000m/10,000ft in the Natal/Lesotho border area and around

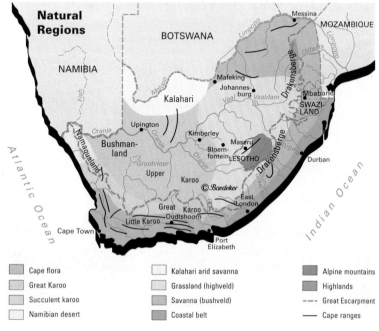

3500m/11,500 in Lesotho itself. The mountainous character of the Drakensberg is at its most pronounced in the border region between the province of KwaZulu/Natal and the kingdom of Lesotho, with South Africa's highest peak, Champagne Castle (3377m/11,080ft). This is an area of great natural beauty, with sharp mountain ridges, sheer rock walls, deeply indented canyons and hundreds of high waterfalls, which is now increasingly being opened up to tourism. Here too there are a number of nature reserves and National Parks (e.g. Royal Natal National Park, Giant's Castle Game Reserve), established to preserve the natural environment and protect its flora and fauna.

The Great Escarpment forms a major obstacle to communications between the central plateau and the coastal regions. In KwaZulu/Natal, for example, there is a stretch of 250km/155 miles in which there is only one road through the Drakensberg. The main route for road and rail communications between the coastal plain and the interior plateau is on the west side, in the Great Karoo, where on an 80km/50 mile stretch the escarpment is rather gentler. In this area the Drakensberg splits into a number of smaller ranges.

Below the Great Escarpment in the Western and Eastern Cape Pro-   Cape ranges
vinces are the Cape ranges, a number of parallel chains of hills, with foldings and faults reflecting sharp tectonic movements in the Meso-zoic era (Swartberg, Langeberg, Baviaanskloof and Tsitsikamma ranges). These hills reach heights of between 1500m/4900ft and over 2000m/6500ft, with Mt Seweweekspoort (2326m/7632ft) as the highest peak. The best known hill is Table Mountain (1087m/3566ft) at Cape Town, with foothills falling steeply down to the sea.

The term Karoo (a Hottentot word for a stony desert area) is applied to   Karoo
three different areas. The Great Karoo is a very arid stony semi-desert

The Olifants River in the south-western Cape

Prairie country in the Orange Free State

lying at altitudes of 600m/2000ft to 900m/2950ft between the Great Escarpment and the northern Cape ranges.

The Little Karoo is an arid depression between two parallel ranges of hills running east–west to the north of Cape Agulhas. The Upper Karoo in the west of the Northern Cape Province, with Bushmanland to the north, is the lowest (900–1200m/2950–9700ft) and driest part of the central plateau, an almost waterless expanse of desert and semi-desert.

Western coastal terraces

Between the interior plateau and the west (Atlantic) coast extends the arid terraced landscape of Namaqualand. This narrow coastal plain, an inhospitable region hostile to settlement and communication, is traversed by dry river beds and in many places crusted with salt.

KwaZulu/Natal coastal plain

Between the Great Escarpment and the Indian Ocean, in northern KwaZulu/Natal, is the only broad coastal plain in South Africa. The southern continuation of the Maputo coastal plain in Mozambique, it has numerous rivers flowing down from the Drakensberg into the Indian Ocean. Along the flat coast are numbers of sandy beaches.

Rivers

The hills of the Great Escarpment are the most important watershed for the South African rivers. The largest river systems are the Orange (Oranje) River (2400km/1500 miles long), which flows west from the Drakensberg into the Atlantic, with its largest tributary, the Vaal, and the Limpopo, which forms the northern boundary of South Africa for many miles. With their sharp variations in flow they are not navigable, any more than the numerous shorter rivers, mostly with a considerable gradient, which flow down from the Great Escarpment into the Indian Ocean. All these rivers, however, are of great importance as sources of water for domestic and industrial use, the generation of power and irrigation in the arid interior.

While the rivers flowing through the Cape provinces into the Atlantic are all relatively small, the Orange River, which flows into the Atlantic at Oranjemund, on the frontier with Namibia, is South Africa's most important river by far. It rises in the Drakensberg at an altitude of over 3000m/10,000ft, flows through Lesotho and then forms the boundary between the Orange Free State and the Northern Cape Province. After being joined by its largest tributary, the Vaal, it continues through the Northern Cape, flowing through deep gorges at many points, and then forms the frontier with Namibia down to its mouth. With its irregular flow, frequent rapids, waterfalls and sandbanks it is unsuitable for navigation.

The shortage of water on the central plateau is illustrated by the fact that the Orange River, with a total length of 2340km/1455 miles and a catchment area of something like a million sq.km (386,000 sq. miles), has no perennially flowing tributaries on the 1200km/750 mile stretch between its junction with the Vaal and the Atlantic. The Molopo in particular, coming from the Kalahari basin, with its tributaries the Nossop and the Auob, has enough water to reach the Orange only at intervals of several years. The largest and most abundantly flowing tributary of the Orange River is the Vaal (1250km/775 miles long), which rises in the northern Drakensberg and is the most important source of water for the Witwatersrand industrial agglomeration.

The most important South African river flowing into the Indian Ocean is the Limpopo (1600km/1000 miles long), which rises on the Witwatersrand and describes a great arc along the frontiers with Botswana and Zimbabwe before flowing through Mozambique to reach the sea north-east of Maputo. Of the many short rivers, abundantly supplied with water, which flow down from the Drakensberg to the Indian Ocean the best known is the Tugela, with its canyon and its great falls (948m/3110ft).

Climate

The climatic characteristics of different parts of South Africa are shown in the climatic diagrams on page 16, based on data from nine typical weather stations. The blue columns show annual rainfall in millimetres month by month in accordance with the blue scale on the right. Temperatures are shown in the orange band, the upper edge of which shows average maximum day temperatures and the lower edge average minimum night temperatures in accordance with the red scale on the right.

Climatic diagrams

The climate of South Africa is determined by its latitude, the seas round its coasts and the altitude of the interior. Four climatic regions can be distinguished:

General

■ the east coast, which is wet throughout the year;
■ the eastern highveld, which is wet in summer;
■ the Cape region, which is wet in winter; and
■ the north-west, which along with an area on the south coast at Mossel Bay separates the wet-in-summer and the wet-in-winter regions.

Since South Africa lies in the southern hemisphere its seasons are the reverse of those in Europe and North America. A European visitor to South Africa moves out of summer into winter, and vice versa; thus Christmas falls at the beginning of summer.

Most of South Africa lies at a relatively high altitude, with extensive upland regions around and above 1000m/3300ft. Since temperatures

Climate

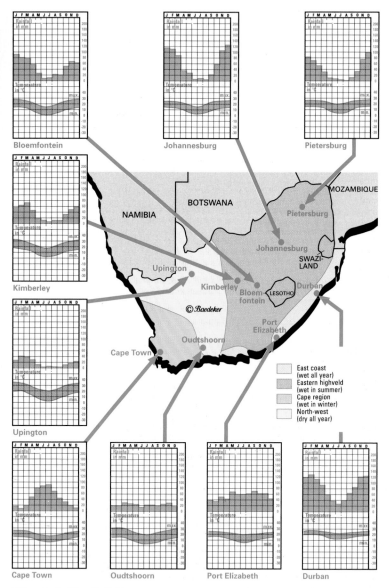

Climate in South Africa
Nine typical weather stations

Hours of sunshine per day												
Station	Jan.	Feb.	Mar.	April	May	June	July	Aug.	Sep.	Oct.	Nov.	Dec.	Year
Cape Town	10.9	10.5	9.1	6.9	5.9	6.0	5.7	6.4	7.2	8.9	9.9	11.1	8.2
Durban	6.5	6.7	6.2	6.8	7.7	6.9	6.9	6.9	5.8	5.2	5.7	6.0	6.4
Johannesburg	8.2	7.8	7.4	8.3	9.0	9.0	9.1	9.7	9.2	8.7	9.1	9.0	8.7
Nice/F	4.8	5.9	6.3	8.1	8.8	10.4	11.7	10.5	8.8	6.5	5.1	4.4	7.6
Upington	11.8	10.5	9.7	9.7	9.1	9.1	9.2	10.0	10.6	10.8	11.6	11.8	10.3

fall by at least 0.5°C/0.9°F for every 100m/330ft in height, it is considerably colder on the highveld than in the lowlands, and, with a greater range of temperature variation in the interior, it can be distinctly cold at night. Visitors should therefore be provided with warm clothing, particularly if they are camping.

South Africa is a dry land: over 65% of its area there is less than 500mm/20in. of annual rainfall, so that productive agriculture is possible only with the help of irrigation, and some 21% has less than 200mm/8in. – desert, or at best semi-desert which is inhabited only by nomads.

South Africa is a sunny land. As can be seen from the following table (which includes Nice, on the south coast of France, for purposes of comparison), the sunniest part of the country is the desertic northwest, followed by the interior plateau and the Cape region.

East Coast (wet throughout the year)

The east coast has a climate which is wet throughout the year and hot in summer. Moisture from the Indian Ocean is carried over the land by east winds – the south-eastern trade winds, which are at their strongest during the southern summer in the north. As a result rainfall is higher at this time of year.

Durban and Port Elizabeth weather stations

At the Great Escarpment air is forced to rise and thus becomes cooler. The water vapour which it carries with it then condenses, clouds and mist or fog are formed and discharge their moisture in the form of rain; at higher levels in the Drakensberg there may also be snow during the winter. Rainfall decreases from north to south: Durban has 1003mm/39½in. in the course of the year, East London 860mm/33¾in. on 81 days, Port Elizabeth 641mm/25¼in. on 74 days. Rainfall is also more evenly distributed over the year towards the south. Catastrophic summer rain-storms, too, are a greater menace in the north: thus between January and March Durban once had 170mm/7in. of rain within 24 hours, Port Elizabeth 100mm/3¾in., while in Natal in October 1987 there were devastating floods.

During the summer months the average air humidity is regularly over the 80% mark. It is sultry, and the sea breezes on the beaches are then pleasantly refreshing. The duration of sunshine increases from north to south: Durban has 2352 hours of sunshine over the year, Port Elizabeth 2818 and East London, half way between them, 2710.

Temperatures on the coast also fall from north to south. The average annual temperature at Durban is 21.4°C/70.5°F, at East London 18.3°C/64.9°F, at Port Elizabeth 17.6°C/63.7°F. Night minimum temperatures in particular are lower in the south (note the sag in the temperature band of the Port Elizabeth climatic diagram); and while the average figure for Port Elizabeth falls just below the 10°C/50°F mark there can be individual extremes as low as freezing point.

The coast north-east of Port Elizabeth is frost-free. The changes in temperature and rainfall from north to south are due not only to differences in latitude but also to marine currents. The warm Agulhas Current which flows along the east coast not only raises the temperature of the air but also increases its water vapour content. The onshore trade winds carry this air over the land, bringing warmth and moisture (just as the Gulf Stream does in Europe). As a result the east coast is markedly warmer than the west coast, with the cold Benguela Current. The average annual temperature at Durban is 7°C/12.5°F higher than at Port Nolloth on the west coast, which lies in the same latitude.

On the south coast, to the west of Port Elizabeth, rainfall is distributed over the year; farther west, in the Cape region, it is higher in winter than in summer.

Eastern Highveld (wet in summer)

Bloemfontein, Kimberley, Johannesburg/Pretoria and Pietersburg weather stations

The highveld has markedly lower rainfall than the east coast, since the air masses which are blown over the Great Escarpment by east winds have already discharged their rain. As the plateau gradually slopes down towards the west rainfall becomes steadily lower until the climate becomes desertic in character. Thus Bloemfontein (alt. 1422m/4666ft) has an annual rainfall of 564mm/22¼in. (on 77 days in the year), Kimberley (alt. 1197m/3927ft) 431mm/17in. (on 50 days) and Upington (alt. 809m/2654ft) 204mm/8in. (on 24 days). Thus the rainier areas are in the east, while towards the west periods of drought become increasingly likely and more severe.

Most of the rain falls in the summer months; and this is also the case farther west, though on a correspondingly smaller scale. During the day the rain falls mainly in the form of short and violent thundery showers.

There are long hours of sunshine, particularly in winter. At Johannesburg between May and August nine to just under ten hours of sunshine per day are normal (see table).Temperatures on the interior plateau are determined by the high altitude and lower rainfall. The altitude leads to considerably lower temperatures than in the lowlands, particularly in winter and during the night (see the temperature bands in the climatic diagrams; depending on altitude, they are on average 6–10°C/11–18°F lower).

Since the plateau rises to the north-east, the climate becomes no warmer towards the Equator. Pietersburg (alt. 1230m/4036ft), in latitude 24°, has the same average annual temperature (17°C/63°F) as Cape Town (alt. 10m/33ft), in latitude 34° south.

The low humidity of the air produces considerable variations in temperature between day and night (reflected in a broad temperature band in the climatic diagram). Average temperature differences of between 13°C/23°F and 16°C/29°F in winter and between 12°C/22°F and 14°C/25°F in summer are normal. Thus in Johannesburg temperatures between April and September may fall below freezing point; in Bloemfontein there may still be below-zero temperatures in October (in July and August the temperature may fall to −7 or −8°C/+18 or 19°F). Conversely, in summer the temperature may rise above 30°C/86°F.

Cape Region (wet in winter)

Cape Town weather station

A small area in South Africa within a radius of just under 300km/185 miles round Cape Town has a climate of Mediterranean type, with its highest rainfall in winter and its dry period in summer. When the southern hemisphere's west wind zone moves so far north during the winter that its outliers reach the southern tip of Africa rainfall, driven by the west winds, may extend over the land. This occurs almost solely to the east and south of Cape Town. Farther east (Oudtshoorn weather station and Mossel Bay, on the coast) the winter rainfall decreases to such an extent that rainfall is uniformly low throughout the year. Still farther east (Port Elizabeth) rainfall again increases and the period of maximum rainfall moves to summer. To the north of Cape Town rainfall also decreases and the climate gradually takes on a semi-desertic and then a desertic character.

Cape Town has mild, rainy winters, with 322mm/12½in. of rain falling on 38 days. Table Mountain is more frequently shrouded in cloud (the "tablecloth"), and there may also be a brief covering of snow on the peaks in the Cape ranges. The summer months (November to March) have 65mm/2½in. of rain on 12 days. The total annual rainfall is 508mm/20in. on 62 days. There are long periods of sunshine, with at least 6 hours daily in winter and 11 hours in summer (see table).

Variations in temperature over the day are lower than on the interior plateau, thanks to the moderating influence of the sea. Maximum day temperatures are around 26°C/69°F in summer, while night minimum temperatures in winter fall below the 10°C/50°F mark. Between May and August there may be occasional night frosts.

Marine currents give rise to considerable temperature differences over short distances. At Muizenberg in False Bay, under the influence of the warm Agulhas Current, the average annual temperature is 16.6°C/61.9°F, while at Cape Town, under the influence of the cool Benguela Current (see below), it is only 12.8°C/55°F.

North-West (dry throughout the year)

North-western South Africa, with a narrow wedge reaching down to the south coast, has areas of semi-desertic (Oudtshoorn weather station) and desertic climate (Upington weather station).

Oudtshoorn and Upington weather stations

The very regular average distribution of rainfall over the year conceals extremes in particular years, when the rainfall in a month may be many times the average. Thus at Oudtshoorn one January had 119mm/4¾in. of rain instead of the average 18mm/⅗in. Extremes of this kind always occur during the summer months January to March. The maximum rainfall within 24 hours may well amount to a third of the average annual rainfall. Thus Oudtshoorn once had 107mm/4¼in. of rain in 24 hours in January, and Upington 119mm/4.7in. in April. At the other extreme, there is no month which has not occasionally been completely or almost completely rain-free (e.g. 1 or 2mm at Oudtshoorn). With low air humidity and little cloud cover, temperature variations over the day are extreme, averaging 16–17°C/29–31°F. Night frosts occur at Oudtshoorn between May and August, at Upington until October. From about 200km/125 miles north of Cape Town it is so arid that the desert reaches right to the Atlantic. From about latitude 32° south northward into Namibia the climate is arid and misty (Port Nolloth on the Atlantic coast, for example, has an annual rainfall of only 63mm/2½in.).

Mist forms when moisture-laden masses of air are driven over the cool Benguela Current by onshore west winds. The Benguela Current, coming from the Antarctic, flows northward up the west coast, producing temperatures which are considerably lower than on the east coast. The air masses cool down over the cold water, and the moisture they carry condenses and gives rise to mist, which at night can reach 30–35km/19–22 miles inland. Rough surfaces may become quite wet, providing "watering-places" for insects. As the day warms up the mists disperse and the land remains rainless and desertic. The small amounts of water to be found in river beds farther inland come from thunder showers which occasionally come in from the east and, very rarely, give the rivers a brief flow of water.

Flora and Fauna

Sandstorms, usually coming from the south, are frequent in summer, when the temperature difference between the heated land and the cool sea is particularly great. When they blow in from the east the air becomes still warmer as it falls down to the coast, producing temperatures which may be as high as 40°C/104°F.

Flora and Fauna

"A world in one country"

The vegetation of South Africa is mainly influenced by the great climatic differences within the country, which give rise to great variety – from evergreen wet forests to desert vegetation adapted to extreme aridity and cold-resistant mountain flora. The slogan with which the tourist authorities seek to attract visitors to South Africa, "A world in one country", is particularly true in relation to the country's vegetation, with some 22,600 species of flowering plants, including 730 species of trees. The following six main vegetation zones can be distinguished.

Flora

Forests

Only just under 1.5% of South Africa's area is forest-covered, although the area of forest is at present being increased, particularly in KwaZulu/Natal, by afforestation programmes designed to produce timber. The country's forests are mainly confined to the coastal regions and are of different types. In the Cape ranges and along the coasts of the Cape provinces sparse deciduous forests predominate, extending along rivers in the form of gallery forests and reaching up to higher, drier levels. In the savanna areas, too, most rivers are edged by tall, dense gallery forests. In wetter areas in the Eastern Cape Province there are

Protea – South Africa's national flower   *Lilies*

The red disa, a famous species of orchid

Flowering steppe country in Namaqualand

remnants of evergreen forest (e.g. Ficus species) and palms of the Phoenix genus. The largest surviving areas of evergreen wet forest are in the Tsitsikamma National Park, extending for some 175km/110 miles between George and Humansdorp (on the coast to the west of Port Elizabeth). The trees range up to 40m/130ft in height, and some of them are of great age. Among the species represented are ironwood, yellow-wood, stinkwood and kamassi, with ferns and lianas at lower levels in the forest. In the subtropical zone of KwaZulu/Natal and on inaccessible mountainsides exposed to the south-eastern trade winds there still survive expanses of evergreen wet forest. The formerly extensive forests in the wet and hot coastal plain of KwaZulu/Natal have now been reduced to a few remnants by the expansion of cultivation. In addition to various species of palm they consist of mahogany, ebony, ironwood, species of strelitzia and mangroves (on the coast); orchids are common.

Savanna (bushveld) is the typical form of vegetation on the central plateau, with its low rainfall and dry winters, at heights of up to around 1000m/3300ft. Savannas are the natural form of vegetation particularly in the Northern and Eastern Transvaal and at lower levels (up to around 800m/2625ft) in the Eastern Cape region and Natal uplands, though large areas of savanna have now given place to agricultural land (mainly grazing for cattle). Characteristic features of savanna country are an undergrowth of tall grass (up to 1m/40in. in height) and bushes, together with isolated trees, mostly of no great height but deeply rooted, which are adapted to long periods of drought in winter; they include commonly found species of acacia, spurges, baobabs, species of aloe, fever-trees, mopane and fig trees.

Savanna

In particularly arid areas, for example on the fringes of the Karoo and the Kalahari, thorny bushes and trees (e.g. camel-thorn bushes) predominate. These are the areas known as thornveld.

Flora and Fauna

Bush and
grass steppe

To the south-west the savanna, with increasing altitude and climatic conditions gradually becoming more extreme (cold winters, aridity), gives place to bush and grass steppeland (grassveld), which covers the eastern part of the plateau in south-western Transvaal and the Orange Free State. With the exception of some acacias (e.g. giraffe acacias on the southern fringe of the Kalahari) and imported willow and eucalyptus acacias, trees are almost entirely absent because of the winter dry frosts which last for many months. In this area the plateau takes on the aspect of an endless expanse of grassland relieved only by areas of macchia-like bush vegetation: low-growing shrubs whose leaves and branches are protected against evaporation by hairs or a layer of wax. In wetter areas the grass grows to a height of over 1m/40in., elsewhere to no more than 40–60cm/15in.–2ft. In stock-farming country the natural grass vegetation has frequently been replaced over large areas by grass sown to provide grazing. Grass vegetation also predominates at higher altitudes in the Drakensberg. Up to about 1400m/4600ft there are hill meadows with a wide range of species and above this, where soil and relief permit, alpine pastures.

Dry savanna,
desert steppe,
semi-desert

Towards the west, with still increasing aridity, the bush and grass steppe merges into "karoo vegetation" – dry savanna, desert steppe and semi-desert – covering most of the Northern Cape Province, where average annual rainfall falls from around 400mm/16in. to under 120mm/5in. and in some years rain is totally lacking. In addition to old-established expanses of dry grassland vegetation which provide only a scanty and sporadic ground cover there grow in sheltered and wetter situations (e.g. along rivers with an occasional flow of water) shrub-like tamarisks, acacias and other low-growing scrub plants which, thanks to their small leaves, lignified stems and widely branching roots, can survive months of extreme drought. There are also succulents, which can absorb water deposited by the air (dew) and store it for months in nodes, stems or leaves.

Desert

Real desert is found in the north-west of the Northern Cape Province, in a 120km/75 miles wide strip running parallel to the coast and along the Namibian border (the lower course of the Orange River). Here, with an average annual rainfall of under 100–120mm/4–5in. – and even this cannot be relied on – there is practically no vegetation. Exceptions are plants adapted to drought conditions, such as stone flowers ("flowering stones") and a few creeping plants which live on sand dunes on dew deposited during the night. In depressions and wadis with more moisture there may be some thorny shrubs; and the well-known kokerboom (quiver-tree), a species of aloe, can occasionally be found.

Desertification

Both the desert and the desert steppe have long been extending their area at the expense of the grass steppe and the savanna. The cause of this process of desertification is generally agreed to be the introduction of a grazing economy on the European pattern. With excessive numbers of cattle the grassland is so badly over-grazed that it is unable, particularly in the regularly recurring years of drought, to regenerate. The over-felling of trees to provide fuel and building timber has accelerated this development and led to severe damage by erosion in the heavy rains which occur from time to time.

Cape flora

The south-western Cape region centred on Cape Town, with its Mediterranean climate of hot dry summers and cool to warm wet winters, has developed in the course of the earth's history a distinctive flora which in many respects is unique. It is much the smallest of the six vegetation zones but is the one which offers, within its small area, the greatest variety. It has some 8500 species of plant, very many of which are endemic (i.e. found in nature only here and nowhere else).

This Cape vegetation is known in South Africa as fynbos. The main characteristic of fynbos vegetation is its adaptation to the arid summers. The predominant species are evergreen schlerophyllous (hard-leaved) plants, including some 600 species of Erica and 400 species of Proteales, among them 85 proteas, numerous species of asters, straw-flowers, cranesbills, and a variety of bulbous and rhizomatous plants (lilies, irises, gladioli, sword lilies, freesias, orchids, etc.). There are, however, few native trees, which tend to be rare and are mostly confined to small and inaccessible areas of sanctuary: for example the Clanwilliam cedar, to be found only in the Cedarberg Mountains.

Special mention must be made of the protea, South Africa's national plant. This is a very special family of shrubs with a thick fire-resistant bark enabling them to survive unscathed the grass fires which are frequent during periods of drought. Proteas grow to heights of between 1 and 3m (3 and 10ft), rarely to 5m/16ft; the flowers resemble thistles and come in many shades of colour – red, pink, yellow, white, silver, greenish. The various species of protea grow in hill and mountain regions which are neither dry nor too wet all over the country, from the southern Cape region by way of the Orange Free State to KwaZulu/Natal and the Transvaal. | Protea

The abundance and beauty of South African flora can be seen and enjoyed in many botanic gardens, which are usually also important centres of botanical research and environmental studies, The following are among the most important. | Botanic gardens

The Kirstenbosch National Botanical Gardens, situated 12km/7½ miles from Cape Town on the south-eastern slopes of Table Mountain, were established in 1913. With an area of some 530 hectares/1300 acres and ranging in height between 100 and 1000m (330 and 3300ft), they offer a variety of habitats for different species. This side of Table Mountain has an abundance of rain, providing favourable conditions of growth and enabling more than 1400 species of plant to flourish. Other gardens well worth visiting are the Karoo National Botanical Gardens at Worcester (Western Cape), with the flora of arid and semi-desertic regions; the Orange Free State National Botanical Gardens in Bloemfontein; the Natal National Botanical Gardens in Pietermaritzburg, with the subtropical flora of KwaZulu/Natal; the Lowveld National Botanical Gardens, on the Crocodile River, at Nelspruit (Eastern Transvaal), with the local lowland flora; the Witwatersrand National Botanical Gardens at Roodepoort, with the flora of the highveld; the Harold Porter National Botanical Gardens at Betty's Bay (Cape region), with the flora of the winter-rain zone; the Pretoria Botanical Gardens; and the Municipal Botanical Gardens, Durban.

Fauna

As a result of the extension of cultivation South Africa'a formerly abundant big game (elephants, rhinos, giraffes, antelopes, zebras, hippopotamuses, lions, leopards, cheetahs, etc.) is now largely confined to a few large National Parks (see Practical Information). Baboons and vervet monkeys are still to be found in the wetter mountain regions, and many species of antelope (eland, oryx, springbok, waterbuck, impala, kudu, blue wildebeest, sable antelope, etc.) live (mainly in reserves) in areas of savanna, steppe and semi-desert which have not been brought into cultivation. The gazelle is the heraldic animal of South Africa. Among smaller mammals are hyenas, jackals, big-eared foxes, aardwolves, Cape foxes and various species of wild cat. | Big game

South Africa has more than 850 species of birds, including some species found nowhere else, such as the sunbird, found in the south- | Birds

*The Addo Elephant National Park in the Eastern Cape:
the last retreat of the African bush elephant*

western Cape region, which have long curved bills, finely pointed for puncturing flowers and thus fertilising them. Other rare birds are the weaver birds and the long-legged secretary bird. The blue crane is South Africa's national bird. The world's largest bird, the flightless ostrich, protected and to some extent artificially reared, lives in the Little Karoo (Oudtshoorn). Here too and in the Kalahari can be seen one of the largest birds with the capacity of flight, the gompou (related to the great bustard), which can weigh up to 20kg/44lb.

Reptiles and amphibians

South Africa has some 300 species of snake (including pythons, mambas, tree snakes and puff adders) and 200 species of lizards (geckoes, monitor lizards, chameleons, etc.). Crocodiles are now found only in game reserves and the Kruger National Park. South Africa's twelve species of tortoise and turtle, including the leatherback turtle found in northern Natal, which can weigh up to half a ton, are now much reduced in numbers.

Insects

South Africa's insects include around 800 species of butterflies and moths, some of them highly colourful. The mounds erected by termites are a characteristic feature of the arid parts of the country. Some species of insect which carry diseases, such as the tsetse fly (a carrier of sleeping sickness), have been eliminated, but the anopheles fly, which transmits the malaria parasite, is still found in some marshy areas.

Protection of wild life; National Parks

As a result of the spread of the Bantu peoples and later of white settlement the habitats of many animal species were much reduced. The larger animals in particular, which were numerous in South Africa until the 18th century, were deprived of their former means of subsistence and at times were in danger of extinction, like the white

A zebra in the world's most famous game reserve, the Kruger National Park

rhinoceros and various species of antelope. Now there are numerous projects and organisations concerned with the protection of endangered species, following the passage of the National Parks Act of 1926, which provided a statutory basis for the establishment of game reserves in National Parks. Tere are now 17 National Parks and a National Lake Area in various parts of the country, controlled by the National Parks Board, which are among South Africa's most popular tourist attractions. The most important are the following:

The Kruger National Park, some 450km/280 miles east of Johannesburg, is one of the world's most famous game reserves. It is home to 137 species of mammals, 493 species of birds, 112 species of reptiles and 49 species of fish. Among the mammals are the "big five" (the elephant, the rhinoceros, the buffalo, the lion and the leopard), as well as cheetahs, giraffes, hippopotamuses, baboons, impalas, kudus, wildebeests and wild dogs.

The Kalahari Gemsbok National Park in the Northern Cape province, together with adjoining reserves in Botswana, is the habitat not only of the antelope from which it takes its name and of wildebeests, gazelles and zebras but also of the carnivores (lions, leopards, hyenas, vultures) which find their prey here.

The Addo Elephant National Park to the north of Port Elizabeth is the last retreat of some 120 surviving South African bush elephants, as well as rhinos and bonteboks.

The Umfolozi and Hluhluwe Game Reserves in Zululand, to the north of Durban, are the last retreat of the white rhino, and also the home of South Africa's other species of rhinoceros, the black rhino.

In the Mountain Zebra National Park in the Great Karoo live the last 200 mountain zebras.

Augrabies Falls National Park, round the waterfall of that name on the Orange River, is the home of monkeys, antelopes, various species of wild cats and birds (including the fish eagle).

There are also bird reserves, particularly on the Atlantic coast and offshore islands. Among the species found here are penguins, cormorants, pelicans and gannets.

The Tsitsikamma National Park, on the Indian Ocean, has an underwater nature trail for snorkellers.

Game farms

In addition to the National Parks and public and private game reserves, which provide shelter for 95% of South Africa's fauna on only 6% of its area, there are game farms which rear various species of wild animal, such as royal cheetahs (De Wildt, near Pretoria), ostriches (Oudtshoorn, 60km/37 miles north of George) and crocodiles (Oudtshoorn, Scottburg near Durban and on the Tongaat River).

Political Structure

Constitution

After the first free general election in the history of South Africa in April 1994 the country's new constitution, the "admission ticket to democracy", came into force on April 27th 1994. Politicians of all colours belonging to nineteen different parties had spent exactly one year, ten months and 29 days in Kempton Park, a suburb of Johannesburg, working out the "mechanism for a peaceful transfer of power after three and a half centuries of oppression" (B. Grill). The present constitution is a transitional one, in force only until 1999, when it will be replaced by a definitive constitution. During this period of transition amendments can be made to the constitution only by a two-thirds majority.

In the drafting of the constitution it was an important principle that all parties, peoples and parts of the country should be involved in the processes of political decision. This protection of minorities is secured by the federal system and the requirement that all parties with over 10% of total votes should be represented in the government. In accordance with this provision a "government of national unity" was formed, including representatives of the three main parties, the African National Congress (ANC) led by Nelson Mandela (see Baedeker Special, p. 30), the National Party (NP) headed by F. W. de Klerk and the Inkatha Freedom Party (IFP) led by Chief Mangosuthu Buthelezi.

The transitional constitution also includes a Bill of Rights.

In May 1996 the South African Parliament adopted a new constitution, providing for majority rule rather than the power-sharing of the transitional constitution, with a Bill of Rights. The new constitution was to come into effect over the next few years, with all of its provisions becoming effective with the general election scheduled for 1999.

The new system of government is on three levels – national, provincial and local. At the national level there will be a bicameral Parliament elected by proportional representation, The National Assembly, with power to make laws, will have 350–400 members and the National Council of Provinces, which will oversee provincial powers, will have 90 members.

A party with more than half the national vote will have power to select the President, who will be appointed by the National Assembly. The Cabinet will then be appointed by the President. (This differs from the transitional constitution, which guaranteed minority parties positions in the Cabinet.) The Bill of Rights enshrines the right to adequate housing, food, water, education and health care and bans discrimination on the basis of race, gender, sexual orientation, age, pregnancy or marital status. In addition it effectively bans the death penalty and includes a provision giving the right to abortion.

The constitution will give the provinces exclusive powers in specific areas (e.g. provincial planning, sports, recreation, highways, etc.). On most issues, however, the constitution demands cooperation between the different levels of government.

Ndebele women at Nelson Mandela's swearing-in ceremony

Under the present constitution the South African legislature consists of two chambers, a National Assembly of 400 members elected by proportional representation and a Senate consisting of ten representatives of each of the country's nine provinces. Each province has its own parliament, also elected by proportional representation. The distribution of powers and functions between the national Parliament and the central government on the one hand and the provincial parliaments and governments on the other has not yet been finally settled. Also still to be decided are the functions of the local (communal) authorities and the future role of the tribal chiefs, who still play an important part in the life of the black population in country areas.

Legislature

Nelson Mandela, elected Executive President on May 9th 1994 at the first sitting of the National Assembly, is both head of state and head of the government. His decisions must be supported by a majority of the Cabinet, and he can appoint ministers only after discussion with their parties.

President

The transitional constitution also provides that parties with at least 80 seats in the National Assembly (that is, with 20% of total votes) are entitled to nominate a deputy president.

The Cabinet is composed of representatives of all parties which have obtained at least 5% of total votes in an election.

Cabinet

The national flag, which, like the constitution, is provisional until 1999, was selected from among 7000 suggestions. It shows a Y lying on its side, in six different colours. At least some of the colours also appear in the symbols of all South Africa's political parties. The flag is thus an expression of a concern to promote unity and reconciliation.

Flag

Political Structure

Coat of arms

In the country's coat of arms, granted by King George V on September 17th 1910, an antelope and a springbok support an escutcheon displaying in its four quarters a female figure with an anchor, running wildebeests, an orange-tree and a trek wagon — all symbols of the former provinces of the Union of South Africa (Cape Province, Natal, Orange Free State and the Transvaal). The escutcheon stands on a field of grass with protea flowers, and the helmet surmounting it bears a lion holding fasces. The original motto "From unity comes strength" is still the motto of the modern Republic.

National anthem

During the transitional period until 1999 South Africa has two national anthems: the old "Stem", written in 1918 by the poet and politician Cornelius Jakob Langenhoven and set to music in 1928 by M. L. de Villiers, and the anthem of black South Africa, "Nkosi Sikelel' iAfrika". The first line of this and the refrain were written by Enoch Mankayi Sontinga in 1897, lines 2 to 8 by Sek Mqhayi (1875–1945).

Justice

South African lawcourts are independent. An important innovation in the new constitution is the establishment of a Constitutional Court to handle disputes between citizens and the government. Thus Parliament no longer stands above the law, as in the British tradition, but the legislature and the executive must submit to the authority of the constitution.

Police

The police force (South African Police, SAP) of 120,000 men, roughly half of whom are whites, is under the authority of the various provinces, but the chief of police is appointed by the central government.

Army

The National Defence Force was formed by the amalgamation of the old South African Defence Force (SADF), various underground movements and the armies of the former homelands. Blacks now make up a third of the country's armed forces of around 75,000 men.

Republic of South Africa
Provinces since 1994

ZA
Car
nationality plate

Province	Capital	Population 1993	Area in sq.km. (sq. miles)	Density pop./ (sq.km) (sq. mile) 1993	Proportion of GDP
Western Cape	Cape Town	3,620,000	129,400 (50,000)	28.0 (72.5)	13.2%
Northern Cape	Kimberley	764,000	363,400 (140,300)	2.1 (5.4)	2.2%
Eastern Cape	King William's Town	6,665,000	170,600 (2,573,400)	39.1 (101.3)	7.5%
Orange Free State	Bloemfontein	2,805,000	129,400 (1,083,000)	21.7 (56.2)	7.1%
North-West	Mmabatho	3,507,000	118,700 (45,800)	29.5 (76.4)	6.9%
KwaZulu/Natal	Pietermaritzburg	8,549,000	91,500 (35,300)	93.5 (242.2)	14.7%
Eastern Transvaal	Nelspruit	2,839,000	81,800 (31,600)	34.7 (89.9)	8.3%
Gauteng*	Johannesburg	6,847,000	18,800 (7,250)	365.0 (945.4)	36.9%
Northern Transvaal	Lebowakgomo	5,121,000	119,600 (46,200)	42.8 (110.9)	3.1%

* Formerly PWV (Pretoria/Witwatersrand/Vereeniging Gauteng)

Parties

The National Party, mainly consisting of Boers, was established in 1912 and from 1948 to 1994 was continuously in power. In 1969 a breakaway group on the right formed the Herstigte Nasionale Party (Restored National Party). The introduction of a three-chamber Parliament by the Botha government led in 1982 to a further split, with the formation of the Conservative Party under the leadership of Dr Andries Treurnicht, which strongly opposed any improvement in the legal status of the Coloured and Indian population. The most militant advocate of "separate development", as apartheid was originally called, was the Afrikaner Weerstandsbeweging (Afrikaner Resistance Movement), founded by Eugene Terre'Blanche in 1973 as a cultural association.

The largest opposition party in Parliament, which until 1994 was wholly white, was the Democratic Party, formed in 1989 by the amalgamation of the Progressive Federal Party and other opposition groups. Its leading figure was Helen Suzman, the "grand old lady of South African liberalism".

The South African Communist Party, founded in 1921, dissolved itself in 1950, shortly before being banned by the government. The ban was lifted in 1990.

The most important organisation representing the interests of the black population was the African National Congress (ANC: see Baedeker Special, p. 30), from which the more radical Pan-Africanist Congress split off in 1959.

The third major black movement is the Inkatha Freedom Party, originally founded in 1928 as a Zulu cultural organisation and now led by Chief Mangosuthu Buthelezi (see Famous People).

The largest and most important organisation representing the interests of the coloured population is the Labour Party, founded in 1902. An earlier predecessor was the Natal Indian Congress, one of whose founding members was Mahatma Gandhi (see Famous People).

Administrative structure until 1993–94 (see map on p. 65)

With the coming into force of the new constitution in 1994 the country's administrative structure was also reformed; but since the old structure inherited from the early settlement and colonial periods is still reflected in literature and in everyday life a brief description may be helpful.

The African National Congress (ANC)

When President F. W. de Klerk, under intense domestic and foreign political pressure, began the process of dismantling the policy of apartheid this was a moment of destiny for South Africa's oldest political party, the African National Congress (ANC), which had been banned for three decades, and its legendary leader Nelson Mandela, who had been imprisoned for thirty years.

The origins of the ANC go back to 1912, when black intellectuals and others with an interest in politics founded in Bloemfontein the South African Native National Congress (renamed African National Congress in 1923) in order to combat racism, tribalism and ethnic rivalries. Tribal differences, said one of the participants, were aberrations which were at the root of all their troubles, their backwardness and their ignorance. "We must think in wider political categories," he declared, "because we are a single people." The first meeting of the Congress opened with a prayer and a hymn by the Xhosa composer

Soweto on May 3rd 1994: ANC supporters celebrating Nelson Mandela's election victory

Enoch Sontonga, "Nkosi Sikelel Afrika" ("God bless Africa"), which became the ANC anthem and is now one of South Africa's two national anthems.

The ANC's aim then and in subsequent decades was the union of all blacks, a say in political debate for the black majority and the improvement of their living conditions. Not only were blacks denied the vote: from 1913 onwards, under the Natives Land Act, they were required to live only in black reserves and were prohibited from acquiring property outside these areas. Until the Second World War the ANC, a mainly urban and middle-class body, confined its activity to petitions, protests, meetings and newspapers. As with other similar organisations, however, this brought no political results: indeed the legislation discriminating against blacks became steadily more restrictive. At last in 1943, stirred to action by the Atlantic Charter (1941) in which Roosevelt and Churchill declared a free world order to be an Allied war aim, the ANC for the first time called for full civil rights for black South Africans, but received a blunt rebuff from the government of J. C. Smuts.

Thereafter the ANC became more radical. 1944 saw the foundation, by a group of activists including Nelson Mandela, of the ANC Youth League, which called for more vigorous methods than the moderate forms of action of the past. The aim was no longer to achieve integration into the political system created by whites, but rather liberation from that system: in other words, the abolition of all racial discrimination. From 1948 onwards the ANC responded to the ever more repressive apartheid laws of the new government with boycotts, strikes and – on the model of Gandhi's non-violent resistance – civil disobedience. In 1952, when white South Africa was celebrating the 300th anniversary of Jan van Riebeeck's landing, tens of thousands of blacks, for the first time, mounted a counter-demonstration.

On June 26th 1955 3000 representatives of all South African races – black, coloured, Indian and also white members of the newly founded Liberal Party – met in the township of Soweto outside Johannesburg in a national congress against apartheid. The congress adopted a Freedom Charter calling for equal rights for all races which remained the basis of the ANC's political programme into the nineties. Following the congress the South African government arrested 156 leading members of various resistance movements and charged them with high treason. The trial lasted five years, at the end of which all the accused were acquitted. One of the accused, Chief Luthuli, president of the ANC, received the Nobel Peace Prize in 1960.

The great alliance of 1955 soon fell apart, mainly because of the lack of agreement about future action. Tensions also developed within the ANC between pluralists and Africanists. The pluralists called for equal rights for all races, while the Africanists, going against what had hitherto been ANC policy, aimed at black leadership in a South Africa liberated from white domination. In 1959 the Africanists, led by Robert Sobukwe, split off from the ANC and founded the Pan-Africanist Congress (PAC).

For 1960 the ANC and PAC planned large-scale campaigns against the hated pass laws, and on March 21st in that year the PAC held a peaceful demonstration outside the police office in Sharpeville (Transvaal). Feeling threatened, the police fired into the crowd, and 68 demonstrators were killed. The massacre aroused international horror and condemnation. After the Sharpeville incident there were strikes and demonstrations throughout South Africa in which more people were killed. The government took ruthless action. On April 8th 1960 it banned the ANC and PAC, which thereafter worked underground and from abroad. In reaction to the government's action the ANC and PAC, which had hitherto held to the principle of non-violence, no longer flinched from armed conflict. Both parties established military wings. The ANC founded Umkhonto we Sizwe ("Spear of the Nation") headed by Nelson Mandela, who after the exiling of Luthuli and the imprisonment of Sobukwe had become president of the ANC and the new leader of black resistance. This organisation carried out some spectacular attacks, but until 1963 the police were able to defeat its efforts. In that year Nelson Mandela, who had been arrested in 1962 and condemned to five years in prison, was given a life sentence for sabotage on the basis of material found by the police in Umkhonto's headquarters. For a time it seemed that the government had broken the black resistance movement. Activists were arrested, and often imprisoned without trial. Many of them died in police custody, and executions reached record heights. In the early seventies new organisations were established, some of which, on the model of the Black Panther movement in the United States, sought to create a "black consciousness". When the government decided to make Afrikaans, seen as the language of the white oppressors, a language of instruction in black schools, some 20,000 school children in Soweto demonstrated against this measure on June 16th 1976. The police fired indiscriminately into the crowd of young people and two of them were killed. Thereupon there were riots and bloody confrontations with the authorities throughout South Africa, and the government was unable to regain control of the situation until the end of 1977. It banned all organisations which in its opinion had anything to do with the disturbances, including the Black Consciousness movement. Steve Biko, its best known leader, died in prison in 1977 as a result of the torture to which he had been subjected. Many young people now joined the ANC and PAC, offering to take part in the armed struggle, and were trained in African guerrilla camps. Their activities were confined, however, to a few sensational attacks: in general the police and the secret service remained in control.

Under the leadership of Oliver Tambo the ANC was recognised by the Organisation of African Unity as the representative of the South African people, and there was increasing international support for the ANC and Nelson Mandela.

Early in 1990 President de Klerk – the "Gorbachev of Africa", as "The Economist" called him – called off the ban on the ANC, the PAC and the Communist Party, against fierce opposition from his own ranks and the far-right white members of the ANC, released Mandela from prison and initiated a dialogue with his former opponent. Although the Inkatha party, under the leadership of Chief Buthelezi, prime minister of KwaZulu, disputes the ANC's claim to be the sole voice of black South Africa, it enjoys the support of 70% of the black population. In December 1992 Mandela and de Klerk were jointly awarded the Nobel Peace Prize for their efforts to reconcile the white and black peoples of South Africa; and in South Africa's first free parliamentary election in April 1994 the ANC proved to be the strongest party, with 62% of the votes.

In the 19th century the Union of South Africa was divided into the Cape Province, the Orange Free State and the provinces of Natal and the Transvaal. Within these provinces, originally established by the Boers or the British colonial authorities, were various settlement areas for Bantu tribes established under the Natives Land Act of 1913 (see History).

One of the consequences of the system of racial segregation (apartheid) introduced in 1948 was the division of the four provinces into "white" heartlands and the "homelands" of the Bantu population, which were to be guided towards internal self-government and eventually to independent status and separation from white South Africa. In the early 1990s there were four homelands (the TBVC states of Transkei, Bophuthatswana, Venda and Ciskei), declared to be independent, and six so-called self-governing states (KwaZulu, Gazankulu, Lebowa, Quaqua, KaNgwane and KwaNdebele), which continued to be regarded as parts of the four provinces.

New
administrative
structure

The final abolition of apartheid in 1993–94 was accompanied by a far-reaching reorganisation of provincial government. In place of the former four provinces, the four "independent" black states and the six self-governing black homelands nine new provinces of mixed race were established, on the basis of which the first free election for all South Africans was held in 1994. Each province had a parliament of between 30 and 100 members and its own constitution.

There is still controversy, however, over the extent of the provinces' powers. On the one hand there are those who advocate a strong centrally directed state (the African National Congress and the Pan-Africanist Congress) and on the other those (the National Party, the Inkatha Freedom Party and the Democratic Party) who prefer a federal model giving the provinces extensive powers of self-government.

The Provinces

The Western Cape Province lies on the Indian and Atlantic Oceans, extending in a wide arc round its capital, Cape Town. It has a population of some 3.6 million, or about 9% of South Africa's total population. They speak mainly Afrikaans, with coloureds in the majority. The province has a wide range of processing industries, a well developed services sector (tourist centre, communications hub) and a productive agriculture (intensive fruit and vegetable growing). The Western Cape contributes over 13% of the country's gross domestic product.

The Eastern Cape Province consists of a large region in the hinterland of the south coast round Port Elizabeth, most of it intensively cultivated by white farmers, and the former homelands of Ciskei and Transkei, in which subsistence farming predominates. It also includes the district of Umzimkulu, an enclave in the neighbouring province of KwaZulu/Natal. The interim capital of the province is King William's Town, though Port Elizabeth and East London are also in contention. The province, with around 16% of the country's total population, has a strongly Xhosa character. The GDP per head, at less than half the national average, is the lowest in the whole of South Africa. In view of its economic weakness the Eastern Cape will be dependent on outside financial help for some time to come.

The Northern Cape Province, with Kimberley as its interim capital, is the largest in area of all the South African provinces, but, mainly in consequence of its extreme aridity, has only about 1.8% of the country's population. Its main sources of income are extensive pastoral farming and mining, contributing 2.2% of South Africa's GDP. It has no major economic, educational or administrative centre. The regional language is Afrikaans.

The North-West Province is a largely semi-arid region with a population of some 3.5 million (8.1% of total population), mostly Tswanas. The economy of the province depends mainly on extensive stock-farming and mining (platinum). Tourism and the entertainment industry have good prospects for growth. The province contributes just under 7% of the country's GDP – below the national average per head. There are a number of towns with scope for development. The provincial capital is Mmabatho, administrative centre of the former homeland of Bophuthatswana.

The Orange Free State coincides broadly with the old province of the same name. It includes the former homelands of Quaqua and Thaba'Nchu (Bophuthatswana). It has a range of processing industries and has good natural resources, making it potentially an important agricultural and mining region. The population of some 2.8 million (6.8% of the national total), mostly speaking South Sotho and Afrikaans, produce 7.1% of South Africa's GDP. Its main economic centres are round Bloemfontein (the provincial capital), Welkom (gold-mining) and Sasolburg (coal processing).

The multi-lingual and multi-ethnic province of Gauteng, formerly known as PWV (Pretoria/Witwatersrand/Vereeniging), is South Africa's strongest economic region, with a population of just under 7 million (17% of the national total). It consists of three differently structured regions. The Pretoria area is still the administrative metropolis of South Africa, a traffic hub and centre of service industries, with major industrial developments (electrical engineering, automobile manufacture). The Witwatersrand, with the provincial capital, Johannesburg, is the main mining and financial centre. Round the towns of

Population

Vereeniging and Vanderbijlpark, in the south of the province, the processing industries (e.g. metalworking, chemicals) and electricity generation predominate. The province produces 37% of South Africa's GDP. It is also the main centre of white settlement in South Africa, with over 40% of the white population concentrated in a relatively small area.

Northern Transvaal

The Northern Transvaal consists of the agricultural region in the north of the old province of the Transvaal, the northern part of Kruger National Park and the former homelands of Lebowa, Venda and Gazankulu. The interim capital is Lebowakgomo. The province's infrastructure is deficient in the extreme, particularly in the former homelands. With almost 13% of the country's population, the Northern Transvaal produces only 3% of the national GDP, and GDP and annual income per head are the lowest in the whole of South Africa. The development of the region will call for huge investment and will inevitably take a long time. Ethically and linguistically the population is very mixed, speaking North Sotho, Shangaan/Tsonga, Venda and Afrikaans.

Eastern Transvaal

The province of Eastern Transvaal, which includes the former homelands of KwaNgwane and KwaNdebele and part of Bophuthatswana, is a region of great scenic beauty in the east of the country. It has no large towns; the interim capital is Nelspruit. Its economy centres on electricity generation, mining and agriculture (it is one of the country's most important fruit and vegetable growing areas). GDP per head is below the national average. Its main prospects of economic growth lie in tourism (southern part of Kruger National Park and adjoining areas). The population is just under 3 million, mostly speaking Swazi, Zulu and Afrikaans.

KwaZulu/Natal

To the south of the Eastern Transvaal is the province of KwaZulu/Natal. Well supplied with water, it has a population of over 8.5 million (over 21% of South Africa's total population), mostly Zulus. The establishment of this province amounted in practice to the extension and consolidation of the old Zulu kingdom, and under the 1944 constitution the Zulu king retained extensive powers.

The main centre of population and the province's economic and administrative centre is the Durban/Pinetown area, which also has the main concentration (79%) of South Africa's Asian population. The provincial capital is Pietermaritzburg.

The province contributes 14.7% of the national GDP, but there is still a great need for economic development, mainly in the rural areas. The infrastructure in the Zulu villages is particularly poor. The province's problems are aggravated by the high rate of population growth among the Zulus and the lack of employment opportunities.

Population

The population of South Africa in 1944 was 40,285,000, giving an average density of 33 inhabitants per sq. kilometre (85 per sq. mile). The density varies considerably according to geography and economic development, ranging between 365 inhabitants to the sq. kilometre (945 to the sq. mile) in the central industrial region of the Transvaal on the Witwatersrand and just over 2 to the sq. kilometre (5 to the sq. mile) in the Northern Cape province. The largest towns are Johannesburg (with Soweto, around 2 million), Cape Town (1.9 million), Pretoria (800,000), Durban (700,000) and Port Elizabeth (600,000).

Capitals

Since the establishment of the Union of South Africa in 1910 the country has had three capitals. Pretoria is the seat of government and

Table: Population (in thousands) of South African towns in 1985 Census (according to Central Statistical Office, Pretoria)

	White	Black	Coloured	Asian	Total
Cape Town	543	282	1069	18	1912
Johannesburg/Randburg	516	914	122	58	1609
East Rand	399	588	33	17	1038
Durban/Pinetown/Inanda	308	123	60	491	982
Soshanguve	432	351	21	18	823
Port Elizabeth/Uitenhage	173	299	172	7	652
West Rand	233	387	19	8	647
Vanderbijlpark/ Vereeniging/Sasolburg	168	352	15	5	540

administrative capital, Cape Town the seat of Parliament and parliamentary capital, and Bloemfontein, centrally situated, the judicial capital.

The most important demographic characteristic of the Republic of South Africa, distinguishing it from all the other African states, is its mixed ethnic composition. The population consists of four main ethnic groups – whites, coloureds (of mixed blood), Asians and blacks. Under the apartheid legislation in force from 1948 to the early nineties every inhabitant of South Africa was officially assigned to one of these groups, and this determined his political rights, his choice of residence and profession, his education, and so on.

Composition of population

Whites, who until 1944 were politically, economically and culturally dominant, make up some 17% of the total population. Around nine-tenths of them live in towns – in the cities (see table above) and in medium-sized and small country towns; only about 10% live in the country, mostly as farmers. Some 56% of the whites are Afrikaans-speaking Boers, descendants of the Dutch settlers who established themselves in South Africa from 1652 onwards. Around 37% are English-speaking, descendants of the British settlers who began to come to South Africa in 1795. The others are of German, French, Portuguese, Italian and other origins.

Whites

The coloureds (in Afrikaans kleurlinge), who make up around 10% of the total population, are mainly descended from unions between whites and the native population of the Cape region (Hottentots and Bushmen) and to a lesser extent Malay slaves and Bantus. They live mainly in the Cape Town area and the southern Cape region. Culturally they are close to the whites. 90% of them speak Afrikaans and are Christians.

Coloureds

Among the coloureds are some 200,000 Cape Malays, descendants of slaves brought to the Cape 350 years ago from the Dutch colony of Batavia and the East Indies by the Dutch East India Company. In Cape Town alone there are some 60,000 Cape Malays. Many bear names such as February, April or September – the dates when the slaves were sold to their new masters. They are strict Muslims.

The Griqua, mainly descendants of European men and Hottentot women, who speak a modified version of Afrikaans, are another independent group who at one stage briefly established an independent state.

The Asians (about 3% of the total population) are mostly of Indian descent and now live mainly as traders and shopkeepers in the Durban region. They were brought to Natal from 1860 onwards by British settlers to work as contract labourers on the sugar plantations. Most of

Asians

Xhosa huts in the former homeland of Ciskei

Parliament House, Cape Town

A township near Cape Town: endless rows of little brick houses

them speak English, though some Indian languages (mainly Tamil, Hindi, Gujarati and Urdu) are still spoken.

The small Chinese community is descended from Chinese workers who were brought to South Africa in much larger numbers around the turn of the century to work in the mines. Most of them had returned to China by 1910, after increasing numbers of blacks were employed in the mines. In the 1920s there was a further wave of Chinese immigrants, whose descendants now live mainly in and around Johannesburg, working in trade. They all speak English and Afrikaans, though still retaining their home languages.

Most of the Asians are Hindus (70%); 20% are Muslims and 10% Christians.

Of the native population who had settled the country (very sparsely) before the coming of the Bantu peoples (from East Africa) and the Europeans (from the colony on the Cape), the Bushmen (San) and Hottentots (Khoikhoi), there survive only some 55,000, mainly in the inhospitable regions of the Northern Cape (see Baedeker Special, p. 92).

Hottentots and Bushmen

The largest population group in South Africa (69% of total population) is the blacks, who moved from Central Africa into the southern part of the continent from the 11th century onwards. Like the whites, they are by no means a homogeneous group. Nine different Bantu peoples are now distinguished, all subdivided into numerous tribes: the Zulus alone have over 200 different tribes. The most numerous of these peoples is the Zulus (9.1 million), followed by the Xhosa (7.4 million), the North Sotho (3.7 million), the Tswana (3.1 million), the South Sotho (2.6 million), the Tsonga (1.5 million), the Swazis (1.2 million), the Venda (680,000) and the Ndebele (290,000).

Blacks

Young Zulu women

The black population live partly in tribal communities, mainly in country areas, and partly in the "townships" (separate black settlements or black districts set apart for blacks in "white" towns). In recent decades the numbers of black inhabitants in districts of towns declared "white" under apartheid legislation have steadily increased as a result of the movement of workers into these districts. The failure of the apartheid policy of keeping the black and white populations apart is shown by the fact that in 1985 the "white" areas, in addition to 4,572,000 whites, had a population of 8,365,000 blacks and that more blacks lived in the "white" areas than in the black townships. The largest "black" town in a "white" area was Soweto (South-West Township), a district of Johannesburg with a population of over a million.

Since the original tribal areas do not coincide with national or provincial boundaries, large numbers of Swazis, South Sotho and Tswana live outside South Africa in the independent states of Swaziland, Lesotho and Botswana.

Density of population

The density of population varies considerable from area to area. The most densely populated areas are the rapidly growing conurbations in the industrial and mining regions and the ports (Cape Town, Durban, Johannesburg, Witwatersrand), as well as some of the traditional settlement areas of the Bantu population, some of whom live by subsistence farming while others are commuters or seasonal workers in the large conurbations.

Some 40% of the black population still live in these country areas in the former homelands. The semi-arid or completely arid regions of the central and northern Cape region, on the other hand, with a scattered population of white farmers practising pastoral farming, are very sparsely populated, and many of them are losing population through emigration.

Venda women

The social structure of the population varies between different population groups. In terms of economic activity, life-style, standard of living and social relationships the life of the white and much of the mixed-blood and Indian population is very much on the European pattern. The black population still lives to some extent in kinship and tribal communities (which are now also responsible for social insurance) in traditional village structures; the urban black population, however, though frequently living in districts segregated by tribe, are more Europeanised; and the numerous male migrant workers frequently provide a link between rural and urban structures. As a result of the migration of workers many villages have relatively high proportions of women, children and old men.

Social structure

The rate of population growth in South Africa is high, though here again there are differences between different population groups. The most rapidly growing group is the Bantu population, with a birth rate which between 1970 and 1992 fell only from 41.2 to 35.0 per 1000 (death rate 9.8 per 1000). The birth rates of the other population groups are much lower (for the whites the rate is 12.0 per 1000). Age structures differ accordingly: in 1990 37.1% of the population were under 15, but the figure for the black population was 45%.

Population growth

Migration has led in recent years to substantial increases in population, though because of the high proportion of illegal immigrants from neighbouring countries it is difficult to get precise figures. The number of illegal black immigrants is estimated at a million. Officially recruited migrant workers, mainly employed in mining, are not given the status of immigrants but after working for a certain period (usually 24 months) must return to their home country (Lesotho, Swaziland, Botswana, Namibia, Malawi, Mozambique, etc.). The number of these

Immigration from neighbouring states

foreign migrant workers has fallen sharply in recent years because of high unemployment among the native population. Other immigrants into South Africa, particularly in the nineties, have been refugees from the civil wars in Mozambique and Angola, though many of them have since been repatriated. There was a net increase in the white population in the 1970s through immigration from Europe (mainly Britain) and from Zimbabwe after it became independent. In the eighties white immigration fell because of South Africa's increasing political and economic problems; but the large-scale departure of whites which many feared would follow the abolition of apartheid has not so far occurred.

Language

The diverse composition of the population of South Africa is reflected also in its diversity of languages. Under the 1944 constitution the country's previous two official languages (English and Afrikaans) gave place to eleven officially recognised languages. In addition to Afrikaans, the language of the Boers (and also the mother tongue of most of the coloured population), which is derived from Dutch, and English, spoken by 36% of the whites and most of the Asians, these are Zulu, Xhosa, North and South Sotho, Tswana, Tsonga, Swati, Venda and Ndebele.

Zulu, Xhosa, Swati and Ndebele belong to the Nguni language group, North and South Sotho and Tswana to the Sotho group; the Tsonga people are connected with both language groups, while the Venda have a language of their own. The numbers speaking the various languages in 1993 are shown in the following table:

Language	No. of speakers	Per cent
Zulu	9,105,702	22.4%
Xhosa	7,443,661	18.3%
Afrikaans	5,919,112	14.5%
North Sotho	3,703,993	9.0%
English	3,428,133	8.4%
Tswana	3,155,323	7.7%
South Sotho	2,593,221	6.4%
Shangaan/Tsonga	1,489,262	3.7%
Swati	1,268,669	3.1%
Venda	682,648	1.7%
Ndebele	290,406	0.7%
Others	1,635,578	4.0%
Total	40,715,708	100%

It should be noted that much of the population of South Africa is bilingual, as are the schools (either Afrikaans and English or one of these together with one of the mother tongues of the majority black population in the area).

Other languages spoken include Portuguese (1.2%), German (0.9%), Dutch, Greek, Italian, French (under 1%) and a number of Indian languages (Gujarati, Hindi, Tamil, Telugu).

See also Practical Information, Language

Religion

There is complete freedom of religious belief in South Africa. Just under 80% of the population profess Christianity. The churches with the largest numbers of members are the 4000 independent black churches, whose proportion of the total Christian membership rose between 1960 and 1991 from 19.7% to 33.4%. After this come the five main Christian denominations, the Dutch Reformed Church (14%), the Roman Catholics (10%, four-fifths of them black), the Anglicans, the Methodists and the Lutherans, whose proportion of the total fell between 1960 and 1991 from 61% to 45%. In addition there are numerous other churches and splinter groups.

During the period of apartheid organised religious life, like South African society, was divided. One section of the church (the Kairos group) took the view from the late eighties that the church could not be merely a mediator but must support the cause of the disadvantaged; and this identification with the resistance movement went so far that an ANC spokesman was able to claim that God was with the ANC.

At the other end of the spectrum there stood for many years the reformed churches of Dutch Calvinist origin, the smaller Nederduitsch Hervormde Kerk van Afrika, the members of which were almost exclusively Boers, and the Nederduitse Gereformeerde Kerk (NG Kerk). For many years the NG Kerk, as the "state church", played a major part in justifying and stabilising the apartheid system, which it saw as a policy of separate development, and had close links with the country's ruling elite. (More than half the government ministers in office during that period came from pastors' families, and many were theologians.) In accordance with this policy there were within the NG Kerk four independent churches, each catering for a different race. In the present situation, however, the reformed churches are concerned with reconciliation and the quest for means of overcoming the consequences of apartheid.

Reformed churches

Independent African churches began to emerge at the end of the 19th century as a reaction to colonialism. "The 'churches without whites' sought to give their adherents in spiritual terms what they has lost in material and intellectual terms: cultural identity, self-respect, human dignity" (B. Grill). The most important of these churches are the Zion Christian Church (ZCC), whose emblem is a silver star on a felt or fabric ground, and the Nazareth Baptist Church.

Independent African churches

The Zion Christian Church was founded in Zion City Moria (Transvaal) in 1910 by Engenas B. Lekganyane, the son of an agricultural labourer. The Nazareth Baptist Church was founded in 1911 by Jesaiah Shembe, a Zulu who is now revered as a Messiah; its main centre is Ekuphakameni, north-west of Durban. Many of the communities included under the general term of Zionist churches were formed under the influence of the Pentecostal Mission from Zion City, USA, and have common features. In particular they are ready to accommodate traditional religious beliefs: medicine men and shamans are taken seriously and prophecy, rites of initiation and purification, taboos, the driving out of devils, etc., are interwoven with Christian beliefs.

South Africa also has 120,000 Jews (the descendants of German, British and Eastern European immigrants over the last two centuries) and 500,000 Hindus and Muslims.

Other beliefs

Education and Science

Education and employment are two central problems in South Africa – consequences of the separate education which existed until the abolition of apartheid. In 1972 expenditure on the education of white children was 18 times as much as for black children, and in 1992 it was still four times as much. Until 1944 there were sixteen different ministries of education dealing with educational provision for different races and in different regions and homelands. (Since 1989 it has been government policy to achieve the ethnic integration of the school system.)

School attendance was compulsory for white, coloured and Indian children between the ages of 7 and 16; compulsory schooling for black children was introduced in 1981 and extended in stages. At present some 80% of black children of school age attend school. While the state schools are still largely divided by race, many private schools are open to all races (as some of them have been for many years). Among the principal problems are lack of accommodation (there is a shortage of 59,000 classrooms), an inadequate pupil/teacher ratio and poor teacher training facilities for black schools. The situation is particularly bad in country areas in the former homelands. In the towns education has for many years been periodically disrupted by disturbances and violence.

Although South Africa spends what is by international standards a great deal of money on education, three-fifths of the population can still neither read nor write. The demand for education has now enormously increased. In 1970 35,000 white children took their "Matric", the school leaving certificate, after twelve years of schooling, compared with 5000 non-white children; in 1991 the numbers were 64,000 and 140,000 respectively. In 1992 4% of children achieved marks qualifying them for admission to university.

The twelve school years are divided into four stages. The first nine years are spent in the junior primary, senior primary and junior secondary stages, and these are followed by three years in the senior secondary stage, with a wide range of subjects at higher, normal and lower level.

After the secondary stage there are trade schools and various other forms of educational provision, including a number of correspondence schools.

South Africa has seventeen universities and twelve technical and teacher training colleges. In 1993 there were 330,000 students at universities, 137,000 at technical colleges and 93,000 at vocational colleges. The number of black students has increased considerably in recent years; the numbers at technical colleges, for example, rose from 17.6% of the total in 1990 to 31.1% in 1993.

Economy

South Africa is the only industrial state in Africa. This classification, however, is fully appropriate only in the areas of white settlement and economic activity: the former Bantu homelands must still be regarded as under-developed agricultural regions. In 1992 the Republic's gross national product per head was US $2670, putting it above the states of eastern and south-eastern Europe and making it the most prosperous country in Africa after oil-exporting Libya.

Condition of
population

Some 45% of South Africans live in poverty. While the 5 million white South Africans take the availability of housing, water, electricity and schools for granted, the black population are very far behind in these respects. There is a shortage of 3 million houses, and another 3 million households are without electricity, as are 86% of all black schools and 17,000 health centres. 12 million people have no drinking water and 21 million have no hygienic toilet facilities.

Minerals and industries

INDUSTRY
- 🏭 Oil refineries
- △ Synthetic fuel production
- ⚒ Iron and steelworks
- ⚒ Copper production
- ⚒ Tin production
- ⚒ Aluminium production
- ✿ Metalworking and engineering
- 🚗 Automobile industry
- ✝ Aircraft industry
- ⚒ Cement production
- ⚒ Chemical industry
- ◉ Tyre manufacture
- 📖 Papermaking

- ◊ Textiles
- ⚒ Leatherworking
- ⚒ Foodstuffs industries
- ⚒ Sugar refineries
- ↔ Oil pipeline

POWER STATIONS
- Nuclear
- Thermal
- ● Hydro-electric

MINERALS
- 🪨 Coal
- 🪨 Iron
- △ Vanadium
- ⊙ Chromium

- ◎ Manganese
- ● Gold
- ○ Silver
- ▥ Platinum
- ⊠ Copper
- ◇ Tin
- U Uranium
- ▽ Diamonds
- ▱ Asbestos
- ⌣ Kaolin
- ∧ Magnesite
- ☆ Rock salt
- ▪ Graphite
- + Mica
- ⊖ Phosphates
- ✕ Antimony

The unemployment rate among black South Africans is 55% and among whites up to 21%, and the under-employment rate is 57%. The labour market can absorb only 5% of the annual 400,000 school leavers, and as a result some 45% of young black people, 12% of whites, 40% of coloureds and 29% of young people of Indian origin are unemployed.

Since the end of the 19th century the basis of the South African economy has been mining, which contributes over 60% of the country's foreign currency and almost 9% of the gross domestic product. It provides employment for around half a million people in more than 900 mines and quarries.

South Africa's resources of minerals are among the richest in the world, and the working of its minerals is becoming increasingly diversified. While in 1940 more than 90% of mining output consisted of gold and diamonds, by 1990 this proportion had fallen to around 30%. South Africa is the leading world producer of gold, platinum, chromium and vanadium and one of the six or eight leading producers of diamonds, coal, iron, manganese, nickel, uranium and phosphates, with lesser outputs of other minerals. With the exception of oil, natural gas and bauxite it meets all its own mineral needs and is of major and

Unemployment

Mining

43

Rock-crushing machinery in a Randfontein gold-mine

sometimes market-dominant importance as an exporter. Some 70% of the country's exports by value is accounted for by mining products (30% by gold alone).

Given the international demand for minerals and South Africa's large reserves, mining is likely to continue making a major contribution to the country's economy. During the 1980s the output and export of coal, iron and platinum increased. Gold-mining, on the other hand, declined, since the fall in world prices meant that many mines working at great depths could no longer operate profitably. Annual output fell from around 1000 tons in 1970 to 600 tons in 1992.

Industry

After mining, the most important element in the South African economy is industry: together they account for almost half the gross domestic product and employ a third of the working population. In addition remittances from migrant workers in mining and industry make a substantial contribution to the economies of South Africa's small neighbouring states.

The most important industrial regions are the Witwatersrand and the Johannesburg/Pretoria agglomeration (some 50% of industrial output) and the Durban/Pietermaritzburg/Richards Bay, Cape Town, Port Elizabeth and East London conurbations.

South Africa's industry is closely bound up with mining (processing of raw materials, semi-finished products) on the one hand and oriented towards the production of consumption goods for the domestic market and for export on the other. The country's increasing international isolation because of the policy of apartheid, accompanied by sanctions and trade boycotts, particularly from the 1960s onwards, meant that its industries, which had made great strides before the Second World War, developed still further, so that South Africa is now self-sufficient in most fields. However the international economic sanctions, together with the lack of foreign investment and the withdrawal of foreign firms, led to an increasing shortage of capital, the ageing of industrial installations and difficulties in gaining admission to export markets. Industry supported the demand within South Africa for the abolition of apartheid, since it hoped that the involvement of the black population in the country's economic life on a basis of equality would open up wider market opportunities. During the seventies and eighties, because of the shortage of labour, South African industry played a leading part in the stage-by-stage abolition of the statutory "job regulation" scheme which protected white workers against black competition.

An important basis for the industrialisation of South Africa is its abundant resources of energy in the form of large deposits of high-quality coal, which meet some 85% of the country's commercial energy needs and is also used in fuel production by hydrogenation. Since the OPEC ban on the supply of oil to South Africa in 1973 its share in primary energy production has fallen to 10%. South Africa's rich supplies of uranium are used to fuel the only nuclear power station in Africa, at Cape Town. The scope for the production of hydro-electricty is limited by the irregular flow of South African rivers, but South Africa is a participant in a hydro-electric project at Cabora Bassa in Mozambique and is involved in projects in Lesotho. It is now an exporter of power, supplying almost all its neighbouring states. In the 1980s offshore deposits of oil and natural gas were discovered in the Indian Ocean.

Two very different forms of agriculture are practised in South Africa. On the one hand there are the highly mechanised "white" farms (some 80,000 in number, mostly of considerable size), highly specialised in production for national and global markets: grain, potatoes, vegetables, fruit, tobacco; on the Indian Ocean also wine (see Baedeker Special, p. 471), citrus fruits, sugar-cane, etc. On the other there is the subsistence farming of the former black homelands, with numbers of small holdings using traditional methods of farming. The land ownership legislation which was repealed in 1991 prohibited the Bantu population from acquiring land in "white" areas, leading to sharp increases in population and reduced availability of agricultural land in black settlement areas.

Agriculture

In view of the great variability of rainfall and frequent years of drought intensive agricultural development is possible only with the help of artificial irrigation using water from reservoirs and rivers (almost 10% of irrigated area). Thanks to irrigation arable farming has been extending far into the semi-arid regions; but the arid climate means that over two-thirds of agricultural land in the "white" areas can be used only for extensive cattle- and sheep-farming (central and northern Cape, western Orange Free State).

In spite of yields which vary sharply according to weather conditions South Africa is self-sufficient in almost all forms of agricultural produce. Agriculture contributes between 5% and 7% of GDP and accounts for some 25% of the value of exports. As a result of overmanning in Bantu agriculture it employs a relatively high proportion (around 15% in 1990) of the working population.

South Africa's transport infrastructure is well developed, and in many parts of the country is up to European standards; there are dense networks of roads and railways (24,000km/15,000 miles). The railway system is of particular importance for commuter and goods traffic (transport of raw materials) and for transit traffic from neighbouring inland states to South African ports. During the last 20 years there has

Transport
Roads and
railways

45

Ostrich farm near Oudtshoorn

Vineyard on the Cape

been a considerable increase in car ownership: in 1992 there were 11 cars per 1000 inhabitants.

In spite of South Africa's peripheral situation it has excellent facilities for international seaborne trade. The leading ports are Richard's Bay (with an annual throughput of more than 50 million tons), Saldanha Bay, Durban, Cape Town and Port Elizabeth.

Seaports and airports

The largest international airport is Johannesburg.

South Africa has an excellent infrastructure for tourism, the major tourist attractions being the National Parks. Although domestic tourism has long been well developed, it was only during the 1980s that foreign visitors began to come in substantial numbers: in 1993 there were around 3 million visitors, 600,000 of them from overseas (the majority from Britain, with 24% of visitors, followed by Germany with 16.9%). There are now 1267 hotels, with some 46,000 rooms. Tourism brings in very considerable amounts of money, but – what is almost more important – provides employment: it is estimated that every eleven tourists provide one additional job. At present around 450,000 people work in the tourist trade. While tourism is, world-wide, the most important earner of foreign currency, in South Africa it takes only fourth place. It is expected, however, to increase at an annual rate of anything up to 20%.

Tourism

Increasing domestic political tensions resulting from the government's apartheid policy and international pressure led in the second half of the eighties to an economic recession accompanied by increased government borrowing and inflation. Inflation has now largely been brought under control; but the future development of the national economy, after the abolition of apartheid and the introduction of equal voting rights for the whole population, will depend mainly on the economic policies of the ANC, the majority party now in government. Until 1992 the ANC leadership called for the transformation of South Africa into a socialist country, but the advocates of a market economy now appear to be in the ascendant. Most of the 38 articles in the South African constitution concerned with economic matters are designed to ensure an independent and responsible financial policy, the main instruments in which are a state bank of issue (whose independence is guaranteed in the constitution), an independent audit department and detailed regulation of the national finances. Three basic rights enshrined in the constitution are freedom of economic activity, freedom to work and freedom to own property. In addition to the right to strike and to form associations and employers' right to lockout workers every South African is entitled to "fair working conditions". Everyone has the right to acquire, own and dispose of property. Anyone who has been expelled from his property since 1913 under apartheid laws can claim restitution from the state. The law on the restitution of land rights passed at the end of 1994 provides for the return of land expropriated by the state. Where such land is now privately owned the land will not be returned to the previous occupier but instead appropriate compensation will be paid.

Prospects for the future

Early indications suggest that the new policy is likely to be successful. For the first time in two decades the rate of inflation has fallen to single figures: it is now 9%. Considerable problems, however, still lie ahead: there are shortages of jobs, of housing (over 3 million dwellings), water and drainage services, electricity, infrastructure and medical services. Moreover the government of national unity has promised to introduce free compulsory schooling and to develop a social insurance system within five years. The cost of this development programme is to be met mainly by strict financial discipline and new principles on government expenditure, with priority given to economy and no increases in taxation. The success of the government of national unity, and indeed the success of the new constitutional order, will be judged by the government's ability to bring about perceptible improvements in the living conditions of millions of South Africans.

History

Bartolomeu Diaz sails round the Cape of Good Hope.	1486
The first white settlers, led by Jan van Riebeeck, land in Table Bay and establish the first European supply base on the Cape.	1652
First armed conflict between whites and blacks – to be followed by eight further "Kaffir wars" until 1878.	1779
Formal cession of the Cape territory to Britain.	1814
Abolition of slavery in British colonies.	1833
Start of the Great Trek	1835
Discovery of the first diamonds.	1867
First Anglo-Boer War.	1888–81
Discovery of gold on the Witwatersrand; foundation of Johannesburg.	1886
Second Boer War.	1899–1902
The British colonies and Boer republics are brought together in the Union of South Africa.	1910
The Pass Laws lay the foundations for the territorial separation of races.	1913
South Africa takes part in the First World War.	1914–18
Afrikaans becomes a second official language, after English.	1915
South Africa takes part in the Second World War.	1939–45
The National Party wins a general election. Beginnings of apartheid.	1948
Demonstrations against the Pass Laws in Sharpeville, with 69 dead.	1960
South Africa becomes a republic and leaves the Commonwealth.	1961
Professor Christiaan Bernard performs the world's first successful heart transplant operation in the Groote Schuur Hospital in Cape Town.	1967
Schoolchildren's rising in Soweto; 176 dead.	1976
The homelands of Transkei, Bophuthatswana, Venda and Ciskei are separated from South Africa and established as "independent" states.	1976–81
Coloureds and Asians are given the vote, but the black majority are still excluded, leading to bloody riots.	1984
General state of emergency declared, with more rigorous censorship of the press; stronger economic sanctions against South Africa.	1986

F. W. de Klerk becomes President.	1989
On February 2nd President de Klerk declares a general amnesty for political prisoners and lifts the ban on political organisations. Nelson Mandela and many others are released from prison. Discussions begin between the National Party, the ANC and other groups (CODESA).	1990
Far-reaching repeal of apartheid laws.	1991
A majority of white electors vote in a referendum for the continuation of de Klerk's policy of reform.	1992
Mandela and de Klerk are jointly awarded the Nobel Peace Prize (December 10th).	1993
First general election in South Africa on the principle of "one man – one vote", won, as expected, by the ANC.	1994
New constitution providing for a majority-rule government is adopted by Parliament, to come into full effect by 1999.	1996

Chronology

Prehistory

Finds of fossil bones in caves at Taung, Sterkfontein, Makapan and other sites show that some 2 to 3 million years ago there were hominids living in South Africa: early forms of man (Australopithecus) representing a stage of development between ape and man. Other excavations (at Sterkfontein, Kromdraai and Swartkrans) have yielded remains of later forms related to Australopithecus – representing extinct sub-species or the next stage of development – which, some 1½ million years ago, made stone implements and knew the use of fire.

Early man

Then in the late 1960s anthropologists discovered 80,000-year-old remains of modern man (Homo sapiens) in the Klasies River Mouth Caves, on the south coast between Cape Town and Port Elizabeth. The most recent discoveries, at the beginning of 1994, push the age of our species still further back into the past, with the discovery in the same caves of fragments of two upper jawbones some 100,000 years old: the earliest known remains of Homo sapiens, who may have spread throughout the world from his origins in South Africa.

Other finds at Fish Hoek and the Echo Caves, between 75,000 and 50,000 years old, include bones and implements similar to those used in the Stone Age in Europe and rock drawings thought to be up to 28,000 years old.

The rock drawings are believed to have been the work of the Bushmen or San (see Baedeker Special, p. 90) who along with the Hottentots or Khoikhoi are among the oldest inhabitants of southern Africa. These two related peoples are grouped together as the Khoisanids. The origin of the name Hottentot used by Europeans is explained by Augustin de Beaulieu in an account of his travels between 1620 and 1622: "On meeting us their usual greeting is a song accompanied by a dance, containing the word 'Hautitou' at the beginning, in the middle and at the end." This account was confirmed by Jón Ólafson in 1623: "In

Bushmen and Hottentots

◀ *Bushman rock painting*

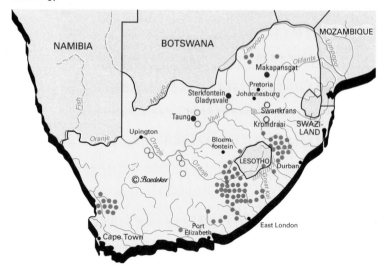

Rock paintings and drawings

FIND SPOTS
- ● Rock paintings (mainly cattle)
- ○ Rock drawings (mainly cattle)
- ● Rock paintings (mainly sheep)
- ○ Rock drawings (mainly sheep)
- ⬭ Numerous rock paintings

Hominids

FIND SPOTS
- ● Australopithecus robustus
- ○ Australopithecus africanus

their dance, as they pronounced the word 'Hottentot', they cracked their fingers.''

There are different opinions about the origins of the Khoisanids. An earlier theory was that they originally lived in East Africa and from there moved south-west until they reached the Cape. According to a more recent view they were tribes of hunters and gatherers with a culture of Neolithic type who lived in northern Botswana around 500 B.C. The Khoikhoi then took to a nomadic life, herding cattle which they had either bought or stolen from black peoples. The Bushmen, however, continued to live as nomadic hunters and gatherers. At some point they moved south, perhaps because of over-population or shortage of grazing land, or perhaps because of the influx of black peoples. At the beginning of the 17th century Bushmen and Hottentots occupied the whole coastal area from Namibia to East London.

The black peoples of South Africa

The largest native population groups in Africa at the present day are the Bantu (so named by a German scholar after the word for "man" in their language), the negroes and the Hamites. In prehistoric times the negroes were already practising arable farming in the tropical forests of Africa. The Hamites, with their cattle and sheep, moved from the East into North Africa and gradually spread from there. From the encounter between these two groups originated the Bantu, a third ethnic group which took over the cattle-herding culture of the Hamites. The Bantu moved southward in separate groups in quest of land where they could settle and graze their livestock. The earliest traces of settlement, dating back to the 2nd–5th centuries A.D., were found in the Transvaal and Natal; they were left by farming peoples with an Iron Age culture. There are few remains of their settlements since they were built of perishable materials (grass, wood, clay). It is established, however, that from around 500 B.C. the peoples of western and central

Africa knew the art of working iron and other metals. Steel was used to make mattocks, axes and blades for knives, spears and razors, while softer metals were used in bracelets and beads. Much fired pottery has also been found. In 1932 archaeologists discovered the remains, dated to about A.D. 1200, of mine-workings and a trading centre on the hill of Mapungubwe, near the mining town of Messina in the northern Transvaal; here the finds included glass beads, ivory carvings and goldsmith's work, including a small rhinoceros carved from wood and covered with hammered gold sheet.

From the 11th century onwards the Bantu moved south in successive waves. The Nguni (a group which includes the Xhosa, the Zulus, the Swazis and the Ndebele), coming from the north, spread eastward to the coast. Some 500 years ago the Sotho moved west, the North Sotho (Pedi) settling in the northern and eastern Transvaal, the South Sotho (Basotho) in Lesotho and the Orange Free State, the West Sotho (Tswana) in Botswana. The third group, the Ovambo-Herero, moved into what is now Namibia. Some 300 years ago the fourth Bantu group, the Venda, appeared in the northern Transvaal, and during the 19th century the fifth group, the Tsonga, moved from Portuguese territory on the east coast into the Transvaal. The various groups lived in their own communities herding cattle and growing grain and vegetables. As a result of contacts between the Bantu and the Khoisanids the click sounds of the Khoisan languages were taken over into the Xhosa and Zulu tongues. (Map, p. 56)

The Age of Discovery (1488–1652) and the First European Settlements

From the 15th century onwards Portuguese navigators looking for a sea route to India sailed down the West African coast. In 1485 Diego Cão reached the Namibian coast to the north of present-day Swakopmund and erected a cross there (Cape Cross). Three years later, in 1488, Bartolomeu Diaz landed in Walvis Bay and later in Lüderitz Bay. He then sailed round the "Cape of Storms", soon to be renamed the Cape of Good Hope. On February 3rd he and his crew sighted land near what is now Mossel Bay, "which we called Angra dos Vaqueiros because we saw so many cows being guarded by their herds", as the historian João de Barros reported. The farthest point reached on this voyage was the mouth of the Great Fish River.

On July 8th 1497 Vasco da Gama set out on a further voyage of exploration. On November 22nd he rounded the Cape of Good Hope, and on Christmas Day reached the south-east coast, which he called the Terra do Natal ("Natal" = "Christmas"). Finally on May 20th 1498 he reached Calicut on the Malabar Coast. The Portuguese had thus discovered the sea route to India, and thereafter they regularly sailed to Asia, with Mossel Bay and Mombasa as important ports of call where they replenished their supplies of water and food and conducted trade by barter. They were not, however, interested in establishing any permanent settlements. In 1503, as a result of a navigational error, Antonio de Saldanha discovered Table Bay, which for more than a century bore his name (now commemorated by rocky Saldanha Bay, 100km/60 miles north). In the course of the 16th century the Portuguese encountered competition from the English and Dutch, who had begun to establish overseas trading companies and trading posts.

In 1605 the first ships of the British East India Company put in at the Cape and declared the land on Saldanha Bay "as far as the territories of the nearest Christian prince" to be a British possession; and in 1613 the East India Company captured a Hottentot chief named Xhoré and carried him off to Britain. These were, however, isolated incidents which had no permanent consequences.

In 1647 a Dutch vessel, the "Nieuw Haerlem", was shipwrecked in Table Bay on the way home from the East. The surviving members of First settlements the crew built a fort at the foot of Table Mountain and lived there for over a year before being rescued. After their return to Holland Leendert Janszen and Jan van Riebeeck (see Famous People) urged the Dutch East India Company (Vereenigde Oost-Indische Compagnie) to establish a permanent base on the Cape (see Quotations).

In 1650 the East India Company agreed to the proposal, and appointed van Riebeeck commander of the enterprise. On Christmas Eve of 1651 he sailed from Texel with five ships, the "Drommedaris", the "Reijger", the "Goede Hoop", the "Walvis" and the "Oliphant". On April 6th 1652 the first two of these ships arrived at the Cape, and van Riebeeck, accompanied by 90 persons, including eight women, founded Cape Town, the first permanent European settlement in South Africa. At first it was no more than a victualling point for trading vessels on their way to India. The settlers were expected to produce "vegetables, meat, water and other necessary supplies for the company's ships so that they could heal their sick". In 1657, to improve the supply of foodstuffs, the first nine "vryburgers", former employees of the East India Company, were given land to farm in the surrounding area, forming the nucleus of the new colony. When Jan van Riebeeck left South Africa in 1662 Cape Town had four streets and 200 white inhabitants.

In 1666 work began on the construction of the Castle of Good Hope, now the oldest surviving building in South Africa. Thereafter the colony grew rapidly. In 1679 Stellenbosch, the second settlement on the Cape, was founded by Simon van der Stel (later governor of the Cape Colony). New settlers now came in from Holland, Germany and France: the first Boers (Dutch *boeren,* farmers). Among the French were many Huguenots, who had left France after the revocation of the Edict of Nantes in 1685. Around 1700 the white population of the Cape was 1147 (402 men, 224 women and 521 children); by 1707 the numbers had risen to 803 adults and 820 children, and by 1743 to around 4000 adults. The labour force was increased by slaves brought in from West and East Africa and Dutch colonies in the East Indies. From the earliest days there were marriages between settlers, slaves and the native population, ancestors of the "coloureds" of the present day. The population lived on Table Bay and in the neighbouring areas of Stellenbosch, Paarl, Drakenstein, Franschhoek and Roodezand (now Tulbagh). The expansion of the colony was at the expense of the native population, who were expelled from their grazing land and water points, exterminated or incorporated in the colony as forced labourers. Until 1795 the colony was governed by officials of the Dutch East India Company, who were not permitted themselves to own any land. The Company controlled the whole life of the colony, from the prices of foodstuffs to the trade in ivory, skins, leather, ostrich eggs and slaves.

Advance into the interior

In the early 18th century the growing of wine and wheat became unprofitable as a result of over-production and price-fixing by the Company, and increasing numbers of farmers turned to cattle and sheep, which required less capital and less labour. The "trekboers" – semi-nomadic cattle-herders – moved along the south coast into unoccupied territory in quest of new grazing land for their herds. In 1779, at the Great Fish River, they came into contact with the Xhosa, who themselves were slowly moving into the south of the country and were known to the white settlers as Kaffirs. This led to the first of the nine bloody Kaffir Wars (the last ending in 1878) in which the Xhosa resisted the north-eastward advance of the whites. "Armed with weapons and a very narrow Calvinist interpretation of the Bible, the Boers pressed on. According to their reading of the Old Testament they had not only the right but the duty to gain control of the land and its people, to subjugate the black 'pagans' and treat them as slaves. The relative prosperity which they achieved as a result was, in their Calvinist view, pleasing to God and a visible measure of their Christianity" (T. Roth).

South Africa and the British

In 1782 the Dutch East India Company, now in low water, paid out its last dividends. Its downfall was brought about by wars, corruption among its officials and growing tensions between the administration and the population of the colony. Popular discontent (with heavy taxes, the distribution of land, the prices of agricultural produce, etc.), the realisation that the Company was unable to offer adequate protection in outlying areas and the influence of republican ideas from Europe (French Revolution, 1789) led dissatisfied Boers in Swellendam and Graaff-Reinert to rise in rebellion, establish "revolutionary national assemblies" and declare free republics in their territories.

Last years of the East India Company

Moreover by the end of the 18th century, after four devastating wars between Britain and Holland, France and Britain had emerged as the leading powers in Europe and now competed for dominance in the oceans of the world. The Cape, strategically situated on the main sea routes, now became a tempting prey. In July 1795 a British force landed at Muizenberg, and six weeks later compelled the two independent republics to surrender. This also marked the end of the Dutch East India Company's authority, though it continued formally to exist until 1798. Major-General Craig now took over the government of the colony as "commandant of the town and settlement on the Cape of Good Hope". The laws and customs of the colony remained unchanged, and no new taxes were imposed. The existing monopolies were abolished and all restrictions on internal and external trade removed.

The population at this stage consisted of some 18,000 whites, 15,000 Khoikhoi and 22,000 slaves. 5000 of the settlers lived in Cape Town, 1000 in Stellenbosch and the rest as nomadic trekboers in the country areas.

In 1799 the third war between the Boers and the Xhosa broke out on the eastern frontier of the colony, with many Khoikhoi supporting the Xhosa.

After the Peace of Amiens in 1802 the Cape Colony was returned to Holland, and, under the influence of the French Revolution, many reforms were introduced. Legislative and executive powers were transferred to a four-member Council of Policy, at least two members of which had to be vryburgers. Local administration was also improved. The four existing districts (Cape Town, Stellenbosch, Swellendam and Graaff-Reinet) were increased to six (with the addition of Tulbagh and Uitenhage). The state took over responsibility for education from the church. Other measures were designed to promote the development of agriculture: wine experts from the Rhineland were brought in to develop wine production, and merino sheep were imported from Spain to improve the quality of wool. But the problem of relationships between the settlers and the Xhosa – both cattle-herders – who had come up against one another at the Great Fish River, remained unsolved.

Interlude of Dutch rule

The various Bantu peoples were not united: even within one people the various tribes, mostly small and weak, were in a constant state of feud. Then around 1785, in what is now KwaZulu/Natal, was born Shaka (or Chaka), son of the Zulu chief Senzangakona (see Famous People). After becoming chief in 1816 this "black Napoleon of Africa" had within a short time and with inconceivable cruelty conquered other Nguni tribes and established a kind of military monarchy. Thie period of war and of the flight of whole tribes, lasting into the mid 19th century, became known to the Nguni as the Mfecane (the "Crushing") and to the Sotho as the Difaqane. Great areas of territory were devastated and largely depopulated, and whole tribes disappeared (see Quotations). New and powerful groups arose in their place, among them the Ndebele, the Swazis and the South Sotho (Basotho), who

Displacements of population

founded the kingdom of Basutoland (now Lesotho) in the highland region.

In 1828 Shaka was murdered by his half-brother and successor. Opinions about him are still divided. To some he is the founder of a modern state, to others a power-hungry dictator.

The British Colony and the Boer Republics

After the French defeat at Trafalgar in 1805 Britain was again un-disputed master of the oceans. In 1806 it reoccupied the Cape Colony, which then had a population of around 26,000 whites, 20,000 Khoikhoi and 30,000 slaves.

The British colonial administration soon introduced a series of measures on relationships between the races. In 1807 the carrying of slaves on British ships was prohibited, and this was followed in 1809 by the Hottentot Laws which declared the Khoikhoi to be British subjects. Forced labour was now banned.

The years 1825–28 saw the introduction of British currency, the British administrative and legal systems, the establishment of English as the official language of the colony and the recognition of free non-whites as having equal rights with whites. During this period over 4000 English, Scottish and Irish families came to South Africa, settling in the territories disputed between the Xhosa and the white settlers (from Bushman's River to the Great Fish River and from Grahamstown to the coast) and thus forming a kind of buffer between the two groups.

In 1833 slavery was abolished in all British overseas possessions. In the Cape Colony this brought freedom to 59,000 slaves.

The Great Trek

Many of the Boer population saw these and other measures, reflecting a more liberal policy aimed at giving the population equal rights, as a

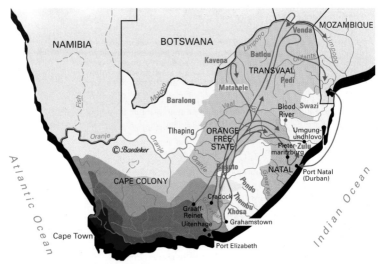

The Settlement of South Africa

CAPE COLONY				BOER STATES
1700		1775		
1725		1814		Great Trek
1745		1835		(1835–38)
		1848		

threat to their way of life. The situation was aggravated by drought and shortage of land. Further grounds for the hostility between the British authorities and the Boers which was to inform the history of South Africa throughout the 19th century lay in the discontent of settlers in the frontier areas. Although the conflict with the Bantu peoples was becoming increasingly violent, the Boers were given no direct protection and no tax reductions or compensation for damage or loss of property. This led some 6000 dissatisfied Boers (a fifth of the white population), the voortrekkers, to leave the Cape Colony between 1835 and 1841 in a series of treks under the leadership of Louis Trigardt (Trichardt), Hans van Rensburg, Andries Hendrik Potgieter, Gert Maritz, Piet Uys and Piet Retief. Originally spontaneous, these treks developed over the next few years into a massive movement of population with far-reaching effects on the history of South Africa.

After crossing the Orange River some of the Boers moved north while others turned east towards Durban and farther into Zulu territory. Large areas were either depopulated or occupied by tribes too weak to put up any resistance – a consequence of the movements of population brought about by Shaka (see above). In February 1838 Dingane, Shaka's successor, received Piet Retief and 70 voortrekkers in his capital, Mgungundhlovo, and a treaty was negotiated under which the new arrivals would be allowed to settle in the land south of the river Tugela. The Zulu king, however, did not carry out the agreement: Retief and his people were murdered and the other voortrekker encampments were attacked. This led to a series of bitterly fought battles, with many dead.

A turning-point came under the leadership of Andries Pretorius of Graaff-Reinet, who was elected commander-in-chief of the voortrekkers on November 25th 1838. On December 15th he launched a counter-attack. With a force of 470 men he confronted Dingane and his army of 12,500 men on the Buffalo River. In spite of their numerical superiority the Zulus were defeated by the settlers, equipped with rifles and two small cannon, in the battle of Blood River (as the Buffalo River was thereafter known), which left more than 3000 Zulu dead.

Battle of
Blood River

In 1839 the Boers founded the republic of Natal, with Pietermaritzburg as its capital. It survived only a short time, being annexed by Britain in 1842 and incorporated in the Cape Colony.

Foundation of
Boer republics
Natal

From Natal the Boers set off again in a trek northward, founding a number of small independent states. In 1848 Britain had occupied the territory between the Orange River, the Vaal and the Drakensberg, but in 1852, after tough negotiations, the Sand River Treaty was signed, recognising the independence of the Boer state of the Transvaal (known from 1857 as the South African Republic), and this was followed in 1854 by the recognition of the Orange Free State.

Transvaal

Orange Free State

After the end of the eighth frontier war between the Boers and the Xhosa, in 1853, the Cape Colony was granted a constitution and a limited degree of self-government (as previously granted to Canada in 1840 and to the Australian states in 1850). The vote was granted, without distinction of class or colour, to all male British subjects over the age of 21 with an income over £50 a year or land yielding over £25 a year. Thus in practice the black population, who greatly outnumbered the whites (in Natal, for example, there were 19 times as many blacks as whites) were deprived of the vote.

Cape Colony

Under British rule the Cape Colony continued to grow in size. The Ciskei (to the west of the Kei River), which had been declared British territory in 1847, was incorporated in the Cape Colony in 1865 as British Kaffraria, and in 1871 Basutoland (now Lesotho), which had been annexed two years previously, also became part of the colony.

By the middle of the 19th century the Xhosa had suffered from eight frontier wars and a cattle plague brought in from Europe which had killed thousands of beasts. In their despair they clung to the prophecies of a sixteen-year-old Xhosa woman named Nongqawuse who had promised her people the resurrection of all their herds and the destruction of the whites. On February 18th 1857 she prophesied that two suns would rise and a whirlwind would sweep the white settlers into the sea, and called for the killing of all cattle and the burning of all food supplies as sacrificial offerings. This was done: at least 200,000 cattle were slaughtered, and as a result more than 40,000 Xhosa starved to death and another 30,000 fled to other parts of the country in quest of food. Nongqawuse was arrested and imprisoned on Robben Island; she died in 1898 somewhere in the eastern Cape, where she had been living in exile. The depopulated region was reoccupied by 2300 ex-soldiers, veterans of the Crimean War, and 4000 German immigrants.

After the ninth Kaffir War (1877–78) the Cape Colony annexed most of the territory between Kaffraria and Natal. Then in 1894, during the prime-ministership of Cecil Rhodes, most of the area between the Kei River and Natal was incorporated in the Cape Colony. In 1885 the territory to the south of the Molopo River was taken under British protection as the Crown Colony of Bechuanaland, and ten years later this was also incorporated in the Cape Colony.

In 1856 Natal became an independent colony with a limited degree of self-government. After a Zulu rising in 1879 the Zulu chief Cetshwayo

The battle of Ulundi (1879)

or Cetewayo was defeated in the battle of Ulundi, after which his country became a British Crown Colony (1887) and in 1897 was in-corporated in the colony of Natal. Tsongaland, which had been annexed in 1895, also became part of Natal. In 1893 the colony was given its own government, under which non-whites were almost com-pletely denied the vote. This applied particularly to the Indians who had been brought in from 1860 onwards to work on white-owned sugar plantations. At the end of their period of contract labour they had the choice between returning to India and staying in South Africa, and many chose to stay. In addition many Indians, mainly traders and shopkeepers, immigrated on their own account. Around 1870 there were 30,000 Indians in Natal, and by 1904 there were 101,000 Indians, outnumbering the 97,000 whites. In 1894 they established the Natal Indian Congress, one of the founders of which was Gandhi (see Famous People).

When the Orange Free State was founded in 1854 all non-white inhabi-tants were excluded from citizenship. Thereupon 3000 Griqua (Hotten-tots), led by their chief Adam Kok, moved eastward and founded East Griqualand (1861–63).

Orange Free State

In a series of conflicts with the Basotho the Boer state enlarged its territory by taking in large areas in the Sotho country. After the British annexation in 1868, however, the Boers were compelled to withdraw to the west of the Caledon and Basutoland came under the administration of the Cape Colony. At this time the boundaries of present-day Lesotho were established.

After the discovery of diamonds on the Orange River in 1869 the territory became a very valuable colonial possession, and fortune-hunters moved into the area from all over the world. There was now a fierce conflict over the mining rights between the British colonial ad-ministration on the Cape, the Boers and the local peoples, the Griqua

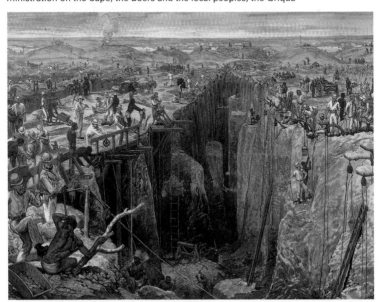

Diamond mine on the Orange River (print of 1872)

and the Tswana (a Bantu people). In 1871 Britain occupied the diamond fields and established the Crown Colony of West Griqualand. In 1884, after the payment of compensation (£90,000, a ridiculously low sum) to the Orange Free State, it was incorporated in the Cape Colony.

Transvaal

After the voortrekkers had crossed the Vaal and defeated the Ndebele under the leadership of Mzilikazi (1837) there were established between the Vaal and the Limpopo a number of Boer republics (Potchefstroom, Zoutpansberg, Utrecht, Lydenburg) which were recognised by Britain in 1852. In 1860 they amalgamated to form the South African Republic (Zuid-Afrikaansche Republiek) under President Marthinus Pretorius (1818–1901), with Pretoria as its capital. In the constitution adopted in 1860 it was laid down that there could be no equality between whites and non-whites either in the state or in the church. Unsolved domestic political problems (differences of opinion between political leaders) and above all external political problems (frontier wars with African tribes) gave Britain a pretext, in 1877, for occupying the Transvaal. After unsuccessful negotiations with the Cape Colony and the British government and various skirmishes the conflict ended in the battle of Mt Amajuba (600m/2000ft), in which the Boers defeated the British garrison (February 1881). Under the treaty of Pretoria in August 1881 the Transvaal was granted self-government but remained under British sovereignty. Its first President was Paul Kruger (1825–1924: see Famous People).

Gold rush

In 1886 the world's largest deposits of gold were discovered on the Witwatersrand, 50km/30 miles from Pretoria, and gold-seekers flocked into the area from all over the world. The gold-diggers' encampment developed into Johannesburg, which grew rapidly into a large city. The Transvaal's population of 85,000 was soon supplemented by twice as many incomers (uitlanders), leading to considerable tensions. Moreover the gold was a great temptation to the British. Under Cecil Rhodes (1853–1902), prime minister of the Cape Colony, the dreams of a united South Africa under British rule revived, and a plan was hatched for a coup d'état to overthrow the government in Pretoria and incorporate the Transvaal in the Empire. The British authorities counted on the support of the dissatisfied uitlanders. The leadership of the enterprise

The Jameson raid

was entrusted to Dr Leander Starr Jameson, an adventurer who headed the British administration in Rhodesia and had previously directed the occupation of Rhodesia. The attempted coup, which took place in December 1896, failed: Jameson was arrested and Rhodes was compelled to resign as prime minister. Anti-British feeling in the Boer republic reached its nadir, and in 1897 the Transvaal and the Orange Free State entered into a defensive alliance. During the next two years the conflict became still more acute. The new governor of the Cape Colony, Sir Alfred Milner, pursued with greater determination than ever a policy of uniting southern Africa, while the Boer republics sought to preserve their independence. War finally broke out on October 11th 1899.

The Boer War (1899–1902) and the Union of South Africa

Some 52,000 Boers now faced a heavily armed British force with a total strength of 448,725 men, commanded by Lord Roberts and later by Lord Kitchener, and after some initial victories they were defeated. After the fall of Bloemfontein, Johannesburg and finally Pretoria the war appeared to have ended. In fact, however, there were a further two years of guerrilla warfare, a war of attrition in which 34,000 Boers, 22,000 British troops and 15,000 blacks lost their lives.

Britain reacted with a scorched earth policy. The Boers' farms were burned down and their wives and children interned in concentration

British bombardment of a Boer laager at Paardeberg (1900)

camps, where many of them died from under-nourishment and poor hygienic conditions, including no fewer than 22,000 children. Barbed wire fences were erected across the country in order to hamper the operations of the Boer commandos.

Peace was finally signed at Vereeniging on May 31st 1902, and the Boer republics of the Transvaal and Orange Free State became British colonies. All four colonies (the Cape, Natal, the Transvaal and the Orange Free State) and the territories of Basutoland, Bechuanaland, Swaziland and Southern Rhodesia were now under British rule.

Growth, Change and Polarisation – the Union of South Africa

The country had been devastated by the war, with at least 30,000 farmhouses destroyed and large areas depopulated. Many of the impoverished and now landless Boers moved into the towns to begin a new life; but there the leading positions in the economy, the administration and the cultural field were mainly occupied by Britons, and they were obliged to compete for jobs with cheaper black labour. As a result there came into being numerous nationalistic Boer organisations demanding, among other things, that whites should get the better jobs and the higher rates of pay.

Reconstruction

The postwar years were devoted to the reconstruction of the country, including the return and resettlement of the population and the construction of new roads, railways and public buildings. Gold-mining profits contributed towards the country's recovery. Shortages of labour were made good by bringing in workers from abroad, including 62,000 Chinese. Between 1903 and 1907 the value of gold production rose by 117% to £27,410,000.

Progress was also made in reconciliation between the Boers and the British. In 1906 the Transvaal and in 1907 the Orange Free State were granted internal self-government. The right to vote, however, remained restricted, and almost 80% of the population of South Africa was left without any voice in the political process. Only the Cape Colony had 15% of non-white voters.

Union of
South Africa

With the union – strongly supported by Britain – of the four colonies of Natal, the Cape, the Transvaal and the Orange Free State on May 31st 1910 there came into being the Union of South Africa, a state within the British Empire with a population of 1.2 million whites and 4.6 million non-whites. Pretoria (Transvaal) became the seat of government, Cape Town (Cape Colony) the seat of Parliament and Bloemfontein (Orange Free State) the seat of the Supreme Court. In the first constitution of 1910 the right to vote was confined to whites; only in the Cape province was there a more liberal law, in force since 1853, tying the right to vote to property, income and education and thus enabling small numbers of the more prosperous blacks and coloureds to vote. The blacks lost this right in 1936, the coloureds in 1956.

Domestic policy

In the country's first election a majority was won by the South African Party (SAP), a coalition of Botha's party Het Volk, the Orangia Union and the Afrikaner-Bond in the Cape Colony. The first prime minister was a former Boer general, Louis Botha (see Famous People). Differences of view between Botha, who favoured a fusion of the English-speaking and the Boer population and the full incorporation of South Africa in the British Empire, and James B. M. Hertzog (1866–1942), who wanted to see the two population groups as equal partners in a state independent of Britain, led to the resignation from the government of Hertzog and other Boer nationalists and to the foundation of the National Party (NP).

First race
segregation laws

Immediately after the establishment of the Union of South Africa the first racial segregation laws were introduced.

The Mines and Works Act of 1911 regulated the working conditions of black miners, and "job reservation" arrangements banned black workers from skilled jobs, which were reserved for whites. In 1977 there were still 158,000 jobs on the "reserved" list.

The Native Labour Law regulated the entry of migrant labour for work in the mines and declared any breach of contract (i.e. a strike) a criminal act.

The Natives Land Act of 1913 prohibited blacks from acquiring land outside specified areas, laying the foundation of the later homelands policy (see below). 70% of the South African population were thus confined to 7.5% of the country's total area – land with the most infertile soils and with no minerals.

The Riotous Assemblies Act of 1914 provided a legal basis for the banning of political meetings and strikes.

South Africa
becomes
an industrial state

In the years between the two world wars, in both of which South Africa was involved on the Allied side, the country developed from a group of colonial territories into a powerful industrial state.

In 1920 the Union of South Africa, as a member of the League of Nations, was given the mandate over the former German colony of South-West Africa (now Namibia), which had been conquered by South African troops in 1914–15.

1922 was a bad year for white workers, whose jobs and pay were threatened by the more numerous and cheaper black workers. The prospect of dismissals led to a strike by 22,000 workers and miners and to the foundation of the South African Communist Party (SACP).

In 1924 the opposition National Party came to power. Its programme, briefly summarised, was the creation of a national Christianity and the protection of the race and culture of the Boers by a continuation of the race segregation policy.

In 1925 Afrikaans became the country's second official language, alongside English.

In subsequent years the rights of the black population were further restricted by a series of laws. The Urban Areas Act of 1923 provided the legal basis for the establishment of black urban districts and townships, the best known of which is Soweto. The Group Areas Act of 1950 provided for the establishment of residential districts for coloureds and Asians.

In order to provide a more effective control over the movement of blacks into the towns the much hated Pass Laws which had been in force since the early 19th century were tightened up. Under these laws non-white men were obliged to carry a pass book at all times. In this "book of life" all frontier crossings and employers' names had to be entered; and without a job a black could not have a pass. Any black without a pass could be arrested by the police and assigned to a white farmer as a slave labourer. In 1952 the law was extended to women.

Under the Immorality Act of 1927 sexual relations between people of different races were made a criminal offence, and this was followed in 1949 by the Prohibition of Mixed Marriages Act.

In 1933 a coalition government formed by the National Party and the South African Party came to power, and a year later the two parties amalgamated. In protest against this development a group headed by the pastor and newspaper publisher D. F. Malan, leader of the nationalists in the Cape province, left the National Party and formed the "Purified National Party", forerunner of the present National Party. Nationalist groups sprang up throughout the country, including in particular the Afrikaner Broederbond, an influential secret society to which from 1948 onwards all prime ministers and most Boer members of parliament and senior officials belonged.

In 1936 the NP/SAP coalition passed the Natives Representation Act, which established a National Council for the representation of non-whites. The Council had only advisory powers, but it provided a pretext for the repeal of the more liberal electoral law of the Cape province.

In the same year the Natives Land Act of 1913 was amended to increase the areas in which blacks could acquire land to 13% of the country's total area.

After the outbreak of the Second World War Prime Minister Hertzog tried to pursue a policy of neutrality, but when pro-British feeling became predominant he resigned in favour of Jan Christiaan Smuts (1870–1950), and on September 6th 1939 South Africa entered the war on the Allied side. Altogether 186,218 white South Africans volunteered for service in the armed forces, at first in East and North Africa and from 1943 in Italy. In addition 24,975 women and 123,131 non-whites served in non-combatant posts.

Apartheid and Resistance

Resistance to white domination began to find expression in the 19th century, and in 1909 a Native Convention met in Bloemfontein with the object of putting forward proposals for the improvement of the new constitution of the Union of South Africa. The conference made no headway, however. In 1912 a group of black intellectuals, including a young lawyer named Pixley ka Isaka Seme, founded the South African Native National Congress (renamed the African National Congress in 1923: see Baedeker Special, p. 30) to fight against racial segregation, tribalism and ethnic rivalries. Its President was a US-trained theologian, Dr John Langibale Dube. The Congress called for the vote for black South Africans and the repeal of the racial segregation laws. In

"Whites only" bench in a Durban street in 1962

1913–14 Mahatma Gandhi led a march organised by the Natal Indian Congress (founded 1894) from Natal to the Transvaal and achieved some improvements for his Indian countrymen.

After the First World War the Industrial and Commercial Workers Union (founded in 1917) was for a time the moving spirit in a black protest movement, while the ANC mounted campaigns against the increasing restrictions on the rights of black South Africans.

There were differences of view within the ANC about whether change could be achieved with or without violence. The All-African Convention which brought together 400 representatives of non-white population groups at Bloemfontein in 1936 likewise failed to produce any binding political programme. While the younger members of the ANC became more radical, others, particularly the older members, advocated taking advantage of such small opportunities for giving the black population a voice in political discussion as had been offered by the government.

1948–61	The land available to black South Africans had long been insufficient to meet the needs of the population, and increasing numbers moved into the large cities in search of work, adding to the population of the already overcrowded slum quarters. Riots and wildcat strikes by black workers and their increasing politicisation fuelled the anxieties of many whites in face of the black majority. Against this background the National Party won 40% of the votes and 70 out of the 150 parliamentary seats in an election in 1948. They formed an alliance with the Afrikaner Party (9 seats) and thus gained a parliamentary majority which was to last until 1994.
Architects of apartheid	The governments led by D. F. Malan (1948–54), J. E. Strijdom (1954–58) and H. F. Verwoerd (1958–66) were the real architects of apartheid. The word *apartheid,* taken over from Dutch, means "separateness,

segregation''. Its central lie lay in the promise to "create a world in which blacks and whites can live separately but with equal rights" (R. Malan). In the words of Nelson Mandela, "The premise of apartheid was that whites were superior to blacks, coloureds and Indians, and apartheid was designed to ensure white predominance for all time to come. As the nationalists say, 'Die wit man moet altyd baas wees' ('The white man must always remain boss')".

The main pillars of apartheid were the Natives Land Act of 1913, which prohibited the blacks from possessing or acquiring land outside speci- fied areas; the Population Registration Act of 1950, which divided the population of South Africa into whites, blacks, Indians and other coloureds; and the Group Areas Act of the same year, which provided that people could live and work only in the areas assigned to them. Hundreds of other laws provided for the application of the principles of apartheid in everyday life.

Pillars of apartheid

The theory of apartheid, never put into practice in good faith, was that all black South Africans should "return" to their "traditional" areas of settlement and there enjoy self-determination in the practice of their political rights.

The homelands policy

The government established ten "homelands" or "Bantustans" for the Bantu peoples who made up 75% of the country's population. The areas thus set apart, totalling 13% of South Africa's area, were mainly in the Northern and Eastern Transvaal, the Eastern Cape and Natal. They were much fragmented – the Zulus, for example, were assigned ten separate regions – and economically were not viable. The law also permitted compulsory transfers of population, and putting it into effect

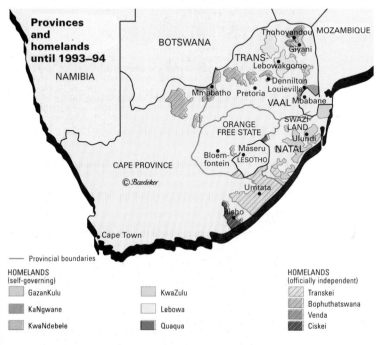

Provinces and homelands until 1993–94

NAMIBIA

BOTSWANA

MOZAMBIQUE

Thohoyandou

Givani

TRANS-

Lebowakgomo

Dennilton

Mmabatho   Pretoria   Louieville

VAAL   Mbabane

ORANGE FREE STATE

SWAZI-LAND

Ulundi

Maseru

Bloem-fontein   LESOTHO   NATAL

CAPE PROVINCE

© Baedeker

Umtata

Bisho

Cape Town

—— Provincial boundaries

HOMELANDS (self-governing)

☐ GazanKulu
☐ KaNgwane
☐ KwaNdebele
☐ KwaZulu
☐ Lebowa
☐ Quaqua

HOMELANDS (officially independent)

☐ Transkei
☐ Bophuthatswana
☐ Venda
☐ Ciskei

involved moving some 3.5 million people from all over South Africa into their "homelands".

In the rest of South Africa (87% of the country's area) blacks could live and work only for specified periods as migrant workers. This was the means by which the dream of a 100% white South Africa was to be realised.

The Pass Laws provided an instrument of control, and any contravention was a criminal offence, for which 1,200,000 blacks were sentenced over a period of ten years.

Economically and politically the homelands remained dependent on Pretoria (two-fifths of the South African budget went on the homelands); the only exception was Bophuthatswana with its productive platinum mines.

Political structures within the homelands were conceived as a mingling of modern and traditional elements. Their parliaments consisted of both elected and appointed members, and the chiefs, as traditional wielders of authority, played a major part in administration. Over the years, however, there were recurring reports of inadequate financial control, corruption, mismanagement and heavy burdens of debt. The Ciskei, Venda, Lebowa, Gazankulu and Quaqua homelands were among the poorest regions in South Africa.

Only four of the homelands accepted the "independence" offered by Pretoria – the Transkei (1976), Bophuthatswana (1977), Venda (1979) and the Ciskei (1981), the so-called TBVC states. Their inhabitants thus lost their South African citizenship. These "independent" states were not recognised internationally, and their population were thus in practice stateless. Chief Buthelezi, prime minister of the KwaZulu homeland and the largest Zulu population group (see Famous People), refused the offer of independence and thus contributed significantly to the failure of the homelands policy.

The Separate Amenities Act of 1953 introduced racial segregation in hospitals, schools, churches, public transport and public lavatories and on park benches.

The Bantu Education Act passed in the same year regulated the education of blacks, which was of a lower standard than for whites; expenditure on the education of blacks was only a twentieth of expenditure on white education.

In 1956 the coloured population, who had hitherto had the vote, now lost it. The Pass Laws were still further tightened up, prohibiting blacks from moving out of the areas assigned to them except to work or with special permission.

Sophiatown
6km/4 miles west of Johannesburg was the township of Sophiatown, one of the few places in the Transvaal where Africans owned property. "Despite the poverty Sophiatown had a special character; for Africans, it was the Left Bank in Paris, Greenwich Village in New York, the home of writers, artists, doctors and lawyers. It was both bohemian and conventional, lively and sedate" (Nelson Mandela, "Long Walk to Freedom").

When neighbouring white residential districts needed room to expand they laid claim to this conveniently situated area. Accordingly the decision was taken, under the Group Areas Act of 1923 (extended to coloureds and Asians in 1950), which provided for the segregation of residential and business districts by race, to evacuate Sophiatown. 60,000 people were removed from their homes and resettled in seven different "ethnic groups" at Meadowlands, 20km/12½ miles away. Bulldozers razed Sophiatown to the ground, and on its ruins was built a new "white" suburb, characteristically named Triomf. Later Cape Town's "District Six" suffered the same fate.

Growing resistance
From 1949 onwards the ANC organised strikes, acts of public disobedience and protest marches against the government's race policy.

Within a short time its membership had risen from 7000 to over 100,000.

In 1955 a number of other organisations joined the ANC in a congress which adopted the Freedom Charter, calling for a non-racial and democratic South Africa, which has remained central to the ANC's policy into the nineties. Three months later the police carried out the largest roundup in South Africa's history, arresting over 156 activists.

The preamble of the Freedom Charter is as follows:

Freedom Charter

"We, the people of South Africa, declare for all our country and the world to know:

That South Africa belongs to all who live in it, black and white, and that no government can justly claim authority unless it is based on the will of the people;

That our people have been robbed of their birthright to land, liberty and peace by a form of government founded on injustice and inequality;

A photograph that went round the world:
the schoolchildren's uprising in Soweto in 1976

67

That our country will never be prosperous or free until all our people live in brotherhood, enjoying equal rights and opportunities;

That only a democratic state, based on the will of the people, can secure to all their birthright without distinction of colour, race, sex or belief;

And therefore we, the people of South Africa, black and white together – equals, countrymen and brothers – have adopted this Freedom Charter. And we pledge ourselves to strive together, sparing nothing of our strength and courage, until the democratic changes here set out have been won."

The PAC and Sharpeville

In 1959 the government introduced regulations on the consumption of alcoholic liquor. Bars for black people were established, selling only a type of beer which was of nutritional value and low in alcohol. Home brewing of beer, traditionally a task for women, was prohibited. This led to further unrest.

In the same year a group of blacks led by Robert Sobukwe left the ANC and founded the Pan-Africanist Congress (PAC), believing that the ANC was too moderate and that white intellectuals and communists had too much influence on its policies. Soon afterwards, on March 21st 1960, the PAC organised a demonstration against the hated Pass Laws at Sharpeville (near Vereeniging). 15,000 peaceful demonstrators gathered in front of the police station, demanding to be arrested. 75 policemen then fired into the crowd, killing 69 Africans and wounding at least 180, including women and children, most of whom had been shot in the back.

The Sharpeville massacre aroused world-wide horror and indignation, and there were demonstrations against the apartheid regime in many European countries. The South African government declared a state of emergency and passed a series of emergency laws, including a law against illegal organisations under which they banned the ANC and the PAC and arrested their leaders. Both organisations thereafter continued to operate underground and from abroad.

In the early 1960s the French, Belgian and British colonies in North Africa became independent, and Britain condemned apartheid with increasing vigour. The South African government then revived an old plan and raised the question of independence from Britain. In October 1960 a referendum in which only whites could vote decided by a narrow majority (52.3%) in favour of a republic, and a few months later (March 15th 1961) South Africa left the British Commonwealth. In an election in 1961 Verwoerd's National Party obtained 105 out of the 156 parliamentary seats (the United Party had 49 seats, other parties 2).

The Republic of South Africa 1961–89

After Verwoerd's murder in 1966 the South African government's existing policies were carried on by his successors as prime minister, J. B. Vorster (1966–78) and P. W. Botha (1978–84), known as the "Great Crocodile".

Within South Africa apartheid had made the Boers rich. Blacks worked on average for 15 more hours a week than whites for wages which were 16 times lower. "Privileged" blacks lived in the townships, the rest in over-populated slums. Over 500,000 miners lived in hostels, separated from their families, working as contract labourers and earning only a fifteenth of the wages of white miners.

In the previous twenty years more than 2 million people had been compulsorily moved from their homes and resettled elsewhere and 4 million had been arrested for contraventions of the Pass Laws, and there were over 7000 political prisoners. The ANC, although banned, gained in influence, and its president, Albert Luthuli (1898–1967), was awarded the Nobel Peace Prize in 1961.

The main leader of the movement was Nelson Mandela (see Famous People), who along with other leading ANC figures had been sentenced to life imprisonment in 1963 in the Rivonia trial.

In 1966 Lesotho, Botswana and Swaziland were granted independence by Britain.

The Roman Catholic bishops condemned apartheid. In 1966, after a series of bloody conflicts, the United Nations withdrew South Africa's mandate over German South-West Africa, but instead of leaving the territory the South African army continued fighting the South-West Africa People's Organisation (SWAPO) until Namibia became independent on March 21st 1990.

In 1972 the ANC and PAC were given observer status at the United Nations, from which South Africa was expelled in 1974.

In 1974 the former Portuguese colonies of Angola and Mozambique became independent. South Africa now saw itself surrounded by ever more independent countries.

In 1980 Robert Mugabe became the first elected prime minister of Zimbabwe (formerly Rhodesia).

In 1976 the government decided that Afrikaans should become a language of instruction in black schools as well as English. Since many teachers and pupils had little knowledge of Afrikaans, which in any case was regarded as the language of the oppressors, there were protest demonstrations at a number of schools in Soweto (South-Western Township), a black settlement 20km/12½ miles south-west of Johannesburg. The police opened fire on a large crowd of children, killing 23 and wounding 220. The subsequent unrest spread to other cities and continued for eight months.

1976: Soweto uprising

In September 1977 Steve Biko, founder of the South African Students' Association, died in police custody in consequence of the torture to which he had been subjected. He was the leader of a new black generation, the Black Consciousness movement, which, on the model of the Black Power movement and the Black Panthers, sought to promote a black consciousness and break away from the non-violent methods of earlier organisations.

1977

In 1978, according to the official statistics, there were 19 million blacks living in their homelands. In actual fact there were no more than 9 million at the most, with the rest living on the outskirts of industrial towns. There was nothing for them in the homelands. Seven-tenths of the population lived below the poverty line, and in some of the homelands half the children under five died of under-nourishment; in others half the children did not live to the age of ten.

The homelands

Under the system of separate development (later renamed multinational development) some of the homelands (the TBVC states: see p. 64) were given independent status by the South African government between 1976 and 1981, but received no international recognition.

In reaction to the death of Steve Biko in 1977 and the banning of numerous black organisations in the same year the Security Council of the United Nations imposed an arms embargo on South Africa (September 1977). In 1979 Sweden became the first industrial nation to pass a law banning investment in South Africa. Increasing numbers of South African firms, concerned about the possibility of further sanctions and believing that further deterioration in the country's economic and financial situation could be warded off by recognising black trade unions, began to press the government to initiate a process of reform. Another important argument for a change in existing arrangements was the increasing shortage of skilled black workers as a result of apartheid (which meant that blacks had inadequate training or none at all).

Sanctions and lack of skilled workers

Pieter W. Botha, who became prime minister in 1978, promised to establish a "clean" administration and to get rid of some particularly vexatious apartheid laws.

In 1979 a new labour law permitted the establishment of black trade unions, and in 1985 these joined to form the Congress of South African Trade Unions (COSATU).

On September 1st 1984 a new constitution, which had been approved by the white population in a referendum held in the previous year, came into force. This gave Indians and coloureds the vote in separate parliaments of their own, though there was a white veto on all their parliamentary proceedings.

In 1984 the black Anglican Bishop Desmond Tutu (see Famous People) was awarded the Nobel Peace Prize.

The majority black population of South Africa was still denied the vote, and this led to bloody riots throughout the country. Powerful umbrella organisations were now formed, among them the United Democratic Front (UDF), established in 1983, a body close to the ANC which brought together over 600 anti-apartheid organisations.

1985

In 1985 the bans on mixed-race marriages and sexual relations were lifted, and in 1986 the hated Pass Laws and the separate courts for blacks and whites were abolished. In the same year blacks were given full rights of property ownership, and hotels and restaurants and some cinemas and theatres were thrown open to blacks.

In 1985 P. W. Botha offered Nelson Mandela, who had been a prisoner since 1962, release from prison if he "unconditionally rejected violence as a political instrument". Mandela refused. As he said in a speech read on his behalf by his daughter, "I am surprised at the conditions the government wants to impose on me. I am not a violent man . . . It was only then, when all other forms of resistance were no longer open to us, that we turned to armed struggle. Let Botha show that he is different from Malan, Strijdom and Verwoerd. Let him renounce violence. Let him say that he will dismantle apartheid . . . Let him guarantee free political activity so that people may decide who will govern them . . .

What freedom am I being offered while the organisation of the people remains banned? . . .

Only free men can negotiate. Prisoners cannot enter into contracts . . . I cannot and will not give any undertaking at a time when I and you, the people, are not free. Your freedom and mine cannot be separated. I will return." (Nelson Mandela, "Long Walk to Freedom").

Probably Botha's initiative came too late. Moreover neither he nor the National Party was genuinely prepared to share power, still less to give it up. Against this background – the blacks having been given a modest degree of freedom of opinion, of assembly and consequently also of action – riots and unrest broke out in earnest. The first township to explode was Sebokeng, and thereafter the disturbances spread rapidly. The South African economy was in deep recession, and the price of gold had fallen steeply. There were widespread strikes involving 37% of the working population. A state of emergency was again declared, continuing until 1990. Hundreds of leading figures in the UDF were imprisoned; within a period of three months in 1986 more than 20,000 activists were arrested and ANC headquarters in the front-line states were bombed. All meetings and other activities of anti-apartheid organisations were banned, and the security laws and press censorship became much stricter. When international sanctions against South Africa were intensified and the withdrawal of international finance continued Botha halted the reforms. White hardliners mobilised round the Conservative Party (CP) founded in 1982 by Pastor A. Treurnicht (known as "Dr No") and the Afrikaner Weerstandsbeweging (AWB, Afrikaner Resistance Movement), originally established in 1973 by Eugene Terre'Blanche as a cultural organisation.

In 1986 war broke out between supporters of the UDF and ANC on the one hand and the conservative Inkatha Party of Chief Buthelezi, President of the KwaZulu homeland (see Famous People), on the other. "Necklacing" (putting a car tyre soaked in petrol round the victim's body and then setting light to it), which had been used as a punishment for "traitors", was now applied to opponents. In addition to the fighting between the ANC and Inkatha there were also conflicts between supporters of the ANC and the Pan-Africanist Congress (PAC) in the towns of the Eastern Cape. The whites took advantage of this violence between blacks for their own purposes: this was the notorious "Third Force". There were riots and disturbances all over the country. In May 220 people were killed in the Cape province, 194 in Soweto and 117 in KwaNdebele; and the year's toll of deaths was over 3000. The funerals of the victims in turn gave rise to demonstrations and in the end were prohibited.

The state of emergency and the emergency legislation remained in force. The whites were divided, and there was widespread anxiety about the future. The secret services were given unlimited powers, and opposition activists were ruthlessly hunted down by every means, including bomb attacks.

The efforts of a young lawyer named Cyril Ramaphosa and others led to the foundation of a miners' trade union, and in mid 1987 the miners went on strike, calling for an improvement in safety conditions in the mines. This was the biggest strike ever by black workers, and work was at a standstill in 40 mines for several months. The police again intervened, and many miners were injured and arrested. 40,000 workers were dismissed and sent back to their homelands.

In 1988 Namibia (formerly South-West Africa) became independent. South Africa and Cuba reached an agreement with Angola under which their troops were withdrawn from Angola. The first free elections were held in Angola in November 1989, and in 1990 it became independent.

On July 18th 1988 Nelson Mandela celebrated his 70th birthday in prison, where he had been confined for 26 years. There were demonstrations calling for his release in Cape Town, Johannesburg and London.

Turning-Point at the Cape

In 1989 the ANC, UDF and COSATU formed a grand coalition against the policy of racial segregation. Their principal demand was "one man, one vote".

International pressure on South Africa increased. The economy was crippled by sanctions, and banks and foreign capital withdrew from the country in the face of the prevailing violence.

P. W. Botha was now losing influence within his own party, and on August 15th, only three weeks before the official end of his term of office, he was succeeded as State President by F. W. de Klerk (see Famous People), who was confirmed in office in a parliamentary election held soon afterwards, which was boycotted by Indians and coloureds out of solidarity with the 21 million voteless blacks.

In a historic speech at the opening of Parliament on February 2nd 1990 President de Klerk initiated a new stage in the development of South Africa. He lifted the bans on the ANC, PAC, UDF and Communist Party, relaxed restrictions imposed under the state of emergency and announced the release of Nelson Mandela and other political prisoners. In June the state of emergency which had been in force for four years was brought to an end, and in October racial segregation was abolished in schools, hospitals and other public institutions.

Miracle at the Cape

After the first free and democratic election in the history of South Africa at the end of April 1994 the world took a fresh look at the changed South Africa. One head of government after the other visited the country which had for decades been outlawed by the international community. After the repeal of the legislation enforcing apartheid race relations in South Africa immediately became less tense, though racist attitudes did not disappear over night. The Republic of South Africa, which until 1989 had for many people been a symbol of the repression of human rights, now had a constitution which in this respect was an example to the rest of the world.

The status of the new African President and Nobel Prize winner Nelson Mandela as a moral leader was now still further enhanced. His policy of national reconciliation, given expression in a coalition government of national unity and in his striving to reach agreement with political opponents, previously at bitter odds, before important decisions were taken led to a visible détente in relationships between South Africans of all colours and convictions. Parallels were frequently drawn between South Africa after the abolition of racial segregation and Germany after the reunion of Eastern and Western Germany: both countries, in their different ways, sought reconciliation, rapprochement, amnesty, compensation and restitution of property.

Visitors to the "new" South Africa who go about the country with eyes and ears open will encounter and will themselves experience conflicting feelings. They will be constantly surprised by the readiness of the victims of apartheid to forgive those responsible for their wrongs, whether from Christian conviction, tolerance of suffering or perhaps mere apathy. After the transfer of power there was no iconoclastic urge to destroy the symbols of the previous regime. A year after the change the portraits of arch-proponents of apartheid were still hanging in the corridors of the Parliament building. Visitors will be no less surprised in their encounters with whites. They will rarely come across an avowed supporter of apartheid: no one, it seems, was in favour of the policy.

The political and legal transformation of South Africa has been accompanied by no less radical economic, cultural and social changes. The country's economy, which under the government of the National Party had been largely state-directed, became more market-led, though previously many observers had believed that it would go in the opposite direction. After years of isolation and cultural boycott South Africa's culture re-established contact with the outside world. This produced a mutual fertilisation, but also led to the introduction into South Africa of some of the more vapid features of television and pop culture. The strict and often ridiculous censorship was abandoned. During the years of resistance there had developed on the stage and in literature a tradition of protest which produced a level of artistic achievement and a variety which have not always been attained in other countries with a comparable history and of comparable size. In many fields – in television and the press, in the churches, in sports policy – there were almost complete changes of attitude between 1990 and 1995. Little that had previously been received wisdom, it seemed, still remained valid.

The tourist trade, too, took on a new lease of life: visitors were attracted by the combination of exoticism with an excellent infrastructure, of scenic variety and beauty with reasonable prices, empty sandy beaches and, particularly between September and May, a settled and usually warm and sunny climate.

But South Africa still had some problems after the change. Politically motivated violence increased, particularly in the Johannesburg region. In some

Mangosuthu Buthelezi, F. W. de Klerk and Nelson Mandela

parts of KwaZulu/Natal it declined but did not disappear altogether, and the bloody struggle for power between the ANC and the Inkatha Freedom Party continued. Until the new democratic government established its authority, too, lawlessness spread in the public service. Though a foreign visitor is unlikely to see much of this, except perhaps in newspaper headlines, he will become aware in Johannesburg of an increase in crime and will regulate his behaviour accordingly. The engaging friendliness of South Africans, always greeting visitors with a smile, is accompanied by an inefficiency – encountered even in the tourist trade – resulting from years of isolation and lack of training. Visitors who, apart from the scenic beauties of the country, want to understand something of its "soul", with all its internal contradictions, reflected, for example, in the juxtaposition of luxurious residential districts and the townships with their corrugated iron huts and matchbox houses – not usually on the tourist route – have a number of possibilities. There are a number of small tourist agencies, mostly black, and humanitarian aid organisations which offer trips to the townships (best not visited by unaccompanied foreigners), with unvarnished accounts of their way of life. Perhaps the best places for a frank discussion, across racial divides, of the situation in South Africa are the racially integrated jazz spots, theatres, dance shows and bars to be found in the "artists' quarters" and near the universities in the cities. There a visitor is likely to find people ready to respond to a friendly approach. Younger black South Africans are often more fluent in English than their elders, who have usually been denied a good education. In conversations of this kind visitors will be repeatedly surprised by the degree of goodwill and the readiness for reconciliation shown by the people they talk to, although almost all the younger ones, if you ask them about their lives, will have a story to tell of an experience with violence, often at the hands of the police.

1991	Further apartheid laws were repealed, including the Population Registration Act and the Group Areas and Land Acts.

After discussions between de Klerk, Mandela and other black organisations the Convention for a Democratic South Africa (CODESA) was set up to work out a new constitution. Other matters for discussion were the future of the homelands and the increase in violence between different black groups, which since the 1980s had led to the death of over 15,000 people.

1992   In a referendum of white voters 68.7% voted in favour of the continuation of de Klerk's reforms.

1993   On April 10th 1993 Chris Hani, a leading member of the ANC and secretary-general of the South African Communist Party, was shot by a militant white right-winger.

Violence in the black townships increased. In July it became known that there had been secret payments from government funds to the conservative Inkatha Party and that Zulu fighters had been armed by the police.

On December 6th 1993 a transitional constitution was adopted, to remain in force for a maximum of five years from the date of the first free election (April 27th 1994). A Transitional Executive Council (TEC) was established, with representatives of all the parties and organisations involved in the negotiations except members of the "Freedom Alliance" (the Conservative Party led by Andries Treurnicht, the Afrikaner Volksfront led by General Constand Viljoen, Chief Buthelezi's Inkatha Party and the governments of the homelands of Bophuthatswana, Ciskei and KwaZulu). This marked the formal end of 341 years of exclusive white rule. The Council had to prepare for and to supervise the first election for the whole population on April 27th, and it was now involved in all government decisions, with a right of veto.

With the adoption of the transitional constitution all laws passed by the four "independent" homelands of Transkei, Ciskei, Bophuthatswana and Venda and the six other homelands were superseded, and all inhabitants of the homelands were entitled to vote in the election in April 1994.

1994   In January South Africa was invited to rejoin the Commonwealth.

On March 1st South Africa handed over to Namibia the port of Walvis Bay and twelve uninhabited islands off the Namibian coast, an area of 1124sq.km/434sq. miles with a population of just under 40,000 which had been administered by South Africa for 84 years.

In March the refusal by Lucas Mangope, President of the homeland of Bophuthatswana, to allow its 2.5 million inhabitants to take part in the election in April led to violent disturbances. The situation was aggravated when a private army of 5000 white right-wingers offered to "help" Mangope. With the support of the homeland's army and police, which had been kept out of action by Mangope, and the intervention of South African troops, the Mangope government was overthrown, and a temporary president was appointed by the South African government to rule the homeland until the election.

Amendments to the transitional constitution (increased rights of decision for the future new provinces and recognition of the kingdom of KwaZulu) opened up the way for Inkatha, the Conservative Party and the Afrikaner Volksfront to take part in the election.

In South Africa's first free election, in April, 22.7 million people were entitled to vote and there were candidates from 18 political parties. As expected, the ANC and Nelson Mandela won a majority, with 62.7% of the votes. De Klerk's National Party had 20.4%, Inkatha 10.5% and all other parties less than 3%. The ANC fell just short of a two-thirds majority, and it was not equally successful in all parts of the country; but even in the province of KwaZulu/Natal, the Inkatha stronghold, it gained 50.3% of the votes. This marked the end of 342 years of predominance by the white minority in South Africa. On April 27th the transitional constitution, giving all South Africans equal rights, came into force.

On May 9th Nelson Mandela was elected President of South Africa – both head of state and head of the government – by a unanimous vote of the National Assembly. For the next five years South Africa was to be governed by a government of national unity of which the three main parties (ANC, National Party, Inkatha) were members.

In May the Security Council of the United Nations called off the last remaining sanctions against South Africa, including the arms embargo.

South Africa now rejoined the international community, becoming the 53rd member of the Organisation of African Unity (OAU), the 109th member of the Non-Aligned Movement (NAM) and the 51st member of the Commonwealth. The Republic now has relations on various levels with 135 countries and is a member of ten international organisations.

The Constitutional Court was established in Johannesburg (February). 1995 South Africa thus made the transition, as provided in the temporary constitution, from the British to the European continental system under which the legislature and executive are no longer above the constitution but are subject to it. Demobilisation of armed forces of ANC (Umkhonto we Sizwe) and Pan-Africanist Congress (August).

Visits to South Africa by Queen Elizabeth II (March) and Pope John Paul II (September).

New constitution adopted by Parliament (May). It will take effect over 1996 the next three years, coming fully into operation with the next general election, scheduled for 1999. It sets up a majority-rule government with a bill of rights.

After the adoption of the constitution the National Party withdrew from the government of national unity, undertaking in future to play the part of a responsible opposition.

Famous People

This section contains brief biographies of notable people who were born, lived or worked in South Africa or died there.

Louis Botha
(1864–1919)
Politician

In recent years there have been two prominent South African politicians named Botha – P. W. Botha, State President 1984–89, and R. F. Botha, foreign minister 1977–94. The first bearer of this old Boer name, however, was Louis Botha, first prime minister of the Union of South Africa after its foundation in 1910 and one of the fathers of apartheid.

Born in Greytown (Natal), Botha later became a farmer in the Boer republic of Transvaal, where he also took a part in political life. In 1897 he was elected to the Volksraad (National Council) of the Transvaal. In contrast to Paul Kruger (see below) he advocated a more moderate attitude to the uitlanders (mostly British) living in the Transvaal. During the Boer War (1899–1902), however, he showed his military skills. He proved a successful commander-in-chief, who distinguished himself particularly in guerrilla warfare. But when the defeat of the Boers seemed inevitable he was among those who pressed for an armistice with Britain. On May 31st 1902, along with other generals, he signed the Peace of Vereeniging, which established British dominance in southern Africa. Lord Milner became governor of the formerly independent Boer republics of the Transvaal and the Orange Free State, seeing it as his principal task to anglicise South Africa still further. The result of this policy, however, was to reawaken Boer national feeling. In 1905 the first postwar Afrikaner party, Het Volk (The People), was established in the Transvaal, headed by five Boer generals, including Botha. The Liberal government which came to power in Britain in 1905 granted the former Boer republics domestic self-government. Het Volk then won a parliamentary election in the Transvaal and Botha became prime minister. Under the constitution which his government now adopted non-whites were given no political influence.

The next objective was the union of all four South African colonies – the Transvaal, the Orange River Colony (the former Orange Free State), the Cape Colony and Natal. On May 31st 1910, exactly eight years after the Peace of Vereeniging, the four colonies became the Union of South Africa, a Dominion within the British Empire with its own government. Louis Botha was elected its first prime minister.

The establishment of the Union was followed by the initiation of the apartheid regime which was to last until 1994. Non-whites were denied any participation in political decisions, and the government sought at once to introduce racial segregation under statutory powers. Under the Mines and Works Act of 1911 non-whites were allowed to perform only unskilled labour, and the Natives Land Act required blacks to live only in specified reserves assigned to them. Soon after the Boer War Botha, impressed by the moderation of the British government, sought to achieve a rapid and comprehensive reconciliation with Britain. This policy, however, was not universally popular with his fellow-countrymen. When the First World War broke out South Africa, as a British Dominion, was automatically involved in the war; but Botha had first to quell a rebellion among Boer soldiers against taking part in the war before he could carry out the British request to occupy German South-West Africa. On July 9th 1915 the German forces in South-West Africa, faced with superior numbers, were compelled to surrender, though one general held out until the end of the war.

Louis Botha died suddenly on August 28th 1919 at Rusthof (Transvaal).

Although Chief Buthelezi's hostility to Nelson Mandela and the African National Congress brought South Africa, shortly before the country's first democratic election in 1994, to the brink of civil war, the two men had not always been enemies. In his student days he was a member of the Youth League of the ANC, and during Mandela's imprisonment he repeatedly pressed for his release and refused to negotiate with the government.

Mangosuthu Gatsha Buthelezi (b. 1928) Politician

Buthelezi, born on August 27th 1928 in Mahlabatini (Natal), is connected with the Zulu royal house through his mother, Crown Princess Magogo. In 1953 he became chief of his clan and in 1957 of his home district. In 1972 he became head of government of the homeland of KwaZulu, but vigorously opposed the South African government's plan, under its apartheid policy, to give KwaZulu independence, which would have made Zulus living there foreigners in their own country.

In 1975, with the approval of the ANC, he brought about the revival of a traditional cultural organisation founded many years before under the patronage of the Zulu king, the National Cultural Liberation Movement (Inkatha yeNkululeko yeSizwe), modelling it on the ANC, taking over the ANC's colours (black, gold and green) and thus seeking to appeal to all blacks. It almost looked as if the ANC, which had been banned in 1961, might regain a foothold in South Africa through the medium of Inkatha, the unity party of the semi-autonomous state of KwaZulu. The exiled leadership of the ANC saw it that way, though Buthelezi did not. Buthelezi had several meetings with leaders of the ANC, but no agreement could be reached. Their views were too far apart: Buthelezi rejected the armed struggle and criticised the school-children's uprising in Soweto in 1976. He ran campaigns against international sanctions and disapproved of the idea of a single unified South African state. The tensions between the two parties became more acute from 1983 onwards. Verbal attacks developed ever more frequently into bloody confrontations between militant supporters of the two parties. The conflict spread from Natal into the townships round Johannesburg and then into the city itself, and finally developed into a regular civil war which by the end of 1994 had claimed over 15,000 lives. For years Buthelezi was the darling of European Liberals and of economists, combining as he did a policy of non-violent resistance to apartheid with a belief in a free market economy. Outside South Africa he had meetings with many leading world statesmen; but his opponents (mainly black African politicians) accused him of collaboration and tribalism. At the same time he repelled old friends, including conservative British and German politicians, when from 1992 onwards he sought to establish closer relations with white right-wing extremists.

The alliance between President de Klerk and Nelson Mandela was a heavy blow for Buthelezi. He feared defeat in the election to be held in April 1994, since opinion polls indicated that many Zulus, seeing the ANC as the winning party, intended to vote for it. He called on Zulus, therefore, to boycott the election, enlisting the support of the the Zulu king Goodwill Zwelethini, the supreme traditional Zulu authority, in spite of the fact that the king was under a duty to maintain political neutrality. One of his strongest arguments was the fact that the Swazi and Sotho peoples had sovereign kingdoms of their own (Swaziland and Lesotho), while the Zulus, the largest people in South Africa with a population of 9 million, were a dependent part of the Republic. Shortly before the election, however, de Klerk and Mandela managed to persuade the Inkatha leader to take part in the election by agreeing to recognise the status of the Zulu kingdom as a constitutional monarchy in an amendment to the constitution. In the election held in April 1994 the Inkatha Freedom Party gained 10.5% of the votes, making it the third strongest party in South Africa, after the ANC and the National Party. Buthelezi became minister of home affairs in Mandela's government – another indication, perhaps, of Mandela's capacity for bringing about integration.

Johnny Clegg
(b. 1953)
Musician

Johnny Clegg is a phenomenon in the South African music scene. He is known in South Africa as the "white Zulu" – not without reason, for he is undoubtedly one of the leading forerunners of the cultural encounter between whites and blacks.

He was born in Rochester (Kent) in 1953. His mother was a cabaret singer, his stepfather a South African journalist. Soon after his birth the family emigrated to Zimbabwe, where the foundations of his later career were laid. His father introduced him to the Kwela music of Africa at an early age, and he learned the language of the Ndebele before he spoke English. In the late fifties the family moved to South Africa. At the age of 14 Johnny ran away from home and became friends with a Zulu named Mzila, who for two years instructed him in the music and dances of the Zulus, the largest population group in South Africa. The police of the apartheid regime did not like this, and Johnny was arrested for the first time at the age of 15. From 1970 onwards he teamed up with a Zulu named Sipho McHunu and the two of them gave performances as a musical duo. Their music showed a mingling of western-style features with black South African rhythms. In 1976 their first LP, "Woza Friday", was issued, and soon afterwards, against apartheid regulations, they formed a band of white and black musicians called Juluka. Producing a total of seven LPs, they gained one platinum record and five golds. In 1982 Clegg gave up his teaching posts in ethnology at the Universities of Natal and the Witwatersrand to devote himself to the band. In 1985, after successful tours in the United States, Canada, Britain, Scandinavia and Germany, the band broke up and Clegg began a career as a soloist. In 1986 he founded the Savuka band, which combined European and Zulu musical language and tradition in gripping rhythms. The themes of their songs were African village life, unemployment, arrest and tribal conflicts. In 1987 Savuka issued the LP "Third World Child", in 1988 the album "Shadow Man". Their third disc, "Cruel, Crazy, Beautiful World" (1989) rapidly gained a place in the hit parades. In France Clegg ranks as a superstar, and French newspapers talk of the Clegg generation and of "Zuluma-nia". In South Africa itself, however, the "white Zulu" (the title of a French biography) became famous only after he had made his name abroad.

Mohandas
Karamchand
Gandhi
(1869–1948)
Leader of the
Indian
independence
movement

Mohandas Karamchand Gandhi, known as the Mahatma ("Great Soul"), the leading figure in the Indian independence movement, spent his formative years in South Africa.

Gandhi was born on October 2nd 1869 in the Indian town of Porbandar. After studying law in London (1888–91) he set up in practice in India, but in 1893, seeking better professional prospects, he moved to the British Crown Colony of Natal, where he discovered what it was like not to belong to the white ruling class. On a railway journey from Durban to Pretoria he was ejected from a first class compartment because non-whites were not permitted to travel first class. The conclusions Gandhi drew from the memorable night he spent in Pietermaritzburg station were to change the history of the world. In 1884 he became one of the founders of the Natal Indian Congress, which put up the first organised resistance to British rule and provided a model for later forms of action by black South Africans (e.g. the burning of passes). Soon Gandhi was recognised as the political leader of the Indian population of South Africa. In September 1906 he persuaded the British Secretary of State for the Colonies to withdraw an ordinance on the registration of Indians in South Africa. The new government of the Transvaal reacted by passing a law on the recording of fingerprints. Thereupon Gandhi organised a mass demonstration and called on his Indian fellow-countrymen to oppose the new law by non-violent passive resistance. The Transvaal police made numerous arrests, including Gandhi himself. In January 1908 Gandhi reached a temporary agreement with Jan Smuts, the Boer general who was later to become prime minister of South Africa, but this fell a long way short of solving the "race question" in South Africa.

Gandhi's experience in fighting for the civil rights of Indians in the Transvaal served him in his later struggle for the independence of India. In 1914, after an absence of 21 years, he returned to India, became leader of the Indian nationalist movement and directed Indian resistance to British rule. Influenced by the old Indian doctrine of *ahimsa* (non-violence), the Sermon on the Mount and the ideas of Tolstoy, Gandhi, a strict and ascetic Hindu, called on his followers, under a policy of *satyagraha* (literally "reliance on truth") involving non-violent resistance, civil disobedience and refusal of cooperation, to join in an economic boycott in order to break the British monopoly of trade, particularly in salt. In addition to Indian independence from Britain Gandhi sought to achieve a social renewal in India, the relaxation of the caste system and the peaceful coexistence of Hindus and Muslims; but after India became independent he was unable to prevent the division of the country. On January 30th 1948 he was shot by a fanatical Hindu.

Although Nadine Gordimer, a Nobel Prize winner and an active member of the Congress of South African Writers (COSAW), has a strong political commitment she refuses to be regarded as a political writer.

Nadine Gordimer
(b. 1923)
Writer

She was born in the mining town of Springs, near Johannesburg, the daughter of a Lithuanian watchmaker who had emigrated to South Africa and an English mother. As a small girl she was a keen dancer and later a great reader. Her literary success began in 1952 with the publication of her second volume of short stories, "The Soft Voice of the Serpent and Other Stories". Her novels and short stories, written in English and very much in the European literary tradition, are inseparably bound up with her country. They are not sensational; the sorrows of the world are not loudly proclaimed and there is no attempt to lecture her readers. But in her quiet understated way she conveys the disunity and the conflict known as apartheid ("The Conservationist", 1974) and raises the question of a white commitment to reform ("Burger's Daughter", 1979). She does not describe the policy itself but shows the effect of the policy on people, their life under apartheid, the guilt feelings of white liberals, the penetration of the all-powerful ideology of racial discrimination into all aspects of life. She is thus in the same tradition as other South African writers such as Alan Paton, Athol Fugard, Breyten Breytenbach, André Brink and John Coetzee.

Although she was persecuted by the censorship and some of her books were banned she remained in South Africa. She has sometimes been blamed for staying there and for the fact that she joined the ANC only after the ban on it was lifted.

Nadine Gordimer has won many literary prizes for her work, including the Italian Malaperte Prize, the German Nelly Sachs Prize, the Scottish Arts Council's Neil Gunn Fellowship, the French Grand Aigle d'Or and the Benson Medal of the Royal Society of Literature. In 1991 she was awarded the Nobel Prize for Literature.

She completed her eleventh novel, "None to Accompany Me", at the end of 1994. This centres on the loneliness of exiles returning to South Africa, the mistrust, the old loyalties and the unfulfilled expectations.

F.W. de Klerk
(b. 1936)
Politician

With his historic speech in Parliament on February 2nd 1990 State President de Klerk, the "Gorbachev of Africa", astonished his country and the whole world. He announced three important decisions: the unbanning of the African National Congress (see Baedeker Special, p. 30), the Pan-Africanist Congress and the South African Communist Party; the release of Nelson Mandela and other political prisoners; and the introduction of full voting rights for non-white population groups. The speech was the beginning of the end for apartheid.

De Klerk, the son of an old-established conservative family of South African politicians, was born in Johannesburg. After studying law he married Marike Willemse, a convinced supporter of the apartheid regime, in 1959. He became a member of the National Party, which had been in power since 1948, and in 1972 he was elected to the all-white South African Parliament. In 1978 he became minister of postal services and telecommunications, and later minister of home affairs and of education.

In the late eighties South Africa was internationally isolated and the economy was crippled by sanctions. State President Botha had lost the confidence of his government and resigned as leader of the National Party in February 1989 and as President in August of that year. He was succeeded in both posts by de Klerk, who took office as President on August 15th 1989. Until then de Klerk had been regarded at best as a mediator between the Verligte, the more open-minded members of the National Party, and the Verkrampte, the rigid supporters of apartheid. In his early months in office he had spoken of a "softly, softly" approach and a cautious rapprochement and had had a number of preliminary discussions with Nelson Mandela, who was still a prisoner; but there had been nothing to suggest a major change of policy. In the meantime the de Klerk family hit the headlines in a domestic capacity when Marike de Klerk forbade her son to marry a coloured girl.

In the 1990 election de Klerk presented himself as a reformer, outlining a picture of a "new South Africa" – though at first few people really believed in his transformation.

The new parliamentary session began on February 2nd, when de Klerk caused a sensation with his opening speech. He reduced the powerful influence wielded by the army and the police and repealed 46 apartheid laws; then in December negotiations began between the government and 19 organisations, mainly black. In March 1992 he held a referendum of the white population on his policy. Over 85% of those eligible voted, and of these 68.7% voted in favour of the continuance of the policy of reform.

The peace process was overshadowed by a wave of violence, which the police and the security forces did little to control. After a massacre of ANC members in June 1992 the ANC broke off negotiations and called a general strike. Up to this point de Klerk had remained silent, but now he was compelled to act. Although he disclaimed any personal responsibility, he was prepared to concede that there had been inappropriate behaviour by individual members of the security forces. In the end a number of them were discharged, giving an indirect confirmation of the complaints that had been made.

On December 10th 1993 de Klerk and Nelson Mandela were jointly awarded the Nobel Peace Prize for their work in bringing about a peaceful end to the apartheid regime – a bold decision at a time when the peace process was still far from complete. South Africa's first free election was held on April 27th 1994, and de Klerk became one of the two deputies to President Mandela in the government of national unity, representing the 5 million whites on whom the country still depends. His declared aim for the second election to be held in 1999 is to enter the new Parliament as the country's second strongest political force.

The history of South Africa in the late 19th century was dominated by two men: Cecil Rhodes (see below), prime minister of the Cape Colony, and his opponent Paul Kruger, President of the Transvaal, popularly known as Oom Paul (Uncle Paul).

Paul Kruger
(1825–1904)
Politician

Kruger was born in Vaalbank, near Colesberg in Cape Province. The founder of the family, a German named Jacob Krüger or Kröger, had come to the Cape in 1713 as a mercenary in the service of the Dutch East India Company. Paul Kruger was an authentic voortrekker who as a boy had taken part in the Great Trek to Natal (1834–40) and in 1848 moved to the western Transvaal. He distinguished himself in the battle of Vegkop, when Ndebele warriors attacked a voortrekker encampment.

In 1864 he became commandant-general of the Boer republic of the Transvaal, which had become self-governing in 1852. Under his leadership the Transvaal and the Orange Free State, the second self-governing Boer republic, rebelled against British rule and in 1881 achieved independence. In 1883 Kruger was elected President of the Transvaal. He was an ardent nationalist and a strict Calvinist, and this led him to compare the history of the Boers with that of the Israelites: a view influential in the rising Boer nationalist movement. Kruger resolutely resisted British attempts to reincorporate the gold-rich Transvaal in the colonial Empire. In 1895 Cecil Rhodes planned a rising by the uitlanders of Johannesburg, who after the discovery of gold on the Witwatersrand had flocked to the area in large numbers, with the object of overthrowing the Transvaal government and incorporating the territory in the Empire. The rebels were to have the support of a British force of 660 men waiting on the frontier, led by a close confidant of Rhodes's, Dr Leander Starr Jameson. The "Jameson Raid" was a failure, and after suffering heavy losses the invading force was compelled to surrender to the Boers (December 29th 1895–January 2nd 1896). Britain then resorted to stronger measures, stationing troops on the frontiers of the two Boer republics and disseminating anti-Boer propaganda claiming voting rights for uitlanders in the Transvaal and the Orange Free State. Kruger offered to negotiate but was rebuffed; then on October 9th 1899 sent Britain an ultimatum calling for the withdrawal of British forces from his frontiers within 48 hours. The time limit expired with no response, and on October 11th Kruger declared war on Britain. When during the Boer War (1899–1902) Kruger realised that defeat was certain he handed over his office to his Vice-President and travelled to Europe in October 1900, seeking in vain for support from Germany and other European states. He never returned

Famous People

to South Africa, and died in Switzerland on July 14th 1904. His body was returned to Pretoria for burial.

Kruger National Park Krugerrand

Kruger's name is associated with two South African institutions, the Kruger National Park and the Krugerrand. In 1898 Paul Kruger, a great nature-lover all his life, established the Sabie Nature Reserve to protect the once rich animal life of the area, and this was later enlarged to become the Kruger National Park. The Krugerrand is a South African gold coin, first minted in 1967, containing one troy ounce of fine gold. Originally popular with investors, it was later displaced, as a result of the apartheid policy, by similar coins such as the Canadian Maple leaf, the Australian Nugget, the Chinese Panda and the American Eagle.

Miriam Makeba (b. 1932) Singer

Miriam (originally Zenzile) Makeba, the "empress of South African song", is one of the best known and most respected representatives of the anti-apartheid movement. Born in Prospect, near Johannesburg, she became a trained nurse. In 1957, at the age of 27, she appeared in the film "Come Back, Africa", which was shot in Sophiatown, a black suburb of Johannesburg, later razed to the ground to make way for the white residential district of Triomf. Her rejection of the apartheid regime, clearly manifested in the film, led to her expulsion from South Africa. Her exile began in the United States, where, promoted by Harry Belafonte and other impresarios, she won international fame with her songs "Pata Pata", "West Winds" and the "Click Song". In 1968 she married the black American civil rights activist Stokely Carmichael and later the musician Hugh Masekela. For a time she represented Guinea, to which she had found her way in the eighties, as a special envoy at the United Nations. In 1987 she made a triumphant comeback on Paul Simon's Graceland tour. In the same year the American writer James Hall published a book on Miriam Makeba, now the best known singer in South Africa. In Hall's book she describes her life, her career as a singer and her fight against apartheid. She has now returned to live in South Africa.

Nelson Rolihlahla Mandela (b. 1918) Politician

Nelson Mandela, for long regarded by the South African government as Public Enemy No. 1, spent more than a quarter of a century behind South African bars as prisoner No. 0221141011. Then, after South Africa's first free election (and the first election in which he himself had ever voted), he became the first black President of South Africa. Mandela, whose original first name Rolihlahla literally means "pulling the branch of a tree", but colloquially means "troublemaker", was born in Mvezo, a tiny village in the district of Umtata, capital of the Transkei. His father was a chief and the principal adviser to Jongintaba, king of the Thembu, a Xhosa tribe. When he was deprived of his chieftainship as a result of a dispute Rolihlahla and his mother moved to Qunu, a nearby village where they would have the support of friends and relations. On the boy's first day at school he was given the "civilised" name of Nelson. After the death of his father the young Mandela's education, sponsored by Jongintaba, continued at the village primary school, the Clarkebury Institute, the Wesleyan College and the University of Fort Hare, which until 1960 was the only higher educational institution for blacks in South Africa. After taking part in student protests he was sent down from the university. To escape a traditional marriage which was planned for him he fled to Johannesburg, where he worked in a lawyer's office, studying law in the evenings by correspondence, first at the University of South Africa and then at the University of the Witwatersrand. In 1943 he marched in support of the Alexandra bus boycott, a protest against the raising of fares. "This campaign had a great effect on me. In a small way I had departed from my role as an observer and become a partici- pant" (Mandela, in his autobiography, "Long Walk to Freedom"). His politicisation could not be dated to any particular point in time: it was the result of "a steady accumulation of a thousand slights, a thousand indignities and a thousand unremembered moments" which "produced in me an anger, a rebelliousness, a desire to fight the system that imprisoned my people". In 1944 he joined the African National Congress (see Baedeker Special, p. 30), and along with Walter Sisulu, Oliver Tambo and others founded the ANC's Youth League.

In 1952 Mandela and Tambo established the first black legal practice in South Africa. Mandela, as a resolute opponent of apartheid, soon became a symbolic figure to the oppressed black majority. After his call for non-violent contravention of the race laws in 1952 the government banned him from all political activity, but he continued to be active in the ANC. Between 1956 and 1961 he was put on trial for high treason but was acquitted.

On June 14th 1958 he married as his second wife Winnie Nomzamo Madikizela (see below), a black social worker. After the Sharpeville massacre in 1961 the ANC was banned, and Mandela went under- ground. From there he organised a three-day general strike, which was bloodily repressed. For Mandela, as for others, this marked the end of the phase of non-violent resistance, and he founded the military wing of the ANC, Umkhonto we Sizwe ("Spear of the Nation"), which carried out sabotage operations against the apartheid regime. In 1962 Man- dela was again arrested, accused of terrorism, attempted revolution and communist activities and sentenced to five years in prison. He was thus already in prison when he and other co-accused were given life sentences in the Rivonia Trial in 1964. He spent most of his time in prison on Robben Island, a small island in Table Bay which became a kind of study centre, while Mandela became the world's most famous political prisoner, the subject of campaigns for his release not only in South Africa but round the world.

In 1985 President Botha made a speech in Parliament offering Man- dela his freedom subject to certain conditions which Mandela rejected: there was no freedom, he said, under apartheid.

Then on February 11th 1990, responding to both internal and exter- nal pressures, President F. W. de Klerk announced the release of Man- dela after 28 years in prison. Thereafter these two men, de Klerk and Mandela (at first Vice-President of the ANC, now unbanned, and from July 1991 its President), worked together for the abolition of apartheid, the creation of a democratic state and the reconciliation of all South Africans. For their efforts they were jointly awarded the Nobel Peace Prize in December 1993. Mandela thus became South Africa's third black Nobel prizewinner, after Albert Luthuli (c. 1898–1967; Zulu chief and from 1952 President of ANC; Nobel Prize 1962) and Desmond Tutu (see below). The ANC emerged from the 1994 election as the strongest party in Parliament, and on May 10th 1994 Nelson Mandela succeeded de Klerk to become South Africa's first black President.

Famous People

Winnie Mandela
(b. 1934)
Civil rights
activist

Winnie Mandela, born Nomzamo Winnifred Madikizela in Bizana, Transkei, became popular within South Africa and outside it mainly because she was the wife of Nelson Mandela. Like her husband, whom she married in 1958, she belongs to the chiefly family of the Thembu tribe. She was named Winnifred by her father, a Wagner enthusiast. After training at the Jan Hofmeyer of Social Work in Johannesburg she became South Africa's first black social worker. In 1958 she became an active member of the African National Congress. While her husband was in prison she made a name for herself – internationally as well as in South Africa – as an uncompromising opponent of the apartheid regime, continuing her husband's struggle on her own account. She spent some time in prison, and between 1976 and 1985 was banished to the remote township of Brandfort in the Orange Free State after becoming head of a parents' association during the Soweto school children's uprising of 1976. After her return to Soweto the "Mother of the Nation" (Mama Wetu), as she was called by her supporters, was frequently involved in rather dubious incidents and increasingly lost the sympathy and support of the black population and the ANC. The release of her husband in February 1990 enabled her to make a brilliant comeback, but in May 1991 she was again in trouble. At the beginning of 1989 a 13-year-old boy named James "Stompie" Moeketsi Seipei, known as the "Little General" of an army of children in the Tumahole district of Soweto, was tortured and killed by her bodyguard. She was brought to trial, accused of abduction and of being accessory to torture and sentenced to six years in prison, but was then released on bail. In November 1992 she resigned all her positions in the ANC to avoid further damage to its image. In spite of this she remained extremely popular in Soweto, and indeed, with the help of the "Civics" (township associations), achieved a second political comeback when the Women's League of the ANC elected her as their President. In May 1994 President Mandela, who had separated from her "for personal reasons" in April 1992, appointed her deputy minister for art, culture, science and technology.

She continues, however, to be surrounded by controversy. She belongs to the populist left wing of the ANC, which finds its support among the young people and the poor of the townships, for whom the pace of change in South Africa is too slow, and which on occasion incites its supporters to action against the government (leading in one recent case to a split within the ANC Women's League). At the beginning of 1995 she was again under suspicion, when the government prosecution service accused her of corruption and embezzlement. Thereupon Nelson Mandela dismissed her from the government. In spite of all this, and in spite of the divorce in 1996, there are those who believe that Winnie Mandela has not given up her political ambitions. Only time will tell.

Mbongeni Ngema
(b. 1955)
Composer and
author

The composer, author, director and choreographer Mbongeni Ngema, born in Verulam, near Durban, in 1955, is one of South Africa's most popular black artists. His songs and musicals are not only part of contemporary black culture: travelling round the globe, they were also "ambassadors" of the oppressed majority of South Africa.

At the age of eleven Mbongeni Ngema, who had begun to play the guitar as a child, was separated from his parents and was brought up by relatives in a village in Zululand. He came to the theatre more or less by chance, standing in for an actor who had fallen ill in a production given in a gold-mine. Thereafter he devoted himself exclusively to the theatre, writing plays which were performed by amateur companies in churches and hospitals and on football pitches in the townships. He met Gibson Kente, the great black theatrical magician whose productions in the black settlements attracted enthusiastic audiences and who became one of Ngema's first teachers. He also discovered the classics of theatrical literature, Stanislavsky, Brook and Grotowski. With Percy Mtwa, a fellow actor, he created a

South African version of the New Testament, "Woza Albert!", which was performed in the legendary Market Theatre in Johannesburg and achieved international success. Ngema then formed his own company, Committed Artists, and wrote his next play, "Asinamali", on a theme taken from everyday life in South Africa, a rent strike in a township near Durban. This too was an international success: it was produced on Broadway and brought its author numerous prizes as well as the first nomination for the Tony Award for his work as a composer, choreographer and director.

The next production was "Sarafina", his first musical, the subject of which was the schoolchildren's rising in Soweto. It played on Broadway for two years, toured America for a further two years and finally was made into a film, starring Whoopi Goldberg and Leleti Khumalo (now Ngema's wife). A second production had to be put together for a European tour, with its premiere in the Vienna Festival in 1989. "Sarafina" was followed in 1990 by the musical "Township Fever", the subject matter of which was again provided by political developments in South Africa, in this case one of the largest and most effective strikes in the history of the country.

His most recent production is "Magic at 4 – the Music of Freedom", which has also been performed abroad. Its co-producer was Mannie Manim Productions, in collaboration with the Vienna Festival and the Ludwigsburg Palace Festival. "Magic at 4" is a musical about the conflicts in a society which is just coming into existence and a song of hope for peaceful co-existence.

The modern history of South Africa began in 1652 with the foundation of Cape Town by Jan Anthoniszoon van Riebeeck.

Van Riebeeck was born in the little town of Culemborg, to the east of Rotterdam, and, like his father, went to sea. At the age of 16 he accompanied his father on voyages to Greenland and Brazil, and in 1639 entered the service of the Dutch East India Company as a clerk. He soon rose to become a merchant, but in 1647 was called back to Holland, suspected of having traded for his own profit in Japan. By chance he was in one of the five ships – the "Coninck van Polen" – which brought the surviving crew members and the cargo of the wrecked "Nieuw Haerlem" (see History and Baedeker Special, p. 158) back to Holland. When the East India Company decided to establish a supply base on the Cape of Good Hope van Riebeeck volunteered his services and was accepted. In offering to go to the Cape he had only one object in mind – to return to the East. Barely two weeks after his arrival at the Cape he reminded his superiors of this; but in fact he was to remain at the Cape for ten years.

On April 6th 1652 two of his fleet of five ships anchored in the fine natural harbour of Table Bay; the others arrived later. In addition to his wife and four-month-old son he had with him ninety men, women and children. His instructions from the East India Company were explicit: he was not to found a colony, merely to establish a supply base for ships sailing to the East Indies, with a fort to defend it. Van Riebeeck's people set to work at once and built a fort, a supply station, a hospital and accommodation for voyagers to the East Indies. In order to ensure the food supply of the settlement of Kaapstad (Cape Town) van Riebeeck put a proposal to the directors of the East India Company for granting land to "free burghers" who would cultivate the land and sell their produce to the Company at fixed prices. The Company took some time to consider the proposal but finally agreed. This marked a change in European policy in Africa. It was no longer a matter of governing and exploiting the native population: instead European settlers set out to conquer land and make a new home for themselves. Under van Riebeeck's rule there were two important developments. Tensions between the settlers and the native population of Hottentots, and after bloody fighting the Hottentots withdrew into the interior of the country. The other development was the introduction of slavery: from 1657 onwards slaves were brought in from East Africa, Madagascar, India

Jan van Riebeeck
(1619–77)
Merchant

and Indonesia to work for the settlers. When van Riebeeck left the Cape on board the "Mars" on May 7th 1662 to take up a new appointment as commandant at Malacca in the Far East Kaapstad was a little town with four streets and some 200 white inhabitants.

Cecil Rhodes
(1853–1902)
Politician

The principal opponent of "Oom Paul" (Paul Kruger: see above), President of the Transvaal, was Cecil John Rhodes – British South African diamond king, statesman, protagonist of British imperialism, "representative of God and of the devil" (Mark Twain) and "rogue of genius" (Robert Rotberg).

Rhodes was born in Bishop's Stortford (Hertfordshire), the son of a clergyman. In 1870 his parents sent him to live on his brother's farm in Natal to cure a serious lung infection. In the 1870s he returned for a time to England to study law in Oxford. Then from 1878 onwards he acquired a considerable fortune in the diamond business in Kimberley, and in 1880 established the De Beers Consolidated Mines Company (see Baedeker Special, p. 272).

Rhodes was not only a shrewd businessman but a ruthless practitioner of power politics. Determined to make his dream of travelling from the Cape to Cairo by sleeping car a reality, he instigated the conquest of Bechuanaland (now Botswana) in 1884. Then in 1889 he established the British South Africa Company, with a royal charter, which subsequently acquired the territories of Northern and Southern Rhodesia (now Zambia and Zimbabwe), so named in Rhodes's honour in 1895. He then turned his attention to the Boer republics, intent on incorporating the Transvaal and the Orange Free State in a British colonial empire extending from the Cape to the Mediterranean. Here chance came to his aid: gold was discovered on the Witwatersrand, in the Transvaal near Johannesburg. The lure of gold drew many British prospectors, who in due course claimed the right to vote in their new country. When the Boers refused Rhodes, who had become prime minister of the Cape Colony in 1890, mobilised against the Boer republics and whipped up opinion against them in the South African press. He also planned a rebellion by the uitlanders (foreigners) in the Transvaal, aided by a British force commanded by his friend Dr Leander Starr Jameson. The "Jameson Raid" was abortive, and Jameson's men were compelled to surrender to the Boers. After this fiasco Rhodes resigned as prime minister.

During the Boer War Rhodes took part in the defence of Kimberley in 1899–1900. His prospects of recovering the premiership of the Cape Colony were now good, but shortly before the end of the war he died in Muizenberg (now part of Cape Town). He left most of his fortune to Oxford (Rhodes House) for the establishment of Rhodes scholarships.

Shaka
(c. 1789–1828)
Zulu chief

Every year thousands of Zulus, wearing traditional costume and armed with spears and shields, assemble in the little town of Stanger, 68km/42 miles north of Durban, on September 22nd, the anniversary of the death of Shaka, the legendary Zulu king and "black Napoleon of South Africa".

Shaka (or Chaka) was born about 1789, the son of a Zulu chief named Senzangakona. Like other Zulu boys, he herded his father's sheep from the age of six; and when, one day, one of his sheep was killed by a wild dog, he and his mother were disowned by his father. Becoming the butt of other children's jokes, Shaka is said as a result to have conceived a burning desire to gain fame and power. Serving under Dingiswayo, chief of the Mtetwa, he rose from the ranks to become commander of one of the chief's regiments. After his father's death in 1815 Dingiswayo helped him to become chief of the Zulus, then a small people, and after Dingiswayo's death he also became chief of the Mtetwa. Within a very short time Shaka managed to weld more than a hundred fragmented Zulu tribes into a powerful Zulu nation, rigidly centralised both politically and militarily, and thus establish an auto-cratic military monarchy headed by himself. New forms of military technology contributed to the success of his campaigns of conquest. One of his innovations, for example, was the assegai, a short stabbing weapon which was more effective in hand-to-hand combat than the traditional long-shafted throwing spear. He organised his subjects in groups of 1000 men and women, who lived in camps while training for his campaigns. He also introduced a new attacking tactic, drawing up his forces in a half-moon formation, with experienced and battle-tried warriors in the centre and younger men on the flanks to encircle the enemy. His impis (regiments) now rapidly defeated and conquered the neighbouring tribes. Shaka's wars and the ruthless cruelty of his rule led to the mass migrations of population known to the Sotho as the Difaqane and to the Zulus as the Mfecane (see History and Quotations; a ten-part television series co-produced by the South African state television corporation, "Shaka Zulu", depicted these events). In 1824 Shaka established friendly contacts with Europeans in what is now Durban, but he now increasingly developed into a bloodthirsty despot. When his mother died in 1827 he compelled the whole Zulu people to take part in gruesome funeral ceremonies. He also tried to get rid of the traditional tribal council and extend his own power. On September 25th 1828 he was murdered by his half-brothers Dingane and Mhlan-gane on the spot now marked by his gravestone, to which thousands of Zulus make the pilgrimage once a year to do honour to the man who made them a people of proud warriors.

Joe Slovo, chairman of the South African Communist Party, was for decades the bitterest enemy of the apartheid regime. To supporters of the regime he was the "red devil", the "wire-puller of terrorism"; but to the black population of South Africa he was a loved and respected figure.

Joe Slovo
(1926–95)
Politician

Joe Slovo was born in a Jewish ghetto in Lithuania. When he was nine his family emigrated to South Africa, and at the age of sixteen he became a member of the South African Communist Party. During the Second World War he fought on the Allied side in North Africa. After the banning of the African National Congress in 1960 he played a major part in building up the military wing of the ANC, Umkhonto we Sizwe (Spear of the Nation: see Baedeker Special, p. 30). In 1963 he went into exile in Mozambique, where he continued to work for the ANC and the Communist Party. In 1977 he established an ANC operations centre in Maputo, capital of Mozambique. In 1982 his wife Ruth First, a writer as well as a politician like himself, was killed in Maputo by a letter bomb, probably intended for him. In 1985 he became the first white man on the ANC executive. In 1986 he was appointed general secretary of the South African Communist Party, a post which he resigned in 1991 on learning that he had cancer. At the first meeting between leaders of the ANC and President de Klerk and other government representatives in 1990 he surprised the government side by his moderation and readi-ness to compromise. He was the originator of the proposal to enshrine in the constitution a time-limited coalition of the main parties in a government of national unity. That he still held to his communist ideals, however, was made clear by the red socks which he ostenta-tiously wore at the meeting.

Slovo was no rigid dogmatist. In his political essay "Has Socialism Failed?" he took a critical look at communism, and he once admitted in an interview that in his visits to Moscow he failed to understand the political situation in the Soviet Union. After the first free election in April 1994 he became minister of housing, and contrived, after lengthy negotiations, to persuade the banks to support housing development with huge credits and to grant loans to developers who could offer no security: a necessary precondition for the success of the new government's housing policy. In December 1994 President Mandela presented him with the Isithwalandwe order, the ANC's highest distinction. On January 6th 1995 he died of cancer of the bone-marrow in his home in Johannesburg. He was probably the only white man to be loved and respected by South Africa's poorest blacks, and dozens of black settlements in South Africa are named after him (e.g. Slovo Park).

J. R. R. Tolkien
(1892–1973)
Writer

J. R. R. Tolkien, whose fantastic stories made him a cult figure in the "hippie generation" of the late 1960s, was born in the South African town of Bloemfontein but moved to England in 1896. After studying at Oxford and taking part in the First World War he taught at various British universities. From 1920 to 1925 he taught English in Leeds, and from 1925 to 1959 was professor of Germanic philology and literature at Oxford. Inspired by his study of Old and Middle English and Celtic and Germanic myths, he wrote novels as well as scholarly works ("Beowulf", 1936). In "The Hobbit" (1937), originally conceived as a children's book, an introduction to the world of the Anglo-Saxon and Nordic sagas, he created a realm of fantasy inhabited by human-like creatures with a language of their own. In the trilogy "The Lord of the Rings" (1954–55), which brought him an international reputation, he developed the story of the Hobbits still further. The three books describe, in the style of old legendary stories, the fantasy world of Middle Earth with its struggle between good and evil. Although Tolkien claimed that his trilogy was a "historical report", it was frequently seen as a utopian or allegorical work. It became a cult book among young people and inspired the fantasy literature which proliferated in the seventies and eighties.

Tolkien died in Bournemouth (Hampshire) on September 2nd 1973. Five years after his death "The Lord of the Rings" reached wide cinema audiences as an animated cartoon film.

Desmond Tutu
(b. 1931)
former Archbishop

Desmond Tutu was born in the mining town of Klerksdorp (Transvaal), where his father, a Xhosa, taught in a Methodist primary school. Although Tutu was baptised as a Methodist he was brought up as an Anglican, his parents having changed to that church. After studying at the University of Johannesburg he became a teacher in a high school in 1954. In 1957 he gave up his profession in protest against government legislation which put black students at a disadvantage compared to whites, entered the Redemptorist order and trained as a priest in St Peter's Theological College in Johannesburg. After further theological studies at King's College in London (1962–66) he taught in the Federal Theological Seminary in Alice (Eastern Cape) from 1967 to 1969 and at the National University of Lesotho in 1970–71. From 1972 to 1974, back in England, he was assistant director of the Theological Educational Fund of the World Council of Churches in Bromley (Kent). He returned to South Africa in 1975 as Dean of Johannesburg, and in the following year became Bishop of Lesotho. In May 1976 he hit the headlines when he wrote an open letter condemning President Vorster's government for the bloody repression of the Soweto uprising. As secretary-general of the South African Council of Churches (1979–84) he publicly denounced the policy of apartheid and called on the international community to impose sanctions. Twice the government withdrew his passport. His fight against apartheid endeared him to the black population of South Africa and won him wide recognition abroad. He received a number of honorary doctorates and prizes, and in 1984 was awarded the Nobel Peace Prize for his non-violent opposition to the apartheid regime. In November 1984 he became Anglican Bishop of Johannesburg, the first black to hold the post, and two years later Archbishop of Cape Town and head of the Anglican Church of South Africa. In 1987 he was elected President of the All Africa Conference of Churches.

The political maxim of this valiant churchman was mediation. He sought to put an end to apartheid by negotiation, combined with international sanctions, and he strove also to mediate between the rival black groups which were increasingly ready to resort to violence. When President de Klerk lifted the ban on the ANC and released Nelson Mandela from prison Tutu at first withdrew from politics, but soon afterwards returned to his role as a mediator when conflicts between ANC and Inkatha supporters endangered the process of democratisation and the election planned for April 1994. After the ANC's victory in the election and the end of apartheid Tutu again returned to his place in the pulpit. He retired in 1996.

Art and Culture

Bushman Drawings, Folk Art and Fine Art

Bushman drawings

The earliest works of art in South Africa are the rock paintings and engravings of the Bushmen (San). The origins of this old-established people of hunters and gatherers are unknown, as are the origins of their art. Some of their drawings may be as much as 30,000 years old, ranking them among the oldest in the world (see Baedeker Special, p. 92).

The drawings are found at thousands of sites, often in caves, over a wide area extending from the Limpopo to the Cape (see map, p. 51). Drawings on sandstone or granite are mostly to be found in hilly regions and river valleys, engravings or incised drawings in open country. Usually they are in remote areas and difficult of access, and subject to damage by weathering, vandalism and ignorance. All Bushman drawings are protected national monuments. They are particularly numerous in the eastern and north-eastern Cape and the southern Drakensberg, varying in style from region to region. In one cave in the Giant's Castle Game Reserve (see Drakensberg) alone there are over 700 rock drawings of animals. Later the Bushmen, confronted by European settlers advancing from the south and the Bantu peoples moving in from the north-west, withdrew into the inhospitable Kalahari. Copies of their art can be seen in various museums.

The rock drawings are difficult to date, since for religious reasons the Bushmen stuck to particular themes and to their particular artistic canon. They may date from prehistoric times or may be only a few centuries old. The more recent drawings can be dated more accurately, since they depict Europeans and the animals they brought in.

Folk art

Lydenburg head

Until a few years ago the policy of apartheid and the cultural boycott, with different aims, produced the same result: the false impression that though there is important tribal art in West and Central Africa there is little or none in South Africa. With the purchase and the return of collections from abroad a rich tradition has been revealed in woodcarving and the making of glass beads. Since the early nineties three South African museums in particular have displayed fine collections of woodcarving (mostly elegant everyday objects – head supports, spoons, pots, staffs, etc.) and glass beads: the Johannesburg Art Gallery (Brenthurst and Horstmann collections), the National Gallery in Cape Town (glass beads from the Eastern Cape and a collection of traditional art acquired from the United States in 1994–95) and the museum in Ulundi (KwaZulu/Natal), with a collection of Zulu glass beads.

Some notable works of art, such as the Lydenburg heads (richly decorated terracotta heads of about A.D. 1500; now in South African Museum, Cape Town, but seldom on display), show that South African history did not begin with the arrival of white settlers, as until recently South African schoolbooks maintained.

History of
folk art

African art is mainly of religious origin. The commonest forms of expression are figures of ancestors, spirits and animals and fetishes, together with sacred vessels and symbols of rank and dignity (staffs, sceptres, pipes, fly-whisks). Sculpture served as a medium for establishing contact with the world of spirits: it had to be so beautiful that the spirit liked it and agreed to dwell within it. The spirit then became involved in human life and granted fertility, wealth, children, advice or protection. It was the same with animal figures or a fetish, an object

South African Museum, Cape Town

enriched with magical substances and consecrated by the medicine-man which protected a supplicant in all conceivable situations. Masks gave visible and palpable form to the souls of the dead and the various protective spirits and enabled mythic events to be re-enacted. Both ancestor figures and masks were consecrated, and when the initiate donned the mask the divine force entered into him. Among the favourite materials used were wood, worked with a hatchet or a knife, which in the climate of South Africa was particularly perishable, and clay, which was only lightly fired and was therefore fragile.

Other techniques and materials, too, have a long tradition behind them, and are still used in the manufacture of typical craft products in some parts of the country. Among them are pottery, basketwork and woven fabrics with particular decorative techniques, woodcarving, leatherware and wrought-iron. Great attention was, and to some extent still is, paid to personal adornments, hair-styles and dress. Clothing in particular was elaborately ornamented with embroidery, dyes, appliqués and openwork decoration.

The Zulus and Ndebele in particular are famed for their imaginative and decorative beadwork. The beads were originally made from a mixture of clay and goat's milk, pierced with holes and dried. Later they were made from grass, animal hairs or string. From the 17th century Portuguese traders brought in coloured glass beads. Over the centuries the women developed patterns formed, depending on the method of threading, of horizontal, vertical or diagonal lines.

Beadwork

The richly coloured art of the Ndebele, which finds expression in wall painting, beadwork and garments, has become widely known outside South Africa through various exhibitions and publications. The geometric patterns and symbols painted on the walls of the forecourt of a

Ndebele art

Bushman Drawings

In James Uys's film "The Gods Must be Crazy" a group of San (the scientific name for Bushmen) try to get rid of what they see as an important product of civilisation, a cola bottle fallen from the sky which has given rise only to hatred and envy among them. Unfortunately the life of the San in this promising satirical production (South Africa, 1980) serves merely as a background for a lively comedy of love and action of no great depth. In two later sequels, numbered II and III, the San are still no more than stage properties in comedies of very similar type. One good thing about these three light entertainment films, however, was that they drew the attention of cinemagoers in Europe, the United States and elsewhere to the existence of this people, now threatened with extinction, to whom South Africa and the world owe important treasures of art.

It is now generally accepted by scholars that the 3000 rock drawings in South Africa (see map, p. 52), Lesotho, Zimbabwe and Namibia were the work of the San.

The San were hunters and gatherers who were thoroughly familiar with the characteristics and habits of animals. The depiction of mammals, particularly the larger ones such as the eland, was a central theme of their paintings. Representations of human figures, depicted either naked or clad in elaborate robes, were equally common. Some can be identified as men, others as women; differences in physique can also be distinguished. It is notable, however, that whereas the animals are usually depicted realistically the human figures are stylised: the artists were concerned with their actions and movements rather than with their personal characteristics. The San are seen hunting and gathering to gain their subsistence, dancing and taking part in ritual ceremonies, enjoying peaceful family life, engaged in conflict within their own group or with another group, encountering Khoikhoi tribes, other black peoples and white settlers, and riding (a practice taken over from the whites).

All these works of art are relatively small: the figures are seldom more than about 30cm/1ft high, and only two life-size representations of human figures are known.

Unfortunately there is no satisfactory method of establishing the age of most of the rock drawings. Since the pigments used in the paintings are mostly of mineral origin and thus millions of years old, radiocarbon dating methods are of little help. Recently some success has been achieved by bombarding the patina with atomic particles. A painted stone from Namibia is believed to be about 28,000 years old, while paintings in the south-western Cape depicting horses and encounters with whites show that this art was still being practised in the 19th century. Some white settlers who had shot a Bushman found a bag on his belt containing ten different pigments, some metallic and some from plants, together with a mixture of quicklime and animal blood.

It is believed that most of the surviving drawings and paintings date from the last 2000 years. Unfortunately almost all of them, apart from those now preserved in museums, are exposed to weathering (by rain, wind or pressures within the rock), and some have been destroyed by vandals.

The generally accepted view is that the rock pictures were the work of medicine-men (shamans) in a state of trance. An important ritual practice of the Bushmen was to dance themselves into a trance, which was believed to liberate supernatural forces. It is the function of the medicine-man, shaman or invoker of spirits (half the men and a third of the women) to take in these forces in their trance so as to protect the San from the powers of darkness, cure the sick and settle conflicts.

While in a state of trance – that is, during his stay in the world of spirits – the shaman experiences physical and visual hallucinations. He feels that he is changing into various animal forms, that he is being killed by some other person, and so on. The shamans used to express the experiences they had undergone in their trance in the form of images. The rock paintings are thus a symbolic and metaphorical form of art which seeks to represent not immediate reality but rather trance states and the world of spirits, gods and ancestors. The origin of the name Bushman which is applied to the San is not certainly established. In the 17th century the Dutch term *bosjesman* or *bossieman* meant a deserter or a bandit, a vagrant living in the bush. The name seems to have been applied at an early stage to certain native tribes. The San are naturally small – hardly any of them are more than 1.60m/5ft 3in. in height – and yellow-skinned. They have high cheekbones and slit eyes: reason enough for the Dutch to equate them with Chinese and name one of their territories Chinafeld.

Anthropologists believe that the San are related to the Khoikhoi (Hottentots). There are two accounts by travellers explaining the origin of the term Hottentot: they reported that on encountering white men the natives danced, sang and pronounced the word "Hottentot". Probably all these tribes were originally hunters and gatherers; then the Khoikhoi took to nomadic stockherding, with longhorn cattle and fat-tailed sheep. The Khoikhoi ("men of all men", the term applied by the Hottentots to themselves) called all those who continued to live by hunting and gathering (that is, the Bushmen) San. Modern anthropology also refers to these tribes as Khoikhoi and San. The terms Khoisan, covering both tribes, reflects the linguistic and ethnic relationship (in morphology, phonetics and the use of click sounds) between the dialects of the San and the Khoikhoi.

There is no agreed view about the origins of these peoples, the oldest known inhabitants of South Africa. It is supposed that they moved from the north of Botswana into southern Africa; but it is not known when or why they did so. When the Dutch first landed in South Africa in the early 17th century the San and the Khoikhoi occupied the whole coastal region between Namibia and the present-day town of East London. Since they were shy and peaceable peoples – the "harmless people", as they are called by the anthropologist Elizabeth Marshall – and preferred to avoid all confrontations, the Bushmen withdrew ever farther into the inhospitable Kalahari Desert in face of the incomers, both white and black, who were pushing forward into their territory. The Khoikhoi either died out or were absorbed into other population groups.

Small numbers of San have survived into our own time in the Kalahari and one or two areas in Namibia. In quite recent years some Bushmen have also settled in the Swartberg, in the privately owned Kagga Kamma Nature Reserve. The reserve, which belongs to a Paarl wine-producer, lies 260km/160 miles north of Cape Town and can be visited (accommodation available; address PO Box 7143, North Paarl 7623, tel. 02211/63 83 34). Like their ancestors, the San live by hunting and gathering. The women look for edible tubers, berries and water, while the men hunt both big game and small. Their principal weapons are bows strung with animal tendons and poisoned arrows. The San live in small family groups; there are no larger units. Apart from hunting dogs they have no domestic animals. Their dwellings are grass huts, each with its own hearth.

Their principal divinity is Kaggen, a cunning character who appears in many forms, from an eland to a vulture. San legends describe him variously as stupid or wise, benevolent or a tormenting spirit.

The future of this people is very uncertain. They seem likely to succumb to the advance of civilisation and disappear for ever. All that will then remain of them will be their rock drawings, perhaps a few nature films describing their way of life – and the film comedies mentioned at the beginning of this section.

house can be seen in the Ndebele settlement area north-east of Pretoria. The mineral pigments originally used gave place from 1945 onwards to synthetic paints. The forms and colours of the Ndebele painters were taken over by the contemporary artist Esther Mahlangu, whose work has been exhibited in Washington and Paris. On the occasion of the 75th anniversary of the BMW automobile firm she painted a BMW in Ndebele style (see Baedeker Special, p. 356).

The applied art of Afrikaans-speaking whites finds expression mainly in their architecture (see below), furniture and silverware. Furniture and domestic utensils can best be seen in the Cultural History Museum and at Groot Constantia in Cape Town. Since its rebuilding in 1995 the Cultural History Museum in Pretoria, whose strong point is white domestic culture, has extended its displays. In Pretoria and many small towns there are museum houses illustrating the way of life of the Afrikaners.

Fine art

So far South Africa has produced no artist of international standing. For many years South African art was confined to traditional forms. Landscape painting, for example, was popular and much practised, beginning with the early paintings of the Cape by Thomas Bowler (1812–69) and Thomas Baines (1820–75). Among the best known names in the first half of the 20th century were Jacob Hendrik Pierneef (1886–1957) and Irma Stern (1904–66), whose work is displayed in a museum of her own in Cape Town, with portraits and views. She and Maggie Laubser (1886–1973), who had both studied in Weimar and Berlin, brought modern art trends to South Africa.

A good overview of the increasingly "political" art of recent years can be had in the National Gallery in Cape Town and the Johannesburg Art Gallery. Many other museums, for example in Pretoria and Stellenbosch, have good collections of South African art.

There are numerous private galleries, though only a few of them offer work of outstanding quality. The object of the Biennale, a large art exhibition held for the first time in Johannesburg in 1995, is to re-establish the link – interrupted in recent years – between the art of South Africa and the rest of the world.

The best collections of European art are in the Johannesburg Art Gallery and, in Cape Town, in the William Fehr Collection (Rust-en-Vreugd, Castle of Good Hope) and the Old Town House.

Until the early nineties the art of black South Africans was neglected. After decades of the Eurocentric purchasing policies of the large museums and private collections (of which there are several of some importance in South Africa) there were large gaps to be filled, and the resultant demand drove up prices. Among the artists who have been rediscovered are Gerard Sekoto (1913–93), the "father of township art", who died in exile in Paris, and Ernest Macoba (b. 1910). Township art developed in the late fifties and sixties in the overcrowded suburbs of South African cities. Young black artists produced expressive representational works, mainly scenes of everyday life. This art found admirers outside South Africa and is now well represented in museums, art galleries and private collections.

In recent years sculptors from the north, particularly from Venda, have attracted much attention. Jackson Hlungwani produces powerful large-scale sculpture in wood on mystical and Christian themes. Frequently the boundary between the colourful paintings of black artists, with a leaning towards naïve art, and "airport art" (designed for tourists, and largely consisting of derivative work produced on a mass scale), is a fairly fluid one.

The largest collection of black art is to be seen in the museum of Fort Hare University, remotely situated in Alice (Eastern Cape), where most of the leading black politicians of southern Africa were students.

Films and Photography

South Africa was one of the first countries in the world to make films and to have cinemas. Its first feature film was produced in 1905 and its first cinemas opened in Johannesburg and Durban in 1905, followed soon afterwards by a travelling cinema. War reporters filmed some of the battles in the Boer War. South Africa appeals to film-makers with its highly developed infrastructure, variety of scenery, well known authors and competent technicians; and yet the quality of its output falls short of film productions in West and North Africa. The reasons for this seem to be the long established system of state subsidies for the making of films, the censorship under apartheid and the absence of a film culture. Like the political life and culture of South Africa, its film industry is in process of radical change. There are problems and different production methods and markets for both whites (English- or Afrikaans-speaking) and blacks.

The market is dominated by two cinema chains, offering correspondingly little variety. South African films are rarely shown. The "Weekly Mail" runs an annual film festival in Johannesburg (Market Theatre) and Cape Town (Labia and Baxter Cinemas), with European

Films

95

and African films, and also provides a platform for "alternative" South African films. Feature films of good quality have been more frequently shown on television since the end of the apartheid regime. Private television services in South Africa, in particular the M-Net subscription channel, have contributed to the growth of the South African film industry.

Among commercially successful films of some quality have been productions by Jamie Uys ("The Gods Must Be Crazy": see Baedeker Special, p. 90) and film versions of books by Athol Fugard (who himself appeared in "The Road to Mecca") and Alan Paton. Anant Singh (producer) and Darrell Roodt (director) have produced a number of feature films in recent years which have been both of good quality and commercially successful ("Sarafina"). Many foreign anti-apartheid films (e.g. "Cry Freedom") were devoted to the resistance movement, frequently from an over-simplified foreign white liberal point of view. Two township films by young German/South African film-makers, such as Oliver Schmitz's "Mapantsula" and Michael Hammon's "Wheels and Deals", caught the atmosphere more tellingly, skilfully combining politics, gangsterdom, everyday life and humour. They were shown in South Africa only after achieving international acclaim. One of the leading documentary film-makers is Jürgen Schadeberg ("Have You Seen Drum Lately?", "Voices from Robben Island"), who brings to life the history and atmosphere of the 1950s.

Photography

Jürgen Schadeberg was also the leading photographer of the fifties. He worked for "The Drum", a periodical mainly read by blacks, on which the best black photographers of the next generation learned their trade. Schadeberg's photographs, which have been published in volume form, depict the atmosphere and culture of black South Africa before the wave of oppression. Schadeberg, Magubane and David Goldblatt were among the pioneers of the earlier period. A new generation of young photographers was marked by the unrest in the townships, in which some of the best of them were killed. Among South African photographers with an international reputation are Paul Weinberg and Steve Hilton-Barber, the latter of whom has worked in the remoter country regions of black South Africa. There are regular exhibitions of photography in the large Bensusan Museum of Photography within Museum Africa, Johannesburg.

Architecture

There is no distinctively South African architecture, since native traditions have been ignored and buildings and styles from Europe and America taken as models. The "Cape Dutch" style, fine examples of which are to be seen in Stellenbosch, Paarl, Franschhoek and Tulbagh, near Cape Town, as well as in Cape Town itself, was likewise based on a foreign model. The houses are built on a compact, symmetrical and rectangular plan, usually in the form of a T, H or U. Characteristic features are the thick whitewashed walls, curving gable and large square hall entered from a raised veranda extending along the whole length of the house. The roof was originally thatched, but in the mid 18th century pitched roofs gave place to flat roofs (e.g. in Rust-en-Vreugh House in Cape Town).

Towards the end of the 18th century two European artists came to Cape Town to work for the Dutch East India Company. Anton Anreith (1754–1822), a skilled German sculptor and woodcarver, arrived in South Africa in 1776; examples of his work include the pulpit of the Groote Kerk in Cape Town and the pediment frieze on the wine-cellar at Groot Constantia. Louis-Michel Thibault (1750–1815), who came to South Africa in 1783 as a military engineer with the French occupation forces, designed Groot Constantia and the Koopmans-De Wet House in

A fine example of Cape Dutch architecture on a wine estate near Tulbagh

Cape Town. They both followed the Cape Dutch tradition, though refining it with new ideas and new features.

After South Africa became a British colony the Georgian style gradually established itself in Cape Town, to be followed by the more ornate and exuberant style of the Victorian period. Towards the end of the 19th century the discovery of gold and diamonds drew many foreign architects to South Africa.

The dominant figure in the late 19th and early 20th century was Sir Herbert Baker (1862–1946), the architect favoured by Cecil Rhodes, for whom he built Groote Schur (1890) in traditional Cape Dutch style. Among the best known of his other buildings are the Rhodes Memorial in Cape Town (1905–08), Government House (1905 onwards), the Railway Station (1908) and the Union Buildings (1910–13) in Pretoria, and the Supreme Court in Johannesburg (1911). J. M. Solomon, one of his successors, designed the campus of the University in Cape Town.

From 1925 onwards South African architecture was much influenced by foreign trends, in particular the "International" style with its asymmetrical layouts, simple cubic forms, horizontally articulated façades, white facing and absence of ornament. Examples of this style include Munro House in Pretoria (McIntosh, 1932) and Harris House (Hanson, Tomkin and Finkelstein, 1933) and Casa Bedo (Cowin and Ellis, 1936) in Johannesburg. In layout they are reminiscent of Mies van der Rohe, with their wide eaves and hipped roofs of Herbert Baker and Frank Lloyd Wright. The Casa Bedo provided a model followed by many houses over the next twenty years.

The influence of Louis Kahn (1901–74) and the American school is predominant in contemporary South African architecture. The skylines of the great South African cities, with their office blocks and other modern buildings, are like those of cities in the western world. Among the most impressive of these new buildings are the Carlton Centre (Skidmore, Owings and Merrill, 1966–72), the Standard Bank (Philip

Dowson, 1971) and the Diamond Building (Helmut Jahn, 1984) in Johannesburg.

South African Literature

Even before Nadine Gordimer (see Famous People) was awarded the Nobel Prize for literature in 1991 books by South African authors were to be found in bookshops all over the world. An indication of the range of talent in South Africa was the feeling among many people familiar with South African literature that other writers such as John Coetzee (b. 1940), André Brink (b. 1935) and Breyten Breytenbach (b. 1939) were at least equally worthy of the prize. In the early days of apartheid Alan Paton's novel "Cry, the Beloved Country" (1948; filmed for the second time in 1995) had drawn the world's attention to the racial discrimination practised in South Africa. Until the publication of Nelson Mandela's autobiography ("Long Walk to Freedom") in 1994 it was the biggest seller in South African publishing history. The novels of Alan Paton (1903–88) as well as his political role mark him out as one of the great South African liberals.

English-language literature in South Africa is much divided. There are writers in exile, like Alex Guma and Christopher Hope, others who, like Gordimer, Coetzee and Brink, stayed in South Africa and others again, like Don Mattera and Wally Serote, who returned from exile, bringing with them the scars and the experiences of both worlds. Another division is between "white" and "black" writing. In recent years the quest for a common South African identity has begun. Meanwhile the world has learned to judge South African literature by aesthetic as well as political standards.

Still older are the poems and legends of the Khoisan (see Facts and Figures, Population) and their depiction of the conquest of South Africa by Europeans, which were recorded for the first time by the German philologist Wilhelm Bleek (1827–75), one of the founders of African studies ("Comparative Grammar of South African Languages", 1862–69).

African Literature

The black peoples of South Africa originally had no written languages and transmitted their epic poems orally. The first written documents in African languages were produced by two missionaries, Bishop J. W. Colenso (1841–83) and Robert Moffat (1795–1883), who translated various texts for mission schools from English into Zulu and Tswana. The Xhosa priest and writer Tiyo Soga (1829–71) translated Bunyan's "Pilgrim's Progress" (1866), the first work of world literature in Xhosa. In addition to his own writings, based on African models, he produced a grammar of the Xhosa language.

After further translations of world literature and against the background of the national movement which had recently come into being Thomas Mofolo (1875–1948) published his historical novel "Chaka" (1910; see Famous People, Shaka, and Quotations). He and the Zulu scholar Benedict Wallet Vilakazi (1906–47) are thus the front runners in the development of an independent black literature. Many works by black writers have been translated into English.

The writings of Sol T. Plaatjes (1876–1932) were also politically motivated. He sought to depict for European readers the consequences of the Natives Land Act of 1913 on his black fellow-countrymen. This inspired a literature of social realism and protest, mainly in English. Among important representatives of this trend are R. R. R. Dhlomo (1906–71), H. I. E. Dhlomo and Modikwe Dikobes (b. 1913; "The Marabi Dance", written 1946, published 1973). P. Abrahams and E. Mphahlele depicted in their works life in the overcrowded city slums.

The "African Drum" (later simply the "Drum"), a magazine financed by
white opponents of apartheid, began to appear in 1951. It published
mainly short stories, and sought to promote African literature by various means, including regular literary competitions (for which in 1957
alone it received no fewer than 1600 entries). At first its main themes
were African folk traditions and the problems of farmers; but this was
not to the taste of the magazine's mainly urban readership and, in a
change of policy, the "Drum" went in for cover girls, dealt with such
subjects as gang warfare in the townships and crime and published
articles on the blacks in the United States and on jazz. This change was
gradually also reflected in the short stories it published. They were
now set in the cities rather than the country, and the treatment was
lighter. The "Drum"'s final breakthrough came when it began to publish political articles: a change of direction which also influenced the
choice of the literary works it published. Soon all the progressive
forces in South Africa were gathered under its banner, including Eze-
kiel (later spelt Es'skia) Mphahlele, Bessie Head, Bloke Mdisane, Nat
Nakasa, Lewis Nkosi, the satirist Caesey Motsisi and the musicians
Todd Matshikiza, Hugh Masekela and Miriam Makeba. The stories
were concerned with everyday life in the townships and depicted the
living conditions of blacks under apartheid, but also dealt with conflicts
between different population groups and with criminals, alcoholics,
etc.

In the late fifties and early sixties the political situation in South
Africa worsened, and this was again reflected in the literature of the
time. Many writers now left the country and others were banned from
writing or persecuted for their political commitment and compelled to
flee. Many exiled black writers published autobiographies describing
the conditions which had led them to leave South Africa and their
experiences in exile. Among them were Peter Abrahams ("Tell Freedom", 1954), Mphahlele ("Down Second Avenue", 1959; "The Wanderers"), Bloke Modisane ("Blame Me on History", 1963), Alfred
Hutchinson ("Road to Ghana", 1960), Todd Matshikiza ("Chocolates
for my Wife", 1961), Noni Jabavu ("Drawn in Colour", 1960; "The
Ochre People", 1963) and Albert Luthuli, who was awarded the Nobel
Peace Prize in 1962. The exodus of writers — a fate they shared with
artists and intellectuals — led to a separation between literature in exile
and literature in South Africa.

Alex La Guma, a writer who was a representative of the ANC, wrote
novels and short stories while in exile, all concerned with the problems
of South Africa ("A Walk in the Night", 1962; "Time of the Butcher-
bird", 1979). Denis Brutus, who campaigned for the exclusion of South
Africa from the Olympic Games, published volumes of poetry ("Sirens,
Knuckles and Boots", 1963; "Letters to Martha and Other Poems from
a South African Prison", 1968). Keorapetse Kgositsile, leaving South
Africa in 1960, joined the Black Power movement in the United States, a
move which is reflected in his poetry. Bessie Head, who went into exile
in Botswana in 1963, published novels and short stories based on the
story of her own life ("When Rain Clouds Gather", 1969; "Serowe,
Village of the Rainwind" (1981) and recorded much material that had
previously been handed down orally ("The Collector of Treasures",
1977: see Quotations).

In South Africa itself there was at first the silence of the grave. Then
in the 1970s the growth of the Black Consciousness movement was
reflected in the literature of the period. Instead of the earlier strident
literature, sometimes criticised as mere "agitprop", works were now
produced which criticised life in South Africa and political conditions in
a more restrained, more personal and more indirect way. A volume of
poems by Oswald Mbuyiseni Mtshali, "Sounds of a Cowhide Drum"
(1971), sold over 16,000 copies in a year and encouraged others to
write poetry. There followed poems by Mongane Wally Serote (b.
1944), Sipho Sepamla, James Matthews and Mafika Gwala.

The violent repression of the schoolchildren's protest in Soweto in June 1976 aroused enormous horror and indignation, but it also gave a new impulse to literature. Many black writers seized on the theme, producing poems, short stories, short plays and essays which were published in the magazine "Staffrider" (founded in 1978) and by various newly established publishing houses. Numbers of novels were also devoted to the theme: Miriam Tlali's "Amandla", Sipho Sepamla's "A Ride on the Whirlwind", Mbulelo Mzamane's trilogy "The Children of Soweto", the anthology "One Day in June" and works by Matshikiza, Modisane, Don Mattera, Ahmat Dangor and Farouk Asvat.

In the eighties apartheid and the living and working conditions of the black population were still important themes, treated in short stories and autobiographies: e.g. Miriam Tlali's "Murial at Metropolitan", Ellen Kuzwayo's "Call Me Woman" (1985), Don Mattera's "Memory is the Weapon", Godfrey Moloi's "My Life", the autobiography of Maggie Resha, a member of the ANC (1992), and Nelson Mandela's autobiography ("Long Walk to Freedom", 1994).

COSAW

The multi-racial Congress of South African Writers (COSAW), which has close links with the ANC, was founded in 1987 and by 1993 had around 1000 active members, among the best known of whom is Nadine Gordimer. An important objective of the Congress, in addition to the promotion of literacy in the population, is the support and encouragement of young writers (to which the Congress's own publishing house, Cosaw Publishing, also contributes).

The three oldest and best known opposition publishing firms in South Africa are David Philip, now concentrating on the reappraisal of history, the Ravan Press (founder of the magazine "Staffrider") and Skotaville Publishers, which until 1993 was the only black publishing house in South Africa. These last two regard the education of the black population as their main field of activity, publish many children's books, schoolbooks and textbooks, and take part in discussions on the school curriculum, schoolbooks and manuals.

Afrikaans Literature

Afrikaans became a written language only in 1875. The first literary works were produced after the Boer War, which had led to an upsurge of national feeling. The predominant themes were the historical experiences of the Afrikaners and the assertion of their identity as a people. Among the pioneers were J. F. E. Celliers, C. Louis Leipholdt (1840–1947) and C. J. Langenhoven (1873–1932), author of the South African national anthem, "Die Stem" (see Quotations). In the 1930s doubts about the traditional values of the Boers (Eugene N. Marais, 1871–1936; Toon van den Heever, 1894–1956) and irony and humour (C. J. Langenhoven; J. van Melle, 1887–1953) found their way for the first time into Afrikaans prose literature. The Dertiger group ("Men of the Thirties") explicitly broke free of the limitations of nationalist and religious themes and brought about a renewal of literature in Afrikaans. Among the most importamt representatives of this group were the brothers W. E. G. Louw and N. P. van Wyk Louw (1906–70; "Dias", 1952; "Germanicus", 1956), M. U. Krige (1910–87; "Alle paaie gaan na Rome", 1949) and Izak David du Plessis (1900–81). Thereafter D. J. Opperman (1914–85). P. Blum and Ingrid Jonker (1933–65) brought fresh life to the imagery and content of Afrikaans literature. S. V. Petersen (1914–87; "Die Kinder van Kain", 1960; "Suiderkruis", 1965) depicted for the first time the social and political situation of the coloureds in South Africa.

In the early sixties the Sestiger, a group of liberal writers, gave Afrikaans literature new impulses. At first the group tended to be concerned with literary innovation and were influenced by European and American models. In the seventies writers began to give expression to criticisms of the ruling structures of the apartheid society – as English-language writers had long done. Important authors in this period included André Brink and Breyten Breytenbach (see below), Etienne Leroux (b. 1922), Elsa Joubert, John Miles, Koos Prinsloo (b. 1957), Adam Small, the first black political author writing in Afrikaans, and Dalene Mathee (b. 1935).

The climate for Afrikaans literature has improved markedly in the last few years with the end of censorship, new literary prizes, the "self-liberation" of many Afrikaners and a proliferation of new translations of Afrikaans novels into European languages and of European classics into Afrikaans. A more important factor is the new view of Afrikaans, even within the ANC, as an African language and a language of liberation rather than of oppression.

The leading Afrikaans poet, Breyten Breytenbach (b. 1939; "A Season in Paradise", 1977) continues to live in exile in Paris. For many people he was a symbol of resistance to attacks on freedom and imagination, and his arrest and imprisonment in 1975, accused of "terrorism", was seen by a generation of writers, whose leading spirit he was, as a signal for turning away from their state, the "poisoned paradise". The novelist and literary scholar André Brink (b. 1935) said, like Athol Fugard, that he would "dry up" without his South African milieu. A stay in Paris converted him from the son of a conservative Boer family into a rebel. He became the third Afrikaans literary troublemaker (after Breytenbach and Coetzee) and was put forward half a dozen times for the Nobel Prize for literature. Among his best-known novels are "A Dry White Season" (film, 1989), "The Wall of the Plague", "The Ambassador", "On the Contrary" and "Rumours of Rain". Like J. M. Coetzee (see below), Brink teaches literature at Cape Town University.

Literature in English

Only a few representatives of English-language literature in South Africa can be mentioned here. The first was Lady Anne Barnard (1750–1825), who depicted in her diaries and letters life in the Cape Province under British rule. Thomas Pringle (1789–1834; "African Sketches", 1834), a Scot, wrote works of social criticism in prose and verse. The first South African novel was written by Olive Schreiner (1855–1920), the daughter of a German missionary and an English mother, who regarded herself as one of the earliest South Africans. In her novel "The Story of an African Farm", published in 1883 under the pseudonym Ralph Iron, she described life in the Karoo. The dog stories of Sir Percy Fitzpatrick (1862–1931) in "Jock of the Bushveld" (1907), written on the basis of his own experiences, were immensely popular. Race problems were taken as a literary theme for the first time in the novels of Sarah Gertrude Millin (1899–1968; "The Dark River", 1919; "God's Stepchildren", 1924). Finally South African literature made its international breakthrough with Alan Paton (1903–88) and his novel "Cry, the Beloved Country" (1948), an attack on the inhuman apartheid laws. The best known woman writer is undoubtedly Nadine Gordimer (see Famous People), who has been writing for over fifty years, producing novels, short stories and essays. In her short stories she depicts the consequences of apartheid and a society in process of radical change.

J. M. Coetzee (b. 1940; "Waiting for the Barbarians", "In the Heart of the Country", "Life and Times of Michael K": see Quotations), another of South Africa's leading authors, is a difficult writer, an unwavering prophet of the Apocalypse. He depicts the reality of life in South Africa as surreal and absurd; most of his characters are awkward, unheroic and inadequate.

Wilbur Smith (b. 1933), who lives in Cape Town and in the Seychelles, is an enormously successful author who makes no claim to produce great literature. The 24 novels he has published so far have sold more than 60 million copies. His tales of adventure and love are frequently set in South Africa.

Less known outside South Africa are such writers as Peter Wilhelm (b. 1943), Rose Zwi, Lionel Abrahams (b. 1928) and Stephen Gray (b. 1941). Abrahams and Gray are also critics and editors. Another notable South African writer, active particularly as a dramatist, is Athol Fugard (see below).

Music, Theatre, Dance

South African theatre, jazz, ethnopop and contemporary dance developed under the shadow of the cultural boycott of the apartheid regime, largely unknown to the outside world, but with the lifting of the boycott has now triumphantly appeared on the world's stages. In the jazz bars and art galleries of Johannesburg and Cape Town white, black and coloured South Africans met naturally and uninhibitedly, at a time when that was still unusual, and thus contributed to the revolutionary change in South African society. The characteristic features of South African theatre and music are its unrestrained energy and zest for life. The combination of African verve, rhythm and physical control with "European" discipline and technique created works of art which have increasingly attracted attention in the West.

The great change that took place between 1990 and 1995 affected not only politics, society and the economy but also South African art. Theories, art forms, organisation, finance and international links all underwent radical change. After years of cultural emptiness and aridity, the result of the international boycott and of a rigid and often absurd censorship, international superstars were once again seen in

Dorothy Masuke   *Abdullah Ibrahim*

Kippie's: the mecca of jazz fans in Johannesburg

South Africa, and also – what was of greater significance for the country's discovery of itself as part of Africa – the great musicians of the continent such as Manu Dibango and Salif Keita. The singer Miriam Makeba (see Famous People), the pianist Abdullah Ibrahim (Dollar Brand) and the trumpeter Hugh Masekela returned after long years of exile, while others remained for the moment in their new home countries, like the writer Breyten Breytenbach, the painter Gerard Sekoto (d. 1993) and the actor Anthony Sher. Almost all of them, however, acknowledged their South African roots.

The National Arts Festival held annually in June/July in the remote university town of Grahamstown – perhaps the largest festival of the kind after the Edinburgh Festival – brings together all the leading figures in the South African arts: theatre and cabaret, opera, jazz, dance, art exhibitions. Here South African theatre and art are displayed in a range, a concentration and a quality to be found nowhere else. During the ten days of the festival the little town is so overcrowded that accommodation must be booked long in advance.
    The Roodepoort International Eisteddfod (singing and dance) is held in alternate years in Roodepoort, near Johannesburg.

Art festivals

South African tunes and singers are well known from Africa to Europe, even though those who hear them often do not know where they come from. Ethnopop (pop based on tribal music) and jazz in particular have achieved international success. Musicians like Johnny Clegg (see Famous People) resisted the apartheid regime after their own fashion. Music, said Clegg, had pushed back boundaries; it was a purifying force.
    South Africa was and is one of the world's great jazz nations. It is said that more jazz records per head of population are sold in South Africa

Ethnopop and jazz

than anywhere else in the world. The influence of township rhythms is unmistakable, as is the sound of the penny whistle which was popular in the 1950s. Alongside veterans such as Miriam Makeba, the "empress of African song", the equally famous singer Dorothy Masuka and the African Jazz Pioneers, the traditional group of the earlier generation, younger groups now came to the fore, achieving their international breakthrough in the mid nineties. Among them are the Bayete group, much influenced by Zulu music, and Tananas, who combine many different styles and musical traditions. Some young musicians, among them the saxophonist McCoy Mrubata and the percussionists Vusi Khumalo and Lulu Gontsana, frequently perform in Europe. Even before the return of Abdullah Ibrahim – ranked in the jazz reference books as Africa's leading jazz musician – Cape Town had developed its own jazz and musical scene, with such figures as the saxophonist Winston Mankunku and Basil "Mannenberg" Coetzee. There too were formed marimba bands such as Amampondo, playing Xhosa music, the traditional sounds of the Eastern Cape.

Bayete are not the only group influenced by Zulu music. Several groups and individual musicians inspired by Zulu traditions and sometimes developing them into ethnopop have achieved great international success, like the Ladysmith Black Mambazo group (which became known in Europe and America through their contribution to the "Graceland" album of the American pop star Paul Simon), Mahlathini and the Mahotella Queens, who sing without instrumental accompaniment. A superstar who is particularly popular in France is Johnny Clegg (see Famous People), the "white Zulu", who performed with Juluka, South Africa's first mixed-race band, and later with Savuka, combining strong rhythms with catchy tunes. Clegg is more frequently to be seen and heard in Europe than in South Africa, though he continues to live in Johannesburg. Little known to white South Africans but familiar to blacks in the beer halls are the Soul Brothers, David Masondo and Moses Ngwenya, whose delicate and tuneful music has sold more than ten million records. They sing in Zulu of beautiful women, street gangs, conflicts in the community but above all of love. After buying back the copyright of their own music they founded the first record company run exclusively by blacks. Another musician influenced by Zulu traditions is the reggae singer Lucky Dube, whose reputation stands high even in the Caribbean homeland of reggae.

Jazz bars

These various groups can be heard in numerous jazz bars, particularly in Johannesburg, the cultural heart of South Africa. An old-established centre is Kippie's, in the Market Theatre complex, named after the saxophonist Kippie Moeketsi. There are also many new bars in the Yeoville, Melville, Rosebank and Orange Grove districts.

Cape Town's jazz bars are in the port quarter, the Waterfront, though here jazz tends to be played as background music to a meal. In the Observatory student quarter and on Long Street there are many cosy little jazz bars. For information about times and places consult the "Weekly Mail".

A wide range of CDs and cassettes is available, and many songs and musicians of the 1950s are being reissued. Good South African jazz and ethnopop, however, is – apart from successful groups such as Mango Groove and Savuka, with Johnny Clegg – not always easy to find: many white South Africans are ignorant of or indifferent to the "black" culture of their country, and this is frequently reflected in "white" shops.

Alongside the groups mentioned there are popular musicians producing rather shallow "township bubblegum": for example Yvonne Chaka Chaka and Brenda Fassie, who are among the most popular singers in Africa.

In South Africa more frequently than elsewhere music and dancing feature in theatrical performances. The musicals "Sarafina" (1988), which ran for more than a year on Broadway and was made into a film, with Whoopi Goldberg, and "Township Fever", by the composer Mbongeni Ngema (see Famous People), drew the attention of the outside world to the injustice and oppression of the apartheid regime with its rousing music and emotional content.

After many years during which South African theatres, in particular Johannesburg's Market Theatre, were dominated by protest drama, there was a return in the nineties to classic European plays. Innovative attempts were made to reconcile Europe and Africa. A notable feature was the collaboration between William Kentridge, one of South Africa's leading artists, and the Handspring Puppet Company which brought Büchner's "Woyzeck" and Goethe's "Faust" Part II to southern Africa in a combination of drama, puppet theatre, video film and music.
   South Africa's leading dramatist is Athol Fugard (b. 1932), who is, after Shakespeare, the playwright most frequently performed in the United States. "Time" judged him to be the greatest living dramatist writing in English. His plays for studio theatres – "The Island" (1974), "The Road to Mecca" (1985), "Bushman and Lena" (1969), etc. – are performed all over the world. Almost all of them are set in Athol Fugard's home area in the Eastern Cape and the Karoo steppeland and are yet timeless and independent of place. His works, reflecting his own experience, depict victims (often of racialism) and characters in despair. Many see his "Sizwe Bansi is Dead" (1973) as the inception of black protest theatre.

Another form of resistance in the theatre was political cabaret. A leading figure in this field, who has also had considerable success outside South Africa, is Pieter-Dirk Uys (b. 1945), who has an almost legendary reputation and the status of a licensed jester. In his assumed character as Evita Bezuidenhout, the "most celebrated white South African woman", he freely criticises anyone and everyone, both in the old and in the new government. Nelson Mandela has said that Uys helped to bring about the end of apartheid by the gentle but sharp mockery and wit which led to a change of heart in Afrikaans-speaking whites.

The centre of non-racist theatre and a meeting-place for intellectuals and artists was for many years the Market Theatre in Johannesburg. It stands in a complex (guarded by security men) which also includes Kippie's jazz bar, galleries, a flea market on Saturdays, Museum Africa, studios for the training of actors and artists, the headquarters of various artists' trade unions, the Dance Factory (contemporary dance) and a concert hall. It carried on the traditions of the Space Theatre in Cape Town (later closed), at which in the seventies many leading South African actors learned their trade. After the end of apartheid the Market Theatre lost its dominant position, at any rate for a time. By then the Municipal Theatre in Cape Town, better equipped financially and technically, had lost the stigma acquired during the apartheid period; and many whites, concerned about inner city crime, avoided the Market Theatre. In Cape Town too there was a changed relationship between the state-run Nico Malan Theatre with its opera house in the city centre, which until a few years ago was boycotted by blacks and coloureds, and the independent Baxter Theatre near the University. The reputation of the "Nico" owed a great deal to the work of Marthinus Basson, the country's most daring director, who put on notable productions, mainly of plays in Afrikaans. The Market and the Baxter, like numbers of other theatres, received no state subsidies under the apartheid regime. There are state-run theatres in the old provincial capitals of Durban, Pretoria and Bloemfontein and in Port Elizabeth.

Glossary of Geographical and Political Terms

Dance and ballet	There is an old and deeply rooted tradition of dance in South Africa, as in the rest of Africa. It began with tribal dances and the miners' "gum-boot dance", which are still danced, and not merely for the benefit of tourists. Cape Town University – the first university in the world to have a department of ballet – was one of the nurseries of dancers in leading British ballet companies, and some of the best dancers in Britain are still South Africans. In South Africa itself, however – in Pretoria and Cape Town – ballet stagnated because of the country's isolation. The distinguished choreographer John Cranko (1927–73) received his first training in Cape Town, but at the age of 19 he left South Africa. Before his death he directed that his works should be performed in South Africa only after apartheid was abolished. In 1990 his hope was fulfilled.
	Matters are very different with contemporary dance, which, after – and perhaps before – jazz, became in the mid nineties the most exciting form of stage entertainment. There was a veritable explosion of dance. In 1993 there were two dance festivals in South Africa, the annual Dance Umbrella in Johannesburg, held in February/March in the theatre of the Witwatersrand University, with around a hundred new productions, and the National Arts Festival in Grahamstown: in 1994 there were six. In Soweto alone there are between 300 and 400 dance groups. The leading dance groups – the Free Flight Dance Company and Moving into Dance of Johannesburg, for example – frequently perform in Europe. Perhaps even more markedly than the theatre, contemporary dance is a reflection of the nation's state of mind.
Opera	The first "African" opera, "Enoch, Prophet of God", was given its first performance in 1995 in the first African Opera Festival in Cape Town. The composer, Roelof Temmingh, and the librettist, Michael Williams, set out to produce an alternative to the classic European arts – opera, symphony, ballet – which were expensive to produce, particularly since the change of government led to a fresh look at the arrangements for state promotion of the arts; and they also believed that account should now be taken of the artistic interests of black South Africans. Michael Williams had previously created three short "African" operas. "Enoch" is based on an actual event in 1921, a battle between the police and a religious sect. The opera combines traditional African sounds with contemporary music and choral singing.
	Choral music has a long and rich tradition among black South Africans. Handel's "Messiah" has recently been translated into Zulu and performed. Black South Africana have also recently shown increased interest in classical music, previously confined to Johannesburg, Cape Town and Durban and their symphony orchestras. The Soweto String Orchestra also gives performances outside South Africa.

Glossary of Geographical and Political Terms

ACWU	African Commercial Workers' Union: the first black trade union in South Africa, established in 1922.
Afrikaans	The language of the Afrikaners; a variant form of Dutch.
Afrikaner	The Boers call themselves Afrikaners or Afrikanders. They are the descendants of the early Dutch and German settlers, who were mostly farmers (in Afrikaans *boeren*).

An association of extreme right-wing groups.	Afrikaner Volksfront
An ANC slogan: "Power is ours!".	Amandla ngawethu!
African National Congress: the best-known black political organisation in South Africa. See Baedeker Special, p. 30.	ANC
Racial segregation. See History.	Apartheid
African People's Organisation.	APO
Afrikaner Weerstandsbeweging (Afrikaner Resistance Movement), an extreme right-wing organisation founded by Eugene Terre'Blanche in 1973.	AWB
The name given to South Africa by blacks, after the Arabic name for the unexplored territory south of Zanzibar.	Azania
An organisation founded in 1978 which had close ties with the Pan-Africanist Congress (PAC), then banned.	Azanian People's Organisation
A member of the largest linguistic group in Africa, the Bantu speakers.	Bantu
See Homelands.	Bantustan
The old name of Lesotho.	Basutoland
Black Consciousness Movement, formed in the 1970s to promote political consciousness among black South Africans.	BCM
Meat dried and cured in the sun.	Biltong
The Afrikaners (in Afrikaans, "farmers"). The term is also applied to the police, specifically the security police.	Boers
Shop selling alcoholic liquor.	Bottle store
Grill, grilled meat; a barbecue party.	Braai, braaivleis
An Afrikaner secret society.	Broederbond
Convention for a Democratic South Africa: the first formal forum, set up in December 1991, for negotiations between the government, the ANC and other South African parties. Altogether 18 delegations took part in the negotiations.	CODESA
South Africans of mixed blood.	Coloureds
Congress of South African Trade Unions, formed in 1985 by non-racist unions, with a total membership of 1.2 million. It has staffing links with the ANC.	COSATU
Conservative Party, which split off from the National Party in 1982 under the leadership of Dr A. Treurnicht.	CP
Reservoir, artificial lake formed by a dam.	Dam
Democratic Party, formed in 1989 by the amalgamation of the PFP and other opposition groups.	DP
A lingua franca, a mingling of various Bantu languages, English and Afrikaans, mainly spoken by migrant workers in the South African mines.	Fanagalo

Glossary of Geographical and Political Terms

Fynbos	The characteristic vegetation of the south-western Cape.
Great Escarpment	The escarpment in which the central highlands fall down to the coastal plains.
Homelands	Reserves for the black peoples of South Africa, established under the apartheid regime; also called bantustans. See History, p. 64.
IFP	See Inkatha Freedom Party.
Indaba	Originally an assembly of Zulu chiefs; now also applied to political and other meetings.
Inkatha Freedom Party	A conservative party established in the former homeland of KwaZulu. See Famous People, Mangosuthu Gatsha Buthelezi.
Kaffir	A pejorative term (from Arabic *kafir*, "unbeliever") originally applied to Xhosa-speaking peoples in southern Africa, later also to other Bantu speakers.
Karoo	A geological formation taking in the periods designated Carboniferous to Permian in Europe. It covers most of southern Africa, including the Upper, Great and Little Karoo.
Kleurlinge	The Afrikaans term for coloureds (see above).
Khoisanids	The oldest known inhabitants of South Africa, the Khoikhoi (Hottentots) and Bushmen (San).
Kloof	Ravine (Afrikaans).
Koppie	A small hill.
Kraai	Strictly speaking an enclosure for livestock, which could also enclose fields and huts; also applied to a round village containing huts.
Laager	A close circular formation of ox-carts, a defensive structure used by the voortrekkers for protection against Zulu attacks.
LP	Labour Party, formed by the coloureds in 1902.
Mayibuye iAfrika!	An ANC slogan: "Come back, Africa!".
Mealie pap, millipap	A kind of maize porridge made with water or milk.
MK	See Umkhonto we Sizwe.
NACTU	National Council of Trade Unions: an association, formed in the 1960s, of trade unions sympathetic to the ideas of the Pan-Africanist Congress (PAC). It has some 400,000 members.
NEC	National Executive Committee.
NIC	Natal Indian Congress.
NP	National Party: a nationalist party, founded in 1912, which was in government continuously from 1948 to 1994.
Ompad	Afrikaans for a road diversion.
PAC	Pan-Africanist Congress: an organisation founded in 1959, when it broke away from the ANC, rejecting the ANC's multi-racial approach. It appealed mainly to young people. Its armed wing was the Azanian People's Liberation Army (APLA). The declared objective of the PAC was to break white predominance and establish a government African

in origin, socialist in content and democratic in form. The delegates abjured communism in all its forms and considered both whites and Indians as "foreign minority groups" or "aliens" who had no natural place in South Africa.

Sea-snails, which cling so firmly to the rock that they have to be broken off.	Perlemoen
Progressive Federal Party. Between 1961 and 1974, when Helen Suzman was its representative in Parliament, its parliamentary representation rose to seven. The PFP's objectives were to establish a National Congress and an integrated system of administration with universal, qualified voting rights. In 1988 it was absorbed into the newly established Democratic Party (DP).	PFP
An establishment providing overnight accommodation in nature and game reserves.	Rest camp
Afrikaans for river.	Rivier
A round hut with a conical roof; originally a Xhosa dwelling, now frequently applied to a holiday hut.	Rondavel
South African Broadcasting Corporation (state-controlled).	SABC
South African Confederation of Labour, established in 1956; represents only white members.	SACLA
South African Communist Party, founded in 1922.	SACP
South African Coloured People's Organisation.	SACPO
South African Police.	SAP
South African Congress of Trade Unions.	SACTU
South African Indian Congress.	SAIC
Nature healers or medicine men or women skilled in the use of herbs, who are much respected. After making a diagnosis they prescribe the right *muti* (traditional medicine).	Sangoma
A hut where drinking takes place (a term taken over from Ireland). Until the ban on the drinking of alcohol by blacks was lifted in 1993 the shebeens were illegal; the term is now applied to beer halls and clubs in the townships.	Shebeen
The South African barracuda (Afrikaans).	Snoek
Afrikaans for a shallow river.	Spruit
South West African People's Organisation.	SWAPO
Transitional Executive Council: an all-party body which governed South Africa in the last four months before the election in April 1944.	TEC
A district on the outskirts of a town inhabited by blacks, overcrowded and in consequence run-down.	Township
A "guerrilla dance" performed by blacks in demonstrations and other mass events.	Toyi-toyi

Glossary of Geographical and Political Terms

Tsotsi	A gangster or hooligan in the townships.
UDF	United Democratic Front: a democratic movement, founded in 1983, which was composed of over 600 anti-apartheid organisations and had close ties with the ANC.
Uitlanders	"Foreigners": an Afrikaans name for the whites, mostly English-speaking, who flocked to the Transvaal during the gold rush.
Umkhonto we Sizwe (MK)	"Spear of the Nation": the military wing of the ANC, established in 1961.
UWUSA	United Workers' Union of South Africa, founded in 1986, with a membership of some 270,000 Zulu workers.
Vlei	Marsh (Afrikaans)
Voortrekkers	Boers who went on the Great Trek of 1835, opening up the interior of South Africa.
Veld	An Afrikaans term for open country, usually open grassland.
Xhosa	One of the Nguni peoples. See Facts and Figures, Population.
ZAPU	Zimbabwe African People's Union.
Zulus	The Zulus are one of the largest of the Nguni peoples. See Facts and Figures, Population.

Quotations

The soil in the said valley is very good and fertile, and during the dry season it would be possible without difficulty to supply the gardens with as much water as was needed. Everything grows as well there as anywhere on earth. From daily experience we know what can be done at the Cape not only for the sick but also for the healthy among the ships' crews on their way to India, perhaps only with some sorrel or two or three cattle, for there is a sufficiency of everything there, including fish; and there are many hartebeests and steenboks. At certain times of year there are numbers of whales and seals. Beyond the Table Mountain and on its slopes there is timber in plenty . . .

Others will say that the natives are wild men and cannibals from whom no good can be expected and that we must be ever on our guard. But these are but frightening tales. It is true that some seamen and soldiers have been killed by them, but our people will always keep silent about the reason for that. Doubtless they killed our people when they had stolen their cattle and not because they wanted to eat them. If the fort that is to be built gets a good commandant who is well disposed to the natives and pays thankfully for all the goods he buys, then there will be nothing to fear.

From a report by Janszen to the Dutch East India Company dated July 26th 1649

*Leendert Janszen
Merchant
(1649)*

Mynheer Cloete took us into the wine-press hall; where the whole of our party made wry faces at the idea of drinking wine that had been pressed from the grapes by three pairs of black feet; but the certainty that the fermentation would carry off every polluted article settled that objection with me. What struck me most was the beautiful antique forms, perpetually changing and perpetually graceful, of the three bronze figures, half-naked, who were dancing in the wine-press and beating the drum (as it were) with their feet to some other instrument in perfect time. Of these presses there were four, with three slaves each. Into the first the grapes were tossed in large quantities, and the slaves danced on them softly, the wine running out from a hole at the bottom of the barrel, pure and clear – this was done to slow music. A quicker and stronger measure began when the same grapes were danced on over again. The third process gone through was that of passing the pulp and skins through a sieve, and this produced the richest wine of the three; but the different sorts were ultimately mixed together by Mynheer Cloete, who told us it has been the practice of his forefathers to keep them separate and sell them at different prices, but he found the wine was improved by mixing.

A visit to the wine-growing estate of Groot Constantia in the 1790s; from the diary of Lady Anne Barnard, wife of the secretary to Lord Macartney, governor of the Cape Colony. Quoted from Hugh Johnson's "The Story of Wine", Mitchell Beazley, London, 1989.

*Lady Anne
Barnard*

Nkosi Sikelel' iAfrika	God Bless Africa	
Nkosi, sikelel' iAfrika	Lord, bless Africa;	
Malupakam'upondo lwayo;	May her spirit rise high up;	
Yiva imitandazo yetu	Hear Thou our prayers	
Usisikelele.	And bless us.	

*God Bless Africa
Mankayi Sontonga
(1860–1904)*

Quotations

Yihla Moya, Yihla Moya,   Descend, O Spirit,
Yihla Moya Oyingewele.   Descend, O Holy Spirit.

Die Stem
Cornelius Jacob
Langenhofen
(1873–1932)

Uit die blou van onse hemel, uit die diepte van ons see,
Oor ons ewige gebergtes waar die kranse antwoord gee,
Deur ons vêr veriate viaktes met die kreun van ossewa –
Ruis die stem van ons geliefde, van ons land Suid-Afrika.
Ons sal antwoord op jou roepstem, ons sal offer wat iy vra:
Ons sal lewe, ons sal sterwe – ons vir jou, Suid-Afrika.

Out of the blue of our sky, out of the depth of our sea,
Out of our eternal mountains, where the echo resounds,
Where the creaking of the ox-wagons sounds far over the plain,
There is heard the much loved voice of our land, South Africa.
We shall obey thy call; we are there, ready for sacrifice.
We will live, we will die – always for thee, South Africa!

From 1938 to 1958 South Africa had two national anthems, "God Save
the King/Queen" and "Die Stem" ("The Voice"). From 1958 to 1994,
there was only one, "Die Stem". There are now again two, "God Bless
Africa" and "Die Stem".

Thomas Mofolo
(1876–1948)

Soon after the killing of the cowards Chaka sent an expedition southward. He finished off the remains of the Maqwabe, and then fought
with the Mafuze, Bathembu and the Machunu. Those were the first
nations to be scattered by Chaka with his combined forces, made up of
local and drafted foreign armies. He killed them without mercy and set
their villages alight together with their crops; but instead of returning
home with his enormous booty, he stopped there for several months.
While stationed there, he went on the rampage, slaughtering people,
while incorporating the young into his armies.

When he left there he continued south, crossing the Thukela, and he
scattered the Mabomvu and Bakwamachibisa. He had those peoples'
cattle driven homewards while he himself pressed on. By this time
there was often no need for him to fight because the people dreaded
him so that whenever they saw his armies advancing they immediately
ran away. Afterwards even the mere mention of his name was enough,
and whenever the alarm was raised that Chaka was on the march the
men would immediately forsake their villages and flee. His fame
spread far and wide: whenever there was a group of men the talk was
always about Chaka, in the courtyards the women's talk was about
Chaka, in the pasture grounds the herdboys' talk was about Chaka.

These nations which were fleeing from Chaka destroyed the weaker
ones who were in their way, took away their cattle and their sorghum –
everything. Other nations on the onward path, which had not yet heard
about Chaka, blocked the way and fought against the ones which were
fleeing from Chaka; that is to say that those who were running away
were attácked from all sides, by Chaka from the rear and, in front, by
the people of the country through which they were running. But since
they had to flee from Chaka, they joined together into a large army, and
they easily trampled over all the little nations which stood in their way,
venting their rage on them. All the nations joined in the stampede of
the southern flight, and they killed each other with such viciousness
that sometimes they waded through the blood of the slain. Often when
Chaka came upon the people he found them already broken, tame and
lacking the strength to fight, and he would simply finish them off.
Those whom Chaka killed with his armies were far outnumbered by the
victims of those fleeing from him. And that was the beginning of the
difaqane and of the wandering bands; it was through Chaka that these
things began.

From Thomas Mofolo's book "Chaka", first published in 1926 (though it existed in an earlier version by 1908); new English translation by Daniel P. Kunene, published by Heinemann, London, 1981.

As the railway lines spread and knotted and ramified all over Southern Africa, along them, at short distances of a few miles, sprang up little dorps that to a traveller appear as insignificant clusters of ugly buildings, but which are the centres of farming districts perhaps a couple of hundred miles across. They contain the station building, the post office, sometimes a hotel, but always a store.

Doris Lessing (b. 1919)

If one was looking for a symbol to express South Africa, the South Africa that was created by financiers and mine magnates, the South Africa which the old missionaries and explorers who charted the Dark Continent would be horrified to see, one would find it in the store. The store is everywhere. Drive ten miles from one and you come on the next; poke your head out of the railway carriage, and there it is; every mine has its store, and many farms.

It is always a low single-storeyed building divided into segments like a strip of chocolate, with grocery, butchery and bottle-store under one corrugated iron roof. It has a high dark wooden counter, and behind the counter shelves hold anything from distemper mixture to toothbrushes, all mixed together. There are a couple of racks holding cheap cotton dresses in brilliant colours, and perhaps a stack of shoe-boxes, or a glass case for cosmetics or sweets. There is the unmistakable smell, a smell compounded of varnish, dried blood from the killing yards behind, dried hides, dried fruit and strong yellow soap. Behind the counter is a Greek, or a Jew, or an Indian. Sometimes the children of this man, who is invariably hated by the whole district as a profiteer and an alien, are playing among the vegetables because the living quarters are just behind the shop.

For thousands of people up and down Southern Africa the store is the background to their childhood.

From "The Grass is Singing", Michael Joseph, London, 1950.

This is not Hendrik's home. No one is ancestral to the stone desert, no one but the insects, among whom myself, a thin black beetle with dummy wings who lays no eggs and blinks in the sun, a real puzzle to entomology. Hendrik's forebears in the olden days crisscrossed the desert with their flocks and their chattels, heading from A to B or from X to Y, sniffing for water, abandoning stragglers, making forced marches. Then one day fences began to go up – I speculate of course – men on horseback rode up and from shadowed faces issued invitations to stop and settle that might also have been orders and might have been threats, one does not know, and so one became a herdsman, and one's children after one, and one's women took in washing. Fascinating, this colonial history: I wonder whether a speculative history is possible, as a speculative philosophy, a speculative theology, and now, it would appear, a speculative entomology are possible, all sucked out of my thumb, to say nothing of the geography of the stone desert and animal husbandry. And economics: how am I to explain the economics of my existence, with its migraines and siestas, its ennui, its speculative languors, unless the sheep have something to eat (for this is not finally an insect farm); and what have I provided for them but stone and scrub? It must be the scrub that nourishes the sheep that nourish me, the bleached scrubgrass, the grey scrub-bushes, dreary to my eye but bursting with virtue and succulence to the sheep's. There is another great moment in colonial history: the first merino is lifted from shipboard, with block and tackle, in a canvas waistband, bleating with terror, unaware that this is the promised land where it will browse

J.M. Coetzee (b. 1940)

113

generation after generation on the nutritious scrub and provide the economic base for the presence of my father and myself in this lonely house where we kick our heels waiting for the wool to grow and gather about ourselves the remnants of the lost tribes of the Hottentots to be hewers of wood and drawers of water and shepherds and body-servants in perpetuity and where we are devoured by boredom and pull the wings off flies.

J. M. Coetzee, "In the Heart of the Country", Secker & Warburg, London, 1977

Sindiwe Magona
(born c. 1944)

"Wanted, coloured housemaid. Cleaning, no cooking. R30 p.m. Apply Astoria Restaurant, Cape Town." Thus read the advertisement. Un-deterred by not being coloured, my dire financial need giving me unaccustomed courage and making me glib of tongue, eager to please, I applied for the job. The interview was deliberately impressive; Mr Paporokolus, the owner of the posh Astoria, interviewed me himself. A man of few words – English words – he expressed his expectations in this simple manner – "No smoking, no drinking, no boy-friend. Polish floor, machine; Washing, machine. No cooking, *You*", pointing signi-ficantly at my person, "eat food from the Astoria. Thirty rand a month," he added expansively. With an expressive shrug of shoulder – accom-panied by spread hands, this tall, bony yet pleasing-looking gentleman delivered his "who in her sane mind could refuse such?" offer. I accepted with alacrity, aware that I was far from the only maid looking for a job. I would have accepted the job anyway; however, the obvious frills made it seem sent by heaven especially to me.

I was about to eat from the Astoria! . . .

How soon our blessings pale when the drudgery of toil, sweat and unrelieved long hours unmitigated by any appreciation, understand-ing or occasional word of kindness or praise begins to take its toll. Mrs Paporokolus, an immigrant like her husband, seemed to have chosen her new country because it answered a deep need within her being, struck a chord within her soul. She had heard that in South Africa the black people do not enjoy the protection of the law; that the workers, especially the domestic servants, were at the mercy of their employers . . . She had been bent on getting her money's worth from her servant, me . . .

It wasn't long before this lady had contradicted her husband on virtually every clause of the verbal contract we had agreed upon: NO – she did not want me to use the polisher. "Girls" scratched the legs of the furniture by letting the polisher bump against them. I went on all fours using a hand-brush to polish her already shiny floors. NO – the laundry was to be done by hand. The new Bendix, according to her husband the best and most expensive washing-machine then avail-able, was for her to use when between maids.

Yes, she wanted me in the kitchen at six o'clock so I could wake up the children at seven o'clock, at which time their freshly squeezed orange juice was to be ready, their lunches packed, their uniforms awaiting them in their dressing-rooms. Madam was not the least concerned that I, barely five or so years older than the children, had not left her kitchen the night before till the wee hours of the morning. The Astoria closed at midnight. As my food came with the Greek waiters who returned about 1am every night, that is when I had dinner. Also, my supper did not change for all the time I worked in this home. For years after I had left the employ of the Paporokoluses of the Astoria I could not eat curry. That is all the food I got out of the famous Astoria! Every night, for fifteen months. I lo–oo–ve curry, but . . .

From "To my Children's Children", published in South Africa in 1990; The Women's Press, London, 1991.

When I come into the world I am black;
When I grow up I am black;
When I am ill I am black;
When I go out in the sun I am black;
When I am cold I am black;
When I die I am black.
But you . . .!
When you come into the world you are pink;
When you grow up you are white;
When you are ill you are green;
When you go out in the sun you are red;
When you are cold you are blue;
When you die you are grey.
And yet you have the cheek to call *me* a coloured?

Published in a German magazine in 1977

Unknown
South African
poet

"Hey, what do you think you're doing, Brille?"
The prisoner swung round, blinking rapidly, yet at the same time sizing up the enemy. He was a new warder, named Jacobus Stephanus Hannetjie. His eyes were the colour of the sky but they were frightening. A simple, primitive, brutal soul gazed out of them. The prisoner bent down quickly and a message was quietly passed down the line: "We're in for trouble this time, comrades."
"Why?" rippled back up the line.
"Because he's not human," the reply rippled down, and yet only the crunching of the spades as they turned over the earth disturbed the stillness.
This particular work span was known as Span One. It was composed of ten men and they were all political prisoners. They were grouped together for convenience as it was one of the prison regulations that no black warder should be in charge of a political prisoner lest this prisoner convert him to his view. It never seemed to occur to the authorities that this very reasoning was the strength of Span One and a clue to the strange terror they aroused in the warders. As political prisoners they were unlike the other prisoners in the sense that they felt no guilt nor were they outcasts of society. All guilty men instinctively cower, which was why it was the kind of prison where men got knocked out cold with a blow at the back of the head from an iron bar. Up until the arrival of Warder Hannetjie, no warder had dared beat any member of Span One and no warder had lasted more than a week with them. The battle was entirely psychological. Span One was assertive and it was beyond the scope of white warders to handle assertive black men. Thus, Span One had got out of control . . .
Trouble began that very day between Span One and Warder Hannetjie.

"The Prisoner who Wore Glasses"; from "Tales of Tenderness and Power", Heinemann, London, 1990.

Bessie Head
(b. 1937)

Although we were roused at 5.30, we were not let out of our cells until 6.45, by which time we were meant to have cleaned our cells and rolled up our mats and blankets. We had no running water in our cells and instead of toilets had iron sanitary buckets known as "ballies". The ballies had a diameter of ten inches with a concave porcelain lid on the top that could contain water. The water in this lid was meant to be used for shaving and to clean our hands and faces . . .
Like everything else in prison, diet is discriminatory. In general, Coloureds and Indians received a slightly better diet than Africans, but it was not much of a discrimination . . .

Nelson Mandela
(b. 1918)

After inspection we would work in the courtyard hammering stones until noon. There were no breaks; if we slowed down, the warders would yell at us to speed up . . . After lunch we worked until 4, when the guards blew shrill whistles and we once again lined up to be counted and inspected. We were then permitted half an hour to clean up. The bathroom at the end of our corridor had two seawater showers, a saltwater tap and three large galvanised metal buckets, which were used as bathtubs. There was no hot water. . . We would sometimes sing while washing, which made the water seem less icy. In those early days, this was one of the only times when we could converse.

Precisely at 4.30 there would be a loud knock on the wooden door at the end of our corridor, which meant that supper had been delivered. . . We again received mealie pap porridge, sometimes with the odd carrot or piece of cabbage or beetroot thrown in — but one usually had to search for it . . . For supper, Coloured and Indian prisoners received a quarter loaf of bread (known as a *katkop,* that is, a cat's head, after the shape of the bread) and a slab of margarine. Africans, it was presumed, did not care for bread as it was a "European" type of food . . .

No cry of "lights out" was ever given on Robben Island because the single mesh-covered bulb in our cell burned day and night.

From "Long Walk to Freedom" (1994)

Suggested Routes

South Africa is a land of striking contrasts, with semi-deserts in the west of the country, luxuriant subtropical forests in the east, coastal regions, mountains, rivers, lakes and lagoons, steppeland and bush, sleepy-looking small towns and large and bustling cities. With its excellent road system it is easily explored by car. The longer distances can be travelled by air, leaving more time for sightseeing.

In this section three round trips are suggested. Two start from Johannesburg, the first requiring at least four weeks, the other three. The third starts from Cape Town and concentrates on the west of the country. All three routes take in the most important sights in South Africa and will introduce visitors to the splendours of this land which claims, with every reason, to be "a world in one country".

The marginal rubrics give an at-a-glance indication of the course of the routes. In these routes the names of places which are the subject of a separate entry in the A to Z part of the guide are given in **bold** type. Most the places mentioned in the guide – towns, villages, regions, isolated features of interest, etc. – are included in the index at the end of the guide, making it easy to find the description of any notable sight. An overview of the routes is given in the map on the facing page, and they can be followed in detail on the large map enclosed with this guide.

1. Grand Tour (4 weeks; 7000km/4350 miles)

The route, starting from Johannesburg, runs north-east to the Kruger National Park and, after a side trip into the Transvaal Drakensberg, continues into north-eastern KwaZulu/Natal, where there are other interesting nature reserves. Then by way of Durban, after a trip into the Natal Drakensberg, it turns south-west and follows the famous Garden Route to Cape Town. The return to Johannesburg, with a possible stopover in Kimberley, can be either by air or by car.

The starting-point is ★★**Johannesburg**, South Africa's leading industrial city, with its gleaming skyscrapers and its wide range of cultural attractions. A visit to Gold Reef City will give an impression of life in the great days of the gold rush.

Main route

The route continues on N 1 to the much quieter city of ★★**Pretoria**, the garden city of South Africa and its seat of government, with a population consisting largely of civil servants. The Voortrekker Monument recalls the story of the Great Trek.

N 1 continues to **Pietersburg**, capital of the Northern Transvaal, where the route turns east to the little town of ★**Tzaneen** with its luxuriant subtropical vegetation. Then on by way of Gravelotte to **Phalaborwa**, at the gates of the Kruger National Park. Since the ★★**Kruger National Park** covers a large area, with a great variety of scenery, at least two or three days should be allowed for exploring it from end to end. Accommodation is available in state-run camps and luxurious privately owned game farms (on the west side of the park).

Leaving the park by the Paul Kruger Gate, the route continues on R 536 via Hazyview to **Sabie**, with the largest expanse of planted forest in the world. From here a side trip can be made into the ★★**Blyderivierspoort Nature Reserve**, centred on the grandiose Blyde River Canyon. This is one of the most beautiful areas in South Africa, best seen from the fine panoramic highway. A visit to ★**Pilgrim's Rest**, a little turn-of-the-century mining town, is a must.

Blyde River Canyon

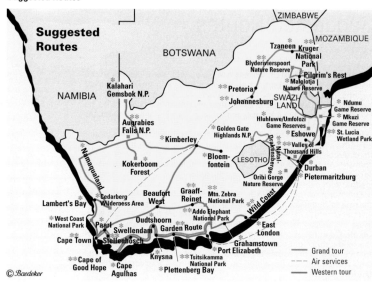

Suggested Routes

ZIMBABWE
MOZAMBIQUE
BOTSWANA
Tzaneen Kruger National Park
Blyderivierspoort Nature Reserve
Pilgrim's Rest
NAMIBIA
Kalahari Gemsbok N.P.
Malolotja Nature Reserve
Pretoria
Johannesburg
SWAZILAND
Ndumu Game Reserve
Mkuzi Game Reserve
Augrabies Falls N.P.
Hluhluwe/Umfolozi Game Reserves
Eshowe
St. Lucia Wetland Park
Golden Gate Highlands N.P.
Kimberley
Bloemfontein
LESOTHO
Valley of Thousand Hills
Kokerboom Forest
Natal-Drakensberg
Durban
Pietermaritzburg
Oribi Gorge Nature Reserve
Beaufort West
Graaff-Reinet
Mtn. Zebra National Park
Wild Coast
Lambert's Bay
Cedarberg Wilderness Area
West Coast National Park
Oudtshoorn
Addo Elephant National Park
Garden Route
East London
Paarl
Swellendam
Stellenbosch
Grahamstown
Cape Town
Port Elizabeth
Cape of Good Hope
Cape Agulhas
Knysna
Tsitsikamma National Park
Plettenberg Bay
© Baedeker

Grand tour
Air services
Western tour

North-eastern KwaZulu/Natal

The road into north-eastern KwaZulu/Natal with its nature reserves runs via Sabie and Nelspruit to Barberton, another old mining town. From there there are two possible routes. One runs through the kingdom of **Swaziland** by way of Pigg's Peak, Mbabane and Big Bend to Golela, where it joins N 2. The other runs via Badplaas (R 33) and Amsterdam to Piet Retief (R 29), continuing through the hill country of Zululand to Pongola and Mkuze, where there is a choice between a number of magnificent game reserves, notably the ★**Hluhluwe Game Reserve**, situated on the first ranges of hills in the interior, and the ★Umfolozi Game Reserve, separated from it by a corridor only 8km/5 miles wide. The main attraction in these reserves, which are among the oldest in Africa, lies in the large numbers of rhinos. To the north-east is the ★★**St Lucia Wetland Park**, a paradise for bird-watchers, which extends for 3km/2 miles into the sea.

Near the little town of Mkuze is the ★**Mkuzi Game Reserve**. For those whose appetite for game reserves is still not satisfied there are also the Kosi Bay Reserve (sandy roads, rivers to be forded: four-wheel-drive vehicles only) and the ★**Ndumu Reserve** (80km/50 miles north of Mkuze). These two reserves, lying only a short distance from the frontier with Mozambique, are relatively little visited.

The route continues south-west on the coast road (N 2) through Zululand, home of South Africa's largest people. This is the home country of Chief Mangosuthu Buthelezi (see Famous People), whose rivalry with the ANC brought South Africa to the verge of civil war before the first free election in 1994.

At Empangeni take R 34 and then R 68 for ★**Eshowe**. The Zulu kraal called Shakaland, originally built as a setting for the television series "Shaka Zulu", is now an open-air museum in which visitors can learn about the traditions and way of life of the Zulus and their legendary chief Shaka (see Famous People).

Then via Gingindlovu or Mtunzini back to the coast road and on to Umhlanga Rocks, a popular bathing resort 12km/7½ miles north of

Golden Gate Highlands National Park

The Swartberg Pass road

Durban. Visitors interested in sharks can look in at the ★Natal Sharks Board (see Baedeker Special, p. 212).

Durban

★★**Durban**, South Africa's "sun capital", is the country's most popular holiday resort, well provided with hotels, night clubs and fun fairs. The population is a mix of Zulus, people of British origin and Indians. For a touch of exoticism, visit the Indian Market. In the Aquarium and Dolphinarium you can see more than a thousand species of fish.

From here an excursion can be made to the beautiful ★★Valley of a Thousand Hills and to ★**Pietermaritzburg**, once chief town of the voortrekkers' republic and now capital of KwaZulu/Natal. The Natal Museum has interesting displays on the history of the region. (The round trip from Durban to the Valley of a Thousand Hills and Pietermaritzburg and back to Durban is about 200km/125 miles.)

Natal Drakensberg

From Durban or Pietermaritzburg the route continues on N 3 via Howick, Nottingham Road with the ruins of its fort, **Estcourt** and Winterton into the grandiose ★★**Drakensberg**, the "Alps" of South Africa, which for part of the way form a natural frontier between South Africa and the independent kingdom of **Lesotho**. This is magnificent country for nature-lovers and walkers, with spectacular mountains rising to over 3000m/10,000ft, waterfalls, wild flowers and many Bushman drawings (see Baedeker Special, p. 90). One of its high spots is a natural amphitheatre formed by huge crags in the Royal Natal National Park.

Golden Gate Highlands National Park

From here a side trip can be made to the ★Golden Gate Highlands National Park with its bizarre rock formations. It can be reached on R 74 via Bergville, skirting the Sterkfontein Dam, and shortly before **Harrismith** turning into R 712, signposted to Phuthaditjhaba, and then following the signposts to the park.

Back in Durban, there are a number of possible routes for continuing the grand tour. Visitors travelling by car can continue on N 2, which between Durban and Port Edward runs along the Hibiscus Coast. Those who have plenty of time at their disposal will find beautiful scenery and lonely beaches on the Wild Coast; but since this route runs through the former homeland of Transkei it is advisable to check by local enquiry that the area is safe. An alternative possibility is to take a domestic flight from Durban to East London or Port Elizabeth.

East London

★**East London**, South Africa's only river port, was until the beginning of the 19th century a frontier town between the white settlers and the Xhosa.

Port Elizabeth

The route continues by way of **Bisho**, chief town of the former homeland of Ciskei, **King William's Town** and ★**Grahamstown**, once a military outpost, round which German settlers established themselves in the 1820s, to ★**Port Elizabeth**, one of South Africa's largest ports and a centre of the automobile industry. Its main attractions are the museum complex on Humewood Beach, a snake park, an oceanarium and above all the ★★Addo Elephant Park (75km/47 miles north), Since there are more than 300 elephants in the park there is a good chance of seeing some even on a brief visit. Overnight accommodation is available in bungalows.

Garden Route

To the west of Port Elizabeth is Humansdorp, starting-point of the famous ★★**Garden Route**. 225km/140 miles long and bordered by chains of hills for most of the way, it offers an ever-changing landscape of great scenic beauty.

On the way visitors can see the little forest trail at Storms River and the Paul Sauer Bridge. Beyond Storms River it is a good idea to turn off into a secondary road which runs over Bloukrans Pass to Coldstream and Nature's Valley and is much more beautiful than N 2 (a toll road).

Cape Dutch house in Swellendam

★★Tsitsikamma National Park with its gigantic old trees also includes Tsitsikamma Coastal National Park, an underwater nature trail for experienced snorkellers. This is the starting-point of the famous Otter Hiking Trail (41km/25 miles; advance booking necessary, since the trail is booked up a year in advance), which along with the Tsitsikamma Hiking Trail (61km/38 miles) makes a popular round trip.

The former fishing village of ★**Plettenberg Bay** is now one of the best known bathing resorts on the Garden Route. Then on, passing lakes and lagoons, through the Knysna Forest to ★**Knysna**, another well known bathing resort. Beyond the idyllic little town of Wilderness it is worth leaving the main road to enjoy a superb view of the town's long white beach. At the foot of the Outeniqua Mountains is **George**, the largest town on the Garden Route.

From here a side trip can be made to **Mossel Bay**, where Bartolomeu Diaz landed in 1488 after rounding the southern tip of Africa.

★**Oudtshoorn**, which lies some miles inland, is the centre of ostrich farming in South Africa. A visit should be paid to one of the ostrich farms and also to the Cango Caves with their magnificent stalactites and stalagmites. There is also an attractive run over the Swartberg Pass to Prince Albert.

Oudtshoorn

The route continues on N 2. From ★**Swellendam** a side trip can be made to the most southerly point in Africa, ★**Cape Agulhas**.

★★**Cape Town**, the "mother city" of South Africa, lies at the foot of majestic Table Mountain. A day or two should be allowed for seeing the city, one of the most fascinating in the world. The city itself, in which whites and coloureds form the majority of the population, has a great deal to offer, including the Victoria and Alfred Waterfront with its many excellent restaurants, bars and shops and numerous museums and exhibitions; and it is also a good base for excursions in the sur-

Cape Town

rounding area, including trips along the north-west Atlantic coast to the ★**West Coast National Park** (description in Route 3), to the wine-growing region round ★**Paarl**, Franschhoek and ★★**Stellenbosch**, and round the ★★Cape peninsula (described in the entry on Cape Town in the A to Z section of the guide).

Wine tour

The following is a suggestion for a "wine tour". From Cape Town N 1 runs north-east to ★**Paarl**, which is of interest not only as a wine-growing centre. The town played an important part in the development of the Afrikaans language. The route then continues on R 303, passing the Victor Vester Prison, in which Nelson Mandela was confined for many years. Franschhoek ("French Corner"), the next wine town, was founded in 1688 by Huguenot refugees from France. R 45 then runs over the Franschhoek Pass and down to the Theewaterskloof Dam; then over the Viljoens Pass on R 321 to Elgin and Grabouw. N 2 continues over the Cole Pass, opened by Governor Sir Lowry Cole in 1830, to **Somerset West** and Strand, a popular bathing resort. Then comes ★★**Stellenbosch**, South Africa's second oldest town, known as "Oak Town" because of the numerous oak-trees in the area. With its white-painted houses in Cape Dutch style and the most famous university in South Africa, it is well worth a visit.

Return to Johannesburg

The return to Johannesburg can be by air, perhaps with a stopover in ★**Kimberley**, from which an excursion can be made to the Boer strong-hold of ★**Bloemfontein** (description in Route 3).

The route by road – for visitors with sufficient time at their disposal – is on N 1 via **Paarl**, **Matjiesfontein**, **Beaufort West**, **Bloemfontein** and **Kroonstad**.

2. Shorter Tour (3 weeks; 5000km/3100 miles)

This route is suggested for visitors who have less time at their disposal but want to see the main sights and places of interest in the east and south of the country. Since it largely follows the same course as Route 1, it is not shown separately on the map on p. 118.

It is also possible to fly direct from Johannesburg to the Kruger National Park, having previously booked accommodation in one of the camps. From there the route continues into the Drakensberg, first in the Eastern Transvaal and then in Natal; then via Pietermaritzburg to Durban.

From Durban the tour can be continued by air to East London or Port Elizabeth and from there on the Garden Route to Cape Town. The return to Johannesburg is by air, with a possible stopover in Kimberley.

Main route

By car, starting from ★★**Johannesburg**, the route runs by way of ★★**Pretoria** and **Middelburg** to Waterval Boven. From there it is possible either to take R 36, which runs via **Lydenburg** to ★**Pilgrim's Rest**, or to continue on N 4, turning soon after Shagen into R 37 for **Sabie**. After passing through the ★★**Blyderivierspoort Nature Reserve** the road comes to **Phalaborwa**, a gateway to the ★★**Kruger National Park**.

Then on R 40 via **Nelspruit** in the direction of Barberton, turning off shortly before that town into R 38, which runs via Badplaas and Carolina to join N 11 at Hendrina. Just to the south of Ermolo N 11 becomes R 36 again, returning to its original number south of Volksrust.

N 11 continues by way of Newcastle to **Ladysmith** and a few miles beyond this runs into N 3 coming from Durban – the main route to the Natal ★★**Drakensberg**. From this road side roads (sometimes un-surfaced) run west to various holiday resorts, between which there is usually no direct connection.

In the Blyde River Canyon

The route continues on N 3 by way of **Estcourt**, Howick and ★**Pieter-maritzburg**, from which a side trip can be made into the ★★Valley of a Thousand Hills (see Route 1), to ★★**Durban**. From here there are a variety of possible excursions to coastal towns north and south of Durban, for example to ★**Eshowe** to learn about the Zulus and their traditions (see Route 1).

On to Durban

From Durban it is possible to fly either to ★**East London** or direct to ★**Port Elizabeth** (a good solution if you are pressed for time). Then, after a visit to ★★Addo Elephant Park, the ★★**Garden Route** (described in Route 1) begins at Humansdorp and continues to ★★**Cape Town**.

Western Tour (3 weeks; 4000km/2500 miles)

This route, starting from Cape Town, runs in a wide arc along the Atlantic coast and into Namaqualand. It then runs north-east by way of Upington into the Kalahari and then to Kimberley and, if desired, Bloemfontein. On the return route, at Beaufort West, there is a choice between the direct road to Cape Town and a longer route via Graaff-Reinet to two National Parks and Port Elizabeth, and then along the coast of the Indian Ocean and on the Garden Route (described in Route 1) to Cape Town.

After seeing the sights of ★★**Cape Town** and the surrounding area (see Route 1) take the coast road by way of **Bloubergstrand** (from which there is the most photographed view of the city against the backdrop of Table Mountain) to the ★**West Coast National Park**, at the south end of Saldanha Bay (100km/62 miles from Cape Town). The National Park takes in part of Langebaan Lagoon, an extensive swamp area and one of the world's most important bird reserves.

Main route

West Coast National Park

Suggested Routes

In the Cedarberg Mountains

Cedarberg
Mountains

The route continues by way of the agricultural market town of Vredenburg to the fishing town of **Lambert's Bay**, an important fish-processing centre on the "Crayfish Route". From here a road runs inland to **Clanwilliam**, on N 7. To the south of the town are the Cedarberg Mountains, a region of rugged hills and wooded gorges with a varied flora and fauna. The Cedarberg Wilderness Area attracts large numbers of walkers.

Namaqualand

The main route continues north to Springbok, capital of ★**Namaqualand**. This apparently inhospitable region is transformed in August and September, during the rainy season, into a paradise of flowers.

Augrabies Falls
National Park

From Springbok R 64 runs north-east to ★★**Augrabies Falls National Park**, where the Orange River, South Africa's mightiest river, plunges down 260m/850ft into a gorge. The park has a varied flora and fauna, including the aloe tree or kokerboom and other species of aloe, wild olives and acacias.

Kalahari Gemsbok
National Park

R 64 continues to **Upington**, from which R 360 runs north to Twee Rivieren, gateway to the ★**Kalahari Gemsbok National Park** in the semi-desertic Kalahari between the rivers Auob and Nassob. Self-catering accommodation is available in three camps (advance booking essential). In addition to herds of springbok, gemsbok and eland the fauna of the park includes the black-maned Kalahari lion, ostriches and over 170 species of birds.

117km/73 miles south of Upington on R 27, near **Kenhardt**, is the ★Kokerboom Forest.

Kimberley

From Upington R 64 runs east via **Griquatown** to the legendary diamond-mining town of ★**Kimberley**, once famed for the world's richest hoard of buried treasure. Most of the mines have now been closed down, but an open-air museum centred on the Big Hole, the largest man-made hole in the world, recalls the town's diamond-mining days.

From Kimberley an excursion can be made to ★ **Bloemfontein**, South Africa's judicial capital. Ironically, it was in this Boer stronghold that the African National Congress (see Baedeker Special, p. 30), the largest black party, was founded in 1912.

Bloemfontein

If time permits it is well worth while to visit the Golden Gate High-lands National Park (on N 1 to Winburg, N 5 via **Bethlehem** to Kestell, then follow signposts: see Route 1).

The return to Cape Town is on N 12 from Kimberley or N 1 from Bloemfontein. The two roads join at Three Sisters, some 80km/50 miles north of **Beaufort West**, the chief town in the Karoo and birthplace of the famous heart surgeon Christiaan Barnard. To the west is the ★ Karoo National Park, with the unique flora and fauna of the semi-desertic Karoo.

Return to Cape Town

There are now two possible return routes to Cape Town. The direct road runs via **Matjiesfontein**, a little Victorian oasis, and ★ **Paarl**. The alternative is on the Garden Route.

From Beaufort West R 61 runs east to ★★ **Graaff-Reinet**, founded in 1786, which has numerous museums and handsome buildings in Cape Dutch style. Within easy reach of Graaff-Reinet is the ★★ Mountain Zebra National Park, home of the last mountain zebras and other species. It lies to the west of Cradock (from Graaff-Reinet on N 9 to Bethesdaweg, then south-east on R 61 to shortly before **Cradock** and from there follow signposts). From Cradock N 10 runs south towards the coast. 75km/47 miles north of Port Elizabeth is the ★ Addo Elephant Park (see Route 1), with over 300 elephants. The road reaches the coast of the Indian Ocean at ★ **Port Elizabeth**, from which the famous ★★ **Garden Route** (see Route 1) runs west to Cape Town.

Return by Garden Route

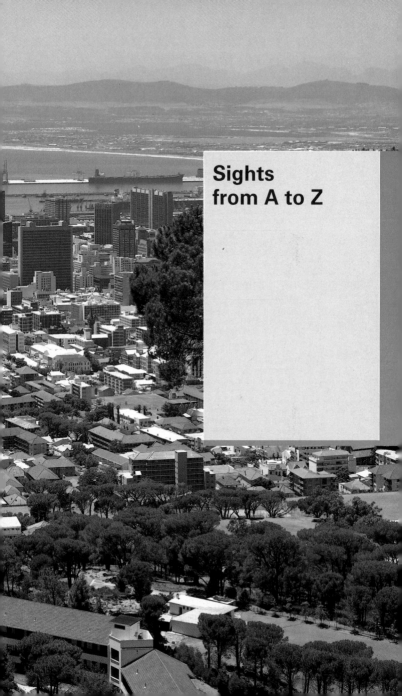

Sights
from A to Z

Sights from A to Z

Aliwal North J 7

Province: Eastern Cape
Altitude: 1416m/4646ft. Population: 34,000
Distances: 207km/129 miles from Bloemfontein, 380km/236 miles from
   East London, 690km/429 miles from Johannesburg, 1070km/665 miles
   from Cape Town

Situation and
characteristics

The town of Aliwal North, famed for its warm mineral springs, lies on the
south bank of the Orange River, near the Lesotho border.
   The name of the town, which was founded in 1849, commemorates the
victory of Sir Harry Smith, governor of the Cape Colony from 1847 to 1852,
over the Sikhs at Aliwal (India) in 1846. The "North" distinguishes it from
Aliwal South, the old name of Mossel Bay.

Sights in and around Aliwal North

Museums

There are displays illustrating the history of the town in Buffelsvlei Farmhouse (near the spa establishment) and the Old Library (1876). The old
church (1864) is also a museum (opened 1987), after previously serving as a
market hall, a cinema and a warehouse.

Aliwal Spa

Two hot springs have a daily flow of over 2.5 million litres (550,000 gallons)
of water at a temperature of 34.4°C/93.9°F, coming from a depth of 1280m/
4200ft, which is used in the treatment of arthritis and rheumatism. The
extensive spa complex includes two large swimming pools.

Buffelspruit
Nature Reserve

On the Krasi River, 2km/1¼ miles from the town, is the Buffelspruit Nature
Reserve (open: October to April daily 10am–6pm, May to September daily
11am–4.30pm), in which numerous species formerly found in this area
have been re-established, including springboks, elands, ostriches, zebras
and oryxes.

Amanzimtoti M 7

Province: KwaZulu/Natal
Altitude: 5m/16ft. Population: 27,000
Distances: 27km/17 miles from Durban, 660km/410 miles from East London

Situation and
characteristics

Amanzimtoti, situated on the Umbogintwini River to the south of Durban, is
the first of the many holiday resorts which lie along the 160km/100 miles of
coast between Durban and Port Edward. The town owes its name to the
story that when the great Zulu king Shaka (see Famous People) drank the
water of the Umbogintwini for the first time in 1828 he exclaimed "Kanti
amanza mtoti!" ("The water is fresh!").
   The town has grown considerably in recent years and is now almost a
suburb of Durban (see entry). It attracts some 300,000 visitors a year.
   The most popular part of the 7km/4½ mile long sandy beach, interrupted
here and there by rocky promontories, is the Nvoni Rocks area, which
among other facilities has a seawater swimming pool.

◀ Cape Town the "mother city" of South Africa

Sights in Amanzimtoti

At the end of Umdoni Road, surrounded by Ilala palms, is the Amanzimtoti Bird Sanctuary (area 4.5 hectares/11 acres; open: daily 6am–6pm), which is home to large numbers of exotic birds. The best observation points are the viewing platforms at the upper end of the pool.

★ Amanzimtoti Bird Sanctuary

Outside the town, on the river Umbogintwini, is the Ilanda Wilds Nature Reserve (area 14 hectares/35 acres), in which live some 300 different species of birds. More than a hundred species of trees and shrubs can be seen on well laid-out nature trails.

Ilanda Wilds Nature Reserve

Sunshine Coast

The coastal region between Amanzimtoti and Mtwalume, 40km/25 miles south, is known as the Sunshine Coast. To the south of this, between Hibberdene and Port Edward, is the Hibiscus Coast (see Port Shepstone). This whole stretch of coast is one of the country's most popular holiday regions. It is best avoided during the school holidays, particularly at Christmas and Easter, when many South Africans come here for a break. There is plenty of accommodation for visitors: few hotels of the highest standard but numerous more modest establishments and innumerable holiday apartments. The beaches farther south, in the Western and Eastern Cape, are even more beautiful and are less crowded.

Between June and August huge swarms of sardines can regularly be observed off the coast here. They normally live in the cold water off the south and south-west coasts of Africa, but in the spawning season move to the coastal waters off Durban which are warmed by the Benguela Current. The current carries the sardines, followed by hungry predators, close to the coast.

Sardine swarms

A few miles south of Amanzimtoti is Kingsburgh (pop. 26,000), a town formed by the amalgamation of five small seaside resorts. The long sandy beaches (altogether 8km/5 miles in length) and the coastal lagoons, with nets to keep out sharks, offer safe bathing.

Kingsburgh

Each of the five parts of Kingsburgh has its own individual character. Nearest Amanzimtoti is Doonside, a little settlement with a shady beach and a modern apartment block: an ideal place for a relaxing holiday. Warner Beach is a friendly little resort situated on a lagoon which is a favourite haunt of sailing and motorboating enthusiasts. Winklespruit offers good sailing waters and good fishing, and there are pleasant walks in the dense forest bordering the beach. Illovo Beach, at the mouth of the river Illovo in a sugarcane-growing area, also has good fishing. Karridene appeals to walkers, with long beach and forest walks.

In Umgababa visitors will find numerous stalls selling Zulu craft products (woodcarving, pottery, etc.) – as well as imported kitsch.

Umgababa

The next place of any size on the Sunshine Coast is Umkomaas (pop. 2000), at the mouth of the Mkomazi River, which rises in the Drakensberg at a height of 3000m/10,000ft. Umkomaas is a centre of the cellulose industry, and accordingly is not particularly attractive as a holiday resort. It does, however, have a beautifully situated 18-hole golf course.

Umkomaas

An attempt in 1881 to establish a port at the mouth of the Mkomazi was frustrated by the strong currents and sandbanks off the coast. The town of Umkomaas was founded in 1902. Its name, derived from that of the river, means "place of the whale-cows": the female whales used to come to the shallow water at the mouth of the river to produce their young. The Zulu chief Shaka is said to have observed this on one occasion and to have named the river accordingly.

Augrabies Falls National Park

★Croc World
South of Umkomaas (4km/2½ miles north of Scottburgh) is Croc World, a crocodile-breeding farm with over 2000 crocodiles and snakes (open: daily 9am–5pm; feeding times 11am and 2pm, Sun. 3pm). A particular attraction is the glass tunnel running through the snake house. There is a restaurant in which visitors can sample crocodile meat.

Scottburgh
The bleak coast at Scottburgh (pop. 7000) is popular with fishermen. On the main beach there is a seawater swimming pool, and there is also a golf course.

★Vernon Crookes Nature Reserve
The Vernon Crookes Nature Reserve (area 2200 hectares/5400 acres; open: daily 8am–7pm) is reached on R 612, which runs inland from the coastal town of Park Rynie, passing through Umzinto (15km/9 miles west of Scottburgh). In this gentle upland region, declared a nature reserve in 1973, live porcupines, blue wildebeests, antelopes and gazelles, zebras and black-backed jackals. Two artificial lakes attract large numbers of birds. The area is worth visiting for its fascinating vegetation, seen at its best in spring. Good walking. Simple self-catering accommodation.

Ifafa Beach
Ifafa Beach (pop. 400), at the mouth of the river Ifafa, has a sheltered bathing beach and a lagoon with good fishing. Water-skiing is practised here, and there is rowing (against the stream) on a long stretch of the river.

Mtwalume
At the south end of the Sunshine Coast is Mtwalume, with a rocky beach which offers good fishing. There is a seawater swimming pool.

Augrabies Falls National Park

E 6

Province: Northern Cape
Distances: 130km/80 miles from Upington, 530km/330 miles from Kimberley

Situation and characteristics
The Augrabies Falls in north-western South Africa, near the frontier with Namibia, are one of the country's great natural wonders. The National Park established in 1967 to protect them (area 820sq.km/320sq. miles) is a region of extreme aridity with an annual rainfall of only 107mm/4¼in. The vegetation is sparse, consisting mainly of euphorbias and kokerbooms. Only on the banks of the Orange River, which flows through the National Park, is there denser tree cover.

★★Landscape
The Orange River plunges in a series of cascades (the main fall 56m/184ft high), almost 150m/500ft across, into a granite gorge enclosed by rock walls up to 240m/800ft high, with a total length of 18km/11 miles. In the language of the Hottentots, who held the falls in awe as a sacred place, the name Augrabies means "place of the great noise"; and indeed the falls, which rank among the six largest in the world, fully justify their name.

The best view of the falls is from a 20m/65ft long suspension bridge spanning the Orange River at the main fall.

Wild life
Among the animals living in the park are antelopes, gazelles, porcupines, leopards, baboons and vervet monkeys. The black rhinoceros, now relatively rare, was established here in 1985. There are over 140 species of birds, including Verreaux's eagle, which can frequently be seen at the falls. The black stork breeds in the gorge.

When to go
The park is open from sunrise to sunset throughout the year. The best time to go is in summer, when there is more water in the river; the falls are particularly spectacular in late summer. During the summer, however, visitors must be prepared for temperatures of up to 40°C/104°F.

The Augrabies Falls on the Orange River: a spectacular sight in a desert landscape ▷

Badplaas

Facilities

There are very well equipped chalets in the National Park's camp, a camping site, a restaurant, a cafeteria and a visitor centre. Although it is preferable to spend at least two days in the park, even a day trip is very rewarding. It is also possible to stay in Upington (see entry) and from there visit the Kalahari Gemsbok National Park (see entry).

Roads

An asphalt road 12km/7½ miles long runs through the park, with short side roads going off it to particular viewpoints and other sights.

Hiking trail

The Klipspringer Hiking Trail, 26km/16 miles long, runs through the gorge. The hike takes three days (overnight accommodation available in huts). In summer the trail is closed because of the great heat.

Badplaas   M 4

Province: Eastern Transvaal
Altitude: 1063m/3488ft
Population: 22,000
Distances: 75km/47 miles from Barberton, 300km/186 miles from Johannesburg

Situation and
characteristics

Badplaas ("Place of the Baths"), one of South Africa's best known thermal resorts, is set against the fantastic backdrop of the greenish-blue Hlumo Hlumo Mountains. The spa complex is equipped with bungalows, a camping site and four beautiful medicinal pools situated in a valley.

Badplaas
Nature Reserve

In the Badplaas Nature Reserve (area 35,000 hectares/86,450 acres), which is reached from the road to Barberton, live large numbers of animals, mainly species of antelope. There are numerous hiking and riding trails in the park, which is open throughout the year; horses can be hired at local stables.

Barkly East   K 8

Province: Eastern Cape
Altitude: 1800m/5900ft
Population: 14,000
Distances: 120km/75 miles from Aliwal North, 210km/130 miles from Umtata

Situation and
characteristics

Barkly East lies 120km/75 miles south-east of Aliwal North, with which it is connected by rail, in the Witteberg, a mountainous region often dubbed the South African Switzerland. At this altitude temperatures fall below freezing point on an average of 81 nights in the year. In winter it is a popular skiing area, in summer a paradise for walkers and trout-fishers. This is also a sheep-farming area, and Barkly East is an important centre of the woollen industry.

The town, named after Sir Henry Barkly, was founded in 1874. Its high altitude presented the railway engineers with considerable problems: the line between Lady Grey and Barkly East has an average gradient of 2.8% and eight hairpin bends.

Surroundings of Barkly East

Rhodes

65km/40 miles north-east of Barkly East is Rhodes, which depending on the time of year, is a winter sports centre (season March–September) or a base for walks in the surrounding area.

Maclear (pop. 13,000), 110km/68 miles east of Barkly East, was founded in 1876 and named after the astronomer Sir Thomas Maclear, who lived for 40 years on the Cape. There is skiing here in winter and good trout-fishing in summer.

Maclear

From Barkly East a magnificent scenic road runs over the Barkly Pass to Elliot (pop. 11,000), 60km/37 miles south. The region is famed for its Bushman rock paintings (notably on Denorbin Farm). From Elliot there are attractive excursions in summer to Lake Thomson, a reservoir situated in a nature reserve, and the Gilli Cullum Falls (18km/11 miles).

Elliot

Barkly West   H 6

Province: Northern Cape
Altitude: 1766m/5794ft
Population: 11,000
Distances: 32km/20 miles from Kimberley, 210km/130 miles from Bloemfontein, 416km/258 miles from Upington, 440km/273 miles from Johannesburg

In 1869 the first diamonds were found at Barkly West in the river gravel of the Vaal. There was an immediate rush to the diggings (which still attract hopeful prospectors). The first settlement established by the diamond-miners was called Klipdrift. Later there was fierce dispute over the ownership of this valuable land, which was claimed by the Griqua, a Hottentot tribe, and the Tswana, a Bantu people, both of whom lived in the area, and by the Boers of the Orange Free State and the Transvaal and the British.

Situation and characteristics

Finally the British authorities assigned the territory to the Griqua; but in 1870 they bought it back and established a new colony, Griqualand West, of which Klipdrift became the capital. The town was given its present name in 1873 in honour of Sir Henry Barkley, Governor of the Cape.

Between June and September the Barkly West police station issues permits for diamond-prospecting – though the prospectors are more likely to find semi-precious stones (tiger's eyes) than diamonds. On Saturday mornings in particular the town still has a little of the atmosphere of the old diamond-mining days, and diamond dealers come to negotiate with the treasure-seekers for the purchase of their week's booty.

Diamond-hunting

Sights in and around Barkly West

In the Mining Commissioner's office are displayed numerous prehistoric artifacts found during the diamond-mining operations as well as photographs of the town's diamond-mining heyday (open: Mon.–Fri. 8am–4.30pm).

Mining Commissioner's Museum

On the outskirts of Barkly West, on the Kimberley Road, is the Canteen Koppie Nature Reserve (area 7 hectares/17 acres). There were once diamond diggings here, but the area has now reverted to its natural vegetation cover of grass, bushes and trees.

Canteen Koppie Nature Reserve

10km/6 miles north-west of Barkly West, on the south side of the Vaal, is the Vaalbos National Park (area 22,500 hectares/55,600 acres), established in 1986, which is of particular interest for its vegetation. The name Vaalbos is derived from the camphor tree which flourishes here. In addition to the local species of animal (antelopes, giraffes) buffaloes and rhinos have been reintroduced here. The park has at present no tourist infrastructure.

Vaalbos National Park

Beaufort West   F 8/9

Province: Western Cape
Altitude: 915m/3000ft
Population: 26,000
Distances: 460km/285 miles from Cape Town, 605km/375 miles from East
   London

Situation and
characteristics

Beaufort West lies on N 1, the main road from Cape Town to Johannesburg,
in the Great Karoo, of which it is the principal town. This is a stock-farming
region, and Beaufort West is a merino-breeding centre.

The town was founded in 1814. It was the birthplace of Sir John Charles
Molteno, a wealthy sheep-farmer who became prime minister of the Cape
province, and the famous heart surgeon Christiaan Barnard. Many prizes
and distinctions won by Barnard are displayed in the town's Museum,
which stands near the little parsonage in which he lived as a child. Also of
interest is the old Stadhuis, the first municipal building.

★Karoo National Park

To the north-west of the town is the Karoo National Park (area 33,000
hectares/81,500 acres), which covers much of the Nuweveldberg range
(825–1911m/2707–6270ft). It was established in 1979 to protect the unique
flora and fauna of the Karoo. A number of species have been reintroduced
here (mountain zebras, springboks, kudus, wild cats). The Springbok Hiking Trail (a 3-day walk: advance booking necessary) runs through the park,
and there are also many shorter walks, for example om the Fossil Trail
400m/440yd), which lets visitors see the fossils on their original find-spots.

The Karoo National Park is open throughout the year (though the Springbok Hiking Trail can be used only between February and September) and

The barren plains of the Karoo are carpeted with flowers after heavy rain

has accommodation for visitors. The main gate, reached on a minor road branching off N 1, is open in summer 7am–7pm, in winter 8am–6pm.

The Great Karoo (or Karoo *tout court*) is a predominantly level semi-arid region with a scanty vegetation cover and a number of precipitous hills up to 2000m/6560ft in height. With an area of around 500,000sq.km/193,000sq. miles, it occupies a third of the total area of South Africa. The Karoo begins in the south (just north of the Garden Route) as the Little Karoo, which then becomes the Great Karoo, followed, far to the north, by the Upper Karoo, which again, on the border with Namibia and Botswana, is continued by the Kalahari.

Great Karoo

The first inhabitants were nomadic Bushmen, who found in the Karoo ample grazing for their flocks and herds as well as for wild animals. They also gave the region its name, from a term in their language meaning the "great drought". The wealth of game formerly to be found here attracted European sportsmen and later farmers, both of whom left an enduring mark on the ecological equilibrium of the Karoo. First the predators were exterminated, and then large areas of the Karoo were enclosed. The herds of livestock over-grazed the grassland and the fences restricted the free movement of the surviving wild animals. The flora and fauna of the Karoo were irreparably changed. In more recent years, however, when the economic value of a healthy natural environment is recognised, nature reserves have been established in which the landscape can be preserved for its inhabitants.

The climate is unpredictable, with wide daily and seasonal variations in temperature, ranging between over 40°C/104°F and −7°C/+19°F. Most of what little rain there is falls in February and March, and then the vegetation is transformed. Normally the Karoo has a cover of low woody scrub, interspersed with succulents, aloes, mesembryanthemum, stonecrop, euphorbias and *Stapelia*, which can store water in their thick leaves and their roots. After a brief shower of rain the grasses recover first and the Karoo becomes green; several days of rain, and the Karoo becomes a paradise of bloom. The seeds of these "one-day flowers of the desert", which can sometimes remain inactive for years, then suddenly germinate, producing a marvellous carpet of blossom.

Bethlehem

K 5/6

Province: Orange Free State
Altitude: 1747m/5732ft
Population: 60,000
Distances: 180km/112 miles from Bloemfontein, 235km/146 miles from Johannesburg, 400km/250 miles from Durban

Bethlehem lies 235km/146 miles south of Johannesburg on the shores of Loch Athlone, an artificial lake created by a dam on the river Jordaan. Situated in a large maize-growing area, it rapidly developed into the economic and administrative centre of the eastern Orange Free State. Bethlehem is also a popular holiday resort, a convenient stopover on the way to the Drakensberg (see entry) and a good base for visiting the Golden Gate Highlands National Park (see Clarens).
The Maize Fair is held annually in October.

Situation and characteristics

The first voortrekkers came to this area around 1840, driven from their homes by the British conquest of the Cape. In 1864 they founded the town of Bethlehem on the site of the Pretoriuskloof farm, naming it after the place of Christ's birth and naming the river after the Jordan.

History

135

Sights in and around Bethlehem

Museum

The Municipal Museum, housed in the former church (1906) of the Nazareth Mission, displays everyday objects from Boer households. In its garden is an old steam engine which ran between Cape Town and Mafeking around the turn of the century. The museum is open: Mon. 10am–12.30pm, Tues., Wed., Fri. and Sat. 10am–12.30pm and 2.30–5pm, Sun. 2.30–5pm.

Other notable buildings

Other notable buildings in Bethlehem are the Strapp Shops (corner of Church and Louw Streets), the Anglican church of St Augustine, The Dutch Reformed Moederkerk in Church Square and the Tuishuis (12 Church Street), now occupied by a restaurant.

Pretoriuskloof Nature Reserve

The Pretoriuskloof Nature Reserve, on the banks of the Jordaan in the centre of the town, is an oasis for small animals, particularly for various species of birds.

Loch Athlone Resort

The Loch Athlone Resort, a holiday village, lies on the banks of the Jordaan, here dammed to form Loch Athlone, 3km/2 miles from Bethlehem. It is well equipped with hotels and holiday apartments, a camping site for tents and motor caravans, a floating restaurant and a variety of sports facilities. Round the lake run waymarked hiking trails. The resort is a good base for long walks, for example on the 36km/22 mile long Houtkop Hiking Trail.

Wolhuterskop Nature Reserve

6km/4 miles from Bethlehem on the Fouriesburg road is the Wolhuterskop Nature Reserve (area 800 hectares/2000 acres), home to various species of antelope and gazelle and large numbers of birds. The 15km/9 mile long Wolhuterskop Hiking Trail runs through the park, starting from the entrance to Loch Athlone Resort.

Church, Bethlehem

Bethulie   J 7

Province: Orange Free State
Altitude: 1589m/5214ft
Population: 13,500
Distances: 75km/47 miles from Aliwal North, 200km/125 miles from
    Bloemfontein

The little town of Bethulie, situated 200km/125 miles south of Bloemfontein   Situation and
between two large nature reserves, the Hendrik Verwoerd Dam Nature   characteristics
Reserve to the west and the Tussen-die-Riviere Game Farm to the east, is
the agricultural market centre of the region, in which intensive sheep-
farming is the predominant activity.

Bethulie was founded in 1829 by the London Missionary Society and taken   History
over four years later by the Paris Missionary Society, who gave it its present
name ("chosen by God").

Sights in and around Bethulie

Pellissier House, named after the first French missionary in Bethulie,   Pellissier House
houses an exhibition on the missionaries who worked here and on the
history of the region.

The D. H. Steyn Bridge, a combined road and rail bridge which spans the   D. H. Steyn Bridge
Orange River at Bethulie, is the longest bridge in South Africa
(1152m/1260yd).

The Bethulie Dam offers facilities for a variety of water sports. Adjoining it   Mynhardt Game
is the Mynhardt Game Reserve (area 160 hectares/395 acres), established   Reserve
in 1937, in which live various species of antelopes and gazelles (accommodation for visitors).

15km/9 miles south-east of Bethulie, between the Orange and the Caledon   Tussen-die-Riviere
Rivers, is the Tussen-die-Riviere Game Farm (area 21,000 hectares/52,000   Game Farm
acres), which was established in 1972 as a home for various species of
antelopes and gazelles, zebras and rhinos. From September to the end of
April it is run like any other game reserve and is open daily from sunrise to
sunset. During the winter, however, hunting is permitted in order to regulate the stocks of game.

South-west of Bethulie is the Hendrik Verwoerd Dam, an artificial lake over   Hendrik Verwoerd
100km/62 miles long, with an area of 374sq.km/144sq. miles, which was   Dam
created in 1971 by the damming of the Orange River. The fourth largest
artificial lake in Africa, with a dam 90m/300ft high and a maximum capacity
of 5958 million cubic metres (1314 billion gallons), it is part of the Orange
River Project, a large and complex irrigation scheme for the distribution of
water from the river. In 1975 the 82.5km/51 mile long Orange River Fish
Tunnel was opened. The world's longest water tunnel, with a diameter of
5.35m/17½ft, it conveys water from the Hendrik Verwoerd Dam into the
valley of the Fish River and thus ensures an adequate water supply for Port
Elizabeth. The lake offers excellent facilities for water sports.

On the north side of the lake is the Hendrik Verwoerd Dam Nature Reserve   Hendrik Verwoerd
(area 36,500 hectares/90,000 acres). Here live many species of game, in-   Dam Nature
cluding wildebeests and the largest population of springboks in South   Reserve
Africa. In the western part of the park is a holiday centre with various types
of accommodation for visitors, sports facilities, a shopping centre and a
restaurant.

Bisho

Province: Eastern Cape
Altitude: 530m/1740ft
Population: 10,000
Distances: 60km/37 miles from East London, 125km/78 miles from Grahamstown

Situation and characteristics

Bisho, 60km/37 miles north-west of East London, was capital of the Ciskei, declared an "independent homeland" in 1982. (Ciskei, in which 97% of the population were Xhosa, had been granted domestic self-government in 1972). This state, which was not recognised outside South Africa and was not economically viable, was reincorporated in the Republic of South Africa when the transitional constitution came into force on April 27th 1994.

The town was founded only in the 1970s, succeeding Zwelitsha, 15km/9 miles south, which had previously served as the administrative centre of the Xhosa people.

The town

The townscape of Bisho is dominated by a number of modern office and government buildings. Befitting its role as one-time capital of Ciskei, it has a large airport.

Surroundings of Bisho

King William's Town

6km/4 miles from Bisho is King William's Town (see entry), which was never within the territory of Ciskei.

Peddie

53km/33 miles from Bisho on N 2, the road to Grahamstown (see entry), is Peddie, which during the Kaffir Wars of the mid 19th century was frequently the scene of bitter fighting between the Xhosa and the white conquerors. An outlook tower erected in 1841 stands on the site of a fort which was a military base during the Kaffir Wars.

Hamburg, Kiwane Resort

A number of side roads (sometimes unsurfaced) run south from N 2 into a coastal strip some 25km/15 miles wide fringed by beautiful beaches. The little town of Hamburg lies on the estuary of the Keiskammer River, which here forms a lagoon. As the town's name suggests, it was founded in 1857 by German settlers who set out to establish a port at the mouth of the river. The project was frustrated by the silting-up of the harbour, but thanks to its beautiful beach Hamburg has developed into a popular holiday resort. 6km/4 miles east is Kiwane, a small holiday village with a camping site and simple bungalows.

★Shipwreck Hiking Trail

Along the Ciskei coast, between the Great Fish River to the south-west and the Ncera River to the north-east, runs the 64km/40 mile long Shipwreck Hiking Trail. The sections of the trail between the Great Fish River and the Bira River (22.5km/14 miles) and between Hamburg and Kiwane (6km/4 miles) are particularly attractive.

Although in the past many ships ran aground on this stretch of coast, the Shipwreck Hiking Trail fails to live up to its name: not a single wreck is anywhere to be seen.

Stutterheim

42km/26 miles north of Bisho on R 346 is Stutterheim (pop. 38,000). Outside the town to the east is the Bethel mission station, established by German missionaries in 1837. In 1857 more German settlers came to the area – members of the German Legion, which had fought on the British side in the Crimean War. The town is named after their commander, Richard von Stutterheim.

Stutterheim is a good base for hikes into the beautiful forest country round the town, with many native species of trees (yellowwood, stinkwood, wild fig, etc.).

Bloemfontein

Province: Orange Free State
Altitude: 1392m/4567ft
Population: 233,000
Distances: 170km/106 miles from Kimberley, 398km/247 miles from Johan-
nesburg, 634km/394 miles from Durban, 677km/421 miles from Port
Elizabeth, 1004km/624 miles from Cape Town

Bloemfontein, the "city of roses" and Boer stronghold, is capital of the
Orange Free State and its economic and cultural centre. As the seat of the
Court of Appeal of the Supreme Court it is also South Africa's judicial
capital. Thanks to its central situation it has developed into a hub of road
and rail traffic, with the largest railway workshops in the country. It is a
university town (university founded 1855) and above all an administrative
centre: over 40% of the employed population work in state, semi-state or
social organisations and other offices. Apart from this the main contribution is made to the town's economy by light industry (furniture, glass,
foodstuffs).

Bloemfontein lies in the central plain of the highveld, a semi-arid region,
with Naval Hill rising above it to the north-east. Predominantly a modern
city, with a number of historic buildings, monuments and museums, it is a
good centre from which to explore the Orange Free State and a convenient
stopover on a journey between the Cape and the adjoining provinces. It is
not a place for a long stay.

The Bloemfontein Rose Festival is held annually in the third week in
October.

Situation and characteristics

The J. B. M. Hertzog Airport, 8km/5 miles east of the city, has regular flights
to Johannesburg and Cape Town. There is no bus service between the
airport and the city, but many car rental firms have desks at the airport and
there are also taxis. The railway station is in Maitland Street.

Airport, railway station

The first large voortrekker encampment north of the Orange River was
established about 1836 near the present-day settlement of Thaba'Nchu. In
1840, a little to the west, a Boer named Johannes Brits built a farm which he
called Bloemfontein ("Flower Fountain") after a nearby spring surrounded
by a profusion of flowers. A year later the British authorities bought his
farm for £37 and established a garrison and an administrative centre on the
site. Bloemfontein developed into a small town, which in 1854 became
capital of the newly founded Orange Free State, then with a population of
just 12,000. It now extended from the banks of the Bloemspruits River to the
Bloemfonteinberg (Naval Hill), north-east of the town. During the Boer War
there was hard fighting for possession of Bloemfontein, and the town was
bombarded by British artillery on the Bloemfonteinberg. After the establishment of the Union of South Africa Bloemfontein became the third
capital of the country, after Pretoria and Cape Town.

The discovery of gold in the Welkom–Odendaalsrus–Virginia area in
1946 – large deposits ranking with those of the Witwatersrand among the
richest in the world – brought an economic boom to the Orange Free State
and to Bloemfontein.

Ironically, this Boer stronghold was also the birthplace of the African
National Congress. Leaders of the black population met here in 1912 to
protest against the establishment of the Union of South Africa, which
denied them the vote, and founded the South African Native National
Congress, predecessor of the ANC.

Bloemfontein was the birthplace of the writer J. R. R. Tolkien (see
Famous People), though he spent only the first four years of his life here. He
died in Bournemouth, England.

History

Bloemfontein fully justifies its name of "Flower Fountain", with numerous
parks and gardens encircling the city centre. The main business and

The city

Bloemfontein

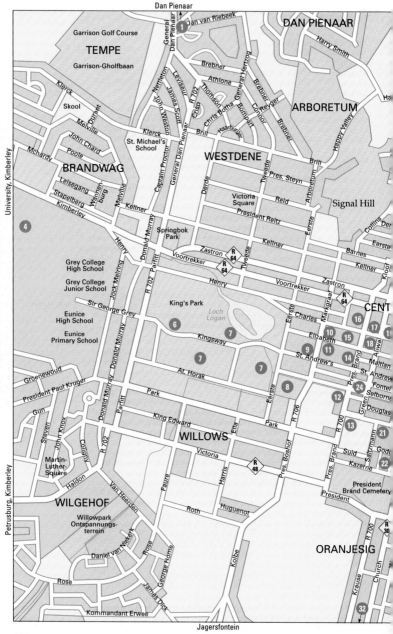

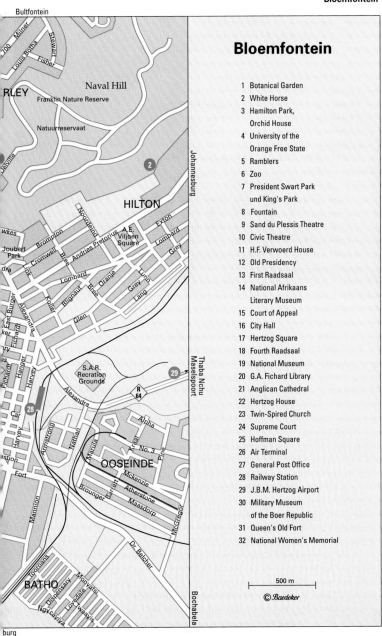

Bloemfontein

1 Botanical Garden
2 White Horse
3 Hamilton Park,
  Orchid House
4 University of the
  Orange Free State
5 Ramblers
6 Zoo
7 President Swart Park
  und King's Park
8 Fountain
9 Sand du Plessis Theatre
10 Civic Theatre
11 H.F. Verwoerd House
12 Old Presidency
13 First Raadsaal
14 National Afrikaans
   Literary Museum
15 Court of Appeal
16 City Hall
17 Hertzog Square
18 Fourth Raadsaal
19 National Museum
20 G.A. Fichard Library
21 Anglican Cathedral
22 Hertzog House
23 Twin-Spired Church
24 Supreme Court
25 Hoffman Square
26 Air Terminal
27 General Post Office
28 Railway Station
29 J.B.M. Hertzog Airport
30 Military Museum
   of the Boer Republic
31 Queen's Old Fort
32 National Women's Memorial

500 m

© Baedeker

Fourth Raadsaal, Bloemfontein

shopping street is Maitland Street, which runs west into President Brand Street, in which most of the buildings described below are situated.

Sights in the City Centre

Walking tour

The bustling hub of the city's life is Hoffmann Square, in which are the Tourist Information Office and the Head Post Office. The square, originally the town's market square, was given its present aspect in the 1970s. It is a convenient starting-point for a tour of the main sights, a walk taking about an hour.

Twin-Spired Church

To the north of Hoffmann Square is the Twin-Spired Church, the only Dutch Reformed church in South Africa with two spires, built in 1880 on the model of Bamberg Cathedral in Germany. It is also known as the President's Church, having been the scene of historically important ceremonies, including the swearing-in of several Presidents of the Orange Free State.

★National Museum

To the west of the church, at the corner of Charles and Aliwal Streets, is the National Museum (open: Mon.–Sat. 8am–5pm, Sun. 1–6pm), which has a large collection of fossils and archaeological material, including the famous Florisbad Skull and one of the largest known dinosaurs. The ethnological section has interesting displays on the life of the Bushmen, and there are also exhibitions on the history of the Orange Free State.

City Hall

Opposite the National Museum, at the corner of Charles and Brand Streets, is the City Hall (by Sir Gordon Leithe, 1935), which is decorated with Italian marble and intarsia work in Burmese wood.

Court of Appeal

The tour continues down Brand Street, which runs south from Charles Street. The first building on the right is the Court of Appeal of the Supreme

Court of South Africa, a Neo-Classical building erected in 1929. The court rooms have stinkwood panelling and magnificent carved decoration.

Opposite the Court of Appeal is the Fourth Raadsaal, one of the city's handsomest buildings. The foundation stone was laid by President F. W. Reitz in 1890 and the building was completed in 1893. It is a Renaissance-style building in red brick with a prominent dome and a portico of Ionic columns. The last session of the Parliament of the old Boer republic of the Orange Free State was held here before the occupation of Bloemfontein by British forces in March 1900. It is now the seat of the Provincial Council of the province of Orange Free State. In front of the building is a monument (by Coert Steynberg) to Christiaan de Wet, a general during the Boer War.

★Fourth Raadsaal

Immediately south of the Fourth Raadsaal are the Waldorf Building, built in 1928 for an insurance corporation and now occupied by offices and flats, and the Jubileum Building and Hall, once the headquarters of the Dutch Reformed Church in the Orange Free State.

Waldorf Building

On the other side of the street, housed in the handsome Old Government Building (1908), is the National Afrikaans Literary Museum (open: Mon.–Fri. 8am–12.15pm and 1–4pm, Sat. 9am–noon), a treasurehouse of African literature, with manuscripts, books, photographs and other items belonging to well-known South African writers. In the same building are the Afrikaans Music Museum (musical instruments) and the Theatre Museum (theatrical costumes). In the Sculpture Garden are busts of famous poets and authors who wrote in Afrikaans.

★National Afrikaans Literary Museum

Farther along Brand Street are the Fire Station (1926) and opposite it the Supreme Court (1906).

Fire Station, Supreme Court

This stately Victorian building (1885) on the west side of Brand Street was the residence of three Presidents of the Boer republic of the Orange Free State. It now houses a museum (open: Tues.–Fri. 10am–noon and 1–4pm, Sat. and Sun. 1–5pm) devoted to the terms of office of the three Presidents – P. J. H. Brand (1864–88), P. W. Reitz (1888–95) and M. T. Stein (1896–1900) – as well as pictures and furniture. The building is also a cultural centre used for art exhibitions, small theatrical performances and concerts.

Old Presidency

In St George's Street, to the east of Brand Street, is the First Raadsaal (1849), the city's oldest building. This thatched cottage was originally a school, then the meeting-place of the Volksraad and later a church. It is now a museum on the history of Bloemfontein (open: Mon.–Fri. 10.15am–3pm, Sat. and Sun. 2–5pm).

★First Raadsaal

From St George's Street Saltzman Street runs south. Off this, on the left, is Goddard Street, in which is Hertzog House, residence from 1895 to 1924 of J. B. M. Hertzog, a Boer general who became President of the Union of South Africa. It is now a museum (open: Tues.–Fri. 9am–4pm). During the 1914 rebellion Hertzog's friends posted themselves in the branches of the tree outside the dining room window to protect him. Among them was a future President of South Africa, C. R. Swart.

Hertzog House

Near the east end of St George's Street is the Anglican Cathedral. Construction of the church began in 1850, but the extension at the west end was completed only in 1885. The bell-tower had to be pulled down in 1964.
   From the Cathedral Gordon Street runs north to return to the starting-point of the tour in Hoffman Square.

Anglican Cathedral

Sights Outside the City Centre

A stone column with the city's coat of arms marks the site of the spring from which Bloemfontein takes its name.

Fountain

Bloemfontein

Sand du Plessis Theatre

The Sand du Plessis Theatre in Markgraaf Street, opened in 1985, with 950 seats, is the venue throughout the year for opera, ballet, drama and concerts.

Opposite the theatre is the H. F. Verwoerd Building, with brilliant stained glass windows composed of over 17,000 pieces of glass.

President Swart Park, King's Park

The city centre is bounded on the west by two parks, President Swart Park and the King's Park. In President Swart Park are the Free State Stadium, with seating for 35,000 spectators, the venue for major sporting events, as well as a heated swimming pool, tennis courts, playgrounds and a camping site.

In King's Park, which was opened by the Prince of Wales in 1925, is a rose garden with over 4000 rose bushes. An arts and crafts market is held here on the first Saturday in every month.

The western part of the King's Park is occupied by Bloemfontein Zoo (open: daily 8am–6pm, to 5pm in winter). The most unusual inhabitant is a "liger", a cross between an African lion and a Bengal tiger.

★ Naval Hill

To the north-east the central area extends almost to Naval Hill, which is reached on a street branching off Union Avenue. Since 1930 this low hill has been occupied by the Franklin Nature Reserve (area 250 hectares/620 acres), with antelopes, zebras and giraffes (open: daily 8am–5pm).

From Naval Hill there is a fine view of the city. Also on the hill is the former Lamont Hussey Observatory, now converted into a theatre. The large white sculpture of a horse on the east side of the hill was set up during the Boer War and served as a landmark for the British cavalry.

★ Orchid House

The Orchid House in Hamilton Park, at the foot of Naval Hill, has the largest collection of orchids in South Africa (open: Mon.–Fri. 10am–4pm, Sat. and Sun. 10am–5pm).

View of Bloemfontein from Naval Hill

In a Cape Dutch mansion in Harry Smith Street, north-west of the Orchid House, is the Oliewenhuis Art Gallery (open: Mon.–Fri. 8am–5pm, Sat. 10am–5pm, Sun. 1–5pm).

Oliewenhuis
Art Gallery

From the city centre Church Street runs south to the Queen's Fort, originally established on this site in 1848 and rebuilt shortly before the outbreak of the Boer War. It is now occupied by the Military Museum, which illustrates the role of the South African army in the two world wars. There are also displays of weapons, including the legendary Mauser, and photographs of the 1914 rebellion (open: Mon.–Fri. 8am–4pm).

Military Museum

This 37m/120ft high obelisk on the south side of Bloemfontein commemorates the 26,000 women and children who died in British concentration camps during the Boer War. In the base of the monument is an urn containing the ashes of Emily Hobhouse, an Englishwoman who campaigned for better treatment of the internees.
  The adjoining War Museum of the Boer Republics is dedicated to the Boer forces which took part in the Boer War. The exhibits include weapons and other objects of the period. The Museum, in Monument Road, is open: Mon.–Fri. 9am–4.30pm, Sat. 9am–5pm, Sun. 2–5pm.

National Women's
Memorial

Surroundings of Bloemfontein

10km/6 miles north-west of the city centre, reached by way of General Dan Pienaar Drive, are the Botanical Gardens (area 45 hectares/110 acres; open: daily 8am–6pm), where visitors can get a general picture of the vegetation of the highveld. Also of interest are the petrified tree trunks many millions of years old. Part of the area is a carefully tended park, with a lake, but in by far the larger part the natural vegetation has been left as it was.

★Botanical
Gardens

At Maselspoort, 22km/14 miles north-east of Bloemfontein on the Modder River, is an attractive holiday centre, with a wide range of leisure activities and a variety of accommodation for visitors.

Maselspoort

35km/22 miles north-west of Bloemfontein, also on the Modder River, is the Soetdoring Nature Reserve. Within its area of 4117 hectares/10,170 acres, which includes Krugersdrif Dam, live large numbers of water birds and other wild life, including lions and cheetahs which have recently been reintroduced.

Soetdoring
Nature Reserve

Bloubergstrand   D 10

Province: Western Cape
Altitude: 57m/187ft
Population: 700
Distances: 25km/16 miles from Cape Town, 55km/34 miles from Malmesbury, 71km/44 miles from Wellington

This little town on the west coast, 25km/16 miles north of Cape Town, takes its name ("Blue Hill Beach") from a 330m/1080ft high hill which has a bluish tinge when seen from the sea.
  In 1806 British forces landed near here and captured the settlement after tough resistance by the Dutch defenders. Later Bloubergstrand developed into an important fishing centre. It is now a favoured – and expensive – residential suburb of Cape Town.

Situation and
characteristics

Visitors come to Bloubergstrand to enjoy the most famous and most frequently painted and photographed view of Table Mountain and Cape Town. The view is equally impressive during the day and at night, when Table Mountain is floodlit. Bloubergstrand is not to be recommended to bathers: there are often cool sea breezes, and the temperature of the sea makes it suitable only for the hardy. Surfers, on the other hand, will find

★★View of
Table Mountain

145

One of South Africa's most photographed sights: Table Mountain, seen from Bloubergstrand

excellent conditions for their sport, and a major international surfing competition is regularly held here.

Surroundings of Bloubergstrand

Robben Island

On clear days the view extends to Robben Island, the notorious prison island (see Cape Town, Surroundings).

Melkbosstrand

From Bloubergstrand a road runs north along the coast through a landscape of dunes, with magnificent views. In spring the country is carpeted with flowers. 10km/6 miles from Bloubergstrand is Melkbosstrand, a quiet little place which is a favourite picnic spot for the people of Cape Town. A marvellous array of shells can be found on the beach – though in summer, when the wind blows from the south-east, it is no great pleasure to walk along the beach.

Blyderivierspoort Nature Reserve   M 3

Province: Eastern Transvaal

Situation and
★★topography

The Blyderivierspoort Nature Reserve lies on the edge of the plateau of the Eastern Transvaal Drakensberg, one of the most beautiful regions in South Africa. Here the highveld falls steeply down from a height of more than 2000m/6500ft above sea level to the lowveld, a fertile region of subtropical climate at heights of no more than 150 to 600m (500 to 2000ft) above sea level. The central feature of the reserve is the Blyde River Canyon, a spectacular gorge.

The Blyderivierspoort Nature Reserve is a favourite staging-point on the journey from Johannesburg to the Kruger National Park. At least two days should be allowed for seeing the natural beauties of the area, using one of

The Blyde River Canyon, hewn from the rock of the Drakensberg over millions of years

the two camping sites within the reserve or one of the hotels in the surrounding area as a base.

The reserve, which has an area of 22,667 hectares/55,987 acres, can be explored by car on a panoramic road, from which side roads branch off to various magnificent viewpoints. The floor of the gorge can be reached only on foot.

Varying climates and altitudes create very varied vegetation patterns. In areas of high rainfall (like the Blyde River Canyon, with an average of 2000mm/80in. of rainfall in the year, compared with only 500mm/20in. in the lowveld) are dense forests, the result of large-scale reafforestation schemes. The ancient rocks, mainly dolomite and quartzite, are frequently covered by coloured lichen. In addition to giant ferns and rare orchids the flora includes species of Erica and Protea. The reserve is also home to many species of animals, including all the species of monkeys commonly found in South Africa and many different species of birds.

Flora and fauna

The Blyde River rises in the Drakensberg to the south of Pilgrim's Rest and in its northward course joins up with the Treur River at Bourke's Luck Potholes. It then flows through the grandiose canyon and finally joins the Olifants River.

Blyde River

The names of the Blyde and Treur Rivers mean "joy" and "sorrow", reflecting an event in Boer history. In the winter of 1844 the voortrekkers set out from the Cape Colony seeking a route to the sea which was not under British control. An expedition led by Andries Hendrik Potgieter headed for Delagoa, leaving their women and children, with the unwieldy trek wagons, on the malaria-free hills of the Transvaal Drakensberg, near Graskop, to await the return of the men. When the agreed time for their return was long past with no sign of them the women thought that something must have happened to the expedition and named the river by which they were camping the Treurrivier, the "River of Sorrow". Soon after

147

setting out for Ohrigstad they were overtaken by Potgieter and his men, who had found the route to the sea they had been looking for but had taken longer than expected to find it. The river where they had met was then named the Blyderivier, the "River of Joy".

Hiking trails

Round Blyde River Canyon are well waymarked hiking trails, ranging in length from an hour or two to several days.

Two long hiking trails run through the nature reserve. The Blyderivierspoort Trail (65km/40 miles; 5 days) runs from God's Window to Swadini (overnight accommodation in huts). The Fanie Botha Trail (80km/50 miles; 5 days), named after a former minister of forestry, runs from the Ceylon Forest Station, 13km/8 miles west of Sabie (see entry), to God's Window, where it joins the Blyderivierspoort Trail.

In view of the limited capacity of the mountain huts it is essential to book in advance. Further information about these and other trails can be obtained from the Regional Director, Eastern Transvaal Department of Forestry (Private Bag, Sabie 1260, tel. 01315/4 10 58).

★★Scenic Route

This scenic route takes visitors travelling by car through the Eastern Transvaal Drakensberg. The first section of the route runs along the edge of the Blyderivierspoort Nature Reserve, with parking places from which visitors can make short trips on foot into the reserve. The second part is also rewarding, though less spectacular. The roads are well made and for most of the way allow fairly rapid travel.

Graskop

The little town of Graskop (pop. 15,000), a timber and forestry centre, is a good base from which to explore the Blyderivierspoort Nature Reserve.

Pinnacle

3km/2 miles north of Graskop on R 532 a side road (R 534) goes off on the right (in 15km/9 miles rejoining R 532). 1.5km/1 mile along R 534 a road on the right leads in 200m/220yd to a parking place above the precipitous scarp of the Drakensberg. From here there is a view of the Pinnacle, a free-standing granite crag rising out of a densely wooded gorge.

★★God's Window

The next stop (a must!) is at God's Window, a viewpoint at an altitude of 1829m/6000ft from which the prospect extends northward over the Blyde River Canyon, eastward over the lowveld, 1000m/3300ft below, and the Kruger National Park to the Mozambique border and westward over forest-covered mountains.

From the parking place there is a well laid-out track to other viewpoints. One particularly rewarding trip (following signs to the Rain Forest) is on a path which winds its way through evergreen tropical rain forest.

Lisbon Falls

R 534 runs in a wide arc to rejoin R 532. Just under a kilometre (¾ mile) south on R 532 a side road (2km/1¼ miles) goes off on the right to the Lisbon Falls, where the river plunges down in a series of steps to a depth of 92m/300ft.

Berlin Falls

1km/⅔ mile north of the R 534/532 junction a side road (2km/1¼ miles) goes off to the Berlin Falls (80m/260ft high), named after a farm which once stood here.

★★Bourke's Luck Potholes

The route continues on R 532, going north. 27km/17 miles from the junction with R 534, at the confluence of the Treur and Blyde Rivers, are Bourke's Luck Potholes. There was once a small gold-mine here called Bourke's Luck. There are now paths and bridges leading to viewpoints from which the potholes can be seen. They were formed at a time where the river had a stronger flow of water and carried down great quantities of sand and detritus which in the course of many million years carved the softer basement rock into the bizarre formations to be seen today.

Bourke's Luck Potholes, at the junction of the Blyde and Treur Rivers

There is a small visitor centre (open: daily 7.30am–4.45pm; kiosk) which gives information about the origin of the canyon and its flora and fauna. For those who want a closer view there are two trails, each 5km/3 miles long, starting from the Bourke's Luck Potholes, the Interpretative Trail and the Bushman Nature Trail.

The next stretch on R 532, running parallel to Blyde River Canyon, offers particularly spectacular views. Another magnificent viewpoint is the Three Rondavels View Site, reached on a side road (3km/2 miles) which goes off R 532 on the right 13.5km/8½ miles beyond Bourke's Luck Potholes. Above the 700m/2300ft deep gorge rear the Three Rondavels and Maripeskop (1944m/6378ft), the highest peak in the Transvaal Drakensberg, named after a Pulana chief named Maripe who in the early 19th century fled with his tribe to the mountain, from which he successfully beat off attacks by the Swazis.

★★Three
Rondavels

Far below, at the inflow of the Ohrigstad River, glitters an artificial lake created by the damming of the Blyde River.

R 532 then continues along the edge of the Blyderiviersoort Nature Reserve for a few miles, passing Odendaal Camp, a well equipped holiday village, and then turns west to join R 36. Here there is a choice of routes. To the north are a beautiful pass and a reptile park; the direct route runs south.

The road to the north (signposted to Tzaneen), which was opened in 1959, leads to the Abel Erasmus Pass (1224m/4016ft), climbing 700m/2300ft with numerous bends and fantastic views.

Abel Erasmus
Pass

50km/30 miles north of the junction of R 532 with R 36, on R 527, is the Swadini Reptile Park (open: daily 9am–5pm; cafeteria), with snakes, lizards and crocodiles from the region and from all over the world. Interesting presentations and commentaries and, for those so inclined, the chance of

★Swadini
Reptile Park

Blyderivierspoort Nature Reserve

The Three Rondavels, three crags in the Blyde River Canyon resembling conical-roofed native huts

handling a snake (under supervision) make a visit to this park a memorable experience.

★Echo Caves

The road running south from the junction, signposted to Lydenburg, comes in 1km/¾ mile to the Echo Caves (on the right of the road), an extensive system of stalactitic caves in the local dolomite. Material found in the caves shows that they were occupied by Stone Age man. Rock paintings and other objects from the caves are displayed in the Museum of Man (open: daily 8am–5pm).

Ohrigstad

The road continues through a rugged landscape, with red soil in which fruit, vegetables and tobacco are grown. 23km/14 miles beyond the Echo Caves it comes to Ohrigstad. A village was established here in 1845 but was abandoned soon afterwards because of epidemics of malaria. This fertile valley was reoccupied only in the 20th century, after the elimination of the mosquitoes. There are some ruins of the original village.

Ohrigstad Dam
Nature Reserve

18km/11 miles beyond Ohrigstad R 36 runs into R 533. A short distance along this road to the east a side road (4km/2½ miles) goes off on the right to the Ohrigstad Dam. Round the lake is the Ohrigstad Dam Nature Reserve, a popular camping and picnicking area.

Mount Sheba
Nature Reserve

6km/4 miles farther east a side road (10km/6 miles) goes off to the Mount Sheba Nature Reserve, which has preserved its natural forest cover (see Pilgrim's Rest).

Pilgrim's Rest

15km/9 miles beyond the road to the Ohrigstad Dam is Pilgrim's Rest (see entry). From here it is 14km/8½ miles to Graskop, the starting-point of this scenic route.

Bredasdorp   E 10

Province: Western Cape
Altitude: 164m/538ft
Population: 10,000
Distances: 170km/106 miles from Cape Town, 176km/109 miles from Mossel Bay

Bredasdorp lies in a fertile agricultural and sheep-farming region some 30km/19 miles from Cape Agulhas (see entry), the most southerly point in Africa. The town is named after Michiel van Breda, a breeder of merino sheep who became its first mayor in 1838.
    A Wild Flower Show is held here annually in August.

Situation and characteristics

Sights in and around Bredasdorp

The Shipwreck Museum (open: Mon.–Fri. 9am–4.45pm, Sat. 9am–2.45pm, Sun. 10.30am–12.30pm) is small but of great interest. It charts the numerous ships which have foundered on this treacherous coast – among them the British troopship HMS "Birkenhead", which sank in 1852 with the loss of 450 men – and displays a great variety of material recovered from the wrecks – ships' figureheads, gold and silver coins, nautical equipment, etc. The oldest objects come from the "Nieuw Haerlem", which sank in 1647. In another hall is a collection of old vehicles and furniture.

Shipwreck Museum

At the end of Van Riebeeck Road is the Bredasdorp Nature Reserve (area 800 hectares/2000 acres). The flora of the reserve includes many species of Protea and Erica and the red Bredasdorp lily, and it is home to many small mammals and birds. From a 368m/1207ft high hill there are fine views of the town and surrounding area. The park is open throughout the year, but the best time to visit it is in September and October, when large numbers of spring flowers are in bloom.

Bredasdorp Nature Reserve

24km/15 miles south-east of Bredasdorp is the fishing village of Arniston or Waenhuiskrans. Some of the old fishermen's cottages have been carefully restored, and a luxurious modern holiday village has been built in the same style. Arniston's great attraction is a long, lonely sandy beach.
    The village takes its name from a British ship which was wrecked on the nearby cliffs in 1815 with the loss of 372 lives. Its other name of Waenhuiskrans comes from a huge sea-cave 2km/1¼ miles south (accessible only at low tide). There are many striking rock formations, the result of erosion by the sea, along this stretch of coast.

★Arniston/ Waenhuiskrans

50km/30 miles north-east of Bredasdorp on the Wydgeleë road is the De Hoop Nature Reserve (area 40,000 hectares/100,000 acres; open: daily 7am–6pm), which was established in 1956.
    The reserve takes in a picturesque stretch of coast and its beautiful hinterland. It is an area of fynbos, the characteristic Cape vegetation, with 1400 species of plants, including 25 extremely rare and endangered species, 63 species of mammals (50 of them on land and 13 in the sea) and 40 species of reptiles. Between June and September right whales, who come here to mate, can be observed close to the coast.
    There is a camping site within the reserve as well as cottages to let.

★De Hoop Nature Reserve

Burgersdorp   J 8

Province: Eastern Cape
Altitude: 1580m/5184ft
Population: 15,000
Distances: 52km/32 miles from Aliwal North

Caledon

Situation and characteristics	Burgersdorp, in the north of the Eastern Cape, was founded in 1847 and is now a centre of stock-farming and the woollen industry. When the Governor of the Cape Colony, Sir Peregrine Maitland, refused to allow the town to be named after him the townspeople named it Burgersdorp, the "burghers' village". It was the seat of South Africa's first theological university, which was later moved to Potchefstroom.
The town	Burgersdorp is a quiet little country town with a number of buildings which have been declared national monuments, among them the old prison and the church. The former parsonage is now a museum. In Burger Square is the Taal (Language) Monument, erected in 1892. The town played an important part in the promotion of the Afrikaans language in South Africa.
Die Berg Nature Reserve	Near the town is Die Berg Nature Reserve (area 425 hectares/1050 acres), with many species of game. From the reserve there is a footpath to the J. L. De Bruin Dam, which has excellent facilities for water sports.

Caledon   E 10

Province: Western Cape
Altitudde: 324m/1063ft
Population: 7000
Distances: 85km/53 miles from Worcester, 100km/62 miles from Cape Town

Situation and characteristics	Caledon lies in an intensively cultivated agricultural region in which arable farming and sheep-rearing are the principal sources of income. The town grew up round its mineral springs, which were frequented by the first European settlers in the 18th century and are still used for medicinal purposes. There are seven springs, with a total daily flow of 900,000 litres (200,000 gallons) of water containing iron and other minerals; six of them are hot, with temperatures around 50°C/122°F, and one is cold. A new hotel was opened in 1990.

Sights in and around Caledon

Caledon Museum	The Municipal Museum in Krige Street (open: Mon.–Fri. 8am–5pm, Sat. 9am–noon) displays relics of Victorian times.
Anglican church	The 19th century Anglican Holy Trinity Church is a scheduled national monument.
★Venster Kloof Nature Garden	The Venster Kloof Nature Garden (area 56 hectares/138 acres; open: daily 7.30am–5pm), established in 1927, is part of a nature reserve on the Swartberg, a hill to the north of the town. It takes its name from a rock in the shape of a window (*venster*). It contains many native species of trees, but is mainly known for its profusion of wild flowers. A large Wild Flower Show is held here annually in September.
Christiaan de Wet Walking Trail	The 10km/6 mile long Christiaan de Wet Walking Trail runs through the surrounding country.
★Salmonsdam Nature Reserve	40km/25 miles south-east of Caledon is the Salmonsdam Nature Reserve (area 846 hectares/2090 acres; open daily 7am–7pm), which is reached by way of R 316 and R 326 (signposted to Stanford). This area of typical Cape fynbos vegetation can be explored on three well waymarked trails, respectively 3km/2 miles, 5km/3 miles and 8km/5 miles in length. If you are lucky you may see antelopes and gazelles as well as various species of birds.

Calvinia   E 8

Province: Northern Cape
Altitude: 1020m/3347ft
Population: 7000
Distances: 330km/205 miles from Cape Town, 472km/293 miles from
   Upington

Calvinia, an isolated little town at the foot of the Hantamsberg
(1673m/5489ft), is a possible base for a trip through Namaqualand (see
entry), north-west of the town. The surrounding area is famed for its show
of blossom in spring.

Situation and
characteristics

   The town, founded in 1848 and named after the Swiss Reformer John
Calvin, is second only to Harrismith as a centre for the breeding of merino
sheep. This breed of sheep, famed for the fineness of its wool, originally
came from Spain. In 1789 King Charles V of Spain presented a number of
merinos to William V of Holland, and six of these came to the Cape, where –
to the displeasure of the Spanish – they flourished magnificently. The
progeny of the original six provided the basis of South Africa's merino-
breeding industry.

Sights in Calvinia

Calvinia's Museum (open: Mon.–Fri. 8am–1pm and 2–5pm, Sat. 8–noon) is
housed in a former synagogue (a relic of the time when the population of
the area included a high proportion of Jews). The Museum's collection
illustrates the history of European settlement and sheep-farming and also
includes archaeological finds from the surrounding area and old furniture
and photographs.

Calvinia Museum

This restored historic building, with 17th and 18th century furniture, now
functions as a guest house; tel. 0273 41 1606.

Bothasdal

2km/1¼ miles north of Calvinia, at the foot of the Hantamsberg, is the
Akkerendam Nature Reserve (area 2300 hectares/5680 acres), established
in 1962. Two hiking trails run through the reserve, which is open throughout the year. The Karebook Trail, which runs along the foot of the Hantamsberg, is a short walk of 3km/2 miles; the Steerboom Trail takes 7 hours.
Both trails allow visitors to discover the marvellous flora of the Hantamsberg. The fauna of the reserve includes various species of antelope.

Akkerendam
Nature Reserve

Surroundings of Calvinia

70km/43 miles west of Calvinia on R 27 is Nieuwoudtville (alt. 719m/2359ft;
pop. 1000), in a sheep-farming region in which corn and rooibos tea are
also grown.

Nieuwoudtville

   The Nieuwoudtville Wild Flower Reserve (area 115 hectares/284 acres) is
particularly attractive in spring. If the winter rainfall has been sufficiently
abundant 300 species of wild flowers bloom here.

   On the beautiful road from Nieuwoudtville to Louriesfontein are the
100m/330ft high Nieuwoudtville Falls, which are particularly impressive
after rain, and the bizarre Kokerboom Forest.

From Nieuwoudtville a track runs 10km/6 miles south to the Oorlogskloof
Nature Reserve (area 5070 hectares/12,520 acres), the main attractions of
which are its Bushman paintings and a number of interesting rock formations. A 46km/29 mile long hiking trail runs through the reserve; to walk the
whole trail takes 3 or 4 days, spending the nights in mountain huts, but it is
also possible to walk along selected sections. The reserve can be visited
only by appointment (Oorlogskloof Nature Reserve, Private Bag, Nieuwoudtville 8180).

Oorlogskloof
Nature Reserve

Tankwa Karoo
National Park

The Tankwa Karoo National Park (area 27,064 hectares/66,848 acres), 95km/59 miles south of Calvinia, was established to safeguard and restore the natural splendour of the semi-desertic landscape of the Karoo. After a rare fall of rain the area becomes a sea of flowers. It is planned to develop leisure facilities in the park.

Cape Agulhas   E 10

Province: Western Cape
Distances: 30km/19 miles from Bredasdorp, 170km/106 miles from Cape Town

Situation and
★characteristics

Cape Agulhas (lat. 34°50′ S) is the southernmost point in the Republic of South Africa and on the African continent. Here, at the "Cape of Needles", the Atlantic and the Indian Ocean meet.

Origin of name

There are different explanations of the name "Cape of Needles". One view is that it was so called because at this point the compass needles of the early Portuguese navigators pointed due north; others think that the name refers to the sharp reefs off the coast.

Topography

The scenery at South Africa's southern tip is not particularly spectacular. The shingle beaches have a very gentle gradient, and offshore extends the Agulhas Bank. For a distance of 250km/155 miles the sea is nowhere deeper than 110m/360ft, and then it suddenly plunges steeply down into the depths. The sea in this area is one of the most productive fishing grounds in the world.

Lighthouse on Cape Agulhas, the most southerly point in Africa, where the Atlantic and the Indian Ocean meet

The lighthouse, now a museum (open: Mon.–Fri. 9.30am–4.30pm, Sun. 9.30–11.30pm), was built in 1848 and is the second oldest in South Africa. A radio beacon warns shipping rounding the Cape.

Lighthouse

Surroundings of Cape Agulhas

5km/3 miles east of the cape is the little settlement of Agulhas, with modern holiday apartments and a few shops. The coast at this point is rocky and not particularly attractive.

Agulhas

8km/5 miles north-east of the cape is Struisbaai, which has a beautiful beach for bathers, fishermen and shell collectors.

Struisbaai

The fishing village of Hotagterklip, 2km/1¼ miles north of Struisbaai, is a favourite subject with South African painters. Some of the old fishermen's cottages have been restored and are now protected as national monuments.

★Hotagterklip

Cape of Good Hope

See Cape Town, Surroundings

Cape Town · Kaapstad

D 10

Province: Western Cape
Altitude: 12m/39ft
Population: 780,000 (conurbation 1.9 million)
Distances: 1402km/871 miles from Johannesburg, 1004km/624 miles from Bloemfontein, 1753km/1089 miles from Durban, 962km/598 miles from Kimberley, 769km/478 miles from Port Elizabeth

Cape Town (in Afrikaans Kaapstad), situated at the south-western tip of the African continent, is for many people one of the world's most beautiful cities, thanks mainly to its magnificent setting against the majestic backdrop of Table Mountain. But Cape Town has much else to offer: there are a number of front-rank sights in the city itself and its immediate surroundings, and the beaches on the Cape Peninsula and in False Bay are among the most beautiful in South Africa. At least a week should be allowed for exploring the attractions of Cape Town.

★★Situation and characteristics

Cape Town is the second largest city in South Africa (after Johannesburg – and excluding Soweto from the definition of a city) and the oldest European settlement in southern Africa, Parliament sits here during the first half of the year (in Pretoria during the rest of the year). Cape Town is also chief town of the Western Cape Province, with numerous government offices, the see of Roman Catholic and Anglican bishops and a major cultural centre, with two universities, technical colleges and many state and private schools.

It is the only town on the African continent south of the Equator in which whites and people of mixed race form the majority of the population. Peculiar to the Cape are the Cape Malays, the descendants of slaves brought in from Indonesia, with cultural traditions of Islamic stamp.

Cape Town plays an important part in the economy of South Africa. The commercial and fishing port, with ultra-modern loading and discharging facilities, is the largest in the country after Durban. Most of South Africa's fruit exports are shipped from here.

Economy

Cape Town's industrial areas lie mainly to the north and east of the city. Its industries include oil processing, concrete factories, the production of

155

View of Cape Town from Table Mountain

fertilisers and chemicals, textiles and the clothing industry, electronics and various light industries.

Many banks, insurance corporations, printing firms and publishers have their headquarters in the city. Tourism is now one of the most important sources of income.

Transport

Cape Town is the starting-point of two important roads: N 1, which runs north-east for 2000km/1240 miles, passing through Johannesburg and ending at Messina, on the frontier with Zimbabwe, and N 2, which runs up the coast of the Indian Ocean into Swaziland.

Cape Town's D. F. Malan International Airport is less than a half-hour's drive south-east of the city. There are regular bus services between the South African Airways terminal in Adderley Street and the airport.

The railway station is in Adderley Street. There are frequent services to the outer districts on the Cape Peninsula to the south, to the False Bay coast as far as Simon's Town and to the outer districts to the north as far as Bellville. Cape Town is also the departure point of the luxurious Blue Train which runs between Cape Town, Johannesburg and Pretoria (see Practical Information, Railways).

There are also regular services by luxuriously equipped buses from Cape Town into the interior of the country.

Climate

Summer is warm and dry, and sometimes hot; winter is like a northern April, with low temperatures, rain and cold winds. The climatic pattern is influenced by the two marine currents which meet on the south-west coast of Africa: the warm Agulhas Current, coming from the Equator, which flows along the east coast, and the cold Benguela Current, coming from the icebergs of the Antarctic, which washes the west coast.

During the summer Cape Town is regularly visited by the "Cape doctor", a strong south-east wind which blows away the city's dust and exhaust gases. South-easterly winds are also responsible for the celebrated "tablecloth". The wind drives warm, moist air masses from False Bay against Table Mountain; the air then condenses, and a layer of cloud covers the plateau like a blanket of cottonwool.

The oldest traces of human settlement on the Cape were left by the Hottentots (Khoikhoi) and Bushmen (San), living as herdsmen and as hunters, gatherers and fishermen. The first European to round the Cape, in 1488, was the Portuguese navigator Bartolomeu Diaz. In 1503 his countryman Antonio Saldanha became the first European to climb Table Mountain. The colonisation of South Africa, however, began only on April 6th 1652, when a Dutch merchant, Jan van Riebeeck, landed in Table Bay. He and his companions established on behalf of the Dutch East India Company a supply base for the company's ships sailing to India. The site was well chosen: springs under Table Mountain supplied fresh water, the soil was fertile, and increasing areas of land were developed by settlers from Holland, Germany and France. Cape Town became known as the "tavern of the seas". For many years to come the history of Cape Town, the "mother city", as it is still known today, was identical with the history of South Africa.

    The little "vleck van den Kaap", the little village on the Cape, developed in the course of time into a town of traders, officials and craftsmen which from 1806 to 1910 was capital of the British Cape Colony. More recently, as the seat of Parliament, it has been one of South Africa's capitals.

    Great things are also planned for the future. Cape Town is putting forward a claim to host the Olympic Games in the year 2004.

History

Its situation makes Cape Town one of the world's most fascinating cities, but the city itself is less impressive than its situation. The regularly laid out central area extends between Table Bay, with the harbour, to the north and Table Mountain (1000m/3280ft) to the south. Within this area many historic old buildings have been preserved. The appearance of the city has been much enhanced by the completion, in recent years, of the Victoria and Alfred Waterfront. The formerly unattractive harbour area is now a lively entertainment quarter.

    The "better" suburbs, almost exclusively occupied by whites – among them Goodwood, Parow and Bellville – extend north-eastward from the city centre along N 1, the road to Paarl. To the south, along the coast between Sea Point and Hout Bay, are a series of attractive bathing resorts. In contrast to these are the ugly 19th century industrial and housing areas (Saltriver, Woodstock, etc.) in the harbour area. Along the north-western edge of the central area is the Malay quarter with its mosques, renovated 18th and 19th century houses and 1950s apartment blocks.

    The black population live in the area known as Cape Flats, extending south-east from the city centre to False Bay. Between N 2 and False Bay are townships such as Athlone, squatter camps like Crossroads and the satellite towns of Mitchell's Plain and Khayelitsha. There are also large townships on the north side of Table Bay and near the big industrial plants, such as Atlantis and Philadelphia.

★Townscape

Sights in City Centre

The tour described in this section begins in the harbour area, on the Victoria and Alfred Waterfront, where there is adequate parking. The tour can be shortened by starting from the Castle of Good Hope and after seeing the rest of the central area taking a taxi to the Waterfront, or alternatively the Waterfront Bus, which runs between the railway station and the harbour (with a stop at the entrance to the Victoria and Alfred Hotel).

Walking tour

Cape Town's artificial harbour is the fourth busiest South African port (after Richard's Bay, Saldanha and Durban), with an annual turnover of 5.9 million tons. Since it lies on solid rock and cannot be deepened, it has a depth at low tide of only 12m/40ft.

Table Bay, Harbour

Occupation of the Cape

Phoenicians sailing in the service of the Egyptian Pharaoh Necho (reigned 609–594 B.C.) are believed to have been the first to round the southern tip of Africa. Later, around 520 B.C., Carthaginians led by Hanno are said by Herodotus (5th century B.C.) to have sailed round it from east to west. Many centuries later two brothers from Verona, Vadino and Ugolino Vivaldi, are said to have rounded the Cape in 1291; but there is no conclusive evidence of any voyage round the Cape of Good Hope before the end of the 15th century. The first navigators who are known on the basis of firm evidence to have sailed round the southern tip of Africa are the Portuguese. During the 15th century many Portuguese seamen sailed ever farther down the west coast of Africa in the quest for a sea route to India. In 1488 Bartolomeu Diaz sailed round the Cape without realising it, since he was then battling with a severe storm. It was only on his return voyage that he discovered the "Cape of Storms", as he at first called it. Soon afterwards the name was changed to Cabo de Boa Esperanza (Cape of Good Hope). The name may reflect the hope that after three-quarters of a century of Portuguese expeditions down the west coast of Africa the sea route to the fabulous land of India had at last been found. (It is not known with certainty who gave this name to the cape: some Portuguese sources say it was Bartolomeu Diaz, others that it was King John II of Portugal.)

Ten years after Bartolomeu Diaz's voyage Vasca da Gama reached India by way of the Cape. Thereafter the Portuguese regularly sailed to Asia, with Mossel Bay as one of their most important ports of call. In view of the strategic importance of the Cape it is surprising that the Portuguese never established a settlement there; but until the end of the 16th century they had no serious competitors on the route to India. The Cape in any case was of little economic importance. There was only a certain amount of barter between ships' crews and the natives (the Khoikhoi or Hottentots). And an incident in 1510, when the Viceroy of India, Francisco de Almeida, was involved in an armed conflict with the Khoikhoi in which he and all his companions were killed, may well have inhibited any plans for establishing a settlement.

Similar considerations probably prevented the English from establishing any permanent settlement at the southern tip of Africa. From the end of the 16th century onwards England and Holland controlled the world's oceans. In 1605 officers of the (English) East India Company declared the Saldanha Bay area a British possession; but no garrison was left behind, and the declaration remained an empty gesture. In 1613 one of the managers of the East India Company, Sir Thomas Smythe, had Xhoré, a chief of the Xhora-Khoikhoi tribe which then occupied the Cape, kidnapped and carried back to Britain, with the idea of teaching him English and inducing him to reveal secrets, particularly about the whereabouts of gold in his country. The enterprise produced little result; but Xhoré became a great admirer of Britain during the six months he spent in the country. His attitude changed when Sir Thomas Smythe, with ten prisoners who had been condemned to death, tried to establish a base on Table Bay. The Xhora tribe had no trouble in disposing of these undesirable incomers, but the incident led to a change in the relationship between the natives and the whites. Their previous peaceable attitude now gave place to caution, if not to outright hostility. They had realised that the Europeans were no longer interested in trade but were out to take their land away from them.

For the moment at least Britain abandoned any attempt to occupy the territory on the Cape. In 1618 British and Dutch commercial houses discussed the possibility of establishing a joint settlement, but without result. In 1620 an English captain took possession of the land for the British crown, but the king would have nothing to do with it. The colonisation of the southern tip of Africa began only a generation later – as a result of a navigational error.

In 1647 a Dutch ship on the way back from India, the "Nieuw Haerlem", ran aground in Table Bay, and the crew had to stay there for a year until they were able to return home in another Dutch vessel. Back in Holland, two members of the crew put in a report on the suitability of Table Bay as a site for a settlement, and the directors of the Dutch East India Company, which had the world's mightiest commercial fleet and dominated trade with the East Indies, thereupon decided to establish a supply station on the Cape of Good Hope. It was a difficult and thankless task, and the directors thought it might suit a young man named Jan van Riebeeck

Jan van Riebeeck and his men landing in Table Bay in 1652

Baedeker Special

who had been suspected of trading in the Far East for his own profit rather than that of the Company. Since his reputation had previously been unblemished and the charges against him had not been substantiated the directors resolved to entrust the task to him. He was commissioned to establish at the Cape a fort, a supply station, a hospital and accommodation for seamen sailing to and from the East Indies; and on April 6th 1652 van Riebeeck, with his wife and 90 men, women and children, landed at the Cape and founded a settlement. In order to improve the colony's food supply and its defence against the natives he received permission from the Company in 1655 to grant land round the colony to "free burghers" who would cultivate it. Conflicts with the natives over the possession of land continued, and in 1659 the conflicts developed into war, in which the Khoikhoi suffered an annihilating defeat. Thereafter they withdrew into the interior of the country.

When Jan van Riebeeck left South Africa in 1662 there were four small forts and – almost as a foretaste of apartheid – a hedge of bitter almond protecting the livestock and the crops of the free burghers, the forefathers of the Boers, against the natives.

Under the apartheid regime April 6th 1652, the day on which van Riebeeck landed at the Cape, was regarded as "the beginning of civilisation on the African continent" and "the foundation of the nation". The anniversary was celebrated as a public holiday for the last time in 1944, just before South Africa's first free election; the annual ceremony of laying wreaths at the monument to Jan van Riebeeck in Cape Town had been quietly dropped some years before.

Fishermen still land their catches in the Victoria and Alfred Basins, while deep sea trawlers and cruise ships use the Duncan and Ben Schoeman Docks, constructed in the 1930s. The port's principal export is fruit, and Cape Town has one of the world's largest deep-freeze depots. On the east side of the harbour is the largest dry dock in the southern hemisphere, the Sturrock Dock, which can easily accommodate two large vessels at the same time. The Royal Cape Yacht Club is also based in the harbour, which because of the excellent wind conditions here is the starting-point of the Cape to Rio race.

Harbour tours

Various firms run harbour tours, day trips and longer evening cruises. There is also the Penny Ferry (daily from 10am to 6pm, in winter to 5pm), a rowing boat service which takes visitors from one quay to another in 4 minutes.

★★Victoria and Alfred Waterfront

The Victoria and Alfred Waterfront is an entertainment quarter with something of the atmosphere of Fisherman's Wharf in San Francisco and London's Soho. It extends round two inner harbour basins, constructed in 1860, and named after Queen Victoria and her second son Alfred (later Duke of Edinburgh). Only a few years ago this was a rather squalid and rundown fishing harbour: it is now one of Cape Town's leading attractions, lively and bustling all day and much of the night. It now draws more than 13 million visitors per year, attracted by its numerous shops, bars, jazz spots, restaurants and hotels, its two theatres (including the Dock Road Theatre, housed in a former power station), a drama school, cinemas and museums.

Victoria and Alfred Waterfront: Cape Town's entertainment and shopping centre, pulsating with life until late at night

Wherever possible old buildings have been preserved and restored: a three-storey warehouse has become a luxury hotel, a pumping-station now houses a bar and a former prison is now the Business School of Cape Town University. The area is developing all the time and the newest attraction is the Two Oceans Aquarium, a fascinating underwater world. For information on special or daily events tel. 418 2369.

The South African Maritime Museum, on the Alfred Basin (Dock Road), has sections devoted to the history of the port and plans for future development, the fishing industry, shipping lines and shipwrecks. The collection includes many ship models. The Museum is open daily 10am–5pm.

South African Maritime Museum

Also part of the Museum are a number of old ships, moored in various parts of the harbour, which are open to visitors. In front of the comfortable Victoria and Alfred Hotel is the "Alwyn Vincent", a steam tug launched in Venice in 1859. The SAS "Somerset" is the only surviving submarine-net guardship in the world.

The "Victoria" is a reconstruction of a sailing ship of 1770, built by a group of treasure-hunting divers who in the last few years have discovered more than 40 wrecks off the coasts of South Africa and recovered large numbers of coins and other objects. The ship contains a small museum of objects recovered from wrecks, and there are audio-visual presentations on the work of the divers. Open: daily 9am–6pm.

"Victoria"

To the south of this is the Fisheries Museum (open: Tues.–Sun. 10am–4pm), which has a collection of ship models, fishing equipment and an aquarium. Here too there are audio-visual presentations.

Fisheries Museum

161

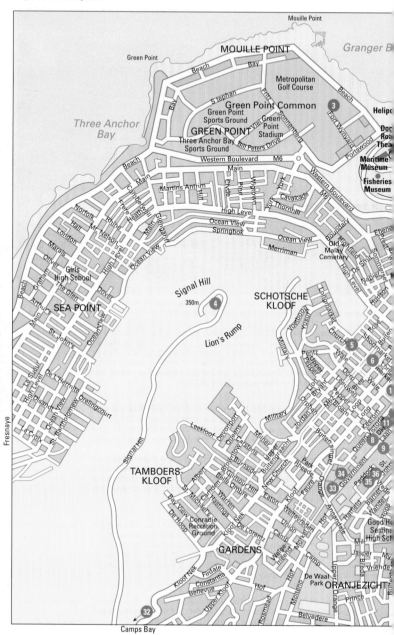

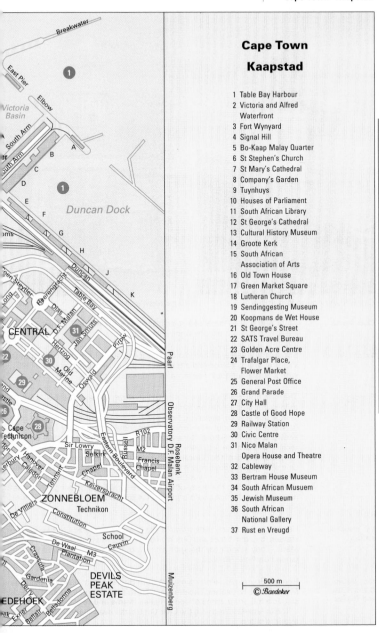

Cape Town

Kaapstad

1 Table Bay Harbour
2 Victoria and Alfred
  Waterfront
3 Fort Wynyard
4 Signal Hill
5 Bo-Kaap Malay Quarter
6 St Stephen's Church
7 St Mary's Cathedral
8 Company's Garden
9 Tuynhuys
10 Houses of Parliament
11 South African Library
12 St George's Cathedral
13 Cultural History Museum
14 Groote Kerk
15 South African
   Association of Arts
16 Old Town House
17 Green Market Square
18 Lutheran Church
19 Sendinggesting Museum
20 Koopmans de Wet House
21 St George's Street
22 SATS Travel Bureau
23 Golden Acre Centre
24 Trafalgar Place,
   Flower Market
25 General Post Office
26 Grand Parade
27 City Hall
28 Castle of Good Hope
29 Railway Station
30 Civic Centre
31 Nico Malan
   Opera House and Theatre
32 Cableway
33 Bertram House Museum
34 South African Musuem
35 Jewish Museum
36 South African
   National Gallery
37 Rust en Vreugd

500 m
© Baedeker

Clock Tower on the Waterfront

Cape Town's City Hall

Clock Tower	At the entrance to the Alfred Basin is the Clock Tower (1887), which houses a small shipping museum (open: Sat. 2–5pm).
Victoria Wharf	Should the weather be bad visitors can spend some time very pleasantly in Victoria Wharf, a large and attractive shopping centre completed in 1991, with luxury boutiques, banks, cafés and restaurants.
Foreshore	The road from the Victoria and Alfred Waterfront to the city centre, 1km/-01-mile south-east, is not an attractive route for pedestrians, but there is a shuttle bus service, departing from the Victoria and Alfred Hotel. This area between the harbour and Strand Street, now traversed by freeways, is known as the Foreshore. It was created between 1937 and 1945 on land reclaimed from the sea, using sand dredged from the sea-bottom during the construction of the Duncan Dock. The site was built up in the late fifties. One of the oldest buildings is the 26-storey Sanlam Building, which at the time of its construction was the tallest building in Africa. It now no longer stands out among the many other high-rise buildings housing oil companies, municipal offices, Safmarine (the largest South African shipping line), etc.
Van Riebeeck statues	Heerengracht, which runs towards the town centre, leads to two bronze statues (by John Week and Dirk Wolbers) of Jan van Riebeeck and his wife Maria. They stand near the spot where van Riebeeck is believed to have landed on April 7th 1652.
Nico Malan Opera House and Theatre	Hertzog Boulevard, which runs east from Heerengracht, leads to the Nico Malan Opera House and Theatre, Cape Town's most modern theatre, which stages a full programme of opera, ballet, drama and concerts. The theatre is linked with the Civic Centre, the headquarters of municipal administration.

Castle of Good Hope: the balcony from which the Governors addressed the townspeople and announced important decisions

To continue the tour, return to Heerengracht and follow it and its continuation, Adderley Street, running south-west. Adderley Street, the city's principal shopping street, runs past the railway station (1970) and tourist information office and comes to the Golden Acre shopping centre (1978). During the construction of the centre the remains of a water reservoir of 1663 were discovered and were incorporated in the new building. On the ground floor is the High Water Mark, showing where the coastline of Table Bay ran in 1663. There are more shops in the underground mall between the Strand Concourse and Adderley Street.

Adderley Street, Golden Acre

One sight that should not be missed is the Castle of Good Hope, to the east of Adderley Street. This is the oldest surviving stone building in South Africa, built in 1666–79 as the residence of the Governor and for the protection of the early settlers – though in fact the castle, which is in the form of a five-pointed star, was never exposed to attack.

★Castle of Good Hope

The main gate leads into an inner courtyard. The range of buildings with an elaborate columned balcony, originally used for ceremonial and official occasions, now houses the William Fehr Collection (open: daily 10am–4pm). The collection includes pictures, porcelain, fine glass, ceramics and furniture of the 17th–19th centuries from South Africa, Europe and Asia.

Other parts of the castle can be seen only on conducted tours (daily at 10am, 11am, noon, 2pm and 3pm). Visitors are shown various prisons and store-rooms (in which archaeological finds are displayed) and taken up on to one of the bastions. Much of the castle is closed to the public, since it is the provincial headquarters of the South African army. Changing of the guard Monday to Friday at noon.

This square between the Castle and City Hall was originally laid out in 1710 as a parade ground. It is now a car park, except for one corner where there

Grand Parade

are flower and fruit stalls. A flea market is held here on Wednesdays and Saturdays.

City Hall

On the south-west side of the square is the City Hall (1905), a striking mix of Italian Neo-Renaissance and British colonial style. The 60m/200ft high bell-tower, with a carillon installed in 1923, was modelled on London's Big Ben.

Groote Kerk

Now return to Adderley Street, at the south end of which is the Groote Kerk (Great Church), the oldest and best known church in South Africa. The first church on this site, built in 1678, was rebuilt in 1703 and again in 1836. The bell-tower dates from 1703. The Groote Kerk is the mother church of the Nederduitse Gereformeerde Kerk (NGK) of South Africa. The pulpit was carved by Anton Anreith.

Cultural History Museum

The building next to the Groote Kerk was erected in 1679 to house the Dutch East India Company's slaves and was converted by Thibault and Anreith in 1809 to accommodate the Supreme Court. It is now occupied by the Cultural History Museum (installed here in 1966), which contains Egyptian, Greek and Roman antiquities, collections of stamps, coins and weapons and a 19th century pharmacy. Of particular historical interest are the "post stones" under which outward-bound seamen left letters in the hope that ships sailing in the opposite direction would pick them up and carry them home. In the courtyard is a reproduction of Jan van Riebeeck's grave. The Museum is open: Mon.–Sat. 9.30am–4.30pm.

St George's Cathedral

Diagonally opposite the Cultural History Museum is the Neo-Gothic St George's Cathedral (by Sir Herbert Baker, 1897–1901), was the seat of Archbishop Desmond Tutu, former head of the Anglican Church in South Africa and winner of the Nobel Peace Prize.

South African Library

The continuation of Adderley Street is Government Avenue (Laan), which is lined by tall oak-trees. This popular pedestrian promenade links the city centre with the suburbs at the foot of Table Mountain. At the near end, adjoining the Cathedral, is the South African Library (established 1812), a reference library of some 400,000 books, including a copy of every book published in South Africa. The books can be consulted but not borrowed. The Library is open: Mon.–Fri. 9am–6pm, Sat. 9am–1pm.

Houses of Parliament

Opposite the Library is the imposing façade of the Houses of Parliament (main entrance in Parliament Road). The original building, in which parliamentary sittings were first held in 1814, has been much altered and extended since then. Here the South African Parliament meets between the end of January and the end of June; during the rest of the year it meets in Pretoria. Its debates are open to the public (apply to Room 12; foreign visitors muct produce their passport). When Parliament is not sitting there are conducted tours of the building on Mon.–Fri. at 11am and 2pm (for information tel. 4 03 29 11).

Tuynhuys

The adjoining Tuynhuys was built in 1751. As the official residence of the State President, it is not open to the public.

★Company's Garden

On a site now occupied by the Botanical Gardens (area 5.5 hectares/13½ acres; entered from Government Avenue) the first white settlers laid out vegetable and fruit gardens in 1652. With their exotic trees and flowers, rose garden, aviaries and ponds, the gardens are an oasis of peace in the heart of the city. Under shady trees is a café where visitors may like to rest and relax after their sightseeing.

Other attractions are the scented garden for blind people, a sundial of 1782 and a reproduction of a slave bell of 1855. There are monuments to Sir George Gray, Governor of the Cape Colony from 1845 to 1862, and Cecil Rhodes (see Famous People). The figure of Rhodes shows him pointing northward – reflecting his ambition to extend British influence from the

The Company's Garden in the heart of the city

Cape to Cairo. The monument was designed by Sir Herbert Baker, a British architect who came to South Africa in 1892 and received many commissions from Rhodes.

At the south-west end of the gardens, in Queen Victoria Street, is the South African Museum (open: daily 10am–5pm), which was established in 1825. It has an extensive and varied natural history collection, including archaeological finds, stuffed or reconstructed South African animals and remains of dinosaurs. Dioramas give a vivid picture of what southern Africa looked like millions of years ago. A special department is devoted to the native peoples and their cultures, with particular emphasis on the life of the Bushmen and examples of their art.

★South African Museum

Attached to the Museum are an exhibition on the development of printing and a planetarium.

To the east of the South African Museum is the South African National Gallery (open: Mon. 1–5pm, Tues.–Sun. 10am–5pm), which is mainly devoted to South African artists but also contains works by British, French and Dutch masters of the 17th–20th centuries.

South African National Gallery

Close by, at 84 Hatfield Road, is the Jewish Museum (open: Dec.–Feb. on Tues. and Thur. 11am–5pm, Wed. 9.30am–12.30pm, Sun. 10am–12.30pm, Mar.–Nov. 2–5pm), founded in 1861. It occupies the oldest synagogue in the country (1862) and displays a collection of Jewish art and exhibits illustrating the history of Jews in South Africa.

Jewish Museum

At the south-west end of Government Avenue is Bertram House, a brick-built Georgian mansion of 1820 which is now an outstation of the South African Museum (open: Tues.–Sat. 9.30am–4.30pm), with a collection of period furniture, ceramics, silver and other objets d'art.

Bertram House Museum

South African National Gallery

St George's Street	To continue the tour the best plan is to return along shady Government Avenue, turn left at the Groote Kerk and immediately right into St George's Street, a pleasant pedestrian precinct with trees, fountains, benches and numerous shops, enlivened by street musicians and other performers.
★Green Market Square	To the left, reached by way of Longmarket or Shortmarket Street, is Green Market Square, which from 1710 onwards was the town's market square. In this atmospheric little cobbled square, with a number of Art Deco buildings as a backdrop, a small flea market is held every day of the week except Sunday.
★Old Town House	On the west side of Green Market Square is the Old Town House (1755), a building in Cape Dutch style which originally housed the town guard. In 1804 it was taken over by the municipal authorities and later accommodated a lawcourt and police station. It now displays a collection of pictures presented to the state by Sir Max Michaelis in 1914, consisting mainly of works by 17th century Dutch and Flemish masters, including Frans Hals, Jan Steen, Jacob van Ruysdael and Jan van Goyen (open: daily 10am–5pm).
South African Association of Arts	Close by, at 35 Church Street, is the South African Association of Arts, which has a collection of contemporary South African art (open: Mon.–Fri. 10am–5pm, Sat. 10am–1pm). The display is changed every three weeks.
Sendinggestig Museum	From Green Market Square Longmarket and Shortmarket Streets run north-west. In this area, at 40 Long Street, is the Sendinggestig Museum (open: Mon.–Fri. 9am–4pm), housed in an old mission church of 1802.
Riebeeck Square, St Stephen's	In Riebeeck Square, where the first settlers on the Cape set up their camp, is St Stephen's Church. Originally a theatre and opera house, it was converted into a Dutch Reformed church in 1839.

To the north-west, at the foot of Signal Hill, is Bo-Kaap, the old Malay quarter, bounded by Rose, Wale, Chiappini and Shortmarket Streets. The picturesque flat-roofed two-storey houses in this area, colour-washed in a variety of colours, are still mainly occupied by Malays, the descendants of slaves who were brought to the Cape from the East Indies in the second half of the 17th century and later mostly became craftsmen of various kinds. They have preserved their Islamic traditions: there are a number of small mosques in the area, and the muezzin's call to prayer is heard five times a day. One of these mosques, the Masjid Korhaanol in Longmarket Street, has remained almost unchanged since it was built in 1886. Some of the houses (most of which date from the 19th century) have been renovated in recent years.

★Bo-Kaap

The Bo-Kaap Museum at 71 Wale Street, in a house dating from 1763, illustrates the Muslim way of life on the Cape in the 19th century (open: Tues.–Sat. 9.30am–4.30pm).

Bo-Kaap Museum

The return to the city centre is by way of Strand Street, in which is the Lutheran Church, one of the oldest Protestant churches in South Africa, consecrated in 1787. The bell-tower was added in 1818. The pulpit and choir screen were carved by Anton Anreith.
    The church forms an attractive group with the former parsonage, the Martin Melck House, at 96 Strand Street.

Lutheran Church

Another notable building in Strand Street is the Koopmans-de Wet House (No. 35), built in 1701 on a U-shaped ground-plan, with a façade by Louis Thibault (1771). The original interior has been preserved and gives a vivid impression of the life-style of a successful 18th century businessman. The period furniture is the work of both European and South African craftsmen. The house is open Tues.–Sat. 9.30am–4.30pm.

★Koopmans-de Wet House

Sights outside the City Centre

Green Point Lighthouse

Green Point Common, on the north side of Cape Town, west of the Victoria and Alfred Waterfront, is an extensive open space with a variety of sports facilities, including a golf course. It lies within the Green Point district at the foot of Signal Hill.
    On the common, near the sea, is Fort Wynyard, built in 1861 by R. H. Wynyard. To the east of this (in Portswood Road, in the City Hospital complex) is the Cape Medical Museum (open: Mon.–Fri. 9am–4pm).

Green Point Common

From here Beach Street runs west to Green Point Lighthouse (1824), the oldest lighthouse in the country.

Green Point Lighthouse

To the south of Green Point Common, in Antrim Road, is the Herring Bequest Institute, with a fine collection of furniture, porcelain, musical instruments and books (open: Mon., Wed. and Fri. 8.30am–8pm, Tues. 2–8pm, Thur. and Sat. 8.30am–1pm).

Herring Bequest Institute

From Signal Hill (350m/1150ft), to the west of the city centre, there is a good view of the city and Table Bay. It is worth driving up after dark to see the shimmering sea of lights that is Cape Town at night. The approach to the hill is from the south by way of Signal Hill Street, which branches off Kloof Nek Road.

★Signal Hill

Every day (except Sunday) at noon a cannon (actuated by an electronic impulse from the Observatory) fires a single shot. In earlier days this "noon gun" served to give the exact time to ships anchored in the bay.

Rust-en-Vreugd

South-east of the city centre, near the intersection of Buitenkant and Roeland Streets, is Rust-en-Vreugd, a mansion in Cape Dutch style built in 1778 with a magnificent façade. It houses a further section of the William Fehr Collection (see Castle of Good Hope), including watercolours, African paintings and antiques (open: Mon.–Fri. 9.30am–4pm).

St Mary's Cathedral

At the corner of Roeland and St John Streets is St Mary's Cathedral, the oldest Roman Catholic church in South Africa.

South African Air Force Museum

In the eastern district of Ysterplaat (reached on N 1 and then M 5) is the South African Air Force Museum (entrance in Piet Grobler Street; open: Mon.–Sat. 8.30am–12.30pm and 1.30–4.15pm), which illustrates the history of the South African Air Force from the 1920s to the recent past, with the main emphasis on the two world wars.

Groote Schuur Hospital

South-east of the city centre, reached on N 2/M 3 or M 4, is the Groote Schuur Hospital, established in 1932, which became world-famed in December 1967, when Christiaan Barnard (b. 1922 in Beaufort West), a surgeon working in the hospital from 1958 to 1983, performed the world's first heart transplant.

Observatory

To the east, in the Observatory district, is South Africa's oldest observatory, which dates from 1821. Since the construction of the South African Astronomical Observatory in the Karoo the Cape Town Observatory has been used only by amateur astronomers.

Mostert's Mill

Soon after the junction where N 2 branches off, M 2 (here called Rhodes Drive) runs past Mostert's Mill, a windmill dating from 1792 which is still in working order (open: daily 9am–3pm).

Irma Stern Museum

A little way east of Mostert's Mill, in the pleasant suburb of Rosebank (Cecil Road), is the house in which Irma Stern, an artist of German origin, lived from 1928 until her death in 1966. It is now a museum (open: Tues.–Sun. 10am–1pm and 2–5pm), with over 200 of her works as well as antiques and other objets d'art.

University of Cape Town

To the west of Rhodes Drive, on the Groote Schuur estate, is the campus of the University of Cape Town. The name Groote Schuur comes from a granary (*schuur*) built here in 1657. The site was acquired in 1891 by Cecil Rhodes (see Famous People), who left it to the state.

The University buildings are picturesquely situated below Table Mountain and Devil's Peak. The University, founded in 1918, developed out of the South African College established in 1829. It has some 15,000 students.

Groote Schuur

To the south-east, beyond Rhodes Drive, is Groote Schuur, the official residence of the State President. It stands on the site of the 17th century granary, which later gave place to a grand country house. When this was burned down in 1896 Rhodes commissioned the celebrated architect Sir Herbert Baker to build a new house in Cape Dutch style.

Woolsack

Within the University campus is the Woolsack, a house built by Cecil Rhodes for Rudyard Kipling, who was a friend of his; the architect was again Sir Herbert Baker. The writer and his family spent the summer months here from 1900 to 1907.

Josephine Mill, Rugby Museum

To the south is the Newlands district, regarded as one of Cape Town's "best" residential areas. Here, in Boundary Road, is the Josephine Mill (1818), Cape Town's only surviving watermill (open: Mon.–Fri. 9am–4pm).

Also in Boundary Road is the Rugby Museum (open: daily 9.30am–4pm), with a lovingly assembled collection of rugby memorabilia.

From the Newlands district it is only a short distance to the famous Kirstenbosch Botanical Gardens (see below).

Kirstenbosch Gardens

★★Table Mountain

Table Mountain (1087m/3566ft), the flat-topped hill to the south of the city centre, is the great landmark and emblem of Cape Town. Its summit plateau is frequently covered by a layer of clouds, the "tablecloth" (see p. 156). Since weather conditions here are very changeable it is advisable to arrange your trip to the summit, either on foot or by road, immediately you see it clear of clouds. The ascent is rewarded by an immense prospect of Cape Town and the Cape Peninsula. At weekends Table Mountain is floodlit after dark. The best view, and the best place from which to take a photograph, is from the road up Signal Hill (see p. 169).

Table Mountain, built up from massive beds of sandstones and slates, forms the northern end of the Cape Peninsula. It is flanked on the east by Devil's Peak (1001m/3284ft) and on the west, beyond a wide depression, by the Lion's Head (669m/2195ft). It extends southward as a broad plateau and then falls steeply down to Orange Kloof (200m/650ft). To the east it rears above the suburb of Newlands and the Kirstenbosch Botanical Gardens; to the west, in the crags known as the Twelve Apostles, it looms over the bathing resorts on the Atlantic coast.

Situated as it is between the Atlantic and False Bay, Table Mountain has a mountain climate with high rainfall. Most of the annual rainfall of 1400mm/55in. occurs in the winter months, between May and September. Two reservoirs on Table Mountain (the source area of many streams) contribute to Cape Town's water supply. The particular climatic conditions

Situation and characteristics

The approach to Table Mountain   *A café on the summit*

From Table Mountain the view extends over the whole of the Cape Peninsula

have produced a very varied flora (over 2200 species) and fauna. Sir Edmund Hillary, the celebrated climber, called Table Mountain one of the world's natural wonders. But it is threatened by soil erosion, the loss of native plants and invasion by alien species, uncontrolled bush fires and large numbers of visitors. In order to stop this deterioration the Table Mountain Nature Reserve was established, taking in, in addition to Table Mountain itself, Signal Hill and adjoining areas.

Cableway

A cableway installed in 1929 runs up Table Mountain, covering the distance of 1244m/1361yd in 7 minutes. Subject to weather conditions – it does not operate in high winds – the cableway runs daily: 7am–10.30pm between Dec. and mid-Jan.; 8am–9.30pm end of Jan. to end of Apr.; 8.30am–5.30pm May–Oct.; 8am–9.30pm Nov. (for information tel. 24 51 48).

The lower station of the cableway is reached by car from the city centre by way of Buitengracht and Kloof Nek Road. There is a bus service from Adderley Street to Kloof Nek Road, from which the cableway company runs buses to the station.

Climbing
Table Mountain

There are said to be more than 350 different routes, in varying degrees of difficulty, for the ascent of Table Mountain. The first European to climb the mountain (Antonio da Saldanha, in 1503) went by way of the Platteklip gorge. Depending on starting-point, the climb takes between 2 and 4 hours.

There are guided climbs to the summit. Further information can be obtained from the tourist information office in Cape Town or from John McDonnell (tel. 45 25 03), who (weather permitting) leads small groups on Tuesdays and Thursdays.

The plateau

At the upper station of the cableway is a café/restaurant with a small viewing terrace. This is the starting-point of three short walks which give visitors some impression of the gigantic scale of the landscape. The Tortoise Walk (waymarked with a tortoise symbol) takes only 5–10 minutes;

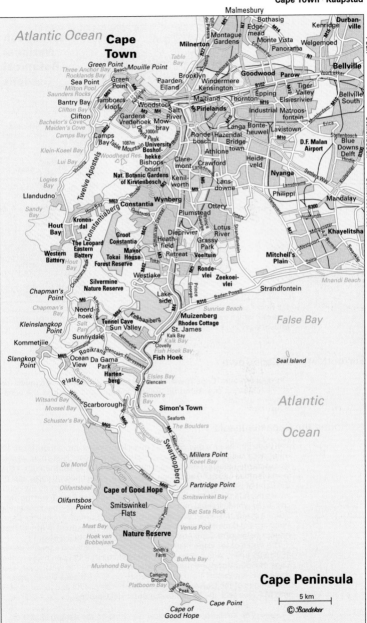

Cape Town · Kaapstad

Atlantic Ocean **Cape Town**

Malmesbury

Paarl

Stellenbosch

Somerset West

Cape Peninsula

5 km

© Baedeker

173

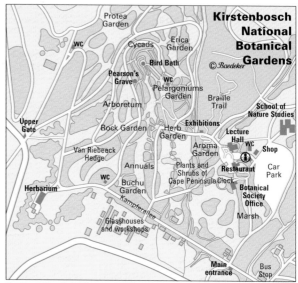

the Rock Dassie Walk, named after the comical little brown animals (rock hyraxes) which swarm round the restaurant, takes 10–20 minutes; and the Klipspringer Walk takes between 30 and 45 minutes.

Surroundings of Cape Town

The country round Cape Town is of great beauty and charm. Two musts for all visitors are a trip round the Cape Peninsula and a visit to the wine-growing districts.

★★Round the Cape Peninsula

The Cape Peninsula alone, 52km/32 miles long and no more than 16km/ 10 miles wide, would be sufficient justification for a visit to Cape Town. Along its coasts are miles of beaches of white sand, and at its southern tip is the world-famous Cape of Good Hope. Cape Point, a few hundred yards east of the Cape of Good Hope, has been recognised by geographers as the point where the Atlantic and the Indian Ocean meet – making Cape Town the only city in the world situated on two oceans. Here the Atlantic's cold Benguela Current meets the Indian Ocean's warm Agulhas Current. But neither Cape Point nor the Cape of Good Hope is the most southerly point in Africa: that honour belongs to Cape Agulhas (see entry), farther to the east.

The sights of the Cape Peninsula are described below in a tour of some 150km/95 miles, which runs down the east coast of the peninsula to the Cape of Good Hope and returns to Cape Town along the west coast. The route runs south-east from the city centre on M 3 (Rhodes Drive), passes the campus of the University of Cape Town (see p. 170) and turns off M 3 into M 63 to reach the Kirstenbosch Botanical Gardens.

The Kirstenbosch Botanical Gardens, on the eastern slopes of Table Mountain, are among the most beautiful in the world ▶

★★Kirstenbosch
National Botanical
Gardens
(Map p. 172)

The site of the Kirstenbosch Botanical Gardens was bequeathed to the state by Cecil Rhodes in 1902. The first director of the Botanical Gardens when they were established in 1913 was Harold Pearson, whose grave is in the gardens. Within this hill area of 528 hectares/1304 acres (some 60 hectares/150 acres of which are cultivated) are over 20,000 native South African species of plants which are collected, grown and studied here. The number of species that can flourish here, however, is limited by the cool, damp winters: this area has an annual rainfall of almost 1500mm/60in., spread over an average of 140 days in the year.

Of particular historical interest are a hedge of wild almond-trees planted by Jan van Riebeeck in 1660 and an avenue of camphor and fig trees planted by Cecil Rhodes in 1898. The flowers, shrubs and trees are so arranged that there is a show of blossom and colour throughout the year. The main flowering season is from mid August to mid October; the red disa, a species of orchid known as the "pride of Table Mountain", is in flower along the banks of streams and in shady gorges from January to March; and the protea, South Africa's national flower, is in glorious bloom from May to October.

Particular attractions in the Kirstenbosch Gardens are a scented garden in which visitors can touch the flowers, a herb garden, a protea garden and a rock garden. The Bird Bath (a pool in the shape of a bird created by Major Christopher Bird in 1811) is the central feature of a shady area in which 70-year-old yellowwood trees grow. At least an hour is required to stroll round the almost level lower part of the gardens, and there are shorter paths round the adjoining wooded area on the slopes of the hill. A general impression of this area can be got on the 500m/550yd long Braille Trail, which runs through a marshy wooded area with an abundance of birds.

The restaurant in the Kirstenbosch Gardens serves refreshments and meals on a shady terrace, and there is a shop selling beautiful and unusual plants. The gardens are open: April to August from 8am to 6pm,

The Wine Cellar, Groot Constantia

September to March 8am to 7pm; there are conducted tours on Tuesdays and Saturdays at 10am.

The wine-making estate of Groot Constantia is reached from the Kirstenbosch Gardens by taking M 63, going south-west, and then turning left into M 41. The direct route from Cape Town is on M 3 to the Plumstead/Constantia/Hout Bay exit and then on M 41.

★★Groot
Constantia

Groot Constantia, the oldest and best known wine-making estate in South Africa, lies surrounded by vineyards in the Constantia valley, a 20-minute drive from the centre of Cape Town. The estate was presented to Simon van der Stel, governor of the Dutch colony, by the Dutch East India Company in 1685 so that he could find, by trial and error, which agricultural products did best on the Cape. In due course he built a mansion in which he lived from 1699 until his death in 1712. In 1778 Hendrik Cloete, grandson of one of the earliest settlers, bought the house and part of the estate and commissioned Louis Thibault and Anton Anreith to enlarge and embellish the building. At this time, too, the Wine Cellar (which is actually on ground level) was built. Cloete also extended the vineyards, since his wines soon gained a reputation in Europe as well as in South Africa. The spread of phylloxera on the Cape 1860 ended the great days of wine production, and in 1885 the whole estate was sold to the colonial authorities.

Groot Constantia is now a state-owned wine-making estate. The mansion, one of the finest examples of Cape Dutch architecture, became a museum in 1926 and now displays valuable 18th and 19th century furniture and a collection of porcelain. The Wine Cellar of 1791, which has a pediment on the façade with figural decoration by Anton Anreith, is now used for exhibitions and congresses. There is a small museum (open: daily 10am–5pm) illustrating the history of wine-making on the Cape and the production and storage of wine. Adjoining the main house, and fitting beautifully into the general ensemble, is the Jonkershuis, now a popular restaurant (open: daily 9am–5pm; reservations tel. 7 94 62 55). Rather

The picturesque little beach huts of Muizenberg and Kalk Bay

more rustic in style is the "Tavern" restaurant (open: daily 10am–6pm, Sat. to 10pm), housed in a building in which wine was formerly stored and bottled.

The wines produced on the Groot Constantia estate can of course be sampled in these restaurants, but they can also be tasted and bought in the new and modern wine-cellar (open: daily 10am–5pm; conducted visits of wine-cellar hourly from 11am to 3pm).

Constantia Uitsig

Visitors who find Groot Constantia too crowded can book a luxurious suite on the privately owned wine farm of Constantia Uitsig, reached by way of M 42 (reservations tel. 7 94 65 00, fax 7 94 76 05), where there is a restaurant popular with local people as well as visitors.

Muizenberg

M 41, going east, runs into M 4, which leads to the north-east coast of the Cape Peninsula. Muizenberg is the first of a series of bathing resorts on False Bay whose long sandy beaches attract large numbers of Cape Towners, particularly at weekends (Muizenberg is connected with Cape Town by fast electric trains). The town grew out of a military post established in 1743 and became fashionable when Cecil Rhodes bought a holiday home here. He was followed by many prosperous citizens, and Muizenberg became a classic example of a South African bathing resort, with numbers of holiday homes which were occupied for only a few weeks in the year. Short-term inhabitants of a town have no great interest in its public buildings and institutions, and as a result the townscape of Muizenberg is not particularly attractive.

The town does, however, have three interesting museums, all on Main Road, on the southern outskirts of the town. The Natale Labia Museum, a branch of the South African Gallery, has a collection of furniture and works of art (open: Tues.–Sun. 10am–5pm; closed Aug.). Rhodes Cottage, in which Cecil Rhodes died on March 26th 1902, is now a museum with many mementoes of Rhodes (open: Tues.–Sun. 10am–1pm and 2–5pm). The Muizenberg Museum Complex, opened in 1990, consists of a Police Museum (open: Mon.–Fri. 8am–4pm, Sat. 9am–1pm, Sun. 2–5pm), a Library built in 1910, the 18th century Posthuys, the Post Office of 1911 and the Railway Station of 1912–13, a red-brick building now housing shops and a restaurant.

Rondevlei Bird Sanctuary

5km/3 miles north-east of Muizenberg, reached by way of Prince George Drive (M 5), is the Rondevlei Bird Sanctuary (established 1952), an area of dunes with a saltwater lake which is home to more than 200 species of birds. The birds can be watched at close range from observation points equipped with telescopes. Attached to the sanctuary are a research station and an information centre with a small museum (open: daily 8am–5pm).

Seal Island

Off Muizenberg, to the east, is little Seal Island (area 2 hectares/5 acres), with a population of some 50,000 seals. In summer there are boat trips to the island from Kalk Bay and Gordon's Bay.

Silvermine Nature Reserve

On the south-western outskirts of Muizenberg, reached on a road which branches off at Kalk Bay or on Ou Kaapse Road (M 64), is the Silvermine Nature Reserve (open: daily 8am–7pm, to 6pm in winter). The flora of this hilly region is among the most beautiful on the whole Cape Peninsula. The reserve (area 2158 hectares/5330 acres), which extends westward from the crest of the hills above Kalk Bay and the Muizenberg range to the east of this as far as Mt Nordhoek (756m/2480ft), is the home of antelopes, gazelles, steppe lynxes, porcupines and genets. There are many attractive footpaths leading up hill and down dale to superb viewpoints. In the late 17th century Governor van der Stel hoped to find silver in this area: his hopes were disappointed, but they have given the reserve its name.

Kalk Bay

In the busy harbour of Kalk Bay the fishing boats can be seen every day coming in with their catches. The place originated in 1795 as a military outpost, and in 1806 it became a whaling station, but when the number of whales in False Bay fell sharply whaling ceased after only five years. Since then Kalk Bay has developed into a bathing resort.

The next place of any consequence on this tour of the Cape Peninsula is Fish Hoek, another popular bathing resort, which grew up round a farm established in 1818 by Lord Charles Somerset. Somerset laid down that no alcohol should be served on his estate: this regulation was adopted by the municipal authorities, and the sale of alcohol is still prohibited in Fish Hoek.

Fish Hoek

In Peers Cave was found the skull of a man who lived more than 15,000 years ago. The access road to the cave branches off M 65, which runs across the peninsula from Fish Hoek to the west coast, 3km/2 miles from Fish Hoek. The last bit of the way must be done on foot.

Peers Cave

Simon's Town (pop. 6000), 6km/4 miles south of Fish Hoek at the end of the electric rail line from Cape Town, took its name from Governor Simon van der Stel. Thanks to its sheltered situation it became in 1741 the winter port for Cape Town and 1957 the main base and training centre of the South African Navy. The harbour is also used by many fishing boats and yachts. In the section of St George's Street between the railway station and Jubilee Square, known as the Historical Mile, there are a number of fine 18th and 19th century buildings.

Simon's Town

The former Governor's residence (1777) is now occupied by the Simon's Town Museum (open: Tues.–Fri. 9am–4pm, Sat. 10am–1pm). The Martello Tower, built by the British authorities in 1796 as a powder magazine, also houses a small museum. In the old parsonage at 2 Church Street, now the Stem Pastorie Museum (open: Mon.–Sat. 9.30am–4.30pm), Pastor M. L. de Villiers composed the South African national anthem in 1921.

The coast road runs down to the south end of the Cape Peninsula, which was declared a nature reserve in 1939 in order to protect the flora and fauna against overdevelopment (open: daily dawn to dusk).

★Cape of Good Hope Nature Reserve

Within this area of 8000 hectares/20,000 acres, with a coastline of 40km/25 miles, live a great variety of animals, including antelopes, bonte-

The Cape of Good Hope

boks, ostriches, warthogs, mountain zebras, lynxes, otters and baboons. The baboons tend to force their attentions on visitors, who should on no account feed them. Off the coast can be seen whales, dolphins and seals. The reserve also contains some 1200 species of plants typical of the Cape, including proteas and various types of heath. But it is not so much the flora and fauna that attract more than 400,000 visitors to the south-western tip of Africa every year as the grandiose scenery and the feeling that they are standing on one of the world's great historic spots (see Baedeker Special, p. 248).

The main road runs south through the nature reserve to Cape Point, where the Atlantic and the Indian Ocean meet. The road ends at a large parking area (souvenir shop, restaurant) from which it is a few minutes on foot or in a shuttle bus to Cape Point. There are two lighthouses here. The older one, erected in 1860, stands at a height of 249m/817ft above sea level. On a clear day its light can be seen at a distance of 67km/42 miles, but in bad weather it is frequently lost in cloud. A new lighthouse was therefore built in 1919 almost 100m/330ft lower down. It is a vital landmark for the more than 20,000 ships which sail round the Cape every year, making this one of the busiest shipping lanes in the world.

From Cape Point a hiking trail runs west to the Cape of Good Hope, and there is also a motor road. Bartolomeu Diaz, who in 1488 became the first European to round the rocky promontory at the south-western end of the Cape Peninsula, originally called it the Cape of Storms; for there are almost always strong winds here, during the summer months usually blowing from the south-east: wind speeds of up to 40km/25 miles an hour are normal, and on occasion they may reach 120km/75 miles an hour. Below the high, steep cliffs are rocks and shallows. Near the information centre is a cross commemorating Bartolomeu Diaz, and farther east, near Buffelsbaai, is another cross honouring Vasco da Gama, who rounded the Cape of Good Hope in 1497 in his quest for a sea route to India.

Kommetjie

Leaving the nature reserve, M 65 runs west and comes in 20km/12½ miles to the little fishing town of Kommetjie, which because of the prevailing strong winds attracts surfers rather than bathers. Its long sandy beach also offers excellent opportunities for bird-watchers.

★Chapman's Peak Drive

From Kommetjie M 65 runs inland to join M 6, which turns north-west and returns to the Atlantic coast beyond Noordhoek. This is the starting-point of Chapman's Peak Drive, one of the world's most impressive corniche roads, which runs for 10km/6¼ miles, with numerous bends, along the rocky face of Chapman's Peak. At its highest point the road reaches a height of 160m/525ft above sea level; and since the rock exposed by the blasting of the road out of the cliff face has not yet oxidised the reddish and yellowish strata of Table Mountain sandstones can be seen above the Cape granite. There are numerous parking places from which visitors can enjoy the view over Hout Bay, extending as far as the Sentinel (331m/1086ft).

Hout Bay

Chapman's Peak Drive ends at the little town of Hout Bay, in the bay of that name. Once surrounded by dense forest (*hout* = "wood"), Hout Bay is now an important fishing port (particularly crayfish). The fishermen's catches, fresh from the sea, are sold on Mariners' Wharf. From here there are cruises to Cape Town (2–3 hours; advance reservation advisable, tel. 7 90 10 40) and in summer to Duiker Island, a seal and bird reserve. The Hout Bay Museum in St Andrew's Road is devoted to the history of the town and the fishing industry (open: Tues.–Sat. 10am–12.30pm and 2–4.30pm).

World of Birds

On the northern outskirts of the town, in Valley Road, is the World of Birds (open: daily 9am–6pm), a bird reserve with over 3000 indigenous and exotic birds, including ostriches, cormorants, pelicans, penguins, parrots, eagles and various kinds of water bird. Special features are the large walk-through aviaries.

Chapman's Peak Drive: magnificent views at every turn of the road

Adjoining Hout Bay, and now almost continuous with it, is the bathing resort of Llandudno, with exclusive villas lining the slopes of the hill. A beautiful and relatively sheltered beach attracts day visitors as well as residents. A footpath runs south to Sandy Bay, one of South Africa's few legal nudist beaches.

Llandudno

The coast road continues past the Twelve Apostles, south-western outliers of Table Mountain.

Twelve Apostles

Numbers of holiday homes and the occasional higher apartment block are indications that the road is nearing Cape Town. The beaches of Camps Bay and Clifton, divided into small sections by rocks, tend to be crowded in good weather. In Kloof Road, Camps Bay, is the Round House, originally used by Lord Charles Somerset (see Fish Hoek) as a hunting lodge and now a restaurant, with fine views over the little town (reservations, tel. 4 38 23 20).

Camps Bay, Clifton

The tour of the Cape Peninsula ends at Sea Point, a populous suburb of Cape Town. Between the modern high-rise blocks there still survive some handsome Victorian buildings. Strung along the 3km/2 mile long seafront promenade are a succession of hotels, restaurants and night clubs.

Sea Point

★Through the Winelands

In the valleys in the hills round Cape Town vineyards extend as far as the eye can see, and amid the vineyards can be glimpsed whitewashed mansions with the characteristic Cape Dutch gables. Names such as La Dauphinée and La Provence recall the French settlers who brought wine-growing to the Cape. Well-drained but rather thin soils, warm and sunny summers, cool winters with a sufficiency of rain and frequent new blends have made

Llandudno, which has one of the finest beaches on the Cape Peninsula

the grapes resistant and given the wines made here their particular quality, enabling them to stand comparison with good French wines (see Baedeker Special, p. 471).

From Cape Town there are a number of "wine routes" which allow visitors to see various wine-making estates, sample their wines and, during the vintage, observe the processes of wine-making. Many wineries also have good restaurants. A useful guide is the brochure "Wine and Dine" produced by the Captour travel agency (Adderley Street, tel. 4 18 52 14).

Stellenbosch	The wine route nearest Cape Town starts from Stellenbosch (see entry), only 40 minutes' drive away. The country's oldest wine route, it runs through the heart of the Winelands.
Franschhoek, Paarl	Rather farther away are the signposted wine routes starting from Franschhoek (see Stellenbosch) and Paarl (see entry).
Groot Constantia	Those who have only limited time at their disposal but would like to see something of wine-making on the Cape can visit the state-owned wine estate of Groot Constantia on the Cape Peninsula (see p. 177).
Other wine routes	Other wine routes with their own particular character are those round Wellington (see Paarl), Worcester, Robertson and Tulbagh (see entries). There is also a wine route along the west coast, north of Cape Town (wineries at Vredendal and elsewhere).

Other Sights round Cape Town

Bloubergstrand	From the bathing resort of Bloubergstrand (see entry), 25km/15 miles north of Cape Town, there is the most famous view of Table Mountain and the city.

In Table Bay, 10km/6 miles off Bloubergstrand, is Robben Island (area 6sq.km/2½sq. miles), which was already used as a prison island by the Portuguese. Here, over the centuries, were confined rebellious slaves, Asian rulers who opposed the Dutch East India Company, African chiefs who fought the white conquerors and political prisoners. Nelson Mandela (see Famous People) spent twenty years here as prisoner No. 466/64. The island was also a leper colony and had a psychiatric hospital, a naval station and a nature reserve. There are still some 700 prisoners on the island. Its future use has not been settled: proposals range from making the prison a tourist attraction – offering visitors the thrill of sleeping in Nelson Mandela's cell – to establishing a centre for the study of South African history.

Robben Island

From the Waterfront in Cape Town there are boat trips to the island. Book well in advance tel. 021/2 411 1006. Boats are not, however, allowed to dock on the island.

Durbanville, 20km/12½ miles north-east of central Cape Town, is one of the oldest settlements in the Western Cape. It is named after Sir Benjamin D'Urban, Governor of the Cape from 1834 to 1838. Durbanville is the starting-point of a wine route.

Durbanville

The town's principal sight is the Rust-en-Vrede Pottery Museum, in the Cultural Centre in Wellington Road. It occupies a building of 1850 in Cape Dutch style which was originally a prison and later the residence of the Governor and a school. The Museum displays work by modern South African artists and a collection of African pottery (open: Mon.–Fri. 9.30am–4.30pm, Sat. and Sun. 2–4.30pm).

False Bay extends for some 30km/19 miles along the coast of the Indian Ocean between Cape Point, at the southern tip of the Cape Peninsula, and Cape Hangklip. Round the bay are a number of very popular holiday resorts, including Muizenberg (see p. 178) and Strand (see Somerset West). When the sea on the Atlantic coast is uncomfortably cold bathers can enjoy warmer water in False Bay, which is washed by the warm Agulhas Current.

False Bay

Ceres   D 9

Province: Western Cape
Altitude: 502m/1647ft
Population: 13,000
Distances: 100km/62 miles from Cape Town, 165km/103 miles from Clanwilliam

Ceres, situated on the Dwars River in a very fertile valley, is named after the old Roman goddess of agriculture. The little town is surrounded by hills up to 2000m/6560ft in height. The scenery in this area is so picturesque that it has been called the Switzerland of South Africa. The town's prosperity depends mainly on its plantations of fruit, and after the harvest the crop is processed in one of the largest canning plants in the whole country. Ceres is also a popular holiday resort, and there are a number of holiday complexes in the area offering a wide range of leisure activities.

★Situation and characteristics

Sights in Ceres

One of Ceres's industries in the past was the manufacture of horse-drawn carriages. The Transport Riders' Museum in Orange Street (open: Mon. 2–5pm, Tues.–Fri. 9am–1pm and 2–5pm, Sat. 10am–noon) has a collection of material on the history of the town, including a few old carriages.

Transport Riders' Museum

The Ceres Bergfynbos Reserve (area 30 hectares/75 acres) on the western outskirts of the town was established to protect the indigenous flora (open: daily 8am–5pm). There are paths leading to beautiful viewpoints and to caves with prehistoric paintings.

Ceres Bergfynbos Reserve

Surroundings of Ceres

★ Gydo Pass

A drive over the Gydo Pass (1018m/3340ft) – named after a species of euphorbia which covers the slopes of the Skurweberg – opens up magnificent views. The road runs north from Ceres and comes in 10km/6 miles to the Prince Alfred Hamlet, which depends for most of its income on fruit-growing. 3km/2 miles beyond it the ascent to the pass begins, and the summit is reached in another 7km/4½ miles. (The pass is sometimes closed on a few days in winter.) The road (now asphalted almost all the way to Citrusdal) then winds its way down from the pass, through beautiful lonely country, only occasionally passing a few houses. 110km/68 miles from Ceres it comes to Citrusdal (see entry).

Mitchell's Pass

Another rewarding trip is over Mitchell's Pass, on a road originally built in 1846 by Andrew Bain and improved in more recent times, which runs through the Rex River Mountains (2249m/7379ft) to Wolseley (pop. 6700), 18km/11 miles from Ceres.

Kagga Kamma

In the Swartberg range is the privately run Kagga Kamma game reserve, in which visitors can observe bushbucks and springboks and see bizarre rock formations. The owner of the reserve has given 40 Bushmen an area of land on which they can live on their own. Visitors can enter the village only with the agreement of the Bushmen; tel. 022/11 63 83 34.

Citrusdal   D 9

Province: Western Cape
Altitude: 275m/902ft
Population: 2800
Distances: 112km/70 miles from Lambert's Bay, 180km/112 miles from Cape Town, 210km/130 miles from Calvinia

Situation and characteristics

Citrusdal, founded in 1916 in the fertile valley of the Olifants River, is a good base for excursions into the Cedarberg range.

The area round Citrusdal is South Africa's third largest fruit-growing region. During the harvest, between May and October, more than 2 million crates of oranges and other fruit, with a total weight of over 80,000 tons, are packed in Citrusdal. Most of the crop is destined for export.

The town

Citrusdal itself has no sights of outstanding interest and is not a place where visitors will want to stay long. On Hex River farm, to the north of the town, is the oldest orange-tree in South Africa, said to be over 200 years old. The local museum, in Church Street, has a collection of material on the history of the town.

The Baths

16km/10 miles south of Citrusdal, on a farm called The Baths, are hot mineral springs (43°C/109°F), with swimming pools and accommodation in a handsome Victorian house.

★ Cedarberg Wilderness Area

The Cedarberg (in Afrikaans Sederberg) is a range of hills extending for some 100km/60 miles between Clanwilliam to the north and Ceres to the south and reaching its highest point in the Sneeuberg (2028m/6654ft). The range is named after the Clanwilliam cedars which were originally common in this area but are now reduced to a few trees at higher and inaccessible levels, most of them having been felled for timber. The Cedarberg is famed for its wooded gorges, its bizarre rock formations coloured red by iron oxides, its caves with their Bushman paintings and its varied flora. At the highest levels in this area visitors may be lucky enough to come across the white snow protea which grows here and nowhere else.

Landscape near Citrusdal

71,000 hectares/175,000 acres of this region between Citrusdal and Clanwilliam (see entry) are now under statutory protection as the Cedarberg Wilderness Area. A permit is required to enter the area, within which there are numerous hiking trails. Permits can be obtained from the Algeria forest station (open: Mon.–Fri. 8am–1pm and 2–4.30pm); and since only a limited number of visitors are admitted at any one time it is advisable to apply in plenty of time (tel. 02682/34 40). The Algeria station is reached by way of N 7, turning off 27km/17 miles north of Citrusdal into a narrow road to the east, which crosses the Olifants River and goes over the Niewoudts Pass (590m/1936ft). In the valley beyond this is the forest station, where detailed directions and further information can be obtained. Accommodation is available in two converted farmhouses and on camping sites. Rooms are also available in farmhouses outside the wilderness area, and there is also plenty of room for campers.

Getting there; facilities

The best time for a visit to the Cedarberg is between September and April. Most of the rain (and sometimes snow) falls between May and September.

Two beautiful roads run through the Cedarberg: R 303 between Citrusdal and Ceres (see entry), now asphalted for almost the whole way, and R 364 between Clanwilliam and Calvinia (see entry), also almost completely asphalt-surfaced.

Roads through the Cedarberg

Clanwilliam   D 8

Province: Western Cape
Altitude: 75m/245ft
Population: 3000
Distances: 160km/100 miles from Calvinia, 220km/137 miles from Cape Town, 225km/140 miles from Garies

Clanwilliam, situated in the fertile valley of the Olifants River, is an attractive little town with a number of buildings in Cape Dutch style which draws visitors not only for its own sake but also for its nearness to the Cedarberg range (see Citrusdal).

Situation and characteristics

There were a few settlers in this area as early as 1732. The little town was founded in 1820, and is thus one of the oldest in the country. A common plant in the surrounding area is the rooibos ("red bush"), whose dried leaves are used to make rooibos tea, a tannin-free tea rich in vitamin C which is now widely exported. The rooibos tea factory can be visited by previous appointment (Rooibos Tea Board, Rooibos Avenue, PO Box 64, Clanwilliam, tel. 0268/64). Other agricultural products of the area are vegetables, citrus fruits, corn and tobacco.

A few of Clanwilliam's earliest buildings have survived, among them the prison and the house of an Irish settler.

The town

Surroundings of Clanwilliam

Clanwilliam Dam, an artificial lake created by the damming of the Olifants River, is a popular resort, particularly in summer (fishing, water sports of various kinds). The Olifants River, whose water irrigates the plantations between Citrusdal and Clanwilliam, rises in the hills north-west of Ceres and flows into the Atlantic to the west of Klawer. When the first white man reached the river in 1660 he encountered a herd of elephants: hence the name Olifants (Elephants') River.

Clanwilliam Dam, Olifants River

The Ramskop Nature Reserve (open: daily 7am–5pm), on the shores of the lake, is famed for its profusion of wild flowers.

Ramskop Nature Reserve

North of Clanwilliam R 364 winds its way up to the Pakhuis Pass. 37km/ 23 miles from Clanwilliam a side road runs south to Wuppertal. In 15km/ 9 miles a poor track goes off on the left to the Bidouw Valley, which is famed for its bizarre rock formations and the splendour of its flowers in spring (August and September).

★Bidouw Valley

18km/11 miles south of the turn-off for the Bidouw Valley is Wuppertal, a little town of whitewashed thatched houses set against a magnificent scenic backdrop, originally a mission station founded by the Rhenish Mission in 1832. Here, as in Clanwilliam, rooibos tea is manufactured and widely exported. An individual souvenir which may appeal to some visitors is a pair of *velskoene*, comfortable walking shoes.

★Wuppertal

Clarens

K 6

Province: Orange Free State
Altitude: 2477m/8127ft
Population: 1200
Distances: 40km/25 miles from Bethlehem, 60km/37 miles from Harrismith,
80km/50 miles from Ficksburg

The little town of Clarens is a convenient staging-point from which to visit the Golden Gate Highlands National Park, near the Lesotho border. The town, founded in 1912, is named after Clarens in Switzerland, where Paul Kruger, former President of the Transvaal, died in exile in 1904. A number of artists live in the town, and there are also a few holiday homes.

Situation and characteristics

Cinderella Castle in Naaupoort Street, a house built from more than 55,000 beer bottles, contains a private collection of precious stones, small objects

Cinderella Castle

◄ *Bizarre sandstone formations in the Golden Gate Highlands National Park*

carved from steatite and pictures of scenes from well-known fairytales. There is also a small souvenir shop and a children's playground.

★ Golden Gate Highlands National Park

The Golden Gate Highlands National Park is best reached by way of Clarens: the road from Harrismith is not yet completely asphalt-surfaced. The road from Clarens, which runs east from the town, comes in 18km/ 11 miles to the park and continues through it, following the valley of the Caledon River, is open throughout the year and is toll-free.

The park, one of the most attractive nature reserves in the country, lies at the foot of the Maluti Mountains. Established in 1962, it has an area of 12,000 hectares/30,000 acres and ranges in height between 1892m/6208ft and 2770m/9088ft. The local sandstones, variously coloured by iron oxides, have been carved into bizarre shapes by erosion. The Golden Gate from which the park takes its name consists of two 100m/330ft crags flanking the road through the park which shimmer in gold at sunset.

The numerous caves in the hills were occupied in earlier days by the Bushmen, and during the Boer War sheltered many Boer families seeking to avoid the British concentration camps.

Flora and fauna

This area has an annual 800mm/32in. of rain and, in winter, snow. The flora includes many grasses and other plants characteristic of mountainous regions as well as numerous lilies and irises.

In the park live many indigenous animals exterminated by European settlers and now reintroduced, including many species of antelope, zebras and warthogs. There are 100 different species of birds, among them the majestic lammergeier and the black eagle.

Holiday villages

There are two holiday villages in the park. The road from Clarens comes first to the well-equipped Brandwag camp, at the foot of a sandstone crag, with a hotel, chalets and various sports facilities. 1km/³⁄₄ mile beyond this is the Glen Reenen camp, with simpler accommodation in rondavels and a camping and caravanning site.

Walks

A number of hiking trails run through the park (which can also be explored on ponyback: information from information bureau in Brandwag camp). The Rhebok Hiking Trail (21km/13 miles) leads to the summit of Mt General-alskop (2757m/9046ft; overnight accommodation in mountain hut).

Other Sights round Clarens

Phuthaditjhaba

Farther east on R 712, which runs through the Golden Gate Highlands National Park, is Phuthaditjhaba, formerly capital of the homeland of Qwa-Qwa (a name which means "whiter than white" – referring to the white patches on Mt Qwa-Qwa formed by the droppings of the Cape vultures which nest here). Qwa-Qwa was the smallest South African homeland, with an area of only 1300sq.km/500sq. miles. Now reincorporated in the Republic of South Africa, it has a population of 190,000 Bakwena and Balokwa, two South Sotho tribes.

In Phuthaditjhaba visitors can buy local craft products, including tapestries, baskets, copper and pewter utensils and glassware.

Witsieshoek
Mountain Resort

Visitors who would like to stay longer in this area will find comfortable accommodation in Witsieshoek Mountain Resort, 25km/15 miles south of Phuthaditjhaba. This is the starting-point of the Metsi Matso Hiking Trail (a 2-day walk).

Fouriesburg

36km/22 miles south-west of Clarens on R 711 is Fouriesburg. The road runs along the Lesotho border, with spectacular views of the mountains. The Brandwater Hiking Trail (65km/40 miles) begins and ends in Fouriesburg (overnight accommodation in caves).

Colesberg

Province: Northern Cape
Altitude: 1428m/4685ft
Population: 3500
Distances: 226km/140 miles from Bloemfontein, 778km/483 miles from
  Cape Town

Colesberg is situated in the Karoo, half way between Johannesburg and
Cape Town on N 1. It is an attractive little place which makes a good
stopover on a journey between the two cities. Like the neighbouring town
of De Aar, Colesberg was originally no more than a railway junction. It was
officially founded in 1829 and named after the then Governor of the colony,
Sir Galbraith Lowry Cole.

Situation and characteristics

A few buildings survive from Colesberg's early days, including six lovingly
restored houses in Bell Street. There is also a fine Dutch Reformed church
of 1866.
  There is a museum of local history, housed in a former bank of 1860.
Among the exhibits is a window-pane with the initials "D. P.", scratched on
the glass with one of the first diamonds found in South Africa.

The town

Cradock

Province: Eastern Cape
Altitude: 1020m/3347ft
Population: 37,000
Distances: 227km/141 miles from Aliwal North, 240km/150 miles from Port
  Elizabeth

The little country town of Cradock was originally a military base, established in 1813 and named after the then governor, Sir John Cradock. Its
situation on the banks of the Great Fish River attracted many farmers, and
the settlement soon developed into the centre of an intensively cultivated
agricultural area. It received its charter as a town in 1837. There are a variety
of leisure facilities (a swimming pool, a camping site, holiday houses, etc.)
round the Karoo Sulphur Springs.

Situation and characteristics

Sights in Cradock

In the centre of the town is a Dutch Reformed church (1867) modelled on
London's St Martin-in-the-Fields.

Church

The Great Fish River Museum, housed in a former parsonage of 1825,
illustrates the history of settlement in the 19th century with a varied collection of material, including furniture and domestic equipment (open: Mon.–
Fri. 9am–1pm and 2–4pm, Sat. 9am–noon).

Great Fish River Museum

The house once occupied by Olive Schreiner now contains a small
museum (open: Thur.–Tues. 8am–12.45pm and 2–4pm) commemorating
the well known South African writer, born in Wittebergen (now in Lesotho)
in 1855, the daughter of a German Methodist missionary. At the age of 15
she became a governess in a Boer family on the fringes of the Karoo. From
1881 to 1889 she lived in England, where her "Story of an African Farm"
was published. Throughout her life she was concerned in her novels and
short stories with the problems of her country and rebelled against Victorian racism and imperialism. As a result of her political opposition to

Olive Schreiner House

Cradock

A mountain zebra in the Mountain Zebra National Park. The smallest
species of zebra, it differs from other zebras in having a white,
unstriped area on the belly

Cecil Rhodes she was interned during the Boer War. Olive Schreiner died in Cradock in 1920 and was buried in Buffelkop, to the south of the town.

Van Riebeeck
Karoo Garden

In addition to succulents and various kinds of shrubs, the flora in the Van Riebeeck Karoo Garden includes wild pomegranate trees.

★★Mountain Zebra National Park

The Mountain Zebra National Park (area 6536 hectares/16,144 acres; open: October to April daily 7am–7pm, May to September daily 7am–6pm), established in 1937, lies on the northern slopes of the Blankberg range (up to 2000m/6560ft), 24km/15 miles south-west of Cradock. It is one of the finest National Parks in South Africa, on account both of its unique fauna and its magnificent scenery. It is also an area of archaeological interest in which remains of Palaeolithic man have been found, and there is a cave containing Bushman paintings, reached on a well signposted road.

Flora and fauna

The park was established to ensure the survival of the mountain zebra. Standing only 1.25m/4ft high, with a reddish-brown nose and a white belly, the mountain zebra is in grave danger of extinction. In 1960 there were some 50 of them left, but the herd in the National Park has now risen to over 200. Every year, too, a number of mountain zebras are given to other parks, so that the total stock is now estimated at 600.

In addition to the mountain zebra other animals of the savanna live in the park, among them springboks, bonteboks and kudus, as well as caracals, jackals, mongooses and many species of birds.

The vegetation is typical of the Karoo, with the addition of wild olives, sumach and thorny acacias.

From the ranger's house there are roads to different parts of the park, and there are also a number of short walks and trails, as well as the 31km/ 19 mile Mountain Zebra Trail (overnight accommodation in mountain huts).

Roads and trails

Within the park there are various types of accommodation for visitors, as well as a shop and a restaurant.

Darling   D 9

Province: Western Cape
Altitude: 79m/259ft
Population: 3600
Distances: 70km/43 miles from Cape Town, 65km/40 miles from Vreden-burg, 120km/75 miles from Ceres

Darling lies in the sandveld, as the 20–30km/12–18 mile wide coastal strip north of Cape Town is called. The town was founded in 1853 and named after the then Governor of the Cape, Charles Darling.

Situation and characteristics

Darling is famed for its show of colour in spring, when the fields are carpeted with flowers. South-east of the town is the Darling Flora Reserve, and there is another flora reserve on the Yzerfontein road (R 315). (The fields of flowers belong to farms and can be visited only at particular times: information from tourist office in Church Street.)

The high point of Darling's year is the Wild Flower Show, held annually in the third week in September. Apart from its spring display of blossom Darling has no great features of tourist interest.

Sights in and around Darling

The Butter Museum in Main Road (open: Mon.–Fri. 7.30am–12.30pm) tells the whole story of butter manufacture.

Butter Museum

5km/3 miles from Darling on the Burgerspan road is the Hildebrandt Monu-ment, commemorating the most southerly battle of the Boer War.

Hildebrandt Monument

Mamre, 17km/10½ miles south of Darling, was originally a Moravian mis-sion station established in 1808. With its old houses in Cape Dutch style it is a jewel of a little town. There is a restored watermill which can be visited on weekdays from 9am to 5pm and on Sundays from 2 to 5pm.

Mamre

25km/15 miles north-west of Darling is the West Coast National Park (see entry).

West Coast National Park

Drakensberg   K–M 3–7

Provinces: Northern Transvaal, Eastern Transvaal, KwaZulu/Natal; also Lesotho

The Drakensberg is a chain of hills extending for 1000km/620 miles from the Kruger National Park in the north to the eastern border of the kingdom of Lesotho in the south. It is the eastern and scenically most spectacular part of the Great Escarpment which girdles the interior plateau of South Africa and separates it from the coastal regions.

Location and ★★topography

Within the Drakensberg range are the highest mountains on the African continent after Kilimanjaro, with numerous peaks rising above 3000m/10,000ft. They were formed in the late Palaeozoic era, some 300 million years ago, when massive deposits of the Karoo Series were built up throughout the whole of southern Africa. These can still be seen in the Drakensberg. When the African continent came into being in the Mesozoic era huge masses of lava were thrust up from the earth's interior and cooled

Drakensberg

The "Amphitheatre" in the Royal Natal National Park:
one of the most spectacular natural features in the Drakensberg

to form black basalt which covered the light-coloured sandstone to a depth of up to 1400m/4600ft and at one time extended as far as the east coast of South Africa. In the most recent period of the earth's history, the Neozoic era, this basalt layer has been steadily eroded by wind and water and the Great Escarpment has gradually moved farther inland.

Transvaal Drakensberg

The Transvaal Drakensberg, with peaks rising to 2286m/7500ft, lies in northern South Africa, to the west of the Kruger National Park, separating the highveld from the fertile lowveld, which lies 1000m/3300ft lower down, with hills ranging only between 150 and 600m (500 and 200ft). This part of the range consists of older rocks, mainly dolomites and quartzites.

The Transvaal Drakensberg, which has increasingly been opened up for tourism in recent years, has many natural beauties to attract visitors – described in the entry on the Blyderivierspoort Nature Reserve.

Natal Drakensberg

The name Drakensberg was originally applied only to the 100km/60 mile long range of mountains extending between the Mont-aux-Sources and the Underberg in KwaZulu/Natal and Lesotho. This range, one of South Africa's most popular holiday regions, is now known as the Natal Drakensberg. The Boer settlers called the range the Drakensberg, seeing the form of the hills as resembling a recumbent dragon. In the Zulu language the mountains, with their jagged crest, are called Qathlamba, the "Rampart of Raised Spears".

The Natal Drakensberg reaches heights of 3377m/11,080ft in Champagne Castle and 3482m/11,424ft in Mt Thabana Ntlenyana (in Lesotho). To the east the mountains fall almost vertically down to 1000m/3300ft. Below this steep escarpment is the Little Berg, a range of hills, some of them bizarrely shaped, ranging in height between 1800 and 2000m (5900 and 6600ft).

Climate

During the winter (April–September) there are frequently falls of snow (there are no ski-lifts). The driest months are June and July. In winter,

Sterkfontein Dam

Harrysmith

Little Switzerland

Ladysmith

Dumbe 2089

Mgodotwa 1463

Geluksburg

Jagersrust
Drakensville
Holiday Resort
Drakensberg

R 212

Manchester
Ford
Carbineers

Malikeng
The Cavern
Mahai
Camping Site
Mont-Aux-
Source
KwaMiya

Hunters
Rest

Mkukwini

Spioen
Kop Dam

N3

1 Visitor
Centre
Tendele
Camp
Seqomeni
Zwelisha

Ekombe

Ntenjwa
Camp

Springfield

Woodford

Bergville

Wen-
kommando

Tugela

Colenso

Busingatha
Mnguni
1991

Mount Amery
3180
Mole Hill
2447

Hoffenthal
Mission

Nkunzi
1621

Winterton

Emmaus
Mission

Kelvin Grove
Et Caravan Park

Winston
Churchill

Bloukrans

North Peak
3153

Cathedral Park

Woodstock
Dam

Lookout
Tower

The Little Berg
2083

Cayley
Lodge

The Nest

Gert
Maritz

Frere

N3

Est-
court

LESOTHO

Drakensberg

Elephant
Pyramid

3004

Meteorological
Station

Dragon
Peak

Berghaven
Holiday
Cottages

Meteorological
Station

Lookout
Tower

Museum

Natal
Drakensberg

Khubelu

Senqu

3280

Ndedema
2
Buttress
3338

Champagne Castle
3377

Forest
Station

Champagne
Valley
White Mountain
Resort

Boshi

Wembesi

Sobabi

Edashi

Agricultural
Research Station

Vechdrift
Dam

15 km

© Baedeker

Ranger's
House

Mahlutshini

KwaMankonjane

Bannerman Hut

Giant's
Castle
3

KwaMkhize

1 Royal Natal
National Park,
Amphitheatre
2 Ndedema Gorge
3 Giant's Castle
Game Reserve
4 Kamberg
Nature Reserve
5 Loteni
Nature Reserve
6 Vergelegen
Nature Reserve
7 Mzimkulwana
Nature Reserve

Mountaineer's Hut

Giant's Castle
3315

Glengarry
Park

Forest
Station

Kamberg
2095

Trout
Bungalow
Fort
Nottingham

Mothatong

4

Kwantabamnyama

Settler's
Homestead
Museum

5

Kwazulu/
Natal

Nzinga

Impendle

Pingpong
Cutting

Forest
Station
6

Bucklands
Farm

Nkothweni
Mzumbe

Mkomazi

Linakeng

Sani Pass

Hodgson's Peak
3257

7

Kwathunzi

Cibelichle

Kamensi

Smilobha

Mashai

Little Bamboo
2421

Sani
Pass

Mkhomazana

Mkomazi

Ndonyela

Mkomazi

Linotsing

Forest
Station

Forest
Station

Himeville

Lookout
Tower

Durban
Pietermaritzburg

Drakensberg
Garden

Wintershoek
2356

Underberg

Sangwana

R 617

Mountain
Park

Bulwer

Technical
College

Sehlabathebe

Park
Lodge
Ngoangoanat
Gate

Bushman's
Nek

1940

Grainger's Kop
1684

Rwaqanyane

Hlabeni
1727

Forest
Station
Donny-
brook

Coleford Nature
Reserve

Coleford

Mooi River

though the nights are cold, there is plenty of sunshine during the day, and in sheltered valleys it can be quite mild, with temperatures of just under 20°C/68°F. In summer it is usually warm, with temperatures between 15 and 30°C (59 and 86°F), but almost every day there are violent thundery showers (frequently with hail). Most of the annual rainfall of between 1000 and 1700mm (40 and 67in.) occurs between January and March. After cloudbursts the rivers and streams are swollen and the roads may sometimes become impassable at short notice.

Flora and fauna

The slopes of the Drakensberg are covered with grass, interspersed below 2000m/6600ft with tufted grass, sclerophyllous (hard-leaved) plants and proteas, and above 2800m/9200ft with low-growing plants like Erica and strawflowers. In sheltered valleys and gorges there are dense forests of mountain cypresses, tree ferns and yellowwood trees. Altogether there are more than 800 different species of flowering plants, including 63 orchids.

Bushman drawings

In numerous caves and rock overhangs in the area, particularly in the Giant's Castle Game Reserve, more than 20,000 rock paintings have been preserved, depicting wild animals and scenes of hunting and fighting. The oldest of these date back some 2000 years; the last Bushmen lived in the Drakensberg in the early 20th century (see Baedeker Special, p. 92).

Tourism; nature parks

The Natal Drakensberg is a popular holiday region throughout the year and has excellent facilities for visitors. There are three tourist areas: the Royal Natal National Park in the north; the central highlands round Cathedral Peak, Champagne Castle and the Giant's Castle Game Reserve; and the southern highlands, with the Loteni, Kamberg and Mzimkulwana Nature Reserves. The central and southern regions are due to be combined to form the Natal Drakensberg Park.

Sights in the Natal Drakensberg

Getting there; accommodation

The main access route to the Natal Drakensberg is N 3, which runs from Johannesburg (400km/250 miles away) via Pietermaritzburg to Durban (150km/95 miles away) on the Indian Ocean. From this road various side roads run west to the different holiday areas in the Drakensberg.

Good centres from which to visit the northern highlands are Harrismith (see entry) and Bergville; the central area can be reached from Bergville, Winterton, Estcourt (see entry) or Mooi River; and the best route to the southern highlands is by way of Pietermaritzburg (see entry), Underberg and Himeville.

Accommodation for visitors is available in the towns mentioned and – much to be preferred – in holiday centres in the Drakensberg itself. There are numbers of holiday camps in which huts can be rented, and comfortable hotels like the Karos Mont-aux-Sources Hotel, the Sani Pass Hotel and the Drakensberg Sun Hotel. Most of the hotels and holiday camps offer a range of sports facilities.

The best way to explore this mountain country is on foot. There are hiking trails in all grades of difficulty, most of which do not call for mountaineering skills. Before undertaking a hike of some length visitors should enter their names in the camp register. The best months for long trips in the mountains are April and May: in summer many streams turn into raging torrents which are impossible to cross. In many areas it is possible to join organised hill walks or to explore the region on horseback.

Mont-aux-Sources

Mont-aux-Sources is the name both of a mountain (3282m/10,768ft) and of a popular holiday centre near it (Karos Hotel Mont-aux-Sources) in the northern Natal Drakensberg. The name was originated by two French missionaries who discovered that several tributaries of the Orange and Tugela rivers rose on the mountain.

★★Royal Natal National Park

Between the Mont-aux-Sources Hotel and the mountain from which it takes its name extends the Royal Natal National Park, which along with the adjoining Rugged Glen National Park has an area of 8800 hectares/22,000 acres. This grandiose mountain region was declared a National Park in 1906: the "Royal" was added after a royal visit in 1947. The most striking scenic feature in the Royal Natal National Park is the Amphitheatre in the southern part of the park. This is a mountain wall 5km/3 miles long which at some points falls vertically down for more than 500m/1640ft. The best place for a photograph is Tendele camp, and the best time is in the morning: in the afternoon the rock face is in shadow. At its west end is the Sentinel (3165m/10,384ft, at its east end the Eastern Buttress (3047m/9997ft. The Tugela River plunges down 800m/2625ft in a series of cascades, forming South Africa's highest waterfall.

The vegetation in the National Park is very varied. Among the commonest species of animals are black wildebeests, mountain reedbucks, rheboks, blesboks, klipspringers and baboons. Over 180 species of birds have been recorded, including crowned eagles, bearded vultures, Cape vultures and jackal falcons.

There are more than 30 waymarked hiking trails in the National Park. An attractive short walk is the 4km/2½ mile long Otto Walk; the longest route is the Mont-aux-Sources Trail, a round trip of 45km/28 miles which calls for fitness but not mountaineering skills. This begins in the centre of the park, runs through the Tendele camp and past the Mahai Falls and finally climbs to the crest of the Amphitheatre on two chain ladders with 100 steps. One of the finest walks, not unduly strenuous (22km/14 miles there and back), is to the Tugela Gorge, where the Tugela flows through a narrow tunnel. Detailed information about the various walks can be obtained in the visitor centre on the road into the National Park (1km/¾ mile beyond the entrance). where there is also a small museum.

★Cathedral Peak

40km/25 miles west of Winterton is Cathedral Peak Hotel, in a beautiful setting in the Mlambonja valley, on the edge of Cathedral Peak State Forest, which offers a wide range of attractive walks and climbs. Above the hotel

View from Cathedral's Peak Hotel of the mountain scenery of the Drakensberg

complex rear Cathedral Peak (3004m/9856ft), Mt Bell (2930m/9613ft), the Outer Horn (3006m/9863ft) and the Inner Horn (3005m/9859ft). From the hotel a gravel track runs up Cathedral Peak – a relatively easy climb. From the summit there are overwhelming views.

Another attractive trip is a drive to Mike's Pass, which also affords magnificent views. From the hotel take the Winterton road and in 3km/2 miles turn into a road on the right.

★Ndedema Gorge

From Mike's Pass walkers (and riders) can find their way down into the 5.5km/3½ mile long Ndedema Gorge, in which is the Sebayeni Cave, with around 4000 Bushman rock drawings. The oldest date from between 970 and 1230, the latest from between 1720 and 1820. Further information about visiting them can be obtained in the hotels.

★Cathkin Peak, Champagne Castle

South of Cathedral Peak are Cathkin Peak (3181m/10,437ft), somewhat apart from the main mountain chain, and Champagne Castle (3377m/11,080ft), one of the highest peaks in the Drakensberg. There are many good walks and climbs in this area (Monk's Cowl State Forest). The hotels (Cathkin Park Hotel, Champagne Castle Hotel, the Nest, El MIrador, Drakensberg Sun Hotel, etc.) and the Dragon Peaks Park (a caravan park with some chalets for hire) offer other sports and entertainment facilities.

★★Giant's Castle Game Reserve

The Giant's Castle Game Reserve (area 34,600 hectares/85,460 acres), established in 1903, is one of the most impressive features in the southern Natal Drakensberg; the fastest access route is from Estcourt (see entry) or Mooi River. It lies below a 35km/22 mile long basalt wall around 3000m/10,000ft in height which extends from Champagne Castle (3377m/11,080ft) in the north to Giant's Castle (3315m/10,877ft) in the south. Through the reserve flow Bushman's River (a good fishing stream) and the Little Tugela River. Most of the vegetation consists of grassland, but there are some remnants of mountain rain forest, particularly in the

A scene from the life of the Bushman in the Giant's Castle Game Reserve

north and south of the reserve. In spring and summer there is a profusion of wild flowers.

The reserve was established in 1903 to protect the last herds of elands, which since then have considerably increased in numbers. Among other animals in the reserve are bushbucks, blesboks, red hartebeests, klip-springers and baboons.

Among the principal attractions of the Giant's Castle Game Reserve are the large numbers of Bushman rock drawings, which have been found at more than 50 different sites. In the Main Cave (2km/1¼ miles from Main Camp, reached on an easy track) there are around 500 drawings (guided tours; small museum), and in the Battle Cave (near Injasuti camp) 1000.

Accommodation for visitors is available in hutted camps in and on the outskirts of the reserve, which are also the starting-points of hiking trails in various grades of difficulty, including a circular route to the summit of Giant's Castle (3315m/10,877ft). From this "roof of South Africa" there are breathtaking views of the surrounding area. Those who would prefer to explore the reserve on horseback can hire horses at the Hillside camp.

The Kamberg Nature Reserve (area 2230 hectares/5510 acres) lies south-east of Giant's Castle, at the foot of the Drakensberg (access on N 3, exit via Mooi River or near Nottingham Road, going west). The Mooi River, a good fishing stream, flows through a region of varied scenic beauty in which several species of antelope live. More than 30 species of orchid (flowering between December and March) are found in the reserve. There is accommodation for visitors in a self-catering hutted camp (suitable for disabled people).
Kamberg Nature Reserve

On the south-west side of the Kamberg Nature Reserve is the Mkhomazi State Forest, and beyond this again is the Loteni Nature Reserve (area 3984 hectares/9840 acres; accommodation in self-catering huts). The Loteni River is an excellent trout stream which draws many anglers. The reserve is also home to many different species of birds, reedbucks, elands and bushbucks. The Settlers' Museum has a collection of agricultural implements, furniture and domestic equipment used by the early settlers.
Loteni Nature Reserve

A few miles south is the Vergelegen Nature Reserve (area 1150 hectares/2840 acres), lying at an altitude of 1500m/5000ft in the source area of the Umkomaas River (accommodation available in huts).
Vergelegen Nature Reserve

The Mzimkulwana Nature Reserve (area 22,751 hectares/56,195 acres) is most easily reached by way of Himeville, 14km/9 miles south-east. It contains many endangered species of plants and animals (Verreaux's eagle, martial eagle, Cape vulture, striped jackal, etc.).
Mzimkulwana Nature Reserve

Through the Mzimkulwana Nature Reserve runs the road to the Sani Pass. The only way through the Natal Drakensberg between the Royal Natal National Park to the north and Bushman's Nek to the south is over this spectacular pass (2895m/9498ft), which lies on the frontier between South Africa and Lesotho. (Only vehicles with four-wheel drive are allowed on the 8km/5 miles of road between the two frontier posts; on foot it takes between 2 and 3 hours.) To the north of the pass is Mt Thabana Ntlenyana (3482m/11,424ft), the highest peak in southern Africa. The pass takes its name from the San (Bushmen), who fled over this pass to escape from their white and black persecutors.

At the foot of the pass on the South African side is the comfortable Sani Pass Hotel. Near the hotel is the starting-point of the Giant's Cup Hiking Trail (60km/37 miles), which ends at Bushman's Nek; it should present no difficulties to experienced walkers.
★Sani Pass

A good centre from which to explore the southern Natal Drakensberg is the little town of Underberg (pop. 1000). The Himeville Nature Reserve, 6km/4 miles north, lies in a good trout-fishing area.
Underberg, Himeville Nature Reserve

Dundee

Coleford
Nature Reserve

20km/12½ miles south of Underberg is Coleford Nature Reserve, which has an area of 1272 hectares/3142 acres, mostly hilly grass steppe and swamp. The fauna includes black wildebeests, blesboks, oribis, reedbucks and other species of antelope.

Dundee   L 5

Province: KwaZulu/Natal
Altitude: 1442m/4731ft. Population: 22,000
Distances: 380km/236 miles from Durban, 330km/205 miles from Johannesburg

Situation and
characteristics

Dundee, a coal-mining centre in KwaZulu/Natal, lies in the Midlands, the hilly region between the Drakensberg and the Natal coast on the Indian Ocean. The area was occupied by man in the Stone and Iron Ages. In more recent times voortrekkers and Zulus, Boers and the British, and the British and Zulus came into conflict with one another here, and a number of bitter battles were fought in the area (see Ulundi).

Sights in and around Dundee

Talana Museum

Outside the town, on the road to Vryheid, is the Talana Museum, which consists of a number of separate buildings spread over an area of 8 hectares/20 acres. The homestead of Peter Smith, founder of the town, has been preserved and now contains, in addition to its original furnishings, a collection of material on the military history of the region. An old miner's cottage has been re-erected here. The museum is open on weekdays and weekend afternoons.

Rorke's Drift

50km/30 miles from Dundee on R 68 is Rorke's Drift, scene of a battle in 1879 in which 100 British soldiers held two Zulu regiments at bay after the British defeat at Isandhlwana (see below, Interpretation Centre open: daily 8am–5pm). There is also a world-renowned Zulu craft centre here (open: Mon.–Fri. 8am–4pm, Sat. 10am–3pm).

Isandhlwana

70km/43 miles from Dundee on R 68 is Isandhlwana, with a monument commemorating a battle in January 1879 in which a small British force was overwhelmed by an army of 17,000 Zulu warriors.

Blood River

27km/17 miles north-east of Dundee a road goes off R 33 and comes in 20km/12½ miles to the Blood River Monument. It stands in a wide plain, now peaceful farming country, which was the scene of a bloody battle on December 16th 1838, when a massive army of Zulus attacked a party of 464 voortrekkers who had set up their laager here. More than 3000 Zulus were killed in the slaughter, and their blood stained the water of the river, now called Blood River. No voortrekkers were killed.

Chelmsford
Nature Reserve

35km/22 miles north-west of Dundee on R 621 is Chelmsford Nature Reserve (area 6015 hectares/14,857 acres). Within the reserve is a reservoir with facilities for a variety of water sports, as well as holiday chalets for hire and a camping site. Among the game to be seen here are antelopes, gazelles, rhinos, black wildebeests and zebras.

Newcastle

The reservoir in the Chelmsford Nature Reserve supplies water to Newcastle (pop. 40,000), 25km/15 miles away. The town, situated at the foot of the Natal Drakensberg, was founded in 1864 and named after the Duke of Newcastle, then colonial secretary. It is now an important centre of steel production.

The rivers in the surrounding area are well stocked with fish. A favourite excursion from Newcastle is to the falls on the Ncandu River, 16km/10 miles from the town on the road to Mullers Pass.

Voortrekker Monument at the Blood River

Durban   M 7

Province: KwaZulu/Natal
Altitude: 5m/16ft
Population: 800,000 (Greater Durban just under 1 million)
Distances: 80km/50 miles from Pietermaritzburg, 588km/365 miles from
   Johannesburg, 634km/394 miles from Bloemfontein, 1753km/1089 miles
   from Cape Town

Durban is the third largest city in South Africa, of importance as an industrial centre and above all as a port. Thanks to its subtropical climate, its long
beaches, the warm water of the Indian Ocean and an excellent infrastructure it can also claim to be South Africa's pleasure capital; and with more
than 2 million visitors every year it is the country's leading holiday resort.
The city owes its cosmopolitan air, however, not so much to its visitors as
to the ethnic variety of its population. Almost half the inhabitants are
Asians, mainly Indians, and about 200,000 are white. Under the apartheid
regime most of the black population was relegated to the townships surrounding the city.

Situation and
characteristics

The port of Durban is the most important in South Africa and one of the
largest on the continent. It brings in supplies for the mining and industrial
areas on the Witwatersrand and exports mainly sugar, fruit and maize. It
has over 15km/9 miles of quays and a storage capacity of 317,265cu.m/
414,967cu.yd. Thanks to its port Durban has developed into an important
industrial centre (sugar, textiles, dyestuffs, chemicals, foodstuffs).

Port

Louis Botha International Airport lies 15km/9 miles south of central Durban.
There is a shuttle bus service from the air terminal in the city centre (corner
of Smith and Aliwal Streets) to the airport.

Airport

199

Durban

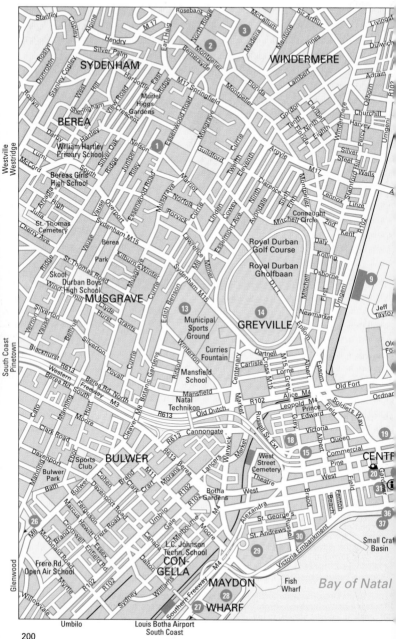

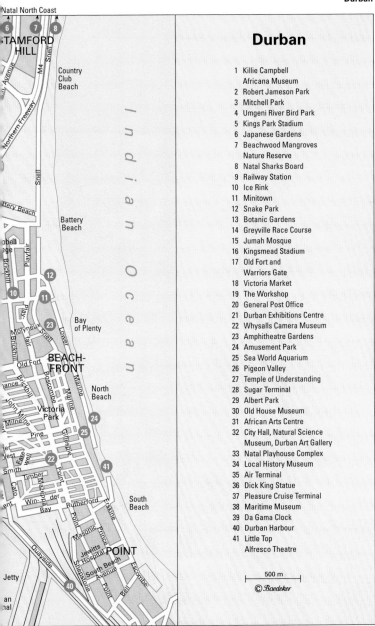

Durban

1 Killie Campbell
   Africana Museum
2 Robert Jameson Park
3 Mitchell Park
4 Umgeni River Bird Park
5 Kings Park Stadium
6 Japanese Gardens
7 Beachwood Mangroves
   Nature Reserve
8 Natal Sharks Board
9 Railway Station
10 Ice Rink
11 Minitown
12 Snake Park
13 Botanic Gardens
14 Greyville Race Course
15 Jumah Mosque
16 Kingsmead Stadium
17 Old Fort and
   Warriors Gate
18 Victoria Market
19 The Workshop
20 General Post Office
21 Durban Exhibitions Centre
22 Whysalls Camera Museum
23 Amphitheatre Gardens
24 Amusement Park
25 Sea World Aquarium
26 Pigeon Valley
27 Temple of Understanding
28 Sugar Terminal
29 Albert Park
30 Old House Museum
31 African Arts Centre
32 City Hall, Natural Science
   Museum, Durban Art Gallery
33 Natal Playhouse Complex
34 Local History Museum
35 Air Terminal
36 Dick King Statue
37 Pleasure Cruise Terminal
38 Maritime Museum
39 Da Gama Clock
40 Durban Harbour
41 Little Top
   Alfresco Theatre

500 m

© Baedeker

The city's bus services are run by the Durban Transport Management Board (DTMB). The central bus station is between Commercial and Pine Streets. There is an information bureau (open: weekdays 7am–4.30pm, Sat. 8.30–11am) at the corner of Gardiner and West Streets.

The DTMB's Mynah shuttle service runs between the North and South Beaches and Albert Park by way of Smith Street (returning on West Street) and also to the Botanical Gardens. There is a bus every 5 minutes on weekdays between 6.30am and 5.25pm; less frequently at other times.

Bus services

DTMB also runs city tours, harbour tours and a variety of excursions (reservations and starting-point at pavilion on Marine Parade).

Excursions are also run by SARtravel, starting from 477 Smith Street.

Information about tours and excursions, accommodation, events in the city, etc., can be obtained from the Greater Durban Marketing Authority (head office at 160 Pine Street, tel. 3 04 49 34).

Sightseeing tours and excursions; information

On Christmas Day in 1497 Vasco da Gama discovered the bay which he called Port Natal ("Christmas" in Portuguese); but the first settlement here was established only in 1823 by a few British traders. Although it lay in Zulu tribal territory the Zulus accepted its existence as a place for trade, mainly in ivory. The settlement developed, and the town was officially founded in 1835 and named after the then Governor of the Cape, Sir Benjamin D'Urban.

History

The first voortrekkers reached the area in 1837 and founded Pietermaritz-burg, 80km/50 miles north-west of Durban. This further white intrusion gave rise to increasing Zulu resistance, and there were bloody massacres, in the course of which Durban was abandoned. After their victory over the Zulus at Blood River (December 16th 1838) the Boers established the first voortrekker republic of Natal, of which Durban was a part. This provoked British resistance. A British force was defeated in the battle of Congella in 1842 and then besieged in their fort (the Old Fort in Durban) for a month; but they were saved by the arrival of reinforcements brought in by Richard King in an adventurous 600-mile ride from Grahamstown. The voortrekkers were defeated and withdrew to the north, settling in what is now the Orange Free State and the Transvaal.

In May 1843 Natal was incorporated in the Cape Colony, and thereafter Durban prospered.

In 1860 the first Indians arrived, brought in as contract labourers to make good the shortage of manpower to work the rapidly expanding sugar plantations. Their numbers grew rapidly, and by 1883 there were more than 30,000 Indians in Natal, many of whom remained in the country after their contracts expired. Among the immigrants was Mahatma Gandhi, a young lawyer who arrived in 1893 and for 21 years fought for the rights of the Indian minority in South Africa (see Famous People).

The first railway line in South Africa, between Durban and Cape Point, was opened in 1860.

Durban is a modern city with wide streets, tall office and apartment blocks and many parks and gardens. Only a few old Victorian buildings survive amid newer developments. The "liveliest city in the country", Durban is well worth seeing, but if you are thinking of staying in this area you should be aware that the seafront is one long succession of hotels and that the parks and places of entertainment are almost always crowded: for a quieter and more restful stay the seaside resorts north and south of the city are to be preferred.

The city

A good starting-point for a walking tour of the city is the "Golden Mile", the coastal boulevard (now with traffic-calming measures). The liveliest spot is at the junction of West Street with Marine Parade. The main

◀ *Besides modern Durban with its high-rise office blocks and hotels the older Durban with its temples, mosques and bazaars can still be discovered*

shopping and business streets are West Street and Smith Street, parallel one-way streets running east–west. They lead to the Indian business quarter round Grey and Victoria Streets, on the west side of the city (about 2.5km/1½ miles from the seafront).

Erskine Parade, the southward continuation of Marine Parade, leads to the Point district, the old harbour quarter on the north side of the port, which is bounded on the south side by the promontory known as the Bluff.

To the north-west, on the slopes of Berea Hill, is the elegant suburb of Berea, and to the west the poor district of Pinetown.

Beach Front

Beaches

Between the Blue Lagoon to the north, into which the Umgeni River flows, and the Point district to the south extends Durban's 8km/5 mile long Beach (Beach Front). The magnificent boulevard which runs along the coast, once a busy freeway, has in recent years been closed to through traffic and made more pedestrian-friendly.

The main beaches, from north to south, are the Blue Lagoon, Laguna, Tekweni, Country Club, Oasis, Dunes, Battery, North, South and Addington Beaches. There are life guards on duty on these beaches from 8am to 5pm, and it is advisable to bathe only within the marked-out areas. Some sections are reserved for bathers, while others are for surfers.

Golden Mile

In the section of the seafront called Marine Parade, with Snell Parade to the north and Erskine Parade to the south, are numerous high-rise hotels and blocks of flats, restaurants and bars. With its striking skyline and constant hustle and bustle, the Golden Mile is very reminiscent of Miami Beach.

Rickshaw men

Near the Sea World Aquarium stand Durban's much photographed rickshaw men in their colourful costumes and imposing headdresses. In the

The gaily bedecked rickshaw men who offer their services on Durban's Beach Front

1930s there were still hundreds of them plying all over the city: now there are only 10–20, offering short trips along the Beach Front.

The Little Top Alfresco Theatre on South Beach is the venue, during the holiday season, of a variety of events for the entertainment of holiday-makers, including beauty and talent contests.

Little Top Alfresco Theatre

The Sea World Aquarium contains over 1000 different species of fish and other marine animals, from brightly coloured tropical fish to turtles, crusta-ceans and beautiful shellfish. One of the principal attractions is the shark pool. The aquarium is open daily from 9am to 9pm. Feeding times are 11am and 3pm; the sharks are fed only Mon., Wed. and Fri. In the Dolphinarium there are performances by trained dolphins, seals and penguins daily during the season, with fewer performances at other times of year. Tel. 031/37 40 79 for more details.

★Sea World

Beyond Sea World, to the north, is a small amusement park, with round-abouts, swimming pools and a chair-lift.

Amusement park

In the Amphitheatre Gardens, with their subtropical plants, ponds and fountains, a flea market is held on the last Sunday in the month and an art market on alternate Sundays.

Amphitheatre Gardens

Minitown, on Snell Parade, is a miniature city with replicas of Durban's best-known buildings on a scale of 1:25. All the models, including the ships and buses, were made in Minitown itself. The first model was completed in 1963. Minitown is open: Tues.–Sat. 9.30am–8.30pm, Sat. 9.30am–5.30pm.

Minitown

To the west of Minitown, at the corner of Somtseu Road and Sol Harris Crescent, is an ice rink (closed Tues. except during school holidays); skates can be hired.

Ice rink

At the north end of Lower Marine Parade is Fitzsimon's Snake Park (open: daily 9am–4.30pm), with around 120 different indigenous species of snakes, including mambas, cobras and puff adders, as well as crocodiles, iguanas and tortoises. At weekends and during the holiday seasons there are various demonstrations. Attached to the park are a snake research institute and a serum-collection station.

Snake Park

In Gillespie Street, which runs parallel to Marine Parade, is The Wheel, a modern shopping and entertainment complex, with more than 140 shops, restaurants, bars and cinemas. Over the entrance is a Ferris wheel.

The Wheel

City Centre

Whysall's Camera Museum, near the intersection of West and Point Streets, illustrates the development of photography from 1841 to the pre-sent day with over 3800 photographs and a collection of old cameras (open: daily 9am–12.30pm).

Whysall's Camera Museum

In the Diamond Cutting Works at 223 West Street (conducted tours Mon.–Sat. at 10am and 2pm), visitors can watch diamond-cutters at work. The sales office is open during normal business hours.

Diamond Cutting Works

The most imposing building in central Durban, between West and Smith Streets, is the City Hall, with its conspicuous copper-covered dome. Built in 1910, it was modelled on the City Hall in Belfast (Northern Ireland). In addition to municipal offices it houses the Municipal Library and the Natural Science Museum (open: Mon.–Sat. 8.30am–5pm, Sun. 11am–5pm).

★City Hall

Durban

Durban's City Hall, modelled on that of Belfast

Art Gallery

Durban Art Gallery, South Africa's second largest art museum, is also in the City Hall (same opening times as Natural Science Museum). It has works by both European and South African artists, including Corot, Utrillo, Lely, Constable, Lewis, Orpen, Rodin and Dalou, as well as collections of ceramics, ivories, silver and glass.

Francis Farewell Square

In front of the City Hall is Francis Farewell Square, the original nucleus of the city, where two British traders, Henry Fynn and Francis Farewell, are said to have established their first camp in 1824.

Local History Museum

Behind the City Hall is the former Courthouse (1863), now occupied by the Local History Museum (entrance in Aliwal Street; open: Mon.–Sat. 8.30am–5pm, Sun. 11am–5pm), which illustrates the history of Zululand and the European settlement of Natal.

Natal Playhouse Complex

Opposite the City Hall, at 231 Smith Street, is the modern Natal Playhouse Complex, with five houses for opera, concerts, drama and ballet. The façades and walls of two old movie theatres were incorporated in its construction. (For information about programmes, consult the brochure "Durban for All Seasons"; for reservations, Computicket, tel. 3 04 27 53.)

African Arts Centre

The African Arts Centre at 35 Gardiner Street sells Zulu arts and crafts (jewellery, baskets, wood and stone sculpture, pottery, woollen carpets, brightly coloured textiles, etc.).

Post Office

Along Gardiner Street to the north, at the corner of West Street, is the General Post Office. Built in 1885, it was Durban's first town hall.

St Paul's Church

In Church Square, to the east of the Post Office, is St Paul's Church (1909).

Exhibition Centre

To the north of the Post Office, at the corner of Soldiers Way (Gardiner Street) and Pine Street, is the old railway station, in use from 1894 to 1980,

206

which has been converted into the Durban Exhibition Centre. It has more than 11,000sq.m/118,400sq.ft of covered exhibition space and 15,000sq.m/18,000sq.yd of grounds, together with restaurants, bars and a large car park for 1000 vehicles. There are permanent exhibitions with audio-visual displays in Hall 4.

Another old station building in Commercial Road has been converted into the Workshop, an attractive shopping centre with restaurants and cafés.

Workshop

To the north of the city centre, set in beautiful gardens, is the Old Fort, in which the British population of Durban took refuge in 1824 during the month-long siege of the town by the voortrekkers. Adjoining is Warriors' Gate, which contains a small collection of militaria (open: Warriors' Gate Tues.–Sat. 8.30am–5pm, Sun. 11am–5pm; Old Fort Mon.–Fri. 10am–5pm).

Old Fort;
Warriors' Gate

On the east side of the Old Fort is Kingsmead Stadium, the venue of international rugby matches and track and field events and the finishing point of the Comrades' Marathon.

Kingsmead
Stadium

Indian Quarter

The main shopping area of the Indian quarter is Grey Street, which runs north from West Street.

Grey Street

At the corner of Queen and Grey Streets is the Jumah Mosque, which South Africans claim to be the largest and finest mosque in the southern hemisphere (visitors must take their shoes off before entering). A fifth of the Indians living in Durban are Muslims.
In Albert Street (between Queen Street and Commercial Road), concealed behind a Baroque façade, is a small Oriental bazaar with a variety of colourful shops.

Jumah Mosque

At the west end of Victoria Street is a new Indian market (open: Mon.–Sat. 6am–6pm, Sun. 10am–4pm), built in 1973 after a fire. Although the modern building lacks the charm of the old market stalls, it is still a fascinating mix of Africa and the Orient. There are around 180 stalls selling exotic spices, basketwork and brassware, wood articles and woodcarving, as well as meat, fish, fruit and vegetables. The souvenir stalls display, of course, a great deal of rubbish, but it is possible, with a bit of luck, to find some very attractive items.

★Victoria Market

The Port Area

Durban's port, the largest and most important in South Africa (and the ninth largest in the world, with an area of 1854 hectares/4579 acres, is enclosed by two promontories, each extended by a pier – the Point, at the end of the Golden Mile, to the north and the Bluff, a 4km/2½ mile long range of dunes, now covered with buildings, to the south. To enable the harbour to accommodate large vessels it was dredged out to a depth of 12.80m/42ft.
Large passenger and cruise ships berth at the Ocean or Marine Terminal at the north end of the harbour basin. Close by are the offices of the port administration.

On the busy Victoria Embankment, near the end of Gardiner Street, is a statue commemorating Dick King (Richard Philip King), who brought reinforcements to Durban during the 1842 siege (see History).

Statue of
Dick King

Near the statue is the Pleasure Cruise Terminal, departure point for harbour cruises and longer excursions. To the west is the Royal Natal Yacht Club.

Pleasure Cruise
Terminal

To the east of the statue, housed in three small ships, is the Natal Maritime Museum (open: Mon.–Sat. 8.30am–4pm, Sun. 11am–4pm).

Natal Maritime
Museum

Durban

A visit to Durban's Indian Market, with its aroma of exotic spices and incense, is an experience not to be missed

Da Gama Clock	Nearby is the Da Gama Clock, a richly decorated bell-shaped iron structure topped by a clock, a gift from the Portuguese government on the 400th anniversary of the discovery of Port Natal by Vasco da Gama in 1497.
Albert Park	Between St Andrews Street and the Victoria Embankment is Albert Park, in which are a keep-fit trail and a jogging route, and, for the less energetic, a huge chessboard.
Old House Museum	At 31 St Andrews Street, on the east side of Albert Park, is the Old House Museum, a grand Victorian mansion furnished in period style (open: Mon.–Sat. 8.30am–5pm, Sun. 11am–5pm).
Maydon Wharf	The south-westerly continuation of the Victoria Embankment is Maydon Wharf, which leads to the container port, with the Sugar Terminal, the Graving Docks and the Fishing Jetty used by the deep-sea fishing fleet.
Sugar Terminal	The Sugar Terminal is one of the largest of its kind in the world, capable of handling up to 800 tons of sugar an hour. The three silos have a storage capacity of over 520,000 tons of sugar. There are daily guided tours of the terminal (by appointment, tel. 3 01 03 31).

Sights outside the City Centre

Killie Campbell Africana Museum	The Killie Campbell Africana Museum, housed in Dr Killie Campbell's old home at 220 Marriot Road (corner of Musgrave Road), on Berea Hill north-west of the city centre, contains his important library of works on the history of Zululand and Natal, the Mashu Ethnology Collection of Zulu arts and crafts, and fine furniture. (Open: Tues. and Thur. 8am–11pm.)
★Botanic Gardens	Durban's Botanic Gardens are a must for every visitor. They lie on the slopes of Berea Hill, on the north-west of the city centre (open: daily

9.30am–5pm). In 20 hectares/50 acres of gardens grow a great variety of plants and trees, including some very rare species. Some specimens are very old, the Botanic Gardens having been established as long ago as 1849. Particularly notable features are the majestic avenue of palms and the orchid house with its glory of tropical colour (closed between 12.30 and 2.30pm). Other attractions are the herb garden and a special garden where blind visitors may touch the plants. Everywhere the twittering of birds is heard: at least fifty different species are permanent residents of the gardens. There is a shady self-service café.

Greyville Racecourse, north-east of the Botanic Gardens, is South Africa's most famous racecourse, and the sporting and social event of the year is Rothman's Durban July Handicap on the first Saturday in July. Within the racecourse circuit is the Royal Durban Golf Course.

Greyville Racecourse

Mitchell Park, in the Windermere district (to the north of the racecourse), is one of the city's oldest parks, with old trees, beautiful flowerbeds and a minizoo. There is a bird house containing large numbers of indigenous, exotic and rare birds. In the park (open: daily 8am–5pm) there is also a restaurant.
    Adjoining Mitchell Park is Robert Jameson Park, which in September has a glorious display of more than 200 different roses.

Mitchell Park

In the northern district of Virginia (Tinsley Road) are the Japanese Gardens, with curving wooden bridges, ponds, waterfalls and Japanese lanterns.

Japanese Gardens

In the Riverside district, on the north bank of the Umgeni River, is the Umgeni River Bird Park (open: daily 9am–5pm). On a network of paths running through the park visitors can observe a variety of indigenous and exotic (from South-East Asia and Australia) species of birds, including lories, cockatoos and aras.

★Umgeni River Bird Park

Between King George V Avenue and Princess Alice Avenue (to the west of the city centre) is the Pigeon Valley nature reserve, a pleasant area for walkers and bird-watchers.

Pigeon Valley

This Hare Krishna temple lies in south-western Durban (reached on N 2, heading for the South Coast: Chatsworth Centre exit). There are conducted tours of this "spiritual wonderland" (by appointment, tel. 43 33 28). Within the complex is a vegetarian restaurant.

Temple of Understanding

Sights to the South of Durban

15km/9 miles south-west of Durban is the Kenneth Stainbank Nature Reserve (area 214 hectares/529 acres; open: daily 6am–6pm), which contains a variety of indigenous plants, numerous birds, antelopes and rhinos.

Kenneth Stainbank Nature Reserve

The 160km/100 mile long south coast of the province of KwaZulu/Natal, between Durban and Port Edward, is one of the country's most popular holiday regions, with a highly developed tourist infrastructure, which draws visitors (mainly South Africans) throughout the year. All along the coast one bathing resort follows another. The stretch of coast between Amanzimtoti and Mtwalume is known as the Sunshine Coast (see Amanzimtoti), the section between Hibberdene and Port Edward as the Hibiscus Coast (see Port Shepstone).
    The resorts are linked with one another and with Durban by the N 2 motorway, the old coast road and a railway line, which run through evergreen subtropical forests, passing banana and sugarcane plantations and hills gay with hibiscus trees in blossom.

Sunshine Coast, Hibiscus Coast

Sights to the West of Durban

This municipal nature reserve (area 50 hectares/125 acres; open daily from sunrise to sunset) lies near Westville, on the western outskirts of the

Palmiet Nature Reserve

North and south of Durban are magically beautiful beaches

expanding Durban conurbation. There are a number of short hiking trails which allow visitors to see the park's flora (mainly of indigenous plants) and its large numbers of birds.

Marianhill monastery

The Marianhill monastery, in the slum quarter of Pinetown, 10km/6 miles west of the city centre, was founded in 1882 by a Trappist abbot, Franz Pfanner, and was taken over in 1909 by the Marianhill missionary order. It has developed into an important training centre for blacks.

Krantzkloof Nature Reserve

The Krantzkloof Nature Reserve (area 6sq.km/2¼sq. miles) lies 25km/ 15 miles north-west of Durban (reached on M 13, signposted to Pietermaritzburg, turning off at Kloof into a road running east). Near the entrance to the reserve the Umgeni River plunges into a deep wooded gorge.

★★Valley of a Thousand Hills

The Valley of a Thousand Hills, a beautiful region of gently rounded hills created since the Mesozoic era by the gradual recession of the Great Escarpment, extends along the Umgeni River between its outflow into the Indian Ocean, to the north of Durban, and the Nagle Dam to the east of Pietermaritzburg, which supplies Durban with water.

Leave Durban on M 13, signposted to Pietermaritzburg, and 10km/ 6 miles beyond Kloof (from which there is a road to the Krantzkloof Nature Reserve: see above) turn off into R 103, the old road between Durban and Pietermaritzburg, which runs along the southern edge of the Valley of a Thousand Hills, with magnificent views. After passing Hillcrest and Botha's Hill it comes to Phe-Zulu, a typical Zulu village where visitors can see something of the traditional Zulu way of life (daily between 9am and 4pm), including performances of tribal dances and a visit to a witch doctor. There are similar opportunities for visitors in nearby Assagay Park, which also has crocodiles, snakes and lizards as tourist attractions.

At Cato Ridge R 103 rejoins N 3. From here it is 40km/25 miles to Pietermaritzburg. 4km/2½ miles before the junction a road runs north to the

A Zulu sorceress in the Valley of a Thousand Hills with her assistant.
She uses tiny animal bones to foretell the future

Nagle Dam (18km/11 miles). The lake lies at the foot of the Natal Table
Mountain (960m/3150ft), from the summit of which there are magnificent
views.

Sights to the North of Durban

There are numerous bathing resorts on the coast north of Durban, sometimes called the Dolphin Coast, but in general this stretch is less developed
for tourism than the Sunshine and Hibiscus Coasts to the south of the city.
   For a round trip through this region, take M 3 (known as Shaka's Way
after the great Zulu king), running close to the coast, as far as Stanger,
returning to Durban on R 102, farther inland.

Dolphin Coast

18km/11 miles from Durban on M 4 is Umhlanga Rocks (pronounced
Umshlanga), with many comfortable hotels, a variety of restaurants and
large shopping centres. With long sandy beaches interrupted by stretches
of rocky coast and protected by shark nets, Umhlanga Rocks is a popular
but not unduly crowded bathing resort.

★Umhlanga
Rocks

Visitors who want to know more about sharks (see Baedeker Special, p.
212) should look in at the Natal Sharks Board, a research institute established in 1964 on a hill 2km/1¼ miles west of Umhlanga Rocks. As a result of
its work the 250km/155 mile long coast between Port Edward in the south
and Zinkwazi in the north has now more than 400 nets protecting bathers
against sharks. There are audio-visual presentations and conducted tours
of the laboratories on Tuesdays at 9am, Wednesdays at 9 and 11am and
2.30pm and Thursdays at 9am, and also on the first Sunday in the month at
2.30pm.

★Natal Sharks
Board

South Africa's Sharks

In the waters off South Africa's coastline of almost 3000km/1865 miles – from the frontier with Mozambique on the south-western Indian Ocean to the mouth of the Orange River on the south-eastern Atlantic – there are something like 100 different species of shark. After Australia, South Africa has the highest officially recorded number of attacks by sharks on humans. Rigorous safety precautions, however, have enormously reduced the danger for swimmers and surfers on the beaches of South Africa.

The large number of shark species in South African waters – including representatives of all the eight main groups (orders) of sharks, consisting of 30 families and more than 350 species worldwide – is due to the two currents which flow along the South African coasts, providing different habitats for sharks and other marine creatures. On the west coast, which is washed by the cold Benguela Current, are found species of shark which like cold water, while on the east coast, with the warmer Agulhas Current, there are tropical species.

Of the hundred or so species of sharks in South African waters only just over twenty can be regarded, because of their size, as possibly dangerous. Only four species, however, are a real danger: the great white shark, the sand tiger shark, the smooth-hound (known in South Africa as the Zambezi shark) and the white-point reef shark. The great white shark, which belongs to the mackerel-shark family, has long – and certainly since Steven Spielberg's film "Jaws" (1974–75) – been regarded as the killer shark *par excellence*. Many zoologists who have studied the sharks do not share this view, and indeed suggest that the so-called "killers" have an inhibition on attacking humans. Although the great white shark is recognised to be the most dangerous species of shark, they are in fact very slow to attack humans. It has frequently happened that a swimmer, surfer or diver who has been seized by a shark has been at once released. It looks as if humans are sometimes attacked in error, having been mistaken for seals, the great white shark's favourite prey. South African divers have told of encounters with great white sharks – predators up to 8m/26ft long and weighing anything up to 2 tons – which have shown no signs of aggression. Between 1926 and 1990 123 attacks by great white sharks were recorded worldwide, 25 of them resulting in the death of the victim, of which only six took place off the South African coasts – no doubt because there are relatively few great white sharks in South African waters.

Very different is the case of the smooth-hound or Zambezi shark, which can be up to 4m/13ft long. In the warm waters off Natal it heads the statistics for attacks on humans. A number of shark attacks in South Africa are also attributed to the sand tiger shark, a predator up to 6m/20ft long which some zoologists regard as the most dangerous of the tropical sharks. It is omnivorous: the contents of the stomach of a sand tiger shark that has been killed resembles a junk-heap, with car tyres, car registration plates, tin cans and so on. The white-pointer shark is a danger only on the high seas – for example to shipwrecked mariners. This species of shark, which can be up to 4m/13ft long and lives in large packs, does not approach bathing beaches.

Encounters with other species of shark can also be dangerous. Caution is necessary, for example, in dealing with all three species of hammerhead shark. Many attacks by sharks, however, are the result of some confusion, threat or unsought provocation and with luck will end with only minor injuries. The giant nurse sharks, for example, are peaceable creatures, but will attack when they feel themselves disturbed and threatened by thoughtless or reckless divers. Underwater fishers using harpoon guns should be careful what they are about: a fish which has been harpooned and is bleeding and struggling may attract sharks; and many an underwater hunter seeking to hold on to his catch has had an unpleasant surprise. But it is not only swimmers, divers and surfers who face attack from sharks: there have also been attacks on boats (mostly fishing boats) by great white sharks and in a few cases by Mako sharks, a deep-sea species up to 3.5m/11½ft long.

Most attacks by sharks have been on the east coast, between Cape Town and Mozambique; on the west coast with its colder water practically no attacks have been reported. One reason for this is that the more dangerous species of sharks prefer warmer water, which will have more fish; another factor may be that on the east coast attacks by sharks have been more systematically recorded. Three-quarters of all incidents recorded took place on the beaches of Natal. The most frequent attacks are said to have been on the beach of the Amanzimtoti holiday centre, 30km/19 miles south of Durban, near the rocky promontory of Inyoni Rocks.

Between 1940 and 1960 there were 43 attacks by sharks on the coasts of Natal, just under half of them ending fatally. These attacks gave rise to a regular hysteria, reaching its peak in April 1958, when, after two people had been killed, holidaymakers fled from the beaches, creating traffic chaos on the roads. There were now increasing calls for protective measures. As early as 1907 the city of Durban had sought to protect bathers by erecting a semicircular protective cage, 200m/220yd in diameter, which lasted for twenty years; but by 1928 it had been destroyed by erosion and battering by the waves and had to be pulled down. In the late fifties, when the shark panic reached its peak, attempts were made to kill the sharks by depth charges and hand grenades launched from naval vessels and police boats. This had a precisely opposite effect: the explosions did little damage to the sharks but more of them were attracted by the fish that had been killed. Thereafter, learning from the example of Australia, the authorities began systematically to protect bathing beaches by installing shark nets (with Durban setting the example in 1952). In 1964 a kind of shark police was established, with responsibility for beach security (that is, for the installation of nets to protect bathing beaches and inlets) throughout Natal. The Natal Sharks Board (as the shark police is now called) has a fleet of boats, 5.5m/18ft long and manned by a crew of six, which set up, monitor and repair a double ring of nets just outside the coastal surf. Each of the nets, which do not form a continuous line but are anchored in overlapping rows, is 107m/350ft long and 6.1m/20ft high. Weather permitting, the nets, which have a total length of 44km/27 miles, are checked daily, and every three weeks are hauled up for cleaning and replaced. The Natal Sharks Board has now extended its activities to beaches outside Natal. In addition it conducts research into sharks and dolphins in the institute at Umhlanga Rocks and carries on educational and publicity work with exhibitions and audio-visual presentations. The Board's netting programme has enormously reduced the danger from sharks. Between 1986 and the end of 1994 there was only one shark attack resulting in the death of the victim. Now, however, there is increasing concern about the ecological consequences of the netting policy. For not only are some 1500 sharks caught in the nets every

Baedeker Special

year, 85% of them suffering an agonising death, but the nets also catch many other large marine creatures such as tunny, dolphins and whales. An effective and more environment-friendly alternative now being introduced is an electromagnetic field produced by sending electric shocks through two cables anchored on the sea bed. When large and dangerous sharks approach the beach they are compelled by the electric field to turn tail and swim out to sea, unharmed. This "eddy current electrode system" has been successfully tested and is due to come into operation shortly. In other respects too there has been some rethinking of ecological policies. The White Shark Research Institute in Cape Town (Victoria and Alfred Waterfront, PO Box 50775) is concerned to protect not only the great white shark but all other shark species and has devoted a considerable publicity effort to overcoming prejudices against sharks. The great white shark is now high on the South African list of endangered species and under statutory protection.

Umhlanga Lagoon Nature Reserve	Immediately north of Umhlanga Rocks is the Umhlanga Lagoon Nature Reserve (area 26 hectares/60 acres). Various trails run through this area of wooded dunes with their rich bird life.
Umdloti	The bathing resort of Umdloti, at the mouth of the Mdloti River, has one of the finest beaches in the area. The river takes its name from a wild tobacco plant which grows along its banks.
Tongaat Beach	Farther north is Tongaat Beach, with a hotel and numbers of holiday apartments. The beaches are protected by shark nets. The nearby Crocodile Creek crocodile farm is open daily to visitors 10am–4.30pm.
Ballitoville	Another popular bathing resort is Ballitoville (or Ballito for short), 45km/28 miles north of Durban. It has a beautiful beach protected by shark nets.
Shaka's Rock	Shaka's Rock also has hotels and a sheltered beach, and there is a beautiful hiking trail running parallel to the coast. This is said to have been a favourite spot of the Zulu king Shaka.
Salt Rock	Just beyond this is Salt Rock, a quiet little resort with a hotel and a camping site. On the coast are piers and towers built for the benefit of anglers. Salt Rock Country Club has a wide range of sports facilities, including a boccia pitch, tennis courts, billiard tables and swimming pools.
Stanger	The coast road continues past two other quiet resorts, Sheffield Beach and Blythdale Beach, from which a road runs inland to Stanger (pop. 26,000), founded in 1873 on the site of Shaka's last royal kraal, Kwadukuza ("Place of the Missing One"). A monument in a small garden marks the spot where the great Zulu ruler (see Famous People) was murdered in 1828. Annually on September 22nd, a day of great significance to the Zulus, they meet here to do honour to Shaka. Stanger is now a busy commercial and administrative centre, mainly inhabited by Indians, for one of South Africa's most important sugar-producing areas.
Tongaat	From Stanger R 102 runs south and comes in 30km/19 miles to Tongaat (pop. 50,000), another important centre of the sugar industry.

Tongaat was founded in 1849 by British immigrants. The town, named after the Tongaat River, was originally called Victoria. It preserves a few buildings from its early days. Also of interest is the Shree Marriamen, a tiny Hindu temple on the main street. The golf course, fringed by palms and surrounded by green fields of sugarcane, attracts golfers from far and wide.

15km/9 miles south of Tongaat is Verulam (pop. 30,000). Founded in 1850 by Methodists, it is the oldest town in the province, with a majority of Indians in the population.

Verulam

South of Verulam a road branches off R 102 and runs west to the Phoenix Park Settlement, where Mahatma Gandhi (see Famous People) established a farm during his stay in Natal. His house now contains a small museum on his life and work.

Phoenix Park Settlement

East London   K 9

Province: Eastern Cape
Altitude: 36m/118ft
Population: 135,000
Distances: 135km/84 miles from Grahamstown, 310km/193 miles from Port
    Elizabeth, 780km/485 miles from Kimberley, 982km/610 miles from
    Johannesburg, 1079km/670 miles from Cape Town

East London, on the estuary of the Buffalo River, which here flows into the Indian Ocean, is the only river port of any economic importance in South Africa, handling mainly wool (auctions in Wool Exchange from May to September) and other agricultural products. Its main industry, after food-stuffs and textiles, is car manufacture. In recent decades, however, East London, handicapped by its situation between the former homelands of Transkei and Ciskei and faced by strong competition from Durban and Port Elizabeth, has increasingly fallen into decline. In the nearby black settlements of Mdantsane and Zwelithsa up to 70% of the population are unemployed.

Situation and characteristics

Of all this, however, visitors to East London see little. Situated as it is on one of the most beautiful stretches of coast on the Indian Ocean, with long, broad, clean and unfrequented beaches, East London is now a very popular holiday resort which attracts visitors throughout the year.

In 1688 a ship anchored at the mouth of the Buffalo River looking for survivors of a shipwreck. Then in 1752 Ensign Beutler undertook a voyage of exploration in the region and reported the discovery of a river which the natives called Konka ("buffalo"). Presumably this area, on the borders of Xhosa country, was thought to be unsafe, for it was more than eighty years before another British ship put in here in 1836, this time with supplies for troops stationed in the region. During the Kaffir Wars the port rapidly gained in importance as a supply base. In 1848 it was occupied by British forces and named East London.

History

In 1857 and 1858 almost 5000 discharged mercenaries of the British German Legion found a haven here and settled with their families in the surrounding area. Hence the many German place-names (Hamburg, Potsdam, Braunschweig, etc.) round East London; hence also the origin of the German Market in which the settlers sold their produce. The market is still held on Fridays and Saturdays in Beacon Bay, on the north side of East London; but now it is mainly African women who sell their wares there. East London was granted its municipal charter in 1880.

From the air terminal at the railway station there are regular bus services to Ben Schoeman Airport, 12km/7½ miles from the city centre, which links East London with all the principal South African cities.

Transport

215

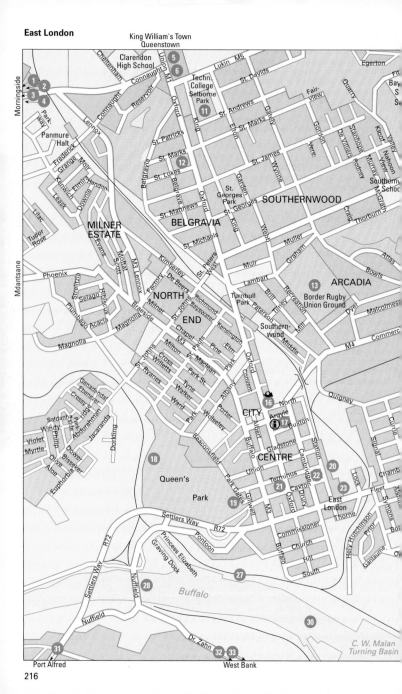

East London

C. W. Malan Turning Basin

Buffalo

Queen's Park

MILNER ESTATE

NORTH END

BELGRAVIA

SOUTHERNWOOD

ARCADIA

CITY CENTRE

Border Rugby Union Ground

St. Georges Park

Clarendon High School

Technical College Selborne Park

East London

Port Alfred

West Bank

King William's Town
Queenstown

Morningside

Mdantsane

216

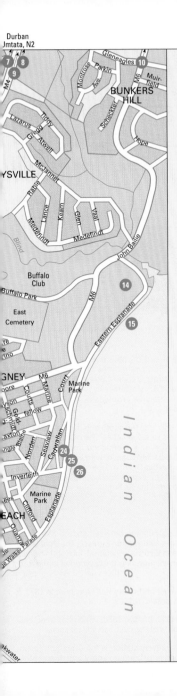

East London
Oos London

1 Amalinda Fisheries Station
  and Nature Reserve
2 Reptileworld
3 Umtiza Forest Reserve
4 Bridle Drift Dam
  and Nature Reserve
5 Guild Theatre
6 East London Museum
7 Calgary Farm
8 Mpongo Game Reserve
9 Soffiantini Castle
10 Nahoon Beach
11 Selbourne Park
   Tennis Stadium
12 Ann Bryant Art Gallery
13 Jan Smuts Ground
14 Marina Glen
15 Eastern Beach
16 General Post Office
17 City Hall
18 Queen's Park
   Botanical Garden and Zoo
19 Gately House
20 Railway Station
21 Satour Office
22 Air Terminal
23 Lock Street Jail
   Shopping Centre
24 German Settlers' Memorial
25 Aquarium
26 Shipwreck Bay
27 Deep Sea Fishing
   and Pleasure Cruises
28 Buffalo Bridge
29 Orient Beach
30 Port
31 Ben Schoeman Airport
32 Powder Magazine
33 St Peter's Church
34 East London Yacht Club

500 m

© Baedeker

View of East London

The town	With its pleasant residential suburbs and its public parks and gardens, East London has a well-cared-for look. The central area is small and can be easily explored on foot. The main street is Oxford Street. It is 5km/3 miles long, but only the section between Argyle Street in the north and Fleet Street is really busy. There is an attractive promenade, the 2km/1¼ mile long Esplanade, along the seafront.
★Beaches	Between the mouth of the Buffalo River to the south and the Nahoon River to the north are the city's three finest sandy beaches. The nearest to the city centre is Orient Beach, with a playground, a paddling pool, a children's slide and minigolf. Adjoining is the Eastern Beach, with water warmed by the Mozambique Current. At Nahoon Beach, on a large lagoon 8km/5 miles north of the city centre, are an amusement park and a camping site, and an offshore reef provides ideal conditions for surfing.

Sights in East London

City Hall	East London's City Hall is a striking building between Oxford Street and Argyle Street (in which is the Visitors' Information Bureau). The clock tower was added on the occasion of Queen Victoria's Diamond Jubilee. In front of it is an equestrian monument commemorating those who fell in the Boer War.
Railway station	The railway station, to the south-east of the City Hall, was built in 1877. It contains a steam engine made in Britain in 1903.
Lock Street Jail Shopping Centre	Beyond the station was the town jail, built in 1880, which has been converted into a shopping centre. Some of the cells can still be seen.
Aquarium	On the seafront to the east of the railway station is the Aquarium (open: daily 9am–5pm), with a large pool containing a variety of fish and other

East London's City Hall, with a monument commemorating the Boer War

marine creatures, from sea-horses and brightly coloured coral fish to great white sharks. The popular favourites are the penguins and the trained seals, which perform daily at 11.30am and 3.30pm. Feeding times are at 10.30am and 3pm.

A short distance away, also on the Esplanade, is the German Settlers' Memorial, by the South African sculptor Lippy Lipshitz, commmemorating the German settlers who came to East London in 1857–58. On the monument are five bronze panels depicting their departure from Germany, their voyage to South Africa and their arrival in East London.

German Settlers' Memorial

The coast round East London has a tragic record. A total of 82 ships have been wrecked here, 46 of them off the Esplanade alone. The most recent was the "Oranjeland", wrecked on August 13th 1984. Commemorative plaques on the Esplanade mark the spots where six ships came to grief. There are organised diving expeditions to the wrecks (information from tourist information bureau; diving certificate required).

Shipwreck Bay

On a hill to the west of the city centre is the Queen's Park Botanical Garden (area 34 hectares/84 acres; open: daily 9am–5pm), with a small zoo. Ponies can be hired for children.

★Botanical Garden and Zoo

At the entrance to the park is a colonial-style mansion built for John Gately in 1878, one of the oldest buildings on the east bank of the Buffalo River. It is now a museum, furnished with period pieces which belonged to the Gately family (open: Sat. and Sun. 3–5pm).

Gately House

Along Oxford Street to the north is the Ann Bryant Art Gallery, in a handsome house showing a mingling of Cape Dutch and Victorian styles. It contains a collection of older and modern South African art, together with some pictures by British artists (open: Mon.–Fri. 9.30am–5pm, Sat. 9.30am–noon and every third Sun. of month).

Ann Bryant Art Gallery

East London

★East London
Museum

At the north end of Oxford Street is the East London Museum (established 1931), perhaps the most interesting natural history museum in the country, with numbers of unusual exhibits (open: Mon.–Fri. 9.30am–5pm, Sat. 9.30am–noon, Sun. 11am–4pm).

The star attraction of the museum is the coelacanth, a fish with limb-like fins which until it was caught in the Chalumna River, near East London, in 1938 was believed to have become extinct more than 50 million years ago. (There are now known to be between 200 and 300 of these "prehistoric" fish in the waters off the Comoro Islands in the Indian Ocean; the specimen caught here had presumably been carried south by the current.) The museum also has numerous specimens of mammals, birds, reptiles and amphibians, as well as a dodo's egg. There is an anthropological section with material on the culture of the Xhosa.

Amalinda Nature
Conservation
Station

On the north-western outskirts of the city (reached on Connaught Avenue, going west, and its continuation M 5, signposted to King William's Town) is the Amalinda Nature Conservation Station (area 134 hectares/331 acres), with a fish hatchery and research centre. The reserve, mostly coastal forest and thornveld, is home to many species of birds and antelopes.

Soffiantini Castle

In Beacon Bay (to the north of the city), above the Nahoon valley, is Soffiantini Castle, a mock Italian castle erected by an Italian immigrant.

The port

The port installations lie to the south of the city centre at the mouth of the Buffalo River. On a tour of the harbour (run by the Greater East London Publicity Association) visitors will be shown the "dolos" – a type of breakwater constructed by an engineer named Eric Merrifield in 1961, formed from interlocking concrete blocks. Similar structures are now used in harbour construction worldwide.

Here, at the East London Yacht Club, is the finishing point of the annual Vasca da Gama Regatta, which starts from Durban.

Buffalo Bridge,
Powder Magazine

The Buffalo Bridge (completed in 1935), a two-level road and rail bridge, leads to the south bank of the river. A little way east is the Powder Magazine, all that remains of Fort Glamorgan, built in 1848 to protect the settlement against Xhosa attacks.

St Peter's

500m/550yd east of the Powder Magazine, in the West Bank district, is St Peter's Church (1857), now protected as a national monument.

Surroundings of East London

★Beaches

To the south of East London, along the coast of the former homeland of Ciskei (see Bisho), are superb unfrequented beaches.

Umtiza
Forest Reserve

15km/9 miles west of East London is Umtiza Forest Reserve, a 724 hectare/1788 acre expanse of dense coastal forest which is home to large numbers of birds, monkeys and antelopes. Three roads (respectively 2.5km/1½ miles, 6km/4 miles and 10km/6 miles long) run through the reserve. It can be entered only with a permit issued by the reserve office (tel. 0431/46 35 32).

Bridle Drift
Dam and
Nature Reserve

25km/15 miles west of East London is the Bridle Drift Dam, an artificial lake formed by a dam on the Buffalo River (reached by way of Mount Coke Road). The lake and surrounding area are now a nature reserve with an area of 580 acres/1435 acres. There are facilities for surfing and boating on the lake (canoes available for hire), and in the nature reserve visitors can observe antelopes and gazelles, as well as large numbers of water birds.

Reptileworld

Above Bridle Drift Dam is Reptileworld (open: daily 10am–5pm), a reptile farm on which a variety of reptiles (mainly crocodiles and snakes) are bred.

There are regular presentations of the animals, and it is also interesting to watch them being fed. From the tea garden there is a fine view of the Buffalo valley.

The Mpongo Game Reserve is a small private game park in the Mpongo valley, 30km/19 miles north-west of East London, with various steppe animals, including lions, as well as large numbers of birds. The park can be explored by car, on organised hikes and on horseback. There is a camping site and a restaurant.

Mpongo
Game Reserve

On Calgary Farm, 35km/22 miles from East London on the Macleantown road, visitors can see a collection of horse-drawn carriages and an old smithy (open: Wed.–Sun. 9am–4pm).

Calgary Farm

This small nature park (open: Mon., Wed. and Thur. 7.30am–1pm and 2–4.30pm, Sun. 11am–1pm and 2–4.30pm), with large numbers of water birds, lies 20km/12½ miles north-east of East London at the little coastal town of Gonubie.

Gonubie
Nature Reserve

Eshowe   M 6

Province: KwaZulu/Natal
Altitude: 520m/1705ft
Population: 15,000
Distances: 216km/134 miles from Durban, 220km/137 miles from Dundee

Eshowe lies in a beautiful sugar-growing area to the west of N 2, which here runs parallel to the north coast of KwaZulu/Natal. It is an attractive town and a good stopover on a journey into the Zulu heartland.
    In 1860 the Zulu king Cetshwayo or Cetewayo established his royal kraal in this area before moving to Ondini (see Ulundi). During the Zulu Wars both Eshowe and Ondini were destroyed. After the annexation of Zululand and its incorporation in the province of Natal the British authorities built a number of forts in the region, including Fort Nongqai in Eshowe. The town became the administrative centre of the newly conquered territory in 1887.
    An agricultural show held here annually in June draws large numbers of visitors.

★Situation and
characteristics

Sights in Eshowe

Fort Nongqai now houses the Zululand Historical Museum (open: daily 10am–5pm).

Fort Nongqai

On the outskirts of Eshowe, at the end of Kangelia Street, is the Dlinza Forest Nature Reserve (area 200 hectares/500 acres; open: daily 7.30am–5pm), home to many small mammals. Some of the trails in the park are said to have been made by British troops stationed here in 1879 after the end of the Zulu Wars.

Dlinza Forest
Nature Reserve

★Into the Zulu Heartland

A very attractive trip from Eshowe is to Empangeni (see Richard's Bay). 6km/4 miles north of Eshowe on R 68 an unsurfaced road goes off on the right, running through what were formerly favourite Zulu hunting grounds, now covered with sugar-cane plantations. 27km/17 miles from Eshowe is a monument marking the site of KwaBulawayo, once the "capital" of the legendary Zulu king Shaka (see Famous People). According to the account of an ivory trader who visited it in 1824 it consisted of several thousand huts.

KwaBulawayo

221

15km/9 miles north of Eshowe a road branches off R 68 on the left and comes in 4km/2½ miles to Shakaland, originally established as the setting for a film on the legendary Shaka. After the completion of the film the set was converted into a typical Zulu village, now an open-air museum with presentations of Zulu life. Here visitors get a vivid impression of the way of life and customs of the Zulus, and can stay in traditional Zulu huts run by the Protea hotel chain.

Shakaland

The road to Shakaland passes the Zulu village of KwaBhekithunga, famed for its rich variety of arts and crafts.

KwaBhekithunga

Stewart's Farm, like Shakaland, appeals to visitors as a typical Zulu village – this time a "real" and not a manufactured village. It is reached on a road (R 34) which branches off R 68, north of Eshowe, at Nkwalini and comes in 30km/19 miles to the village. Stewart's Farm seeks to preserve traditional Zulu tribal life, illustrating it for visitors with various exhibitions and presentations.

Stewart's Farm

A visit to Dingane's Kraal, 85km/53 miles from Eshowe, is an experience not to be missed. Leave Eshowe on R 68 and, 5km/3 miles beyond Melmotte, turn into R 34, signposted to Vryheid. From this road, 5km/3 miles beyond the intersection with R 66, a road goes off on the left to Dingane's Kraal. Here, at Umungundlovo, Dingane, Shaka's half-brother and successor, established his royal kraal in 1828. It consisted of more than 2000 huts, accommodating up to 20,000 warriors. Here in 1838 the Boer leader Piet Retief met Dingane to conclude a treaty but was murdered on Dingane's orders along with 70 of his men. Some of the huts have been reconstructed, and there is a small museum and a monument commemorating the murdered Boers. At least as rewarding for visitors is the magnificent scenery in this area.

★Dingane's Kraal

Estcourt

L 6

Province: KwaZulu/Natal
Altitude: 1484m/4869ft
Population: 40,000
Distances: 140km/87 miles from Dundee, 190km/118 miles from Durban

Estcourt is a small industrial town on the Bushman River in an intensively cultivated farming area. Although the town itself has no outstanding features of interest, it is a good centre for visiting the Drakensberg (see entry). Estcourt is one of the oldest towns in Natal, a voortrekker settlement having been established in this area in 1838.

Situation and characteristics

Sights in and around Estcourt

Fort Durnford, established in 1874 by Major Anthony Durnford, is now a museum.

Fort Durnford

Wagendrift Dam, 5km/3 miles south-west of Estcourt, offers good fishing and water sports.

Wagendrift Dam

At the end of Wagendrift Dam is the Moor Park Nature Reserve, in which there are zebras and various species of antelope.

Moor Park Nature Reserve

◀ *Excursions from Eshowe into the Zulu heartland will allow visitors to see scenes from everyday Zulu life – sometimes laid on for their benefit*

Weenen Nature Reserve	30km/19 miles north-east of Estcourt is Weenen Nature Reserve (area 5000 hectares/12,500 acres). A number of hiking trails run through the reserve, which is home to rhinos, buffaloes, giraffes and various species of antelope.
Mooi River	Mooi River (pop. 13,000), 30km/20 miles south of Estcourt on the river of that name, is another good centre for trips into the Drakensberg. A favourite recreation area with the people of Mooi River is the Craigburn Nature Reserve (area 330 hectares/815 acres), on the road to Greytown, within which is a small artificial lake (fishing, boating; picnic spots).

Ficksburg   K 6

Province: Orange Free State
Altitude: 1834m/6017ft
Population: 30,000
Distances: 110km/68 miles from Bethlehem, 185km/115 miles from
    Bloemfontein

Situation and characteristics	The little town of Ficksburg, founded in 1867, lies on the frontier with Lesotho, surrounded by plantations of cherry-trees and asparagus fields. It is particularly attractive when the cherry-trees are in blossom in spring (September and October; Cherry Trail running through the plantations – information from tourist office) and during the annual Cherry Festival in November. Ficksburg has preserved its original character, with handsome sandstone buildings and well cared for parks and gardens. The surrounding area was populated at an early period – no doubt because of its agreeable climate – as is shown by the numerous Bushman paintings in nearby caves and rock overhangs.

Sights in and around Ficksburg

General J. I. J. Fick Museum	This sandstone-built museum commemorates General John Fick, after whom the town is named. Other sections are devoted to the development of the town and the history of the Sotho people.
Meulspruit Dam	The Meulspruit Dam, 5km/3 miles from Ficksburg, has facilities for water sports and fishing, picnic spots and a camping site.
Imperani Hiking Trail	Meulspruit Dam is the starting-point of the Imperani Hiking Trail, a two-day circular walk through the Imperani Hills, in which there are large numbers of Bushman drawings in caves and rock overhangs.
Hoekfontein Game Farm	15km/9 miles north-east of Ficksburg on the Fouriesburg road (R 26) is Hoekfontein Game Farm, which offers comfortable accommodation for visitors and opportunities of seeing white rhinos, hippopotamuses, zebras and various species of antelope.
Clocolan	Clocolan, 35km/22 miles west of Ficksburg, was founded in 1906. Its name comes from the Sotho term Hlohloloane, meaning "ridge of the battle". From here there are views, particularly fine in winter, of the Maluti Mountains to the east of the town. At the Steunmekaar Dam, 1km/¾ mile from the town, are a camping site and facilities for various sports. There is also accommodation for visitors in a holiday village on the slopes of the Tanjiesberg (10km/6 miles from Clocolan), which offers pony-trekking in the surrounding area.

Fort Beaufort   J 9

Province: Eastern Cape
Altitude: 486m/1595ft
Population: 15,000
Distances: 77km/48 miles from Grahamstown, 125km/78 miles from
    Queenstown, 150km/93 miles from Cradock

Fort Beaufort lies 100km/62 miles from the coast of the Indian Ocean on the
borders of the former homeland of Ciskei. Founded in 1822 as a military
outpost of the Cape Colony, it is now a citrus fruit growing and sheep-
farming centre.

Situation and
characteristics

   Fort Beaufort was the scene of an incident which sparked off the seventh
frontier war, the "Axe War". In 1846 a Xhosa stole an axe from a shop in the
town; a group of British soldiers and volunteers thereupon attacked the
Xhosa settlement of Queen Adelaide; and this in turn led to a bloody
conflict which ended only in 1847.

Surroundings of Fort Beaufort

37km/23 miles west of Fort Beaufort is Adelaide (pop. 10,000), founded in
1834 as a garrison town and named after William IV's wife Queen Adelaide.
It is now the centre of a corn and citrus fruit growing and sheep-farming
area. Its Heritage Museum has a fine collection of porcelain, glass and
silver.

Adelaide

Alice, 23km/14 miles east of Fort Beaufort, was founded in 1847 as a
mission station and military post. The Municipal Museum has a display of
traditional Xhosa dress. Outside the town, housed in an old British fort, is
Fort Hare University, established in 1916 as a college for blacks and promoted to university status in 1970. Among its students have been Nelson

Alice

Fort Beaufort has three museums illustrating its eventful history

Mandela, Oliver Tambo, Robert Mugabe and Kenneth Kaunda. It has now more than 3400 students.

★Hogsback,
Katberg

A few miles east of Alice a road runs north to Hogsback, 50km/31 miles north-east of Fort Beaufort. The town lies at an altitude of 1300m/4265ft in the beautiful Amatola Mountains. Hogsback and the little town of Katberg, 27km/17 miles east, are popular holiday resorts in summer and winter, but the best time of year here is between June and September. (On some days during the year there may be snow, but most of the rainfall occurs in summer, when thunderstorms and mist are to be expected.) Round Hogsback are dense forests – good walking country. The beautiful scenery in this area is said to have given J. R. R. Tolkien (see Famous People) the inspiration for his "Lord of the Rings".

Part of the forested area round Hogsback is now the Auckland Nature Reserve, with a population of antelopes, gazelles, porcupines and reedbucks. Birds to be seen here include both predators and songbirds (among them the African golden oriole). The most striking natural features are the Madonna and Child Falls and the Kettlespout.

Tsolwana
Game Reserve

50km/31 miles north of Fort Beaufort (and west of Sada) is Tsolwana Game Reserve (area 10,000 hectares/25,000 acres), established in 1979, which lies at heights of between 1300 and 1800m (4265 and 5900ft) in a relatively rainless area. After rain does fall, however, a luxuriant vegetation comes to life. The fauna includes rhinos, giraffes, mountain zebras and various species of antelope. The reserve can be explored by car on unsurfaced roads or on conducted walks; there is accommodation for visitors in old farmhouses.

Garden Route   F–H 10

Provinces: Western Cape, Eastern Cape

Situation and
characteristics

The Garden Route (in Afrikaans Tuinroete) is the name given to a 200km/125 mile long stretch of National Highway 2 (N 2), which runs for a total distance of 2000km/1250 miles, close to the coast of the Indian Ocean for most of the way, between Cape Town and Swaziland. The stretch of coast between Mossel Bay in the west and the mouth of the Storms River in the east is one of the classic South African tourist attractions, perhaps the most famous tourist route in the country. It is particularly busy in December and January.

★★Topography

The Garden Route runs along a narrow coastal terrace some 200m/650ft above sea level, with the Outeniqua and Tsitsikamma Mountains rising to 1875m/6150ft as a backdrop. It passes through luxuriant tropical and planted pine forests, often reaching down to the coast, and every now and then crosses wild rivers flowing down from the mountains, cutting deep gorges through the basement rocks and in flatter areas (as in Nature's Valley) forming beautiful lagoons. There is a continual alternation between stretches of steep cliffs and gently sloping, empty beaches.

Along the coast are many holiday resorts which attract visitors throughout the year. The climate is generally mild, and water temperatures average around 17°C/63°F. In contrast to the arid steppe-like hinterland, the coastal region has regular rainfall, fostering a wide range of vegetation. In the past the forests were much reduced by felling for timber, slash-and-burn cultivation and overgrazing, but in line with modern ecological thinking nature reserves have been established all along the route. There are now tree and flower reserves, state forests and bird parks, as well as one marine reserve.

★★Along the Garden Route

The Garden Route follows N 2 all the way; but visitors should make a point of turning off the main road into smaller side roads and tracks leading to hidden beauties.

The route runs east from the port and popular holiday resort of Mossel Bay (see entry) on N 2 or on R 102, which runs parallel to it.

Mossel Bay

10km/6 miles from Mossel Bay R 328 runs north over the spectacular Robinson Pass to Oudtshoorn (80km/50 miles: see entry), with its numerous ostrich farms.

Oudtshoorn

Beyond the coastal resort of Great Brak River N 2 and R 102 run rather farther inland, but the scenery is still magnificent, with beautiful views of the Outeniqua Mountains. Side roads run south to the quiet little resorts of Glentana and Herold's Bay, both of which have beautiful beaches and consist mainly of holiday bungalows.

Glentana, Herold's Bay

Beyond this is George (see entry), one of the larger towns on the Garden Route.

George

From George the route continues on N 2, which soon returns to the coast and comes in 10km/6 miles to the holiday resort of Wilderness. Here there are hotels, restaurants and shops, and of course beautiful beaches in the surrounding area. Wilderness is also a good base from which to explore Wilderness National Park.

Wilderness

Wilderness National Park (area 10,000 hectares/25,000 acres) lies on both sides of N 2, extending from the mouth of the Trouw River in the west to Sedgefield in the east. On the north it is bounded by the Outeniqua Mountains, and on the south reaches down at some points to the Indian Ocean. The area is often known simply as the Lakes, for along this stretch of coast

★Wilderness National Park

Long lonely beaches and dense unspoiled forests are among the attractions of the Garden Route

there are a number of lakes, swamps and estuaries linked with one another. The juxtaposition and mingling of salt and fresh water produce a very varied flora and fauna, and the National Park is a paradise for water birds. It contains accommodation for visitors, and there are facilities for water sports in and on the lakes.

★ Goukamma
Nature Reserve

A few miles east of the Wilderness National Park, straddling the estuary of the Goukamma River, is the Goukamma Nature Reserve (open: daily 8am–6pm), established to protect this region of dunes with its distinctive bird life. It is reached from the road to Buffel's Bay; the reserve must then be explored on foot.

Knysna

N 2 then runs past the picturesque lagoons of Knysna (see entry).

Garden of Eden

15km/9 miles east of Knysna is a popular picnic spot known as the Garden of Eden, with a forest nature trail.

Plettenberg Bay

One of the busiest bathing resorts on the Garden Route is Plettenberg Bay (see entry).

★★ Tsitsikamma
National Park

Until 1868 there were no roads to the Tsitsikamma area. Now, for travellers coming from Plettenberg Bay, there is a choice between N 2 (a toll road) and R 102. N 2 shortens the distance between Plettenberg Bay and Humansdorp by 7km/4½ miles, crossing the Bloukrans River on the 460m/500yd long Bloukrans Bridge, 270m/885ft above the river. Just after a little place called the Crags R 102 branches off N 2 into beautiful Nature's Valley (see Plettenberg Bay); it then goes over the Bloukrans Pass and rejoins N 2 6km/4 miles before Storms River. R 102 is one of the most beautiful stretches of the Garden Route, winding its way through unspoiled natural forest and deep and narrow gorges, with spectacular views of the coast.

Beach, Plettenberg Bay   *The Big Tree, near Storms River*

1km/¾ mile after the hamlet of Kleinbos a road branches off N 2 and runs south to Storms River Mouth. Off this road opens the access road to Tsitsikamma National Park.

In the Hottentot language the name Tsitsikamma means "clear water". The National Park, opened in 1964, takes in a narrow strip of land extending for 80km/50 miles along the coast, alternating between rocky and sandy shore. The coastal waters are also included in the park. Thanks to the rain which falls throughout the year (heaviest in May and October, lightest in June and July), the vegetation in the Tsitsikamma National Park is particularly luxuriant. The dense forest, which contains some very ancient trees, is interspersed with ferns and flowering plants; there are many rivers and streams flowing down to the sea from the Tsitsikamma Mountains; and the rocky coast, here falling steeply down to the sea, is covered with fynbos vegetation. The park contains many species of birds, monkeys and the smaller antelopes, and there is also a very varied marine fauna (of particular interest to scuba divers and snorkellers). Dolphins and whales are frequently sighted off the coast.

The park, which is open daily throughout the year, has a variety of accommodation for visitors, together with restaurants and shops. A number of short hiking trails start from the Storms River Mouth rest camp. From the end of the road a boardwalk (1km/¾ mile) leads to the mouth of the Storms River, with signs giving information about the main species of trees in the coastal forest. There is also a narrow path leading to a suspension bridge which crosses the Storms River to a viewpoint on the other side.

For those who want a longer walk there is the 42km/26 mile long Otter Trail between Storms River Mouth and Nature's Valley (with overnight accommodation in four huts along the route). A number of shorter trails start from the Vasselot rest camp (3km/2 miles from Nature's Valley).

1km/¾ mile east of Storms River a signpost on N 2 points the way (500m/550yd) to the Big Tree (Groot Boom), a gigantic yellowwood tree which is said to be 800 years old, making it South Africa's oldest as well as its largest tree. Its crown has a circumference of 33m/108ft and it takes eight people to encircle its trunk.

★Big Tree

At the east end of the Garden Route (3km/2 miles east of the Big Tree) is the Paul Sauer Bridge. The bridge, 190m/210yd long, spans the Storms River at a height of 130m/425ft (restaurant, picnic spots).

Paul Sauer Bridge

From a viewpoint to the west of the bridge there is a fine prospect of the Tsitsikamma State Forest, on the north side of N 2. This expanse of natural rain forest contains many giant trees rising to heights of 50m/165ft or more, some of them with long trailing "beards" of lichen. Mushrooms, toadstools and mosses flourish in the damp conditions. From the Paul Sauer Bridge there is a 4km/2½ mile long hiking trail to the Big Tree (see above).

Tsitsikamma State Forest

George   F 10

Province: Western Cape
Altitude: 226m/742ft. Population: 100,000
Distances: 45km/28 miles from Mossel Bay, 90km/56 miles from Knysna, 438km/272 miles from Cape Town, 1171km/728 miles from Johannesburg, 1319km/820 miles from Durban

George is picturesquely situated on a coastal plateau at the foot of the Outeniqua Mountains, which reach a height of 1579m/5181ft in George Peak, 8km/5 miles from the coast of the Indian Ocean. One of the principal towns on the Garden Route (see entry), with its own airport, it is good centre for excursions in the surrounding area.

The agricultural area round George is intensively cultivated. One of the main crops is hops.

Situation and characteristics

Golden Gate Highlands National Park

The town

George (originally called Georgetown) was founded in 1811 and named after King George III. Anthony Trollope, visiting South Africa in 1877, declared that George was "the prettiest village on the face of the earth". In recent years this "garden city", its broad streets lined by oak-trees, has grown considerably in size.

The town's main street is York Street (the continuation of N 2 coming from Mossel Bay), which runs into Courtenay Street at a T junction.

★★Outeniqua
Choo-Tjoe

An unforgettable experience is a trip on the Outeniqua Choo-Tjoe, a narrow-gauge steam train running on a spectacular line between George and Knysna (see entry). Particularly impressive is the crossing of the Kaaimans River, which at this point, just before it flows into the Indian Ocean, has cut a deep gorge through the rock. Information about the service can be obtained at George railway station, from which the train departs at 8.15am except at weekends and on public holidays (see Practical Information, Railways).

Sights in George

Museum

The George Museum, in the Old Drostdy Building (1813) at the junction of York Street and Courtenay Street, illustrates the history of the region and the local timber industry, and also displays a collection of musical instruments (open: Mon.–Fri. 9am–4.30pm, Sat. 10am–1pm).

SS Peter and Paul

The Dutch Reformed church of SS Peter and Paul, built in 1842, has a pulpit of stinkwood and pillars and dome of yellowwood.

Van Kervel
Nature Reserve

On Caledon Street is the Van Kervel Nature Reserve (area 9 hectares/ 22 acres), with indigenous trees and plants.

Surroundings of George

Outeniqua Pass

From George N 12 runs north through the Outeniqua Mountains to Oudtshoorn (60km/37 miles: see entry). 15km/9 miles from George it comes to the Outeniqua Pass (799m/2622ft). On the way up to the pass there are fine views of the fertile countryside, but beyond the pass the scene changes as the road enters the arid region of the Little Karoo.

Seven Passes
Road

The Seven Passes Road, the old main road between George and Knysna (see entry), part of which is unsurfaced, runs through a lonely landscape above N 2. The views from this road, however, are no more spectacular than those from the faster coast road (see Garden Route).

Outeniqua
Hiking Trail

The Outeniqua Hiking Trail, a 137km/85 mile long ridge walk through the Outeniqua Mountains, runs from the Witfontein forest station near George to the Diepwalle forest station near Knysna. The walk takes eight days.

Golden Gate Highlands National Park

See Clarens

Graaff-Reinet   H 8

Province: Eastern Cape
Altitude: 663m/2175ft
Population: 32,000
Distances: 105km/65 miles from Middelburg, 672km/418 miles from Cape Town, 837km/520 miles from Johannesburg

Graaff-Reinet lies in a bend on the Sundays River at the foot of Spandau Kop, a peak in the Sneeuberg range. Almost the whole of the town is encircled by the Karoo Nature Reserve. This attractive little town, beautifully situated between the foothills of the Great Escarpment and the wide expanses of the Great Karoo, is aptly named the "Gem of the Karoo".

The town is one of the oldest in the Cape Province, founded by Boer settlers in 1786. It was named after the then Governor of the colony, Cornelis Jacob van de Graaff (1785–91) and his wife Cornelia Reinet. Since in the eyes of the settlers the Cape government did not give them sufficient protection against attacks by the local tribes the inhabitants of Graaff-Reinet drove out the landdrost (government administrator) in 1795 and declared the town to be an independent republic. The Cape government reasserted its authority in the following year, but the town remained a centre of unrest. In the mid 19th century many British and German settlers came to the area, and Graaff-Reinet developed into an important economic and commercial centre. Other major sources of income are the breeding of angora goats and merino sheep, followed in recent times by ostrich farming and tourism.

Graaff-Reinet is one of the most attractive towns in South Africa, with over 250 lovingly restored old buildings in the architectural styles of the last two centuries, from modest flat-roofed cottages to gabled mansions in Cape Dutch style and ornate Victorian villas. The main street is Church Street, running north–south.

Sights in Graaff-Reinet

Reinet House, a former parsonage in Cape Dutch style in Murray Street, is now a museum (open: Mon.–Fri. 9am–noon and 3–5pm, Sat. 9am–noon, Sun. 10am–noon), with a large collection of 18th and 19th century furniture

Reinet House, Graaf-Reinet

and furnishings and farming equipment. In the garden is a grapevine planted in 1870.

Old Residency

Diagonally opposite Reinet House, in Parsonage Street, is the Old Residency, a mansion of 1820 which now houses a collection of hunting rifles (opening times as for Reinet House).

★ Old Library

The Old Library, at the corner of Church and Somerset Streets, is now occupied by the Graaff-Reinet Publicity Association and a museum (opening times as for Reinet House). The exhibits in the museum include 19th century clothing, photographs by William Roe, who travelled in South Africa in the second half of the 19th century, paintings and an interesting collection of fossils from the Karoo, the oldest of them dating back more than 200 million years.

Hester Rupert
Art Museum

The Hester Rupert Art Museum, in a former mission church of 1821 in Church Street, displays works by contemporary South African artists (opening times as for Reinet House).

★ Drostdy

The Drostdy, opposite the Hester Rupert Museum, was originally the residence of the landdrost, built in 1806. It has been well restored and is now a hotel, which also incorporates Stretch's Court, a range of trim little houses built in the 19th century for freed slaves.

Groote Kerk

At the north end of Church Street is the Neo-Gothic Groote Kerk (Dutch Reformed Church), built in 1886 on the model of Salisbury Cathedral. It has a collection of valuable church plate, which can be seen on request.

★ Karoo Nature Reserve

The town is surrounded by the Karoo Nature Reserve (area 16,000 hectares/40,000 acres), established in 1975, which takes in Spandau Kop, Van Ryneveld Dam (formed by the damming of the Sundays River) and the Valley of Desolation.

The semi-desertic landscape of the Great Karoo has steadily expanded over the last hundred years and now occupies a third of the area of South Africa. The main factor in this expansion has been overgrazing by sheep. Beasts of prey have been eliminated and the variety of vegetation reduced. The establishment of the Karoo Nature Reserve was designed to put a stop to this development, at least within a restricted area. Various species have been reintroduced, including mountain zebras, black wildebeests and springboks. Since an encounter with some of the larger mammals may be dangerous, visitors are not allowed to leave their cars in the Game Viewing Area. Walking is permitted in certain parts of the reserve subject to previous notification.

Van Ryneveld
Dam, Game
Viewing Area

The area round Van Ryneveld Dam, to the north of Graaff-Reinet, is a bird sanctuary. The Dam itself has an area of 1000 hectares/2500 acres.

To the north of the Dam is the Game Viewing Area (open only at weekends and holiday periods), which among other species contains Cape buffaloes, elands, kudus and springboks.

★★ Valley of
Desolation

The most striking natural feature round Graaff-Reinet is the deep, narrow gorge known as the Valley of Desolation, to the west of the town (reached from Murraysburg road; entrance signposted; always open). The steep access road, climbing to 1500m/4920ft, ends at a parking area from which there are footpaths to various viewpoints. To the south can be seen the Great Karoo, to the east Graaff-Reinet, to the north the Sneeuberg Mountains.

The Valley of Desolation in the Karoo Nature Reserve; ▶
bizarre rock formations created by erosion over millions of years

Grahamstown

Nieu Bethesda

50km/31 miles north of Graaff-Reinet (31km/19 miles on R 57, then side road running north-west) is the little town of Nieu Bethesda, famed for the Owl House, with a collection of work by the eccentric sculptor Helen Martins, who lived a solitary life here (open: daily 9am–4pm).

Grahamstown   J 9

Province: Eastern Cape
Altitude: 540m/1770ft. Population: 56,000
Distances: 127km/79 miles from Port Elizabeth, 160km/100 miles from East London, 854km/531 miles from Durban, 999km/621 miles from Johannesburg

Situation and characteristics

The university town of Grahamstown lies in a sheltered basin 60km/37 miles from the south coast, half way between Port Elizabeth and East London. It is the chief town of the Settler Country, in which white settlers came into conflict with the Xhosa in the early 19th century.

With Rhodes University and many other educational institutions, Grahamstown has developed in recent years into a major cultural centre. It is also the see of an Anglican bishop, and its many churches (said to number more than 40) have earned it the name of "city of the saints". The Grahamstown Arts Festival, famed throughout South Africa, is held annually at the end of June, when the town becomes one gigantic stage hosting a great variety of cultural events.

History

In the 18th century Dutch settlers began to move east from the Cape in search of new land. On the Great Fish River they came into contact for the first time with the Xhosa, a Bantu people who were moving south, also in the quest for land. After the Cape Colony was taken over by Britain in 1806 there was an influx of British settlers, most of whom established them-

Some of the many Victorian buildings in Grahamstown

selves on the east coast. By 1857 there had been eight bloody wars within less than a century in the border region between the Great Fish River and the Bushman River. To protect the frontier between the white and the black population the British built a chain of military posts and forts, including a military base, established in 1812 and named after Col. John Graham, which was to develop into Grahamstown. The settlement flourished, and by 1831 Grahamstown was the largest town in the Cape Colony after Cape Town.

Grahamstown is a trim and attractive place with many historic old buildings in the town centre. The High Street, running east–west, is its central thoroughfare, with Rhodes University at its west end. From here a brief walk will take visitors round the town centre and up Gunfire Hill.

★The town

Sights in Grahamstown

On an island site in the High Street is the Cathedral of St Michael and St George, originally built in 1824 and altered and enlarged in 1853, after Grahamstown became the see of an Anglican bishop. It has the tallest spire in South Africa (53.6m/176ft).

Cathedral

The City Hall, beyond the Cathedral, was built round the bell-tower of 1870.

City Hall

Opposite the City Hall Bathurst Street runs south from the High Street. At the near end, on the left, is the Observatory Museum, in a house occupied from 1850 until his death in 1886 by Henry Carter Galpin, a watchmaker and goldsmith who was also interested in astronomy. Here in 1882 he constructed a camera obscura, still the only one in South Africa. In clear weather, with the help of a mirror on the roof, this shows an image of the whole town and its immediate surroundings.

★Observatory Museum

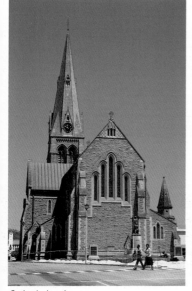

Cathedral and . . .   *. . . University Tower, Grahamstown*

235

Grahamstown

The museum, with a Victorian-style interior, displays old furniture and furnishings and a collection of old telescopes (open: Mon.–Fri. 9.30am–1pm and 2–5pm, Sat. 9am–1pm).

National Literary Museum

To continue the tour of the town, now return to the High Street and follow it south-west (in the direction of the University). In Anglo-African Street, which goes off the High Street on the right, is the National Literary Museum, housed in a building in which the "Eastern Star" was printed – predecessor of the "Star", the Johannesburg daily which now has the biggest circulation in South Africa.

Bannerman House

Farther along the High Street, at the corner of Hemming Street, is Bannerman House, headquarters of the South African Library for the Blind, established in 1918, which supplies books to blind people throughout South Africa.

Rhodes University

At the end of the High Street is Rhodes University, founded in 1904 and named after Cecil Rhodes (see Famous People). The site was formerly occupied by government buildings, which were demolished in 1935 to make way for the new University buildings, except for the old Drostdy Gate, now the entrance to the University campus. The University has some 4000 students.

Albany Museum

Adjoining the entrance to the University, in Somerset Street, is the Albany Museum. The main building, erected in 1899–1902, houses the Natural History Museum (open: Mon.–Fri. 9.30am–1pm and 2–5pm, Sat. and Sun. 2–5pm), which displays material on the history of early man in Africa, one of the three Egyptian mummies in South Africa and geological and ornithological collections. Another section commemorates Dr W. G. Atherstone, who discovered South Africa's first diamond in Grahamstown.

1820 Settlers Museum

Next door is the 1820 Settlers Museum, opened in 1965, with furniture and furnishings, weapons, pictures and historic photographs (opening times as for Albany Museum).

Botanical Gardens

In Lucas Street, which opens off Somerset Street, is the entrance to the Botanical Gardens, established at some time before 1850 and thus among the oldest of their kind in the country. The gardens, which are open all year round, lie on the slopes of Gunfire Hill, extending up to the Settlers Monument. In addition to plants indigenous to the Eastern Cape there are exotic plants and an English-style garden with lavender, forget-me-nots and roses.

Fort Selwyn

Beautiful paths run up through the gardens to Fort Selwyn (built 1835; restored), now a museum (open: by appointment, tel. 0461/22 397). This was one of a chain of forts and signal stations extending to the Great Fish River.

Settlers Monument

A short distance from Fort Selwyn is the Settlers Monument, a modern cultural centre opened in 1974 which includes an art gallery, a number of conference rooms and a theatre. This is the venue of the Arts Festival which has become the major cultural event of the South African year.

A bronze monument at the entrance depicts a settler family in typical early 19th century dress.

Surroundings of Grahamstown

Andries Vosloo Kudu Reserve and Sam Knott Nature Reserve

35km/22 miles north of Grahamstown on R 67 is this 23,000 hectare/ 57,000 acre reserve, with rhinos, hippopotamuses, buffaloes, wild pigs and even a few leopards. Open daily from sunrise to sunset, it can be explored by car.

15km/9 miles south of Grahamstown on R 343 (signposted to Salem) is the Thomas Baines Nature Reserve (area 1000 hectares/2500 acres; open: daily 7am–5pm), home to a variety of game, including rhinoceros and the rare Cape buffalo. The reserve can be explored only by car on a 15km/9 mile long track; walking is prohibited.

Thomas Baines
Nature Reserve

20km/12½ miles south of Grahamstown on R 343 is the little town of Salem, which preserves a number of settlers' houses dating from the first half of the 19th century. Although the name Salem means "peace", the settlement was frequently besieged by the Xhosa in the Frontier Wars. During one of these sieges, in 1834, a settler named Richard Gush, who as a Quaker was opposed to any kind of violence, had taken refuge, along with his wife and children, in the Methodist church. One day he left the village, unarmed, to negotiate with the Xhosa. When he asked what they really wanted they replied that they were hungry. He went back into the village and brought them bread, tobacco, tomatoes and some pocket knives, whereupon the Xhosa called off the siege.

Salem

The former church is now a school.

40km/25 miles south-east of Grahamstown on R 67 is Bathurst (pop. 5200), a little town founded in 1820 in what is now one of the main pineapple-growing areas in South Africa. The fruit was brought to South Africa by Dutch settlers in the mid 19th century, and pineapples were first planted in Natal in 1860. When a farmer from Bathurst saw the fruit at his barber's in Grahamstown he took some plants home and discovered to his surprise that they flourished on his land. South Africa now takes the eighth place among the world's pineapple-growing countries.

Bathurst

The main features of interest in Bathurst are St John's Church (1832), the oldest surviving Anglican church in South Africa, and the Pig and Whistle pub (1831) in Kowie Road, still a popular rendezvous.

On the road from Grahamstown to Port Alfred, near Bathurst, is Summerhill pineapple farm, with a reconstructed Xhosa village (exhibition and sale of Xhosa crafts).

Summerhill Farm

58km/36 miles south of Grahamstown, at the mouth of the Kowie River, is Port Alfred (pop. 25,000), founded in 1820 and later named after Queen Victoria's second son. It is now a popular holiday resort, with magnificent beaches round the town, facilities for all kinds of water sports and a beautifully situated 18-hole golf course.

★Port Alfred

Kowie Nature Reserve (open: daily 7am–5pm) lies 5km/3 miles north of Port Alfred (access from the Bathurst road). A hiking trail (a 2-hour walk) runs through the reserve.

Kowie Nature
Reserve, Bathurst
Conservation Area

Adjoining the reserve is the Bathurst Conservation Area, through which runs a "canoe route", starting from Port Alfred and running 20km/12½ miles up the Kowie River (canoes can be hired).

A steam train, the Settlers' Express, runs between Bathurst and Port Alfred, through beautiful scenery with extensive pineapple plantations.

Settlers' Express

Griquatown

G 6

Province: Northern Cape
Altitude: 1476m/4843ft. Population: 5000
Distances: 70km/43 miles from Postmasburg, 123km/76 miles from
Prieska, 160km/100 miles from Kimberley

Griquatown, situated between Kimberley and Upington in the Northern Cape Province, was once capital of an independent state with its own coinage and flag.

Situation and
characteristics

Harrismith

History
The Griqua were a Hottentot tribe who, under the leadership of Adam Kok (Adam the Cook), a freed slave, migrated from the south-western Cape to the area north of the middle Orange River. Here in 1801 the London Missionary Society established a mission station which developed into the chief town of the self-governing territory of Griqualand. Among the missionaries who worked in the mission station was Robert Moffat (1795–1883), whose daughter Mary (b. 1821) married the African missionary and explorer David Livingstone (1813–73).

After diamonds were found in this area (see Barkly West) Griqualand became a British colony in 1871 and three years later was incorporated in the Cape Colony. At this time the Griqua had split, and in 1862 one group had moved south through the Drakensberg and founded Kokstad and Griqualand East.

Sights
The house once occupied by Robert Moffat and his family is now the Mary Moffat Museum, with personal mementoes of the Moffat family and displays on the history of the London Missionary Society, in particular on the work of Robert Moffat.

Other features of interest are the Raadsaal, seat of Griqualand administration, the Execution Tree on which cattle thieves were hanged and the grave of Andries Waterboer, one of the leaders of the Griqua.

Surroundings of Griquatown

Pannetjie
At Pannetjie, 5km/3 miles from Griquatown, are Bushman rock paintings.

Postmasburg
75km/47 miles north of Griquatown is Postmasburg (pop. 16,000), originally a mission station. Soon after the end of the First World War the discovery of diamonds gave a great boost to the development of the town, and in 1926 considerable deposits of manganese were found in the area. Archaeological discoveries a few miles north-east of the town have shown that there was mining activity here around A.D. 700.

The Postmasburg diamond mine, like the Big Hole at Kimberley, is now filled with water. Fishing is permitted in this 45m/150ft deep artificial lake.

★Roaring Sands
At Witsand, 20km/12½ miles south-west of Postmasburg, an unusual natural phenomenon can be observed. In the dry heat prevalent here the huge travelling dunes (up to 100m/330ft high) in the area produce a strange moaning sound which in periods of extreme heat can increase in volume until it sounds like the howling of a storm. The light-coloured dunes are in marked contrast to the usual reddish sand of the Kalahari.

Prieska
From Griquatown R 386 runs 120km/75 miles south-west to Prieska (pop. 13,000), situated on the banks of the Orange River. The town, founded in 1878, is an agricultural and mining centre with copper mines and rich deposits of tiger's eyes (a semi-precious stone).

From an old fort situated on a hill there are superb views of the Doringberg range and the Orange valley. Other features of interest are the Ria Huisamen Aloe Garden (aloes and succulents) in the centre of the town and Die Bos Nature Reserve (2km/1¼ miles outside the town), populated by large numbers of meerkats and birds.

Harrismith   L 6

Province: Orange Free State
Altitude: 1615m/5299ft. Population: 5000
Distances: 90km/56 miles from Bethlehem, 282km/175 miles from Johannesburg, 306km/190 miles from Durban, 328km/204 miles from Bloemfontein, 1331km/827 miles from Cape Town

Harrismith is an agricultural centre and an important traffic hub, situated at the junction of N 3 (Johannesburg–Durban) with N 5, which runs from Harrismith to Bloemfontein. Harrismith has no particular tourist attractions apart from its Wild Flower Garden, but it is a good centre for excursions to the northern Natal Drakensberg (see Drakensberg) and the Golden Gate Highlands National Park (see Clarens).

Situation and characteristics

Harrismith was originally founded in 1849 near Vrededorp, but subsequently moved steadily nearer the Wilge River, thus solving the problem of water supply. The town was named after Sir Harry Smith, Governor of the Cape Colony from 1848 to 1852. During the 19th century gold and diamond rush Harrismith became a post town and thereafter developed even more rapidly.

History

An important sporting event is the Harrismith Mountain Race, held annually on October 10th, whose origins go back to the Boer War. Near Harrismith is a hill, the Platberg (2377m/7799ft), of which a British officer, Major Belcher, spoke disparagingly, referring to it as "our little hill". Thereupon a citizen of the town, annoyed, bet Belcher that he could not reach the top in an hour. Belcher won the bet and established a prize for all future winners of the race.

Mountain Race

Sights in Harrismith

In a park in the town centre is the Town Hall, a sandstone building erected in 1907. Near it lies a petrified tree, 27m/90ft long, which is believed to be 150 million years old.

Town Hall

5km/3 miles south of the town (signposted from town centre; open: daily 8am–6pm) is the Drakensberg Botanic Garden (area 114 hectares/282

★Drakensberg Botanic Garden

Botanic Garden, Harrismith

The Sirens' Song

On the South African coast, specifically in Walker Bay between Hermanus and Gansbaai, you are sometimes reminded of Odysseus. Odysseus knew what would happen if he allowed himself to be bewitched by the singing of the Sirens. He stopped his companions' ears with wax and had himself tied to the mast when their ship was sailing past the island of the Sirens. Only in this way could they escape destruction; for with their sweet singing the Sirens sought to attract seamen to their island, where they would be killed and eaten.

This episode from Homer's "Odyssey" probably had some foundation in fact, for it was well known to whalers and seafarers in earlier times where the singing came from – from whales. Naturally, too, they told all sorts of tales about their experiences. Scholars wrote these accounts off as seamen's yarns, particularly since it was known that whales had no vocal chords. It was only in the fifties of the 20th century that biologists discovered by chance, during soundings carried out for military purposes off Bermuda and Hawaii, that whales were by no means dumb but could make sounds, and indeed could "sing".

The finest singer among the whales is the humpback whale (*Megaptera novae angliae*), a massive whale with a barrel-shaped body which can reach a length of 19m/62ft and weigh up to 48 tons. Characteristic features are the long flippers (hence the name Megaptera, "long-winged"), which can be a third of the length of the whale's body. Humpback whales live in all the oceans, reaching as far north and south as the edge of the pack ice; formerly they were also found in the Mediterranean. They form small family groups of three to twelve and travel on long seasonal migrations. In summer they live in the polar regions, where at that time there are huge populations of the tiny organisms known as krill on which they feed. In winter they move to tropical and subtropical regions, where their young are born. Since for this purpose they prefer sheltered, warm and shallow water, their "nursery" areas are near the coast; and accordingly every year the humpback whales make the long journey from the Antarctic to the east coast of South Africa.

Why the humpback whale sings is not known; but certainly it produces the longest and most complex sequences of sounds of all whales; possibly, indeed, of all animals. It can properly be called singing, since it consists of a particular sequence of different tones, ranging from a moaning sound to grunting, roaring, sighing and high-pitched squeaking and chirping, which can last for ten minutes or more, after which the whole sequence is exactly repeated – a process of repetition which can last for several hours. All the whales in a particular area of the sea sing the same "songs" at the same time. Changes are made only very slowly. The songs do, however, differ from place to place: the humpback whales of Hawaii have different songs from their counterparts in South African waters. It seems that only male whales sing – perhaps as a warning, a declaration of dominance in a particular territory or a mating call. The singing of the humpback whales is most frequently heard in the warmer regions of the sea, where mating and calving take place; in their feeding grounds in colder seas they appear to sing only fragmentary songs. The humpback whale is popularly known as the "clown of the seas", and Herman Melville describes him in "Moby Dick" as the most playful of the larger whales. Certainly he flings himself into the air, almost clear of the water, more frequently than other whales. These acrobatic feats are most commonly performed in the whales' feeding grounds. When a whale "belly-flops" into the water after a leap of this kind the sound can be heard under water over a wide area: it may, therefore, serve as a form of communication. Another skill possessed by the humpback whales is the use of a net to catch their food: they can create a spiral "net" of air bubbles into which they drive the plankton on which they feed and then swallow them in one large gulp: a fantastic sight when, during this operation, several whales raise their heads out of the water at almost the same time.

But the humpbacks are not the only whales to be seen off the South African coast, particularly in Walker Bay and False Bay and off De Hoop. Every year between May and the end of November numbers of southern right whales (*Eubalaena australis*) come here to mate and produce their young. This is the time when the "whale crier" in Hermanus walks the streets giving information about where the whales can be seen.

The right whale is a massive creature up to 17m/56ft long which at birth is pale and almost colourless and grows steadily darker with age. It has no dorsal fin, and tends to have horny growths infested with parasites on its snout. It was given its name by the old whalers, who regarded it as the "right" whale to hunt for its whalebone and its oil. As a result the southern right whale was decimated and is now rare.

Another species sometimes to be seen in Walker Bay is Bryde's whale (*Balaenoptera edeni*), which reaches a length of 14m/70ft and a weight of 20 tons. It also appears off the west coast of South Africa, though it can be observed only from special viewing points in Walker Bay.

The pygmy right whale (*Caperea marginata*), up to 6m/20ft long, a species confined to the southern hemisphere, is also found off the coasts of South Africa.

The whales so far mentioned all belong to the sub-order Mysticeti (baleen whales), which have whalebone in place of teeth. The other sub-order of whales, Odontoceti (toothed whales), is also represented in South African waters by Layard's whale, the Chinese white dolphin, True's beaked whale, the dark dolphin, Heaviside's dolphin, the common dolphin and the bottle-nosed dolphin.

Not surprisingly, therefore, in the past many South Africans lived by whaling, and between Durban on the east coast and Saldanha on the south-west coast there were numbers of whaling stations. Since 1976, however, South Africa has been concerned to protect whales. Round the coasts there are viewing stations from which visitors can observe these beautiful and still mysterious creatures and listen, like Odysseus, to the song of the Sirens.

acres), with plants from the three different zones in the Drakensberg: the highland zone (1200–1800m/3900–5900ft), the sub-alpine zone (1800–2800m/5900–9200ft) and the alpine zone (2800–3300m/9200–10,800ft). Only part of the area (round the two reservoirs created by British troops during the Boer War) is regularly cared for; the rest of the gardens, through which a hiking trail winds its way, passing impressive rock formations, is left in its natural state.

Surroundings of Harrismith

Sterkfontein Dam

25km/15 miles south of Harrismith is the Sterkfontein Dam, a favourite haunt of water sports enthusiasts and anglers (trout). The road from Harrismith into the northern Natal Drakensberg (see Drakensberg) runs past this reservoir.

Mount Everest
Game Reserve

In a hilly region 20km/12½ miles north-east of Harrismith is the privately owned Mount Everest Game Reserve (area 1000 hectares/2500 acres), home to more than 22 species of game. Visitors are taken round the reserve in open cross-country vehicles. There is accommodation for visitors in holiday houses and huts.

Hermanus   D 10

Province: Western Cape. Altitude: 233m/764ft. Population: 13,000
Distances: 85km/53 miles from Caledon, 108km/67 miles from Bredasdorp, 120km/75 miles from Cape Town

Situation and
characteristics

Hermanus is a popular holiday resort on the Atlantic, 120km/75 miles east of Cape Town. During the main season (December and January) the population of the town is doubled by an influx of holidaymakers and it is practically impossible to find a room free. Hermanus's great attractions are the beautiful sandy beaches to the east of the town and the facilities for all kinds of water sports. The coastal waters, in which some record catches have been made, attract numbers of anglers, and the fishing industry ranks along with tourism as a major source of income.

History

The town takes its name from an itinerant Dutch teacher named Hermanus Pieters who, with his flock of sheep, encamped at a nearby spring in 1830. The original name of the place, Hermanuspietersfontein, was, fortunately, shortened when it gained the status of a town in 1904.

The beginnings of tourism in Hermanus date back to the 19th century: the town's first hotel was opened in 1891, and holiday homes began to be built round the harbour in the early years of the 20th century.

The town

Hermanus consists of a seemingly endless succession of holiday and weekend houses. The heart of the town, however, round the harbour, is quite small. In this area there are a number of restored fishermen's houses, now occupied by restaurants, bars and shops.

Cliff Path

A good general impression of Hermanus can be had from the 10km/6 mile long Cliff Path which runs from the New Harbour to Grotto Beach. Between June and November there are good prospects of seeing whales close inshore.

Sights in Hermanus

Old Harbour
Museum

The Old Harbour Museum (open: Mon.–Sat. 9am–1pm and 2–5pm) has a large collection of material on the history of fishing and whaling in Hermanus, as well as a number of old fishing boats (restored) in use between 1855 and 1961.

The museum also has a collection of photographs, housed in the Old Schoolhouse in Market Square.

On the north-eastern outskirts of Hermanus, centred on the Mossel River, is Fernkloof Nature Reserve (area 1446 hectares/3572 acres), which also takes in the Platberg, a hill to the north. Ranging in height between 63m/207ft and 842m/2763ft, the reserve presents an interesting cross-section of the different types of fynbos vegetation and protea species. There are over 40 different Erica species, offering a succession of flower throughout the year. Over 100 species of birds have been recorded here, including a pair of crowned eagles which bred in the reserve. The visitor centre, 500m/550yd from the entrance to the reserve, is the starting-point of a 40km/25 mile long hiking trail running through the whole of the reserve (picnic areas).

★Fernkloof
Nature Reserve

Hibiscus Coast

See Port Shepstone

Hluhluwe and Umfolozi Game Reserves   M/N 5/6

Province: KwaZulu/Natal
Altitude: 60–600m (200–2000ft)
Distances: 80km/50 miles from Richard's Bay, 280km/174 miles from
  Durban

The Hluhluwe (pronounced Shlu-shlu-we) and Umfolozi Game Reserves in north-eastern KwaZulu/Natal, separated only by a corridor 8km/5 miles wide, are among the oldest game reserves in Africa, the Hluhluwe reserve having been established in 1897. With a total area of 1000sq.km/385sq. miles (including the corridor, which is also a game reserve), this is the third largest game reserve in South Africa.

Situation and
characteristics

The white settlers in the area were at first hostile to the establishment of the reserve, since they considered the game (as host animals of the tsetse fly) responsible for a plague which decimated their herds of cattle. They responded by killing large numbers of game animals – an estimated 100,000 between 1930 and 1950 alone. Since the elimination of the tsetse fly by the use of insecticides from 1945 onwards the animals have largely been left unharmed.

Both reserves can be visited throughout the year. In summer it is very hot, with day temperatures not uncommonly rising above 35°C/95°F, accompanied by high air humidity and frequently also by thunder showers (after heavy rain some of the tracks become impassable). Temperatures are more agreeable in winter. The months May to October, when the vegetation is less dense, are the best times for observing the game.

When to visit

The reserves are in a malaria-risk area.

The fauna in both reserves is almost identical. There are 50 species of mammals, including buffaloes, blue wildebeests, zebras, giraffes, elephants, dwarf antelopes, klipspringers, reedbucks, bush pigs, lions, leopards, cheetahs, spotted hyenas, black-backed jackals, baboons and crocodiles. There are large numbers of rhinoceroses: white rhinos are more commonly seen than black rhinos, which almost always live in impenetrable thickets. There are 400 species of birds.

Fauna

Four rhinos were shot in Umfolozi Game Reserve in December 1994 by poachers seeking rhinoceros horn, one of whom paid for it with his life. Powdered rhinoceros horn is much prized, particularly in the Far East, as a means of increasing male potency. A single horn will fetch as much as £20,000, of which the poachers will get between £1000 and £2500.

The Hluhluwe and Umfolozi Game Reserves are famed for their large numbers of elephants. The white rhino, shown here, is only slightly lighter in colour than the black rhino

In the Umfolozi reserve there are two well equipped hutted camps, the Masinda camp and the Mpila camp. In the Hluhluwe reserve there is the new Hilltop hutted camp (220 beds), with accommodation ranging from modest huts to the luxurious Mtwazi Lodge. There are also privately run camps outside the reserves. Within a few miles of the village of Hluhluwe are the Bonamanzi Game Park camp and Bushlands Game Lodge, where the accommodation includes comfortable "tree houses".

Accommodation

★Hluhluwe Game Reserve

At Hluhluwe an asphalted road branches off N 2 and comes in 15km/9 miles to the main entrance of Hluhluwe Game Reserve. It can also be reached from R 618 on a track which goes off on the right 17km/11 miles beyond Mtubatuba.

Getting there

With an area of only 230sq.km/89sq. miles, the Hluhluwe reserve is less than half the size of the Umfolozi reserve. The landscape, too, is different: it is hilly country which, particularly to the north and along the rivers, is densely wooded, with a distinctly tropical feel.

Topography

The reserve can be explored by car on a 40km/25 mile network of tracks.

Auto Trail

★Umfolozi Game Reserve

R 618 leads to the main entrance to the reserve. Alternatively there is a road from Ulundi to the Cengeni Gate on the west side of the reserve.

Getting there

◄ *Dense forests line the rivers in the Hluhluwe Game Reserve*

Topography

The Umfolozi Game Reserve consists mainly of savanna country, with some areas of dense bush. There are taller trees along the banks of the Mfolozi Emnyana (Black) and Mfolozi Emhlope (White) Rivers, which join within the reserve.

Only about half the reserve can be explored by car. An area of 240sq.km/93sq. miles can be seen only on guided walks. (These walks on Wilderness Trails, led by experienced game wardens, take between 3 and 5 days, with overnight accommodation in tents in the bush; they are usually fully booked months in advance.)

Umfolozi Mosaic
Auto Trail

A tour of the northern part of the reserve on this trail (67km/42 miles) takes 4–5 hours. A leaflet showing the route and the game-watching points can be obtained at the entrance to the reserve.

Johannesburg
K 4

Province: Gauteng
Altitude: 1752m/5748ft. Population: 1,600,000
Distances: 398km/247 miles from Bloemfontein, 472km/293 miles from Kimberley, 588km/365 miles from Durban, 1075km/668 miles from Port Elizabeth, 1402km/871 miles from Cape Town

Situation and
characteristics

Johannesburg (Jo'burg to the white population, E'Goli, the "city of gold", to the blacks), the third largest city in Africa, after Cairo and Alexandria, and the world's youngest city to pass the million mark, lies on the highveld, South Africa's central plateau, on the edge of the Witwatersrand, an 80km/50 mile long range of hills, rich in minerals, which rises only 300m/1000ft above the surrounding country. Johannesburg is steadily expanding to join up with Pretoria to the north and the industrial towns of Vanderbijlpark and Vereeniging to the south, together forming the

From the Carlton Centre there are breathtaking views over Johannesburg

province of Gauteng (until 1994 Pretoria–Witwatersrand–Vereeniging, or PWV for short). The province, with only 2% of South Africa's total area, contains 25% of its population.

It is difficult to establish the exact population of Johannesburg. The white population has remained fairly constant for some years at around 500,000; estimates of the black population range widely between 1 and 2 million (excluding the black ghetto of Soweto, which was separated from Johannesburg in 1983 and has a population of at least 2 million).

Although many gold-mines in and around the city have been closed down, Johannesburg is still the financial and industrial metropolis of South Africa. Most of the country's leading industrial firms have their headquarters here, and 70% of South Africa's industrial production comes from the Witwatersrand area. The city's Stock Exchange is one of the busiest in the world.

Johannesburg has three universities – the (English-language) University of the Witwatersrand, founded in 1922, the Rand Afrikaans University, founded in 1966, and the Vista University in Soweto, whose students are exclusively black – as well as a college of technology and a teachers' training college. In recent years there has been a great flowering of art and culture in Johannesburg, and the city's international cultural scene has sent fresh impulses throughout the country.

For many visitors to South Africa Johannesburg is their first port of call, and many of them stay no more than a day or two before escaping from the city with its grave social problems. Certainly Johannesburg is not a beautiful town, and its architecture has only limited appeal. It has a high crime rate. But it is the South African city with the most stimulating atmosphere. While elsewhere in South Africa white and black people lived separate lives (and still do), in Johannesburg a gradual process of getting together had begun. Here you will meet more blacks of higher social status than elsewhere; here beats the heart of the new South Africa. Against this background it is well worth spending several days in South Africa's largest city. Visitors should, however, bear in mind the high crime rate. It is inadvisable to walk about after dark, when Johannesburg becomes a ghost town. The best way of seeing the sights is by taxi or on an organised tour. And of course it is advisable to dress simply and avoid flaunting an expensive camera. But there is no need to panic: the newspapers may report unpleasant incidents but they have little to say about the 3 million people who survive the day in Johannesburg unscathed.

The Jan Smuts International Airport – the largest in southern Africa – is 25km/15 miles east of the city centre. There are regular half-hourly bus services (5am–10pm) between the airport and the air terminal in the city centre. | **Transport**

Johannesburg has excellent road and rail connections with other South African cities.

Thanks to its altitude, Johannesburg has a very agreeable climate. The winters are relatively cool and dry, with sunny days following ice-cold nights. In summer the temperatures are high, with occasional showers of rain in the afternoon. Average temperatures are 20.3°C/68.5°F in January and 10.2°C/50.4°F in July. Average annual rainfall is 847mm/33⅓in. The number of hours of sunshine per day averages 8.7. | **Climate**

In July 1886 an Australian prospector, George Harrison, discovered by chance the world's largest natural treasure chamber, the Witwatersrand gold-mines. The news of his discovery spread like wildfire, and thousands of hopeful treasure-seekers flocked to the area and pitched their tents round the find-spot. After the richness of the deposits of gold was established the miners dug ever deeper into the earth, steadily improving their mining techniques. | **History**

Although the prospectors' camps continued for years to have a temporary aspect, the settlement's first public buildings were erected in 1888.

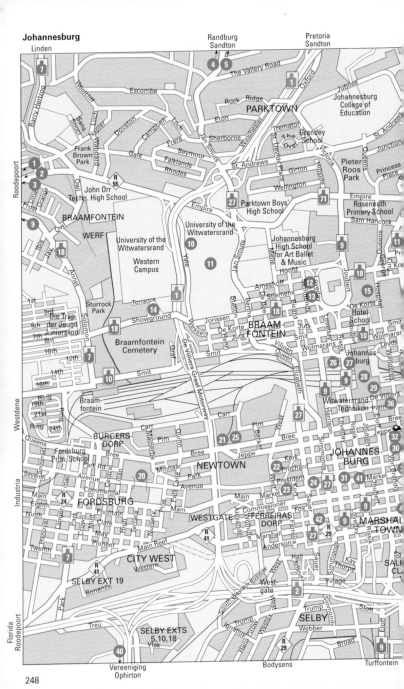

Johannesburg

Johannesburg

1 Botanic Garden
2 Melville
3 Braamfontein Spruit Trail
4 Bernberg Museum
  of Costume
5 Herman Eckstein Park
6 The Wilds/Melrose
  Bird Sanctuary
7 Rockey Street
8 Bezuidenhout Park
9 Rand Afrikaans University
10 Planetarium
11 University of the
  Witwatersrand
12 Civic Theatre
13 Civic Centre
14 Bensusan Museum of
  Photography
15 Adler Museum
16 Johannesburg Art Gallery
17 Joubert Park
18 Strijdom Tower
19 Windybrow Theatre
20 Oriental Plaza
21 Market Theatre Complex
22 Stock Exchange
23 Kwazuli Muti Shop
24 Public Library
25 Museum Africa
26 Air Terminal
27 Bus Terminal
28 Railway Station
29 South African
  Railway Museum
30 Supreme Law Courts
31 City Hall
32 Main Post Office
33 Johannesburg Publicity
  Association
34 Satour
35 Carlton Centre
36 St Mary's Cathedral
37 Diamond Cutting Works
38 Ellispark
39 Rhodes Park
40 Gold Reef City
41 Rissik Street
  Post Office
42 Chamber of Mines
43 Jewish Museum
44 Pioneers' Park

500 m
© Baedeker

Johannesburg acquired a school, a hospital, a theatre and a music hall. In 1888 the famous Wanderers' Club, a sports and entertainment centre for the miners, was opened, and towards the end of the century it had 1500 members, who could practise six different forms of sport. The Turfontein racecourse was opened in 1887.

By the end of the century the owners of the gold-mines – the "randlords", men like Barney Barnato, the Beit brothers, Cecil Rhodes and the Wernher family – had built up their financial empires.

The population of Johannesburg increased at a fantastic rate. Barely six years after the discovery of gold the town had 40,000 white inhabitants, and by 1905 the figure had risen to 150,000. The black population rose from around 60,000 in 1904 to 112,000 in 1911 (plus another 300,000 or so living outside the town). Most of the blacks were employed only as seasonal workers, returning periodically to the agricultural areas from which they came.

Turn-of-the-century Johannesburg still lacked an infrastructure adequate to its population. This was largely due to Paul Kruger, President of the Transvaal, who did not like the idea of an English-speaking town so close to Pretoria. He refused to grant Johannesburg the status of a town, in spite of the fact that within less than twenty years it had overtaken Pretoria both in population and in economic importance. The development of municipal services in Johannesburg began only after the Boer War (during which, on May 31st 1900, it was occupied by British forces). In 1904 it gained the right to elect its own town council, and in the following year it acquired a proper water and drainage system.

In the course of the 20th century the gold workings went ever deeper (down to 3581m/11,750ft at Carletonville). Some uneconomic mines were closed down; but in the early 1990s there were still over 50 gold-mining companies, most of them with several small mines. In addition to gold the mines yield manganese, iron and asbestos, as well as uranium, a by-product of the gold-mining process.

The city

Johannesburg is a city of glaring disparities: here, more sharply than in other cities in the world, inconceivable wealth contrasts with extreme poverty. While over the last hundred years the black population has been relegated to the townships spreading ever farther to the south of Johannesburg, much of the white population lives very comfortably in the northern suburbs of the city. In these districts, concealed behind high walls protected by barbed wire, are attractive villas with beautiful gardens, swimming pools and other amenities, and their shops can stand comparison with boutiques in Rome, Paris or London.

The city centre, laid out on a regular plan, is relatively small, but its high-rise blocks give it a skyline reminiscent of American cities. On weekdays after business hours and at weekends the central area appears to be populated almost entirely by blacks.

Braamfontein Spruit Trail

If you are spending some time in Johannesburg it would be worth while following the Braamfontein Spruit Trail, a walking tour which takes visitors round the main features of interest in the central area and the Randburg and Sandton districts. Information on the exact route can be obtained from the Johannesburg Tourism Association.

Tours of gold-mines and diamond-cutting works

The Chamber of Mines organises conducted tours of gold-mines Tues.– Thur. They usually take a full day and are relatively strenuous (booking essential tel. 4 98 71 00).

Visits to diamond-cutting works, during which the processes of diamond mining, cutting and polishing are explained and demonstrated, are arranged by the Johannesburg Tourism Association, Rotunda, Leyd Street, Braamfontein, tel. 3 37 66 50).

The Cullinan Mine, where the world's largest diamond was found, can also be visited (see Pretoria, Surroundings).

Sights in City Centre

A good starting-point for a tour of the city is the Carlton Centre in Commissioner Street, one of Johannesburg's tallest buildings. On the lower floors are a shopping centre and parking decks; the rest of the building is occupied by offices. From the 50th floor, at a height of 202m/663ft (open: daily 9am–11.30pm), there are fantastic views of Johannesburg and the surrounding area. Adjoining the Carlton Centre is the luxury Carlton Hotel.

★Carlton Centre

A little way south-west of the Carlton Centre, at 29 Kruis Street, is the Jewish Museum (open: Mon.–Thur. 9am–1pm and 2–5pm), with sacred objects and documents illustrating the history of Jews in South Africa from 1920 to the present day.

Jewish Museum

In Rissik Street, at the intersection with Market Street, are two of Johannesburg's few (relatively) old buildings. The Rissik Street Post Office is a brick building of 1897, with an additional storey and tower added in 1902. The Neo-Renaissance City Hall (1910–15) now houses only a few municipal offices (most of the city's administration is now in the Civic Centre).

★Rissik Street Post Office, City Hall

Barclays Bank (90 Market Street) has a small museum on the history of banking (open: Mon.–Fri. 9am–4pm).

National Bank Museum

Along Market Street to the west, at the corner of Simmonds Street, is the Public Library, built in 1935, which in addition to its lending department has a valuable collection of old books.

Public Library

In the same building is the Africana and Geological Museum (open: Mon.–Sat. 9am–5.30pm, Sun. 2–5.30pm). The Africana Museum illustrates the history of the city and the occupation of South Africa by Europeans. The geological section on the first floor has a unique collection of minerals and a quantity of prehistoric material.

Africana and Geological Museum

The Johannesburg Stock Exchange occupies a high-rise building of notable quality in Diagonal Street (the only street in the city centre to cut across the regular grid), which branches off Market Street. There are conducted tours Mon.–Fri. at 11am (booking essential tel. 833 65 80), which include an audio-visual show on the South African economy.

Stock Exchange

Another striking building in Diagonal Street is the Diamond Building, with a façade reminiscent of the facets of a diamond. It was designed by the well-known German-born architect Helmut Jahn (b. 1940), who now lives in Chicago.

Diamond Building

The Kwazuli Muti Shop at 14 Diagonal Street sells herbal medicines and salves used by Zulu medicine-men. Some of the medicines are very curious indeed, made from bones, animal skins and a variety of unidentifiable items. (Open: Mon.–Sat. 7.30am–5pm.)

Kwazuli Muti Shop

The Market Theatre complex in Bree Street, housed in a converted market building, plays a major part in Johannesburg's cultural life. It has four live theatre venues on which some of the finest productions in South Africa are presented. The musical "Sarafina", which later became a Broadway success, had its first performance here. The complex also includes a bookshop, an art and photographic gallery and restaurants. Kippie's Bar is a popular rendezvous, with music by well-known jazz groups in the evenings.

★Market Theatre

In the huge car park opposite the Market Theatre complex a large flea market is held every Saturday.

Adjoining the Market Theatre complex is Museum Africa, installed here in August 1994 (open: Tues.–Sun. 9am–5pm). It has an excellent ethnological department, with reproductions of the huts, tools, domestic equipment,

★★Museum Africa

Johannesburg Art Gallery and . . .   *. . . one of the exhibits*

arts and crafts, dress and toys of the various South African peoples and tribes. The collection of rock art gives a good impression of the intensity and artistic quality of Bushman drawings and paintings (see Baedeker Special. p. 92). Younger visitors will enjoy the nearby Children's Museum, with a dinosaur exhibition and art collections presented in a way that children can appreciate.

On the north edge of the city centre is the Railway Station, the largest in Africa, handling half a million passengers every day.
    In the older part of the station is the South African Transport Museum (open: Mon.–Fri. 7.30am–4pm), with a wide range of exhibits, including old steam engines and model railway layouts.

Railway Station, South African Transport Museum

To the east of the station is Joubert Park, the oldest park in Johannesburg, originally laid out in 1887. It is the only open space of any size in the city centre, with a flower clock, a giant chessboard, a tropical house and a restaurant.

Joubert Park

In Joubert Park is the Johannesburg Art Gallery (open: Tues.–Sun. 10am–5pm), with a collection of works by South African and European artists. One room contains over 2000 prints of the 15th to 20th centuries. Works of sculpture are displayed in the courtyard of the gallery and in Joubert Park. There is a restaurant and a museum shop.

Johannesburg Art Gallery

De Villiers Street leads to Hoek Mall, in which is St Mary's Cathedral (Anglican), an imposing building designed by Sir Herbert Baker (1926).

St Mary's Cathedral

To the south of the Main Post Office, in Pritchard Street, are the Supreme Law Courts. Sittings of the Supreme Court are open to the public.

Supreme Law Courts

◀ *The headquarters of De Beers Consolidated Mines,
   the world's largest diamond producer and dealer*

Johannesburg

Chris Lessing
Boxing Museum

In Kerk Street, near the intersection of Jeppe and Harrison Streets, is the Chris Lessing Boxing Museum (open: Mon.–Fri. 8am–1pm and 2–4.30pm), with cups, boxing gloves, photographs and other mementoes of the "greats" of the ring.

Sights outside the City Centre

Oriental Plaza

On the west side of the city centre, between Bree Street and Main Street, is the Oriental Plaza, a huge shopping centre with more than 300 shops and two excellent Indian restaurants. In this exotic eastern bazaar bargaining over the price is normal.

Bensusan
Museum of
Photography

The Museum of Photography (Raikes Road, in the Braamfontein district; open: Mon.–Sat. 9am–1pm and 2–5pm, Sun. 2–5.30pm) documents the history of photography with a collection of photographs, cameras and other equipment.

Planetarium

The Planetarium, on the campus of Witwatersrand University (Braamfontein district), has presentations in English on Friday at 8pm, Saturday at 3pm and Sunday at 4pm. Up to 9000 stars can be projected on to the 22m/72ft high dome.

Jan Smuts's Study

In one of the university buildings is the room in which Jan Smuts (1870–1950) worked (open: daily 8am–noon and 1–5pm). The furniture came from Smuts's last home in Irene (near Pretoria). Smuts, soldier and statesman, withdrew from public life after the defeat of his United Party in the 1948 election.

Standard Bank
Foundation
Collection

Also on the University campus is the Standard Bank Foundation Collection of African tribal art (masks, headdresses, beadwork, Ndebele fertility dolls, etc.).

Bernberg Museum
of Costume

To the north along Jan Smuts Avenue, which runs past the University campus, is the Bernberg Museum of Costume (corner of Duncombe Road; open: Mon.–Sat. 9am–4.30pm, Sun. 2–4.30pm), with a lovingly assembled collection of clothing and accessories of the 17th to 20th centuries.

★Herman Eckstein
Park,
Johannesburg Zoo

To the north, straddling Jan Smuts Avenue, is the Herman Eckstein Park, part of which is occupied by Johannesburg Zoo (open: daily 8.30am–5.30pm), with more than 300 species of animals (including elephants, lions and many species of monkeys). Some of the animals live in open enclosures separated only by water-filled ditches. Within the Zoo is a lake on which boats can be hired.

In the eastern part of the park is the Museum of Rock Art, an open-air museum with reproductions of prehistoric rock paintings (open: daily 8.30am–5.30pm).

Also in the park is the South African Museum of Military History (open: daily 9am–4.30pm), with a variety of material on the Boer War and the two world wars.

Botanic Garden

To the west of the Herman Eckstein Park, in the Emmarentia district, is the Botanic Garden (open: daily from sunrise to sunset). In summer there is a display of blossom by over 4000 roses. Exotic plants are grown in a hothouse. On the Emmarentia Dam, a small reservoir in the gardens, there are facilities for wind-surfing and sailing.

Civic Centre

To the east of the University campus, between Loveday and Joubert Streets, is the Civic Centre (1978), headquarters of the municipal administration.

Civic Theatre

The Civic Theatre, to the west of the Civic Centre, is one of the city's leading venues for ballet, opera and drama (conducted tours on Tues. and Thur. at 11am and 2pm; tel. 403 34 08 ext 264).

Still farther east, within the South African Institute for Medical Research, is the Adler Museum of the History of Medicine, installed here in 1967 (open: Mon.–Fri. 10am–4pm). As well as the large collection of medical and dental instruments displayed in the main building the museum includes a chemist's shop which originally stood in Beit Street and a medicine-man's herb shop.

Hillbrow is the district of Johannesburg with the highest population density. Particularly in recent years many blacks have moved into Hillbrow and the neighbouring Berea district. Here, in contrast to other parts of the city, black and white people live quite happily side by side, giving the area a lively and multicultural atmosphere. Many shops stay open until late at night, and there is a wide choice of restaurants and bars. (It is not advisable to walk about here after dark.)

Hillbrow

This part of the city is dominated by the 268m/880ft high J. G. Strijdom Tower, headquarters of the South African Post Office. This high-rise block – not an entirely satisfactory example of contemporary architecture – was completed in 1971.

The Windybrow Theatre occupies a building of 1896 in the Hillbrow district (Catherine Street), a typical example of South African architecture of the gold rush period. The theatre has three houses.

Windybrow Theatre

To the north of the Hillbrow district, on Houghton Drive, is this 17 hectare/42 acre park, in which grow many species of protea and wild flowers from Namaqualand (at their best between September and December). There is also a pleasant tea garden. (It is advisable to visit this area only in groups.)

The Wilds

To the north, along M 1 or West Central Street which runs parallel to it, is the Melrose Bird Sanctuary. This area of 10 hectares/25 acres, with its luxuriant vegetation, is an ideal nesting-place for many species of birds (open: from sunrise to sunset).

Melrose Bird Sanctuary

This lively street to the north-east of the city centre is the haunt of young people, artists and students of all social classes and colours. There are numerous shops selling African arts and crafts, way-out clothing and jewellery. The street really comes to life in the evening, when the "scene" in bars and pubs hots up, with jazz, pop and folk music until late at night.

Rockey Street

This spacious park in the Bezuidenhout district, east of the city centre, occupies the site of Doornfontein Farm. The old farmhouse, dating from gold rush days, still survives. Children will be more interested in the miniature railway which runs round the park.

Bezuidenhout Park

To the south, in the Kensington district, is the smaller Rhodes Park, centred on a reservoir (restaurant).

Rhodes Park

3km/2 miles south of the city centre (reached on Rosettenville Road) is Pioneers' Park, through which flows a small stream, the Wemmer Pan (rowing boats for hire). In the south of the park are fountains, with musical accompaniment, which play September to March Tues.–Sun. 7.30–9pm, April to June Tues.–Sun. 6.30–8pm.

Pioneers' Park

In the north of the park is Santarama Miniland (open: daily 10am–4.30pm), with models of well-known buildings in South Africa on a scale of 1:25, miniature railways, a miniature harbour and a cableway. There are a souvenir shop and a restaurant, and for children there are rides in miniature trains and boats.

Also in Pioneers' Park is the James Hall Transport Museum (open: Tues.–Sun. 9am–5pm), with an enormous collection of carriages, veteran cars, steam engines and trams.

James Hall Transport Museum

Johannesburg

★ Gold Reef City   No buildings of the early gold rush period have survived in Johannesburg, but visitors can get some idea of what the town was like in those days in Gold Reef City (6km/4 miles south of the city centre on M 1), with its reproductions of houses, public buildings and shops, the Royal Theatre, an old brewery, a hotel, a Chinese laundry, a tailor's workshop, a chemist's shop, a newspaper office and Johannesburg's first stock exchange. Visitors are also shown round a disused shaft of the Crown Mines, one of the richest gold-mines in the world, which gives a vivid impression of the work of the gold-miners.

Most of the shops and the museum displays in other buildings are open: Tues.–Sun. 9.30am–11pm. There are numerous restaurants which stay open until late in the evening. The Gold Reef City Hotel is not a mock-up of an old gold-miners' tavern but a comfortable modern hotel.

Melville Koppies Nature Reserve   On the western outskirts of Johannesburg, in the Melville district, is the Melville Koppies Nature Reserve (area 80 hectares/200 acres), which contains around 80% of the plant species found on the Witwatersrand. Of these 30 are edible, 113 have medicinal properties, 8 are poisonous, 2 are used in the manufacture of expensive perfumes and 35 are used in magical rituals. Within the reserve is an important bird-watching station, where more than 150 species of birds have been recorded. (Open: Sept.–Apr. Guided tours available; tel. 782 70 64 or 888 48 31.)

Northern Surroundings of Johannesburg

Sandton   Sandton, on the northern outskirts of Johannesburg, is a pleasant residential district in a beautiful setting, with broad tree-lined streets and handsome villas. The town, which now has a population of more than 100,000, was formed in 1966 by combining the Sandown, Bryanston and Sandhurst districts. Visitors to Johannesburg who want to be near the

Gold Reef City: reminders of gold rush days

centre but outside the turmoil of the city will find comfortable accommodation in the Sandton hotels. The town's shopping centre is probably the largest in Africa and the one with the widest range of wares.

On the northern outskirts of Sandton (reached from Johannesburg on N 1 to Alan Dale Road exit, then R 561, going west) is the Lipizaner Riding School, a stud farm established in 1965 which is the only recognised Spanish Riding School outside Vienna. The Lipizaners are the result of a cross between Berber and Arab horses and Spanish and Italian breeds. When born they range in colour between brown and mouse-grey, becoming white only after six to ten years. Lipizaners, the first of which came to South Africa in 1948, are better at performing difficult dressage movements than any other breed. There are demonstrations of their skill, with musical accompaniment, on Sundays at 11am; book at Computicket or tel. (011) 702 21 03.

★Lipizaner
Riding School

In Halfway House, between Johannesburg and Pretoria, is the Transvaal Snake Park, with 150 species of snakes, reptiles and amphibians from southern Africa, as well as crocodiles and tortoises. There are regular presentations of different species of snake (open: daily 10am–5pm).

Transvaal
Snake Park

Half way between Johannesburg and Pretoria, on the west side of N 1, is the Rhino Park, a privately owned nature reserve at the foot of Zwartkop Mountain in which live 20 different species of game. The main attractions are the white rhinos. There is overnight accommodation for visitors, but day visitors are also welcome.

Rhino Park

On the west side of Sandton is Randburg (pop. 120,000), formed in 1959 by the amalgamation of 13 northern suburbs of Johannesburg. The town developed rapidly into a commercial and shopping centre – the Sanlam Centre was one of the first pedestrian shopping malls in the country – but has remained primarily residential. Within the town are 37 parks and gardens and an art gallery (in the town hall in Hendrik Verwoerd Drive) displaying contemporary South African art.

Randburg

The Kleinjukskei Motor Museum in Witkoppen Road displays a large private collection of veteran cars and motorcycles. The oldest model is a Mercedes of 1889, still in working order. Attached to the museum are a picnic area on the Kleinjukskei River and a restaurant (open: Wed.–Sun. 10am–6pm).

Kleinjukskei
Motor Museum

Eastern Surroundings of Johannesburg

Edenvale, 16km/10 miles east of Johannesburg, is a residential area (pop. 30,000) with some industry, founded by mine workers in 1903. Some of the modest houses of gold rush days, built of iron and wood, have survived. In Horwood Street is a large leisure park, with an artificial lake, a roller-skating rink and many picnic areas.

Edenvale

North-east of Edenvale is Kempton Park, an industrial town with a population of 90,000. Here too is the Jan Smuts International Airport, South Africa's largest airport, named after the soldier and politician Jan Smuts (1870–1950), who, after holding various ministerial offices, was prime minister of the Union of South Africa from 1919 to 1924 and again from 1939 to 1948. He played a part in the founding of the United Nations in 1945.

Kempton Park

Boksburg (pop. 250,000) is a densely populated industrial town on the Witwatersrand, 20km/12½ miles east of Johannesburg, founded in 1887 on the land of Leeuwpoort Farm as an administrative centre for the goldfields.
    The privately run Hechter Schultz Museum and Study Centre (seen only by appointment) has collections of ethnographic material on the life of the

Boksburg

Ndebele, Zulu, Xhosa and other peoples as well as beadwork and hunting weapons of the Bushmen.

The La Grange Bird Park on the North Rand Road (open: Mon.–Sat. 8am–noon, Sun. 9am–4.30pm) is populated by many species of birds. Within the park are a picnic area and an attractive tea garden.

On Parsonage Road is Boksburg Lake (sailing, hire of rowing boats). Other attractions are a golf course and a roller-skating rink.

Germiston

20km/12½ miles south-east of Johannesburg is Germiston (pop. 130,000), the most important railway junction in South Africa, with the world's largest gold refinery. The Rand Refinery produces 73% of world output of gold (excluding Russia). The town originated, soon after the first discovery of gold, as a gold-miners' camp on the main seam of gold. (By the time the mine was closed down in 1964 it had yielded 448 tons of gold.) In addition to the gold refinery Germiston now has more than 2000 other industrial installations.

Rondebult
Bird Sanctuary

The Rondebult Bird Sanctuary (area 94 hectares/232 acres; open: daily 8am–5pm) is home to over 150 species of birds, including many water birds. There are a number of viewing posts from which the birds can be observed.

Springs

Springs, now an important craft and industrial centre with a population of over 100,000, was originally founded to house workers in the coal-mines of the surrounding area. Coal-mining later gave place to gold-mining – at one time more gold was produced here than anywhere else in the world – and various industries (paper, cosmetics, glass, etc.).

The first railway line in South Africa, the Rand Tram, ran between Springs and Johannesburg.

Southern Surroundings of Johannesburg

Heidelberg

Heidelberg, 50km/31 miles south-east of Johannesburg at the foot of the Suikerbosrand ("Sugar Hill"; 1903m/6244ft), was founded in 1862 by a German businessman, H. J. Ückermann, who named it after his home town in Germany. After the finding of gold on the Witwatersrand the town enjoyed a period of modest prosperity. It now has a population of 13,000.

Unlike most of the other centres round Johannesburg, Heidelberg is an attractive little town with a number of features of interest and a large nature reserve just outside the town. The Klipkerk (1890) in H. F. Verwoerd Street is a national monument; the vaulted undercroft contains valuable liturgical utensils. The old railway station, a handsome sandstone building of 1895, was restored in 1969 and now houses a Transport Museum (open: Tues.–Sat. 10am–1pm and 2–5pm, Sun. 11am–5pm), with old steam engines, veteran cars and old bicycles.

★Suikerbosrand
Nature Reserve

On the north-western outskirts of Heidelberg is the Suikerbosrand Nature Reserve (area 13,000 hectares/32,000 acres; open: daily 7am–6pm), home to many kinds of game, including zebras, black wildebeests and several species of antelope, as well as more than 200 species of birds. The old Diepkloof farmhouse (1850) has been restored and now houses a visitor centre and museum. This is the starting-point of a number of hiking trails, including the short Cheetah Trail (4km/2½ miles). There is also a tarred track over the highveld with its wide expanses of grassland.

Vereeniging

Vereeniging (pop. 170,000) lies on the Vaal River 60km/37 miles south of Johannesburg. Founded in 1892, it gained a place in history when the treaty ending the Boer War was signed in the town. It subsequently developed into one of the most important centres of heavy industry (coal and steel) and the processing industries (engineering) in South Africa. This development was boosted by the construction of a large electric power station in 1909 and the Union Steel Corporation's steel-processing plant in 1913. The deposits of high-quality coal still remaining to be worked are estimated at 4000 million tons, so that coal-mining is likely to remain the foundation of the town's economy for many years to come.

The Municipal Museum in Leslie Street (open: Mon.–Fri. 10am–4.30pm, Sat. 10am–1pm) has a varied collection, including archaeological material, costumes, weapons and glassware.

In 1938 a dam almost 700m/765yd long was built on the Vaal River to the south-east of Vereeniging, creating a huge reservoir up to 50m/165ft deep, the Vaal Dam, which supplies Johannesburg with water. This is now a popular recreation area, with facilities for swimming and various water sports. On the grassland round the shores of the reservoir there are picnic areas and barbecue sites.

Vaal Dam
Nature Reserve

Immediately south-west of Vereeniging is Vanderbijlpark (pop. 65,000), another industrial town on the banks of the Vaal. It is a regularly planned town with extensive open spaces and leisure facilities, established in 1952 to house the employees of a new iron and steel works.

Vanderbijlpark

130km/81 miles south-west of Johannesburg on the banks of the Vaal is Parys (pop. 46,000), which was founded in 1876. It was given its name by a German who had taken part in the siege of Paris in 1870. It is now a popular holiday resort. The Vaal at this point is up to 1km/³⁄₄ mile wide, with numerous little wooded islands, providing ideal conditions for fishing and boating. In addition to tourism the town's economy depends on the maize, groundnuts and grain grown in the surrounding area.

Parys

Western Surroundings of Johannesburg

Soweto (an abbreviation for South-Western Townships) lies 20km/12½ miles south-west of Johannesburg. Here, within an area of around 100sq.km/40sq. miles, live between 2 and 3 million people, making Soweto by far the largest of the towns round Johannesburg designed to house the black population. Soweto now consists of more than 20 townships. One of the first of these was Orlando East, established in 1934; others are only a few years old.

Soweto

The inhabitants of Soweto are by no means a homogeneous group: ethnically the town is very mixed. Here, within a narrow space, are members of all the different black peoples of South Africa, the largest group by far being the Zulus, with around 33% of the total population. There are few wealthy people in Soweto, and only small numbers in the middle income bracket; and the great majority of the population live in slum conditions. Only a few of the inhabitants have a regular income, and estimates of the number of unemployed range between 50% and 80% of the population of working age.

At one end of the social scale in Soweto there are districts with villas which may have cost the equivalent of several hundred thousand pounds. Below this level there is an apparently endless sea of little box houses consisting of two or three rooms, a kitchen and a bathroom, with a trim and well-kept yard (though refuse piles up on some streets and squares, since it is collected only once a week). Less privileged members of the community live in makeshift shacks of corrugated iron. At the lowest level of the social hierarchy are the inhabitants of the men's hostels, enclosed by barbed wire, who live a bachelor life far from their families. Most of them have not even 2sq.m/22sq.ft of living space, and a single chair and table must sometimes be shared between four men. Given these conditions, it is hardly surprising that unrest and violence are the order of the day in Soweto. The wave of violence began in 1976, when there was an uprising by black schoolchildren against the introduction of Afrikaans as a language of instruction. The unrest, which also spread to other townships, was

No one knows how many people live in Soweto

bloodily repressed by the police. Since then many thousand people have died. More recently the violence was less directed against whites but took the form of attacks by blacks on blacks, leading to bloody massacres. Before the 1994 election there was bitter fighting between ANC supporters and Zulus. There have also been numbers of murders which represented the settlement of private accounts, where the police could do little or nothing.

Soweto has the status of an independent town, though with only limited powers of self-government. Much of it now has electricity, and some streets are asphalted. There are kindergartens, schools and hospitals (the largest of which is the well-equipped Baragwanath Hospital, with 5000 beds); and the Vista University provides higher education for blacks. It is a striking fact that this city of 2 or 3 million inhabitants has no real centre. It has little in the way of facilities for leisure and recreation – a few sports grounds, bars and other drinking-places, two parks littered with rubbish and two cinemas. For such a large population there are very few shops. There are practically no jobs to be had in Soweto itself: some of the population make a living by trade, but the overwhelming majority have to commute by train or minibus to jobs in Johannesburg.

Seeing Soweto

Visitors who want to see Soweto can do so safely only by taking a guided tour. Some may not like the idea of a sightseeing trip of this kind, but they should consider whether they ought not to overcome their reluctance: Soweto is, after all, a part of South Africa, and without seeing it they will not fully realise the scale of the social problems with which the country has to contend. There have so far been no serious incidents on conducted tours of Soweto, and most of the inhabitants show a friendly attitude to white visitors. On these tours, usually in minibuses, visitors are taken round the different parts of Soweto, are shown Winnie Mandela's house and also see the slum quarters. Sometimes the bus stops at some point to give visitors a chance to meet some of the inhabitants.

House in Soweto

The largest company running such tours is Jimmy's Face to Face (the proprietor of which, incidentally, owns one of Soweto's luxury villas). The tour can be booked through various travel agencies or directly in Johannesburg (tel. 3 31 61 09 or 3 31 62 09). Visitors are picked up from their hotel in the city centre or in Sandton. The tour takes between 4 and 5 hours.

Carletonville (pop. 140,000), between Johannesburg and Potchefstroom, lies in one of the most important gold-mining regions in the world. There are a number of townships within the city limits. Among the deepest of the mines is the Western Deep Levels Mine, which reaches down to a depth of 3581m/11,750ft (over 2 miles). Carletonville is also an important agricultural centre; the principal crop grown in the area is maize.

Carletonville

The Abe Bailey Nature Reserve (area 300 hectares/750 acres), 7km/4½ miles north of Carletonville, lies in a stretch of country typical of the highveld. It is noted for the numbers of waterfowl and birds of prey to be seen here. There are also zebras, springboks, black wildebeests and red hartebeests. There are guided one-day tours of the reserve.

Abe Bailey
Nature Reserve

Roodepoort, 10km/6 miles west of Johannesburg, is an industrial town which has grown within a few years to a population of 170,000. Its leisure activities are centred on Florida Lake (bathing, water sports). On the shores of the lake is a bird sanctuary, with a 3km/2 mile long hiking trail running through it.

Roodepoort

On Malcom Street is the National Botanic Garden (open: Mon.–Fri. 7.30am–4.30pm, Sat. and Sun. 8am–5pm), in which some remnants of the original vegetation of the region are preserved. There are 2500 species of succulents from areas ranging between South Africa and the Middle East.

The Roodepoort Museum, on the ground floor of the Municipal Theatre, illustrates the life of the first pioneers on the Witwatersrand, the early finds of gold and the different kinds of auriferous rock (open: Tues.–Fri. 9.30am–1pm, Sun. 2–5pm).

Kalahari Gemsbok National Park

Krugersdorp

Krugersdorp (pop. 140,000), 15km/9 miles north-west of Johannesburg, takes its name from Paul Kruger (see Famous People), President of the Transvaal Republic. The town was founded on the site of a farm in 1887 after the discovery of gold in the area. It became the administrative of the West Rand goldfields and in consequence has a number of imposing public buildings.

The Paardekraal Memorial outside the town marks the spot where the Boers assembled in 1880 to protest against the British annexation of the Transvaal.

Among other features of interest in the town are the African Fauna and Bird Park on Koedol Street (open: daily 9am–4pm) and the South African Railway Society Museum on Rustenburg Road (open: daily 9am–4pm).

★Krugersdorp Game Reserve

In the Krugersdorp Game Reserve (5km/3 miles from the town on the Rustenburg road; area 1400 hectares/500 acres) visitors can get some impression of what the Witwatersrand must once have looked like. Among the game to be seen here are giraffes, rhinos, elands, blue wildebeests, kudus, buffaloes, impalas and baboons. A particular attraction is the 200 hectare/500 acre lion enclosure.

The Krugersdorp reserve, only a 40-minute drive from Johannesburg, is one of the most visited reserves in the Transvaal. There is accommodation for visitors in huts and on a camping site, a cafeteria and a picnic area. There are a number of short hiking trails in the reserve, which is open: daily 8am–5pm.

★Sterkfontein Caves

The Sterkfontein stalactitic caves, 8km/5 miles north of Krugersdorp, consist of six linked underground chambers, with a lake at a depth of 40m/130ft. After their discovery in 1896 the caves were at first used as a limestone quarry, destroying many stalactites and stalagmites. Then in 1936 two students discovered fragments of a baboon's skull in the caves, and thereafter archaeological excavations began, continuing until 1951. These brought to light, along with numerous other bones, the skull of a humanoid creature known as Australopithecus africanus, estimated to be 2 million years old. There are conducted visits (Tues.–Sun. 9am–4pm) to the caves, which have not yet been completely explored. Some of the most important finds from the caves are displayed in the nearby Robert Broom Museum.

★Heia Safari Ranch (Illus. p. 263)

Between Krugersdorp and Randburg is Honeydew (reached from Johannesburg on M 5), set in beautiful hilly country. Near the little town is the Heia Safari Ranch, where visitors can spend the night in luxuriously equipped rondavels or, more modestly, in reproductions of Zulu huts. Every Sunday there is a typical *braai*, when great quantities of meat are grilled over an open fire and there are performances of Zulu tribal dances (the Mzumbe Dance Show). The Zulus live in a reproduction of a Zulu village, which was inaugurated by King Zwelethini in 1988. Visitors not spending the night can go on a stalking tour, on which, with luck, they may see buffaloes, zebras, giraffes, rhinos and antelopes.

★Lion Park

23km/14 miles north of Johannesburg (reached from Krugersdorp on R 28) is the Lion Park (open: daily 8am–4.30pm), which can be explored on 10km/6 miles of roads. Visitors can observe numerous animals from their cars, including lions, zebras, ostriches, wildebeests and various species of antelopes and gazelles. Within the park are a restaurant, a souvenir shop, a swimming pool, picnic areas and barbecue sites.

Kalahari Gemsbok National Park   E 3/4

Province: Northern Cape
Distances: 240km/150 miles from Upington, 580km/360 miles from Johannesburg

There are regular performances of Zulu dances on the Heia Safari Ranch

The Kalahari Gemsbok National Park in the far north-west of South Africa forms along with the adjoining Gemsbok National Park in Botswana a huge nature reserve with a total area of 27,000sq.km/10,400sq. miles, of which the Kalahari Gemsbok National Park accounts for 9600sq.km/3710sq. miles.

Situation and characteristics

Since there are no fences between the two National Parks and animals can roam freely over the whole area, this is one of the last great regions in which animal migrations related to the changing seasons, rainfall and sources of food are still possible.

The National Park was established in 1931 to put an end to the activities of the ruthless poachers who were decimating the game and to preserve the herds of springboks and gazelles from extinction.

Over large areas the inhospitable semi-desertic landscape of the Kalahari has been left unspoiled, with only a few Bushmen ranging from time to time over its endless expanses.

The best way to reach the National Park by car is by way of Upington (see entry), from which it is 240km/150 miles on dirt roads to the park entrance. It is advisable before setting out to enquire about the condition of the roads. An alternative route is from Johannesburg via Kuruman and Hotazel, which involves 300km/185 miles of travel on dirt roads. The easiest way to reach the National Park, however, is by air: there are landing strips at the Twee Rivieren and Nossob camps, where cars can be hired (advance booking essential).

The Kalahari is a semi-desertic region extending over more than 1,000,000 sq.km (380,000 sq. miles) of a basin with no outlet for drainage. Most of the Kalahari lies within Botswana, the western part is in Namibia, and only the southern tip is in South Africa. The endless plains of the Kalahari, covered by a layer of red sand, lie at altitudes of between 800 and 1200m (2600 and 3900ft). The sand, formed by the erosion of huge rock masses, has been driven by the wind into dunes. The reddish colouring of the sand is due to

★Topography

263

The semi-desertic landscape of the Kalahari Gemsbok National Park

the presence of oxides of iron. In the Kalahari Gemsbok National Park areas of dunes in their varying shades of colour alternate with expanses of arid savanna.

There is no permanent surface water. The beds of the rivers Auob and Mossob run through the National Park, but they have had a flow of water on only three occasions in the past hundred years. In the course of many millennia, however, they have carved out impressive valleys.

The Kalahari is not an absolute desert. The part lying within South Africa has an annual rainfall of around 200mm/8in., which supports only a very scanty vegetation. There are some dwarf shrubs, various grasses and succulents adapted to arid conditions. Among the few species of trees are the white-barked shepherd's trees, whose leaves provide shade throughout the year and with their high protein content are a much sought-after source of food. The camel-thorn, which grows in dry river valleys, reaches heights of over 15m/50ft. After rain the desert comes to life with a brief flowering of vegetation. A supply of water for the animals is provided by some 80 windmills along the dry river valleys. Another source of moisture is the tsamma, a melon-like fruit which is 90% water and is eaten both by the animals and the Bushmen.

Fauna

The National Park is named after the gemsbok which is found here in large numbers. Other animals frequently encountered are blue wildebeests, elands and red hartebeests. More rarely seen are black-backed jackals, spotted hyenas, brown hyenas, caracals, leopards, impalas and kudus. The so-called Kalahari lions are not a distinct species but have adapted particularly well to their barren environment and can go without water for weeks at a time. Their main source of food is porcupines.

Among the 215 species of birds which have been recorded in the National Park are 50 birds of prey, including the martial eagle, the tawny eagle and the long-legged secretary bird. Ostriches are frequently seen.

The National Park is open throughout the year. The gates at the three camps are opened at sunrise and closed at sunset.

The hottest months are October to March, when day temperatures of over 40°C/104°F are normal. A pleasanter time to visit the park is between May and September, when the days are warm but the temperature falls sharply at night, sometimes down to −10°C/+14°F. The best time for observing the animals is between February and May, when they are most likely to be seen in dry valleys and at waterholes.

Malaria prophylaxis is advisable, particularly in summer.

There are three camps providing overnight accommodation and food: Twee Rivieren at the south end of the National Park, Mata Mata to the west, on the Namibian border (no crossing point), and Nossob to the north. Each camp has chalets and huts in various price ranges, a camping site, a filling station and shops. The Twee Rivieren camp also has a restaurant and a swimming pool.

Three tracks negotiable by cars run through the National Park, following the dry river beds of the Auob and the Nossob, these two tracks being linked by the Dune Trail. Visitors who would rather not go it alone can join one of the organised trips in cross-country vehicles.

When to visit

Facilities for visitors

Karoo National Park

See Beaufort West

Karoo Nature Reserve

See Graaff-Reinet

Kenhardt   F 6

Province: Northern Cape
Altitude: 973m/3192ft
Population: 3600
Distances: 141km/88 miles from Upington, 148km/92 miles from Brandvlei

Kenhardt lies well off the main tourist routes, 141km/88 miles south of Upington on a seemingly endless plateau, a barren region suitable only for sheep-farming.

Situation and characteristics

The town was founded in the early 19th century, when the governor of the Cape Colony sent a force of 20 soldiers to the area to protect the settlers and the north bank of the Orange River from the native population.

Surroundings of Kenhardt

10km/6 miles south of Kenhardt on the Brandvlei road is the Kokerboom Forest, now a nature reserve. The kokerboom ("quiver tree") is a giant aloe which produces yellow flowers in June. This slow-growing plant with a smooth bark and greyish-green leaves is excellently adapted to arid conditions, being able to store water in its trunk. In the Kenhardt area there are some 700 of these bizarre trees, which grow to a height of 4m/13ft. The Bushmen used to make quivers for their arrows from the wood of the kokerboom: hence its name.

★Kokerboom Forest

12km/7½ miles south of Kenhardt a track branches off the Brandvlei road and runs east for some 60km/37 miles to the Verneukpan, a dried-up salt lake which is a bird-watcher's paradise.

Verneukpan

The bizarrely shaped kokerboom trees, found all over the north-western Cape and south-western Namibia

Kimberley   H 6

Province: Northern Cape
Altitude: 1198m/3931ft. Population: 150,000
Distances: 177km/110 miles from Bloemfontein, 294km/183 miles from
    Welkom, 472km/293 miles from Johannesburg, 530km/329 miles from
    Pretoria, 811km/504 miles from Durban

Situation and
characteristics

Many people still think of Kimberley as the diamond capital of the world, although nowadays there are very few diamond-mines in operation and their output is declining. Yet the extraordinary story of the origins of the city and the fact that the foundations of South Africa's wealth were laid here still draw numbers of visitors from far and wide. Situated on the highveld, on the boundary between the Northern Cape Province and the Orange Free State, Kimberley is a convenient stopover on the road from Cape Town to Johannesburg. It is also easily reached by air; the airport is only 10km/ 6 miles south-west of the city centre (no regular bus services).

In addition to diamonds, a major source of income is stock-farming. Kimberley is also the chief town and administrative centre of the Northern Cape Province.

History

The first diamonds in Kimberley were found in 1869 and 1870 on farms in the area, and this sparked off an unprecedented diamond rush. In 1871 prospectors struck it lucky on a farm belonging to the de Beer brothers and on a neighbouring hill. The hill was then completely dug away, and mining continued ever deeper into the ground, eventually creating the shaft known as the Big Hole. By 1872 there were more than 50,000 diamond-miners in the area, and in the following year the settlement, previously known as the

Big Rush, was given its present name, after the then British colonial secretary, the Earl of Kimberley. Thereafter Kimberley developed at a fantastic rate, and by 1900 the tented settlement had become a flourishing city. Electric street lighting was introduced in 1882, and the town's first trams ran in 1887.

By 1914, when it was closed down, the Big Hole alone had produced 14.5 million carats of diamonds. In the course of time De Beers Consolidated Mines, a company founded by Cecil Rhodes in 1880, had taken over most of the Kimberley diamond mines (see Baedeker Special, p. 272).

Although Kimberley is a city in which incalculable wealth has been produced, the city centre with its narrow (by South African standards) streets does not reflect that wealth. The main office blocks and department stores are round Market Square, from which it is a short walk (or ride on the old-style Kimberley Tram) to the focal point of Kimberley's diamond fever, the Big Hole. Very different from the central area is the grand residential district of Belgravia, south-east of the city centre. Here, in addition to the handsome villas set in gardens, are a number of interesting museums.
The city

An old tramcar of 1913, restored, carries visitors between the city centre (City Hall) and the Big Hole.
Kimberley Tram

There are several jewellers' shops in Jones Street. Visitors who are thinking of buying a diamond should be sure to seek expert advice (see Practical Information, Diamonds). Some shops not only sell diamonds but put on an informative video show on the cutting and polishing of diamonds, and in some cases give visitors the opportunity of seeing a goldsmith at work.
Diamond dealers

City Centre and Big Hole

Kimberley's City Hall, a Neo-Classical building of 1899, is now a national monument. In addition to municipal offices it also houses a tourist information bureau. In front of the City Hall are reproductions of the first electric street lights in South Africa, installed in Kimberley in 1882.
City Hall

To the south of the City Hall, in Chapel Street, is the Alexander McGregor Memorial Museum (open: Mon.–Fri. 9am–5pm, Sat. 9am–1pm, Sun. 2–5pm), a natural history museum with an interesting collection of rocks and minerals and a section on the early history of South Africa.
Alexander McGregor Memorial Museum

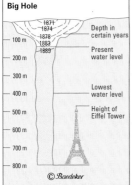

Big Hole

Depth in certain years 1871 1874 1878 1883 1889

Present water level

Lowest water level

Height of Eiffel Tower

© Baedeker

Kimberley's main tourist attraction is the Kimberley Mine Museum (open: daily 8am–6pm), an open-air museum centred on the "Big Hole". The entrance to the museum, in Tucker Street, can be reached on foot by way of either the North or the South Circular Road or by taking the Kimberley Tram from the City Hall.
★★Big Hole, Kimberley Mine Museum

The Big Hole (the Kimberley Mine) is the world's largest man-made hole, with a depth of 800m (half a mile), a diameter of 470m (515yd) and a circumference of 1.5km (just under a mile). Between 1871 and 1914 22.6 million tons of earth and rock were excavated from the mine for a yield of 2722kg/6000lb of diamonds. Visitors can look down from a viewing platform into the mine, now filled with water to 150m/500ft below ground level, and picture what it was like when thousands of men were working in the hole and hauling the rock up to the

Kimberley

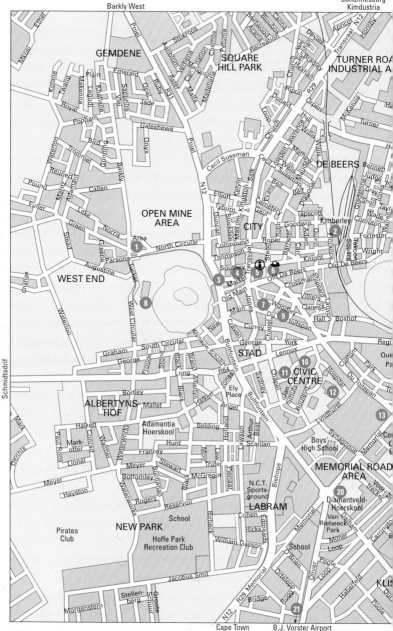

Kimberley

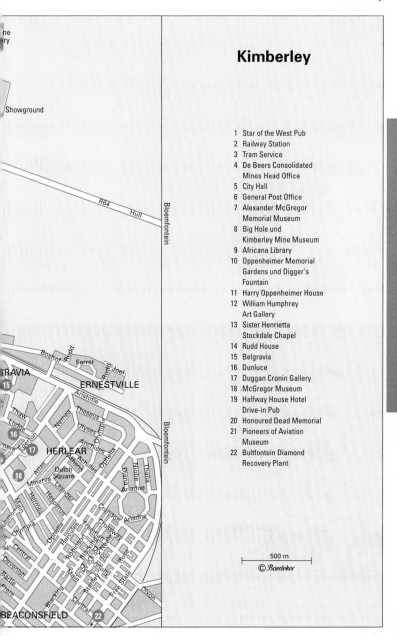

1 Star of the West Pub
2 Railway Station
3 Tram Service
4 De Beers Consolidated
  Mines Head Office
5 City Hall
6 General Post Office
7 Alexander McGregor
  Memorial Museum
8 Big Hole und
  Kimberley Mine Museum
9 Africana Library
10 Oppenheimer Memorial
   Gardens und Digger's
   Fountain
11 Harry Oppenheimer House
12 William Humphrey
   Art Gallery
13 Sister Henrietta
   Stockdale Chapel
14 Rudd House
15 Belgravia
16 Dunluce
17 Duggan Cronin Gallery
18 McGregor Museum
19 Halfway House Hotel
   Drive-in Pub
20 Honoured Dead Memorial
21 Pioneers of Aviation
   Museum
22 Bultfontein Diamond
   Recovery Plant

500 m

© Baedeker

The Big Hole, now surrounded by a museum village . . .

. . . with the old winding-tower and . . .

. . . the Lutheran church

surface with cables. By 1889, when the workings had reached a depth of 400m (a quarter of a mile), opencast mining was no longer possible. Later the work was increasingly mechanised, the first winding tower being installed in 1892.

On the west side of the Big Hole is a museum village of almost 50 buildings (some original and some reproductions), representing Kimberley as it was at the time of the diamond rush. Some of the houses, furnished in the style of the time, can be entered. The first church built in Kimberley was the German Lutheran church of St Martin (1875). Kimberley's oldest house, however, dates only from 1877; it was built of prefabricated parts imported from Britain: a residence of extraordinary luxury at a time when everyone else was living in tents. The "Diggers' Rest" is a reconstruction of one of the 128 bars which the town boasted in its early days. Other houses, shops and workshops line a cobbled street. In the Mining Hall is a collection of photographs and documents from diamond rush days. Opposite it is the Diamond Hall, the exhibits in which include a 616 carat diamond, one of the largest uncut diamonds in the world, and the Eureka, the first diamond discovered in South Africa.

After leaving the Mine Museum it is worth paying a visit to the oldest public house in Kimberley, the Star of the West (to the north of the Museum, at the corner of North Circular Road and Barkly Road). This was the favourite rendezvous of the diamond prospectors from the early 1870s. The interior of the pub has been restored and now looks as it did in the early days of the diamond rush. Its proudest memento is a bar stool said to have been made specially for Cecil Rhodes.
Star of the West

Belgravia

The first houses in the Belgravia district, on the south-east side of the city centre, were built in 1873. The luxurious villas in this district, set in large gardens, were built by those fortunate citizens who had made their pile in the diamond fields. Balgravia is still Kimberley's favoured residential district, with numerous handsome old buildings.

Jan Smuts Boulevard runs round the Oppenheimer Memorial Gardens, in the centre of which is the Diggers' Fountain (five life-size figures holding a diamond sieve).
Oppenheimer
Memorial Gardens

The William Humphreys Art Gallery on Jan Smuts Boulevard, opened in 1952, has one of South Africa's most important art collections, with works by Dutch, Flemish, British and French masters as well as South African artists (open: Mon.–Sat. 10am–1pm and 2–5pm, Sun. 2–5pm).
William
Humphreys
Art Gallery

In Hentrich Street, to the west of the Oppenheimer Memorial Gardens, is the 13-storey Harry Oppenheimer Building (1974), designed by the German architect H. Hentrich, in which all diamonds found in South Africa are graded. Since this can be done only in artificial light, the windows on the south side of the building are so constructed that no sunlight can get in. The building is not open to the public.
Harry
Oppenheimer
House

Farther east is the beautiful Queen's Park. Originally laid out in 1874, it was given its present name in 1953 on the occasion of Queen Elizabeth II's coronation.
Queen's Park

To the south of the park, at 5–7 Loch Road (reached by way of Harley Street), is Rudd House, once the home of the mining magnate H. P. Rudd, whose father was a friend and business partner of Cecil Rhodes. Since 1988 the house has been run by the McGregor Museum, and guided tours are available on application to the Museum (tel. 3 26 45/6).
Rudd House

There are other handsome old villas in Lodge Road, the continuation of Harley Street. At No. 7 is Oppenheimer House, built in 1906 for Ernest
Oppenheimer
House

Sparkling Stones

In the city of Kimberley, in the Northern Cape Province, is the largest man-made hole in the world, half a mile deep and just under a mile in circumference. Digging for diamonds began here in 1871, and the mine was closed down in 1914. Between these two years 22.6 million tons of earth and rock were taken out of the mine, yielding 2.7 tons of rough diamonds, with a total value of many billions of pounds. Kimberley's "Big Hole" is now filled with water, but its heyday is recalled by the museum village on one side of the hole.

It all began in 1866, when a 15-year-old Afrikaner boy named Erasmus Jacobs found an interesting pebble in the bed of the Orange River near Hopetown. This turned out to be a 21 carat diamond (1 carat = 0.2 gram) which became known as the Eureka Diamond. Soon afterwards the "Star of Africa" (83.5 carats), later known as the Dudley Diamond, was discovered.

The real diamond fever set in, however, only in 1869, with the discovery of five veins of diamond-bearing rock in the Kimberley area. Whereas elsewhere diamonds were usually found in superficial deposits, usually along the banks of rivers, at Kimberley the diamonds were in a volcanic chimney of solidified magna reaching far down into the bowels of the earth. It soon appeared that the stores of diamonds in the bluish-black diamond-bearing rock (kimberlite) were sufficient to last for many years, and thousands of fortune-seekers, many of them from abroad, flocked into the area. The town of Kimberley grew up round the largest mine, and in no time it had a population of over 10,000. There are said to have been hundreds of bars and brothels long before the first church or school was built.

The farther the diggers penetrated into the earth, the more expensive and more complicated became the mining process. Accordingly the owners of individual claims joined up to form companies. An adventurer named Cecil Rhodes now came along and bought up as many claims as he could. In 1880 he acquired the claims of the de Beer family, on whose land two large mines had been discovered, and founded the De Beers Mining Company. His bitterest competitor was Barney Barnato, a Londoner, who was determined to bring all the diamond claims under his control and establish a monopoly. In 1888, however, Rhodes bought Barnato's company and founded De Beers Consolidated Mines. Barnato received a cheque for £5,338,650 – then the largest ever issued. Almost all South African diamond mining was now controlled by a single firm.

From the economic point of view Kimberley represented progress in two respects. On the one hand the industrialisation of South Africa now began, and in 1885 the railway lines from the ports of Cape Town, Port Elizabeth and East London reached the mining town in the interior of the country. On the other, South Africa now had an export product which brought in large revenues. On the down side, however, the first signs of the apartheid which was later to become general began to appear in the diamond mines of Kimberley. Black miners were housed in strictly guarded camps and had to submit to body searches to ensure that they did not smuggle out diamonds – indignities to which white workers were not exposed.

In 1902, the year Cecil Rhodes died, Ernest Oppenheimer (1880–1957), the son of a Jewish cigar merchant in Germany, arrived in South Africa to do business on behalf of a London diamond dealer. Like Rhodes before him, he was obsessed by the idea of gaining monopoly control over the production and marketing of diamonds; and by 1929 he had succeeded in amalgamating other diamond companies, including the formerly German-owned companies in South-West Africa (with an output in 1912 of a million carats, or 20% of total

African diamond production), into syndicates and cartels which under the overall control of De Beers, of which Oppenheimer was chairman, for many years controlled the whole of the world trade in diamonds and dictated prices. The South African-based Anglo-American Corporation (founded in 1917) still controls 80% of the world diamond trade through the Central Selling Organisation in London, established by Oppenheimer in 1930. Ernest Oppenheimer was not only the leading figure in the international diamond trade: he was the richest and most powerful man in South Africa, an *éminence grise* whose influence was felt throughout the South African economy.

A gallery in the celebrated Cullinan mine, Pretoria

For the last 70 years the Oppenheimer family has played a decisive part in the world of diamonds. The firm and the Central Selling Organisation are now headed by Nicholas Oppenheimer, the third generation of the family, who followed his father, Harry F. Oppenheimer. Like some other business leaders, the Oppenheimers were against apartheid. They wanted, particularly after the Second World War, to employ skilled workers in their mines, not slaves. During the years of apartheid, therefore, they sought to develop the training of black workers and to improve their living conditions. They promoted black trade unions and were among the first employers to pay black and white workers at the same rates – though this led them to be regarded with extreme mistrust by both sides. The Oppenheimers were happy to see the end of apartheid, for this led to the removal of restrictions to which the South African diamond industry had been subjected for many years.

South Africa is the fifth largest producer of diamonds in the world. There are still large deposits of diamonds in veins of kimberlite at Kimberley, Cullinan (Pretoria) and Postmasburg, where there are underground workings at depths of up to 3000m/10,000ft.

Most diamonds are used for industrial purposes (in drills, stone saws,

273

Baedeker Special

gramophone pick-ups, etc.); only a quarter are cut and polished as gems (brilliants). The vein of kimberlite at Pretoria has yielded some of the finest gem diamonds in the world – the Cullinan, the Transvaal Blue (25 carats), the Premier Rose (139 carats), to mention only a few. The Cullinan diamond was, in its day, the largest rough diamond ever found (3106 carats, or about a pound). It was presented to King Edward VII on his 68th birthday and was split by the Amsterdam diamond-cutter Joseph Asscher into 105 parts (9 large ones and 96 smaller ones); the largest of them is now in the sceptre which forms part of the British crown jewels.

The cutting and polishing of a diamond calls for the highest degree of precision. During the cutting of the Cullinan diamond a doctor and two nurses were in attendance, and Joseph Asscher was under such stress that after the operation was completed he had a nervous breakdown and was confined to bed for three months.

The richest sources of gem diamonds in southern Africa – and in the world – are not the kimberlite pipes of South Africa but the alluvial soils of Namaqualand and the sea bottom off the west coast of South Africa.

Since 1992, as a result of international political changes, the South African giant De Beers, holder of the last raw material monopoly in the world, has been fighting to maintain its control of the world diamond trade. When diamonds from Angola flooded the free market in Antwerp De Beers was faced with a serious sales crisis. And it has also had to contend with competition from the former Soviet Union: Russia has an annual output of diamonds worth 1.5 billion dollars – a fifth of the world market.

Oppenheimer, first mayor of Kimberley and later chairman of De Beers Consolidated Mines. Here in 1908 was born his son Harry, who in 1957 succeeded his father as head of the diamond cartel which controlled some 80% of world production of diamonds.

★Dunluce

At 10 Lodge Road is Dunluce, an outstanding example of Late Victorian architecture. Originally built in 1897, it was acquired by John Orr in 1903 and remained in the hands of the much respected Orr family until 1975. Like Rudd House, it is attached to the McGregor Museum and can be seen at weekends by appointment (tel. 3 26 45/6).

★Duggan Cronin Gallery

At the east end of Lodge Road is Edgerton Road, in which there are two interesting museums. The Duggan Cronin Gallery (open: Mon.–Fri. 9am–5pm, Sat. 9am–1pm and 2–5pm, Sun. 2–5pm) contains a unique collection of photographs of the native peoples of South Africa, taken by A. M. Duggan Cronin between 1919 and 1939. Some of the traditional tribal rites depicted can never be photographed again. The gallery also displays African arts and crafts and a number of rock paintings (originals).

McGregor Museum

A short distance away is the McGregor Museum, housed in a former sanatorium established in 1897 on the initiative of Cecil Rhodes. During the four-month siege of Kimberley by the Boers in 1900 Rhodes lived in two rooms on the ground floor. The building is still furnished as it was around the turn of the century. The sanatorium later became a hotel and still later a school. Since 1971 it has housed the McGregor Museum (open: Mon.–Sat.

Dunluce House, one of the many handsome old villas in Kimberley's Belgravia district ▶

9am–5pm, Sun. 2–5pm; natural history, religious history). The museum also has a section on the history of the town, with particular emphasis on the days of the diamond rush.

Halfway House Hotel

From here the return to the city centre is by way of Du Toitspan Road, in which, at the corner of Edgerton Road, is the Halfway House Hotel (1880). This was the first drive-in pub in South Africa and undoubtedly also the first in the world. In those days the customers rode in and drank in the saddle; nowadays they drive in and drink in the car.

Sights outside the City Centre

Honoured Dead Memorial

The Honoured Dead Memorial is one of the first things visitors will see when coming into Kimberley from the airport. Designed by Sir Herbert Baker, it commemorates those who died in the siege of Kimberley during the Boer War (1899–1900).

Pioneers of Aviation Museum

At Alexandersfontein, 3km/2 miles from the airport, is the Pioneers of Aviation Museum (open: Mon.–Sat. 9am–1pm and 2–5pm, Sun. 2–5pm). The first flying school in South Africa was established at Kimberley in 1913, and the museum is dedicated to these early aviators. The collection includes reproductions of the first aircraft hangar and a biplane used for the training of pilots.

Buitfontein Mine

The Bultfontein diamond mine in Molyneux Road, on the south-eastern outskirts of Kimberley, is still working. There are conducted tours of the surface installations, starting from the visitor centre, Mon.–Fri. at 9 and 11am. Advance booking is required for underground tours (tel. 2 96 51).

Surroundings of Kimberley

Magersfontein Battlefield and Museum

The battlefield of Magersfontein, scene of a British defeat during "Black Week" in the Boer War, lies 30km/19 miles south of Kimberley. There is an observation point from which there are good views of the battlefield and the trenches. There is a small museum with a collection of weapons and uniforms (open: daily 7am–5pm).

Barkly West

The first diamonds in the Kimberley area were found in 1869 at Barkly West (see entry), 30km/19 miles north-west of Kimberley.

Riverton

28km/17 miles north-west of Kimberley, on the banks of the Vaal River, is Riverton, a municipal pleasure resort with accommodation for visitors in various categories and a wide range of sports facilities. There is boating on a 25km/15 mile long stretch of the river and excellent fishing.

King William's Town   J 9

Province: Eastern Cape
Altitude: 533m/1749ft. Population: 25,500
Distances: 60km/27 miles from East London, 121km/75 miles from Grahamstown, 148km/92 miles from Queenstown

Situation and characteristics

King William's Town lies some 50km/30 miles from the coast of the Indian Ocean and a few miles south-west of Bisho (see entry), the former capital of the Ciskei. Unlike Bisho, however, it always belonged to the Cape Province. It is the shopping and administrative centre of the region, with many educational institutions. Its economy is based on various light industries (textiles, leatherworking, the manufacture of footwear, soap and candles, etc.).

King William's Town grew out of a mission station established on the
Buffalo River in 1826. In 1835 the Xhosa destroyed the settlement and
carried off the missionaries. In the hope of pacifying this unsettled area
the Governor of the Cape Province, Sir Benjamin D'Urban, declared it a
separate province named Queen Adelaide, with King William's Town,
refounded on the site of the former mission station, as its capital. The new
province did not last long, however. After being again destroyed in 1846
the town becane in 1847 the administrative centre of British Kaffraria. In
subsequent years it was several times the scene of fighting between Xhosa
and Europeans. It lost its status as a provincial capital in 1865, when British
Kaffraria was incorporated in the Cape Province.

History

Sights in and around King William's Town

The Kaffrarian Museum owes its existence to the Natural History Society
founded in King William's Town in 1884. The first section of the museum
was opened in 1898, and this was followed by a series of extensions, most
recently in 1979, when the old Post Office was incorporated in the complex.
    The main part of the museum is the natural history section. Among the
collections of mammals, birds, fish, reptiles and insects is a female hippopotamus called Huberta which became famous in 1928–31, when she
roamed up and down the coast between St Lucia and King William's Town,
where she was finally shot. There are also sections on the history and way
of life of the Xhosa (Xhosa Gallery in the old Post Office building) and of the
British and German settlers in the region (open: Mon.–Fri. 9am–12.45pm
and 2–5pm, Sat. 9am–12.45pm).

Kaffrarian
Museum

The Missionary Museum of South Africa, housed in a former Methodist
church of 1855, is an outstation of the Kaffrarian Museum and has the same
opening times. It has a comprehensive collection of material illustrating the
history of missionary activity in South Africa.

Missionary
Museum
of South Africa

15km/9 miles north of King William's Town on the Stutterheim road is Pirie
Forest, on the slopes of Mount Kemp (1420m/4659ft). Much of it is a planted
forest, but it also includes some fine specimens of yellowwood trees.

Pirie Forest

Kleinmond   D 10

Province: Western Cape
Altitude: 15m/50ft
Population: 2400
Distances: 44km/27 miles from Caledon, 104km/65 miles from Cape Town

Kleinmond is a small and not particularly attractive town with a fishing
harbour in Sandown Bay, on the coast of the Indian Ocean, but it lies in an
area of great natural beauty, the "flower paradise on the Cape". In Sandown Bay itself there are mile-long sandy beaches (though strong currents
make bathing dangerous), while inland there is beautiful hill country. There
is safe bathing in a lagoon.

Situation and
characteristics

Surroundings of Kleinmond

This nature reserve, to the west of Kleinmond round the mouth of the
Palmiet River, was established to protect the vulnerable ecosystem between the hills and the coast. It covers an area of 400 hectares/1000 acres
containing many indigenous species of trees (the milkwood tree being
particularly common) and rare Erica and Protea species. A number of
hiking trails run through the reserve; especially rewarding is an 8km/5 mile
long coastal trail from which marine life can also be observed. The reserve

Kleinmond Coastal
Nature Reserve

277

is open throughout the year from sunrise to sunset; there is no overnight accommodation.

Betty's Bay

11km/7 miles west of Kleinmond is the little holiday resort of Betty's Bay, named after Betty Youlden, daughter of a landowner in the years before the Second World War. This charmingly situated little place consists almost exclusively of privately owned holiday homes.

At Betty's Bay is the only penguin reserve on the mainland: on Stony Point is a colony of rare jackass penguins.

★Harold Porter
National
Botanic Garden

At the foot of the Platberg (917m/3009ft), to the north of Betty's Bay, is the Harold Porter National Botanic Garden (area 189 hectares/467 acres), which is famed for its beautiful wild flowers. Only 5 hectares/12½ acres of the garden are cultivated; the rest of the area consists of typical Cape fynbos. In January the rare red disa orchids flower here, in March the nerines. Two mountain streams flow through the gardens. During the main flowering season, between October and February, large numbers of birds are attracted to the gardens, including the Cape thrush and various species of woodpeckers and cuckoos. Also to be seen in the gardens are porcupines, mongooses, baboons and (more rarely) leopards. The gardens are open throughout the year daily 8am–4pm.

★Coast road to
Gordon's Bay

The coast road (R44) which runs north from Betty's Bay to Gordon's Bay (40km/25 miles; see Somerset West) is of outstanding scenic beauty. Mile-long sandy beaches alternate with stretches of rugged cliffs, and there are wide views over False Bay (see Cape Town, Surroundings), with the Cape Peninsula in the background.

A side road goes off R 44 to Cape Hangklip (453m/1486ft), at the east end of False Bay, with a lighthouse, a number of holiday houses and a hotel.

Knysna   G 10

Province: Western Cape
Altitude: 50m/165ft
Population: 30,000
Distances: 105km/65 miles from Mossel Bay, 120km/75 miles from Oudtshoorn, 247km/153 miles from Port Elizabeth

★★Situation and
characteristics

Knysna is one of the principal centres on the famous Garden Route (see entry) along the south coast of South Africa. It is delightfully situated between the forest and the sea on a lagoon which offers scope for a variety of water sports. In 1985 this beautiful region of salt lakes and swamps was declared a National Lake Area, and it is now administered by the National Parks Board. Round the lagoon are numerous holiday houses, hotels and guesthouses. On the seaward side the mouth of the lagoon is flanked by two crags, the Knysna Heads. On the two islands in the lagoon, which are linked with the mainland by bridges, are numbers of handsome holiday homes. There are believed to be more than 200 species of fish and other marine creatures in the lagoon, including the rare seahorse (*Hippocampus capensis*). The local oysters are particularly prized by connoisseurs; they can be bought in the Knysna Oyster Company's shop in Long Street.

History

The name of George Rex (1765–1839) keeps cropping up in Knysna. Rumour had it that Rex, who came to this area in 1803, was the illegitimate son of King George III and Hannah Lightfoot. This could never be proved, and is now regarded as historically improbable. Certainly the local people believed that his lavish life-style could be explained in no other way. He owned a large farm and was involved in a variety of other business activities. His supposed royal descent attracted many other settlers, and in 1825 the town of Knysna was officially founded by the Governor of the Cape, Lord Charles Somerset.

The town's harbour, built on the initiative of George Rex, brought Knysna prosperity in the course of the 19th century; but in 1928 the railway superseded ships as a means of transport, and in 1954 the harbour was closed.

Knysna is a lively little town, with its main public buildings, restaurants and shops on its busy Main Road. There are also good shops and restaurants in the attractively laid out Woodmill Lane Shopping Centre in Long Street, which branches off Main Road.

The town

The Outeniqua Choo-Tjoe, a narrow-gauge steam train, runs between Knysna and George (see entry).

Outeniqua
Choo-Tjoe

Sights in and around Knysna

In Queen Street is the Millwood House Museum. This trim little house originally stood in the nearby settlement of Millwood, where gold was discovered in 1876 – a small deposit which was almost worked out by 1895. This house was then taken down and re-erected in Knysna. It is now a national monument. The museum is mainly devoted to the town's founder, George Rex, and to the gold-mining operations in Millwood (open: Mon.– Sat. 9.30am–12.30pm).

Millwood House
Museum

Near the town (take Gray Street, which branches off Main Road, and turn left into Bond Street) is Pledge Park, a small nature reserve with an area of only 10 hectares/25 acres. The park, which is freely accessible, has a fine show of indigenous vegetation and many attractive viewpoints.

Pledge Park

The road running west from Knysna, which turns left immediately after crossing the river and heads for Brenton-on-Sea, runs past the Belvidere Church, a Norman-style chapel built in 1855 for a son-in-law of the legendary George Rex.

Belvidere Church

Millwood House, Knysna

Knysna

★Brenton-on-Sea

6km/4 miles south of the church is Brenton-on-Sea, a charming little seaside resort on Buffalo Bay with magical, endlessly long sandy beaches.

Buffalo Valley Game Farm

To the west of Brenton-on-Sea, in the valley of the Goukamma River, is the privately owned Buffalo Valley Game Farm, with zebras and numerous species of antelopes and gazelles, which visitors can observe from their cars (on a 3km/2 mile long track running through the reserve) or on short guided walks (open: daily 9am–6pm, in winter to 5pm).

Featherbed Nature Reserve

There is a daily ferry service (departing 10am and noon; book by telephone, 0445/2 16 93) from Knysna to the Featherbed Nature Reserve on the Western Head. Here visitors can observe the local flora and fauna; there is a restaurant.

★Knysna Forest

Knysna is surrounded by a wide expanse of forest country. Between George to the west and Humansdorp to the east extends the largest area of forest in South Africa (80,000 hectares/200,000 acres): only 1% of the country's area consists of forest, compared with 25% in the United States. Much of the area is planted forest (pines and eucalyptus), but there are still some stretches of natural "primeval" forest with giant yellowwood trees, some of them between 400 and 800 years old, as well as stinkwoods and the pink-flowered Cape chestnut. There are no longer any of the larger game animals in this area, and the fauna consists mainly of some species of antelopes and large numbers of birds. There are only four surviving elephants, which are rarely sighted. At the end of the 19th century there were around 400–500 elephants in the area; by 1962 the number had fallen to ten. This decline in numbers is due not only to hunting but also to the fact that the planted forests do not form an ideal habitat.

An unspoiled tract of natural forest near Knysna

There are numerous hiking trails through the forest, but it can also be seen by car. One attractive trip, for example, is on R 339 to King Edward's Tree (20km/12½ miles north-east of Knysna: see Elephant Walk, below), returning on a road which runs past the Gouna forest station. There are numerous picnic spots on the road.

The Elephant Walk is a very attractive hiking trail (20km/12½ miles), though the chances of seeing one of the forest's four elephants are slim. The trail (waymarked) starts at the Diepwalle forest station (20km/12½ miles from Knysna on R 339, signposted to Uniondale; maps available at forest station). Experienced walkers can do the Elephant Walk in a day, but it can also be split into three shorter walks. It runs past King Edward's Tree, a 40m/130ft high yellowwood tree which is believed to be at least 600 years old.

Elephant Walk

The Kranshoek Walk starts at the Kranshoek picnic area (27km/17 miles east of Knysna), comes in 2km/1¼ miles to the coast of the Indian Ocean and continues parallel to the coast in the direction of Plettenberg Bay; then in 5km/3 miles turns inland to return to its starting-point (total distance 9km/5½ miles).

Kranshoek Walk

This trail (6.5km/4 miles) is named after a species of tree found only in this area. The starting-point is the old Gouna forest station, 17km/10½ miles north of Knysna. The trail, waymarked with a wild pig symbol, runs past several giant yellowwood trees.

Terblans Walk

The Harkerville Trail, a two-day walk (for fit and experienced walkers only) starting from Harkerville forest station, runs through a beautiful coastal region. Overnight accommodation is available in a hut (advance booking necessary; information from tourist office in Knysna).

Harkerville Trail

This trail leads to the scanty remains of the little gold-diggers' settlement of Millwood (see Millwood House Museum, above). After gold was discovered in Knysna Forest in 1876 prospectors flocked to the scene and a town rapidly came into being, complete with post office, lawcourt, three newspapers, numerous shops and six hotels. The gold seam, however, was quickly worked out and Millwood became a ghost town which in 1893 had a population of only 70. All that now remains of Millwood is a few traces of gold workings and the cemetery. A small museum containing mementoes of the settlement is the starting-point of a 5.5km/3½ mile walk to the surviving remains. The museum is reached by taking N 2, going west from Knysna, and turning off into the Rheenendal road.

Millwood Walk

For other sights within reach of Knysna, see Garden Route, Plettenberg Bay and George.

Garden Route

Kosi Bay Nature Reserve

See Ndumu Game Reserve

Kroonstad   J 5

Province: Orange Free State
Altitude: 1100m/3609ft
Population: 100,000
Distances: 187km/116 miles from Johannesburg, 211km/131 miles from Bloemfontein, 537km/334 miles from Durban, 888km/552 miles from Port Elizabeth

Kroonstad, situated on the banks of the Vals River half way between Johannesburg and Bloemfontein, is an important agricultural and commercial centre and a railway junction.

Situation and characteristics

Kruger National Park

History	The town was founded by voortrekkers on April 20th 1855 and named after Kroon, the favourite horse of Sarel Cilliers, leader of the trek. As a staging point on the main north–south road it grew rapidly, and around 1900 was briefly the capital of the Orange Free State republic.
The town	Kroonstad has preserved a number of handsome old buildings, including the old market hall, the town hall, the post office and the offices of the Standard Bank.

Sights in Kroonstad

Sarel Cilliers Museum	The Sarel Cilliers Museum is on the first floor of the Public Library in Steyn Street (open: Mon.–Fri. 10am–noon and 2.30–6pm and 2nd and 4th Sat. mornings of the month). It contains portraits and documents relating to the Cilliers family, who lived on Doornkloof farm. 45km/28 miles east of Kroonstad. (The farmhouse has been preserved and can be visited by appointment; tel. 0562/22601.)
Kroonpark	Kroonpark is a recreation area on the Vals River, with a large camping site, a restaurant, a swimming pool and landing-stages for boats. It lies in an area of lush green meadows and grazing land.

Kruger National Park   M/N 1–4

Provinces: Northern and Eastern Transvaal
Altitude: 200–900m/650–3000ft
Distances: 400–500km/250–300 miles from Johannesburg

Situation and characteristics	The Kruger National Park is the largest and oldest National Park in South Africa, internationally renowned as one of the world's most important game reserves. It lies in the north-east of the country, extending for 350km/220 miles from north to south, with a maximum breadth of 90km/55 miles and a total area of 19,485sq.km/7523sq. miles. It is bounded on the north by the Limpopo, on the south by the Crocodile River, on the east by the frontier with Mozambique and on the west by a barrier fence. The Kruger National Park has been completely enclosed only since 1975: an 1800km/1100 mile long fence now serves to protect humans from animals and animals from humans.
Getting there	The National Park is a 5–6 hours' drive from Johannesburg. Most visitors enter by the Numbi Gate or the Paul Kruger Gate to the north of it. The fastest route to these gates is on N 4 to Nelspruit and then R 40 and R 538.
	It is also possible to reach the National Park by air. There are flights from Johannesburg, Durban and Nelspruit to airstrips at the Skukuza and Phalaborwa camps (where cars of different categories can be hired).
	Various travel agencies in Johannesburg, Durban and Nelspruit run tours to the National Park in air-conditioned coaches.
Malaria hazard	The Kruger National Park lies in a malaria-risk area. Though the chances of catching malaria here are not particularly high (they are higher in summer than in winter) provided that certain precautions are taken (so far as possible staying indoors after dark, keeping well covered up, using insect repellents, etc.), there does remain a residual risk. Each visitor must decide for himself, after consulting his doctor or an institute of tropical medicine, whether to take a course of antimalarial drugs.
History	The National Park is named after Paul Kruger (see Famous People), President of the Boer Republic of the Transvaal. In 1884 Kruger conceived the

Landscape in the south of the Kruger National Park ▶

Seen from your car: elephants, . . .   *. . . a giraffe, . . .*

idea of creating a game reserve in the Transvaal, the eastern part of which was a favourite hunting ground of both the native population and Europeans. A beginning was made in 1898, when a relatively small area between the Sabi and Crocodile Rivers was declared a reserve. It was subsequently further extended until in 1926 the National Park was opened in its present form.

★Topography

The Kruger National Park occupies an almost level area lying for the most part between 200 and 300m (650 and 1000ft) above sea level, much of it covered by expanses of grassland and scrub, with gallery forests frequently extending along the banks of rivers. Most of the southern part of the park is hilly wooded savanna, with a great variety of species. This alternation between grassland, bush and trees is known in South Africa as bushveld. Altogether almost 2000 different species of plants have been recorded in the National Park, including some 500 different trees and shrubs. Many of the trees have thick cork-like barks which provide protection against savanna fires. What seems at first glance to be a featureless landscape reveals on closer observation an astonishing variety, with a range of different habitats.

The lifelines of the Kruger National Park are the five perennial rivers which flow through it from west to east: the Crocodile, the Sabie, the Olifants, the Luvuvhu and (to some extent) the Letaba. None of these rivers rises in the National Park. Before reaching the park they have been badly polluted by industrial and agricultural wastes. Moreover much of their water has been piped off for irrigation. Thus the Letaba has gradually become a seasonal river. The ecosystem of the Kruger National Park, however, is vitally dependent on these rivers, particularly since rainfall in recent years has been relatively low. Within the National Park there are almost 400 artificially created waterholes which never dry up even during severe drought. In earlier centuries the animals could move elsewhere when water was short, but this for the most part is no longer possible.

... a cheetah and ...   *... antelopes*

The Kruger National Park is remarkable for the exceptional quantity and   ★★Fauna
variety of its game. Visitors who have sufficient time at their disposal can
observe from their car great numbers of animals which otherwise they
would only see behind bars in a zoo. The best times for seeing the animals
are the early morning and late afternoon.

The big game living in the National Park includes 1500 lions, 900 leopards, 7500 elephants, 1500 rhinoceros (mostly white rhinos: there are
only about 200 of the slightly darker black rhinos), 32,000 zebras, 4900
giraffes, 30,000 buffaloes and 125,000 impalas (one of the 17 species of
antelopes represented in the park). In addition there are 114 different
species of reptiles, over 500 species of birds (including 15 species of eagle
alone), and numerous butterflies and moths and other insects. The
National Park is one of the last refuges for many gravely endangered
animal species, including the black rhino, the wild dog and the sable
antelope.

Every year the National Park authorities carry out a thorough census of
the animals in the park and check up on the plants. If it appears that some
animals are increasing too rapidly some of them are culled in order to
maintain the ecological balance in the park. Thus since 1967 some 13,000
elephants have been killed in order to maintain their numbers at the
optimum level of 7500 (on average an elephant consumes 300kg/660lb of
plants a day and in the course of a year can destroy 1000 trees). The flesh of
the animals killed is used to make biltong, a type of dried meat much prized
in South Africa, and their skins and hides are processed for industrial uses.

The climate of the National Park is subtropical. Most of the rain falls in   When to visit
summer, the annual figure being distinctly higher (at 700mm/28in.) in the
south of the park than in the north (400mm/16in.). It can be extremely hot,
with temperatures of around 40°C/104°F on occasion. The best time of year
for observing the animals is in winter, when on most days it is sunny and
pleasantly warm, but much cooler in the evening; frost, however, is rare. In

winter many trees and shrubs have lost their leaves, making it more difficult for the animals to hide. On the other hand the scenery is finer in summer, and there are still plenty of animals to be seen: some animals, indeed, produce their young in summer.

The eight gates of the National Park are opened between 5.30 and 6.30 in the morning, varying according to season, and close between 5.30 and 6.30 in the evening. These opening and closing times apply also to the camps within the National Park.

Driving in the
National Park

The National Park has a network of some 2300km/1430 miles of roads. There are only 900km/560 miles of asphalted roads, but the unsurfaced tracks are usually negotiable by cars without difficulty. (Open cars and motorcycles are not permitted.) All the roads are well signposted; detailed maps can be obtained when entering the park. The condition of all roads and tracks is regularly checked.

Driving within the park is permitted only during the day. There is a speed limit of 50km/31 miles an hour on asphalted roads and 40km/25 miles an hour on other roads. Visitors should allow plenty of time to get back to the camps before dark, remembering that delays are likely to occur (for example if there is a "traffic jam" caused by game blocking the road). Visitors exceeding the speed limit or feeding the animals face the prospect of a fine. It is strictly forbidden for visitors to leave their car except at specially designated places. Most accidents involving big game result from failure to observe these rules.

A particularly attractive trip is a drive through the whole length of the park, observing the striking variations in the scenery. Alternatively you can make one of the camps your base and explore the surrounding area in a series of shorter trips. At least two or three days should be allowed for your stay in the park.

Guided walks
and drives

Visitors can join guided walking tours lasting several days, led by experienced game rangers, with overnight accommodation in simple huts. A place on these walks must usually be booked a year in advance (enquiries to National Parks Board, PO Box 787, Pretoria 0001, tel. 012/3 43 19 91, fax 012/3 43 09 05). At some camps there are shorter (one-day) walks led by rangers.

The various camps also organise guided tours in cars (night trips now also available).

Camps in the Kruger National Park

Rest camps,
private camps,
bushveld camps

Accommodation for the 650,000 visitors who come to the Kruger National Park every year is available in rest camps, privately run camps and bushveld camps. The privately run camps take only parties booked in advance, not individual visitors. Bushveld camps, which have simpler accommodation and facilities than rest camps, are meant for parties, families and individual travellers who want to experience the wilderness in relative isolation; day visitors are not admitted.

The great majority of visitors spending two or more days in the National Park stay in rest camps, which also welcome day visitors. The range of accommodation extends from luxuriously equipped chalets to simple huts for from two to five people. Most of them are air-conditioned and are appropriately and attractively equipped. Almost all of them have a bathroom and cooking facilities, as well as a barbecue. There are also camping sites. All the larger rest camps have restaurants and shops, a filling station, an information centre and first aid facilities.

In this section rest camps are listed and described from north to south. Accommodation in camps can be booked through travel agencies or by direct application to the National Parks Board (see Practical Information, National Parks).

Punda Maria

Punda Maria, in the extreme north of the National Park at the foot of the Dimbo Mountain, is a small and simple hutted camp with a restaurant, shops, a filling station and a nature trail. From the camp there are wide views over the Mopane plain. The camp was originally built in 1919 for the forestry authorities but has been modernised.

The sandveld round Punda Maria is an offshoot of the Kalahari basin. To the north of Punda Maria, on the Luvuvhu River, the dry savanna gives place to gallery forests of tropical aspect. This area, less frequented by tourists, will appeal particularly to bird-watchers: there are excellent opportunities for observation on S 99, a circular route (25km/15 miles) which begins near the camp. At Klopperfontein, 20km/12½ miles north-east of the camp, are a number of giant baobab trees on the edge of a waterhole. Big game can often be seen here. 23km/14 miles beyond this the road comes to the Luvuvhu River (picnic area). There is a bridge from which crocodiles and hippopotamuses can be observed. From here a track runs east along the river to the Pafuri picnic area, with good views of the banks of the river.

The Shingwedzi camp, 73km/45 miles south-east of Punda Maria, is the largest of the three camps in the northern part of the park. Its amenities include a restaurant, a cafeteria, a swimming pool, a shop and video shows.

There are good viewpoints for observing game on the road from Punda Maria to Shingwedzi. A few miles north of the camp elephants, buffaloes and baboons are frequently seen and, more rarely, wild dogs and leopards. 10km/6 miles north of Shingwedzi S 56 goes off the road on the left, following the Mphongolo River, and in 30km/19 miles rejoins the road at the Babalala rest area. Another track runs south-east from Shingwedzi to the Kanniedood Dam, where there is a game observation point.

Shingwedzi

60km/37 miles south of Shingwedzi is the modern and very luxurious Mopani camp, with accommodation in different categories, a restaurant, a cafeteria, a filling station, a shop, a swimming pool and an information centre.

There is an excellent game observation point at the Nshawu Dam, 17km/10½ miles east of Mopani, where herds of elephants gather, particularly after rain.

Mopani

This excellently equipped camp (car hire) lies in a wide bend on the Letaba River. The information centre, which will advise visitors about the animals (particularly elephants) to be seen in the area, has a collection of elephant tusks. Those of a bull elephant known as Shawu, 3.17m/10ft 5in. long, are believed to be the longest ever found in southern Africa.

In the savanna country round Letaba live many species of antelopes and cheetahs. At shady waterholes elephants, buffaloes, zebras and gazelles can be observed. The most beautiful tracks round Letaba are S 46 and S 93 and 44, which run south-east along the Letaba River. The Engelhard Dam to the east and the Mingerhout Dam are also good places for observing game.

Letaba

50km/31 miles west of Letaba on the road to the Phalaborwa Gate is the Masorini Open-Air Museum, where remains of a prehistoric settlement and an iron-smelting plant have been excavated. Thousands of years ago the territory of the Kruger National Park was inhabited by hunters and gatherers. The earliest traces of human occupation – sherds of pottery, copper articles, gold ornaments – date from around 1700 B.C.

Masorini Museum

The Olifants camp, with its magnificent old trees, is one of the finest in the National Park. From the camp itself, situated 100m/330ft above the Olifants River, there are excellent views. If you are lucky enough to get one of the comfortable huts overlooking the river you will be able, with the help of field-glasses, to see game along its banks. The sunrises and sunsets here are spectacular. The camp also has an aquarium, with tanks in which visitors can see the various species of fish which live in the reserve.

10km/6 miles west of the camp is the Nwamanzi Lookout, one of the best game observation points in the National Park.

Olifants

View of the Olifants River from Olifants camp

Balule	Balule, 10km/6 miles south of the Olifants camp, is a small camp with a camping site. It will suit visitors who want to get close to nature (no electricity; no day visitors).
Satara	50km/37 miles south of the Olifants camp is Satara, a modern camp situated in a part of the National Park where large numbers of big game can be seen. Within the camp is a small pond on which birds can usually be observed at close quarters. The abundance of game round Satara is due to the large numbers of waterholes in the area. At the Nsemani Dam, 9km/5½ miles west of Satara, hippopotamuses and waterbucks can frequently be seen, as well as the occasional pride of lions. 16km/10 miles east on S 100 is the Gudzani Dam, where large herds of buffaloes and herds of three or four hundred zebras can be seen. Giraffes are frequently also to be observed. 25km/15 miles north-west of Satara, on the banks of the Timbavati River, is the popular picnic area of Marcoela. On the road south from Satara a track goes off on the right, 15km/9 miles from the camp, to the nearby Nkayapan waterhole, which, particularly in winter, attracts many animals. The road continues, passing bizarrely shaped baobab trees, to the Kumana Dam (on the east side of the road), which is regularly visited by storks.
Orpen	The Orpen rest camp, at the National Park's Orpen Gate, offers only very simple accommodation (no electricity, no restaurant).
Skukuza	Skukuza is the National Park's largest camp, with the park offices, two small museums, several restaurants and shops, a library, a filling station, a police station and an airstrip. At the entrance is a reception area, with a bank, post office and car rental desk. Accommodation is in cottages for two to six people and comfortable straw-thatched huts for two or three people. There is also a large camping site. Altogether Skukuza camp can accommodate up to 600 people. An observation point within the camp overlooks the banks of the Sabie River, where hippopotamuses can sometimes be seen and elephants come down to the river to drink.

Big game are frequently to be seen from the road which runs north-east from Skukuza to Tshokwane, in spite of the fairly busy traffic on the road. The Manzimahle Dam is often frequented by lions. The Olifantsdrinkgat is a waterhole frequently visited, particularly in winter, by elephants, baboons, zebras and lions. It is worth pausing, too, at the nearby Lionpan with its beautiful waterlilies. The Silolweni Dam is the home of one of the largest herds of hippopotamuses in the National Park. A short distance beyond this is Tshokwane, a favourite picnic spot.

From Skukuza a road runs along the Sabie River to the Lower Sabie camp. Big game can almost always be seen in the bush flanking the road, and it is often necessary to brake to avoid giraffes, antelopes, elephants or zebras crossing the road. With its extensive areas of grass and its many trees, the Lower Sabie camp is a pleasant place to stay. The Sabie River, which is dammed at this point, is home to many water birds, and monkeys, elephants, rhinos and buffaloes are frequently also to be seen here.

Lower Sabie

30km/19 miles south is the Crocodile Bridge rest camp, with 20 bungalows, a small shop and a parking area for mobile homes. The grassland in the surrounding area attracts zebras, wildebeests, impalas, kudus, gazelles and large herds of buffaloes. In winter the Crocodile River dries up, leaving only small pools, but these are still an important source of water for animals. If you find a good observation point near one of these waterholes you will not have to wait long to see big game. 6km/4 miles from the camp there is an observation point from which to watch the hippopotamuses which like to wallow in the mud on the banks of the river.

Crocodile Bridge

In the south-west of the National Park, 9km/5½ miles from the Numbi Gate, is the Pretoriuskop camp, the oldest in the park and one of the three largest, with accommodation for 400 visitors, a swimming pool, a restaurant, a shop, a post office and a camping site. Within this area, enclosed by

Pretoriuskop

Zebras, found in large numbers all over the Kruger National Park

289

picturesque granite hills, grow 67 different species of trees and 21 species of shrubs, including the coral tree, which produces its blood-red flowers in August and September. Round Pretoriuskop visitors can sometimes see rare species of animals at close quarters, including wild dogs, cheetahs, leopards and rare species of antelope.

Berg-en-Dal

60km/37 miles south-east of Pretoriuskop is the very comfortable Berg-en-Dal camp, from which there are magnificent views of the hilly surrounding country. In addition to a restaurant, a shop, a swimming pool, an information centre and a filling station it has facilities for conferences of up to 200 people. A short nature trail runs through the camp, from which there are also organised night tours of the surrounding area.

Private Game Reserves

On the western border of the Kruger National Park are a number of private game reserves in which most of the animals living in the National Park can also be seen. In these reserves accommodation for visitors is in exclusive "game lodges", which are markedly more luxurious (and correspondingly more expensive) than the state-run camps; almost all of them have swimming pools. Visitors are taken round the reserves in open-top jeeps, the drivers of which are kept informed by radio of the whereabouts of game. Night trips are also organised, offering the additional thrill of "dinner in the bush".

Timbavati
Nature Reserve

The Timbavati private nature reserve, half way down the west side of the Kruger National Park, occupies an area of unspoiled bushveld some 75,000 hectares/185,000 acres in extent which is home to numerous birds and animals, including some species which are threatened with extinction. A

The owners of the luxurious private game lodges in the Kruger National Park try to let their guests see big game at close quarters

day-and-night safari through the park, accompanied by an armed ranger, gives visitors the thrilling experience of being close to the "real" Africa.

The Ngala camp has first-class air-conditioned accommodation for a maximum of 40 people, with a swimming pool, an airstrip and a conference centre. Also in the Timbavati reserve is the Tanda Tula game lodge, a small and very exclusive establishment accommodating a maximum of 14 people, with three rangers who will arrange individual programmes for visitors. Accommodation is in straw-roofed cottages set round the swimming pool.

Comfortable accommodation is also available in the Motswari (26 beds) and M'bali (14 beds) game lodges.

Beyond the western boundary of the Timbavati reserve is the Klaserie private nature reserve, which occupies an area of 60,000 hectares/150,000 acres (30km/19 miles long by 25km/15 miles across) on both banks of the Klaserie River. The reserve belongs to a group of some 100 owners and can be visited only on a five-day trekking tour (which can be booked in Johannesburg). | Klaserie Nature Reserve

The Tshukudu Game Lodge can be reached from R 40, which runs between the villages of Hoedspruit and Mica. Accommodation (for a maximum of eight visitors) is in comfortable straw-thatched rondavels. Within the reserve's area of 5000 hectares/12,500 acres there are organised tours in cross-country vehicles, with the prospect of seeing at close quarters giraffes, leopards, lions, kudus, zebras and rhinos. | Tshukudu Game Lodge

In spite of its relatively small size (4000 hectares/10,000 acres) this reserve, 30km/19 miles west of the Orpen Gate of the National Park, is a popular safari area. Visitors are accommodated in 16 chalets. | Thornybush Game Lodge

South-east of the Timbavati reserve is the Manyeleti Game Reserve, reached from the road between Acornhoek and the Orpen Gate of the National Park. The Manyeleti reserve, which is less concerned with luxury than with closeness to nature, is famed for its two- and three-day safaris. | Manyeleti Game Reserve

Within the 60,000 hectares/150,000 acres of the Sabi Sand reserve are a number of game lodges which offer not only marvellous opportunities of seeing wild life close-up but also a stimulating mix of adventure and relaxation. | Sabi Sand Nature Reserve

Londolozi Game Reserve, in the centre of the Sabi Sand reserve, is one of the best known tourist attractions in the lowveld, which has several times won the title, awarded by South African travel agencies, of "best game lodge of the year". Accommodation is available in three camps: Tree Camp, with luxurious accommodation for small parties of 2–8 people; Bush Camp, accommodating up to 8 people in local-style stone cottages; and Main Camp, with accommodation for 24 people in luxury chalets with views of the luxuriant vegetation along the river. | Londolozi Game Reserve

The Mala Mala Reserve, which is also part of the Sabi Sabi reserve, is only a few minutes' drive from Londolozi. It is the oldest and most exclusive private camp in the lowveld, with accommodation for up to 50 visitors in tastefully appointed bungalows. The area round Mala Mala, on the Sand River, is well stocked with game (leopards, lions, elephants, rhinos and buffaloes). | Mala Mala Reserve

In the south of the Mala Mala reserve is Kirkman's Camp. From the verandas of the bungalows there are fine views of the river and surrounding area. The central point of the camp is an old farmhouse, furnished in the style of the 1920s, with a recreation room and a restaurant.

Harry's Camp has accommodation for 16 visitors in typical Ndebele cottages.

The territory of the Sabi Sabi Game Lodge lies on the Sabie River, the haunt of numerous hippopotamuses and crocodiles. Sabi Sabi has won a great | Sabi Sabi Game Lodge reputation in recent years for its hospitality and high standard of service. Also within this area is the Bush Lodge, situated amid typical lowveld vegetation, with 24 comfortable straw-roofed chalets. River Lodge has 20 straw-roofed rondavels.

Inyati Game Lodge

Inyati Game Lodge, beautifully situated on the Sand River, with accommodation for 20 visitors, is noted for its individual attention to its guests and its excellently organised game drives. When booking accommodation here you should ask for a room in one of the larger straw-roofed chalets: there are also smaller double rooms which are comfortable enough but not luxurious.

Kuruman   G 5

Province: Northern Cape
Altitude: 1315m/4315ft
Population: 10,000
Distances: 151km/94 miles from Vryburg, 216km/134 miles from Kimberley, 258km/160 miles from Upington

Situation and characteristics

Kuruman lies in arid country on the north-western borders of the Northern Cape Province. It grew up round the source of the Kuruman River, the "Eye of Kuruman", a spring which produces 18 to 20 million litres (4 to 4½ million gallons) of water a day – enough to supply the town with water and irrigate a 6km/4 mile long valley. The economy of the area is based on mining and cattle-farming.

History

In 1821 Robert Moffat founded here what became the best known mission station in the whole of South Africa. Here he baptised the first members of the local Tswana tribe in 1829, translated the Bible into their language, which had never previously been written, and printed the first copies himself on a simple printing-press. From here David Livingstone set out on his journeys of exploration into the interior of Africa, and here too, in the mission church, he married Moffat's daughter Mary in 1838. The mission is now run by the United Congregational Church of Southern Africa.

The town

Kuruman is an attractive little town which preserves some buildings dating from the early days of the mission. The Eye of Kuruman, in a beautiful park, gushes out of a cleft in the dolomitic rock and fills a small pond. The park with its shady trees is an ideal spot for a relaxed picnic.

Sights in Kuruman

Moffat Mission

The mission church, built in 1831, is now a national monument. For many years this simple church, which could accommodate a congregation of 1000, was the tallest building in the Northern Cape. Recently restored, it is now part of a museum complex which also includes the Moffat family home and a schoolhouse.

Kuruman Nature Reserve

1km/¾ mile outside the town is the Kuruman Nature Reserve (area 850 hectares/2100 acres), in which live rhinos, ostriches and various species of antelopes and gazelles. The reserve is open only on Sunday afternoons.

Surroundings of Kuruman

Wonderwerk Cave

In the Wonderwerk Cave, 25km/15 miles south of Kuruman, are notable Bushman paintings. Some of them are over 10,000 years old.

Kathu

Kathu, 50km/31 miles south-west of Kuruman, is the youngest town in South Africa, founded only in 1980. It now has a population of almost

10,000. The town owes its existence to the Iron and Steel Corporation (ISCOR), which erected modern functional buildings here and in the neighbouring settlement of Sishen to house miners working the nearby deposits of iron ore, believed to be the largest in South Africa. Here too was established a nature reserve with an area of over 2000 hectares/5000 acres in which are elands, springboks, gazelles, kudus, impalas, rhinos, red hartebeests, blesboks and steppe zebras (open: daily 7am–7pm, 7am–6pm in winter).

Ladybrand   J/K 6

Province: Orange Free State
Altitude: 1612m/5289ft
Population: 17,000
Distances: 16km/10 miles from Maseru, 71km/44 miles from Ficksburg,
    145km/90 miles from Bloemfontein

Ladybrand lies at the foot of the Patberg, near the western border of Lesotho. The surrounding area, in which grain is now intensively cultivated, was already inhabited in prehistoric times, as is shown by the numerous rock paintings (many of them, unfortunately, poorly preserved). The town, founded in 1867, was named after Lady (Catharina) Brand, wife of Sir Johannes Brand, then President of the Orange Free State.

Situation and characteristics

Ladybrand has a number of handsome sandstone buildings, including the Town Hall, the Dutch Reformed church and the secondary school.

The town

Sights in and around Ladybrand

The Catharina Brand Museum has a collection of interesting archaeological material and rock paintings.

Catharina Brand Museum

3km/2 miles outside the town is Rose Cottage Cave, where Bushman rock paintings and the ashes of a fire lit 50,000 years ago were found.

Rose Cottage Cave

10km/6 miles from Ladybrand is the Modderpoort Cave Church, in which services were held from 1869 onwards. The cave was originally used by the Anglican Society of St Augustine both as a church and as a dwelling. The church now belongs to the Anglican Society of the Sacred Mission.

Modderpoort Cave Church

The Leiehoek Holiday Resort, to the south of Ladybrand, is the startingpoint of the Steve Visser Hiking Trail, a rewarding two-day walk.

Steve Visser Hiking Trail

Ladysmith   L 6

Province: KwaZulu/Natal
Altitude: 1350m/4430ft
Population: 115,000
Distances: 236km/147 miles from Durban, 364km/226 miles from Johannesburg

Ladysmith is a lively town on the main road between Durban and the Transvaal, situated in a thriving agricultural area (maize, soya, barley, fruit and vegetables; stock-farming).

Situation and characteristics

The first European settlers in the area founded the town in 1847, declaring it capital of the Klip River Republic. The "republic", however, lasted only a few months before the area was brought under British control. The town was then named after the wife of Sir Harry Smith, Governor of the Cape.

History

Siege Museum, Ladysmith

During the Boer War (1899–1902) Ladysmith was under siege by the Boers for 120 days before being relieved by General Sir Redvers Buller. A number of important battles were fought round the town (at Wagon Hill, Caesar's Camp, Lombard's Cop and Umblawana Hill).

Sights in and around Ladysmith

Siege Museum

The Siege Museum, adjoining the Town Hall, displays mementoes and documents on life in Ladysmith during the Boer War (open: Mon.–Fri. 8am–4pm, Sat. 8am–noon, Sun. 10–11.30am).

Spioenkop
Nature Reserve

35km/22 miles west of Ladysmith is the Spioenkop Nature Reserve (area 5979 hectares/14,768 acres), in an attractive region of hills and valleys round the Tugela River, which is dammed at this point. This was the scene of a bloody battle during the Boer War (known in English history books as the battle of Spion Kop). A Historic Trail leads to the battlefield.

Within the nature reserve is a 400 hectare/1000 acre game park containing blue wildebeests, zebras, reedbucks, impalas, red hartebeests, blesboks, rhinos and giraffes. Visitors can explore the reserve on foot accompanied by a park ranger. The Spioenkop Discovery Trail (a 2–4 hour walk) introduces visitors to the ecology of the region.

There is accommodation for visitors in the form of attractive chalets, country cottages and a camping site. There are also picnic areas and children's playgrounds, and facilities for water sports on the Spioenkop Dam.

Colenso

25km/15 miles south of Ladysmith is Colenso, in an area which was also the scene of fighting during the Boer War – commemorated by a number of monuments and the Robert Stevenson Museum. From Tugela Drift Nature Reserve (area 98 hectares/242 acres) there is a view of the battlefield of Colenso.

The Bloukrans Monument, 18km/11 miles south of Colenso on R 74, commemorates a bloody battle between Zulus and Boers in 1838.

Bloukrans
Monument

Lambert's Bay   D 8

Province: Western Cape
Altitude: 50m/165ft
Population: 3600
Distances: 158km/98 miles from Vredenburg, 213km/132 miles from Cal-
  vinia, 290km/180 miles from Cape Town

Lambert's Bay is a fishing town, with fish-processing industries, 290km/180
miles north of Cape Town on the west coast of South Africa. There has
hitherto been little tourist development in this area, but this is due to
change, and there is already accommodation for visitors in modest hotels
and guest houses. Many South Africans are attracted to Lambert's Bay by
the busy life round the harbour and the freshly caught fish served in the
restaurants (for example the well-known Muisbosskerm beach restaurant,
5km/3 miles south of the town). A major annual event is the Crayfish
Festival at the end of November.

Situation and
characteristics

The town lies in a 30km/19 mile long coastal strip of very sandy soil in
which only drought-loving plants flourish. In spring, however, this "sandveld" is transformed into a sea of blossom.

The town is named after Sir Robert Lambert, naval officer in charge of the
region in 1820–21. The bay was the scene of the only naval battle of the
Boer War, when General Hertzog's fleet opened fire on a British warship,
the "Sybille".

History

On Bird Island, Lambert's Bay

Sights in and around Lambert's Bay

★Bird Island
From the harbour a causeway leads out to Bird Island, which is occupied by large colonies of cormorants, gannets and of course seagulls. Black-footed penguins can be observed at close quarters. The best time for bird-watching is between September and February, in the early morning or late afternoon.

Eland's Bay
27km/17 miles south of Lambert's Bay on a dirt road is Eland's Bay, which in summer is a surfer's paradise. The little town is not particularly attractive, largely because of the presence of a fish-processing factory, but it has a beautiful beach as well as a hotel, shops and a camping site.

Graafwater
At Graafwater, 30km/19 miles east of Lambert's Bay, agricultural produce from Clanwilliam and fish and seafood from Lambert's Bay are graded and prepared for transport.

22km/14 miles north of Graafwater on the road to Vredendal is a cave known as the Heerenlogement ("Gentlemen's Lodgings"), on the walls of which are scratched the names of more than one hundred and seventy 17th and 18th century travellers who found overnight accommodation here, near a conveniently situated spring.

Lesotho
J–L 6/7

Area: 30,335sq.km/11,712sq. miles
Population: 1,860,000
Capital: Maseru

Location and characteristics
Lesotho – officially the kingdom of Lesotho/Sotho Muso oa Lesotho – is an independent state wholly enclosed by South Africa, bounded on the north and west by the Orange Free State, on the west by KwaZulu/Natal and on the south by the Eastern Cape Province. With an area of 30,335sq.km/ 11,712sq. miles, Lesotho is about the same size as Belgium. The official languages are English and Sotho.

Lesotho, known as the "Roof of Southern Africa", offers visitors the experience of a purely black African state and a fascinating mountain world.

The capital, Maseru, is easily reached from Johannesburg, Bloemfontein and Aliwal North by car. There are daily bus services and flights from Johannesburg.

Topography
The whole of Lesotho lies at heights of 1000m/3300ft and above. but almost everywhere the plateau rises to 2000m/6600ft or more. Through the mountains the Orange River and its tributaries have carved gorges up to 800m/2625ft deep, with innumerable waterfalls at breaks in the gorges. The Maletsunyane Falls (192m/630ft) are the highest in southern Africa. The plateau is bounded on the east by the Drakensberg, with Thabana Ntle-nyana, the highest mountain in southern Africa (3482m/11,424ft), and on the west by the Maluti Mountains (3277m/10,752ft) and the Thaba Putsoa range (3096m/10,158ft). To the west the highland plateau falls down to the lowlands, with hills ranging in height between 1200 and 2000m (3900 and 6600ft), which are traversed by the broad bed of the Caledon River, forming the border with the Orange Free State. This region, amounting to around a quarter of the country's area, is the main area of settlement and economic activity.

Climate
In the lowlands the climate is temperate, with average temperatures ranging between 8°C/46°F in July and 21°C/70°F in January. Average annual rainfall is around 700–800mm/28–31in., most of it occurring in summer.

In the mountains the temperature falls below freezing point in winter (May–September) and there may be falls of snow.

The vegetation at higher altitudes consists of mountain pasture and lower down of grassland. There are trees (for example olives) only in sheltered valleys.

Lesotho has a population of 1,860,000, with an average density of 61 to the sq. kilometre (158 to the sq. mile). Most of the population live in the western lowlands, while large areas on the highland plateau are either very scantily populated or completely empty of population. Four-fifths of the population live in country areas, but increasing numbers of people are now moving to the capital, Maseru.

The rate of population growth has increased over recent decades and is now just under 3% a year – a rate of increase which has led to overpopulation.

Lesotho has one of the most uniform population structures in Africa. Almost 100% of the population belong to the Sotho, a group of Bantu tribes which moved into the region in the early 19th century. There are around 2000 whites and Indians.

43% of the population are Roman Catholics, 30% Protestants and 12% Anglicans. There are also minorities of Muslims and believers in natural religions.

This primarily agricultural country has a low per capita income, though the gross domestic product is rising at an annual rate of around 6%. Foreign debt amounts to about a quarter of GDP, and there is high inflation.

78% of the population are employed in agriculture, the remaining 22% in industry and the services sector. In view of the limited job opportunities in Lesotho – more than a third of the population is unemployed – some 40% of the male population of working age work in South Africa, mainly as miners. These migrant workers bring in almost half Lesotho's gross domestic product – reflecting the country's heavy dependency on South Africa. And now that many mines are closing down in South Africa unemployment in Lesotho has risen.

In spite of the high proportion of the population engaged in agriculture, it contributes only around a fifth of the country's GDP, since most of the farmers produce only subsistence crops. Land is the inalienable property of the nation, administered by the king; but arable land (unlike grazing land) is granted to individual farmers on an annual basis. The principal crops are maize, millet, sorghum, wheat and vegetables. Yields have fallen in recent years as a result of the unfavourable climate, soil erosion and antiquated methods of cultivation and are no longer sufficient to meet the country's needs, so that, particularly for the urban population, food has to be imported, mainly from South Africa. Important contributions to the export trade are made by the rearing of angora goats for the production of mohair wool, of which Lesotho is the world's fourth largest producer, and by sheep-farming; in recent years cut flowers and strawberries have also become useful exports. Since the great majority of the population live by stock-farming, over-grazing has become a major problem.

In the processing industries a dominant place is occupied by subsidiaries of South African firms, which take advantage of low labour costs and state subsidies to develop labour-intensive industries such as carpet-weaving, the manufacture of candles and textile production. Imports consist mainly of foodstuffs, machinery and oil products, while the principal exports are clothing, footwear and wool (mohair) – though imports considerably exceed exports.

Lesotho is a member of the South African Customs Union, which is its most important trading partner after Switzerland and the European Union. Of major economic importance to Lesotho are remittances from Lesothian migrant workers, the tourist trade (mainly concentrated in the capital, Maseru) and various forms of development aid.

One of the world's largest hydro-electric and water supply schemes is at present under way in Lesotho. Six large dams which are being built on the upper course of the Orange/Senqu River will pound 10 million cubic metres

Lesotho

(2.2 billion gallons) of water, supplying electric power for Lesotho and water for Johannesburg.

History

The territory of Lesotho was inhabited in prehistoric times (probably from about 3500 B.C.) by Bushmen who lived by hunting and gathering and have left innumerable rock drawings as evidence of their presence. From the 17th century A.D. they were driven west by tribes practising agriculture and stock-farming. In the 1820s large numbers of refugees fleeing before Shaka's Zulu warriors found their way into the mountainous territory of what is now Lesotho. Almost all of them belonged to the Sotho group of tribes, which around 1830 were welded by Chief Moshoeshoe I into a nation state under his rule. This state, which included not only the territory of Lesotho but considerable tracts of the Orange Free State, came under increasing pressure from the Boers moving north out of the Cape Colony in the Great Trek. Foreseeing military defeat, Moshoeshoe asked in 1867 for British protection, and after much valuable land had been lost to the Boers the rest of his territory was administered from 1868 as part of the British Cape Colony and in 1871 was incorporated in the colony. After a number of rebellions the territory became directly subject to the British crown as the protectorate of Basutoland (1884). In 1903 a National Council was established to advise the colonial administration. When the chiefs were found to be misusing their powers these were restricted by the British government in 1934. During the two world wars Basutoland was on the Allied side but took no part in the fighting.

After the introduction of democratic principles from 1944 onwards the Basutoland Congress Party, with a policy of radical reform, won a majority in 1960, but in 1965, in the country's first direct election, they were defeated by the conservative Basotho National Party, led by Leabua Jonathan, who now became prime minister. On October 4th 1966 (now the country's National Day) Lesotho became independent as a constitutional monarchy under King Moshoeshoe II but remained in the Commonwealth. Its policies were marked by dependence on South Africa, and it took a very cautious line on the question of apartheid. After a coup d'état in 1970, when Prime Minister Jonathan declared a state of national emergency, the 1966 constitution was suspended, the opposition parties banned and the king sent into exile. In 1983 a law was passed ending the state of emergency, establishing new constitutional structures and providing for free elections, but in 1986 this was set aside by a military coup. Political parties were again banned, the prime minister was deposed and a military council took over the government. In 1993 a new constitution came into force. King Letsie III was crowned and a free election was held. Then in 1994 the king unexpectedly dissolved Parliament and dismissed Prime Minister Mokhehle. After demonstrations by Mokhehle's supporters the king abdicated in favour of his father, who had been living in exile in Britain, and a month later Moshoeshoe reinstated Mokhehle as prime minister. Since the abolition of apartheid in South Africa relations between the two countries have returned to normal.

Suggested Routes in Lesotho

Frontier posts, roads

In this section the sights of Lesotho are described in a number of tours by car. There are twelve frontier crossings into Lesotho from South Africa, but only the frontier posts at Caledonspoort (for traffic from Fouriesburg) and Ficksburg Bridge (from Ficksburg) operate round the clock; the others are open only during the day.

The roads in Lesotho have been improved in recent years, but much of the country is accessible only on unsurfaced tracks. Visitors should enquire at the frontier post about road conditions.

Information

The Lesotho Tourist Board (PO Box 1873, Maseru 100, tel. 266 31 28 96, fax 266 31 01 08) offers a range of organised tours. It is advisable to book in plenty of time.

Maseru to Mafeteng and Moyeni/Quthing (180km/112 miles)

Maseru ("Red Sandstone": pop. 110,000), capital of Lesotho and its only   Maseru
large town, lies on the Caledon River in the western lowlands. It was made
the administrative centre of the protectorate of Basutoland in 1869, but at
first its population consisted mainly of traders and shopkeepers.

Maseru has no features of tourist interest but is a good centre for tours in
the surrounding area.

From Maseru the main road runs through a region carved into its present
form by erosion. Farther on the central range of mountains recedes and the
road runs over a sunny plain with fields of maize, herds of cattle, villages,
waterfalls and the "Sotho castles" (sandstone crags, remnants of a plateau
which has been eroded away).

40km/25 miles south of Maseru a side road runs east to the old mission   Morija
station of Morija, founded in 1833 by the Paris Evangelical Missionary
Society and named after the Biblical Mount Moriah. A collection of material
on Basuto culture and archaeological finds assembled by the missionaries
from the early 20th century onwards is displayed in the Morija Museum
and Archives, Lesotho's only museum (open: Mon.–Sat. 8.30am–4.30pm,
Sun. 2–4.30pm).

Farther east is Matsieng, where the royal family live. The group of round   Matsieng
huts above the village was the residence of Letsie I, who chose the site
because of the flat stones shaped by erosion to be found there which could
be used for serving meals: there were, for example, a "soup dish" and a
"meat plate".

Another attractive side trip is on a road which runs east 50km/31 miles
south of Maseru, signposted to Mphaki, and goes over the Matelile Pass to
reach the beautifully situated Malealea Lodge.

The Maluti Mountains in Lesotho, the "Switzerland of Africa"

Lesotho

<table>
<tr><td>Mafeteng</td><td>Mafeteng (the "town of the fat unmarried woman") is a small industrial and commercial town (pop. 13,000) of rather cheerless aspect.</td></tr>
<tr><td></td><td>From Mafeteng the main road continues south-east over a rocky plain and in 40km/25 miles crosses the Makhaleng River. From the bridge there is a view, to the east, of the Thaba Tsoeu range (the White Mountains), famed for a petrified forest.</td></tr>
<tr><td>Mohale's Hoek</td><td>The pretty little town of Mohale's Hoek is a good base for tours in the surrounding area, for example to the Makhaleng Gorge. Farther information can be obtained in the comfortable little Mount Maluti Hotel.</td></tr>
<tr><td></td><td>The main road runs west and then south through an increasingly rugged landscape to the summit of the Mesitsaneng ("Place of the Wild Beans") Pass, from which there are beautiful views. The road then runs down into the wide valley of the Maphutseng River, with magnificent views of the central mountain massif. It continues through a gorge and crosses the Orange/Senqu River on the Seako Bridge, the longest in Lesotho (191m/209yd).
In this area some dinosaurs' footprints have been preserved. For directions about how to find them apply to the Tourist Board in Maseru or one of the local hotels and lodges.
Some 8km/5 miles before Moyeni/Quthing the road comes to the Masitise mission station, with a large church founded by the well-known missionary D. F. Ellenberger. The Cave House here was built under a rock overhang. Here and elsewhere in the district there are Bushman rock paintings.
After passing the Roman Catholic mission station of Villa Maria the road climbs towards Moorosi's Mountain.</td></tr>
<tr><td>Moyeni/Quthing</td><td>Moyeni/Quthing (pop. 6000), founded in 1877, is the chief town of Quthing district. Its double name is due to the fact that the first post station was called Quthing. Moyeni means "place of the wind", for in this area there is always a strong wind blowing.</td></tr>
<tr><td>Excursion to
Qacha's Nek</td><td>From Moyeni/Quthing it is well worth making an excursion to Qacha's Nek (203km/126 miles – a whole-day trip) for the sake of the grand mountain scenery. Two features of interest on the way are some dinosaur footprints (in a fenced enclosure) and a remarkable cave occupied by Bushmen near the village of Pokane.</td></tr>
</table>

Maseru to the Maletsunyane Falls (113km/70 miles)

<table>
<tr><td></td><td>This route runs up from the densely populated lowlands into the Maluti Mountains. An attractive alternative route is from Maseru via Machache into the Blue Mountains (200km/125 miles): see p. 302.</td></tr>
<tr><td>Thaba Bosiu</td><td>To the east of Maseru a track branches off A 2 for the historic settlement of Thaba Bosiu ("Mountain of Night"), originally a small fort established by Moshoeshoe I in 1824, which for many years was capital of the country.
From the hill on which there are remains of the original settlement there are fine views of the Berea plateau and Mt Qiloane.</td></tr>
<tr><td>Roma</td><td>Farther south, on A 5, is the university town of Roma. The town was founded by Moshoeshoe in 1862, and some years later a Roman Catholic mission station was established here, which in 1945 became a college and later still a university.</td></tr>
<tr><td></td><td>The road, at first still asphalted, continues south-east (from here to Semonkong it is 83km/52 miles), but soon (beyond Ngope) degenerates into an</td></tr>
</table>

Fruit-sellers on Bushman's Pass: they may still have to wait some time for a sale, for there are still few tourists in Lesotho ▶

unsurfaced track, running through very beautiful scenery, with villages, fields of maize, herds of cattle and flocks of sheep. In March the country is gay with the blossom of cosmeas and wild peach-trees.

Here too (for example at the village of Ha Mpotu) there are caves containing Bushman paintings. The great expanses of reeds in this area have given the principal river, the Malehlakana, its name ("Mother of Reeds").

Mapeshoane

3km/2 miles south of the road is the village of Mapeshoane, near which is the Helekokoane Cave, with Bushman paintings. 3km/2 miles beyond the turn-off for Mapeshoane a road runs east through the Raboshabane Gorge and past the Mohomeng Cave to the Raboshabane Crag (200m/660ft). The track then climbs steeply on to a grassy plateau. The nearby village of Motlepu is the starting-point for the ascent of Thaba Telle (2533m/8311ft). The road then runs down to cross the Makhalaneng ("Place of the Small Shrimps") River and then climbs again to Nkesi's Pass (2012m/6601ft), from which there is a superb view of Thaba Putsoa (3096m/10,158ft) and the neighbouring mountains.

Beyond the village of Ramabanta there is a magnificent stretch of road with spectacular views of the surrounding mountains in their varying shades of colour.

★Maletsunyane Falls

Near Semonkong ("Place of Smoke") are the Maletsunyane Falls, the highest in southern Africa (192m/630ft). They are a fantastic sight in winter when the water freezes.

Alternative route to the Blue Mountains

The road to the Blue Mountains, which branches off the Maseru–Roma road and runs east, climbs through a region of sandstone crags to the grassy plateau at the foot of the Maluti Mountains. From the plateau there are magnificent views of these mountains and Mt Machache (2884m/9462ft). The road (A 3) now runs down over a hilly plateau, on which sorghum, maize and other cereals are grown.

From the little village of HaNhatsi a track runs north to Ha Boroanna ("Place of the Small Bushman"), where there are very fine rock paintings.

The main road continues past the village of Machache (camping site), climbs steeply to Bushman Pass, runs down into the Makhaleng valley and then climbs again to the Molimo Nthuse ("God Help Me") Pass (2328m/7638ft), with the Molimo Nthuse Lodge. A few miles beyond this is the Basotho Pony Trekking Centre, from which there is a rewarding ride (3–4 hours) to the Qiloane Falls. Soon after this the road climbs to the Blue Mountain Pass (2621m/8600ft) and then runs down into the Likalaneng valley. After going over another pass it enters the wide valley of the Senqunyane River, with the village of Marakabei, where there is a lodge (self-catering). Beyond this the track is in poor condition, and it is therefore better to return to Maseru.

Maseru to Leribe, Butha-Buthe and Oxbow (200km/125 miles)

This route is known as the Roof of Africa Road, although it climbs above 3000m/9850ft only at four passes beyond Butha-Buthe (within Lesotho). Before that it runs parallel to the Caledon River for most of the way.

The main road runs north from Maseru, passing tall sandstone crags rising above the Teyateyaneng River, with interesting caves.

Teyateyaneng

Teyateyaneng ("Rapid Sand"; pop. 14,000) is a busy little town, the commercial centre of the Berea district. It is famed for its knotted carpets.

Beyond the town the road runs over the wide plain between the Caledon River and the Maluti Mountains, passing large fields of maize.

Leribe/Hlotse

The little town of Leribe/Hlotse (pop. 10,000), founded in 1876, has some industry. The name Hlotse ("Dead Meat") is said to have been given to the town because travellers crossing the river threw pieces of meat into the water to distract the crocodiles.

The oldest building in the town is the Anglican church (1877). It is worth paying a visit to the Leribe Craft Centre, originally established by Anglican women missionaries who taught the Basuto women the craft of weaving. Here visitors can see (and buy) a variety of craft products (e.g. ponchos).

From Leribe/Hlotse there is an attractive excursion through beautiful scenery to the Katse Dam, where there is a hotel.

The next stretch of road, going north-east, runs through rugged and impressive sandstone country.

The little town of Butha-Buthe (pop. 7000) is probably so called (the "place where people settled") because it was here that Moshoeshoe united the Basuto peoples in 1823. It is a scattered assemblage of offices and shops. The picturesque little market hall is in the shape of a typical Sotho straw hat.

Butha-Buthe

The road from Butha-Buthe to the frontier crossing at Joel's Drift runs all the way at heights of above 2300m/7550ft. The road to Oxbow, which branches off this road to run east, is one of the most magnificent in the whole of Africa. It runs through the valley of the Hololo River, passing a series of extraordinary sandstone formations. There is a climb of 760m/2495ft to the summit of the Moteng Pass (2835m/9302ft).

★Road to Oxbow

65km/40 miles from Butha-Buthe, at an altitude of 3000m/10,000ft, is the New Oxbow Lodge, a good centre for fishing, walking, pony trekking and skiing (best months are June to August).

Beyond the lodge the track is suitable only for cross-country vehicles, and before setting out it is essential to check on road conditions and weather prospects. The road leads to the almost abandoned village of Letseng-la-Terae, where there is a diamond mine formerly worked by a South African mining company: now only a few individual prospectors still dig for diamonds in conditions of extreme difficulty.

On to Mokhotlong

Mokhotlong ("Place of the Baldheaded Ibis"), chief place in Lesotho's remotest district, is a good base for walks and pony treks into the Drakensberg (see entry) and along the Mokhotlong River. It is essential to take a guide (information in the local hotel).

Mokhotlong

Lichtenburg

J 4

Province: North-West
Population: 21,000
Distances: 65km/40 miles from Mmabatho, 230km/143 miles from Johannesburg

Lichtenburg, an agricultural centre 230km/143 miles west of Johannesburg, had a more eventful existence during its diamond rush in the 1920s. The area has no great scenic or cultural attractions, but the town may be a convenient stopover on a longer journey (there are a few modest hotels).

Situation and characteristics

The town was founded in 1873 on the Elandsfontein farm. It developed at lightning speed after the first diamond was found in the area in 1926 and 10,000 prospectors flocked to the town. The boom lasted only ten years, during which the whole of the level river valley was dug over and the diamond fields were worked out.

History

Sights in and around Lichtenburg

Lichtenburg's municipal museum contains mementoes and documents on the town's diamond rush and on the life of General Jacobus de la Rey, a hero of the Boer War (open: Mon.–Fri. 9am–noon and 2–5pm, Sat. 9am–noon).

Museum

Louis Trichardt

Lichtenburg Nature Reserve	The Lichtenburg Nature Reserve (area 6000 hectares/15,000 acres), on the northern outskirts of the town, has some 40 species of mammals, including rhinos, mountain zebras and water buffaloes. Attached to the reserve is a breeding station (open: daily 8am–6pm, to 5.30pm in winter; no accommodation for visitors).
Diamond fields	To the north of the town, on both sides of the road to Zeerust, are the remains of diamond workings. Here and there can be seen tools left by the miners. There are some houses dating from diamond rush days in Bakerville, 21km/13 miles north of Lichtenburg.
Zeerust, Marico district	The little town of Zeerust, 83km/52 miles north of Lichtenburg, and the neighbouring settlements of Groot Marico and Ottoshoop make up the Marico district. This is a thriving agricultural area in which citrus fruits, tobacco, maize and wheat are grown. It is also famed for the production of mampoer, a schnaps distilled from peaches, apricots and other fruit. There is an annual Mampoer Festival.
	5km/3 miles east of Zeerust is a reservoir with facilities for water-skiing and fishing (picnic area, holiday village).
	The Marico Trail (a two-day walk with overnight accommodation in a hut) runs along the Marico River.

Louis Trichardt L 2

Province: Northern Transvaal
Altitude: 901m/2956ft
Population: 11,000
Distances: 94km/58 miles from Messina, 107km/66 miles from Pietersburg, 440km/273 miles from Johannesburg

Situation and characteristics	Louis Trichardt is magnificently situated in a fertile valley at the foot of the Soutpansberg, in the far north-east of South Africa. With a pleasantly warm climate, a relatively high rainfall (an annual 940mm/37in.) and fertile soils, this is an intensively cultivated agricultural area, with large farms rearing cattle and growing citrus fruits, pears, avocados, pistachios and vegetables.
	Louis Trichardt itself has no sights of outstanding interest, but there are a number of nature reserves in the area which are well worth a visit. Moreover the northern part of the Kruger National Park (see entry) is no more than 140km/87 miles away.
History	The town is named after the Boer leader Louis Trichardt, who set up camp in this area in 1836. He was followed by other settlers, and in 1847 the little township of Zoutpansbergdorp was founded. This attracted ivory and cattle dealers as well as adventurers, who fought among themselves but combined against the Venda, a Bantu people who are believed to have come to this area from Zimbabwe around 800 years ago. The Venda put up fierce resistance to the advance of the European settlers, who in 1867 were forced to abandon the town, which was then destroyed by the Venda. The Transvaal government regained control of the area only in 1898, and in the following year Louis Trichardt was founded as its administrative centre.

Sights in Louis Trichardt

Fort Hendrina	This little fort, near the Municipal Building in Erasmus Street, was built at the end of the 19th century to provide protection for the inhabitants of the town. It can be seen only from outside.
Indigenous Tree Park	The Indigenous Tree Park, adjoining the camping site, has numbers of handsome old trees.

Surroundings of Louis Trichardt

The mountain country round Louis Trichardt can be explored on this 91km/57 mile long trail (which can also be divided into shorter sections). The whole trail takes takes five days, with overnight stops in huts accommodating up to 30 people (information from tourist information bureau in Louis Trichardt).

Soutpansberg Hiking Trail

The Albasini Dam, 18km/11 miles east of Louis Trichardt, has facilities for fishing and various water sports.

Albasini Dam

The Ben Lavin Nature Reserve (area 2500 hectares/6175 acres; open: daily 6am–7pm), 12km/7½ miles south-east of Louis Trichardt, is a good place for a stopover (camping site). The green plains in the reserve are home to giraffes, impalas, wildebeests and zebras, as well as many species of birds.

Ben Lavin Nature Reserve

The road running north from Louis Trichardt winds its way up the slopes of the Soutpansberg to a pass (1524m/5000ft), 10km/6 miles from the town, from which there are superb views of the Soutpansberg (named after a large salt-pan in the western part of the range which supplied salt to the inhabitants of the area from prehistoric times onwards). The road then continues through a fertile valley to Wyllie's Poort, where the old pass road has been replaced by two tunnels.

★Wyllie's Poort

90km/56 miles east of Louis Trichardt on R 524 is Thohoyandou, formerly capital of the homeland of Venda. With an area of 7410sq.km/2860sq. miles and a population of 500,000, Venda was the smallest of the "independent" homelands and, like the others, was not economically viable.
    The town is named after a legendary Venda leader. It was rebuilt after the establishment of the homeland in 1973 and is now a modern African town with a university. There is a small museum devoted to the history of the Venda people. The town caters for tourist needs with a hotel, a casino and the Ditike Craft Centre, where Venda craft products can be purchased.

Thohoyandou

Thohoyandou is a good base from which to explore the surrounding country, which is almost exclusively inhabited by the Venda; organised tours can be booked in the tourist bureau. Here, away from the crowded tourist areas, are expanses of beautiful country, still largely unspoiled. Most of the Venda still live in their traditional villages under the direction of chiefs and medicine-men. Many places are associated with myths and legends of the Venda people. Lake Fundudzi, north-west of Thohoyandou, is said to be the home of a giant snake which is venerated as a fertility symbol; a permit to visit the lake must be obtained through the tourist bureau in Thohoyandou.

Lake Fundudzi

From Thohoyandou a road runs north-west to Wyllie's Poort (see above). Off this road, in the Nzhelele valley, is the site of Dzata, once the chief town of the Venda people, with remains of the walls which surrounded it.

Dzata

Nwanedi National Park lies almost 80km/50 miles north of Thohoyandou on a poor track; there is a better road by way of the village of Tshipise. The National Park, established in 1981, has small stocks of giraffes, zebras and impalas; there is some accommodation for visitors.

Nwanedi National Park

Lydenburg

M 3

Province: Eastern Transvaal
Altitude: 1381m/4531ft
Population: 22,000
Distances: 57km/35 miles from Sabie, 144km/89 miles from Middelburg

Lydenburg lies on the western slopes of the Transvaal Drakensberg, at the foot of Long Tom Pass. This is an intensively cultivated agricultural area,

Situation and characteristics

Lydenburg

*Lydenburg, once briefly the capital of an independent Boer republic,
still preserves some handsome buildings from its early days*

with fields of maize, corn, soya and clover. The waters round Lydenburg are well stocked with fish (particularly trout), and there is a trout farm at Sterkspruit, 12km/7½ miles from the town.

History

The town was founded in 1849 by Boers who had originally settled at Ohrigstad (45km/28 miles north). After a devastating epidemic of malaria in which many settlers died they abandoned their first settlement and moved to this malaria-free site on the highveld, where they founded a new town named Lydenburg ("Town of Sorrow") in memory of the dead.

The town

Lydenburg is a quiet little town with numerous shops and other services catering for the population of the surrounding agricultural area. The Voortrekker School of 1851 in Church Street is the oldest schoolhouse in the Transvaal. The Dutch Reformed church dates from the same period.

Surroundings of Lydenburg

Museum

Outside the town, on the Long Tom Pass road, is the Lydenburg Museum. Its star attractions are the Lydenburg Heads (replicas; originals in South African Museum, Cape Town): seven terracotta heads (six human and one animal) found in nearby Sterkspruit valley. Until recently they were thought to date from the 5th century A.D.; the latest research, however, dates them to around A.D. 1500.

Gustav Klinkbiel Nature Reserve

To the east of Lydenburg, near R 37, is the Gustav Klinkbiel Nature Reserve (area 2200 hectares/5435 acres), with indigenous flora and various species of antelope, as well as remains of an Iron Age settlement. There is a small museum devoted to these earliest settlers in the area.

Sabie

R 37 runs east from Lydenburg, goes over the Long Tom Pass and comes in 53km/33 miles to Sabie (see entry).

For other sights in the Lydenburg area see Blyderivierspoort Nature Reserve.

Malmesbury   D 9

Province: Western Cape
Altitude: 140m/460ft
Population: 16,000
Distances: 109km/68 miles from Citrusdal, 65km/40 miles from Cape Town, 35km/22 miles from Wellington

Malmesbury is the centre of South Africa's largest wheat-growing area, situated in the region north of Cape Town known as Swartland (so called because of the dark colour of its fertile soil), which produces not only wheat but a full-bodied dark red wine. The wine can be tasted and bought at the Swartland Cellars, 4km/2½ miles outside the town.

Situation and characteristics

Malmesbury grew up round a mineral spring which produces sulphurous water at a temperature of 32°C/90°F. The first settlers established themselves here in 1744. The settlement was given its present name in 1829 during a visit by the Governor of the Cape, who named it after his father-in-law the Earl of Malmesbury. The spring is no longer used for medicinal purposes.

History

Surroundings of Malmesbury

To the south of Malmesbury is the Riverlands Nature Reserve (area 1297 hectares/3203 acres), established in 1986, which contains over 500 species of fynbos vegetation.

Riverlands Nature Reserve

40km/25 miles north of Malmesbury is Moorreesburg (pop. 7000), with the Wheat Industry Museum (open: Mon.–Fri. 8am–12.30pm and 2–5pm). Here too is the Langgewens experimental farm, which carries out scientific experiments and trials seeking to develop improved strains of wheat; it can be visited by appointment.

Moorreesburg

Matjiesfontein   E 9

Province: Western Cape
Altitude: 732m/2402ft
Population: 3200
Distances: 55km/34 miles from Touws River, 225km/140 miles from Beaufort West, 240km/150 miles from Cape Town

Matjiesfontein, situated in the Little Karoo half way between Cape Town and Beaufort West, is a charming little town, popular with South Africans for a weekend holiday trip, which is also a convenient stopover for visitors on their way from the interior of the country to Cape Town (the Trans Karoo Train which runs between Cape Town and Johannesburg stops in Matjiesfontein). The barren country round the town is suitable only for sheepfarming; some of the farms are the size of several British or American counties.

Situation and characteristics

In 1880 a Scot named James Logan who had suffered all his life from a lung disease settled in this area and found that the dry air cured his complaint. Thereupon he founded a spa so that others could benefit as he had. This was a great success, and in the late 19th century many notable people came to Matjiesfontein to take the cure, among them the Sultan of Zanzibar, Lord

History

Randolph Churchill (Winston Churchill's father) and the writer Olive Schreiner. Such distinguished visitors had to be provided with every comfort, and accordingly Matjiesfontein became the first place in the country with electricity and running water.

★The town

The whole of Matjiesfontein was declared a national monument in 1975. It preserves many buildings of the Victorian era, including the Lord Milner Hotel, an elegant building in which the guests feel carried back a hundred years, Olive Schreiner's house, the Post Office and an old warehouse. The Mary Random Museum has a collection of Victoriana and material on the Boer War. From 1899 to 1902 the headquarters of the commander-in-chief of the Cape were in Matjiesfontein, with a garrison of 10,000 men.

Surroundings of Matjiesfontein

Sutherland

120km/75 miles north of Matjiesfontein on R 354 is the little town of Sutherland (alt. 1456m/4777ft; pop. 2000). The road runs through a quiet and empty expanse of country with only scanty vegetation. Nevertheless the Great Karoo has a particular charm of its own, and the sunrises and sunsets in this semi-desertic region are a memorable experience (see Beaufort West).

Sutherland, which has preserved a number of buildings of the Victorian period, is one of the coldest places in South Africa. In winter the temperature frequently falls to −6°C/+21°F, and snow is by no means rare. The high altitude and clear air offer ideal conditions for astronomical observations: hence the presence of the South African Astronomical Observatory 14km/8½ miles outside the town.

Messina   L 1

Province: Northern Transvaal
Altitude: 538m/1765ft
Population: 14,000
Distances: 95km/59 miles from Louis Trichardt, 530km/329 miles from Johannesburg

Situation and characteristics

Messina, the most northerly town in South Africa (15km/9 miles from the Zimbabwe border), is a mining town, the largest producer of copper in South Africa. The inhabitants' other main source of income is agriculture. The subtropical climate (with an average annual temperature of just under 30°C/86°F) fosters a luxuriant vegetation and makes it possible to grow fruit and vegetables. The main agricultural activity in the surrounding area, however, is cattle-farming. The town also has some leather-working industries (tanneries, dyeworks).

An annual event in Messina is a large cattle show.

History

As many archaeological finds have shown, the Messina area was already inhabited by man in prehistoric times. The Europeans who moved into this area at the beginning of the 20th century found traces of earlier mining activity everywhere. They discovered that there were still incalculably large deposits of copper here, and copper-mining on a large scale started in 1905. After the completion of the road from Louis Trichardt (see entry) to Messina in 1907 the town flourished as never before.

Surroundings of Messina

Baobab trees, Elephant's Trunk

Messina is famed for the baobab trees which grown in large numbers in this area. These deciduous trees with thick trunks (which can be up to 28m/92ft in girth) and few short branches are statutorily protected throughout South Africa. A particularly fine specimen, known as the Elephant's Trunk, can be seen just outside the town on the road to Malala Drift, and there is another 5km/3 miles from Messina on the Louis Trichardt road.

This reserve on the outskirts of Messina (open: daily 7am–5pm; no accommodation for visitors), with an area of 3700 hectares/9140 acres, is noted particularly for its numerous baobab trees, some 12,000 of which have been counted. The largest of them is 25m/82ft high. 250 other species of trees and shrubs have been identified in the reserve. The fauna is confined to giraffes, wildebeests, antelopes and gazelles.

Messina
Nature Reserve

Tshipise, 40km/25 miles south-east of Messina, is the starting-point for a visit to the Honnet Nature Reserve. Tshipise has a sulphurous spring which supplies water to a number of swimming pools and various spa establishments. There are a hotel, holiday houses, a camping site and a variety of sports facilities.

Tshipise,
Honnet
Nature Reserve

From Tshipise visitors can either join an organised excursion to Honnet Nature Reserve or explore the reserve on foot. The 10km/6 mile long Baobab Trail runs through the reserve, in which, with a bit of luck, you will see not only the mighty baobab trees but giraffes, zebras, antelopes and gazelles.

On Mapungubwe Hill, a flat-topped massif 75km/47 miles west of Messina on R 572, remains of early human settlement have been discovered, including rock drawings, pottery and gold ornaments. The remains of a stone fort date from the 11th century. The Mapungubwe Hill site is being investigated by the University of Pretoria, and visitors are admitted only by prior arrangement.

Mapungubwe Hill

Middelburg

L 4

Province: Eastern Transvaal
Altitude: 1447m/4748ft
Population: 100,000
Distances: 130km/81 miles from Pretoria, 145km/90 miles from
    Johannesburg

Middelburg lies half way between Pretoria and Lydenburg: hence its name. The town was founded in 1866 and developed into an important agricultural, industrial and coal-mining centre. Middelburg itself is of no particular interest, but there are places worth seeing to the north of the town.

Situation and
characteristics

A few buildings survive from the town's early days, among them the White Church, the railway station and the Meyer Bridge, which all date from 1890.

The town

Surroundings of Middelburg

8km/5 miles north of Middelburg on R 35 a road goes off to Fort Merensky (5km/3 miles). The origins of the fort go back to 1865, when Alexander Merensky settled here, charged by the Berlin Missionary Society to establish Botshabelo mission station. The name Botshabelo means "place of refuge". The fort was built by Sotho workmen and shows an interesting mix of African and European ideas. The fort, along with other mission buildings and a Ndebele village, is now an open-air museum (open: daily 9am–5pm).

★Fort Merensky,
Botshabelo
Open-Air Museum

The museum is the starting-point of a number of waymarked hiking trails. Walkers on the Botshabelo Trail (3 hours) are likely to encounter baboons, antelopes and gazelles. The Klein Aasvoelkrans Trail takes 6 hours, the Baboon Trail 8 hours.

45km/28 miles farther north on R 35 is Loskop Dam Nature Reserve. This reservoir was created in 1938 by the construction of a 40m/130ft high dam

Loskop Dam
Nature Reserve

309

An open-air museum near Middelburg introduces visitors to Ndebele culture and the colourful decoration of Ndebele houses

on the Olifants River. Near the reservoir is a lookout from which there are magnificent views of this region of wooded hills. There are bathing and fishing in the reservoir. In the nature reserve surrounding it live rhinos, ostriches, giraffes, zebras, buffaloes, kudus and wildebeests. There is accommodation for visitors in the form of holiday houses and a camping site.

Mkuzi Game Reserve   N 5

Province: KwaZulu/Natal
Altitude: 60–150m/200–500ft
Distances: 60km/37 miles from Hluhluwe, 350km/217 miles from Durban

Situation and
★topography

The Mkuzi Game Reserve (area 34,644 hectares/85,570 acres), established in 1912, is reached from Durban by way of N 2, turning off at an exit (signposted) 35km/22 miles north of Hluhluwe. The reserve is particularly worth visiting for its varied topography and large numbers of birds. It lies in a plain between the Lebombo Mountains on the west and the dense forests bordering the Mkuzi River on the east. Coastal dunes alternate with wooded steppe, gallery forests with open grassland savanna. The original flora has largely been preserved.

★Fauna

Nowhere else in South Africa can such rich bird life within a relatively small area be seen. More than 410 species are represented here, including ten species of heron, cormorants, fish eagles, the rare black-winged plover and saddle-bill storks. Notable among the mammals are the two species of rhinoceros, black and white. There are also large numbers of antelopes (particularly impalas), gazelles, blue wildebeests, giraffes, zebras, hippopotamuses and crocodiles. Elephants are in process of being re-established in the reserve.

In this region, near the east coast of South Africa, it becomes very hot in summer and air humidity is also high. Weather conditions are better in winter, which is also a better time for observing game, since the vegetation is then less dense. The reserve is, however, open throughout the year from sunrise to sunset.

When to visit

It should be borne in mind that there is a malaria risk in this region.

The camp in the reserve has accommodation for visitors in simple huts and rather more comfortable cottages and on a camping site. There is also a filling station. Booking: Natal Parks Board, PO Box 662, Pietermaritzburg 3200, tel. 0331/47 19 81, fax 0331/4 79 61.

Visitor facilities

The reserve can be explored by car on the Auto Trail, a network of tracks with a total length of 80km/50 miles. From the camp an unsurfaced road runs south-east to the Nsumopan, where the reserve's bird life can be observed at close quarters from a viewing platform. The car park is the starting-point of the Mkuzi Fig Forest Walk (3km/2 miles), which crosses a suspension bridge to enter a forest of fig trees. Many of the wild fig trees have a girth of 12m/39ft, and some old trees are 25m/80ft high. The figs ripen at different times on different trees, thus providing food throughout the year for birds and herbivorous animals. If this brief walk gives you a taste for the wilderness you can join an all-day hike led by an experienced game warden.

Drives and hikes

Mmabatho · Mafikeng

H 4

Province: North-West
Population: 13,000
Distances: 280km/174 miles from Johannesburg, 460km/286 miles from Bloemfontein, 1340km/833 miles from Cape Town

Mmabatho, formerly capital of the homeland of Bophuthatswana, has now joined up with Mafikeng to form a single built-up area. Mmabatho was founded only in 1977, when the South African government declared Bophuthatswana, a homeland consisting of a number of separate areas, an independent republic; in 1994, however, it was re-incorporated in South Africa. Mmabatho (a name which in the local Tswana language means "Mother of the People") has the offices of various government agencies, a university (founded 1979), a sports stadium with seating for 60,000 and an airstrip.

Situation and characteristics

Traditional branches of the economy are arable farming (wheat, maize, millet, groundnuts and sunflowers) and cattle-rearing. Mining and industry have gained in importance in recent decades.

Before the first whites crossed the Vaal River in the 1830s much of the territory of the present-day Transvaal provinces was occupied by the Tswana, a Bantu people, who resisted the Boer advance and asked Britain for support. This was not forthcoming until British interests were directly threatened. Britain then established the protectorate of Bechuanaland (now Botswana) and in 1885 made Mafikeng (then called Mafeking), a British settlement founded in 1867, its administrative centre, even though the town lay outside the territory of the protectorate. Mafikeng retained that status until 1965.

History

When the town was besieged by the Boers in 1899–1900 the defence was commanded by Col. Robert Baden-Powell, who established a boys' cadet corps to carry messages and perform other errands. This was the inspiration for the scouting movement which Baden-Powell launched in Britain in 1907.

Mafikeng was incorporated in the homeland of Bophuthatswana in 1980.

The town

The centres of Mafikeng and Mmabatho lie 4km/2½ miles apart. Mmabatho is a town of wide streets and grand official buildings; Mafikeng is rather busier and has preserved a number of historic old buildings, including the Anglican church, which was designed by the famous architect Sir Herbert Baker. The Mafikeng Museum (open: Mon.–Fri. 8am–4pm, Sat. 9am–noon) has interesting material on local history, in particular relics and mementoes of the siege.

Montagu   E 10

Province: Western Cape
Altitude: 223m/732ft
Population: 7500
Distances: 53km/33 miles from Swellendam, 70km/43 miles from Worcester, 170km/106 miles from Cape Town

Situation and characteristics

Montagu would make an attractive stopover for anyone travelling east from Cape Town, and it is within easy reach for an excursion from Swellendam (see entry). To the south of the town is the Langeberg range, to the north the arid landscape of the Little Karoo. Montagu lies in a wine- and fruit-growing area, with apple, pear, apricot and peach trees as far as the eye can see. The nearby thermal springs, with water at a temperature of 43°C/109°F, have been used for 200 years. Montagu has a number of agreeable hotels and a surprisingly wide range of restaurants. It is easy for visitors to forget the time and imagine themselves back in the 19th century.

★The town

Montagu (founded in 1851) is a remarkable pretty little town, with many Cape Dutch and Georgian houses. On Long Street, the town's main street, alone 14 houses have been declared national monuments.

Sights in Montagu

Museum

The former mission church in Long Street now houses the Montagu Museum (open: Mon.–Fri. 9am–1pm and 2–5pm, Sat. and Sun. 10am–noon), with displays illustrating the history of the town and period furniture.

Joubert House

A little way west of the Museum is one of Montagu's finest houses: Joubert House, a Victorian mansion erected in 1853 which is now also a museum (opening times as for Montagu Museum, but closed at weekends).

Lovers' Walk

Lovers' Walk is a charming footpath which runs along the Keisie River for 3km/2 miles to the thermal springs.

Montagu
Hot Springs

On the northern outskirts of the town are the Montagu Hot Springs. The spa buildings round the spring were almost completely destroyed in 1981 by a devastating flood. There is now a comfortable hotel (the Avalon Springs Hotel, with a swimming pool and spa treatment facilities) and more than 100 holiday houses.

Mossel Bay   F 10

Province: Western Cape
Altitude: 76m/249ft
Population: 35,000
Distances: 62km/39 miles from George, 93km/58 miles from Oudtshoorn, 350km/217 miles from Cape Town

The port and holiday resort of Mossel Bay lies at the west end of the beautiful Garden Route (see entry) along the coast of the Indian Ocean. It owes its name to the shells (*mosseln*) which the first Europeans found here in such quantity. Until a few years ago Mossel Bay was one of the most charming places on the Garden Route, with a variety of accommodation for visitors, beautiful beaches within easy reach and a wide range of sports and leisure facilities: now the scene is spoiled by industrial development and the offshore rigs processing the oil and natural gas that were discovered here in the 1980s. But that is only one side of Mossel Bay, which still has its trim villas and holiday houses.

Situation and characteristics

Many of the seafarers who sailed round the Cape anchored in Mossel Bay. The first of them was Bartolomeu Diaz, who set foot on South African soil here in 1488. He was followed in 1497 by Vasco da Gama and in 1501 by the Portuguese Admiral João da Nova, who built a chapel (not preserved) which is believed to have been the first European-style building in South Africa. There was no permanent settlement in the bay until 1787, but thereafter Mossel Bay developed into an important port serving the southern Cape region and the Little Karoo.

History

Sights in Mossel Bay

The 500th anniversary of Bartolomeu Diaz's landing in Mossel Bay was marked by the establishment of a large modern museum complex. The reception and information centre is housed in the Granary (opening times of Granary and museums: Mon.–Fri. 9am–5pm; museums also open Sat. 10am–1pm). The Granary, originally built in 1786, was pulled down in the mid 20th century and rebuilt in its original form in 1986. Facing it is the Maritime Museum, in a building which from 1901 onwards was a grain mill

★Bartolomeu Diaz Museum

In the Mossel Bay museum complex: the milkwood tree used by early seafarers as a "mail-box"

313

and sawmill. The museum's star exhibit is a replica of the caravel in which Diaz rounded the Cape in 1488. The vessel was built in Portugal and sailed into Mossel Bay in 1988. Adjoining this museum is the Shell Museum, with a collection of shells from all over the world on the upper floor and aquarium tanks showing living shellfish in their natural environment on the ground floor. The Munrohoek Cottages, built around 1830 and restored in the mid 1980s, are among the oldest buildings in Mossel Bay (arts and crafts shop).

★Post Office Tree

Outside the Shell Museum is the Post Office Tree, a large milkwood tree beside a spring (still existing) from which ships replenished their water supplies. Mariners sailing east used it as a "letter-box", letters deposited here being collected and delivered by ships on the homeward voyage.

Local History Museum

The nearby Local History Museum in Market Street (open: Mon.–Fri. 9am–1pm and 2–5pm, Sat. 10am–1pm) is also part of the Bartolomeu Diaz museum complex. It is housed in a building of 1858 and a larger extension of 1879.

St Blaize lighthouse

On the Point, a rocky promontory south-east of the town centre, is the St Blaize lighthouse. This is a good place from which to watch whales and dolphins; there is a restaurant and a bar. The St Blaize Trail to Dana Bay (13km/8 miles west) starts at the Bats' Cave, below the lighthouse.

Seal Island

There are excursions from Mossel Bay to Seal Island, home to 2000 seals.

Garden Route

For other places of interest round Mossel Bay see Garden Route.

Mountain Zebra National Park

See Cradock

Namaqualand

C/D 5–8

Provinces: Northern Cape, Western Cape

Location and topography

Namaqualand occupies an area of some 48,000sq.km/18,530sq. miles in the north-west of South Africa, extending from Vanrhynsdorp in the south to the Orange River (here forming the frontier with Namibia) in the north and reaching westward to Pofadder. The southern part of this semi-desertic region is generally flat, the northern part hilly. Rainfall is low throughout Namaqualand – in the coastal areas, washed by the cold Benguela Current, as little as 50mm/2in. annually, and only slightly higher, at up to 200mm/8in., to the east of N 7, which runs through the region from north to south.

★★Wild flowers

The low rainfall nourishes only a sparse covering of vegetation, and in summer the intense heat burns up every trace of green. Visitors travelling through Namaqualand in summer cannot imagine the splendour of blossom that erupts after the winter rains. Between August and October the barren landscape can suddenly be carpeted with flowers. Among the commonest flowers are various species of mesembryanthemum and Compositae (including the Namaqualand daisy). The finest show of blossom is round Springbok, but there are also magnificent displays at various points along N 7. It is not possible to predict exactly when or where the wild flower season will reach its peak, since this depends on the rainfall and climatic conditions, which differ from year to year. Before setting out from Cape Town on the long journey to Springbok it is advisable to ring the "flower hotline" (021/4 18 37 05) to check on the current situation.

After the spring rains the normally barren countryside of Namaqualand is briefly transformed into a sea of flowers

When the first whites settled in Namaqualand in the mid 19th century they came in contact with Bushmen, who were already working the copper ore in the region. The first copper-mine was opened by the new arrivals near Springbok about 1852. The main copper-mining centres are now Okiep and Nababeeb. Namaqualand is also an important diamond-mining area, the first diamonds having been found in 1926 between Port Nolloth and the mouth of the Orange River in Alexander Bay. Diamonds were also found off the coast, and there are now "diamond divers" who, working from boats, suck up the diamond-bearing gravel from the sea floor in pipes. This section of the coast, between Kleinsee and Oranjemund, is a restricted area in which the roads are closed to normal traffic.

Other sources of income in this thinly populated region are fishing and sheep-farming.

Economy

Through Namaqualand

The gateway to southern Namaqualand is Vanrhynsdorp, which is reached from Cape Town on N 7 (300km/185 miles) and is the terminus of the rail line from Cape Town. The town's only tourist attraction is a hothouse containing cactuses and other drought-loving plants. High-quality marble is quarried in the surrounding area.

Vanrhynsdorp

From Vanrhynsdorp R 27 runs west via Vredendal, which is surrounded by irrigated fruit plantations and vineyards, to Strandfontein (78km/48 miles), a coastal town which is a favourite holiday resort for the local farming population (water sports, fishing).

Vredendal, Strandfontein

From Vanrhynsdorp N 7 continues north through an increasingly barren landscape and comes in 190km/118 miles to Kamieskroon, at the foot of the

Kamieskroon

315

Kamiesberg range of grass-covered hills, in an area famed for its show of wild flowers in summer.

Springbok

From Kamieskroon it is 68km/42 miles to Springbok (pop. 8000), "capital" of Namaqualand, named after the springboks which were once common in this area.

★Goegap
Nature Reserve

15km/9 miles south-east of Springbok (most easily reached on R 355) is the Goegap Nature Reserve (area 15,000 hectares/37,000 acres), which is worth a visit even outside the wild flower season. The vegetation in the reserve is typical of Namaqualand, with succulents, shrubs and the bizarre koker-boom tree, and of course a luxuriant show of blossom in spring. Among the larger mammals in the reserve are antelopes and mountain zebras. There is no accommodation for visitors, but there are a number of picnic areas and three short circular hiking trails. The reserve is open daily from sunrise to sunset in August and September; at other times of year it is open only on weekdays.

Port Nolloth

From Steinkopf, 52km/32 miles north of Springbok, a road runs west to Port Nolloth (93km/58 miles), going over the Anenous Pass, from which there are fine views of the coast and the sea. Port Nolloth has a population of around 6000, attracted mainly by the diamonds found in the surrounding area. Other sources of income are fishing (crayfish) and the tourist trade – though the prospects for tourism are restricted by the cold Benguela Current, with a maximum temperature of 16°C/61°F.

Richtersveld
National Park

To the north of Port Nolloth is the Richtersveld National Park (area 162,445 hectares/401239 acres). In order to preserve the delicate ecological balance in this hilly desert region visitors are admitted only in exceptional cases. The area is named after a German missionary who came to this remote region in 1830. There are none of the larger mammals in the National Park, which is of interest mainly for its geological structure and its large numbers of succulents.

Natal Drakensberg

See Drakensberg

Ndumu Game Reserve

Province: KwaZulu/Natal
Distances: 80km/50 miles from Mkuze, 470km/292 miles from Durban

Situation and
★topography

The Ndumu Game Reserve (area 10,000 hectares/25,000 acres), situated in north-eastern Zululand, on the Mozambique border, is one of the most interesting and most attractive in South Africa. It lies on the flood plain of the Pongola River, an expanse of wetland with tropical and subtropical habitats. In summer it is extremely hot in this area, with high air humidity. The rivers which flow through the reserve are lined with gallery forests. There are more than 200 species of trees, including some giant specimens of marula, wild fig trees and the fever tree. Ndumu Hill (115m/377ft) is covered with a forest of acacias.

Fauna

The dense forests and swamps of the reserve are occupied by large numbers of mammals, including hippopotamuses and crocodiles, various species of antelope, cheetahs and zebras. In the wetland areas are large numbers of insects and birds (some 400 species). For many tropical birds from East Africa this is their farthest point south. The animals are sometimes difficult to sight in the dense forest: the best places for seeing them are along the rivers and on the many flood lakes.

The Ndumu Game Reserve is open throughout the year. Between November and March it is oppressively hot; the best time for a visit is between May and July, which are also the best months for bird-watching.

There is accommodation for visitors in a hutted camp (self-catering; provisions can be bought in the village of Ndumu, 5km/3 miles from the reserve; advance booking essential). There are guided walks and land-rover tours of the reserve; individual travellers can tour the reserve only in their car.

Bordering Ndumu Game Reserve on the east is the Tembe Elephant Reserve, home to around 100 elephants. It can be seen only on conducted tours; the numbers of visitors are restricted.

Kosi Bay Nature Reserve

From the village of Ndumu a track runs 70km/43 miles south and then east to the Kosi Bay Nature Reserve (area 10,000 hectares/25,000 acres), on the coast of the Indian Ocean. Here mangrove swamps and swamp woodland surround a freshwater lake and several salt lakes. The fauna includes hippopotamuses, crocodiles and leatherback turtles (an endangered species), as well as 250 species of birds. The sandy and swampy terrain is negotiable only in a four-wheel-drive vehicle. There is simple accommodation for visitors, who can go on guided walks led by game wardens.

Nelspruit

Province: Eastern Transvaal
Altitude: 671m/2202ft
Population: 60,000
Distances: 43km/27 miles from Barberton, 65km/40 miles from Sabie, 355km/221 miles from Johannesburg

For many travellers Nelspruit, situated in the valley of the Crocodile River, is no more than a convenient stopover on the way from Johannesburg to the Kruger National Park (the Numbi Gate of which is only 50km/31 miles away to the north-east). But Nelspruit is also an important agricultural centre. The good soil and temperate climate (warm to hot in summer, pleasantly cool in winter, with no frost) of this area produce rich crops of citrus fruits – a third of South Africa's total exports of oranges come from here – as well as tobacco, litchis, mangoes, avocados, pawpaws, bananas and nuts. Cattle-farming is also increasing in importance.

When the railway (the Eastern Line, running through the valley of the Crocodile River) came to this area in 1892 a station was built on a farm belonging to the Nel family. This was soon followed by shops, a hotel and a police station, and in 1905 Nelspruit was declared a town.

Although Nelspruit has no sights of outstanding interest, it is an attractive town with tree-lined streets and a good base from which to explore the surrounding area.

Sights in and around Nelspruit

On the northern outskirts of Nelspruit (reached by way of R 37) is the Lowveld National Botanic Garden (area 154 hectares/380 acres; open: daily 7am–4.30pm). The Crocodile River flows through the gardens from east to west, forming the impressive Nelspruit Falls; there is a path running along the river. Only a small part of the Botanic Garden (22 hectares/54 acres) is laid out as a garden; in the rest of the area, almost untouched by human hand, grow 500 species of plants native to this area.

Fresh fruit for sale near Nelspruit

★Sudwala Caves

24km/15 miles west of Nelspruit (near the Montrose Falls, where the Crocodile River plunges down 12m/40ft into the Schoemanskloof) R 539 branches off N 4 to run north, leading to the Sudwala Caves. A 600m/650yd long section of this stalactitic cave system, which was occupied by man in prehistoric times, has artificial lighting and is open to visitors (daily 8.30am–4.30pm). The caves have not yet been explored throughout their entire length. There is a constant current of fresh air, the source of which has not been identified, throughout the caves, which have a constant temperature of 17°C/63°F. The caves were used as a munition store by the Boers during the Boer War, and they are said to have been the inspiration for the caverns in Rider Haggard's novels "She" and "King Solomon's Mines".

The Sudwala Caves are worth visiting not only for their magnificent stalactites and stalagmites but also for their beautiful setting, with a lush green wilderness surrounding the entrance to the caves. A good impression of the vegetation of this area can be got on a walk through the nearby Dinosaur Park (open: daily 8am–4.30pm), in which there are almost 40 life-size models of this huge primeval reptiles.

White River

White River (pop. 5000), 19km/12 miles north of Nelspruit, is also a good stopover on the way to the Kruger National Park. It lies 300m/1000ft higher than Nelspruit and has rather less rain – though enough to produce good crops of fruit and vegetables.

Barberton

50km/31 miles south of Nelspruit on R 40 is Barberton (pop. 25,000), which had a brief period of prosperity after gold was discovered here in the late 19th century. By 1888, however, the boom was over and the prospectors turned their attention to the Witwatersrand (see Johannesburg). A number of handsome houses, three of which are open to the public, still bear witness to the town's heyday. Barberton also has a modern museum complex, opened in 1994, which gives a comprehensive picture of the

history, geology, archaeology and ethnology of the region. (Open: Mon.–
Fri. 9am–1pm, 2.30–4.45pm; Sat. 9am–5pm; Sun. 8.30am–noon.)

Nylstroom   K 3

Province: Northern Transvaal
Altitude: 1173m/3849ft. Population: 12,000
Distances: 95km/59 miles from Potgietersrus, 130km/81 miles from
    Pretoria

Nylstroom, 130km/81 miles north of Pretoria and a few miles west of N 1, is   Situation and
the centre of an intensively cultivated agricultural area, producing mainly   characteristics
table grapes, tobacco and groundnuts. The town is said to have been given
its name by the Boers, who in 1866 came upon a spring here which they
believed to be the source of the Nile – a theory which seemed to be
confirmed by the discovery of what they took to be a pyramid. In fact the
"pyramid" was merely a hill which the Bushmen had used as a place of
burial.

Among the town's historic buildings are the Hervormde Kerk (Reformed   The town
Church) of 1889 and Strijdom House, home of Prime Minister J. G. Strijdom, which is now a museum.

Surroundings of Nylstroom

Naboomspruit (pop. 7000), 40km/25 north-east of Nylstroom on N 1, at the   Naboomspruit
foot of the Waterberg range, is another important agricultural centre
(maize, groundnuts, citrus fruits), which also has productive tin-mines and
rich deposits of fluorspar in the surrounding area.
    Naboomspruit is a good base for excursions into the Waterberg, with
beautiful valleys, impressive gorges and a number of thermal springs.

The Nylsvley Nature Reserve (open: daily 6am–6pm; no accommodation   Nylsvley
for visitors), 20km/12½ miles south of Naboomspruit, lies on the flood plain   Nature Reserve
of the Nyl River. In years with a lot of rain 150sq.km/58sq. miles of low-lying
grassland and wooded savanna are flooded, and more than 400 species of
birds then settle here. Various species of antelope can also be observed in
the reserve.

121km/75 miles north-west of Nylstroom (R 517 to Vaalwater, then north-   Lapalala
east on Melk River road) is the Lapalala Wilderness Area, a private reserve   Wilderness Area
taking in 24,000 hectares/60,000 acres of the Waterberg range which is
home to zebras, wildebeests, hippopotamuses, giraffes, antelopes,
gazelles and rhinos. Accommodation for visitors is available in a number of
small camps within the reserve. Canoeing on a 50km/30 mile long stretch of
river; guided hikes led by experienced rangers.

Oribi Gorge Nature Reserve

See Port Shepstone

Oudtshoorn   F 9

Province: Western Cape
Altitude: 335m/1099ft. Population: 52,000
Distances: 59km/37 miles from George, 199km/124 miles from Beaufort
    West, 506km/314 miles from Cape Town

Oudtshoorn

Situation and characteristics

Many visitors following the Garden Route (see entry) make a side trip (70km/43 miles inland) to Oudtshoorn, the world's principal ostrich-breeding centre. Its period of greatest fame was around 1900, when ostrich feathers from Oudtshoorn were sent all over the world. These days of glory are now past, but Oudtshoorn still makes a good living from ostrich farming. Ostrich feathers and ostrich meat find a ready sale, and Oudtshoorn's ostriches have been successfully marketed as a tourist attraction.

Another reason for visiting Oudtshoorn, the largest town on the Little Karoo, is the beauty of the surrounding country. It lies in a fertile valley (tobacco, fruit, vegetables, grain), surrounded by the Swartberg and Outeniqua Mountains.

History

Oudtshoorn was founded in 1847, but its rise to prosperity began in the 1870s, when ostrich feathers were much in demand as a fashion accessory. Between 1880 and 1915 there were anything up to 750,000 ostriches on farms in this area. The ostriches flourished in the warm, dry climate, bringing the "feather barons" unprecedented wealth. After the out-break of the First World War ostrich feathers were no longer in demand in Europe and ostrich farming declined, though it was never entirely abandoned.

The town

Oudtshoorn is a country town of modern aspect, with several large hotels. A number of luxurious mansions (known locally as "feather palaces") have been preserved from the heyday of ostrich farming.

Sights in Oudtshoorn

★★Ostrich farms

A number of ostrich farms in Oudtshoorn offer visitors a conducted tour lasting one or two hours on which they learn all about ostrich breeding. They will be shown round the breeding houses, they will discover how hard the shells of ostrich eggs are (well able to stand the weight of a man) and with luck may see the ostrich chicks emerging from the egg. Other attrac-tions are a ride on an ostrich (not always possible to avoid falling off!) and ostrich races. Tours of this kind are offered, for example, by the Highgate Ostrich Show Farm and the Safari Show Farm (both near R 328, the road to Mossel Bay, some 10km/6 miles south-west of the town centre; open: daily 7.30am–5pm), and the Cango Ostrich Farm, on the road from Oudtshoorn to the Cango Caves.

And when in Oudtshoorn visitors should not miss the opportunity of sampling the delicate lean meat of the ostrich, for example in the Godfather restaurant (61 Voortrekker Road, tel. 22 54 04).

Arbeidsgenot

The house once occupied by C. J. Langenhoven, a lawyer who came to Oudtshoorn in 1899 and composed the South African national anthem here, is now a museum (open: Mon.–Fri. 9am–12.30pm and 2–5.30pm, Sat. 9am–noon).

C. P. Nel Museum

In Oudtshoorn's main street is the C. P. Nel Museum (open: Mon.–Sat. 8.30am–1pm and 2–5pm), housed in a sandstone building of 1907 with a striking bell-tower. Its collections range from artifacts illustrating the cul-ture of the Bushmen to fashionable costumes with ostrich feathers and domestic equipment.

Cango Crocodile Ranch and Cheetahland

On the outskirts of the town (on R 328, the road to the Cango Caves) is the Cango Crocodile Ranch and Cheetahland (open: daily 8am–5pm; restau-rant), with over 300 crocodiles as well as snakes, cheetahs, lions and leopards, ponies and hippopotamuses.

An ostrich farm near Oudtshoorn ▶

The World's Biggest Bird

Oudtshoorn is South Africa's ostrich farming centre. Some ostrich farms welcome visitors, who can thus learn about ostrich breeding at first hand and can even have a ride on an ostrich.

The African mhou or ostrich (*Struthio camelus*) originally came from the steppes of Central Asia. It now exists in four sub-species in the hot and arid savannas of Africa. Some 98% of all farm-bred ostriches – about 250,000 – live in South Africa, and another 8000 in Namibia, Zimbabwe, Tanzania and Botswana. The largest numbers outside Africa are in the hot climatic zones of the United States (30,000), Israel (8000) and Australia (5000). During the 1990s there have been experiments in ostrich farming in colder regions such as Canada, Japan and Europe.

There are now very few wild ostriches in Africa south of the Sahara. Until the First World War South African ostrich farmers made fortunes from ostrich feathers (until the age of 15 ostriches grow a kilogram of feathers – just over 2 pounds – within nine months). Then ostrich feathers went out of fashion and the market collapsed. Recently, after decades of stagnation, ostrich farming has taken on a new lease of life. There is still not much of a market for ostrich feathers, but ostrich eggs are now in demand, either as a souvenir or for eating (one ostrich egg is the equivalent of 24 hens' eggs!).

Ostrich meat is also steadily gaining in popularity (a farm-bred ostrich is ready for eating at the age of 15 months). After being successfully marketed in the United States, France and Switzerland it is now also available in Britain. An ostrich will yield something like 15 kilograms (33 pounds) of steaks. In colour, texture and taste ostrich meat is similar to the best beef and can be prepared in the same way. Like poultry, it has the advantage over red meat of being very lean (1% fat) and low in protein, cholesterol and calories but still delicate and tasty.

The Kalahari truffle is claimed to be the ideal accompaniment to ostrich meat, and this too is now available on the international market.

Even more valuable than ostrich meat is the ostrich's fine-grained hide, which is made into purses, handbags, belts and many other articles.

An adult farm-bred ostrich is thus a very valuable property which can bring in good money. At present some 50,000 birds are sold annually in South Africa, and it is a rising market.

What sort of a bird is the ostrich?

First, the statistics. The ostrich is the largest living bird. It can reach a height of 3.10m/10ft and a weight of 100kg/220lb. Over short distances it can run at up to 80km/50 miles an hour and is thus the fastest living biped, with a stride, when running, of up to 4m/13ft. Because of its very powerful muscles and consequent weight the ostrich can neither fly nor glide.

The female ostrich lays the largest eggs of any bird. A single egg weighs around 1.6kg/3½lb; it is 16cm/6¼in. long by 13cm/5in. across, and the shell is 2mm thick (the thickness of a porcelain cup). A hammer is needed to open an ostrich egg. When the young ostrich emerges from the egg it weighs at least 1kg/2¼lb.

The ostrich also has the longest intestines of any bird. The colon alone is 15m/50ft long (compared with 1.8m/6ft in man, in a state of rest). The male ostrich has a penis which emerges for the purpose of mating and retracts after copulation. (In most species of birds, particularly songbirds, the males – like the females, and the female ostrich – have only a cloaca, a cavity in the pelvic region into which the genital duct opens.)

The loose plumage of the ostrich is black in the male, with the exception of a white ruff round the

Ostrich chicks in an incubator

neck and the white or brownish wing and tail feathers, and brown in the female. The foot has only two toes. Ostriches feed mainly on plants but also eat small animals. They are either monogamous or polygamous, depending on population numbers.

In general ostriches – which can live to the age of 40 – are not aggressive, but if they feel threatened they can become belligerent. An unwelcome intruder will be greeted by a roar, not unlike that of a lion, and if this is not sufficient to get rid of him the ostrich will show his skill as an exponent of the martial arts. A blow with his foot can break an opponent's bones. When it is a question of protecting his young the male ostrich will show no mercy, for he is a very protective father. When he is in his natural habitat, the open savanna, he can be observed holding his wings over the young ostriches running beside him in order to protect them from the sun, while the young scurry to keep up with him.

The female ostrich has nothing to do with the bringing up of her young. She is not allowed to; for as soon as the young ostriches emerge from the egg the male ostrich takes over, chasing the mother away from the young, since he is better able to protect them. He does not have to feed them, for the day after they hatch they are able to forage for seeds and insects on their own. His job is to take them to good feeding grounds and protect them from enemies, of which they have more than enough. One danger which threatens them is dying of cold – a fate which may befall them while still in the egg. The old birds, both male and female, sit on the eggs for 45 or 46 days. There are usually between 21 and 25 eggs in the nest, but there may be as many as 30 or more; and on cold nights the eggs at the edge of the nest may die of hypothermia. The eggs may also fall prey to lions, hyenas or vultures, which are fond of this high-protein food. And occasionally a herd of buffaloes may reduce the brood to scrambled eggs, or a steppe fire to boiled eggs. In the face of all these hazards the success rate of the breeding process is relatively low – statistically, 0.9 ostrich chick per nest, compared with a 75% success rate on ostrich farms.

This is no doubt the explanation for the curious marital habits of ostriches. During the breeding season a male ostrich will have a principal wife and two to four subsidiary wives (the ostrich population has an excess of females over males). He impregnates them all, and they lay up to six eggs each in a single nest. But the females also lay eggs in several neighbouring nests, so that even if the main brood is lost there will still be

Baedeker Special

some eggs in other nests. Thus the polygamy of the male is matched by the polygamy of the female, and as a result there will be many nests with illegitimate "cuckoo's eggs" in them.

After hatching, the ostrich chicks, like all young animals, attract the attentions of predators; and it is remarkable that the male's protective instinct is not confined to his own brood. When a male ostrich with his brood of young ones meets another male similarly accompanied he tries to drive him off and take over his brood. Fathers with as many as a hundred children have sometimes been observed. Sometimes, too, several males with their broods join to form a "creche", the guardians of which may not even be related to the young ones.

Ostriches are not alone in their mating habits and the "maternal" instincts of the male. Similar behaviour patterns are found in other large flightless birds, such as the nandus of South America and the emus and cassowaries of Australia (the cassowaries at least in the bringing up of the young).

And what about the tale that when danger threatens the ostrich buries its head in the sand? The origin of this legend is the female ostrich's way of protecting her brood from attack. She seeks to camouflage the nest with her brownish plumage by lying on top of it, extending her wings and pressing her long neck and head on to the ground so that it looks like a dead branch. Usually the trick is successful: the nest escapes notice and the brood remains unharmed.

Surroundings of Oudtshoorn

★★Cango Caves

27km/17 miles north of Oudtshoorn, at the foot of the Great Swartberg, are the impressive Cango Caves, with magnificent stalactites and stalagmites. Visitors are taken on a conducted tour of the cave system for a distance of 2km/1¼ miles, taking about an hour (tours daily at 9 and 11am and 1 and 3pm). There is a restaurant and a cafeteria.

In earlier centuries the caves, which have a constant temperature of 18°C/64°F, were occupied by Bushmen, who left rock drawings, little of which can now be distinguished, as evidence of their presence. At the entrance to the caves is a tableau depicting the life of the Bushmen. The conducted tour takes visitors into a series of huge chambers with impressive stalactites and stalagmites, the effect of which is enhanced by spectacular lighting effects. The Van Zyl Hall is named after the man who first ventured into the darkness of the caves in 1780. This enormous chamber (70m/230ft long, 35m/115ft wide and up to 17m/56ft high), brilliantly flood-lit, has room for 1000 people. It has excellent acoustics, and concerts are occasionally given here.

Other caves, known as Cango II, III and IV, with a total length of over 2200m/2400yd, were discovered in 1972. To protect their delicate ecological system, they are not open to the public.

★Swartberg Pass

Beyond the Cango Caves the road climbs to the Swartberg Pass. The Swartberg range, which forms the boundary between the Little and the Great Karoo, extends for a length of 200km/125 miles, with heights of up to 2326m/7628ft. Of the three passes through the range the Swartberg is the

An ostrich ride   *In the Cango Caves, near Oudtshoorn*

most spectacular. The road (not completely asphalted, but in dry weather negotiable by ordinary cars without difficulty) was built in 1881–88. After almost every bend there is a magnificent view, and the vegetation is equally fascinating, with a profusion of proteas. Beyond the pass (1568m/5145ft) the landscape changes, and the road eventually enters a narrow gorge with a lush growth of vegetation.

70km/43 miles from Oudtshoorn the road comes to Prince Albert (pop. 4500), named after Queen Victoria's consort. Mountain streams supply an abundance of water for the fruit plantations round the little town (peaches harvested in January, wine grapes in March).

Prince Albert

The Museum in Church Street, once the home of the Haak family, has a collection of Bibles, furniture, domestic equipment, weapons, old vehicles and tools.

Meiringspoort is the lowest (716m/2349ft) and fastest of the three passes in the Swartberg range. N 12 (Oudtshoorn to Beaufort West) runs through a 20km/12½ mile long gorge with folded sandstone formations.

Meiringspoort

35km/22 miles south-west of Oudtshoorn (R 62, signposted to Calitzdorp, and in 12km/7½ miles left into track to Warmbad) is the Gamka Mountain Nature Reserve (area 9400 hectares/23,200 acres), in which the rare mountain zebra can be seen, as well as antelopes, gazelles, caracals and 80 species of birds, including Verreaux's eagle.

Gamka Mountain
Nature Reserve

There is a small visitor centre (open: daily 7am–7pm) which can supply information about walking in the reserve, from short walks to two-day hikes. Cars must be parked at the visitor centre; no accommodation for visitors.

Paarl   D 10

Province: Western Cape
Altitude: 145m/476ft.
Population: 88,000
Distances: 46km/29 miles from Worcester, 60km/37 miles from Cape Town

Situation and characteristics

Paarl lies on the banks of the Berg River in a broad fertile valley under the Paarl Mountain (729m/2392ft). The name Paarl ("Pearl") comes from a large granite crag which gleams like a pearl when it is caught by the sun after a fall of rain. The fruit and vegetables grown in the surrounding area are processed in canning factories in the town.

Paarl is one of the leading wine-producing centres in South Africa, with six wineries round the town and ten wine-making cooperatives. In the town are the headquarters of KWV (Kooperatieve Wijnbouwers Vereeniging), the largest wine cooperative in South Africa (established 1918), which controls almost the whole of South African wine production.

History

The first Europeans settled in this area in 1687, soon to be followed by Huguenot refugees from France, who introduced wine production. The town was officially founded in 1717, making it one of the oldest European settlements in the hinterland of Cape Town.

The town played an important part in the development of Afrikaans as the official language of South Africa. A society was formed in the town in 1875 to regularise the grammar and vocabulary of the language, and the first Afrikaans newspaper, "Die Afrikaanse Patriot", began to appear in Paarl on January 15th 1876.

★The town

Paarl is a quiet and attractive town. Its oldest street (Main Street), 11km/7 miles long and lined by oak-trees, was laid out in 1720; it has preserved a number of historic old buildings.

Sights in Paarl

Strooidakkerk

The Strooidakkerk ("straw-roofed church") in Main Street, built in 1805, is one of the oldest churches in South Africa still in use.

Oude Pastorie

The Oude Pastorie (Old Parsonage) at 303 Main Street, built in 1787 and renovated in 1939, is now a museum (open: Mon.–Fri. 8am–1pm and 2–5pm, Sat. 10am–noon, Sun. 3–5pm), with a fine collection of Cape Dutch antiques, silver, copperware, brass, porcelain and glass, textiles of Huguenot origin and Afrikaner culture.

Afrikaans Language Museum

Close by, in Gideon Malherbe House, is the Afrikaans Language Museum. Here in 1875 was founded the Genootskap van Regte Afrikaners (Association of True Afrikaners), a society for the promotion of Afrikaans, and here too, in the following year, the first Afrikaans newspaper, "Die Afrikaanse Patriot", was published. The Museum (open: Mon.–Fri. 9am–1pm and 2–5pm) illustrates the development of the language.

Kooperatieve Wijnbouwers Vereeniging (KWV)

The KWV Cellars are in a large building in Cape Dutch style in Kohler Street. There are interesting conducted tours (Mon.–Fri. at 9.30 and 11am and 2.15 and 3.45pm; tel. 02211/7 30 08 to reserve a place) which tell visitors all about wine-making and give them an opportunity of sampling the product.

Surroundings of Paarl

Paarl Wine Route

A signposted Wine Route leads to various wineries where wines can be tasted and bought. A map and guide booklet can be obtained from the Paarl Valley Publicity Association, 251 Main Street, tel. 02211/2 38 29.

A gabled house in Paarl   *The Taal Monument*

Prominently situated on Paarl Mountain, to the west of the town centre (reached by way of Jan Philips Mountain Drive), is the 57m/187ft high Taal Monument (open: May to October daily 9am–6pm, November to April daily 8am–8pm). The design of the monument, which was inaugurated in 1975, was the work of the architect Jan van Wyk and the writers C. J. Langenhoven and N. P. van Wyk Louw. It symbolises the contributions made by Africa, the Netherlands and Britain to the development of the Afrikaans language. From the monument there are fine panoramic views.

Taal Monument

A visit to the Taal Monument can be combined with a walk in the Paarl Mountain Nature Reserve (area 2000 hectares/5000 acres). From the Britannia Rock (649m/2129ft) there are beautiful views of the surrounding country.
    Adjoining the nature reserve, finely situated on the slopes of the hill, is the small Meulwater Wild Flower Reserve, with some 200 species of indigenous plants. It is particularly beautiful in late spring, when the flowers are in their many-coloured glory.

Paarl Mountain Nature Reserve

7km/4½ miles east of Paarl, beyond the Berg River and on the fringes of the Klein Drakenstein Mountains, is the famous Nederburg winery. Here every year is held a great wine auction at which South Africa's finest wines are sold. The winery was originally established by Philip Wolvaart, an immigrant of German origin who bought the farm in 1792. The mansion, in Cape Dutch style, was built about 1800.
    The vineyards and winery can be seen by appointment (tel. 02211/ 62 31 04).
    Nearby is the Paarl Rock Brandy Cellar (conducted tours Mon.–Fri. at 11am and 3pm; tel. 62 61 59).

★Nederburg

Laborie, at the foot of Paarl Mountain, was formerly a sumptuous mansion and a famous wine estate; it now belongs to KWV. The wine made here can

Other wineries

be tasted in the house. There are other wineries west and north of the town, among them Fairview and Rhebokskloof.

Wellington

20km/12½ miles north of Paarl, at the foot of Bain's Kloof, is Wellington (pop. 26,000). Situated in a fertile fruit-growing region, it is the main centre in South Africa for the production of dried fruit. There are also a number of wineries in the area where the local wines can be bought.

The first settlers here, in 1688, were Huguenots, who called the area Limiet Valley (the "farthest valley"). Thereafter the settlement grew slowly. It was given its present name in 1840 in honour of the Duke of Wellington.

The Wellington Museum has a collection of material illustrating the history of the town and the valley, with a section devoted to the development of education. There is also a good collection of Egyptian antiquities in the Huguenot University College. Other features of interest are the beautiful Victoria Jubilee Park and the Old Blockhouse, a relic of the Boer War which is now a national monument.

★ Bain's Kloof Pass

From Paarl R 303 runs north-east, through magnificent scenery, to Ceres, going over Bain's Kloof Pass (595m/1952ft). This 30km/19 mile long road, built in 1853, is still one of the finest pass roads in South Africa, offering marvellous views of Paarl, Wellington and Swartland.

Phalaborwa   M 2

Province: Northern Transvaal
Altitude: 445m/1460ft
Population: 11,000
Distances: 114km/71 miles from Tzaneen, 75km/47 miles from Hoedspruit, 200km/125 miles from Skukuza

Situation and characteristics

For many travellers Phalaborwa, which has an airport, is no more than a stopover for a visit to the central part of the Kruger National Park (the entrance gate to which is only 3km/2 miles east). Summer temperatures of around 38°C/100°F and an average annual rainfall of around 457mm/18in. make Phalaborwa a garden city.

Phalaborwa is the commercial, administrative and recreational centre of a mining area which has massive deposits of phosphates, copper and iron. Zirconium, vermiculite, mica and gold are also worked in the area. Some 2000 million years ago tectonic movements in the earth's crust forced a great mass of magma to the surface, creating a treasurehouse of minerals which has brought prosperity to the region. The rich mineral deposits were already being worked in prehistoric times, as is evidenced by a nearby excavation site in the Kruger National Park (see entry).

The town

Phalaborwa's wide streets are lined by trees and gardens; but this is only one side of the picture. The mining areas on the outskirts of the town are like a lunar landscape. A man-made crater with a greater diameter than Kimberley's Big Hole reaches down to well below sea level. The sulphur which is a by-product of the copper-mining process gives the earth a yellowish tinge.

Pietermaritzburg   L 7

Province: KwaZulu/Natal
Altitude: 613m/2011ft
Population: 134,000
Distances: 79km/49 miles from Durban, 509km/316 miles from Johannesburg, 555km/349 miles from Bloemfontein

City Hall, Pietermaritzburg ▶

Pietermaritzburg

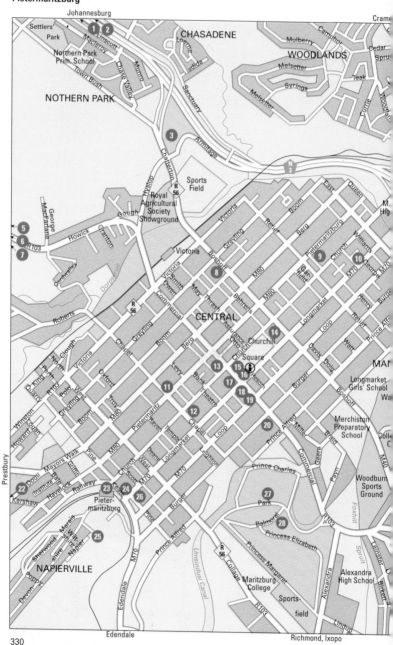

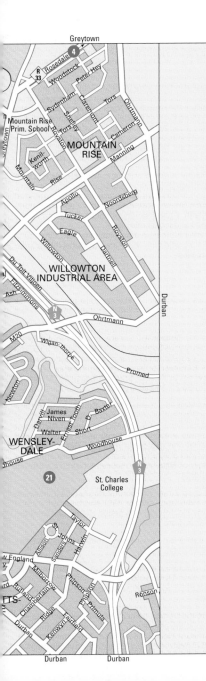

Pietermaritzburg

NORTHERN PARK

1 Howick Falls
2 Midmar Dam and
   Nature Reserve
3 Bird Sanctuary
4 Albert Falls
   Public Resort and
   Nature Reserve
5 Queen Elizabeth Park
6 World's View
7 Wylie Park
8 Voortrekker House
9 Main Muslim Mosque
10 Hindu temples
11 Victorian House
12 St Peter's Church
13 Old Colonial Building
14 Voortrekker Museum
   and Memorial Church
15 City Hall
16 Pietermaritzburg
   Publicity House
17 Tatham Art Gallery
18 Post Office
19 Natal Museum
20 St Mary's Church
21 Scottville Race Course
22 Botanic Gardens
23 Railway Station
24 Old Government House
25 Fort Napier
26 Macrorie House Museum
27 Fleamarket
28 Alexandra Park
29 Comrades Marathon
   House Museum
30 Oribi Airport
31 University of Natal

500 m

© *Baedeker*

Pietermaritzburg

Situation and characteristics	Pietermaritzburg, capital of the province of KwaZulu/Natal, lies in a fertile agricultural region. It is the seat of South Africa's Supreme Court and of the University of Natal, and is also an important industrial and commercial centre.
History	Pietermaritzburg was founded in 1838, after the Boer victory over the Zulus in the battle of Blood River, and named after the two Boer leaders, Pieter Retief and Gerrit Maritz. When the republic of Natal was established in the following year Pietermaritzburg became its capital. After the annexation of the republic by Britain the headquarters of British administration was moved to Pietermaritzburg (1843), a garrison was stationed here and Fort Napier was built. The town later became capital of the British colony of Natal and in 1910 the seat of government of the province of Natal.
★The town	Pietermaritzburg is abundantly supplied with parks and gardens and with historic buildings, now protected as national monuments or museums, and has preserved much of its British colonial architecture and atmosphere. In 1990 Church Street became an attractive pedestrian precinct and shopping mall with a great variety of shops, including a very well-known bookshop, and handsome buildings.
	The city centre can be seen on foot, in a tour starting from City Hall in Churchill Square, immediately adjoining which are the tourist information bureau and car parking facilities.

Sights in the City Centre

City Hall	The City Hall (now a national monument) is claimed to be the largest brick building south of the Equator. It has a 47m/154ft high bell-tower and magnificent stained glass.
Tatham Art Gallery	Opposite the City Hall is the Tatham Art Gallery, installed in 1990 in a building which was occupied by the Supreme Court from 1906 to 1983. The gallery (open: Tues.–Sun. 10am–6pm) has a remarkable collection of work by 19th and 20th century European artists, including pictures by Corot, Sisley and Sickert and drawings by Picasso, Braque, Chagall and Moore, as well as a large collection of South African art.
★Natal Museum	The Natal Museum (open: Mon.–Sat. 9am–4.30pm, Sun. 2–5pm) in Loop Street, to the south of the City Hall, is one of South Africa's five National Museums. The building dates from 1905. The Museum has collections of South African mammals, birds, amphibians, insects and molluscs as well as valuable palaeontological and geological material. The ethnological department has artefacts from different parts of Africa. There are also a room devoted to the history of Natal and a reconstruction of a Victorian street, with houses and shops.
Macrorie House	To the south-west, along Loop Street, is Macrorie House (1862), in which Bishop William Macrorie lived from 1869 to 1891 and installed a small chapel. It is now a museum of Victoriana, with period clothes and furniture (open: Tues.–Thur. 9am–1pm, Sun. 11am–4pm).
Old Government House	Another impressive building is Old Government House (1860), once the residence of the Governor of Natal.
Old Colonial Building	From the railway station, a Victorian brick building, Church Street (partly pedestrianised) runs north-east. The most striking building in this street is the handsome Old Colonial Building of 1899, which housed various offices of the colonial government.
Voortrekker House	This has brought us back to the starting-point of the tour, but there are two other sights still to be seen in the city centre. To the north-west, in Boom Street (No. 333), is Voortrekker House (open: Mon.–Fri. 9am–5pm, Sat. 9am–12.30pm), built in 1847 (restored). This is the only surviving building

Tatham Gallery, Pietermaritzburg

of the pioneering period in Pietermaritzburg, with period furniture. Note particularly the yellowwood ceilings.

A few hundred yards south-east are the Voortrekker Museum and the Church of the Vow, which forms part of the museum complex (open: Mon.–Fri. 9am–4pm, Sat. 8am–noon). The church was built by the Boers in 1841 to commemorate their victory over the Zulus in the battle of Blood River. Beside it is the thatched two-storey house of Andries Pretorius, commander of the Boer forces in the battle. The museum displays mementoes of the voortrekkers, including a replica of a trek wagon. In the forecourt are statues of Pieter Retief and Gerrit Maritz, the Boer leaders after whom the town is named.

Voortrekker Museum, Church of the Vow

Sights outside the City Centre

The town's principal mosque is in Church Street, to the north of the city centre. It can be visited daily 9am–1pm and 1.30–5pm.

Mosque

The two Hindu temples (in Longmarket Street, to the east of the mosque), Sri Siva Soobramoniar and Mariammen, are the religious centres of the town's Indian inhabitants. Annually on Good Friday a festival, with fireworks, is celebrated here.

Hindu temples

In a restored Victorian house south-east of the city centre is a museum illustrating the history of the South African Marathon.

Marathon House Museum

On the south side of the city centre is Alexandra Park (area 65 hectares/ 160 acres), with an abundance of flowers, shrubs, aloes and succulents. It also has a splendid bandstand of 1890. In the annual Art in the Park show in May South African artists display their work. There is a flea market in the park on the first Sunday in the month.

Alexandra Park

Fort Napier	Farther south is Fort Napier, built in 1843 as a British headquarters, which preserves a number of guns and other military exhibits (open: daily 2.30–4pm). The military cemetery dates from the same period as the fort. The garrison church of St George (1897) also displays mementoes of the British garrison.
Wylie Park	In Taunton Road, to the west of the city centre, is Wylie Park, with many indigenous plants, including proteas, and exotic azaleas, which put on a glorious show of blossom in spring.
Botanic Gardens	The Botanic Gardens have separate sections for indigenous and exotic plants. Some of the trees are of great age.

Surroundings of Pietermaritzburg

Queen Elizabeth Park	Queen Elizabeth Park (area 100 hectares/250 acres; open: daily 5am–7pm in summer, 6am–6pm in winter), 8km/5 miles north of the city, has a luxuriant growth of vegetation, including aloes and proteas, and many species of birds. Good walks; picnic spots.
★World's View	World's View is a viewpoint 18km/5 miles north-west of Pietermaritzburg on the old road to Howick (which rejoins N 3 at Hilton). From the top of the hill (1083m/3553ft) there is a magnificent view of the city. The old voortrekkers' road can be seen winding its way up the hill (picnic spots).
★Howick Falls	The impressive Howick Falls, 119m/360ft high (near the town of that name, 25km/15 miles north of Pietermaritzburg), are the most striking feature in the Umgeni Valley Nature Reserve, which attracts thousands of visitors every year. The reserve contains more than 200 species of birds, as well as giraffes, zebras, wildebeests and many species of antelope. There are hiking trails along the river; some accommodation for visitors.
★Midmar Public Nature Reserve	In the Inhluanza Hills, to the west of Howick, is the Midmar Public Nature Reserve (area 2844 hectares/7025 acres), within which is the Midmar Dam, a favourite haunt of water sports enthusiasts and anglers. Visitors can observe – from a boat or a cross-country vehicle – white rhinos, zebras, wildebeests, antelopes and water birds. There is good walking and riding in the reserve, which also has tennis, boccia and squash courts, a swimming pool, a children's playground, camping sites and a restaurant. Accommodation for visitors is available in chalets and huts. Near the reserve is Midmar Historical Village, with an exhibition of mementoes of pioneering days. There is also a smithy, a typical Zulu village, old steam locomotives and agricultural implements.
Albert Falls Nature Reserve	23km/14 miles north-east of Pietermaritzburg, on the road to Greytown, is the Albert Falls Nature Reserve (area 3012 hectares/7440 acres; open throughout the year). Here, in a beautiful setting, is a lake fringed with vegetation, with excellent opportunities for bird-watching, sailing, rowing and picnicking. There are also hiking trails and a riding arena. The fauna consists mainly of zebras and various species of antelope and gazelle. There is accommodation for visitors in two camps with well equipped chalets.

Pietersburg   L 2

Province: Northern Transvaal
Altitude: 1280m/4200ft. Population: 43,000
Distance: 717km/446 miles from Bloemfontein, 117km/73 miles from Louis Trichardt, 206km/128 miles from Phalaborwa, 319km/198 miles from Johannesburg

Pietersburg, capital of the province of Northern Transvaal and its largest town, lies 319km/198 miles north-east of Johannesburg on N 1. It is a favourite stopover on the way to the Kruger National Park and the beautiful Tzaneen region. Founded in 1884, the town rapidly developed into the commercial and administrative centre of an intensively cultivated agricultural area. Round Pietersburg are some of the largest cattle farms in South Africa.

Situation and characteristics

This busy modern town has no sights of outstanding interest, but there are a number of attractive features in the surrounding area. Pietersburg has an excellent tourist infrastructure.

Sights in Pietersburg

Pietersburg has two interesting museums. In Vorster Street is the Irish House Museum, with collections of material illustrating the cultural history of the region.

Irish House Museum

The Dutch Reformed church, recently restored, now houses the Hugh Exton Photographic Museum, with a collection of photographs by the photographer of that name, who lived in Pietersburg. Many of his photographs are of historical as well as artistic interest.

Hugh Exton Photographic Museum

Surroundings of Pietersburg

15km/3 miles south of the town centre is the Pietersburg Municipal Game Reserve (area 3200 hectares/8000 acres; open: daily 7am–6pm in summer, 8am–5pm in winter), with a varied flora and fauna (rhino, zebra. antelopes, gazelles, etc.).

Pietersburg Municipal Game Reserve

Adjoining the Game Reserve is Union Park, with a lake (fishing permitted), picnic spots, a camping site and a number of holiday cottages.

Union Park

9km/5½ miles south of Pietersburg on R 37 is the Bakone Malapa Open-Air Museum (open: Mon. 8.15am–12.30pm, Tues.–Fri. 8.15–11am and 12.30–3.15pm), which is centred on a traditional North Sotho village still occupied by members of the tribe, who sell various craft products to tourists. Background information can be obtained in the visitor centre. Within the museum complex are archaeological sites with remains of iron- and copper-smelting installations, as well as rock paintings of around 1000 B.C.

★Bakone Malapa Open-Air Museum

60km/37 miles from Pietersburg N 1 comes to a column marking the position of the Tropic of Capricorn (lat. 23°27′ south), where the sun is vertically overhead at the summer solstice.

Tropic of Capricorn

Half way between Pietersburg and Potgietersrus, on the north side of N 1, is the Percy Fyfe Nature Reserve (area 3462 hectares/8551 acres), famed as a breeding centre for rare and endangered species of antelope, such as the sassaby, the roan antelope and the sable antelope. The animals bred here are then released in other areas. Visitors can look round the reserve only when accompanied by members of the staff.

Percy Fyfe Nature Reserve

Potgietersrus, 43km/27 miles south-west of Pietersburg, is the centre of an agricultural and mining region in which chromium, platinum, tin and asbestos are worked on a large scale. This attractive little town is named after Pieter Potgieter, a Boer commander who was killed in a battle with supporters of Chief Tlou Makapan in 1854. The town was abandoned for some years but was reoccupied in 1890.

Potgietersrus

Game in one of South Africa's many game reserves

The Arend Dieperink Museum in Voortrekker Road (open: Mon.–Fri. 8am–4.30pm, Sat. 9am–1pm, Sun. 2–5pm) has an interesting collection of material on the history of the region.

On the northern outskirts of the town is the Potgietersrus Nature Reserve and Game-Breeding Centre (open: Mon.–Fri. 8am–4pm, Sat. and Sun. 8am–6pm) with antelopes, gazelles, blue wildebeests, steppe zebras, Hartmann's mountain zebras, impalas and white rhinos, as well as the relatively rare pygmy hippopotamus. Visitors can drive through the reserve in their own car.

Pilgrim's Rest   M 3

Province: Eastern Transvaal
Altitude: 1255m/4118ft
Population: 1600
Distances: 55km/34 miles from Lydenburg, 90km/56 miles from Nelspruit

Situation and characteristics

Visitors staying in the Transvaal Drakensberg region (see Blyderivierspoort Nature Reserve) should not miss the chance of seeing the little town of Pilgrim's Rest, at the foot of the Mauchberg (2115m/6939ft).

History

In 1873 Alec Patterson and William Trafford struck gold in the little stream now known as Pilgrim's Creek, and the news of their find brought other prospectors flocking to the area. Over the years their claims were bought up by mining companies, and eventually the Transvaal Gold Mining Estate was established. Pilgrim's Rest meanwhile grew into a small town with a church, a school and its own newspaper. Mining operations finally ceased in 1971.

Pilgrim's Rest, now preserved in its entirety as a national monument, retains the atmosphere of gold-digging days

In 1972 the town and the gold workings were bought by the provincial government and carefully restored, and this old gold-diggers' town is now an open-air museum, with many houses containing authentic furniture and furnishings, shops, the Royal Hotel (still offering accommodation for visitors), a bank and the office of the "Pilgrim's Rest and Sabie News". A plan of the town showing all the most interesting buildings can be obtained from the information centre in the main street, which is open daily 9am–12.45pm and 1.15–4.30pm. Most of the museums are also open at these times.

★The town

Surroundings of Pilgrim's Rest

10km/6 miles west of Pilgrim's Rest a narrow side road runs south to Mount Sheba Nature Reserve (area 1500 hectares/3750 acres), centred on the 1958m/6424ft high Mount Sheba.

Mount Sheba
Nature Reserve

10km/6 miles from the entrance, in the centre of the reserve, is the Mount Sheba Hotel. There are numerous hiking trails through this region of wooded hills, with a varied flora, impressive waterfalls and beautiful viewpoints. A leaflet on the hiking trails can be obtained from the hotel or the information bureau.

One of the high spots of a visit to South Africa is a drive through the Blyde River Canyon, north-east of Pilgrim's Rest (see Blyderivierspoort Nature Reserve).

Blyde River
Canyon

The road to Sabie runs past the impressive Mac Mac Falls (see Sabie).

Mac Mac Falls

337

Plettenberg Bay   G 10

Province: Western Cape
Altitude: 73m/240ft
Population: 10,000
Distances: 142km/88 miles from Mossel Bay, 210km/130 miles from Port
  Elizabeth

Situation and
★★beaches

Plettenberg Bay has developed into one of the most popular bathing
resorts on the Garden Route (see entry), thanks to the marvellous beaches
which extend for almost 12km/7½ miles round the town, many of them
particularly suitable for children. The sun is claimed to shine on 320 days in
the year at Plettenberg Bay, and the temperature of the sea is around
20°C/68°F throughout the year. These advantages have attracted many
South Africans to build luxurious holiday homes here, while for visitors
there are numerous hotels, guest houses and camping sites. During the
main holiday season in summer the 10,000 inhabitants of the town are
outnumbered by anything up to 50,000 visitors. There are fewer visitors
between February and April, and since during these months weather conditions are usually ideal that is the best time to choose for a visit.

The Portuguese navigator Mesquita da Perestrelo, who anchored in the
bay in 1576, originally named it Bahia Formosa ("Beautiful Bay"). Its present name comes from the governor of the Dutch colony, Joachim van
Plettenberg, who visited the region in 1778.

Surroundings of Plettenberg Bay

Beacon Island

Beacon Island, just off the coast near the town centre, is now linked with the
mainland. A Norwegian whaling station was established on the island in

One of the endless sandy beaches round Plettenberg Bay

1912; it was abandoned in 1920 but some of its buildings remain. In 1972 a new, spectacularly situated hotel was opened on the peninsula, offering magnificent views of the bay and the open sea. Many whales are to be seen here between July and September, when they come to this sheltered bay to give birth to their young.

From Plettenberg Bay a secondary road runs 9km/5½ miles south-east to Robberg Nature Reserve, on a 4km/2½ mile long peninsula at the foot of the Mountain of the Seal. The reserve is a breeding-place for many water birds, and dolphins and whales play off the coast. Within the reserve is a large cave which was occupied by prehistoric man. Information about the local flora and fauna can be obtained from the visitor centre at the car park, which is the starting-point of a number of hiking trails, ranging in length between 2 and 11km (1¼ and 7 miles) and passing many picnic spots. The reserve is open daily 7am–6pm.

★Robberg
Nature Reserve

Keurbooms Nature Reserve (open: daily 8am–6pm) lies 7km/4½ miles north-east of Plettenberg Bay, near N 2. The banks of the Keurbooms River are lined by dense forest, while on the hills fynbos vegetation predominates. In addition to large numbers of birds there are wild pigs, monkeys and antelopes to be seen in the reserve. A short hiking trail (about 1 hour) runs along the river; but it is even better to explore the reserve in a canoe (which can be hired).

Keurbooms River
Nature Reserve

Farther east is Nature's Valley, an idyllic holiday resort lying between the sea and the hills. The whole town lies within a nature reserve. This the starting-point of the Tsitsikamma Hiking Trail and the end-point of the Otter Trail (see Garden Route).

Nature's Valley

Port Elizabeth

Province: Eastern Cape
Altitude: 60m/200ft
Population: 650,000
Distances: 130km/81 miles from Grahamstown, 310km/193 miles from East London, 335km/208 miles from George, 769km/478 miles from Cape Town

Port Elizabeth – usually abbreviated by South Africans to P.E. – is South Africa's fifth largest city and its third largest port. Along with Uitenhage and Kirkwood it forms the industrial and commercial centre of the Eastern Cape. In this "Detroit of South Africa" the most important branch of industry is automobile manufacture, second place being taken by weaving mills. In cultural matters Port Elizabeth can stand comparison with other large South African cities: it has a University, with 5000 students, and a range of other educational institutions including a college of technology.

Situation and
characteristics

But Port Elizabeth is also a popular holiday resort, with an attractive townscape, endlessly long beaches, particularly to the south of the city, and an interesting hinterland.

Originally this was an area of grassland used by a Hottentot tribe as grazing for their livestock. The first Europeans to discover Algoa Bay, in which the city lies, were Portuguese navigators, beginning with Bartolomeu Diaz, who landed at the east end of the bay in 1488. Port Elizabeth, however, was not founded until 1820, when British settlers arrived in Algoa Bay. Sir Rufane Donkin, acting Governor of the Cape, came here to welcome the pioneers and named the new settlement after his wife Elizabeth, who had died young. The place developed only very slowly, receiving its charter as a town in 1861.

History

Although a number of freeways run through the city centre, Port Elizabeth has preserved an attractive aspect, with handsome Victorian buildings as

★The town

339

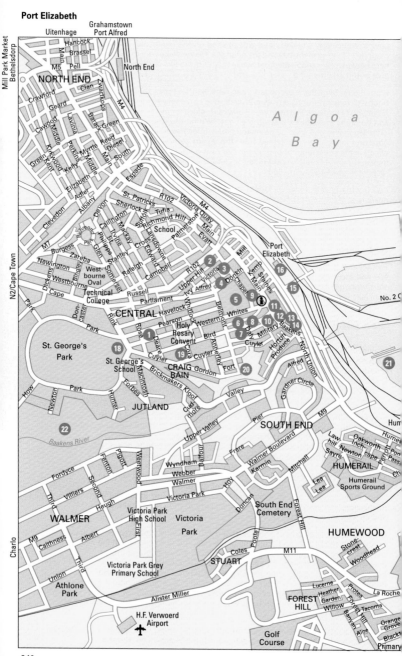

Port Elizabeth

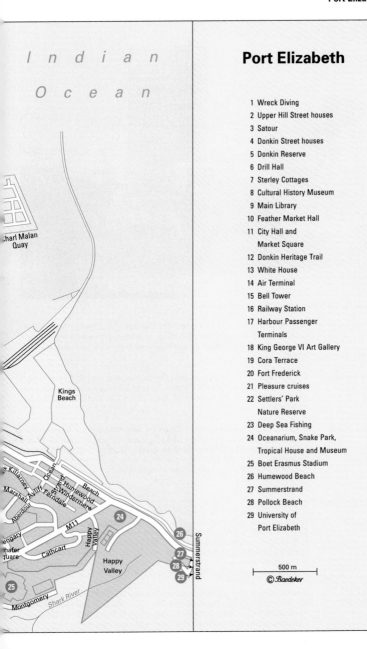

Port Elizabeth

1 Wreck Diving
2 Upper Hill Street houses
3 Satour
4 Donkin Street houses
5 Donkin Reserve
6 Drill Hall
7 Sterley Cottages
8 Cultural History Museum
9 Main Library
10 Feather Market Hall
11 City Hall and
   Market Square
12 Donkin Heritage Trail
13 White House
14 Air Terminal
15 Bell Tower
16 Railway Station
17 Harbour Passenger
   Terminals
18 King George VI Art Gallery
19 Cora Terrace
20 Fort Frederick
21 Pleasure cruises
22 Settlers' Park
   Nature Reserve
23 Deep Sea Fishing
24 Oceanarium, Snake Park,
   Tropical House and Museum
25 Boet Erasmus Stadium
26 Humewood Beach
27 Summerstrand
28 Pollock Beach
29 University of
   Port Elizabeth

500 m
© Baedeker

View of Port Elizabeth from the Donkin Reserve

well as modern high-rise blocks. The central area extends over a level coastal strip of land and the steep hill at its west end on which is the Donkin Reserve. The main shopping and business area is on and around Main Street.

Donkin Heritage Trail

On this 5km/3 mile long route between the City Hall and St George's Park are 43 sights and features of interest. Further information can be obtained from the Publicity Association at the Donkin Lighthouse Building (tel. 52 13 15).

Pleasure cruises

A variety of cruises are on offer, departing from the harbour. A particularly interesting trip is to the island of Santa Cruz, on which there is a large colony of penguins. Also popular with many visitors are diving expeditions to wrecks in the surrounding area, organised by Mike's Diving Shop; participants must have a certificate of competence.

Sights in the City Centre

★Campanile

At the entrance to the harbour, near the railway station, is the Campanile, a 52m/170ft high tower with a carillon of 23 bells (which plays daily at 8.32 and 10.32am and 6.02pm) erected in 1923 in honour of the first settlers. From the viewing platform at the top, reached by climbing 200 steps, there is a good general view of the city. The Campanile is open Mon., Tues. Thur. and Fri. 9am–1pm and 2–4pm, Wed. and Sat. 8.30am–12.30pm.

City Hall, Market Square

From the Campanile a street under the freeway leads to Market Square, the city's historic centre. Opposite the City Hall (1858) is the Diaz Cross, a replica of the cross erected by Bartolomeu Diaz at Kwaahoek in 1488. Every Saturday morning a flea market is held in Market Square.

City Hall

Public Library

North-west of Market Square is the Donkin Reserve, a small park which Sir
Rufane Donkin caused to be laid out in 1820. The lighthouse (1861) is now
occupied by a Military Museum (open: daily 10am–6pm), with a display of
uniforms, medals and weapons. Beside the Museum is a pyramid commemorating Sir Rufane Donkin's wife, after whom the city is named.

Donkin Reserve

On the north side of the park is Donkin Street, a terrace of Victorian houses
built between 1860 and 1870 which have recently been restored and are
now national monuments. They are privately owned and not open to the
public.

★Donkin Street

A short distance farther north is Upper Hill Street, which also preserves
something of the atmosphere of the 19th century.

Upper Hill Street

At 7 Castle Hill, to the south of the Donkin Reserve, is the Cultural History
Museum (open: Mon. 2–5pm, Tues.–Sat. 10am–1pm and 2–5pm), in the
oldest house in Port Elizabeth, built in 1827. It contains period furniture and
other interesting items, including a collection of dolls.

Cultural History
Museum

From here Belmont Terrace runs south to Fort Frederick, built in 1799 to
defend the mouth of the Baakens River. It is now a national monument.

Fort Frederick

Returning along Belmont Terrace and turning left into Bird Street, we come
to Cora Terrace, a row of seven beautifully restored Regency-style houses
built from 1856 onwards. The street is named after the daughter of one of
the original settlers. The houses are privately owned and not open to the
public.

Cora Terrace

Near the west end of Bird Street is St George's Park (73 hectares/180 acres),
In the park are the oldest cricket ground and bowling green in the country,
together with sports fields, tennis courts and swimming pools.

St George's Park

343

Victorian houses in Donkin Street

King George VI Art Gallery

Also within the park is the King George VI Art Gallery (open: Mon.–Fri. 8.30am–5pm, Sat. 8.30am–4.30pm, Sun. 2–4.30pm), with a collection of 19th and early 20th century British art.

Settlers Park Nature Reserve

This 54 hectare/133 acre park lies to the south of St George's Park in the valley of the Baakens River; the main entrance is in How Street, Its beauty is enhanced by indigenous flora, rock pools and grassed areas, and it is home to some 100 species of birds.

Sights outside the City Centre

★Port Elizabeth Museum, Snake Park, Oceanarium

Visitors who have more time at their disposal should pay a visit to this museum complex, situated on the coast to the south of the city centre. The main building contains the departments of archaeology and anthropology. The Oceanarium has a large number of aquarium tanks in which fish and other marine creatures live in near natural conditions, but its great attraction is the dolphin show, presented daily at 11am and 3pm. The Snake Park, one of the finest of its kind, displays a fascinating variety of snakes, crocodiles, lizards and tortoises. The Tropical House, with its lush vegetation, is inhabited by brightly coloured birds. In the Children's Museum all the exhibits can be touched and handled. The museum complex is open daily 9am–5pm.

Happy Valley

With its lush lawns, lily ponds, winding paths and play areas for children, this park, to the south-east of the museum complex, is an ideal place for picnicking or merely relaxing.

In the Addo Elephant Park live the last surviving African bush elephants. ▷ They differ in appearance from other elephants, probably because of many generations of inbreeding. Unusually, the females have no tusks

Surroundings of Port Elizabeth

Apple Express

For railway buffs nostalgic for the days of steam a trip on the Apple Express is a must. The narrow-gauge line on which fruit was formerly transported to Port Elizabeth harbour from the fruit-growing country to the west of the city is now used by steam trains conveying passengers to the beaches south and west of the city. The terminus is at Loerie.

Seaview
Game Park

30km/19 miles west of Port Elizabeth is Seaview Game Park (open: daily 8am–5pm), occupied by large numbers of giraffes, lions, zebras, wilde-beests, antelopes, gazelles, baboons, caracals, steppe lynxes and chee-tahs. The more highly strung animals live in special enclosures. Visitors can observe the animals from cross-country vehicles, or they can walk the Nyala Trail (45 minutes), which winds its way through the scrub. There is a camping site within the park.

Uitenhage

35km/22 miles north of Port Elizabeth is Uitenhage (pop. 202,000), a busy modern industrial city which is famed for its beautiful trees and gardens. It is an important centre of automobile manufacture, metalworking, mechan-ical engineering and railway engineering. The Volkswagen works are the largest car assembly plant in Africa (conducted tours: Tues.–Thur. at 8.45am; booking necessary – apply to Volkswagen of SA, 103 Algoa Road, tel. 041/9 94 41 11).

The old Victorian railway station in Market Street (built 1875; restored) now houses the Railway Museum (open: Mon.–Fri. 10am–1pm and 2–5pm, Sat. 10am–12.30pm, Sun. and pub. hols. 2–5pm), which displays steam locomotives and railway equipment. The Drostdy Africana Museum has a collection of material on African life and culture before the arrival of white settlers. The Cuyler Manor Cultural Museum (open: Mon.–Fri. 10am–1pm and 2–5pm, Sun. 2–5pm), 4km/2½ miles from the town centre, occupies the former home (restored) of a British officer named Jacob Glenn Cuyler.

★★Addo
Elephant
National Park

The Addo Elephant National Park (area 14,551 hectares/35,941 acres; open: daily 7am–8pm) lies 72km/45 miles north of Port Elizabeth between the Zuurberg range and the valley of the Sundays River. It was established in 1931 to preserve the last eleven South African bush elephants from extinc-tion (there are now some 200 elephants in the reserve). The valuable Cape buffalo has also been preserved here. Other animals to be seen in the park include black rhinos and numerous species of antelope (bushbucks, kudus, red hartebeests, elands, Cape grysboks, duikers, etc.). Among nocturnal animals found here are porcupines, anteaters and bush pigs. 185 species of birds have been recorded, including Cape thick-knees, bronze-naped pigeons, ostriches, little swifts, quails, wattled starlings, Cape red-shouldered glossy starlings and kites. The bush in the park consists of low-growing trees and climbing plants. The dominant plant is the spek-boom bush, the elephants' main source of food. The best place to see elephants is at one of the six waterholes in the park. For bird-watchers there is an observation platform at the entrance to the park.

Accommodation for visitors is available in rondavels, cottages, chalets and a camping site, and there are a restaurant and a shop. Day visitors are also welcome. The park can be explored by visitors in their own car. There is also an area surrounded by an elephant-proof fence in which they can walk freely.

★Zuurberg
National Park

The Zuurberg National Park (area 20,777 hectares/51,319 acres) lies in the Winterhoek Mountains 12km/7½ miles north of the Addo National Park. It is a hilly region with deep rocky ravines in which rare and beautiful plants flourish. There are expanses of fynbos scrub, including the low-growing sugarbush. Among the animals to be seen in the park are numerous antelopes and gazelles, including mountain reedbucks and rheboks, as well as baboons, caracals and jackals. Kudus are to be found both within and outside the park. Mountain zebras and hippopotamuses have been re-established here.

Facilities for visitors include hiking trails, pony trekking and a guest house.

Port Shepstone

Province: KwaZulu/Natal
Altitude: 17m/23ft
Population: 9000
Distances: 47km/29 miles from Port Edward, 130km/81 miles from Durban

Port Shepstone, situated at the mouth of the Mzimkulu River, is the chief town and commercial and administrative centre of the Hibiscus Coast, the most southerly stretch of coast in KwaZulu/Natal. The first settlers came here because of the marble in the area, and after building a harbour founded the town in 1882. Until 1901, when the railway from Durban reached Port Shepstone, all the agricultural products of the area had to be sent by ship to Durban.

Situation and characteristics

Port Shepstone's tourist attractions are a very beautiful golf course, fishing and water sports in the sheltered estuary of the river and magnificent beaches within easy reach of the town, which is well supplied with hotels.

The Banana Express, a narrow-gauge steam train, runs through banana and sugarcane plantations to Izotsha and on to Paddock, returning after a 2-hour pause; the whole excursion takes 6 hours.

Banana Express

★Oribi Gorge Nature Reserve

One of the most attractive sights in the Port Shepstone area is the Oribi Gorge Nature Reserve (area 1837 hectares/4537 acres), 21km/13 miles west of the town on the Harding road. The gorge is 24km/15 miles long and 5km/3 miles wide, and at some points has been carved out of the local sandstone by the Umzimkulwana River to a depth of 400m/1300ft. The river is lined by dense forest. In the reserve live leopards, striped woodbucks, baboons, vervet and samango monkeys and blue and grey duikers. The oribi from which the gorge takes its name is rarely if ever seen by the casual visitor. This is also a great place for bird-watchers, with 258 recorded species.

There is accommodation for visitors in the reserve in the form of holiday cottages and huts, and in Fairacres there is the Oribi Gorge Hotel, which has a marvellous view of the gorge. The nature reserve can be explored on 30km/19 miles of tarred road and 35km/22 miles of waymarked hiking trails.

Hibiscus Coast

The Hibiscus Coast is the most southerly stretch of coast in KwaZulu/Natal, extending for 50km/30 miles from Hibberdene in the north to Port Edward in the south. To the north of it is the Sunshine Coast (see Amanzimtoti). It is at its busiest around Christmas, when many South African families come to spend their holidays here and it is almost impossible to find accommodation in the coastal resorts. At many points the coast is edged by evergreen tropical forest. Innumerable rivers and streams flow into the sea along the coast, forming sheltered lagoons at their mouths.

Hibberdene, 80km/50 miles south of Durban, is an attractive bathing resort with long sandy beaches and facilities for a variety of sports. The climate in summer is more agreeable than round Durban, with rather lower temperatures and lower air humidity. To the south of the town is Umzumbe, which also offers good swimming and fishing.

Hibberdene

Port Shepstone

The beautiful beaches of the Hibiscus Coast

Bendigo	The name Bendigo covers the four holiday settlements of Sunwich Port, Anerley, South Port and Sea Park. The South Port beaches are protected from sharks by nets; Sunwich has a bathing beach surrounded by rocks, also with shark nets; Domba Bay and Sea Park attract many anglers; and Anerley has a seawater swimming pool.
Shelly Beach	From Port Shepstone R 61 runs south down the coast to Shelly Beach, a resort famed for its abundance of seashells.
Margate	Margate, a town founded in 1919 and named after the popular English resort, is one of the largest and best-known bathing resorts on the Hibiscus Coast. It has numerous restaurants, discos and night spots, mainly patronised by younger holidaymakers. There is an amusement park, water slides, diving platforms, boccia and bowling greens, a roller skating rink, an 18-hole golf course and good fishing and swimming.
Southbroom	Beyond Margate is Southbroom, with two sheltered lagoons and a beach protected by shark nets. Nearby is the River Bend Crocodile Farm (open: daily), where crocodiles (which had been exterminated in this area by the mid 19th century) are bred and studied.
Marina Beach	Marina Beach is a relatively quiet resort with an immensely long sandy beach which outside the season is largely unfrequented.
Trafalgar	Trafalgar is a resort particularly favoured by surfers. The offshore Trafalgar Marine Reserve was established to protect the unique underwater flora and fauna.
Port Edward	Port Edward, near the boundary of the former homeland of Transkei, is the last place on the Hibiscus Coast.
★Umtamvuna Nature Reserve	This nature reserve on the Umtamvuna River (access road 8km/5 miles west of Port Edward on the Izingolweni road) contains some 1300 species

of plants, including many species of trees and 25 species of orchids, within its area of 3257 hectares/8045 acres. Narrow paths lead to lookout points with magnificent views. Cape vultures, falcons and eagles can be seen on the rock walls of the gorge, as well as duikers and bushbucks. There is no accommodation for visitors in the reserve.

Potchefstroom   J 4

Province: North-West
Population: 97,000
Distances: 49km/30 miles from Klerksdorp, 119km/74 miles from Johannesburg

Potchefstroom, 119km/74 miles south-west of Johannesburg, was the first capital of the Boer republic of the Transvaal, and even after the capital was moved to Pretoria in 1860 it remained an important economic and cultural centre. It now has a university with over 9000 students. The climate (cool, dry winters and warm, rainy summers) fosters a productive agriculture (grain, sunflowers, fruit and vegetables; cattle-farming).

Situation and characteristics

Potchefstroom preserves numerous historic buildings to bear witness to its past, including the Dutch Reformed church of 1866 and the old fort near the railway station. In 1880–81 a British force in Fort Buren was besieged for three months by the Boers.
    In addition to the Municipal Museum and the museum housed in the former residence of President M. W. Pretorius there is the Totius Museum, with mementoes and the library of the well-known Afrikaans writer and poet J. D. Du Toit.

The town

Surroundings of Potchefstroom

49km/30 miles south-west of Potchefstroom is Klerksdorp (pop. 130,000), the first white settlement in the Transvaal (1837). It became a boom town in 1886, when gold was discovered here and 40,000 prospectors flocked to the area. The gold seams, however, turned out to be much less productive than those of the Witwatersrand, and it was only the introduction of improved mining methods after the Second World War that made the workings profitable. The second most important branch of the economy is agriculture.

Klerksdorp

14km/8½ miles north of Klerksdorp is the Faan Meintjies Nature Reserve (open: daily 10am–6pm, in winter to 5pm), an area of more than 1300 hectares/3200 acres of flat grassland and sandy hills which is home to numerous species of antelope, as well as buffaloes, black wildebeests, giraffes, zebras and rhinoceros. There is no accommodation for visitors in the reserve.

Faan Meintjies Nature Reserve

Pretoria   K 4

Province: Gauteng
Altitude: 1370m/4495ft
Area: 632sq.km/244sq. miles
Population: 823,000
Distances: 58km/36 miles from Johannesburg, 456km/283 miles from Bloemfontein, 1460km/907 miles from Cape Town

Pretoria, situated in the fertile valley of the Apies River, at the foot of the Magaliesberg range, is the administrative capital of South Africa and the

Situation and characteristics

Papatso
Pretoria North

Pretoria North

Heu

Paul Kruger

National
Zoological Gardens

R101

Apies

National
Zoological
Gardens

Prinsho
for the
B

Mosco
Margarets

Lave

De Wet

Prinsloo

Bazaar

Belle-Ombre

① ②

Boom

Mogul

Boom

Boom

Andries

Bloed

Brown

Border

Jooste

Boom

D.F. Malan East

D.F. Malan West

Seventh

Potgieter

③

PRETORIA

Paul Kruger

⑥

Struben

Bosman

⑤

Vom Hagen

Struben

N4

Proes

President Burgers

Rieter

Luttig

PRETORIA
WEST

Proes

N4

⑦

⑪

Vermeulen

Ve

Westpark

Christoffel

Ou Kerkhof

Cowie

④

Schubart

Kerk

⑧

⑩

Andries

van der Walt

①

⑫

⑬ ⑭

P

Kerk

Prince's
Park

Pretorius

CENTRAL

⑨

Schoeman

Iscor Club

D.F. Malan

Steenovenspruit

Princess Park

Potgieter

Technical
High School

Bosman

Hamilt
Primary S

Show Ground

M2

Skinner

⑳

Visagie

Paul Kruger

㉑

㉒

Park Lane
Burgers
Park

Minna

Van der Walt

Soutter

Elson

Pretorius Burgers

Pretter

Mitchell

PRETORIA-
WES

M6

Minnaer

㉕

Von Wielligh

Barracks

Artillery Row

Jacob Mare

Andries

㉔

Bosman
Street

Scheiding

Loop

Rhode

Berea
Park

Pretoria

Railway

Clara

Hartbeespoort Dam

Pretoria
of Edu
Spo
Gro

㉓

Skietpoort

Second

SALVOKOP

Fourth

Second

Fifth

Laerskool
Jopie Fopurie

Ben Schoeman

Andries

Magazine Hill

R101

M1

Salvokop

Verw

㉗ ㉘

Valhalla
Verwoerdburg

Johannesburg

Verw

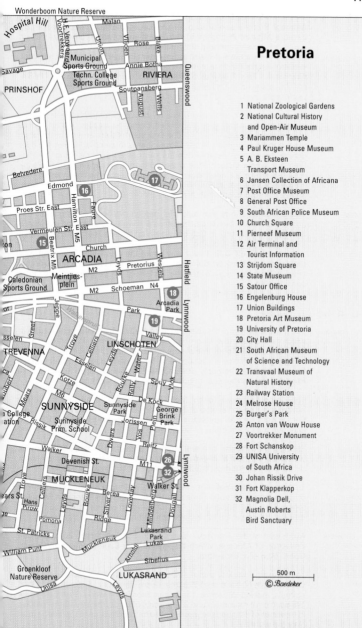

Pretoria

1 National Zoological Gardens
2 National Cultural History
  and Open-Air Museum
3 Mariammen Temple
4 Paul Kruger House Museum
5 A. B. Eksteen
  Transport Museum
6 Jansen Collection of Africana
7 Post Office Museum
8 General Post Office
9 South African Police Museum
10 Church Square
11 Pierneef Museum
12 Air Terminal and
   Tourist Information
13 Strijdom Square
14 State Museum
15 Satour Office
16 Engelenburg House
17 Union Buildings
18 Pretoria Art Museum
19 University of Pretoria
20 City Hall
21 South African Museum
   of Science and Technology
22 Transvaal Museum of
   Natural History
23 Railway Station
24 Melrose House
25 Burger's Park
26 Anton van Wouw House
27 Voortrekker Monument
28 Fort Schanskop
29 UNISA University
   of South Africa
30 Johan Rissik Drive
31 Fort Klapperkop
32 Magnolia Dell,
   Austin Roberts
   Bird Sanctuary

500 m

© Baedeker

seat of government for six months in the year, alternating with Cape Town. Although Pretoria is so close to Johannesburg, the two cities could scarcely be more different. Pretoria, with the largest area of any South African town, is a city of civil servants and diplomats, trim residential districts and beautiful parks and gardens. It is also an important industrial town (iron and steel, automobile manufacture, cement production) and an educational and cultural centre. The University of Pretoria was founded in 1930; and UNISA, the University of South Africa, is one of the largest open universities in the world, with over 100,000 students.

History

The area round Pretoria was originally occupied by the Ndebele, whose women are famed for their skill in decorating the façades of their houses (see Baedeker Special, p. 356). The first voortrekkers arrived in the area, then sparsely populated, in 1827. Pretoria was founded in 1855 by the Boer general Marthinus Wessel Pretorius and named after his father Andries Pretorius, whose victory in the battle of Blood River had made possible the establishment of an independent white settlement in the Transvaal. In 1860 Pretoria became capital of the Transvaal and in 1910 the seat of government of the Union of South Africa.

★The town

This beautiful, sunny and colourful garden city with a tranquil air has numerous historic buildings, museums and well kept parks and gardens. It is at its most beautiful in October when its thousands of mauve-flowered jacaranda trees are in bloom.

It is not difficult to find your way about the city, which is laid out on a regular grid, but visitors doing their sightseeing on foot will discover that even within the city centre the distances to be covered are quite considerable.

Sights in the City Centre

★Church Square

The first settlement grew up round historic Church Square, in the centre of which is a statue (by Anton van Wouw) of President Paul Kruger (see Famous People). Round the square are a number of important buildings, including the Palace of Justice and Sir Herbert Baker's South African Reserve Bank on the north side and the Renaissance-style Republikeinse Raadsaal, the former seat of government, on the south side.

Pierneef Museum

The Pierneef Museum (open: Mon.–Fri. 8am–4pm), in a late 19th century house (restored) in Vermeulen Street, north of Church Square, has a collection of works by the landscape painter Jacob Hendrik Pierneef (1904–75) and personal mementoes of the artist.

Post Office Museum

The Post Office Museum (open: Mon.–Fri. 9am–4pm) in Proes Street (to the west of the Pierneef Museum) is devoted to the history and development of postal services (stamps, telephone, telegraph) in South Africa.

A. B. Eksteen Transport Museum

To the north of the Post Office Museum, in the Forum Building at the corner of Bosman and Struben Streets, is the A. B. Eksteen Transport Museum (open: Tues.–Fri. 10am–4pm, Sat. 10am–noon), which illustrates the history and development of civil aviation and other forms of transport.

Jansen Collection of Africana

North-east of the Transport Museum, in Struben Street, is the Jansen Collection of Africana, which displays mostly Cape furniture and silver. Open: Mon.–Fri. 8am–4pm.

★National Zoological Gardens

To the north of the city centre, in Boom Street, are the National Zoological Garden (area 60 hectares/150 acres; open: daily 8am–5.30pm), with 3500 animals, making this one of the largest zoos in the world. There are some 140 species of mammals and 320 species of birds; the aquarium displays 300 species of fish; and the reptile house has a collection of reptiles from all over the world.

View of Pretoria from the Union Buildings

The National Cultural History Museum (open: Mon.–Fri. 8am–4pm), adjoining the Zoo, has a varied collection which includes Bushman rock engravings, an ethnological section, Cape Dutch furniture, silver and archaeological material.

National Cultural History Museum

The State Theatre complex in Church Street (on the eastern edge of the city centre), built in 1981 in a style which shows the influence of Japanese architecture, has six theatres which stage large and small-scale productions of opera, ballet, drama, chamber music and symphony concerts.

State Theatre

In front of the State Theatre, in Strijdom Square, is a bust (by Coert Steynberg, 1972) of J. G. Strijdom, prime minister of South Africa in the 1950s. Another piece of sculpture in the square is Danie de Jager's "Galloping Horses", symbolising freedom. A market is held in the square every Saturday morning.

Strijdom Square

The Police Museum (open: Mon.–Fri. 8am–3.30pm, Sat. 8.30am–noon), in the Compol Building in Volkstem Avenue (to the south of Church Square), has a collection of weapons used by criminals, uniforms and reconstructions of celebrated crimes.

South African Police Museum

In Skinner Street, to the south of the city centre, is the South African Museum of Science and Technology (open: Mon.–Fri. 8am–4pm, Sun. 2–5pm), with a variety of exhibits on space travel, science and technology.

South African Museum of Science and Technology

A little way south, in Paul Kruger Street, is the City Hall, which has an enormous clock-tower with 32 bells.
   Outside the entrance are statues of Andries Pretorius and his son Marthinus Wessel Pretorius, founder of Pretoria.

City Hall

353

Melrose House, one of Pretoria's handsomest old buildings

★Transvaal Museum of Natural History	This celebrated museum (open: Mon.–Sat. 9am–5pm, Sun. and pub. hols. 11am–5pm), facing the City Hall, has an extraordinary collection of mammals, amphibians, fossils, geological specimens and archaeological material. In the Austin Roberts Bird Hall visitors can see all the 875 species of birds indigenous to South Africa.
Museum of Geological Survey	Adjoining the Natural History Museum is the Museum of the Geological Survey (open: Mon.–Sat. and pub. hols. 9am–5pm, Sun. 11am–5pm), which has a fine collection of precious and semi-precious stones, fossils and geological illustrations.
Burgers Park	South-east of the Natural History Museum is Burgers Park (open: Tues.–Sat. 10am–5pm, Sun. 1–6pm), Pretoria's oldest park, laid out in 1892 and named after Thomas François Burgers, second President of the Transvaal. With its well cared-for lawns, pretty ponds and attractive coffee-house it is a good place to relax after a sightseeing tour.
★Melrose House	In Jacob Mare Street, looking on to Burgers Park, is Melrose House, built by George Heys in 1866. In this handsome Victorian house (open: Tues.–Sat. 10am–5pm, Sun. noon–5pm) the treaty of Vereeniging was signed in 1902. The house with its period furniture is now a museum, which is also used for art exhibitions and concerts.
Paul Kruger Museum	This modest Victorian house in Church Street, to the west of the city centre, the oldest and best known house in the city, was the home from 1883 to 1900 of Paul Kruger (see Famous People). It is now a museum (open: Mon.–Sat. 8.30am–4pm, Sun. 11am–4pm), with mementoes of Kruger and the Transvaal state coach.
Mariammen Temple	A few blocks north is the Mariammen Temple (1905), Pretoria's oldest Hindu temple, dedicated to Mariammen, the goddess of infectious diseases. Visitors are welcome.

Union Buildings, Pretoria

Sights outside the City Centre

The Union Buildings (by Sir Herbert Baker, 1913), set in beautiful gardens, are commandingly situated on Meintjieskop Hill on the east side of the city. This impressive range of sandstone buildings is the seat of government and of Parliament (though in the first half of the year Parliament sits in Cape Town). Here too are housed the state archives.

    In the gardens which slope down in terraces to Church Street are the Delville Wood Memorial, commemorating the South African soldiers who fell in the First World War, statues of the South African prime ministers Louis Botha, J. B. M. Hertzog and J. C. Smuts, and a Police Memorial. For tours tel. (012) 325 2000.

★Union Buildings

To the south of the Union Buildings, in Arcadia Park, is the Pretoria Art Museum (open: Tues.–Sat. 10am–5pm, Sun. 1–6pm), with numerous works by South African artists such as Pierneef, Frans Oerder and Anton van Wouw and the Michaelis Collection of Dutch and Flemish masters.

Pretoria
Art Museum

The Pretoria National Botanic Gardens (area 77 hectares/190 acres; open: daily 8am–5pm), the largest in the country, lie 10km/6 miles east of the city centre. The plants are grouped according to their climatic region (the savannas of the Karoo, the coastal forests, the grassland plains of Namibia). Altogether there are 5000 species of plants, including 300 indigenous species of trees.

★Pretoria
National
Botanic Gardens

The beautifully laid out Magnolia Dell gardens (in Queen Wilhelmina Avenue, to the south of the University of Pretoria) are seen at their best when the magnolias are in bloom in spring. There is a small lake in the gardens. An "Art in the Park" show is held here on the first and last Saturdays in the month.

Magnolia Dell

Women Painters of the Ndebele

In spite of the tragic history of their people – more harshly treated by fate than any other ethnic group in South Africa – the Ndebele have not lost their liking for gay colours. It is the women who, with their works of art inspired by delight in colour and a boundless imagination, have given this divided, maltreated and in a real sense homeless people their sense of identity. Their whole life is imbued with colour – their day-to-day existence, their festivals, their rituals, their dress, their houses. The women regularly, and not merely on festive occasions, wear golden brass rings round their neck, increasing in number over the years and elongating the neck, as well as on their forearms and lower legs. Children

Ndebele beadwork

too wear neck ornaments of this kind, though in their case the rings are of plaited straw, tied so tightly that they can be taken off only with the help of a saw. The strings of beads and the beadwork embroidery worn by the little girls differ from those of adult women and girls being prepared in initiation ceremonies for their life as a woman. When the Ndebele took to settled life the beadwork patterns developed over hundreds of years of nomadic life formed the basis of a form of art which is without its like in Africa: the wall-painting of the Ndebele women.

The characteristic Ndebele dwelling is the umuzi, consisting of a principal house and a number of associated single or double houses with forecourts. The umuzis are built by men and women working together. First they drive wooden poles into the ground; then they fill the spaces between them with walls woven from branches, twigs and straw, which are then faced on both sides with a mixture of clay and cow dung and covered with a temporary straw roof. When the walls have dried out the women set about painting them. Formerly they used to walk for miles to get the clay and mud from which they made the pigments they required – red, brown, ochre, blue, white and black. Now they prefer to buy acrylic paints – less easily washed out by rain – in the supermarket, mixing them with clay to produce the traditional pastel shades. The decorative patterns on house walls are predominantly linear and geometric, based on the patterns used in the much older craft of beadwork, with horizontal, vertical and diagonal lines. But the patterns now also include some of the products of modern civilisation. There are representations of aircraft and automobiles: so at least they appear to be, for there is no limit to what the imagination of the Ndebele women will conceive. The walls are decorated for special occasions like marriages and initiation ceremonies, but sometimes also simply because the women feel like it.

One of the leading Ndebele painters is Esther Mahlangu, who achieved fame beyond the bounds of South Africa when she painted a BMW car on the occasion of the firm's 75th jubilee.

It might be supposed that a people which takes such delight in decoration and in gay colours and is so strongly attached to its traditions had enjoyed a happy and carefree life. But the exact contrary is true. The Ndebele have been worse treated by fate than any other Bantu people in South Africa and are now one of the most widely scattered peoples in the country.

Little is known about the history of the Ndebele. They have no written records, and their traditions have been handed down orally (as have the techniques of house-painting). All that is certain is that by the 16th century they were settled in two groups in the Transvaal – the Ndebele of the northern Tranvaal and the Ndebele of the southern Transvaal – and that they are distantly related to the Ndebele of Zimbabwe, the Matabele. The fatal date in the modern history of the South African Ndebele was 1883. The establishment of a British colony on the Cape had compelled the Boers to move northward into the interior, where they founded the republic of the Transvaal on the territory of the Ndebele. In 1882 the Boers undertook their fourth attempt to wipe out the Ndebele people. The Ndebele, seeing their danger, sought refuge on August 2nd 1882 in the Mabhogo caves near Nomtjarhelo. The Boers blew up part of the cave system with dynamite, and when this failed resolved to starve them out. Finally in July 1883, after a nine month long siege, the Ndebele surrendered. Of the 15,000 people who had entered the caves a year before there survived only 8000 men, women and children. The Ndebele king,

The Ndebele artist Esther Mahlangu with her mother

357

Baedeker Special

Nyabela, was sentenced to 15 years in prison, and the members of his tribe were sent to work on Boer farms.

Thereafter, for many years, the Ndebele led a rootless existence with no civil rights. In 1977 the South African government established the tenth and last of the so-called "homelands", KwaNdebele. The Ndebele hoped that this would make possible the reunion of their people and the rebirth of their culture and identity; but KwaNdebele was not the historic territory of the Ndebele, and it was too small and too poor to support its population. As a result the Ndebele had for the most part to seek a livelihood outside the homeland. In 1986 the South African government proposed to make KwaNdebele an "independent" state, but the 400,000 Ndebele successfully opposed the proposal, since independence would have made them aliens in their own country, without the right to work there. During clashes with government forces 200 Ndebele were killed.

In spite of everything the Ndebele people has survived. Though externally dependent on Pretoria, internally they remain strongly attached to their own values and their old traditions. This is most clearly seen in the spontaneous freehand drawings of the Ndebele women, which give expression not only to individual imagination and fantasy but also to the collective memory of a people which for generations has been submerged.

Austin Roberts Bird Sanctuary	South-east of the Magnolia Dell gardens, in Boshoff Street, is the Austin Roberts Bird Sanctuary (area 11 hectares/27 acres; open: 7am–4pm), named after the South African ornithologist who wrote the best known handbook on the birds of South Africa. Over 100 indigenous species of birds and numerous other animals can be seen here in their natural surroundings. On the edge of the sanctuary is a reservoir, on the shores of which are hides for bird-watchers.
Anton van Wouw House	To the east of the bird sanctuary, at 299 Clark Street, is the former home of the South African sculptor Anton van Wouw, now a museum (open: Tues.–Fri. 10am–4pm, Sat. 10am–noon).
Faerie Glen Nature Reserve	At the eastern end of the city area is the very beautiful Faerie Glen Nature Reserve, with a varied flora (including the umbrella tree) and fauna. It is part of the Moreleta Spruit Nature Trail, an 8km/5 miles long hiking trail which runs from Menlyn Drive to Hardekool Avenue, following a winding course along the banks of the stream through ever-changing scenery.
Fort Klapperkop	6km/4 miles south of the city, reached by way of Johan Rissik Drive, from which there are fine views of Pretoria, is Fort Klapperkop, one of the four forts built to defend the town – though it was never called on to perform that function. It is now a military museum (open: daily 10am–4pm), with exhibits illustrating the military history of South Africa from 1852 to the end of the Boer War.
★Voortrekker Monument	Prominently situated 6km/4 miles south of the city centre is the Voortrekker Monument (open: Mon.–Sat. 9am–4.45pm, Sun. 11am–4.45pm), built in 1949 to commemorate the voortrekkers, the Boers who in the mid 19th century pushed northward into unknown territory. A ponderous square granite structure 40m/130ft high stands on a base 40m square. Steps lead

Voortrekker Monument, Pretoria

up to the Hall of Heroes, with 27 marble reliefs depicting the Great Trek of 1838. Through an opening in the floor can be seen a slab of granite in the vault below with the inscription "Ons vir jou, Suid-Afrika" ("We are for you, South Africa"). The monument is surrounded by a wall depicting ox-wagons – representing the trek wagons which the Boers drew up in a circle to form a defensive laager. There is a museum illustrating this period of South African history. (Open: Mon.–Sat. 9am–4.45pm, Sun. 11am–4.45pm.)

Surroundings of Pretoria

On the northern outskirts of the city is the Wonderboom Nature Reserve (open: daily 7am–6pm), established to protect a fig-tree (*Ficus salicifolia*) over 1000 years old with a trunk 5.5m/18ft in diameter. The branches touching the ground have formed roots. It is said that more than a thousand people can shelter under the branches of this "wonder tree", which has been declared a national monument. The reserve of which it is the central feature has an area of 90 hectares/225 acres, with picnic spots and barbe-cue sites. One of the hiking trails in the reserve leads to a hill topped by a small fort dating from the Boer War.

Wonderboom
Nature Reserve

R 101, running north from Pretoria, comes to the village of Hammanskraal, 12km/7½ miles beyond which is the Papatso craft centre, where local craftsmen (and craftswomen), mainly Ndebele, sell their products. The brightly coloured Ndebele houses are highly photogenic (see Baedeker Special, p, 356).

Papatso

40km/25 miles east of Pretoria is Cullinan, where the largest rough dia-mond ever found, the 3106-carat Cullinan Diamond, came to light in 1905. It was presented to King Edward VII on his 66th birthday and in 1908 was split

★Cullinan

by an Amsterdam diamond-cutter into 105 pieces. The largest of them is now set in the sceptre which is one of the British crown jewels.

The Premier Diamond Mine in Cullinan produces around 1 million carats of diamonds every year, mainly for industrial use. Surface tours: Mon.–Fri. booking essential, tel. (01213) 40081.

Dornkloof Farm

Dornkloof Farm, 16km/10 miles south of Pretoria, was once the home of Jan Christiaan Smuts, prime minister of the Union of South Africa. Still retaining most of its original furniture, it has been restored and is now a museum (open: daily 9.30am–1pm, 1.30–4.30pm, open until 5pm at weekends). Round the house are picnic spots, camping sites and a tea garden.

Hartbeespoort Dam

Hartbeespoort Dam (area 1883 hectares/4651 acres) lies 32km/20 miles west of Pretoria. With the help of a 544km/338 mile network of water channels it irrigates an extensive agricultural area in which tobacco, grain, fruit and flowers are grown.

This is now a popular recreation area (open: Mon.–Fri. 8am–6pm, Sat. to 10pm), with accommodation for visitors, camping sites and amusement parks. There are numerous hiking trails in the Hartbeespoort Nature Reserve (on the south-east side of the reservoir) on which visitors can observe the large numbers of birds and antelopes which live in the reserve.

There is also a small zoo with many mammals, reptiles and birds. A notable feature is a very large aquarium. Cruises on the lake in small steamers.

Rustenburg

To the west of Hartbeespoort (105km/65 miles from Pretoria), at the foot of the Magaliesberg range, is the little town of Rustenburg, a favourite resort of the people of Pretoria. Near the town, in a beautiful hill setting, is the Rustenburg Nature Reserve, an ideal area for long walks.

On the north side of the town is Boekhoutenfontein, Paul Kruger's farm. Some of the old buildings have been preserved, including Kruger's house, built in 1863.

Queenstown   J 8

Province: Eastern Cape
Altitude: 1094m/3589ft
Population: 90,000
Distances: 160km/100 miles from Aliwal North, 195km/121 miles from East London

Situation and characteristics

Queenstown, situated in the narrow corridor between the former homelands of Transkei and Ciskei, is the commercial, administrative and cultural centre of a fertile agricultural region. It has little of tourist interest but, as a modern town with hotels, restaurants and shops, may be a convenient stopover on a long journey. There are two museums with material of local interest.

Sights in and around Queenstown

Walter Everitt Sunken Gardens

Queenstown is a town of parks and gardens. Among the finest are the Walter Everitt Sunken Gardens, with two lakes surrounded by lush vegetation which attract many water birds.

Lawrence de Lange Game Reserve

The Lawrence de Lange Game Reserve (open: daily 8am–5pm) occupies an area of 818 hectares/2020 acres on the slopes of the Madeira Mountain, just outside the town. A 7km/4½ mile long hiking trail runs through the reserve to the summit of the hill, on which, with luck, visitors may see kudus, springboks, blesboks, red hartebeests, black wildebeests, impalas, gems-boks, elands and steppe zebras.

Richard's Bay   M/N 6

Province: KwaZulu/Natal
Altitude: 47m/116ft
Population: 17,000
Distances: 43km/27 miles from Mtubatuba, 91km/57 miles from Melmoth, 200km/125 miles from Durban

Richard's Bay, situated on the Indian Ocean at the mouth of the Mhlatuze River, is one of South Africa's leading ports. The deep-water harbour completed in 1976 was at first used only for the export of coal but now handles almost half the total turnover of South African ports. A 660km/410 mile long railway line links Richard's Bay with the Witbank coalfields. After the new harbour came into use the town's industries developed rapidly (oil pipeline, manufacture of fertilisers, aluminium works).
   Apart from the harbour Richard's Bay has no features of tourist interest, but there are some attractive sights within easy reach of the town.

Situation and characteristics

Surroundings of Richard's Bay

South-west of the town, between N 2 and the sea, is the Umlalazi Nature Reserve (area 1028 hectares/2539 acres), an area of dunes, swamps and mangrove forests. The dense coastal vegetation is relieved by a number of small lakes and a lagoon formed by the Umlalazi River. Among the animals to be seen here are bush pigs, blue, red and grey duikers, striped wood-bucks and a small colony of crocodiles, as well as many species of birds.
   Accommodation for visitors is available in log cabins and on camping sites. There are two hiking trails, picnic areas and boats for hire.

★Umlalazi Nature Reserve

Empangeni, in beautiful hill country 20km/12½ miles inland from Richard's Bay, is the centre of Zululand's sugar industry (see Ulundi). It grew out of a Norwegian mission station established in 1851, and is now a university town and an important railway junction.

Empangeni

15km/9 miles north-east of Empangeni, at a bend on the Enseleni River, is the Enseleni Nature Reserve (area 293 hectares/724 acres). A number of hiking trails (the longest 5km/3 miles long) run through the dense vegeta-tion of the reserve, home to many species of animals, including hippopota-muses and crocodiles.

Enseleni Nature Reserve

Robertson   E 10

Province: Western Cape
Altitude: 209m/686ft
Population: 27,000
Distances: 50km/31 miles from Worcester, 77km/48 miles from Swellen-dam, 29km/18 miles from Montagu

Like the neighbouring towns of Montagu and Swellendam (see entries), Robertson is famed for its wines. There are some 35 major wineries in the surrounding area, producing mainly good dessert wines from muscatel grapes and an excellent brandy. Since Robertson is an attractive town with many parks and gardens, and a good base for walks in the Langeberg hills, it is a favourite holiday place well equipped to cater for visitors.

Situation and characteristics

Sights in and around Robertson

Robertson
Museum

The Museum (open: Mon.–Sat. 9am–noon) has a variety of material on the history of the town as well as a very fine collection of lace.

McGregor

20km/12½ miles south of Robertson is the remote and charming little town of McGregor, where time seems to have stood still. A number of mid 19th century houses in Cape Dutch style have been preserved, set in beautiful fruit and vegetable gardens. There is attractive accommodation for visitors, making this a good place to spend a day or two away from the stresses of modern life.

Royal Natal National Park

See Drakensberg

Sabie   M 3

Province: Eastern Transvaal
Altitude: 1109m/3639ft
Population: 11,000
Distances: 45km/28 miles from Lydenburg, 65km/40 miles from Nelspruit

Situation and
characteristics

The little town of Sabie lies amid dense forests on the slopes of Mount Anderson (2285m/7497ft) and the Mauchberg (2115m/6939ft). It is the principal centre of the timber industry in the region, with the largest paper factory in the country.

Mac Mac Falls, Sabie

Sabie, well equipped with shops, restaurants and filling stations, is a favourite stopover for tourists on their way to the Blyderivierspoort Nature Reserve or the Kruger National Park (see entries).

Sabie occupies the site of a farm acquired in 1880 by H. T. Glynn, who one day during a party challenged his guests to a shooting contest with empty bottles set in front of a rock as targets. Under the hail of bullets fragments of rock splintered off, revealing a seam of gold, which thereafter was worked from 1895 until 1950. Sabie grew up round the gold-mine, and in 1913 was linked by rail with Nelspruit. | History

With its agreeable climate and expanses of forest (otherwise rare in South Africa) the country round Sabie is a popular holiday area for South Africans. Since the forests have mostly been planted within recent years, their attractions for walkers are limited; but there are a number of magnificent waterfalls round Sabie, among them the 68m/225ft high Lone Creek Falls (12km/7½ miles west), the Bridal Veil Falls (8km/5 miles west) and the Horseshoe Falls (1km/¾ mile north). | Walking country

Sights in and around Sabie

The small Forestry Museum in Sabie is informative about the development of timber-working and the various species of trees. | Forestry Museum

14km/8½ miles from Sabie on the Graskop road (R 532) is a parking place from which steps lead up to a lookout point a 5 minutes' walk away from which there is a superb view of the Mac Mac Falls – twin falls which plunge down 56m/184ft into a wooded gorge, forming a crystal-clear lake 2km/1¼ miles downstream. At one time when gold was found here prospectors flocked to the area, including many Scots: hence, it is said, the name of the falls. | ★Mac Mac Falls

From Sabie R 37 runs 53km/33 miles west to Lydenburg (see entry), going over the Long Tom Pass (2149m/7051ft) and following the old voortrekker route through the Drakensberg. The pass got its name during the Boer War, when the Boers defended the pass with long-barrelled guns nicknamed Long Toms. From the pass road there are magnificent views of the surrounding country. | Long Tom Pass

St Francis Bay

Province: Eastern Cape

St Francis Bay, a wide bay extending to the west of Port Elizabeth, was given its name by Manoel Perestrelo, a Portuguese navigator, in honour of St Francis, patron saint of all seafarers. There are a number of bathing resorts round the bay, consisting almost exclusively of holiday homes which are occupied only for a few weeks in the year. The attractions of St Francis Bay are its beautiful beaches and the opportunities it offers for surfers and wind-surfers; the mighty waves, particularly towards the west end of the bay, are a challenge to their skill. Their sport can also be enjoyed by the lookers-on. Shell collectors, too, will find some marvellously beautiful shells here. | Situation and characteristics

Sights in St Francis Bay

The little resort of St Francis Bay, at the mouth of the Kromme River, is favoured by anglers as well as by surfers and shell-hunters. The best fishing is 12km/7½ miles upstream. | St Francis Bay

St Francis Bay

Cape St Francis
At the west end of the bay is Cape St Francis, a flat promontory reaching out into the sea. It is dominated by a 28m/92ft high lighthouse erected in 1876.

Jeffrey's Bay
Within the last few years Jeffrey's Bay has developed into a considerable holiday resort with a population of 7000. The best time for surfers is in winter, when fine regular high waves roll in to the shore.
An attractive footpath winds its way up the river for 3km/2 miles through the little Noorskloof Nature Reserve, in which, with luck, antelopes and vervet monkeys can be spotted.

Seekoei River Nature Reserve
To the south of Jeffrey's Bay, at the little resort of Aston Bay, is the Seekoei River Nature Reserve (open: daily 7am–5pm), established to protect the water birds living round the mouth of the river. Some of the smaller antelopes can also be seen here.

Humansdorp
The little country town of Humansdorp (pop. 54,000), 20km/12½ miles inland, is the supply centre for the resorts at the west end of St Francis Bay. The situation of the town is not particularly attractive: the flat and arid coastal plain offers only limited scope for agriculture, the principal crops being fodder plants and barley. Sheep-farming is also developing.

St Lucia Wetland Park

Province: KwaZulu/Natal

Situation and characteristics
The Greater St Lucia Wetland Park, on the northern coast of KwaZulu/Natal, was formed by the amalgamation of a number of smaller nature reserves. The central feature of this wetland area is Lake St Lucia, South Africa's largest natural inland lake. The unique coastal vegetation and the extraordinarily rich bird life make the park a front-rank attraction for nature-lovers.
The best route to the park from Durban (200km/125 miles south-west) is by way of N 2, turning off at Mtubatuba into a road on the right which leads to the little town of St Lucia (28km/17 miles). From here a track runs north between Lake St Lucia and the sea to Cape Vidal. To see the northern part of the park it is necessary to continue beyond Mtubatuba on N 1 and in 20km/12½ miles take a road on the right signposted to Fanies Island or Charters Creek. The park can also be reached on the road to Hluhluwe, which branches off N 2 still farther north.

★★ Topography
Lake St Lucia is 60km/37 miles long, up to 10km/6 miles wide and only 1–2m/6–12ft deep. It extends parallel to the coast, from which it is separated by a belt of wooded dunes. More than 400 species of plants have been recorded here. The commonest species of trees are white milkwood, campeachy and wild fig; in winter the coral-tree is conspicuous with its brilliant red flowers. The Umfolozi, Mkuzi and Hluhluwe Rivers flow into the lake, which is connected to the sea by a channel 20km/12½ miles long. Freshwater and seawater thus mingle in the lake, producing an ideal habitat for many water birds. Along the coast of the Indian Ocean extends an endlessly long sandy beach. The coastal waters reaching 5.6km/3½ miles out to sea are also included in the reserve. Here the warm Agulhas Current has fostered the growth of coral reefs in which live hosts of colourful fish.
On the landward side the dunes give place to areas of swamp and grassland, with thorny scrub and dry savanna still farther inland.
The ecological equilibrium of this coastal region is under grave threat. The rivers which flow into Lake St Lucia lose much of their water to irrigation schemes, and with a high rate of evaporation there is a danger that the lake will become too saline. Moreover part of the dune area has been destroyed by mining for titanium ore.

The shallow waters of the lake are the home of thousands of flamingos and pelicans; more than ten species of heron are represented here, and there are many other species of water birds. Leatherback and false diamondback turtles come in to the coast to lay their eggs between October and February. There are also large numbers of antelopes of various species, and leopards, buffaloes and rhinoceros can occasionally be seen.

When to visit

The park is open throughout the year. In summer visitors must be prepared for frequent rain and high temperatures. In winter temperatures are more agreeable, but it can be very windy. The best time of a year for a visit is from April to June.

Visitor facilities

Within the St Lucia Wetland Park there are a number of holiday camps (Charters Creek, Fanies Island, Mapelane, St Lucia, etc.), with accommodation in log cabins and holiday cottages; there are also camping sites. Boats can be hired in St Lucia. There are also 2-hour cruises on the lake three times a day in a boat taking 80 passengers, gliding past water birds, crocodiles and hippopotamuses. There is good fishing at many points on the lake.

2km/1¼ miles north of the St Lucia holiday complex is St Lucia Crocodile Centre, where visitors can learn about the breeding and keeping of crocodiles; the animals are usually fed on Saturdays at 3pm.

Excursions, walks

The park can be explored on the road which runs north from St Lucia to Cape Vidal (35km/22 miles). At all the holiday camps there are hiking and nature trails through the wooded dune country and the inland regions. The St Lucia Crocodile Centre is the starting-point of a number of hiking trails; the Mpophomeni Nature Trail (6km/4 miles) begins and ends at the False Bay camp; and there are many more.

Nyalas were originally common in Zululand but were almost exterminated there. They have been re-established in almost all South African game reserves and have now increased in numbers

Surroundings of St Lucia Wetlands Park

★Sodwana Bay
National Park

To the north of the St Lucia Wetland Park, on the shores of the Indian Ocean, is the Sodwana Bay National Park (area 413 hectares/1020 acres). It is reached by turning off N 2 10km/6 miles beyond Hluhluwe into a road signposted to Mbazwana, from which it is 25km/15 miles to Sodwana. After heavy rain the last stretch of road may be difficult to negotiate in an ordinary car. The coastal region is covered with forest. In swamp areas huge wild fig trees flourish. A touch of colour is added by strelitzias or parrot-flowers. In addition to numerous species of birds the fauna includes bush pigs, antelopes and some species of snake. Off the coast are unspoiled coral reefs, a happy hunting ground for divers. There is accommodation for visitors in log cabins and on camping sites.

Other nature
reserves

Farther north, near the Mozambique border, there are two interesting nature reserves, the Kosi Bay Nature Reserve and the Ndumu Game Reserve (see entry). Also very rewarding are the Mkuzi Game Reserve and the Hluhluwe and Umfolozi Game Reserves (see entries).

There are also a number of luxurious private game parks in this area, among them the Phinda Resource Reserve (area 17,000 hectares/42,000 acres), to the west of N 2, between the Hluhluwe and Mkuzi reserves.

Somerset West   D 10

Province: Western Cape
Altitude: 8m/26ft
Population: 29,000
Distances: 35km/22 miles from Cape Town, 73km/45 miles from Caledon

Situation and
characteristics

The little town of Somerset West, prettily situated at the foot of the Heiderberg range, can be taken in on a round trip from Cape Town through the wine-growing areas round Stellenbosch (see entry), Franschhoek and Paarl (see entry).

The town, founded in 1822, grew up round a Dutch Reformed church. It was named after Lord Charles Somerset, Governor of the Cape.

The town

Somerset West is a town of trim villas with many parks and gardens. It preserves a number of old buildings, including the police station, the former parsonage and the church (1820).

Surroundings of Somerset West

Vergelegen

The best known winery in the immediate area of Somerset West is Vergelegen, which is reached from the road to the Heiderberg Nature Reserve. The estate belonged to Governor Van der Stel, who acquired it in 1700. Visitors can see round the magnificent Cape Dutch mansion and taste the wines Mon.–Sat. (tel. 024/51 70 60).

★Heiderberg
Nature Reserve

On the outskirts of Somerset West, at the foot of the Heiderberg (1138m/3734ft), is the Heiderberg Nature Reserve (area 245 hectares/605 acres; open: daily 7.15am–6pm), which was established in 1960. It is famed mainly for its many species of protea and its rich bird life. There are a number of hiking trails through the reserve, the finest of which is one running up through the Disa Gorge (named after the disa orchid, which flowers from December to the beginning of February) to the summit of the hill, the Heiderberg Dome, from which there are fascinating views.

There are 82 species of proteas in South Africa, particularly in the Cape region ▶

Somerset West

Strand

Strand, originally planned as a coastal suburb of Somerset West, soon outstripped the older town, and now has a population of 33,000. The beautiful sandy beaches on False Bay and the facilities for a variety of water sports have made this a popular holiday resort, conveniently situated for the people of Cape Town.

Gordon's Bay

A rather quieter place, 8km/5 miles south-east, is the little fishing town and holiday resort of Gordon's Bay (pop. 3500). The coast here, however, is rocky and more suited for fishing than for bathing. From Gordon's Bay there is a very attractive run along the coast road to Kleinmond (see entry).

Sir Lowry's Pass, Grabouw

From Somerset West N 2 runs south-east and climbs to Sir Lowry's Pass (452m/1483ft), from which there are fine views of False Bay and the Cape Peninsula. From the pass the road continues to Grabouw (30km/19 miles from Somerset West), which along with the neighbouring town of Elgin is the market centre of the largest fruit-growing area in South Africa.

Soweto

See Johannesburg, Surroundings

Stellenbosch   D 10

Province: Western Cape
Altitude: 914m/2999ft
Population: 56,000
Distances: 30km/19 miles from Paarl, 50km/31 miles from Cape Town

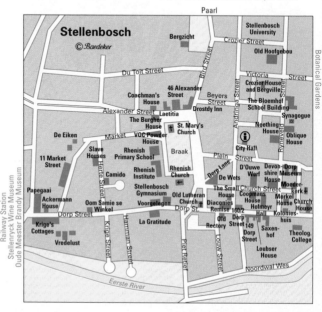

Stellenbosch, situated in a wine- and fruit-growing area, is one of the more interesting of South Africa's smaller towns. Lying so close to Cape Town, with so many attractive sights in the surrounding area, it is a place where visitors could profitably spend some time.

Stellenbosch is the second oldest European settlement (after Cape Town) on the Cape, founded in 1679 by Governor Van der Stel. The first settlers planted wheat, but it was soon realised that, thanks to the good soil and favourable climate of the area, it was possible to produce excellent wine here. This is now one of the most important wine-producing regions in South Africa. Stellenbosch has also been for more than a century a university town and centre of learning.

Stellenbosch is one of the most beautiful towns in South Africa and one of the best preserved of the towns dating from the time of the Dutch East India Company. Most of the town's historic core, round the Braak and along Dorp Street, still survives, with numerous old buildings in Cape Dutch style. A feature of Stellenbosch is its old oak-trees. Gay with colour throughout the year, it has a relaxed and cheerful atmosphere which all visitors will feel as they stroll quietly about the town.

Sights in Stellenbosch

The best starting-point for a walking tour of the town is the central square, Die Braak ("Fallow Field"). This open stretch of grass was originally a military parade ground on which festivals and other events were held (as they still sometimes are). Round the square are a number of historic buildings. Among them is the VOC Powder House, built by the Dutch East India Company (Vereenigde Oost-Indische Compagnie, VOC) in 1777,

Nowhere else in South Africa are there so many attractive little whitewashed Cape Dutch houses than in Stellenbosch

which now houses a small military museum (open: Mon.–Fri. 9.30am–1pm and 1.30–5pm). Near it is the Burgher House, built in 1797 and restored in the 1950s, which is now the headquarters of the Historical Houses of South Africa Society.

At the north end of the square is the little church of St Mary on the Braak (1854), with a bell-tower added in 1884.

★Stellenbosch
University

To the north of the Braak, reached by way of Bevers Street and Andringa Street, is the Neo-Classical Old Hoofgebou (1886), the main building of Stellenbosch University.

Stellenbosch University (the students are known as *maties* and the campus as Matieland) is the oldest and most celebrated university in South Africa. Founded in 1866 as a small grammar school, it was renamed Victoria College in 1887, Queen Victoria's Jubilee year, and raised to university status in 1918. Here the Boer intellectual elite studied and taught, among them future prime ministers, heads of state and ministers (Hans Strijdom, Daniel Malan, Jan Smuts, etc.). Here, it could be said, racism was given an academic consecration. But the University was also the source of progressive ideas: in 1958 a memorandum signed by 28 professors and lecturers called for reforms, some of which found expression in President de Klerk's "Rubicon" speech of 1990. The university refers with pride to the enormous increase in the number of black students between 1989 and 1993 – a percentage increase of no less than 228%; but it should be noted that in 1993 there were still only 151 black students out of a total of 14,387 – just 1.05%.

Botanical
Gardens

A little way east, in Neethling Street, are the University Botanic Gardens (open: Mon.–Fri. 8am–5pm), with indigenous succulents, orchids and cycads, as well as the welwitschias which are common in the deserts of Namibia.

★★Dorp Museum

From the University Ryneveld Street runs south to the Dorp (Village) Museum (open: Mon.–Sat. 9.30am–5pm, Sun. 2–5pm), a group of four houses dating from 1709 to 1850 which have been carefully restored and furnished in the original style, with gardens planted as they would have been at the time. The Schreuder House, built around 1709 by a court messenger of that name, is the oldest in town. The Bletterman House was built about 1789 by Judge H. L. Bletterman, and after his death became the residence of the local judge. The oldest part of Grosvenor House, a two-storey building in Neo-Classical style, dates from 1782; on the left of the main building are the old slaves' quarters, on the right a shed. The O. M. Bergh House was occupied by Oloff Marthinus Bergh until his death in 1866.

Moederkerk

Facing the Dorp Museum is the Moederkerk, a Dutch Reformed church of 1722 which originally had a thatched roof. In 1863 it was remodelled in Neo-Gothic style by the architect Carl Otto Hager.

Dorp Street

Farther south Drostdy Street runs into tree-lined Dorp Street, the old main street of the town, in which are many handsome old whitewashed houses, some of them with elaborate Cape Dutch gables.

The old Lutheran church (1851) now houses the University Art Gallery.

La Gratitude

This house at 95 Dorp Street, built by the Rev. Meent Borcherd in 1798 as a parsonage, has the "All-Seeing Eye" on the gable. It is now privately owned.

Libertas Parva

This finely restored house of 1783 at 31 Dorp Street is now occupied by the Rembrandt van Rijn Art Gallery (open: Mon.–Fri. 9am–12.45pm and 2–5pm, Sat. 10am–1pm and 2–5pm, Sun. 2.30–5.30pm), with works by Irma Stern, Jacob Hendrik Pierneef and Anton van Wouw among other South African artists.

In Libertas Parva Cellar is the Stellenryck Museum of the Distillers' Corporation of South Africa (open: Mon.–Fri. 9am–12.45pm and 2–5pm, Sat. 10am–1pm and 2–5pm. Sun. 2.30–5.30pm), which illustrates the history of wine-making with displays of tools, other apparatus and wines. In front of the museum is an imposing late 18th century German wine-press.

Stellenryck
Wine Museum

This museum (open: Mon.–Fri. 9am–12.15pm and 2–5pm, Sat. 10am–1pm and 2–5pm, Sun. 2.30–5pm), in Old Strand Road (which opens off Dorp Street) has a collection of material illustrating the development of brandy-making on the Cape.

Oude Meester
Brandy Museum

To get back to the starting point of the tour, return along Dorp Street and turn left into Market Street. Opening off this on the right is Herte Street, in which are the "slave houses", actually built by bond labourers after the liberation of the slaves in 1838 and much altered in later times.

Slave houses

Surroundings of Stellenbosch

On the outskirts of the town, on the Cape Town road, is the Stellenbosch Farmers' Winery Centre, which organises presentations on the history of wine-making on the Cape and conducted tours (Mon.–Thur. at 10.30am and 2.30pm, Fri. at 10.30am: to book, tel. 02231/7 34 00).

★Stellenbosch
Farmers' Winery
Centre

The Stellenbosch Wine Route (waymarked by signs showing a white winding road on a green ground, surmounted by a green bunch of grapes on a circular red ground) leads to 23 wineries and five wine-making cooperatives. Beautifully situated amid great expanses of vineyards, these offer wine-tastings and good meals in their restaurants. Further information on the Wine Route is available from the Wine Route office (tel. 021/8 86 43 10).

★Stellenbosch
Wine Route

South-west of Stellenbosch on R 310 is the old-established Neethlingshof winery. In the Cape Dutch mansion is an excellent restaurant. Rather less elegant is the adjoining Palm Terrace (wine tasting and sales Mon.–Fri. 9am–5pm, Sun. 10am–4pm: to book in restaurants, tel. 021/8 83 89 66).

Neethlingshof

An attractive excursion from Stellenbosch is to the Jonkershoek valley, in which is the Assegaaibosch Nature Reserve (area 168 hectares/415 acres; open: Mon.–Fri. 8.30am–4pm, Sat. 9am–6pm). Through the reserve runs a circular hiking trail 2km/1¼ miles long, which also leads to a 5 hectare/12 acre wild flower garden.

Assegaaibosch
Nature Reserve

Beyond this is the Hottentots Holland Nature Reserve (area 25,000 hectares/61,750 acres), which is accessible only on foot, on the Boland Hiking Trail; it can also be reached from Sir Lowry's Pass (see Somerset West). This reserve has an extraordinarily rich flora and a fauna which includes rheboks, springboks and dwarf antelopes; leopards, caracals and jackals are also occasionally to be seen.

Hottentots Holland
Nature Reserve

30km/19 miles east of Stellenbosch is Franschhoek (see below), best reached on R 310. Soon after leaving Stellenbosch the road begins to climb to the Helshoogte Pass (336m/1102ft), from which there are magnificent views. The road then runs down to the Boschendal winery, with a mansion of 1812 which is a superb example of Cape Dutch architecture, now a national monument. The house is furnished in period style and is open to the public (daily 11am–5pm). Here too there are a souvenir shop, the Taphuis (wine tasting) and a restaurant.

★Boschendal

R 310 runs into R 45, which leads to the wine-producing town of Franschhoek (pop. 3400), surrounded by vineyards. As the name ("French Corner") indicates, the town was originally established by French settlers – Huguenots who came here in 1688, seeking refuge from persecution in France.

Franschhoek

Vineyard near Franschhoek

The newcomers included many wine-growers, who soon realised that the soil and climate of this area would enable them to produce first-class wines.

Franschhoek is the starting-point of a wine trail which leads through country of great beauty to a number of wineries in the area.

Huguenot Monument

In gardens at the south end of the town is the Huguenot Monument (by the sculptor Coert Steynberg), erected in 1938 to commemorate 250 years of settlement by the Huguenots. The central figure is a woman holding a Bible in her right hand and a broken chain in the left, symbolising the Huguenots' escape from religious oppression.

Beside the monument is a museum opened in 1965 (open: Mon.–Sat. 9am–5pm, Sun. 2–5pm), consisting of two buildings displaying mementoes and documents on the history of the Huguenots.

★Franschhoek Pass

Beyond the monument the road climbs to the Franschhoek Pass (701m/2300ft), from which there are breathtaking views of the surrounding wine- and fruit-growing country.

The return route to Stellenbosch is on the road to Grabouw, which goes over Viljoen's Pass (525m/1723ft) and finally joins N 2. This runs west to Somerset West (see entry), from which it is 18km/11 miles to Stellenbosch.

Sun City   J 3

Province: North-West
Distances: 140km/87 miles from Pretoria, 160km/100 miles from Johannesburg

Situation and characteristics

Sun City, a huge entertainment complex 160km/100 miles north-west of Johannesburg, draws a daily 25,000 visitors, who travel from Johannes-

View of Sun City

burg by air or by car. It consists of four hotel complexes, of which the fairytale palace called the Lost City is the most exclusive, and offers every conceivable facility for the entertainment of its visitors, including the world's largest gaming casino, cinemas, discothèques, a huge range of water sports and a golf course of international standing. There is a large stadium used for sporting events and pop concerts. This "Las Vegas of southern Africa" lies on the territory of the former homeland of Bophuthatswana (see Mmabatho), surrounded by lush green parkland – an area which in 1977 was still barren savanna steppe.

The concept of Sun City seems to have proved itself. In recent years its hotels have had occupancy rates of 80%, a figure that other luxury hotels can only hope for. In the days when Bophuthatswana was (at any rate in theory) independent of South Africa well-to-do South Africans flocked from their relatively prudish country, in which gambling was strictly prohibited, to the more relaxed atmosphere of this pleasure city over the border, and Sun City has continued to flourish since Bophuthatswana was incorporated in the new South Africa.

Sights in and around Sun City

The hotel and leisure complex to which the name of Lost City was given in 1992. It is supposed to recall a legendary lost African culture – though one that never existed in the form in which it is now presented, an illusion created by the use of the most modern technology. The central feature is the Palace, a luxury hotel with 338 rooms in a mingling of various architectural styles which nevertheless achieves a harmonious effect. Above the hotel rears a 70m/230ft high tower, and in the 25m/80ft high lobby a visitor feels as if he is in a cathedral rather than a hotel – for in the Lost City everything is larger than it is elsewhere. Below the hotel are 25 hectares/60 acres of artificially created tropical rain forest containing

★The Lost City

373

10,000 orchids. The construction of this expanse of "primeval forest" involved the transport to this site of trees weighing up to 40 tons. Streams run through the forest, creating waterfalls up to 16m/50ft high. The shores of the Roaring Lagoon are formed from imported sand, with artificially generated waves (on which surfing is possible) rolling in to the beach. To create the impression of being in the "real" South Africa loudspeakers emit animal sounds throughout the day and night, and every now and then computer-generated programmes create the illusion of an earthquake. Whether you like this fairytale world or dismiss it as Disneyland-style kitsch is a matter which each visitor must decide for himself.

There is restricted access to the Lost City from Sun City's other three hotels.

★Pilanesberg National Park

An alternative to this artificial world is offered by a safari through Pilanesberg National Park, to the north of Sun City (open: April to August daily 5.30am–5pm, September to March 5am–8pm). Visitors not coming from Sun City can reach the park by way of R 510, which runs between Rustenburg and Thabazimbi. The park (area 58,000 hectares/143,000 acres) lies in a hilly region, whose highest point is the Pilanesberg (1687m/5535ft), in the border area between the arid Kalahari and the moist lowveld of the Transvaal.

When the National Park was established in the 1960s the farmers who worked the land here had to be resettled elsewhere. A tall fence was erected round the area and animals from elsewhere in Africa were introduced into the park. Its denizens now include steppe zebras, rhinos, elephants, leopards, giraffes, buffaloes and many species of antelope, as well as 300 species of birds.

The animals can be observed either from your own car on the park's 150km/95 mile network of tracks or on a guided walk. There is accommodation for visitors in chalets and on camping sites.

Sunshine Coast

See Amanzimtoti

Swaziland   M/N 4/5

Area: 17,364sq.km/6704sq. miles
Population: 847,000
Capital: Mbabane

Location and characteristics

Swaziland (known to the Swazis as Ngwane) lies in the south-east of the African continent, bounded on the north, west and south by South Africa and on the east by Mozambique. With an area of 17,364sq.km/6704sq. miles, it is the second smallest state in Africa (after Gambia).

Swaziland is a monarchy, with a parliament whose main function is to advise the king. The head of government is appointed by the king. Political parties are banned.

The official language is Swazi (SiSwati). English is also used to some extent in administration and education.

The most used route from Johannesburg to Mbabane, capital of Swaziland, is on N 4 to Machadodorp and then R 541. Mbabane can also be reached on R 29 to Ermelo and then R 39. The best route from KwaZulu/Natal is on N 2 via Nsoko and Big Bend to Manzini and Mbabane.

Topography

The hilly region in the west of the country (Mt Mlembe, 1862m/6109ft) is part of the Great Escarpment on the edge of South Africa's central plateau (the highveld). Well watered by rain and rivers and densely wooded as a result of afforestation, this is the economic heartland of Swaziland (iron and asbestos working). East of this is a fertile upland region, the middleveld, which in turn gives place to the flat and also fertile lowveld (200–300m/650–1000ft). A natural frontier with Mozambique in the east is formed for 150km/95 miles by the Lebombo Mountains, a basaltic range of hills (around 600m/2000ft) geologically related to the Drakensberg of South Africa which extends northward from northern Zululand for 600km/370 miles to the Limpopo. Swaziland's principal river is the Usutu, which flows into the Pongola River beyond the eastern frontier. The Usutu valley is the most populous part of the country.

In the hilly part of the country the subtropical climate is relatively temperate, with a good deal of rain. The middleveld, with an average annual rainfall of around 1000mm/40in., is Swaziland's main agricultural region. The lowveld is hot and dry, with extensive irrigated areas in which the main crop is sugar-cane.

Climate

Swaziland's eucalyptus and pine forests, mostly the result of afforestation programmes, lie mainly on the highveld, which is otherwise a grassland region. In the rainy middleveld the umbrella acacia is common, while the lowveld with its scanty rainfall is a region of savanna with thorny shrubs.

Vegetation

Swaziland has an average population density of 49 to the sq. kilometre (127 to the sq. mile), the western and eastern regions being more densely populated, with steadily increasing numbers of people moving into these areas from the rest of the country. More than two-thirds of the population live on the land.

Population

95% of the population are Swazis. In addition there are a few thousand of mixed race, some 2000 Europeans, Indians, Pakistanis and 46,000 refugees from Mozambique. The annual rate of population growth, at over 3%, is very high.

The predominant religions are various Bantu faiths and Protestantism (African Apostolic Church).

The economy of Swaziland is heavily dependent on that of South Africa. The most important branch of the economy is the services sector. Many thousand Swazis work in South Africa.

Economy

Although two-thirds of the population work on the land, agriculture makes only a minor contribution to the gross domestic product. Most of the country's agricultural land is devoted to subsistence agriculture, on land granted on lease by the king through the local authorities; the rest is owned by Europeans or by companies. In Swazi eyes stock-farming has more prestige than arable farming, and as a result there are very large numbers of livestock, leading to over-grazing and erosion of the soil. The government seeks by promoting the development of cooperatives to encourage the growing of more basic foodstuffs and produce for the market. In the lowveld, with the help of irrigation, citrus fruits, rice and sugar-cane are grown. The most important agricultural export product is sugar. Other important products are cotton and citrus fruits and, for meeting domestic needs, maize and millet, the traditional staple foods.

Forestry, particularly on the highveld, is of considerable economic importance as a result of large-scale reafforestation projects from the 1950s onwards. Most of the timber felled consists of conifers, mainly pines.

Industry contributes just under a third of the gross domestic product. The processing industries deal mainly with the products of agriculture and forestry, and accordingly a dominant place is occupied by the foodstuffs industries (particularly sugar), timber-working and papermaking. Textiles, metalworking and chemicals are also of some importance. Plans for the further development of industry are hampered by the country's landlocked situation and by the small domestic market. The government seeks to attract investment by offering various incentives such as tax concessions and favourable prices for land.

Mining also makes a contribution to Swaziland's economy. The asbestos plant at Havelock is one of the largest in the world. Coal is worked at Mpaka and on the eastern borders of the country. Other minerals are kaolin, diamonds, gold and tin.

Swaziland's imports, mainly from South Africa, include machinery, transport equipment, fuel and foodstuffs; its principal exports, mainly to South Africa and the European Union, are foodstuffs, animals and timber.

Almost half of Swaziland's electric power is imported from South Africa. It has a number of small coal-fired power stations and hydro-electric stations, and it is planned to develop these sources of energy still further. In the field of tourism the country's main attractions are its game reserves and the mountain scenery of the highveld; most foreign visitors come from South Africa.

History

The Swazis came to what is now Swaziland during the Nguni migration around 1750. In the 19th century great Swazi kings – Sobhuza I (c. 1780–1839), Mswati II (c. 1820–68) – formed the Swazi people ("Mswati's people") from the Swazi upper strata, old established Sotho tribes and other immigrant Nguni groups. Then in the middle of the century the first whites began to appear – adventurers, hunters, traders, missionaries and farmers. When the pressure from these incomers, particularly Boers from the Transvaal, grew steadily greater Mswati asked Britain for protection, which was granted on certain conditions. Mswati's grandson Mbandzeni, who succeeded him as king, was compelled by economic necessity to sell large tracts of territory and grant all mining rights to South Africans. After the British annexation of the Transvaal, in 1881, Britain established Swaziland's independence from the Transvaal and laid down its present frontiers. From 1894 to 1899 it was a protectorate of the Transvaal. Until the accession in 1921 of the legendary king Sobhuza II (b. 1899) the country was ruled by his grandmother, who called on her subjects to buy the country back. During her reign, in 1903, Swaziland became a British protectorate. In the distribution of land by the British authorities the Swazis were allotted mainly arable land. In spite of increasing problems between the colonial authorities and the queen regent Swaziland took part in the First World War on the Allied side. In recognition of this the British authorities bought up land occupied by whites and returned it to the Swazis.

After Swaziland became independent on September 6th 1968 (National Day) King Sobhuza II (1899–1982) remained head of state. In 1972, during a period of political conflict, he suspended the democratic constitution and banned all political parties. In 1978 a new constitution came into force, restricting the two-chamber parliament to a purely advisory role. After Sobhuza's death a regency under two of his widows Mswati II succeeded him as king. In 1989 he appointed Obed Ufanyana Diamini prime minister.

Incwala festival

The Incwala is an impressive religious festival celebrated in December and January and lasting three weeks. It is a kind of fertility ceremony designed to prepare for the new year and as a symbolic renewal of the monarchy.

At the beginning of the celebrations representatives of the Bemanti people bring water from all the main rivers of Swaziland and foam from the sea, gathered at the new moon. Young men then build a royal kraal at Lobamba from branches of the lusekwana tree and other plants. The central ceremonies begin on the first night of full moon and last six days. On the "day of the bull" a bull is killed and offered as a sacrifice. The climax is reached on the following day, the "great day", when the king, clad in his finest robes, symbolically tastes the first fruits of the harvest and there is singing and dancing. On the last day all the ceremonial objects are burned as offerings to the rain gods.

Visitors are welcome at these celebrations except for certain parts of the ceremonies. Photography is not permitted.

Travel Routes in Swaziland

There are twelve frontier crossings, usually open only during the day, between South Africa and Swaziland. European and other visitors require a

A Swazi village

visa, which can be obtained at the frontier. With Mbabane, which has comfortable hotels, as a base, the country can be explored by car. The most important main roads are asphalted, but even the unsurfaced tracks are usually negotiable by an ordinary car. In the remoter parts of the country, particularly during the months of high rainfall (October to March), it is essential to enquire locally about road conditions.

Mbabane – Siteki – Bhalekane – Mbabane (300km/185 miles)

Mbabane (pop. 52,000), Swaziland's capital, was founded by white pioneers. In 1888 Michael Walls set up a shop here, round which a small village soon grew up. The development of the place received a boost after Swaziland became a British protectorate in 1903, when the centre of colonial administration was transferred from Bremersdorp (now Manzini) to Mbabane with its more agreeable climate.

Mbabane has developed rapidly in recent years, and building activity is continuing. It is now a town of widely separated districts, beautiful gardens and tree-shaded streets.

The only feature of tourist interest is the Swazi Market at the south end of Allister Miller Street, the town's main shopping street. The wares offered for sale include not only agricultural produce but all the various craft products of Swaziland, including masks, basketwork and pottery.

A pleasant excursion from Mbabane is a trip up beautiful Pine Valley to the north of the town. The route follows the Umbeluzi River, passing a number of waterfalls. This is good walking and riding country, with agreeable temperatures even in summer.

Ezulwini ("Place of the Sky"), to the south of Mbabane, is a tourist centre, with a large number of hotels and a gaming casino. There are also tennis courts, riding arenas and a thermal spring, as well as numerous shops selling craft products.

Mbabane

Ezulwini

377

Swaziland

★Mlilwane
Wildlife
Sanctuary

Ezulwini is surrounded on the north, west and south by Mlilwane Wildlife Sanctuary, established by Ted and Elizabeth Reilly, who turned their farm at Mlilwane, with the support of King Sobhuza II, into a game reserve and presented it to the state in 1964. The Mlilwane Wildlife Sanctuary, which has now grown to 4500 hectares/11,100 acres as a result of further donations of land, is an area of scrub and grassland surrounded by the Nyonyane ("Place of the Little Bird") Mountains. Originally animals had to be brought to the reserve from far afield, and particular species of plants had to be introduced for them to feed on. The Mlilwane Sanctuary is now home to 470 species of birds and many indigenous mammals, including zebras, rhinoceros, crocodiles, giraffes, hippopotamuses and antelopes. The chance of a visit to the Mantenga Falls should not be missed.

There is accommodation for visitors in chalets and on a camping site. Conducted tours on horseback or by car are available.

★Lobamba

To the south of Ezulwini, in the beautiful Ezulwini valley, is Lobamba Royal Village, with the Royal Kraal, the Parliament Building, the National Museum and other government buildings.

In the large Embo State Palace the king holds audiences, and the magnificent State House, built in 1978, is used mainly for ceremonial and other state occasions; neither of these buildings is open to the public. The Parliament Building (1979) can be visited. The Somhlolo Stadium is the venue of major cultural and sporting events, state celebrations, concerts, dance performances and speeches by the king.

The National Museum (open: Mon.–Fri. 9am–3.45pm, Sat. and Sun. 10am–3.45pm), set in beautiful gardens, has interesting archaeological and historical exhibits on the culture and history of Swaziland, including examples of traditional dress with explanations of their significance and function. Outside the Museum is a Swazi kraal.

Manzini

15km/9 miles east of Lobamba is Manzini, on the Mzimneni River. The town grew up round a shop and hotel established towards the end of the 19th century and in 1890, under the name of Bremersdorp, became the administrative centre of Swaziland under British and Boer rule – a role which it lost to Mbabane a few years later. It was given its present name ("Place on the Water") in 1960.

Manzini (pop. 52,000) is the country's main economic centre, with cotton- and meat-processing factories, a brewery and an electronics factory. In spring its streets are gay with the blossom of jacarandas and flame-trees. It has no features of tourist interest apart from a market selling local craft products.

From Manzini the road runs east. From the last hills of the middleveld there is a wide view over the lowveld, with the Lebombo Mountains in the distance. The road runs through an extensive area of pastureland. After the turn-off for Big Bend it climbs steeply into the Lebombo Mountains, with ever grander views of the lowveld the higher it goes.

Siteki

The little town of Siteki (pop. 1500), set in a park-like landscape with jacarandas and tulip-trees, is the commercial and administrative centre of the Lebombo district. The origins of the town are unknown, but its name ("Place of Many Marriages") suggests interesting possibilities.

Hlane
Game Sanctuary

Returning along the same road and in 13km/8 miles turning into a road on the right running north, we come to the Hlane ("Wilderness") Game Sanctuary. This reserve, the largest in the country (30,000 hectares/75,000 acres), belongs to the king, who hunts here annually. Most of the area is therefore closed to the public.

The reserve is a paradise for nature-lovers, with fine bush vegetation and large numbers of animals, including elephants, giraffes, water buffaloes, zebras and crocodiles.

The little town of Simunye (pop. 4500), on the north-eastern edge of the game sanctuary, was established some years ago for workers in the sugar industry. It has a large new sugar factory.

Simunye

To the east of Simunye is the Mlawula Nature Reserve (area 18,000 hectares/45,000 acres), which extends from the lowveld up into the Lebombo Mountains.

Mlawula Nature Reserve

From the junction at the bridge over the Mbuluzi River a road runs west through large plantations of sugar-cane and citrus fruits, passing Mhlume, which has the largest sugar factory in the country, to Tshaneni ("Place of the Small Stone"). In this area dams have been built to provide water for irrigating the fields. Beyond Bhalekane there is a choice of routes: either the road which runs south via Croyden to return to Manzini or the track which runs north-west to Pigg's Peak (76km/47 miles from Tshaneni), climbing into the hills through marvellous scenery.

Mhlume, Bhalekane

Mbabane – Bunya – Nhlangano – Mbabane (190km/120 miles)

With an area of 65,000 hectares/160,500 acres, mainly pines, Usutu Forest is one of the largest planted forests in the world. The road south from Mbabane via Mhlambanyatsi to Bunya runs through the forest, affording magnificent views of the richly wooded country.

Usutu Forest

Bunya has a paper factory which produces 180,000 tons of paper annually. It can be visited by appointment (tel. 7 43 31).

Bunya

From Bunya the road runs east, turning south at Loyengo into the road to Mankayane, through country of unspoiled natural beauty. After passing the Ngabeni mission and Mtimani Forest it comes to Mankayane, where there are a few shops.

Mankayane

The road now continues south-west to Sicunusa and then south-east, heading for Nhlangano. It runs through the beautiful and well cultivated Grand Valley, from which there are fine views. The Swazis moved into this area in the mid 18th century.
The name of Nhlangano ("Meeting-Place") the chief place in the valley, refers to a meeting here in 1947 between Sobhuza II and King George VI.

Nhlangano

From Hlatsikhulu, 27km/17 miles north of Nhlangano, there is a magnificent view of the Grand Valley. From here the return to Mbabane is by way of Manzini.

Hlatsikhulu

Mbabane – Pigg's Peak (67km/42 miles)

15km/9 miles north-west of Mbabane is Motshane, from which a road runs north-east through some of the most beautiful upland country in Africa. The first part of the road is through an area of grassland and rocky hills, with the Ngwenya and Silotwane Mountains to the west.

Motshane

To the left of the road is the Malolotja Nature Reserve (area 18,000 hectares/45,000 acres); the name means "river with many rapids and waterfalls". In this area are some of the oldest rock formations in the world. The fauna is particularly notable for the many species of reptiles and of birds, and the flora is rich and varied.
In the southern part of the reserve is the Ngwenya Mine (seen by appointment: apply to nature reserve office), probably the oldest mine in the world, in which haematite and smectite were already being worked 45,000 years ago. In more recent times iron ore was worked here, but the mine closed down in the 1970s. There are hiking trails through the reserve, and accommodation is available in numerous camps. In the Komati valley are some interesting Bushman paintings.

★Malolotja Nature Reserve

Nkaba	After passing through the little market town of Nkaba the road enters the valley of the rapidly flowing Komati River, an area of outstanding natural beauty in both form and colour. It climbs up the north side of the valley, passing the plantations of the Swaziland Plantation Company, with a sawmill.
Pigg's Peak	The little town of Pigg's Peak grew up after the discovery of gold here in 1881. Three years later William Pigg struck a gold-mine which for 80 years was the largest in the country. Pigg's Peak is now a timber-working town, with shops, government offices and a craft market.
Excursion to ★Phophonyane Falls	13km/8 miles north-east of Pigg's Peak are the imposing Phophonyane Falls. This beautiful area, with its lush vegetation and rich bird life, has been used as the setting for films. It can be explored on a number of hiking trails. Nearby is the very attractive Phophonyane Lodge, which accommodates visitors in cottages and tents and organises tours of the surrounding area.
Excursion to ★Havelock Mine	At Bulembo, 21km/13 miles west of Pigg's Peak, is the Havelock Mine (named after Sir Arthur Havelock, a former Governor of Natal), one of the five largest asbestos mines in the world. Gold was also found here in 1836, drawing prospectors from far and wide for the next 30 years. After the rediscovery of the asbestos deposits, in 1930, a Canadian firm bought shares in the mine at a horrendous price and began to work the asbestos, which is transported to Baberton on a 20km/12½ mile long cableway running 5m/16ft above the ground.

Manzini – Big Bend – Lavumisha (153km/95 miles)

Manzini	From Manzini this route, the main road to the South African province of KwaZulu/Natal, runs south-east over the lower middleveld to Siphofaneni ("Yellowish-Brown Place"), where there are hot chloride springs. Past the town flows the Usutu River, Swaziland's largest river and at this point a beauty spot, lined by tall fig trees (good fishing). Farther on a side road goes off on the left to the Mkhaya Nature Reserve.
Mkhaya Nature Reserve	The Mkhaya Nature Reserve (area 6250 hectares/15,450 acres) belongs to Ted Reilly and can be visited only by appointment; there is accommodation for visitors in a tented camp. The reserve was established to protect endangered species. Among the animals to be seen here are elephants and rhinos.
Big Bend	At Big Bend, a centre of sugar production, the road turns south. This stretch of road skirting the Lebombo Mountains is particularly beautiful. After running through the little market town of Nsoko it comes in 77km/48 miles to the frontier town of Lavumisha ("Hot Place"), which in summer fully lives up to its name.

Swellendam   E 10

	Province: Western Cape Altitude: 122m/400ft Population: 8500 Distances: 67km/42 miles from Robertson, 72km/45 miles from Bredasdorp, 240km/150 miles from Cape Town
Situation and characteristics	Swellendam lies in a well watered valley under the imposing peaks of the Langeberg Mountains. The third oldest town in South Africa, it is now a busy agricultural centre. A number of handsome old buildings have been preserved from the town's early days.

The territory round Swellendam was originally occupied by the Hassekwa, a Hottentot tribe, who built their kraals here because of the abundance of game in the area. In Bonteboskloof can be seen the graves of the last two chiefs of the tribe, Klaas and Markus Shababa.

Swellendam was founded in 1745 as an outpost of the Dutch East India Company and named after Governor Swellengrebel and his wife Helena ten Damme. During the 19th century, as a centre of wool production, it developed into a flourishing commercial and administrative town.

Swellendam has preserved numerous historic old buildings, including some very handsome villas, in Cape Dutch, Georgian and Victorian style. Most of them are in Voortrek Street and round the Drostdy Museum complex.

History

★The town

Sights in and around Swellendam

The Drostdy, the residence of the landdrost (the district officer of the Cape government), was built in 1747. A handsome house in Cape Dutch style, it is now, after restoration, the principal building in the Drostdy Museum complex (open: Mon.–Fri. 9am–4.45pm, Sat. 10am–4pm). It contains a collection of fine Cape Dutch furniture and domestic equipment. Other buildings in the complex are the old prison, the prison governor's house and Mayville House (1853).

★Drostdy Museum

5km/3 miles north of the town, at the foot of the Langeberg range, is Marloth Nature Reserve (area 11,300 hectares/37,000 acres), which attracts many walkers. There is a 76km/47 mile long hiking trail with five possible overnight stops in huts (though it can be shortened to 54km/34 miles or 48km/30 miles). A permit is required to undertake the walk, and a place must be booked in advance: apply to Trail Director, Private Bag X9605, Cape Town 8000.

Marloth Nature Reserve

The original habitat of the bontebok, a species of antelope (*Damaliscus dorcas dorcas*), was the 56km/35 mile wide plain between the Bot River in the west and Mossel Bay in the east. Until the end of the 18th century this area was grazed by great herds of bontebok, which in the course of the 19th century were reduced to a few dozen. The Bontebok National Park (area 3226 hectares/7968 acres; open: October to April daily 8am–7pm, May to September 8am–6pm), 7km/4½ miles south-east of Swellendam, was established to protect them, and since 1961 their numbers have risen from 60 to more than 300. At excellent place from which to observe them is Lang Elsieskraal, an old Khoikhoi encampment. Among other animals in the park

★Bontebok National Park

The Drostdy, Swellendam; one of South Africa's finest Cape Dutch houses

are rheboks, mountain zebras, dwarf antelopes and grey duikers. There are also 192 species of birds. As for flora, the park has over 470 species of plants, which in spring produce a brilliant show of colour.

The Breede River, which flows through the National Park, is a good fishing stream. Visitors can observe the wild life from their car, and there are two short hiking trails. For day visitors there are picnic areas; for those who want to stay longer there is only a camping site.

Robertson,
Montagu

Within easy reach of Swellendam are the attractive little towns of Robertson and Montagu (see entries).

Transvaal Drakensberg

See Blyderivierspoort Nature Reserve

Tsitsikamma National Park

See Garden Route

Tulbagh

D 9

Province: Western Cape
Altitude: 200m/660ft
Population: 3000
Distances: 60km/37 miles from Worcester, 130km/81 miles from Cape Town

Situation and
characteristics

A trip from Cape Town into the Cedarberg (see Citrusdal) can be combined with a visit to the pretty little town of Tulbagh. The soil and climate of this area favour the growing of fruit and wine, and sheep-farming also makes a contribution to the local economy.

History

The first settlers arrived in the valley of the Little Berg River in 1700 and, finding the land to be fertile, established numbers of farms in the area. In the mid 18th century they built a church, round which the little town of Tulbagh (named after a Governor of the Cape) grew up from 1795 onwards.

★The town

In 1969 an earthquake destroyed much of the old town, but since then the damaged buildings have all been restored in their original form. In Church Street is a row of 32 gabled houses of the 18th and 19th centuries, one more charming than the other.

Wine and
Sherry Route

Tulbagh is the starting-point of a Wine and Sherry Route taking in a series of local wineries. In the town itself wine can be tasted and bought in a number of establishments, among them the Tulbagh Wine Cellar. The Twee Jonge Gezellen winery offers conducted tours.

Sights in Tulbagh

★Oude Kerk
Volksmuseum

The old Dutch Reformed church at 2 Church Street, built in 1743, is now a folk museum (open: Mon.–Fri. 9am–1pm and 2–5pm, Sun. 11am–12.30pm and 2–4.30pm). Attached to the museum are three little houses in Church Street. No. 4 displays historical and geological collections; the Victorian House at No. 14, built in 1892, is furnished in the style of the period; and No. 22 is a typical Cape Dutch house, with a herb garden.

All the old gabled houses in Church Street, Tulbagh, are protected as national monuments

Outside the town, to the west, is the Oude Drostdy, once the residence of the landdrost, the district officer of the Cape government. It now contains a collection of Cape Dutch furniture and furnishings. In the old prison visitors can sample the locally produced sherry (open: Mon.–Sat. 10am–12.50pm and 2–4.50pm).

De Oude Drostdy

Tzaneen   L 2

Province: Northern Transvaal
Altitude: 684m/2244ft. Population: 5500
Distances: 112km/70 miles from Phalaborwa, 121km/75 miles from Louis Trichardt

Tzaneen, situated at the foot of the northern Drakensberg in the valley of the Letaba River, is famed for its magnificent subtropical vegetation. Among the crops grown here are exotic fruits, tea (there are conducted tours of the plantations), nuts, flowers, winter vegetables and potatoes. Tzaneen has developed into a popular tourist centre, both as a stopover on the way to the Kruger National Park and as a base from which to explore the surrounding area. In the town and its immediate surroundings there are a number of comfortable hotels, and it has a wide range of sports facilities, including an 18-hole golf course and a swimming pool of Olympic dimensions. Tzaneen has an agreeable climate in winter, when it is pleasantly warm during the day and there is little rain.

Situation and characteristics

Surroundings of Tzaneen

To the north of Tzaneen is the Fanie Botha Dam Nature Reserve, consisting of the Dam itself and a 300m/330yd wide strip of wooded country round it.

Fanie Botha Dam Nature Reserve

The reservoir attracts large numbers of water sports enthusiasts and anglers, and round it are numbers of attractive picnic spots. The wild life in the nature reserve consists of antelopes and more than 150 species of birds; there is no big game.

Duiwelskloof

Another tourist centre in this area is Duiwelskloof, 18km/11 miles from Tzaneen on R 36 (which runs along the Fanie Botha Dam). In the subtropical climate avocados, mangoes and citrus fruits flourish, and in spring the area is carpeted with flowers. The Duiwelskloof Resort is the starting-point of a number of hiking trails.

★Modjadji
Nature Reserve

It is a pleasant drive from Duiwelskloof to the Modjadji Nature Reserve, 28km/17 miles north-east. The reserve was established in 1985 to protect a species of cycad known as the Modjadji palm (or breadfruit tree). This reaches a height of 3 or 4m (10–13ft), with some specimens as much as 8m/26ft high. Visitors can explore the reserve on a number of hiking trails and, with luck, may see impalas, blue wildebeests, nyalas and kudus.

The reserve lies on the territory of the Lobedu tribe, the chief of which is a woman known as the "rain queen". The female ruling dynasty to which she belongs can be traced back to the 16th century, when, it is said, a princess who had the skill of a rain-maker fled to this area with a group of her supporters. She and her successors were frequently appealed to by other peoples and tribes asking for rain. Rider Haggard's adventure novel "She" (1887) was based on this legend.

★Hans Merensky
Nature Reserve

70km/43 miles north-east of Tzaneen is the Hans Merensky Nature Reserve (area 5185 hectares/12,807 acres), which is bounded on the west by the Letaba River. In contrast to most other nature reserves in South Africa, visitors cannot explore the reserve in their own car. There are organised bus tours, starting from the Eiland Mineral Spa complex, and there are also hiking trails for those who prefer to see the reserve on foot. Among the animals living in the reserve are sable and roan antelopes, zebras, giraffes and kudus. A particular attraction in the reserve is the Tsonga Kraal open-air museum, illustrating the way of life of the Tsonga tribe a hundred years ago.

★Magoebaskloof

From Tzaneen R 71 runs south-west towards the Magoebaskloof, at first running parallel to the valley of the Magoebas River. In 18km/11 miles a road goes off on the right to the Debegeni Falls, which plunge down 80m/260ft to form a small lake (bathing permitted). The main road then climbs to a pass (1432m/4698ft) with the Magoebaskloof Hotel. A few miles beyond this it runs past the Ebenezer Dam, a popular recreation area (boating, fishing). From here it is 5km/3 miles to Haenertsburg, famed for its abundance of trout and its cherry-blossom festival in spring.

The forest country round the Magoebaskloof can be explored on various hiking trails (including walks taking several days, with overnight accommodation in huts): information from tourist office in Tzaneen.

Wolkberg
Wilderness Area

The high hills and deep valleys of the Wolkberg range are part of the Drakensberg chain. This wilderness area (20,000 hectares/50,000 acres) is almost completely unspoiled. It is reached from Tzaneen by taking the road (No. 589) to the New Agatha forest station and continuing from there on foot.

Ulundi   M 6

Province: KwaZulu/Natal
Altitude: 660m/2165ft
Population: 8000
Distances: 100km/62 miles from Eshowe, 316km/196 miles from Durban

Ulundi is the most important town in Zululand and was until 1994 capital of the "non-independent" homeland of KwaZulu, which consisted of ten separate areas of land, occupied by some 3 million Zulus out of the total Zulu population of 5.5 million. This region is now combined with Natal in the new province of KwaZulu/Natal.

Situation and characteristics

Ulundi was founded in 1873 by the great Zulu chief Cetshwayo, and both before and after that date was the scene of important historical events.

After his defeat by the Boers in the battle of Blood River in 1838 the Zulu king Dingane fled to Swaziland, where he was killed in 1840. He was succeeded by Mpane, during whose reign the Zulus lost much of their territory to the Boers and the British (who had recently founded the colony of Natal). During the reign of his son and successor Cetshwayo the Boers in the growing republic of the Transvaal occupied further territory in Zululand; but although Britain declared this seizure of land illegal it gave the Zulus no effective help: it had other plans of its own. In January 1879, on the pretext that Cetshwayo had failed to respond to an ultimatum which was impossible of fulfilment, British troops invaded the Zulu kingdom. At first the Zulus, numerically much superior, successfully resisted the invasion. They defeated a British force in the bloody battle of Isandhlwana, but failed to follow up their advantage at Rorke's Drift (see Dundee) and finally suffered an annihilating defeat in the battle of Ulundi on July 4th.

History

Cetshwayo was taken prisoner, and in his place the British authorities appointed 13 chiefs on whom they could rely. Thereafter the Zulus were split between supporters and opponents of Cetshwayo, a situation of which the British authorities took advantage, dividing the territory of Zululand between the two parties, and in 1887, after repeated outbreaks of fighting between the rival groups, annexed the whole country and sent Dinzulu, Cetshwayo's son and successor, into exile in St Helena in the Cape Province. In 1897 the province of Natal was given responsibility for administering Zululand.

The present Zulu king is Goodwill Zwelethini, but the most powerful Zulu figure is the controversial Mangosuthu Buthelezi (see Famous People).

Apart from one of two places of historical interest the modern town of Ulundi has no tourist attractions. Opposite the Legislative Assembly in the town centre are the grave of King Mpane and a small museum.

The town

Surroundings of Ulundi

The site of Cetshwayo's one-time capital, Ondini, which was destroyed by British forces in 1879, is a few miles south-east of present-day Ulundi (reached from the road to the Umfolozi Game Reserve: see Hluhluwe and Umfolozi Game Reserves). In recent years the site has been excavated and some huts reconstructed. The KwaZulu Cultural Museum has a very interesting exhibition on the history and culture of the Zulus.

Ondini

100km/60 miles south of Ulundi is Eshowe (see entry).

Eshowe

The main battlefields in this area are described in the entry on Dundee.

Dundee

Umfolozi Game Reserve

See Hluhluwe and Umfolozi Game Reserves

Umtata

Province: Eastern Cape
Altitude: 720m/2362ft
Population: 130,000
Distances: 230km/143 miles from East London, 415km/258 miles from
Durban

Situation and characteristics

Umtata was capital of the Transkei homeland, which was given independence in 1976. In 1994 the territory, which is not economically viable on its own, again became part of South Africa.

Umtata and the territory of the former homeland are mainly occupied by Xhosa, a people made up of a number of different tribal communities which have preserved their various traditions and dialects.

The town lies in a hilly region, surrounded by grassland. The land is mostly used for grazing livestock; arable farming is possible only in a small part of the area.

Before contemplating a trip into the former Transkei – which is well worth it for the sake of the glorious coastal scenery – you should enquire locally about possible dangers for tourists. In recent years there have been some acts of violence against whites.

History

The earliest inhabitants of this region were Bushmen and Hottentots, who were driven out by the Xhosa who moved into the area in the 17th century. In the late 18th and the 19th centuries the interests of the Boers, the British and the Xhosa came into conflict, and after the bloody Kaffir Wars, in 1879, the territory was incorporated in the Cape Colony. The Transkei was granted internal self-government in 1963.

The town

Umtata, on the Umtata River, was founded in 1879. It has a number of imposing public buildings, including the Bunga (Parliament Building) and

Umtata, once capital of the Transkei homeland, is a busy commercial administrative centre

the Town Hall (1907). There is also a fine Anglican cathedral. The University, originally founded in 1976 as a branch of Fort Hare University (see Fort Beaufort, Surroundings), now has 4000 students.

Close to the town are two charming nature reserves, the Luchaba Nature Reserve (460 hectares/1136 acres), 5km/3 miles north, and the Nduli Nature Reserve, 3km/2 miles south.

There are also a number of interesting craft centres in the town, including the Hilmond weaving-mill (using mohair wool) and the Izandla pottery, to which a craft school is attached. Both of these are on the Queenstown road (R 61).

★★Wild Coast

The Wild Coast, as the 280km/175 mile stretch of coast between Qolora Mouth in the south and Port Edward in the north is called, is an enchanting succession of quiet inlets and lagoons, bizarre rock formations and caves and beaches of magical beauty. It is called the Wild Coast not for the rugged beauty of the scenery but because of the numerous ships that have come to grief on this stretch of coast with its rocks and shallows.

Along the Wild Coast there are numbers of modest hotels, as well as establishments offering high standards of comfort and amenity (mainly in Coffee Bay and Port St John's). The climate is agreeable all year round, and sea bathing is possible even in winter.

The various holiday areas along the coast are not linked by a coast road but are reached on tracks, mostly unsurfaced, running down to the coast from N 2 through beautiful scenery, in which evergreen rain forests and mangrove swamps alternate with wide expanses of hilly grassland strewn with the round huts of the Xhosa.

Driving at night in the former Transkei is to be avoided.

Xhosa women on their way to church

Umtata

Wild Coast Hiking Trail

A 280km/175 mile long hiking trail runs along the whole length of the Wild Coast. Sections of this can be followed in 3- to 6-day walks; particularly attractive is the 60km/37 mile walk between Port St John's and Coffee Bay (which involves wading or swimming over various rivers and carrying your own provisions).

★Mkambati Nature Reserve

One sight not to be missed is the Mkambati Nature Reserve, near the north end of the Wild Coast; it can be reached from Port St John's or Flagstaff. Here, within a small area, can be found all the various landscape variations of this stretch of coast – dense forests, mangrove swamps, expanses of grassland and lonely sandy beaches. Within the reserve is an impressive gorge on the Msikaba River, best explored in a canoe (which can be hired). There is a camping site and a shop in the reserve.

Port St John's

The largest town and most popular resort on the Wild Coast is Port St John's, 95km/59 miles east of Umtata. Situated at the mouth of the Umzimvubu River, which here forms a very beautiful lagoon, it is surrounded by lush subtropical vegetation. There are a number of hotels offering a variety of sports facilities. Numbers of artists and craftsmen who have settled in the town, attracted by the paradisiac scenery, offer their work for sale.

Hluleka Nature Reserve

At Libode, on the road between Umtata and Port St John's, a side road goes off to the Hluleka Nature Reserve. Here evergreen coastal forests surround the lagoon at the mouth of the Mnenu River.

Coffee Bay

Farther south is the charming holiday village of Coffee Bay, reached on an asphalted road which branches off N 2 18km/11 miles south of Umtata. There are a number of hotels with views of the spectacular coastal scenery. A sheltered lagoon offers safe bathing.

The origin of the name Coffee Bay is not entirely clear. One story has it that a ship ran aground here and lost its cargo of coffee beans. These, it is said, were washed ashore and some of them took root, but the coffee bushes which grew soon died off.

★Hole in the Wall

The famous Hole in the Wall, an offshore rock 8km/5 miles south of Coffee Bay through which erosion has carved a hole, can be reached either by road or on a delightful footpath.

★Dwesa Nature Reserve

The Dwesa Nature Reserve, an area of unspoiled natural beauty, is reached on a road which branches off N 2 at Idutywa. Rhinos, buffaloes and zebras have been reintroduced here, and there are also crocodiles. The real attractions of the reserve, however, are the tropical coastal forest and the lonely coast, on which shell-collectors will gather a rich harvest. There is accommodation for visitors in holiday cottages and on a camping site.

Butterworth

Farther south on N 2 is Butterworth, the oldest town in the former Transkei (founded in 1827 as a mission station) and now its second largest town, with a population of 60,000. It is an industrial and commercial centre, a rather depressing town of huts with corrugated iron roofs.

Mazeppa Bay

From Butterworth a road runs down by way of Kentani to Mazeppa Bay. Many deep-sea anglers come here in August to fish for shark. Other holidaymakers are attracted by the long sandy beaches. A small offshore island is linked with the mainland by a suspension bridge from which there are magnificent views of the coastal scenery.

Qolora Mouth

At the south end of the Wild Coast is Qolora Bay, a holiday resort which draws many visitors with its subtropical vegetation and endlessly long beaches of fine sand.

Upington   F 6

Province: Northern Cape
Altitude: 836m/274ft
Population: 55,000
Distances: 262km/163 miles from Kuruman, 411km/255 miles from
  Kimberley

Upington lies on the west bank of the Orange River in the far north of the   Situation and
Northern Cape Province. To the north the landscape merges into the Kala-   characteristics
hari Desert. It is very hot here in summer: the best time for a visit is between
April and October. Thanks to the town's excellent communications – it has
a modern airport, lies on the railway line from De Aar to Namibia and is an
important road junction point – many visitors stop over here on the way to
Namibia, the Kalahari Gemsbok National Park (240km/150 miles north) or
the Augrabies Falls (130km/80 miles west).
    The town is the commercial and agricultural centre of the north-western
part of the Northern Cape Province. The Orange River, with a perennial
flow, supplies water for the irrigation of an extensive agricultural area. The
main crops are cotton, dates, table grapes and other kinds of fruit, much of
it marketed as dried fruit. The South African Dried Fruit Cooperative has the
second largest and the most modern fruit-processing plant in the world
(conducted tours). The Orange River Wine Cellars are the largest wine-
making cooperative in the country (conducted tours by appointment, tel.
0541/56 51 52 53). The wine harvest is in January and February.

The town – named after Sir Thomas Upington, prime minister of the Cape   History
Colony from 1884 to 1886 – developed out of a mission station established
in 1871. The early missionaries created an irrigation system which provided a basis for the rapid growth and prosperity of the town.

Upington is a surprisingly green town, with broad streets, many shops and   The town
trim residential districts.
    Olyvenhoutdrift, an island in the Orange River, is now a holiday centre,
with a camping site, various categories of accommodation for visitors and
a variety of sports facilities.

Sights in and around Upington

The Kalahari Oranje Museum, housed in a mission building of 1883, has   Kalahari Oranje
collections of material illustrating the natural history and culture of the   Museum
region.

13km/8 miles north of Upington is the Spitzkop Nature Reserve (open: daily   Spitzkop
7am–7pm), centred on a striking granite hill ("koppie"), with antelopes,   Nature Reserve
gazelles, wildebeests, ostriches, steppe zebras and camels.

From Upington R 359 runs south-west, following the course of the Orange   Keimoes
River. In 50km/31 miles it comes to Keimoes (pop. 8500), which is worth a
brief stop to drive up the Tierberg (nature reserve), from the top of which
there are fine views of the oasis of irrigated land round the town.

40km/25 miles beyond Keimoes is Kakamas (pop. 5500). In the Hottentot   Kakamas
language the name means "barren grazing land"; but with the help of
irrigation Kakamas is now a flourishing agricultural centre surrounded by
vineyards, cotton fields and arable land.
    The area is famed for the semi-precious stones to be found here in great
quantity and variety (onyx, amethyst, blue, green and brown tiger's eyes,
etc.).

Augrabies Falls   36km/22 miles from Kakamas is the spectacular Augrabies Falls National
Park (see entry).

Vryburg   H 4/5

Province: North-West
Altitude: 1000m/3280ft
Population: 28,000
Distances: 190km/118 miles from Lichtenburg, 212km/132 miles from
Kimberley

Situation and
characteristics

The country round Vryburg is flat, arid and bare, and few visitors venture
into this "Texas of South Africa" – so called because it is the largest
cattle-farming region in South Africa. For the farmers in the surrounding
area Vryburg is an important shopping and business centre, and it has a
number of factories which process the produce of the region.

Surroundings of Vryburg

Leon Talyard
Nature Reserve

6km/4 miles north of Vryburg on R 378 is the Leon Talyard Nature Reserve
(area 857 hectares/2117 acres), with blue and black wildebeests, steppe and
mountain zebras, antelopes and gazelles, Cape buffaloes and rhinos.

★Barberspan
Nature Reserve

100km/62 miles north-east of Vryburg by way of Delareyville is the Barber-
span Nature Reserve (area 3100 hectares/7660 acres; open: daily
6am–6pm), the largest reserve for water birds in the Transvaal, which has
been declared an International Wetland Area. Some 350 species of birds
have been recorded here. After heavy rain in September and October the
lake which is the central feature of the reserve expands to cover an area of
2000 hectares/5000 acres, with a depth of up to 8m/26ft. It then becomes the
home and breeding area of innumerable coots, various species of ducks
and geese, grebes and many other water birds. The flamingos, however,
prefer a rather lower water level. The lake is also a paradise for anglers and
the scene of fishing competitions. The only accommodation for visitors is a
camping site.

Schweizer-Reneke

70km/43 miles south-east of Vryburg on N 14 is Schweizer-Reneke (pop.
11,000), the centre of an agricultural area (maize, groundnuts; cattle and
sheep farming). North-east of the town is the Wentzel Dam, a popular
recreation area (water sports).

Vryheid   M 5

Province: KwaZulu/Natal
Altitude: 1112m/3648ft
Population: 24,000
Distances: 67km/42 miles from Dundee, 108km/67 miles from Piet Retief

Situation and
characteristics

Vryheid is the largest town on the Northern Natal Battlefields Route, which
takes in various battlefields, the scene of fighting between British forces
and Zulus and between British forces and the Boers (see Dundee).
   Vryheid was briefly the capital of the New Republic proclaimed by the
Boers in 1884, which survived only until 1887, when it was incorporated in
the Transvaal. It has, however, preserved a number of historic buildings
from the period of independence, including the Volksraad and the Lucas
Meyer House, once the home of the State President's widow and now a
museum.

Surroundings of Vryheid

Paulpietersburg (pop. 9000), 50km/31 miles north of Vryheid, is an important coal-mining and forestry centre.

    16km/10 miles from the town is Lurula Natal Spa, with hot springs and various facilities for treatment and recreation.

Paulpietersburg

70km/45 miles north-east of Vryheid, on the Swaziland border, is the Itala Game Reserve (area 30,000 hectares/75,000 acres), which was established in 1972. Beautifully situated in the valley of the Pongola River, it is reached by way of the little town of Louwsburg. Here, in the open bushveld, furrowed by deep valleys, live both species of rhinoceros, impalas, water buffaloes, giraffes, kudus, baboons and numerous other mammals.

★Itala
Game Reserve

Experienced park rangers lead groups of visitors on three-day hikes through the reserve. They can also explore the park in their own car on the 30km/19 mile long Ngubhu Loop Auto Trail. There is a wide range of accommodation for visitors, from a luxury lodge by way of comfortable chalets to a camping site.

Warm Baths (Warmbad)   K 3

Province: Northern Transvaal
Altitude: 1143m/3750ft
Population: 13,000
Distances: 100km/62 miles from Pretoria, 164km/102 miles from Potgietersrus

The spa of Warm Baths (founded in 1921), 100km/62 miles north of Pretoria, is famed for the healing powers of its thermal springs. The area was known to the Tswana as Biele Bela (the "Boiling Place"). The water, containing sodium chlorate, calcium carbonate and other salts, gushes out at a temperature of 62°C/144°F, at the rate of 23,000 litres (5060 gallons) an hour. It is used in the treatment of rheumatic conditions. Every year some 260,000 people come here to seek relief from their ailments.

Situation and
characteristics

Round the springs has grown up a holiday complex with accommodation of various categories, treatment facilities, a restaurant, a café and tennis, squash and badminton courts. People also come here in winter not for medical treatment but to enjoy the pleasure of bathing in thermal water at a temperature of 32°C/90°F.

Adjoining the spa is the Warm Baths Nature Reserve (area 50 hectares/125 acres), with red hartebeests, steppe zebras and impalas among other game.

Warm Baths
Nature Reserve

Welkom   J 5

Province: Orange Free State
Altitude: 1338m/4390ft
Population: 150,000
Distances: 72km/45 miles from Kroonstad, 150km/93 miles from Bloemfontein

Welkom, the second largest city in the Orange Free State, is the centre of the gold- and uranium-mining region in the north-west of the province (which produces around 30% of South Africa's total output of gold). The town was founded in 1947 and laid out as a garden city. The modern business centre is surrounded by extensive parks and gardens, and on the

Situation and
characteristics

outskirts of the city are artificial lakes, formed from water pumped up from the mines, which have become an oasis for water birds.

Surroundings of Welkom

Virginia	The town of Virginia (pop. 95,000), 20km/12½ miles south-east of Welkom on the Sand River, also lives by gold- and uranium-mining. It is the second largest town in the mining region and the fourth largest in the province. The gold-mines, now closed down, have become an attraction for visitors, who can also watch performances of tribal dances there.
Willem Pretorius Game Reserve	50km/31 miles south-east of Virginia by way of Ventersburg is the Willem Pretorius Game Reserve, established in 1962 round the Allemmanskraal Dam. The wide grass-covered plains in the southern part of the reserve are populated mainly by springboks, black wildebeests and other species of antelope. Rhinos, giraffes, buffaloes and impalas live mainly in the hilly northern part. Remains of prehistoric settlements have also been found here. Tourist facilities include holiday cottages, a camping site, a restaurant, a golf course and a swimming pool.
Winburg	Winburg (pop. 8000), 90km/56 miles south-east of Welkom, is the oldest town in the Orange Free State (founded in 1842) and was originally its capital. The leaders of five voortrekker groups met in Ford's Hotel (still in existence) and resolved to found the Free State. The event is commemorated by the Voortrekker Monument (3km/2 miles from the town centre) and a small museum.
Erfenis Dam Nature Reserve	South-west of Winburg is the Erfenis Dam Nature Reserve (area 3308 hectares/8171 acres), with facilities for water sports on the lake, a camping site and picnic areas. A small separate area is home to black wildebeests, red hartebeests, mountain reedbucks, steppe zebras, springboks and blesboks.
Bloemhof Dam	100km/62 miles north-west of Welkom is the Bloemhof Dam, another popular recreation area. The Vaal River has been dammed here to create a huge artificial lake, and the area round the lake has been declared a nature reserve.

West Coast National Park   D 9

Province: Western Cape
Distances: 60km/37 miles from Malmesbury, 110km/68 miles from Cape Town

Situation and topography	The West Coast National Park (area 18,000 hectares/45,000 acres) was established in 1985, taking in the area round the Langebaan Lagoon on the west coast of South Africa and four small offshore islands. It is of international importance for its unique bird life. The National Park is reached from R 27, which runs north from Cape Town. The main entrance is just to the south of Langebaan, and there is another entrance 20km/12½ miles south of Langebaan (signposted from R 27). The climate in this region, influenced by the cold Benguela Current which flows along the Atlantic coast, is raw and dry. The low rainfall (an annual 270mm/10½in.) occurs almost exclusively in winter. Quite frequently there are morning mists. In consequence the vegetation is scanty, consisting mainly of low-growing bushes and succulents. There are large expanses of mud round the shores of the lagoon. In spring, however, the scene changes, and between August and October the barren land is carpeted with flowers.

The West Coast National Park, home to 250 species of birds and, in winter, to many Arctic migrants

Among the numerous birds, of many species, found in the park are cormorants, seagulls, small sandpipers, curlew sandpipers, plovers, gannets and flamingos. This is one of the last retreats of the black-footed penguin, the only African species of penguin. In addition to the indigenous species tens of thousands of migrants come here in summer: some from as far as the Arctic Circle, around 80% from Eastern Europe. ★Fauna

Among mammals in the National Park are bonteboks, elands, springboks, kudus and blue wildebeests.

An asphalted road runs round the lagoon (about 35km/22 miles), with lookouts from which the bird life can be observed. In the old farmhouse of Geelbek, at the south end of the lagoon, is an information centre, the starting-point of a number of nature trails. There are also bird-watching cruises on the lagoon. The National Park is open daily in summer 5.30am–8pm, in winter 7.30am–5pm. There are accommodation for visitors and shops in Langebaan. Visitor facilities

Surroundings of the West Coast National Park

Langebaan, at the north end of the lagoon, has become an increasingly popular holiday resort. Many new holiday homes have been built here, with fine views over the lagoon. Langebaan

To the north of Langebaan extends Saldanha Bay, 10km/6 miles long, with the little town of Saldanha – not a very attractive place for tourists, with port installations and factories dominating the scene. In terms of turnover Saldanha is South Africa's third largest port (after Richard's Bay and Durban), handling mainly iron ore (from Sishen, with which Saldanha is Saldanha connected by rail). It is also a fishing port (crayfish), with numerous fish-processing plants.

Vredenburg   Vredenburg, 13km/8 miles north of Saldanha, is now amalgamated with it. The town was founded in 1875 because of a particularly abundant spring in the neighbourhood. The town's main sources of income are arable farming and sheep-rearing.

Paternoster   The fishing village of Paternoster has been able to preserve a little of its original character, in spite of the fact that it has been drawing increasing numbers of weekend visitors from Cape Town. Some old cottages are available for renting to visitors.

Wild Coast

See Umtata

Wilderness National Park

See Garden Route

Worcester   E 9/10

Province: Western Cape
Altitude: 221m/725ft
Population: 70,000
Distances: 60km/37 miles from Tulbagh, 110km/68 miles from Cape Town

Situation and   Worcester, the largest town in the fertile valley of the Breede River, is easily
characteristics   reached from Cape Town on N 1. In this sheltered valley, surrounded by ranges of high hills, wine and fruit are grown. Worcester is worth a brief visit for the sake of its interesting open-air museum and beautiful Botanic Garden. The town was founded in 1822 and named after the Marquis of Worcester, brother of the then Governor of the Cape, Lord Charles Somerset.

Sights in Worcester

Old Drostdy   One of the handsomest houses in Worcester is the Old Drostdy (1825), once the residence of the landdrost (the government-appointed district officer). Now a national monument, it is occupied by the College of Technology.

Beck House   There are a number of pretty mid 19th century houses in Church Street. One of the finest is Beck House (now a museum), with Victorian furniture.

Afrikaner Museum   Housed in another fine old building is the Afrikaner Museum, with an interesting collection of 19th century surgical and dental equipment and reproductions of surgeries of the period.

★Kleinplasie   Within this open-air museum (open: daily 9.30am–4.30pm) visitors can see
Farm Museum   a Khoikhoi camp, a Boer encampment and a fully equipped 18th century

farm. A variety of activities are demonstrated by people in period costume – spinning wool, grinding corn, making soap and candles, etc.

2km/1¼ miles north of the town centre is the Karoo National Botanic Garden (open: daily 8am–5pm), which was established in 1948. It contains many succulents and other plants from the arid regions of South Africa. Only part of the area of 154 hectares/380 acres is laid out as a garden; the rest has been left in its natural state.

★Karoo National Botanic Garden

**Practical
Information
from A to Z**

Accommodation

See Camping and Caravanning; Hotels; Youth Hostels

Air Services

South Africa has nine state-run airports and more than 200 smaller airports, airstrips and heliports, served by the national airline South African Airways (SAA) and a number of smaller airlines.

Family concession fares: the first adult pays full fare, the second adult and children over 12 60% of the full fare, children under 12 10%.

SAA offer sightseeing flights in a restored JU 52 along the east coast (from Durban, East London, Port Elizabeth, George and Cape Town) and on a number of short routes on the national network. Information from SAA.

SAA Offices outside South Africa

United Kingdom	St George's House 61 Conduit Street London W1R 9FD Tel. (0171) 312 5000
	1 St Ann's Square (4th floor) Manchester M2 7LG Tel. (0161) 839 4436
USA	Suite 1530 9841 Airport Boulevard Los Angeles CA 90045 Tel. 310/641 2825
	901 Ponce de León Boulevard Coral Gables Miami FL 33134 Tel. 305/461 3484
	900 Third Avenue (9th floor) New York NY 10022 Tel. 212/826 0995
Canada	Suite 1500 55 Younge Street, North York Toronto, Ontario M2N 6P4 Tel. 416/512 8870

SAA
SOUTH AFRICAN AIRWAYS

Alcohol

On Sundays and religious festivals alcoholic drinks are usually only served with meals in public bars outside the big cities. Alcoholic drinks may be taken into restaurants and bars not licensed to sell alcohol.

There are different types of licence for serving alcohol in hotels:
Y=wine and beer only with meals
YY=only wine and beer
YYY=wine, beer and spirits
Alcoholic drinks can be bought only in special shops ("bottle stores").

◀ *Venda women in a fruit market in Louis Trichardt*

Beaches

South Africa has a coastline of 3000km/1865 miles, which inevitably varies considerably over this great distance – in the nature of the coast, the temperature of the water and the number of visitors. On the west coast, which is washed by the cold Benguela Current, the water is never warmer than 17°C/63°F, but on the east coast the warm Agulhas Current, coming from the Indian Ocean, provides much pleasanter conditions for bathers.

Along the Garden Route the best time for bathing is from November to April. On the northern coast of KwaZulu/Natal, with its beautiful, lonely beaches, the water is pleasantly warm (up to 24°C/75°F) throughout the year. The Wild Coast too has plenty of beautiful unfrequented beaches for sun-worshippers and bathers. Very different are the beaches round the main holiday resorts: holidaymakers who want a lively holiday with plenty of other people will find what they want there.

Strandfontein (north of Lambert's Bay) is popular with swimmers. McDougall's Bay (near Port Nolloth) is sheltered by reefs and offers good swimming. | West coast

There are beautiful and very popular beaches to the west of Mossel Bay, round Still Bay, Witsand and Infanta, and beyond this at Muizenberg, on False Bay, and Sea Point, a suburb of Cape Town. | Western Cape

On Cape Hangklip, near Hermanus, there are pleasant cliff walks.

In Walker Bay whales can be observed between June and November (see Baedeker Special, p. 240).

Sandy Bay is an unofficial nude bathing beach.

The safest areas for swimmers are King's Beach, Humewood and McArthur (at all of which there are life guards). | Garden Route

Jeffrey's Bay and St Francis Bay are popular with both swimmers and surfers.

Mossel Bay has many sheltered lagoons (Hartenbos, Little and Great Brak Rivers, etc.).

In Herold's Bay (south-west of George, which has sandy beaches) there is a tidal swimming pool, but bathing in the sea is also perfectly safe.

At Sedgefield (on the Swartvlei), Buffels Bay (near Knysna), Plettenberg Bay, Nature's Valley (east of Plettenberg Bay) and round the estuaries of the Bushman and Kariega Rivers there are beautiful sandy beaches, some of them of considerable length.

Some of the beaches in Oyster Bay are relatively unfrequented.

Less suitable for bathing, and accordingly less frequented, are the beaches in the Tsitsikamma Coastal National Park (a steep stretch of coast, with the estuary of Storms River) and Morgan's Bay (cliffs).

On the coast of the former homeland of Transkei, between East London in the south and Port Edward in the north, there is danger from sharks, particularly round the mouths of rivers. There are no shark nets. | Wild Coast

There are good swimming areas between the mouths of the Umngazi and Mzamba Rivers, at Port St John and East London, between Kidd's Beach and the Great Fish River and at Kei Mouth, on the Kei River.

There are tidal swimming pools at Fullar's Bay (East London) and Kidd's Rock.

Almost all the beaches on the KwaZulu/Natal coast are protected by shark nets. | KwaZulu/Natal

To the south of Durban there are very beautiful beaches, safe from sharks, between Port Shepstone and Port Edward.

The finest beaches north of Durban are at Umhlanga Rocks, Umhloti Beach and Ballito (very busy during the main holiday season).

There are many tidal swimming pools in this area (particularly in Thompson's Bay, to the north of Ballito Bay) which are very popular.

To the north of Zinkwazi Beach there are beautiful bathing beaches, which are accessible only in cross-country vehicles; there are no shark nets, so bathers need to keep a careful lookout.

Bathing in inland lakes and lagoons is not safe because of hippopotamuses and crocodiles.

Business Hours

Shops

There are no rigid regulations on shop opening times. The usual opening hours are Mon.–Fri. 8/9am–5pm, Sat. 8.30am–1pm. In small towns shops close between 1 and 2pm. Most shops are closed on Monday mornings.

Many of the large shopping centres, supermarkets, greengrocers and bookshops stay open until 6pm, including Saturdays; some are also open on Sundays.

Banks

Banks are generally open Mon.–Fri. 9am–3.30pm, Sat. 8.30–11am. In country areas they often have shorter hours, with a lunch break.

Banks at the country's three international airports have longer opening hours.

Filling stations

Most filling stations are open round the clock.

Government offices

Government offices and agencies are open Mon.–Fri. 8am–3.30pm.

Museums

Museums are usually open Mon.–Fri. 9am–5pm, Sat. and Sun. 10am–4pm.

Post offices

Post offices are open Mon.–Fri. 8/8.30am–4.30pm, Sat. 8/8.30am–noon. In country areas and in smaller branches they have a lunch break (1–2pm).

Bus Services

The long-distance buses which provide regular services linking the larger South African towns are faster and cheaper than the railways.

National services

Greyhound Cityliner
Reservations:
Cape Town: tel. 021/45 41 25
Durban: tel. 031/37 64 78
Johannesburg: tel. 011/4 03 64 63

Central reservation office for all towns:
Greyhound Cityliner, PO Box 11229, Johannesburg 2000, tel. 011/3 33 21 34

Translux Express
Reservations:
Cape Town: tel. 021/4 05 33 33
Durban: tel. 031/3 61 83 33
Johannesburg: tel. 011/7 74 33 33
Port Elizabeth: tel. 041/5 07 33 33

Central reservation office:
Translux, PO Box 2383, Johannesburg 2000, tel. 011/7 74 33 33

Intercape/Mainliner
Reservations:
PO Box 618, Bellville 7535, tel. 021/9 34 44 00

Regional services

Copper Rose
Route: East London–Port Elizabeth
Reservations: tel. 0431/47 50 55

Garden Line Transport
Route: Mossel Bay–Middelburg/Queenstown
Reservations: tel. 0441/74 28 23

Inter Cape Ferreira Express
Route: Cape Town–Port Elizabeth
Reservations: tel. 021/9 34 44 00

Leopard Express
Route: Port Elizabeth–Grahamstown
Reservations: tel. 0461/2 45 89

Margate Mini Coach
Route: Margate–Durban
Reservations: tel. 03931/2 16 00

Prestige Travel
Route: White River–Johannesburg/Pretoria
Reservations: tel. 01311/3 12 28

Turnkey Travel
Route: Phalaborwa–Johannesburg/Pretoria
Reservations: tel. 01524/44 92

There are also minibus services linking all South African towns. Mostly   Minibus services
used by blacks, they are usually filled to overflowing. Seats cannot be
booked.

Camping and Caravanning

South Africa has over 700 camping sites, which in addition to accommodating tents and caravans often have rooms, chalets and rondavels available
for renting. Most camping sites have swimming pools, shops, sports facilities, children's playgrounds and restaurants.
   Many of the sites belong either to the state Overaal Resorts organisation
or to the private Club Caraville chain.

Overaal Resorts, PO Box 3046, Pretoria 0001, tel. 012/3 46 22 77   Central booking
Club Caraville, PO Box 139, Sarnia 3615, tel. 011/6 22 46 28   offices

An up-to-date list of camping sites, with detailed information about the
sites, can be obtained from Satour (see Information).

Motor caravans can be hired, at a cost per day of the order of £100. They are   Hire of
mostly Mitsubishi microbuses, which are manoeuvrable and well   motor caravans
equipped.

Capricorn Tours and Campers, 39 Elsenham Avenue, PO Box 1530, tel.   Hire firms
   024/55 23 31
Leisure Mobiles, PO Box 3722, Johannesburg 2000, tel. 011/4 77 23 74
Campers' Corner, PO Box 48191, Roosevelt Park 2129, tel. 011/7 87 91 05

Canoeing

River rafting, in canoes or rubber dinghies, is becoming increasingly
popular in South Africa, and a number of organisations run river trips
lasting between four and six days. Though exciting, these trips are not at all
hazardous: participants – who may include children – need have had no
previous experience. The overnight stops are in tents, and cooking is done
on the camp fire.

The following organisations specialise in trips of this kind:

Felix Unite (canoe trips on the Orange, Tugela and Breede Rivers), PO Box 1524, Sandton 2146, tel. 011/4 63 31 67

Oranje River Adventures (in Mohawk Indian canoes), 5 Matapan Road, Rondebosch 7700, tel. 021/6 85 44 75

River Rafters (trips in rubber dinghies on the Orange River), PO Box 1157, Kelvin 2054, tel. 011/82 54 07

River Runners (trips in canoes and rubber dinghies on the Orange River), PO Box 583, Constantia 7848, tel. 021/7 62 23 50

Sunwa Ventures (canoe trips on the Tugela River and Vaal Dam), PO Box 41952, Craighall 2024, tel. 011/7 88 51 20

Car Rental

During the hot summer months it is advisable to hire a vehicle with air-conditioning.

The following four large car rental firms have offices throughout South Africa:

Avis

Freephone reservations in South Africa: tel. 0800 02 11 11
Head office: PO Box 221, Isando 1600, tel. 011/9 74 25 71
Cape Town: 123 Strand Street, tel. 021/24 11 77
Durban: Royal Hotel, Ulundi Place, tel. 031/3 04 17 41
Johannesburg: Prolecon Road, tel. 011/33 45 40

Budget

Freephone reservations in South Africa: tel. 0800 01 66 22
Head office: 494 Wrench Road, Isando EXT 2 1600, tel. 011/3 92 39 29
Cape Town: 63A Strand Street, tel. 021/23 42 90
Durban: 21 Aliwal Street, tel. 3 04 90 23
Johannesburg: Carlton Centre, 130 Main Street, tel. 011/3 31 36 31

Europcar/
Dolphin

Freephone reservations in South Africa: tel. 0800 01 13 44
Cape Town: Dolphin Car, Block C, Roy Beamish Centre, Airport Industria 8050, tel. 021/9 34 22 63
Durban: Louis Botha Airport, tel. 031/3 14 69 06 67
Johannesburg: Jan Smuts Airport, tel. 011/3 94 88 32

Imperial
(formerly Hertz)

Freephone reservations in South Africa: tel. 0800 21 02 27
PO Box 26177, Excom 2023, tel. 011/3 37 23 00
Cape Town: tel. 021/9 34 02 13
Durban: tel. 031/42 46 48

In addition there are smaller firms in many towns with lower rates. The disadvantages are that the cars are mostly well used and that service in the event of breakdown may be less satisfactory.

Chemists

A chemist's shop in Afrikaans is *apteek*.
In all the larger towns there is a rota system under which certain pharmacies are open outside the normal hours for dispensing urgent prescriptions.

Consulates

See Diplomatic and Consular Offices

Crime

In recent years there has been an increasing crime rate in South Africa, particularly in the large cities. Nevertheless it is still a "safe" holiday country.

There are a few obvious precautions that all visitors should bear in mind:
■ Do not carry any valuables or large amounts of money about with you: leave them in the hotel safe.
■ Keep a careful eye on handbags and cameras.
■ Do not walk about on your own after dark.
■ When driving in the cities keep your car windows closed.

Currency

The South African currency unit is the rand (ZAR or R), which is made up of 100 cents (c).

South Africa has recently introduced new notes and coins, but the old currency is still in circulation. Old and new 1c, 2c, 5c, 10c, 20c, 50c and R1 coins and R5, R10, R20 and R50 notes are all in use. New R2 and R5 coins and new R100 and R200 notes were recently introduced.

Visitors may bring into the country or take out of it no more than 500 rand. There are no restrictions on the import of foreign currency in the form of cash or travellers' cheques, but the amount must be declared on entry.

Import and export of currency

South African banknotes and coins

Customs Regulations

Travellers' cheques	It is advisable to carry money in the form of travellers' cheques. Euro-cheques are not accepted except in some banks. Money is best changed and travellers' cheques cashed in banks; the banks at airports are convenient for new arrivals. Some hotels and shops cash travellers' cheques, but at less favourable rates.
Credit cards	Most hotels, shops, restaurants, travel agencies, airlines, car rental firms, etc. – but not filling stations – accept major international credit cards such as American Express, Diners Club, Mastercard, Visa and their affiliates. They may be less acceptable, however, in small shops and in small towns and country areas.
Krugerrands	Krugerrands may be exported from South Africa only by visitors. In the departures hall of Johannesburg's Jan Smuts Airport they can be bought without payment of VAT.
VAT	Value-added tax (VAT) is normally included in the price; the current rate is 14%. Foreign visitors can recover the VAT paid on purchases costing R250 or more which they are taking out of the country. This applies only to goods purchased in certain shops. The shop assistant must give the purchaser a receipt and complete a form (VAT 255) giving the name and address of the purchaser and the shop assistant and a description of the goods purchased, their price and the VAT paid. The VAT can then be recovered on presentation of the form to the VAT authorities at airports, harbours and customs offices.
	Information about the VAT recovery procedure can be obtained from the VAT Refund Administrators, tel. 011/4 84 75 30 or PO Box 9478, Johannesburg 2000. Information leaflets on the procedure to follow are available from VAT Refund Administration offices at the Johannesburg, Durban and Cape Town international airports.
	VAT is not payable on articles such as clothing, jewellery, etc., sent directly by the shop to the visitor's home address.
	When purchasing diamonds and jewellery of precious metals in a shop belonging to the Jewellery Council of South Africa, tel. 011/29 64 41 (Johannesburg), the purchaser is asked to sign a separate credit card voucher for the VAT due. When leaving South Africa he should present this voucher at the Jewellery Council desk (beyond passport control); the voucher will then be returned to the shop and the charge cancelled.
Banks	In the larger towns most banks are open daily 9am–3.30pm, Sat. 8.30–11am. Banks in country areas often have shorter opening hours and a lunchtime break. Banks at the three international aiports of Johannesburg, Cape Town and Durban have longer opening hours.
	Exchange offices at the three international airports open two hours before each international departure and close two hours after each international arrival.
Currency in Lesotho	The unit of currency is the loti (plural maloti), which is made up of 100 lisente. The loti is tied to the South African rand. The rand is also generally accepted.
Currency in Swaziland	The unit of currency is the lilangeni (plural emalangeni), which is at par with the rand. The rand (notes only) is accepted mainly in the larger hotels.

Customs Regulations

Visa	Nationals of countries in the European Union, the United States and Canada need only a passport to enter South Africa; no visa is required.
Entering South Africa	All used personal effects are admitted duty-free. In addition there are the following duty-free allowances for adults: 1 litre of spirits, 2 litres of wine,

400 cigarettes, 50 cigars, 250 grams of tobacco, 250 millilitres of toilet water, 50 millilitres of perfume and gifts to the value of R200.

Further information can be obtained from the Department of Customs and Excise in Pretoria, tel. 012/28 43 08.

Plants and animal products (e.g. sporting trophies) may be taken out of South Africa only with a special licence. Trading in endangered species of plants and animals is prohibited and strictly controlled.

For further information see Shopping and Souvenirs.

Leaving South Africa

All visitors to Swaziland must have a valid passport; visas are issued free of charge at the Mahamba, Luvumisa, Ngwenya, Jeppe's Reef and Matsamo border posts. The best plan is to get a visa in advance in Johannesburg or before leaving home. Information from the Southern African Regional Tourism Council (SARTOC), PO Box 600, Parklands, Johannesburg 2121.

Swaziland has a trade mission in Johannesburg: PO Box 8030, Room 915, Rand Central Building, 165 Jeppe Street, Johannesburg 2000, tel. 29 97 76.

For repeated visits to Swaziland a multiple entry visa is required.

Entry to Swaziland

No visa is required for a stay of up to 30 days.

Entry to Lesotho

Diamonds

Many people think of South Africa as the land of gold and diamonds, and assume that they will be much cheaper there. That is not entirely true, since even in South Africa the price of gold and precious stones is determined by the international market; but it is certainly possible to save money by buying cut diamonds and other gems in a specialist shop in South Africa, since wages are much lower than in Europe or America. Imported jewellery costs almost twice as much after paying import and other duties.

Foreign visitors need not pay value-added tax (VAT; see Currency), but must produce their passport and airline ticket when making a purchase.

On refund of VAT see Currency.

The diamond industry developed in the 16th century, but until the 18th century India was the sole source of supply. Then in 1866 diamonds were discovered in South Africa. The first finds were made at Hopetown, a little place 120km/75 miles south of Kimberley; among them was an 83.5 carat diamond which later became known as the Star of Africa and most recently changed hands at an auction in Geneva for 552,000 US dollars. Then the real diamond rush began with the discovery of diamonds at Kimberley in 1869 (see Baedeker Special, p. 272).

History

Diamonds are among the most valuable precious stones in the world. Their special characteristics are their hardness, their crystalline brilliance and their rarity.

Rough diamonds

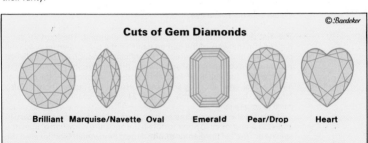

© *Baedeker*

Cuts of Gem Diamonds

Brilliant   Marquise/Navette   Oval   Emerald   Pear/Drop   Heart

Diamonds

Diamonds were formed many millions of years ago. They consist of pure carbon which was compressed and crystallised by the massive pressure exerted by solidifying volcanic rock, with such force that diamonds became the hardest mineral (10 on the Mohs scale of hardness). This means that a diamond can stratch any other mineral but no other mineral can scratch a diamond. Hence the name diamond (from Greek *adamas,* "invincible"). That diamonds are so much sought after, so famous and so valuable, however, is due to their brilliant lustre, the result of their high refractive power, and to the rarity of diamonds, particularly of diamonds of any size.

Diamond-producing areas

Diamonds are found in alluvial gravels, glacial tills and kimberlite pipes (mined at Kimberley to a depth of 2000m/6500ft). The main sources of diamonds are Africa (Zaire, South Africa, Ghana, Sierra Leone, Namibia, Botswana, Tanzania, Liberia, Central Africa, Ivory Coast, Angola), the former Soviet Union (Urals), Australia, South America (Venezuela, Brazil, Guyana), Indonesia and the East Indies.

Uses of diamonds

Only about a fifth of the diamonds found are suitable for cutting and polishing as gem diamonds (brilliants). The remainder are used for industrial purposes (in rock drills, stone-cutting saws, glass-cutters, etc.; for drilling, grinding, scouring and polishing metals and synthetic materials; as sensors in precision instruments, phonograph needles, wire-drawing dies, hardness testers, etc.). Since 1955 it has also been possible to produce synthetic industrial diamonds by the application of extremely high pressures and temperatures.

Value

The value of a gem diamond is assessed on four criteria, the "four Cs": carat (weight), colour, clarity and cut.

Weight

The weight of a diamond is measured in carats (1 carat=0.20 gram), a word which originally came from Arabic by way of Dutch and meant the dried carob seeds formerly used for weighing diamonds in India and gold in Africa. The value of a diamond is not directly related to its weight: a 1-carat diamond is not worth twice as much as one of 0.5 carat but perhaps three times as much, since large diamonds are rarer than small ones.

Colour

The second criterion in assessing the value of a diamond is its colour. The scale ranges from "pure white" by way of "clear white", "white", "slightly tinted white" , "tinted white" and "considerably tinted white" to "yellowish". Colourless diamonds are the most valuable. There are, however, also diamonds in a great variety of colours, some of which are particularly valued.

Clarity

The third criterion is clarity. There are seven internationally recognised degrees of clarity, recognisable under 10-times magnification, ranging from "internally flawless" (with no extraneous inclusions) by way of "very, very small inclusions" and "small inclusions" down to "coarse inclusions" visible with the naked eye.

Cut

The first three criteria apply to the natural diamond. The fourth – cut – depends on the work of the human hand. Of the cuts shown on p. 405 the best known and most favoured is the brilliant. Although cut and polished diamonds are commonly called brilliants, the term properly applies only to those with a full cut in 58 facets. The other cuts shown – marquise or navette, oval, emerald, drop and heart – also have 58 facets. There are also other cuts: baguette (a simple cut with 24 facets), octahedron (16 facets), carré (a square cut).

Facets are the surfaces created by cutting, which must be set at certain angles to one another in order to obtain the optimum refraction of light (the sparkle or "fire" of the diamond). The largest (horizontal) facet is called the "table".

Formerly the rough diamond was cut with a diamond chip and a special knife; nowadays a less risky sawing technique is used. Ths saw is a paper-thin disc of phosphor bronze smeared along the edge with olive oil and diamond grit. The stone is given its final cut, facet by facet, with a castiron disc faced with diamond granules, turning at a rate of 2500 revolutions a minute. The cutting of a rough diamond is a high-precision operation which must take account of the crystalline structure of the stone (that is, the particular pattern in which the carbon atoms are arranged) to ensure that the diamond does not literally explode.

Diplomatic and Consular Offices

South African Diplomatic Offices

High Commission: United Kingdom
South Africa House
Trafalgar Square
London WC2N 5DP
Tel. (0171) 930 4488

Embassy: USA
3051 Massachusetts Avenue NW
Washington DC 20008
Tel. 202/232 4400

High Commission: Canada
15 Sussex Drive
Ottawa, Ontario K1M 1M8
Tel. 613/744 0330

Diplomatic and Consular Offices in South Africa

High Commission: United Kingdom
91 Parliament Street
Cape Town 8001
Tel. 021/4 61 72 20

225 Hill Street
Arcadia
Pretoria 0002
Tel. 012/43 31 21/2932

Consulates:
Southern Life Centre (15th floor)
8 Riebeeck Street
Cape Town 8001
Tel. 021/25 36 70, 25 36 86 and 25 44 75

Fedlife House (10th floor)
320 Smith Street
Durban 4000
Tel. 031/3 05 29 29

c/o Messrs Coopers Theron Du Toit
Suite 7, Norvia House
34 Western Avenue
Vincent 5247
East London

Diplomatic and Consular Offices

Sanlam Centre (19th floor)
corner of Jeppe and von Weilligh Streets
Johannesburg 2000
Tel. 011/3 37 89 40

Room 727, Allied Building
93 Main Street
Port Elizabeth 6001
Tel. 041/55 24 23

USA
Embassy:
Thibault House (7th floor)
225 Pretorius Street
Pretoria 0001
Tel. 012/28 42 66

Consulates:
Broadway Industries Centre
Heerengracht
Foreshore
Cape Town 8001
Tel. 021/21 42 80

Durban Bay House (29th floor)
333 Smith Street
Durban 4001
Tel. 031/3 04 47 37

Kine Centre (11th floor)
Commissioner and Kruis Streets
Johannesburg
Tel. 011/3 31 16 81

Canada
High Commission:
Nedbank Plaza (5th floor)
corner of Church and Beatrix Streets
Arcadia
Pretoria 0083
Tel. 012/3 24 39 70

Diplomatic Offices of Lesotho and Swaziland

Lesotho
High Commission in United Kingdom:
7 Chesham Place
London SW1 8HN
Tel. (0171) 235 5686

Embassy in United States:
2511 Massachusetts Avenue NW
Washington DC 20008
Tel. 202/797 5533

High Commission in Canada:
202 Clemow Avenue
Ottawa, Ontario
Tel. 613/236 9449

Swaziland
High Commission in United Kingdom:
20 Buckingham Gate
London SW1E 6LB
Tel. (0171) 630 6611

Embassy in United States:
3400 International Drive NW
Washington DC 20008
Tel. 202/362 6683

High Commission in Canada:
Suite 1204, 130 Albert Street
Ottawa, Ontario K1P 5G4
Tel. 613/567 1480

Diplomatic Offices in Lesotho and Swaziland

United Kingdom High Commission:
PO Box Ms 521
Maseru 100. Tel. 31 39 61

Lesotho

United States Embassy:
PO Box 333
Maseru 100. Tel. 31 26 66

United Kingdom High Commission:
Allister Miller Street
Mbabane. Tel. 4 25 81

Swaziland

United States Embassy:
PO Box 199
Central Bank Building, Warner Street
Mbabane. Tel. 4 64 41

Distances

The distances between selected towns in South Africa are shown in the
table on the map attached to this guide.

Diving

There are plenty of good diving grounds off South Africa's 3000km/1865
miles of coast. The meeting between the cold Benguela Current on the west
coast and the warm Agulhas Current on the east coast produces a rich
marine fauna and flora, with something like 2000 species of fish; and
whales and dolphins are also occasionally to be seen. The most southerly
coral reefs in the world are off the northern KwaZulu/Natal coast. In addition to its endless variety of plant and animal life, its reefs, sea-caves, rock
overhangs and tunnels there is a special attraction for divers in the wrecks
of ships which have fallen victim to stormy seas off the Cape of Good Hope.

Ocean Divers International: head office in Port Elizabeth, PO Box 5624,
    Walmer 6065, tel. 041/55 65 36; branches in Cape Town, East London,
    Durban, Gordon's Bay, Plettenberg Bay, Port Elizabeth, etc.
Adventure Centre, PO Box 83, Rondebosch 7700, tel. 021/6 80 19 57
Scuba City, Randburg Plaza, 153 Hendrik Verwoerd Drive, Randburg 2194,
    tel. 011/7 87 10 30
Sodwana Bay Lodge Dive School, Leisure Lodges, PO Box 5478, Durban
    4000, tel. 031/3 04 59 77
Blue Water Divers, 114 Victoria Embankment, Durban, fax 021/3 07 27 11
Underwater World, PO Box 2584, Cape Town 8000, tel. 021/4 61 82 90

Diving schools

Baedeker Special

Graveyard of Ships

Even after the occupation of the Cape by white settlers (see Baedeker Special, p. 158) the route round the Cape of Good Hope remained a challenge to the skill of seamen. So far more than 500 wrecks have been located in Table Bay, bearing witness to the sudden end of many a voyage as a result of storms, fog, displacement of cargo or human error. Now a series of lighthouses point the way round the Cape, the one on Cape Point being one of the most powerful in the world, and navigation is simplified by the use of radar. The Maritime Museum in Cape Town plans to establish a Historic Wreck Route, with signs round the coast telling the story of the wrecks and describing diving conditions.

Off the rugged coasts of the Cape Town suburbs of Sea Point, Green Point and Mouille Point alone there are at least ten wrecks. Many ships lie on the Atlantic coast and off Robben Island, the prison island in Table Bay. The oldest remains of ships' timbers, found in a silted-up area near the coast, are thought to have belonged to a Phoenician galley. The wreck of the Dutch East India Company's ship "Oosterland", which just before it sank in 1688 had brought French Huguenots to the Cape, lay undiscovered for 300 years; it was carrying a cargo of peppercorns, indigo dyes, cowrie shells (a form of currency), seamen's shoes and porcelain from China, Japan and Persia. Off Robben Island, 7km/4½ miles from the coast, are two dozen wrecks, including the "Dageraad", which sank in 1694 with seventeen chests of gold and silver on board.

Not all wrecks, however, have been discovered and their cargoes salvaged. And there are still occasional wrecks to add to the toll of the sea. In November a ship which had taken part in the Allied landings in Normandy in June 1944, the South African minesweeper SAS "Pietermaritzburg", sank between Cape Town and the Cape of Good Hope. As HMS "Pelorus" it had been the first vessel to land on the French coast on June 6th 1944; then in 1947 it was handed over to the South African navy and renamed, and was finally withdrawn from service in 1964. Attempts to salvage the wreck were unsuccessful, and it is now a rusty hulk, lying at a depth of 19m/62ft, with its highest point only 4m/13ft below the surface. It is to become an artificial reef and a new attraction for divers.

Diving addresses   Ocean Divers International (see above)
JR Diving, Sodwana Bay, PO Box 38158, Point 4069, tel. 031/29 46 05 (Durban)
Aliwal Cove, PO Box 24, Umkomaas 4170, tel. 0323/3 10 02

Dress

Visitors' clothing should be appropriate to a warm climate. In the holiday regions dress is casual during the day, but for dinner in a hotel or restaurant something a little more formal is usual. In summer (and in KwaZulu/Natal also during the winter months of June–August) something light is required (summer dresses, lightweight suits, shorts). But an anorak or coat of some kind is also needed, since the evenings can be distinctly cool. In the Cape provinces and at higher altitudes (for example on the highveld at Johannesburg) warm clothing is required in winter. Some protection against rain is also necessary: it does not rain often in South Africa, but when it does it is real rain, and then an umbrella and a rainproof coat will prove useful.

Divers can explore South Africa's colourful underwater world

Drinking Water

See Food and Drink

Electricity

City and town power systems are 220/230 volts AC, except in Pretoria, which has 250 volts AC. Plugs have three round pins; the necessary adaptors can be bought in hardware shops and some travel agencies.

Embassies

See Diplomatic and Consular Offices

Emergency Services

Tel. 1 01 11

Police (in all large towns)

The telephone numbers of district hospitals are given at the beginning of local telephone books.

Hospitals

Emergencies: 999
Fire: 3 31 22 22
Hospital (Johannesburg Hospital): 4 88 49 11

Emergency numbers in Johannesburg

Events

<table>
<tr><td>in Cape Town</td><td>Emergencies: 51 51 51
Fire: 4 61 41 41
Hospital (Groote Schuur Hospital): 4 04 91 11</td></tr>
<tr><td>Information</td><td>Addresses and telephone numbers can be obtained by dialling the following numbers:
Cape Town: 021/4 18 50 00
Durban: 031/3 05 38 77
Johannesburg: 011/4 02 50 00</td></tr>
</table>

Events

In this country of many different peoples there is a corresponding variety of events over the year. Satour (see Information) issues twice a year, free of charge, a Calendar of Events all over South Africa. The following list is merely a brief selection.

<table>
<tr><td>January</td><td>January 1st–7th: Cape Coon Carnival in Cape Town (coloureds' street carnival)</td></tr>
<tr><td>February</td><td>Art and Antiques Fair in Cape Town</td></tr>
<tr><td>March</td><td>Shell Festival in Jeffrey's Bay (near Port Elizabeth)
Cape Town Festival (street festival)
Durban Fiesta and Harbour Festival</td></tr>
<tr><td>March/April</td><td>Rand Easter Show in Johannesburg (the largest show of consumer goods in South Africa)</td></tr>
<tr><td>May/June</td><td>Comrades Marathon (Pietermaritzburg to Durban)</td></tr>
<tr><td>June/July</td><td>National Arts Festival in Grahamstown (ten days of drama, opera, dance and jazz)
Zululand Show (with Agricultural Show in Eshowe)</td></tr>
<tr><td>July</td><td>Racing in Greyville Stadium, Durban
Shembe Festival at Ekupakuneni, near Durban (Zulu religious festival, with tribal dances)
Kimberley Steam Festival (presentation of the town's collection of steam locomotives)</td></tr>
<tr><td>September</td><td>Great Train Race (against Apple Express), Port Elizabeth</td></tr>
<tr><td>October</td><td>International Eisteddfod (song and dance) at Roodepoort, near Johannesburg
Bloemfontein Rose Festival
Stellenbosch Wine Festival
Durban Tattoo (Scottish-style festival, with bands and fireworks)
Jacaranda Festival in Pretoria
Cape Craft Exhibition in Cape Town</td></tr>
<tr><td>December</td><td>Rothman's Week Regatta (from Cape Town to Saldanha)</td></tr>
</table>

Fishing

South Africa is a fisherman's paradise. Trout fishing on the country's rivers and lakes is the favourite national sport; but there is also plenty of rock fishing, surf fishing and deep-sea fishing – for the two currents which wash the east and west coasts of Africa and meet at the Cape support a great variety of marine life.

In South Africa you can fish practically all year round. The only restrictions are on trout fishing, which is prohibited in June, July and August.

African Fishing Safaris, PO Box 124, Bergvliet 7945, tel. 021/72 12 72
(deep-sea fishing, trout fishing, tiger fishing)
Bonaventure Fish Africa, PO Box 85450, Greenside 2034, tel. 011/6 46 61 20
(deep-sea fishing, trout fishing, tiger fishing)
Gone Fishing, PO Box 46122, Orange Grove 2192, tel. 011/4 85 11 73
(deep-sea fishing, trout fishing, tiger fishing)
Trout Adventures Africa, 10 Dean Street, Cape Town 8001, tel. 021/
21 26 10 57 (trout fishing)
Critchley Hackle Lodge, PO Box 141, Dullstroom 1110, tel. 01325/4 01 45
(trout fishing)
Mountain Shadows, PO Box 2501, Paarl 7620, tel. 02211/62 31 92 (deep-sea
fishing, trout fishing)
Kaliiso Lodge, PO Box 195, Welgeheuwel 1736, tel. 011 4 75 57 02 (tiger
fishing)
Pongolwane, PO Box 12, Golela 3990, tel. 03843/5 11 23 (tiger fishing)

Firms organising fishing trips

Flying

Visitors with a pilot's licence can charter an aircraft from one of the following firms:

Aircraft charter

Inter-Air, PO Box 18046, Rand Airport 1419, tel. 011/8 27 98 04, and PO Box 259, Lanseria Airport 1748, tel. 011/6 59 15 74
Departure airports: Rand, Lanseria

KwenaAir, PO Box 428, Rivonia 2128, tel. 011/8 03 49 21
Departure airports: Jan Smuts, Lanseria, Rand, Grand Central

Rossair, PO Box 428, Lanseria 1748, tel. 011/6 59 29 80, and PO Box 4711, Halfway House 1685, tel. 011/3 15 58 88
Departure airports: Lanseria, Rand, Grand Central

Speed Air, PO Box 310, Lanseria 1748, tel. 011/6 59 28 85
Departure airport: Lanseria

Aero Club of South Africa, Grand Central Airport, Old Pretoria Road, PO Box 898, Kempton Park 1620, tel. 011/8 05 03 66

Information:

Route: Johannesburg, Pretoria, Kruger Park, Durban, Port Alfred, Oudtshoorn, Cape Town and return. Part-route flights also available.
Information: Court Helicopters (see under Helicopter tours).

Air safaris

Sightseeing flights round Johannesburg in a JU 52 (20-minute flight; on first weekend of month between 10am and 3pm).
Information: South African Airways.

There are also air safaris into Namibia, Botswana, Zimbabwe, Malawi and Mozambique.

Afro Ventures, PO Box 2339, Randburg 2125, tel. 011/7 89 10 78

Organisers of air safaris

Comair, PO Box 7015, Bonaero Park 1522, tel. 011/9 73 29 11

Dragonfly, PO Box 2, Sun City 0316, tel. 01465/2 10 00

Fly Southern Africa Tours, PO Box 201703, Durban North 4016, tel. 031/5 62 85 52

Hamilton Tours, PO Box 1288, Randburg 2125, tel. 011/8 86 15 50

Flying

Safariplan, PO Box 4245, Randburg 2125, tel. 011/8 86 18 10

Wilderness Safaris, PO Box 651171, Benmore 2010, tel. 011/8 84 14 58

Flying schools

Avex Air Training, Grand Central Airport, PO Box 2259, Halfway House 1685, tel. 011/3 15 00 03

Cape Flying Services (Garden Route), PO Box 2535, George 6530, tel. 0441/76 92 17

Lanseria Flight Centre (Johannesburg), PO Box 51, Lanseria 1748, tel. 011/6 59 28 10

43rd Flying School (Garden Route), Private Bag X43, Port Alfred 6170, tel. 0464/4 34 33

Progress Flying School (Port Elizabeth), PO Box 28, Greenbushes 6390, tel. 041/72 16 47

Wonderboom Flying School (Pretoria), PO Box 215, Bon Accord 0009, tel. 012/57 12 51

Gliding

Transvaal, with its stable weather conditions and good thermals, offers particularly good prospects of long flights. There are 23 gliding clubs in South Africa which organise gliding meets and hire out two-seater gliders. The South African gliding championships are held at Vryburg (North-West Province) in December. The Mecca of gliding enthusiasts is Bloemfontein (Orange Free State).

Information

Dick Bradley, PRO Soaring Society of South Africa, PO Box 890, Sloane Park 2152, Transvaal, tel. 011/7 89 13 28
Magaliesburg Gliding Club, PO Box 190, Tarlton 1749, tel. 011/7 16 52 29

The Magaliesburg Gliding Club, PO Box 67, Randburg 2125, tel. 011/7 05 32 01, welcomes visiting enthusiasts.

Hang-gliding

Favourite areas for hang-gliding are the Western and Eastern Cape and the Natal Drakensberg. For the purpose of insurance hang-gliders must be members of the Aero Club (which offers temporary membership to visitors).
There are no official arrangements for hiring a glider, but clubs will usually help out. A recovery service is essential. Essential items of equipment are a water bottle and a radio transmitter. It is advisable not to fly alone.

Addresses

Aero Club of South Africa, PO Box 898, Kempton Park, 1620, tel. 011/8 05 03 66

Hang Gliding and Paragliding Association of South Africa, tel. 011/6 09 16 78

Cape Albatross Club, PO Box 342, Sea Point 8060, tel. 021/4 62 26 60

Helicopter tours

Court Helicopters, PO Box 18115, Rand Airport 1419
Johannesburg: tel. 011/8 27 89 07
Cape Town: tel. 021/25 29 66
Flights in Johannesburg and Pretoria area: from short sightseeing flights to two-day trips.

Dragonfly Helicopter Adventures, PO Box 26, Sun City 0316, tel. 01465/2 10 00
Flights in Eastern Transvaal.

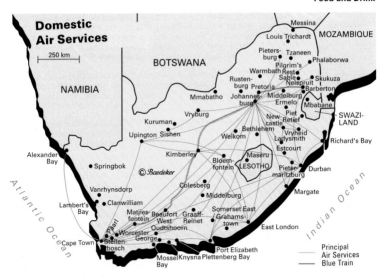

Gold Reef City Helicopters, tel. 011/4 96 14 00
Flights from Gold Reef City over Johannesburg and Soweto.

Bill Harrop's Original Balloon Safaris, PO Box 67, Randburg 2125, tel.   **Hot-air ballooning**
  011/7 05 32 01
Flights round Johannesburg and Pretoria and over the Magaliesberg

Airtrack Adventures, PO Box 630, Muldersdrift 1747, tel. 011/9 57 23 22
Flights to Sun City and Lost City (160km/100 miles from Johannesburg) and
over Pilanesberg Game Park.

Wineland Ballooning, tel. 0211/4 16 85
Flights in Berg River valley, near Paarl.

Parachute jumping is possible at any time of year, but the best months are   **Parachute jumping**
December and January.

Western Province Sport Parachuting, PO Box 7017, Roggebaai 8012, tel.   Addresses
021/5 09 26 65 (Mr Phelps) or 021/4 61 06 77

Pietermaritzburg Parachuting Club, PO Box PO Box 398, Pietermaritzburg
3200, tel. 0331/6 25 34 (Mr John Plessis)

The Free Fall Factory, PO Box 82072, Southdale 2135, tel. 011/4 44 06 56 (Mr
R. McCallum)

Food and Drink

There is no authentic South African cuisine: the South African menu shows
a variety of influences, both European (British, French, Italian, German) and
Asian (Malay, Indian).

Most hotels serve the traditional British breakfast – eggs, bacon, sausages,   Breakfast
toast.

Specialities in and around Cape Town	Malay cuisine predominates in the Cape Town area. Local specialities are *bobotie* (a delicately flavoured curry served with stewed fruits and chutney), *sosaties* (mutton and beef kebabs with small onions) and various kinds of *bredie* (a meat and vegetable stew), the best known of which is *waterblommetjie-bredie,* flavoured by water-hyacinth blossoms.
In Durban	The cuisine of Durban is predominantly Indian, with hot beef, lamb, chicken and fish curries served with sweet-sour chutney. Also very tasty are *samosas* (small triangular pastries with a meat or vegetable curry filling). If the curry is too hot for you, nibble the desiccated coconut that is served with it.
	South Africans have a particular liking for *braaivleis* (grilled meat) – beef, mutton, lamb, pork or *boerewors* (a long, coiled sausage), accompanied by *pap,* a kind of maize porridge. A braaivleis barbecue is a favourite South African meal, which many hotels serve in their gardens.
	A particular South African speciality is biltong – wind-dried meat (beef or, more exotically, kudu, ostrich or elephant) – which is a popular high-protein snack. In its raw state it looks unattractive, but when cooked is mouth-wateringly tasty.
	There are excellent fish dishes to be had in the coastal areas, particularly in and around Cape Town, but also in Johannesburg. Specialities are crayfish, grilled kingklip (a species of cod with firm white flesh), snoek (the South African mackerel) and perlemoen (a large shellfish from the Atlantic).
Sweets	A favourite sweet is *koeksisters*, a small plaited pastry fried in fat and then dipped in syrup.
Fruit and vegetables	With its widely varying climatic zones and soils, South Africa has a varied range of fruit and vegetables, usually available fresh. Thanks to strict controls on quality and freshness, fruit, salads and vegetables are absolutely safe to eat. On the Cape grow grapes, apples, pears and Cape gooseberries (small yellow berries which are used in preserves and cakes). In KwaZulu/Natal and the Eastern Transvaal there are tropical and subtropical fruits and vegetables – bananas, pineapples, pawpaws, avocados, etc. Asparagus in South Africa usually means the green variety: the growing of white asparagus has begun only in recent years.
Drinks	Since tapwater is everywhere safe to drink – the standard of Cape Town's water is one of the highest in the world – the sale of mineral water has made little headway in South Africa. The best known brand of mineral water is Skoonspruit ("Clean Spring"). In view of the high temperatures in South Africa iced water is commonly drunk with meals.
	The local beer is excellent.
	White South Africans like long hard drinks such as brandy and cola. South Africa itself produces many schnapps and liqueurs, e.g. Amarula (a liqueur made from the fruit of the wild marula tree) and Van der Hum (a mandarine liqueur).
	Refreshing soft drinks include fruit juices (e.g. of the liqui fruit) and rooibos tea, which tastes like a mixture of herb tea and black tea.
	First place among South African drinks is taken by the wines of the Cape (see Wine).
	South African coffee differs in taste from European and American coffee: it is roasted in a different way and is mixed with chicory. Better filter coffees are now, however, increasingly being served.

Getting to South Africa

By air	There are frequent flights from London on British Airways, South African Airways, Olympic Airways (via Athens), Air Namibia and Air Zimbabwe (via Harare). The flight takes about 11 hours.

From the United States there are flights by South African Airways (New York to Cape Town, Durban, East London, George, Johannesburg and Port Elizabeth; Atlanta to Cape Town and Johannesburg; Miami to Bloemfontein, Cape Town, Durban, Johannesburg and Port Elizabeth).

From Canada there are flights by Air Canada from Montreal to Cape Town and Johannesburg.

There are now increasing possibilities for travelling to South Africa by sea, sometimes in cargo boats with a number of very comfortable cabins for passengers. Information from the following: **By sea**

Medite Shipping Co. (Medite Travel)
Antwerp: tel. 032/32 34 03 60
Durban: tel. 031/3 01 60 61
Route: Felixstowe (GB), Antwerp (NL) or Livorno (I) to Cape Town (2½ weeks)

Safmarine
London: tel. (0171) 537 6380
Cape Town: tel. 021/4 08 69 11
Route: Southampton to Cape Town (16 days)

St Helena Shipping Co.
Curnow Shipping Ltd, Halston (GB), tel. 013265/63434
Route: Cardiff to Cape Town (3½ weeks)

Noble Caledonia
11 Charles Street, London, W1X 7HB; tel. (0171) 491 4752

Golf

The first golf club was founded in Cape Town in 1885 and is today known as the Royal Cape Golf Club.

There are currently more than 660 clubs throughout the country.

Top class, world standard golf courses are found in all the major tourism centres, such as Cape Town, the Garden Route, Durban, Phalaborwa near the Kruger National Park and Sun City. It is very simple to combine golfing with game viewing, a beach holiday, fishing or shopping trips to the big cities.

South Africa's major golfing events are: the Million Dollar Sun City Classic, which takes place each December at Sun City, the Sunshine Golf Circuit, which is played every November to March at selected clubs throughout the country and South African Airways International Pro-Am in January.

Expect to pay from £6 to £21 for an 18 hole round and £3–£6 for a caddy.

South Africa has produced many famous international golfers including: Gary Player, John Bland, Bobby Locke and Ernie Els.

Some of the well known South African clubs:

Royal Cape, Cape Town: Predominantly a parkland layout and has played host to the South African Open many times. If you want a challenging wind, then this is the course to play in the summer months (December to March) when Cape Town's notorious south-easter hits, even though the temperature can be 30°C.

Royal Johannesburg: A championship course built in 1933 and frequent host to the SA Open. This course is a tree-lined parkland layout, with gentle undulations.

Gary Player Country Club & the Lost City, Sun City: Sun City is a spectacular Las Vegas style complex rising out of the African plain. Sun City has recently opened the spectacular Lost City, a re-creation of an ancient African city set in a tropical rainforest. There are two golf clubs at Sun City,

the Gary Player Country Club opend in 1979 and the £3 million Lost City "desert-style" course opened in 1992. Both courses were designed by Gary Player.

Hans Merensky Golf Club, Kruger National Park: This club backs onto the Kruger National Park and must be the only course in the world where hippos inhabit the water features. Expect to see impala and waterbuck on the course and even lions and leopards have been spotted in the early mornings.

Durban Country Club, Durban: Laid out by the father of South African golf, Laurie B. Waters in 1922. The first five holes have been described as the best start to any golf course in the world and it is where, in 1956, Gary Player won his first South African Open. From the first tee the views across the ocean are stunning, although this means that wind is almost always a factor.

January: South African Open Championship, Lexington PGA Tournament, Johannesburg
February: Sunshine Circuit of various courses
December: Million Dollar Golf Classic, Sun City

Major tournaments

Golf Courses (a selection)

Unless otherwise indicated, all the golf courses listed are 18-hole courses.

Royal Johannesburg Golf Club (two courses), Fairway Avenue, Linksfield North, Orange Grove, Johannesburg 2119, tel. 011/6 40 30 21
Wanderers Golf Club, The Kent, Northlands 2116, tel. 011/4 47 33 11
Houghton Golf Club, 2nd Avenue, Lower Houghton 2198, tel. 011/7 28 10 04
Bryanston Country Club, Bryanston Drive, Bryanston 2021, tel. 011/7 06 13 61
Dainfern Golf Club, Bryanston, Johannesburg 2021, tel. 011/4 65 45 80
Crown Mines Golf Club, Booysens Reserve Road, Crown Mines 2025, tel. 011/8 35 13 17
Roodepoort Country Club, Helderkruin 1733, tel. 011/6 62 14 80
Zwartkop Country Club, Johannesburg–Pretoria road, Verwoerdburg 0157, tel. 011/64 11 44
Glendower Golf Club, Marais Road, Johannesburg 2008, tel/ 011/4 53 10 13
Pretoria Golf Club, Pretoria 0001, tel. 011/79 48 50

Hans Merensky Golf Club, Molengraaf Road, Phalaborwa 1390, tel. 011/59 31

Sabi Country Club (Golf Hotel), Sabie 1260, tel. 011/3 95
White River Country Club (Golf Hotel), Hazyview 1242, tel. 011/2 42
Malelane Golf Club (9 holes), Malelane 1320, tel. 011/23 11

Umhlali Country Club, Umhlali, tel. 0322/7 11 81
Huletts Country Club, Mount Edgecombe 4300, tel. 031/59 53 31
Durban Country Club, Walter Gilbert Road, Durban 4000, tel. 031/23 82 82
Maritzburg Golf Club, New England Road, Pietermaritzburg 3200, tel. 0331/96 23 56
Scottborough Golf Club, Williamson Street, Scottborough 4180, tel. 0323/2 00 41
Selborne Country Club (Golf Hotel), Pennington 1482 (leave N 2 at Sezela), tel. 0323/5 11 33
Port Shepstone Country Club, main South Coast road, Umtentwini, Port Shepstone 4240, tel. 0391/5 01 40
Margate Country Club, Margate 4275, tel. 03931/2 05 71
Southbroom Golf Club, Captain Smith Road, Southbroom 4277, tel. 03931/60 26
San Lameer Country Club, Southbroom 4277, tel. 0393/8 51 44

Gauteng

Northern Transvaal

Eastern Transvaal

KwaZulu/Natal

◄ A golf course with Table Mountain as a magnificent backdrop

Health

Eastern Cape	Wild Coast Country Club (Golf Hotel), Mzamba Beach, Port Edward 4295, tel. 0471/5 91 11
	East London Golf Club, Gleneagles Drive, East London 5200, tel. 0431/35 13 56
	Alexander Golf Club, Clovelly Road, Sunnyridge, East London 5200, tel. 0431/46 36 46
	Fish River Sun Country Club (Golf Hotel), Port Alfred 6170, tel. 0431/61 21 01
	Royal Port Alfred Golf Club, Princess Avenue, Port Alfred, Kowie West 6171, tel. 0464/4 25 00
	Wedgewood Park Country Club, Old Cape Road, Greenbushes, Port Elizabeth 6000, tel. 041/72 12 12
	Humewood Golf Club, Marine Drive, Port Elizabeth 6000, tel. 041/53 21 37
Western Cape	Plettenberg Bay Country Club, Plettenberg Bay 6600, tel. 04457/3 21 32
	Knysna Golf Club, Howard Street, Knysna 6570, tel. 0445/2 23 91
	Fancourt Country Club (Golf Hotel), George 6530, tel. 0441/70 82 82
	George Golf Club, C. J. Langenhoven Street, George 6530, tel. 0441/51 43
	Mossel Bay Golf Club, 17 De Laan, Mossel Bay 6500, tel. 0444/23 79
	Hermanus Golf Club, Main Road, Hermanus 7200, tel. 0283/1 19 54
	Strand Golf Club, Gordon's Bay Road, Strand 7140, tel. 024/53 29 69
	Clovelly Country Club, Fish Hoek, Cape Town 7975, tel. 021/7 82 64 10
	Royal Cape Golf Club, 174 Ottery Road, Wynberg 7800, tel. 021/7 61 65 51
	Milnerton Golf Club, Bridge Road, Milnerton 7441, Cape Town, tel. 021/52 10 47
	Paarl Golf Club, Paarl 7620, tel. 02211/63 11 40
	Stellenbosch Golf Club, Strand Road, Stellenbosch 7600, tel. 02231/32 79
Orange Free State	Bloemfontein Golf Club, Mazelspoort Road, Bloemfontein 9300, tel. 051/33 20 13
	Worcester Golf Club, Worcester 6850, tel. 0231/7 25 42
	Oppenheimer Park Golf Club, Steyn Mine, Welkom 9460, tel. 0171/3 21 31
	Riviera Country Club (Golf Hotel), Riviera Road, Vereeniging 1930, tel. 016/22 28 61
North-West	Gary Player Country Club (Golf Hotel), Sun City 0316, tel. 014651/2 10 00
	Arizona Golf Club (Golf Hotel), Sun City 0316, tel. 014651/7 77 77
Swaziland	Royal Swazi Golf Club (Royal Swazi Sun Hotel), Mbabane–Manzini road, tel. 09268/6 10 01

Health

Malaria	Visitors, at any time of year, to the lower-lying areas in the north, east and west of the Northern and Eastern Transvaal provinces (including the Kruger National Park) and the coastal regions of KwaZulu/Natal north of the 28th parallel must take precautions against malaria; other parts of South Africa are malaria-free. If you are contemplating a visit to any of the malarial areas, therefore, you should consult your doctor, before leaving home, about preventive medication, involving a course of antimalarial tablets, starting a week before departure and continuing throughout your stay and for four weeks after your return.
	This does not give an absolute guarantee of protection. If you develop a fever in spite of this prophylactic medication (the incubation period of malaria can range from 5 days to several years) you should consult a doctor at once.
	In addition you should take precautions against being bitten by the mosquitoes which carry the disease, Sleep under a mosquito net (which works better if impregnated with insecticide). Sleep in properly screened rooms, and use a knockdown spray to kill any mosquitoes in the room. Use insect repellents. Keep arms and legs covered after sunset. Avoid stagnant

water (where the mosquitoes breed), particularly in the evening and at night.

Bilharziasis (schistosomiasis) is caused by a worm which occurs in water and penetrates the skin. With early treatment by effective modern drugs it clears up without difficulty. The best way of preventing the disease is to avoid bathing in fresh water in bilharziasis-infected areas; there is no danger in seawater or chlorinated swimming pools.

Bilharziasis

Help for the Disabled

Considerable efforts are being made in South Africa to meet the needs of disabled people. The following organisations will provide information and help for disabled visitors:

This organisation has an information centre in Durban:
PO Box 1059, Pinetown 3600, tel. 031/72 65 23

Disabled People of South Africa

The Independence Living Centre provides information on transport, sightseeing and accommodation for disabled people. Addresses:
Johannesburg: PO Box 32099, Braamfontein 2017, tel. 011/7 20 65 46
Cape Town: Barkeley Road, Mowbray 7700, tel. 021/6 85 41 00

Independence Living Centre

The National Parks Board provides facilities for disabled people in all its camps. Address:
PO Box 787, Pretoria 0001, tel. 012/3 43 97 70

National Parks Board

South African Airways has facilities for disabled people at its larger airports.

South African Airways

The brochure issued by Satour (the South African Tourism Board), "Where to Stay?", contains information for handicapped people.

Satour

The list of hotels in this guide (see Hotels) indicates which hotels have facilities for disabled people.

Hotels

Hotels

South Africa has a dense network of hotels, in all categories from good to luxury, which can stand up to any international comparison. Hotels, motels and guest houses are classified on the five-star principle, on a scale extending from luxury (five stars) to good comfortable standard accommodation (one star) – though this does not mean that establishments without a star necessarily fall short in terms of cleanliness or comfort.

Hotels, motels, guest houses

It is advisable, particularly during the main holiday season, to book rooms well in advance.

Reservations

The South African Tourism Board (Satour: see Information) publishes annual lists of hotel and other accommodation, with detailed information on hotels, motels and guest houses; bed and breakfast accommodation; accommodation in National Parks; and camping sites.

Information

There are now increasing numbers of houses, particularly in the Cape region, offering bed and breakfast accommodation at very reasonable rates.

Bed and breakfast

Accommodation in National Parks is frequently in rondavels (round huts of traditional type with conical roofs), also at very reasonable rates.

Rondavels

Hotels

Hotel pass

Individual travellers will find it worth while to get a hotel pass – in effect a set of vouchers for hotels in a particular category. Hotel passes can be obtained from travel agencies or from the airline.

Tariffs

Tariffs vary considerably according to season. Many hotels – particularly the large chains such as Protea, Southern Sun, Holiday Inns and Sun International – offer special rates, even during the main season. The rates in the following table (in South African rands) are guide prices per night.

Category	Double room	Single room
★★★★★	R251–300	R251–300
★★★★	R201–300	R201–300
★★★	R151–300	R151–250
★★	R101–250	R101–200
★	R101–200	R100–150

N.B. These rates are likely to be overtaken by current increases in hotel prices.

In this section hotels are listed under provinces. The category is indicated by the number of stars. SP=swimming pool, T=tennis courts, FH=facilities for disabled visitors.

Eastern Cape

Addo

★Zuurberg Inn, Zuurberg Pass, tel. 0426/40 05 83, 7 rooms, SP, T

Aliwal North

★★Thatcher's Spa Hotel, Dan Pienaar Avenue, tel. 0551/27 72, 15 r.
★★Umtali Motel, Dan Pienaar Avenue, tel. 0551/24 00, 33 r.

Edward Hotel, Port Elizabeth

New Masonic Hotel, Stockenstroom Street, tel. 0481/31 15, 24 r.   Cradock

★★★Holiday Inn Garden Court, corner John Baillie and Moore Streets,   East London
tel. 0431/2 72 60, 173 r., SP, FH
★★★Hotel Osner, Esplanade, tel. 0431/43 34 33, 110 r., SP
★★★Kennaway Protea Hotel, Esplanade, tel. 0431/2 55 31, 88 r.
★★★King David Hotel and Conference Centre, 15 Inverleith, tel. 0431/
2 31 74, 43 r.
★★Dolphin Hotel, 85 Harewood Drive, Nahoon, tel. 0431/35 14 35, 33 r.
★★Esplanade Hotel, Beachfront, tel. 0431/2 25 18, 74 r.
★★Hotel Majestic, 21 Orient Road, tel. 0431/43 74 77, 32 r.

★★Savoy Hotel, 53 Durban Street, tel. 04634/3 11 46, 18 r., SP   Fort Beaufort

★★Gonubie Hotel, 141 Main Road, tel. 0431/40 40 10, 24 r.   Gonubie

★★★Drostdy Hotel, 30 Church Street, tel. 0491/2 21 61, 51 r., SP   Graaff-Reinet

★★★Settlers Inn, N 2 Highway, tel. 0461/2 73 13, 52 r., SP, FH   Grahamstown
★★Cathcart Arms Hotel, 5 West Street, tel. 0461/2 71 11, 14 r., SP
★★Graham Protea Hotel, 123 High Street, tel. 0461/2 23 24, 28 r.

★★Hogsback Inn, Main Road, tel. 045/9 62 10 06, 31 r., SP, T   Hogsback

★★★Savoy Protea Hotel, 16 Da Gama Road, tel. 0423/93 11 06, 31 r., SP   Jeffreys Bay

★★Kei Mouth Beach Hotel, Beach Road, tel. 0438/88 00 88, 28 r., SP   Kei Mouth

★★Grosvenor Lodge, 48 Taylor Street, tel. 0433/2 14 40, 15 r.   King William's Town

★★Hotel Middelburg Lodge, Meintjies Street, tel. 04924/2 11 00, 22 r., SP   Middelburg Cape
★★Country Protea Inn, corner of Meintjies and Loop Streets, tel. 04924/
2 11 87, 23 r.

Morgan's Bay Hotel, tel. 043272/62, 26 r., SP   Morgan's Bay

★Sandflats Hotel, 2 Bruton Street, tel. 042/8 51 10 12, 5 r., T   Paterson

★★★victoria Protea Hotel, 7 Albany Road, tel. 0464/4 11 33, 22 r.   Port Alfred
★★Kowie Grand Hotel, corner of Grand and Princes Avenues, tel. 0464/
4 11 50, 25 r.
★Ferrymans Hotel, Beach Road, tel. 0464/4 11 22, 28 r.

★★★City Lodge Port Elizabeth, corner of Beach and Lodge Roads, Sum-   Port Elizabeth
merstrand, tel. 041/56 33 22, 148 r., SP, FH
★★★Holiday Inn Garden Court Port Elizabeth–Kings Beach, La Roche
Drive, Humewood, tel. 041/52 37 20, 132 r., SP, FH
★★★Holiday Inn Garden Court Port Elizabeth–Summerstrand, tel. 041/
53 31 31, 236 r., SP, T, FH
★★★Marine Protea Hotel, Marine Drive, Summerstrand, tel. 041/53 21 01,
73 r.
★★★Beach Hotel, Marine Drive, Summerstrand, tel. 041/53 21 61, 63 r.
★★Edward Hotel, Belmont Terrace, tel. 041/56 20 56, 110 r.
★★Humewood Hotel, 33 Beach Road, Humewood, tel. 041/55 89 61, 65 r.
★★Walmer Gardens Hotel, 10th Avenue, Walmer, tel. 041/51 43 22, 37 r.,
SP

★★Grand Hotel, Cathcart Road, tel. 0451/30 17, 28 r., SP   Queenstown
★★Hexagon Hotel, Cathcart Road, tel. 0451/30 15, 49 r.
★★Jeantel Hotel, Shepston Street, tel. 0451/30 16, 25 r.

★Rhodes Hotel, Miller Street, tel. 045/42/ask for 21, 10 r., T   Rhodes

Hotels

Storms River	★★Tsitsikamma Lodge, N 2, Tsitsikamma, tel. 042/7 50 38 02, 26 r., SP
	★★Tzitzikamma Forest Inn, Darnell Street, tel. 0425/41 17 11, 41 r., SP, T, FH
Venterstad	★★Union Hotel, Kruger Street, tel. 0553/4 00 45, 11 r.

Eastern Transvaal

Belfast	★Belfast Hotel, 103 Vermooten Street, tel. 01325/3 04 61, 14 r.
Dullstroom	★★★★Walkersons Country Manor, Waboomkop Farm, near Dullstroom–Lydenburg road, tel. 01325/4 02 46, 25 r., SP
	★★★Critchley Hackle Lodge, Teding van Berkhout Street, tel. 01325/4 01 45, 19 r., SP, T
	★★Dullstroom Inn, corner of Teding van Berkhout and Nassau Streets, tel. 01325/4 00 71, 11 r.
Evander	★★★Highveld Protea Inn, corner of Rotterdam and Stanford Streets, tel. 0136/2 46 11, 74 r., SP
Groblersdal	★Groblersdal Hotel, 1 Hereford Street, tel. 01202/20 57, 24 r.
Hazyview	★★★★Karos Lodge, Sabie River, Kruger Gate, tel. 01311/6 56 71, 96 r., SP, T, FH
	★★★★Sabi River Sun, Main Sabi Road, tel. 01317/6 73 11, 60 r., SP, T
	★★★Bohms Zeederberg, Hazyview, tel. 01317/6 81 01, 12 r., SP, T, FH
	★★★Hotel Numbi, Hazyview, 16km/10 miles from Kruger Park, tel. 01317/6 73 01, 22 r., SP, T
	★★★Hazyview Protea Hotel, Burgers Hall, tel. 01317/6 73 32, 48 r., SP, T
Kiepersol	★★★★Farmhouse Country Lodge, R 40 to Hazyview, tel. 01317/6 87 80, 14 r., SP
Komatipoort	★★★Border Country Inn, N 4, Lebombo Farm, tel. 01313/5 03 28, 17 r., SP
Lydenburg	★Morgan's Hotel, 14 Voortrekker Street, tel. 01323/21 65, 29 r.
Malelane	★★★★Malelane Lodge, Riverside Farm, tel. 01313/3 03 31, 102 r., SP, FH
Middelburg	★★★Midway Inn, Jan van Riebeeck Street, tel. 0132/46 20 81, 128 r., FH
Nelspruit	★★★Crocodile Country Inn, Schagen (near N 4), tel. 01311/6 30 40, 30 r., SP, T
	★★★Hotel Promenade, Louis Trichardt Street, tel. 01311/5 30 00, 73 r., SP, FH
	★Town Lodge Nelspruit, corner of Gen. Dan Pienaar and Koorsboom Streets, tel. 01311/4 14 44, 106 r., SP, FH
Pilgrim's Rest	★★★★Mount Sheba Hotel, Pilgrim's Rest, tel. 01315/8 12 41, 25 r., SP, T
Volksrust	★★Transvaal Hotel, 57 Joubert Street, tel. 01333/20 78, 16 r.
Waterval Boven	★★★Bergwaters Lodge, Waterval Boven, tel. 013262/ask for 103, 10 r., SP, T
	★★★Malaga Hotel, N 4 Sycamore, tel. 013262/ask for 431, 52 r., SP, T
White River	★★★★Cybele Forest Lodge, tel. 01311/5 05 11, 12 r., SP
	★★★★Hotel Die Winkler, Old Numbi Road, tel. 01311/3 23 17, 57 r., SP, T
	★★★★Pine Lake Sun, Main Hazyview Road, tel. 01311/3 11 86, 68 r., SP, T
	★★★Glory Hill Guest Lodge, R 358 (to Numbi), tel. 01311/3 32 17, 5 r., SP
	★★★Hulala Lakeside Lodge, R 40 (between White River and Hazyview), tel. 01311/5 17 10, 21 r., SP
	★★Karula Hotel, Old Plaston Road, tel. 01311/3 22 77, 37 r., SP, T

KwaZulu/Natal

★★★Little Switzerland Resort, tel. 036/4 38 62 20, 35 r.   Bergville

★★★Rob Roy Hotel, Rob Roy Crescent, tel. 031/7 77 13 05, 37 r., SP   Botha's Hill

★★Landhaus Karin, Sub 42 Middelbosch, tel. 03324/42 74, 5 r., T   Dargle

★★★★Karos Edward Hotel, Marine Parade, tel. 031/37 36 81, 98 r.   Durban
★★★City Lodge Durban, corner of Brickhill and Old Fort Roads, tel. 031/
32 14 47, 161 r., SP, FH
★★★Elangeni Sun, Snell Parade, tel. 031/37 13 21, 446 r., SP, FH
★★★Holiday Inn Garden Court Durban – North Beach, Snell Parade, tel.
031/32 73 61, 270 r., SP, FH
★★★Holiday Inn Garden Court Durban – South Beach, Marine Parade, tel.
031/37 22 31, 380 r., SP, FH
★★★Holiday Inn Marine Parade, Marine Parade, tel. 031/37 33 41, 344 r.,
SP, FH
★★★Palace Protea Hotel, Marine Parade, tel. 031/32 83 51, 76 r., SP
★★★Hilton Hotel, Hilton Road, tel. 0331/3 33 11, 28 r., SP, T
★★Crossways Country Inn (Hilton), 2 Old Howick Road, tel. 0331/3 32 67,
19 r., SP

★★★Sani Pass Hotel, Sani Pass Road, tel. 033/7 02 13 20, 79 r., SP, T Himeville
★★Himeville Arms, Arbuckle Street, tel. 033/7 02 13 05, 13 r., SP, T

★★★★Old Halliwell Country Inn, Currys Post, tel. 0332/30 26 02, 12 r., SP Howick

★★★Karridene Protea Hotel, Old Man South Coast Road, tel. 031/96 33 21, Illovo Beach
23 r., SP

★★Mount Currie Inn, Main Road, tel. 037/7 27 21 78, 34 r.   Kokstad

Holiday Inn Garden Court, Durban

Hotels

Ladysmith	Royal Hotel, Murchison Street, tel. 0361/2 21 76, 70 r., SP
Margate	★★Beach Lodge Hotel, Marine Drive, tel. 03931/2 14 83, 35 r., SP ★★Palm Ridge Guest House, 20 Ridge Road, tel. 03931/7 13 47, 3 r., SP
Mkuze	★★Ghost Mountain Inn, Old Man Road, tel. 035/5 73 10 25, 28 r., SP, T
Mont-aux-Sources	★★★Karos Mont-aux-Sources Hotel, Mont-aux-Sources, tel. 036/4 38 62 30, 72 r., SP, T
Mtunzini	★★Trade Winds Hotel, Hely Hutchinson Street, tel. 0353/40 14 11, 21 r., SP
Newcastle	★★★Holiday Inn Garden Court Newcastle, corner of Victoria and Hunter Streets, tel. 03431/2 81 51, 167 r., SP, FH
Nottingham Road	★★★Rawdons Hotel, Old Man Road, tel. 0333/3 60 44, 25 r., SP, T ★★Nottingham Road Hotel, tel. 0333/3 61 51, 11 r.
Pietermaritzburg	★★★Imperial Hotel, 224 Loop Street, tel. 0331/42 65 51, 60 r.
Richards Bay	★★★Karos Richards Hotel, Hibberd Drive, tel. 0351/3 13 01, 100 r., SP ★★Karos Bayshore Inn, The Gully, tel. 0351/3 12 46, 100 r., SP
Tongaat	★★Westbrook Hotel, 82 North Beach Road, tel. 0322/4 20 21, 24 r., SP
Tweedie	Fern Hill Hotel, R 103 Midmar, tel. 0332/30 50 71, 18 r., SP, T
uMhlali	★★★★Shortens Country House, Compensation Road, tel. 0322/7 11 40, 12 r., SP, T
Umhlanga Rocks	★★★★Beverly Hills Sun, 54 Lighthouse Road, tel. 031/5 61 22 11, 87 r., SP ★★★Oysterbox Hotel, 2 Lighthouse Road, tel. 031/5 61 22 33, 88 r., SP, T
Umzumbe	★★Pumula Hotel, 67 Steve Pitts Road, tel. 0391/84 67 17, 35 r., SP
Uvongo	★★★Brackenmoor Hotel, Lot 2013, tel. 03931/7 51 65, 16 r., SP, T
Vryheid	★★★Stilwater Protea Hotel, Dundee Road, tel. 0381/61 81, 80 r., SP Villa Prince Imperial, 201 Deputation Street, tel. 0381/80 26 10, 4 r., SP
Wartburg	★★★Wartburg Hof Guest House, 53 Noodsberg Road, tel. 033/5 03 14 82, 16 r., SP, FH
Westville	★★★Westville Hotel, 124 Jan Hofmeyer Road, tel. 031/86 63 26, 42 r., SP
Winterton	★★★Drakensberg Sun, Cathkin Park, tel. 036/4 68 10 00, 148 r., SO, T, FH ★★★Cathedral Peak Hotel, tel. 036/4 88 18 88, 90 r., SP, T ★★★Cayley Lodge, Bergvlei, tel. 036/4 68 12 22, SP, T

Northern Cape

Colesberg	★★★Merino Inn Motel, N 1 bypass, tel. 051753/07 81, 70 r., SP ★★Van Zylsvlei Motel, Philippolos Road, tel. 051753/05 89, 18 r. ★Spes Bona, 22 President Kruger Street, tel. 051753/02 10, 4 r.
Groblershoop	★★Groot Rivier Hotel, 15 Main Street, tel. 05472/ask for 14, 9 r.
Kakamas	★★★Waterwiel Protea Hotel, Voortrekker Street, tel. 054/4 31 08 38, 25 r., SP

★★Kamieskroon Hotel, Old National Road, tel. 0257/61 47 06, 15 r.   Kamieskroon

★★★Holiday Inn Garden Court, 120 Du Toitspan Road, tel. 0531/3 17 51,   Kimberley
113 r., SP, FH
★★★Hotel Kimberlite, 162 George Street, tel. 0531/81 19 67, 30 r.
★★Colinton Hotel, 14 Thompson Street, tel. 0531/3 14 71, 10 r., SP
★★Diamond Protea Lodge, 124 Du Toitspan Road, tel. 0531/81 12 81, 34 r.,
FH

★★★Eldorado Motel, Main Stret, tel. 05373/2 21 91, 81 r., SP   Kuruman

★Nababeep Hotel, Main Street, tel. 0251/3 81 51, 27 r., FH   Nababeep

★★Postmasburg Hotel, 37 Main Street, tel. 0591/7 11 66, 22 r.   Postmasburg

★★Kokerboom Hotel, tel. 0251/2 26 85, 28 r.   Springbok
★★Springbok Hotel, Van Riebeeck Street, tel. 0251/2 11 61, 28 r.

★★Oasis Protea Lodge, 26 Schroeder Street, tel. 054/31 11 25, 32 r., FH   Upington

★★Melton Wold Guest Farm, Melton Wold, tel. 0242/ask for 1430, 23 r.,   Victoria West
SP, T

★Williston Hotel, Lutz Street, tel. 02052/5, 24 r.   Williston

Northern Transvaal

★Imp Inn Hotel, Botha Street, tel. 01523/92 53, 21 r.   Duiwelskloof

★★★Bergwater Hotel, 5 Rissik Street, tel. 015516/02 62, 24 r., SP, FH   Louis Trichardt
★★★Clouds End Hotel, tel. 015517/70 21, 38 r., SP, T
★★★Ingwe Ranch Motel, tel. 015517/70 87, 29 r., SP

★★★★Glenshiel Country Lodge, Magoebaskloof, tel. 015276/43 35, 15 r.,   Magoebaskloof
SP, FH
★★★Magoebaskloof Hotel, R 71, tel. 015276/42 76, 60 r., SP, T, FH
★★Troutwaters Inn, R 71, tel. 015276/42 45, 20 r., SP, T

★★★Kate's Hope River Lodge, Kate's Hope Farm, Mt 21, tel. 01553/4 00 86,   Messina
4 r., SP

★★★Shangri La Country Lodge, Eersbewoond Street, tel. 01470/23 81,   Nylstroom
30 r., SP, T

★★★Impala Inn Hotel, 52 Essenhout Street, tel. 01524/56 81, 56 r., SP   Phalaborwa

★★★Holiday Inn Garden Court Pietersburg, Vorster Street, tel. 0152/   Pietersburg
2 91 20 30, 179 r., SP, FH
★★★The Ranch, 22km/14 miles south of Pietersburg, tel. 0152/2 93 71 80,
75 r., SP, T

★★★Protea Park Hotel, 1 Beitel Street, tel. 0154/31 01, 90 r., SP   Potgietersrus
★★Oasis Lodge, 1 Voortrekker Road, tel. 0154/41 24, 20 r.

★★★★★Coach House Hotel, Old Coach Road, Agatha, tel. 0152/   Tzaneen
3 07 36 41, 45 r., SP, FH
★★★Karos Tzaneen Hotel, 1 Danie Joubert Street, tel. 0152/3 07 31 40,
56 r., SP

★★La Rive Hotel, Bergsig Farm, Vaalwater, tel. 0020/ask for Bulgerivier   Vaalwater
311, 8 r., SP

Hotels

Warmbaths   ★★★Mabula Game Lodge, tel. 014734/616/717, 37 r., SP, T

North-West

Boshoek   ★★★Sundown Ranch Hotel, Boeshoek Road, Rustenburg, tel. 0142/
                   73 31 21, 101 r., SP, T

Potchefstroom   ★★★Elgro Hotel, 60 Wolmarans Street, tel. 0148/2 97 54 11, 99 r., SP

Rooigrond   ★★Sehuba Protea Inn, Mafikeng/Lichtenburg road, tel. 01448/6 44, 22 r.,
                   SP

Rustenburg   ★★★Belvedere Hotel, Rhenosterfontein, tel. 0142/9 21 21, 11 r., SP, T
                   ★★★Karos Safari Hotel, Kloof Road, tel. 0142/97 13 61, 131 r., SP, T
                   ★★★Sparkling Waters Holiday Hotel, Rietfontein Farm, tel. 0142/75 01 51,
                   56 r., SP, T
                   ★★Olifantsnek Country Hotel, 184 Machol Street, tel. 0142/9 22 08, 29 r.,
                   SP, T
                   ★★Wigwam Holiday Hotel, Modderfontein, tel. 0142/9 21 47, 100 r., SP, T

Rustenburg/   ★★★Westwinds Country House, Westwinds Farm, Zuurplaat, tel. 0142/
Magaliesburg   75 05 60, 5 r., SP

Vryburg   ★★International Hotel, 43 Market Street, tel. 05391/22 35, 29 r., SP

Zeerust   ★★★Abjaterskop Hotel, Rustenburg Road, tel. 01428/2 20 08, 19 r., SP

Orange Free State

Bethlehem   ★★Park Hotel, 23 Muller Street, tel. 058/3 03 51 91, 42 r., SP

Bloemfontein   ★★★Holiday Inn Garden Court Bloemfontein, corner of Zastron Street
                   and Melville Drive, tel. 051/47 03 10, 147 r., SP, FH
                   ★★★Holiday Inn Garden Court Bloemfontein – Naval Hill, 1 Union
                   Avenue, tel. 051/30 11 11, 126 r., SP, FH
                   ★★Bloemfontein Inn, 17 Edison Street, Hospital Park, tel. 051/22 62 84,
                   33 r.
                   ★★City Lodge Bloemfontein, corner of Voortrekker Street and Parfitt
                   Avenue, tel. 051/47 98 88, 152 r., SP, FH
                   ★★Die Herberg, 12 Barne Street, tel. 051/30 75 00, 48 r.

Boshof   ★★Boshof Hotel, Jacob Street, tel. 053/5 41 00 91 10 r.

Bothaville   ★★Hotel Enkel Den, 13 President Street, tel. 0565/43 41, 19 r., SP

Edenburg   ★★Edenburg Hotel, 2 Church Street, tel. 051742/2 85, 12 r., SP

Ficksburg   ★★★Nebo Holiday Farm, Nebo Farm, tel. 05192/39 47, 10 r., SP
                   ★★Franshoek Mountain Lodge, Franshoek, tel. 05192/39 38, 6 r., SP

Fouriesburg   ★★Fouriesburg Hotel, 17 Reitz Street, tel. 058223/02 07, 13 r.

Frankfort   ★★Lodge 1896, 55A Brand Street, tel. 01613/3 10 80, 10 r.

Gariep Dam   ★★★Verwoerddam Motel, 2 Aasvoël Avenue, tel. 052172/60, 23 r.

Ladybrand   ★★Travellers Inn, 23A Kolbe Street, tel. 05191/4 01 91, 12 r., FH

Reddersburg   ★Hotel Sarie Marais, 22 Van Riebeeck Street, tel. 052122/ask for 138, 12 r.

Sasolburg   ★★Indaba Hotel, 47 Fichardt Street, tel. 016/76 06 00, 27 r., SP

★★Beau Vista Motel, Louw Street, tel. 051712/1 11, 12 r.   Trompsburg

★★Langberg Hotel, Marina Dam, tel. 01334/3 20 80, 14 r., SP   Vrede

★★★Welkom Hotel, 283 Koppie Alleen Road, tel. 057/5 14 11, 82 r., SP, FH   Welkom
★★★Welkom Inn, corner of Tempest and Stateway Roads, tel. 057/
3 57 33 61, 120 r., SP, FH

★★★Maluti Hotel, 22 Hoofh Street, tel. 05542/1 07, 18 r.   Zastron

Gauteng

★★Park Hotel, 18 Church Street, tel. 0122/2 31 05, 10 r.   Bronkhorstspruit

★★City Lodge Jan Smuts Airport, Sandvale Road, tel. 011/3 92 17 50,   Edenvale
161 r., SP, FH

★Town Lodge Jan Smuts Airport, Herman Road, tel. 011/9 74 52 02, 135 r.,   Germiston
FH

★★★★★Carlton Court, Main Street, tel. 011/3 31 89 11, 63 r.   **Johannesburg**
★★★★★Carlton Hotel, corner of Main and Cruis Streets, tel. 011/   Centre
3 31 89 11, 295 r., SP, FH
★★★Holiday Inn Garden Court Johannesburg, 84 Smal Street, tel. 011/
29 70 11, 672 r., SP, FH
★★Springbok Hotel, 73 Joubert Street, tel. 011/3 37 83 36, 82 r.
★★★Holiday Inn Garden Court Johannesburg – Milpark, corner of Empire   Jhb Auckland
and Owl Park Streets, tel. 011/7 26 51 00, 234 r., SP, FH
★★★Protea Gardens Hotel, 35 O'Reilly Street, tel. 011/6 43 66 10, 318 r., SP   Jhb Berea
★★Sunningdales Hotel, 88 Corlett Drive, tel. 011/8 87 68 10, 28 r.   Jhb Birnam
★★★★Parktonian Hotel, 120 De Karte Street, tel. 011/4 03 57 40, 294 r.,   Jhb Braamfontein
SP, FH
★★★Devonshire Hotel, corner of Jorisson and Melle Streets, tel. 011/
3 39 56 11, 63 r.
★★★Capri Hotel, 27 Aintree Avenue, Savoy Estates, tel. 011/7 86 22 50,   Jhb Bramley
49 r., SP
★★★Karos Johannesburger Hotel, corner of Twist and Wolmerans   Jhb Joubert Park
Streets, tel. 011/7 25 37 53, 376 r., SP
★★★Mariston Hotel, corner of Claim and Koch Streets, tel. 011/7 25 41 30,
174 r., SP
★★★Linden Hotel, corner of 7th Street and 4th Avenue, tel. 011/7 82 49 05,   Jhb Linden
25 r.
★★Ascot Hotel, 59 Grant Avenue, tel. 011/4 83 12 11, 25 r.   Jhb Norwood
★★★★Sunnyside Park Hotel, 2 York Road, tel. 011/6 43 72 26, 88 r.   Jhb Parktown
★★Robertsham Hotel, corner of Harry and De Lamere Streets, tel. 011/   Jhb Robertsham
6 80 53 87, 24 r., SP
★★★★Rosebank Hotel, corner of Tyrwhitt and Sturdee Avenues, tel.   Jhb Rosebank
011/4 47 27 00

★★★★Holiday Inn Jan Smuts Airport, Germiston–Pretoria Highway, tel.   Kempton Park
011/9 75 11 21, 365 r., SP, FH
★★★Holiday Inn Garden Court Johannesburg – Airport, 6 Hulley Road,
Isando, tel. 011/3 92 10 62, 230 r., SP, FH

★★★Auberge Aurora, Pappehaai Street, Rant en Dal, tel. 011/9 56 63 07,   Krugersdorp
7 r., SP, FH

★★★★Mount Grace Country House Hotel, tel. 0142/77 13 50, 57 r., SP, T   Magaliesburg
★★★★Valley Lodge, Jenning Street, tel. 0142/77 13 01, 52 r., SP, T
★★★Magliesburg Country Hotel, 41 Main Rustenburg Road, tel. 0142/
77 11 09, 20 r., SP

Hotels

Midrand	★★★★Midrand Protea Hotel, 14th Street, Noordwyk, tel. 011/3 18 18 68, 177 r., SP, FH ★★Constantia Lodge, 239 Old Pretoria Road, tel. 011/3 15 05 30, 20 r., SP ★Town Lodge Midrand, corner of Bekker Road and Le Roux Avenue, Waterfall Park, Vorna Valley, tel. 011/3 15 60 47, 118 r., FH
Muldersdrift	★★★Aloe Ridge Hotel, Swartkop, tel. 011/9 57 20 70, 73 r., SP, T ★★★Heia Safari Ranch, Swartkop, tel. 011/6 59 06 05, 28 r., SP, T
Pretoria Pr Akasia	★★★Bentley's Country Lodge, corner of Main Street and Heatherdale, tel. 012/5 42 17 51, 20 r., SP, T
Pr Arcadia	★★★★Holiday Inn Crowne Plaza Pretoria, corner of Church and Beatrix Streets, tel. 012/3 41 15 71, 241 r., SP, FH ★★★Aradia Hotel, 515 Proes Street, tel. 012/3 26 93 11, 139 r., FH ★★★Best Western Pretoria Hotel, 230 Hamilton Street, tel. 012/3 41 34 73, 127 r. ★★★Karos Manhattan Hotel, 247 Scheiding Street, tel. 012/3 22 76 35, 259 r., SP
Pr Central	★★★Holiday Inn Garden Court Pretoria, corner of Van der Walt and Minnaar Streets, tel. 012/3 22 75 00, 238 r., SP, FH
Pr Die Wilgers	★★★The Farm Inn, Lynwood Road East, at Silverlakes Golf Estate, tel. 012/8 09 02 66, 34 r., SP
Pr Hatfield	★★★★La Maison, 235 Hilda Street, tel. 012/43 43 41, 4 r., SP
Pr Menlo Park	★★★Battiss House, 92 20th Street, tel. 012/48 73 18
Randburg	★★Fleet Street Guest House, 101 Fleet Street, tel. 011/8 86 07 90, 10 r.
Sandton	★★★★★Sandton Sun, corner of Alice and 5th Streets, tel. 011/7 80 50 00, 333 r., SP, FH ★★★★★Sandton Sun Towers, corner of 5th and Alice Streets, tel. 011/7 80 50 00, 232 r., SP, FH

Holiday Inn, Sandton

★★★★Balalaika Protea Hotel, 20 Maud Street, tel. 011/8 84 14 00, 150 r., SP, FH

★★★★Holiday Inn Crowne Plaza Sandton, corner of Graystone Drive and Rivonia Road, tel. 011/7 83 52 62, SP, FH

★★★City Lodge Sandton Katherine Street, corner of Katherine Street and Graystone Drive, tel. 011/4 44 53 00, 159 r., SP, FH

★★★City Lodge Sandton Morningside, corner of Hill and Rivonia Roads, Morningside, tel. 011/8 84 95 00, SP

★★★Holiday Inn Garden Court Sandton, corner of Katherine and Rivonia Roads, tel. 011/8 84 56 60, 157 r., SP, FH

★★City Lodge Randburg, corner of Main Road and Peter Place, Bryanston, West Sandton, tel. 011/7 06 78 00, 123 r., SP

★★★★Karos Indaba Hotel, Hartbeespoort Dam Road, Witkoppen, Four-ways, tel. 011/4 65 14 00, 210 r., SP, T, FH | Sandton Fourways

★★Hotel Drostdy, 52 4th Avenue, Geduld, tel. 011/8 11 63 94, 22 r. | Springs

★★★★Riviera International Hotel and Country Club, Mario Milani Drive, tel. 016/22 28 61, 101 r., SP, T, FH | Vereeniging

★★★★Centurion Lake Hotel, 1001 Lenchen Avenue North, tel. 012/6 63 18 25, 165 r., SP, FH | Verwoerdburg

Western Cape

★★Albertinia Hotel, 61 Main Street, tel. 02934/5 10 30, 16 r., FH | Albertinia

★★Oasis Hotel, 66 Donkin Street, tel. 0201/32 21, 46 r., SP | Beaufort West

★★★Bellville Inn, Cross Street, tel. 021/9 48 81 11, 170 r., SP, FH | Bellville
★The Lodge, corner of Willie van Schoor Avenue and Mispel Road, tel. 021/9 48 79 90, 106 r., SP, FH

★Avalon Bonnievale Hotel, 87 Main Road, tel. 02346/21 55, 16 r., SP | Bonnievale

★★★Cape Rendezvous Protea Hotel and Conference Centre, Brackenfell Boulevard, tel. 9 81 21 71, 97 r., SP, FH | Brackenfell

★Brandvlei Hotel, Main Street, tel. 02702/2, 11 r., SP, FH | Brandvlei

★★★Arniston Hotel, Beach Road, Waenhuiskrans, tel. 02847/5 90 00, 24 r., SP | Bredasdorp
★★Hotel Victoria, 10 Church Street, tel. 02841/4 11 59, 29 r.
★Standard Hotel, 31 Long Street, tel. 02841/4 11 40, 30 r.

★★Brenton-on-Sea Hotel, Agapanthus Avenue, tel. 0445/81 00 81, 29 r. | Brenton-on-Sea

★★★Overberger Country Hotel and Spa, Nerina Avenue, tel. 0281/4 12 71, 95 r., SP | Caledon
★★Alexandra Hotel, Market Square, tel. 0281/2 30 52, 9 r.

★★★★★Cape Sun Hotel, Strand Street, tel. 021/23 88 44, 350 r., SP, FH | **Cape Town**
★★★★Capetonian Protea Hotel, Pier Place, Heerengracht, tel. 021/21 11 50, 169 r., SP | Centre
★★★★Town House Hotel, 60 Corporation Street, tel. 021/45 70 50, 104 r., SP

★★★Holiday Inn Garden Court – Greenmarket Square, 10 Greenmarket Square, tel. 021/23 20 40, 166 r., FH

★★★Holiday Inn Garden Court – St George's Mall, Trustbank Building, St George's Mall, tel. 021/4 19 08 08, 136 r.

Constantia Uitsig Farm, a hotel and wine estate

★★★Tulbagh Protea Hotel, 9 Ryk Tulbagh Square, tel. 021/21 51 40, 56 r.
★★Carlton Heights Hotel, 88 Queen Victoria Street, tel. 021/23 12 60, 57 r.
★★Metropole Hotel, 38 Long Street, tel. 021/23 63 63, 33 r.
★★Pleinpark Travel Lodge, 9 Barrack Street, tel. 021/45 75 63, 28 r.
★★Tudor Hotel, 153 Longmarket Street, tel. 021/24 13 35, 27 r.

Bantry Bay   ★★★★Ambassador by the Sea, 34 Victoria Road, tel. 021/4 39 61 70, 69 r., SP

Camps Bay   ★★★★★Bay Hotel, Victoria Road, tel. 021/4 38 44 44, 70 r., SP, FH

Constantia   ★★★★★The Cellars – Hohenort Country House Hotel, 15 Hohenort Avenue, tel. 021/7 94 21 37, 53 r., SP, T
★★★★Alphen Hotel, Alphen Drive, tel. 021/7 94 50 11, 29 r., SP
Constantia Uitsig, Ladies' Mile EXT, PO Box 32, tel. 021/7 94 65 00, 8 garden suites

Gardens   ★★★★★Mount Nelson Hotel, 76 Orange Street, tel. 021/23 10 00, 159 r., SP, T
★★★Cape Swiss Hotel, 1 Nicol Street Gardens, tel. 021/23 81 90, 44 r.
★★★Helmsley Hotel, 16 Hof Street Gardens, tel. 021/23 72 00, 26 r., SP, T
★★★Holiday Inn Garden Court – De Waal, Mill Street Gardens, tel. 021/45 13 11, 130 r., SP, FH

Mowbray   ★★★City Lodge Mowbray Golf Park, on Raapenburg Road, tel. 021/6 85 79 44, 134 r., SP, FH

Newlands   ★★★★Vineyard Hotel, Colinton Road, tel. 021/6 83 30 44, 118 r., SP, FH
★★★Holiday Inn Garden Court – Newlands, Main Road, tel. 021/61 11 05, 145 r., FH

Sea Point   ★★★★Karos Arthur's Seat Hotel, Arthur's Road, tel. 021/5 34 11 87, 123 r., SP, FH
★★★Centurion All-Suite Hotel, 275 Main Road, tel. 021/4 34 00 06, 70 r., SP
★★★Winchester Mansions Hotel, 221 Beach Road, tel. 021/4 34 23 51, 39 r., SP

Tambours   ★★★Mijlof Manor Hotel, 5 Military Road, tel. 021/26 14 76, 25 r.

★★★★Victoria and Alfred Hotel, Waterfront, tel. 021/4 19 66 77, 68 r., FH   Victoria and
★★City Lodge, at corner of Dock and Alfred Roads, tel. 021/4 19 94 50,   Alfred Waterfront
164 r., SP, FH
★★★Holiday Inn Garden Court – Eastern Boulevard, at corner of Mel-   Woodstock
bourne and Coronation Streets, tel. 021/4 48 41 23, 279 r., SP, FH

★★Cedarberg Hotel, Voortrekker Street, tel. 022/9 21 22 21, 26 r., SP   Citrusdal

★★Strassbergers Hotel Clanwilliam, Main Street, tel. 027/4 82 11 01, 23 r.,   Clanwilliam
SP

★★Huguenot Hotel, Huguenot Road, tel. 022/12 20 92, 12 r., SP   Franschhoek

★★★Far Hills Protea Hotel, N 2, tel. 0441/71 12 95, 48 r., SP   George
★★Hawthorndene Hotel, Morning Glory Lane, tel. 0441/74 41 60, 26 r., SP

★★★Van Riebeeck Hotel, 67 Beach Road, tel. 024/56 14 41, 78 r., SP   Gordon's Bay

★★Houw Hoek Inn, on N 2 between Grabouw and Bot River, tel. 02824/   Grabouw
4 96 46, 33 r., SP, T, FH

★★Greyton Hotel, 36 Main Road, tel. 028/2 54 98 92, 9 r., SP   Greyton

★★★Marine Hotel, Main Road, tel. 0283/70 01 50, 53 r., SP   Hermanus
Mountain Drive Guest House, 66 Mountain Drive, tel. 0283/2 44 52, 4 r.

★★Hout Bay Manor, Main Road, tel. 021/7 90 59 60, 11 r.   Hout Bay

★★Keurbooms Hotel, Keurbooms Road, tel. 04457/93 11, 24 r., SP   Keurboomstrand

★★★Beach House, 13 Beach Road, tel. 02823/31 30, 23 r., SP   Kleinmond

★★★Knysna Protea Hotel, 51 Main Street, tel. 0445/2 21 27, 52 r., SP, FH   Knysna

★★Grand Hotel, Station Street, tel. 02372/38, 13 r., SP   Laingsburg
★★Laingsburg Country Hotel, Voortrekker Street, tel. 02372/9, 23 r., SP

★★★Marine Protea Hotel, Voortrekker Street, tel. 027/4 32 11 26, 47 r.   Lambert's Bay
★★★Raston Guest House, 24 Riedeman Street, tel. 027/4 32 24 31, 5 r., SP

★★Lord Milner Hotel, Logan Road, tel. 02372/ask for 52 03, 38 r., SP, T   Matjiesfontein

★★★Avalon Springs Hotel, Uitvlucht Street, tel. 0234/4 11 50, SP, T   Montagu
★★Montagu Country Inn, Bath Street, tel. 0234/4 11 15, 15 r., SP

★★Samoa Hotel, Central Street, tel. 0264/3 12 01, 16 r., SP   Moorreesburg

★★★Eight Bells Mountain Inn, Ruitersbosch, tel. 0444/95 15 44, 24 r., SP, T   Mossel Bay
★★★Rose and Crown Hotel, 3 Matfield Street, tel. 0444/91 10 69, 10 r.
★★★Santos Protea Hotel, Santos Road, tel. 0444/71 03, 58 r., SP

★★Shrimpton Manor, 19 Alexander Road, tel. 021/7 88 11 28, 17 r., SP   Muizenberg

★★★Holiday Inn Garden Court Oudtshoorn, Baron van Reede Street, tel.   Oudtshoorn
0443/22 22 01, 120 r., SP, T, FH
★★★Riempie Estate, Baron van Reede Street, tel. 0443/22 61 61, 40 r., SP
★★Caves Motel, Baron van Reede Street, tel. 0443/22 25 11, 39 r., SP
★★Feather Inn, 218 High Street, tel. 0443/29 17 27, 24 r., SP
★★Queen's Hotel, Baron van Reede Street, tel. 0443/22 21 01, 62 r., SP, T

★★★★Grande Roche Hotel, Plantasie Street, tel. 02211/63 27 27, 29 r.,   Paarl
SP, T, FH
★★★★Zomerlust Gastehuis, 193 Main Street, tel. 02211/2 21 17, 14 r., SP

Hotels

De Oude Herberg Guest House, Tulbagh

Plettenberg Bay	★★★★Hunters Country House, Pear Tree Farm, tel. 04457/78 18, 30 r., SP
	★★★★Plettenberg Hotel, 40 Church Street, tel. 04457/3 20 30, 26 r., SP
	★★★Formosa Inn Country Hotel, N 2, tel. 04457/3 20 60, 34 r., SP, T
	★★Strombolis Inn, N 2, tel. 04457/77 10, 16 r., SP
	★★Arches Hotel, Marine Way, tel. 04457/3 21 18, 20 r., SP
Prince Alfred Hamlet	★★Hamlet Hotel, Voortrekker Road, tel. 0233/30 70, 5 r.
Robertson	★★Grand Hotel, 68 Barry Street, tel. 02351/32 72, 9 r., SP
Saldanha Bay	★★★Saldanha Bay Protea Hotel, 51B Main Street, tel. 02281/4 12 64, 33 r., SP, FH
	★★Hoedjiesbaai Hotel, Main Road, tel. 02281/4 12 71, 16 r.
Sedgefield	★★★Lake Pleasant Hotel, Groenvlei, on N 2, tel. 04455/3 13 13, 17 r., SP, T
Simon's Town	★★★Lord Nelson Inn, 58 St George's Street, tel. 021/7 86 13 86, 10 r.
Somerset West	★★★★★Lord Charles Hotel, corner of Stellenbosch and Faure Roads, tel. 024/55 10 40, 196 r., SP, T, FH
Stellenbosch	★★★★Lanzerac Hotel, Lanzerac Road, tel. 021/8 87 11 32, 30 r., SP
	★★★Devon Valley Protea Hotel, Devon Valley Road, tel. 021/8 82 20 12, 36 r., SP
	★★★Douwe Werf Herberg, 30 Church Street, tel. 021/8 87 46 08, 25 r., SP
	★★★Guest House, 110 Dorp Street, tel. 021/8 83 35 55, 3 r.
Swellendam	★★★Swellengrebel Hotel, 91 Voortrek Street, tel. 0291/4 11 44, 52 r., SP, T, FH
Tulbagh	★★De Oude Herberg Guest House, 6 Church Street, tel. 0236/30 02 60, 6 r.

★★Vredendal Hotel, 11 Voortrekker Street, tel. 0271/3 10 64, 30 r.   Vredendal
★Maskam Hotel, corner of Church Street and Van Riebeeck Avenue, tel.
  0271/3 13 36, 20 r.

★★Klein Rhebokskloof, Rhebokskloof Farm, Blouvlei, tel. 02211/3 41 15,   Wellington
  5 r., SP

★★★★Karos Wilderness Hotel, N 2, tel. 0441/8 77 11 10, 158 r., SP, T   Wilderness
★★★Holiday Inn Garden Court Wilderness, N 2, tel. 0441/8 77 11 04, 149 r.,
  SP, T, FH
★★Fairy Knowe Hotel, Dumbleton Road, tel. 0441/8 77 11 00, 42 r., T

★★Breede River Lodge, Port Beaufort, tel. 02935/6 31, 14 r.   Witsand/
                                                                 Port Beaufort

★★★Cumberland Hotel, 2 Stockenstroom Street, tel. 0231/7 26 41, 55 r.,   Worcester
  SP, T

Hotels in Lesotho

★Crocodile Inn, Reserve Road, tel. 09266/46 02 23, 25 r.   Butha-Buthe

★Leribe Hotel, Main Street, tel. 09266/40 03 62, 33 r.   Leribe/Hlotse

★★★Malealea Lodge, Wepener 9944, tel. 09266/78 57 27, 9 r.   Mafeteng

★★★★Lesotho Sun, Hilton Road, tel. 09266/31 31 11, 230 r., SP   Maseru
★★Lancers Inn, Kingsway/Pioneer Road, tel. 09266/33 21 14, 21 r.

★Mount Maluti, Hospital Road, tel. 09266/78 52 24, 35 r.   Mohale's Hoek

Mokhotlong, tel. 09266/92 02 12, 16 r.   Mokhotlong

★Orange River, on the hill, tel. 09266/75 02 52, 16 r.   Moyeni/Quthing

New Oxbow Lodge, tel. 0563/22 47, 16 r.   Oxbow

Semonkong Lodge, tel. 0563/27 30   Semonkong

Hotels in Swaziland

★★★★Lugogo Sun, on Mbabane–Manzini Road, tel. 6 11 01   Ezulwini
★★★★★Royal Swazi Sun, on Mbabane–Manzini Road, tel. 6 10 01
★★★Yen Saan, on Mbabane–Manzini Road, tel. 6 10 51

New George, Ngwane Road, tel. 5 22 21/5 20 61   Manzini

★★★Mbabane Inn, Princess Drive, tel. 4 22 21/4 27 81   Mbabane
★★★Swazi Inn, on road to Ezulwini, tel. 4 22 21/4 22 35

★★★★Piggs Peak Protea Inn, 12km/7½ miles north on Jeppe's Reef road,   Piggs Peak
  tel. 7 12 22/7 11 04
Phophonyane Lodge, 13km/8 miles north, tel. 7 13 19

★Siteki, tel. 3 41 26   Siteki

Hunting

The hunting of game is strictly controlled in South Africa, but still attracts numbers of sportsmen and yields an income which goes towards maintaining the game reserves. Hunting is possible throughout the year; from the climatic point of view, however, the best months are March to November.

Information

Satour (see Information) issues a leaflet giving detailed information about the game that can be hunted, the charges to be paid, the preparation and export of hunting trophies, the calibre of gun recommended, the import of sporting guns and ammunition, suitable clothing and the availability of shelters in case hunters get into difficulty.

Information

Detailed information about accommodation, National Parks, sports facilities, car rental, transport, etc., can be obtained from Satour, the South African Tourism Board. Satour also publishes a very informative and useful Travel Guide to South Africa, with maps, brief descriptions of places of interest, photographs, hints for travellers and much else besides.

Satour Offices outside South Africa

United Kingdom
5–6 Alt Grove
Wimbledon
London SW19 4DZ
Tel. (0181) 944 8080

USA
Suite 2040
500 Fifth Avenue (20th floor)
New York NY 10110
Tel. 212/730 2929

Suite 1524
9841 Airport Boulevard
Los Angeles CA 90045. Tel. 310/641 8444

Canada
Suite 2
4117 Lawrence Avenue East
Scarborough
Ontario M1E 2S2. Tel. 416/283 0563

Satour Offices in South Africa

Head office
Head Office, 442 Rigel Avenue South, Erasmusrand 0181, Private Bag X164, Pretoria 0001
Tel. 012/3 47 06 00

Bloemfontein
Sanlam Parkade, Shop No. 9, Charles Street, Bloemfontein 2000
Tel. 051/47 13 62

Cape Town
Tourist Information Centre, 3 Adderley Street, Cape Town 8000
Tel. 021/4 18 52 02

Durban
22 Gardiner Street, P.O. Box 2516, Durban 4000
Tel. 031/3 04 71 44

Johannesburg
Jan Smuts Airport, International Arrivals Hall, Johannesburg 2000
Tel. 011/9 70 12 20
In city centre:
Carlton Centre, Suite 4305
Tel. 011/3 31 52 41

Kimberley
Suite 620, Flaxley House, Du Toitspan Road, Kimberley 8300
Tel. 0531/3 14 34

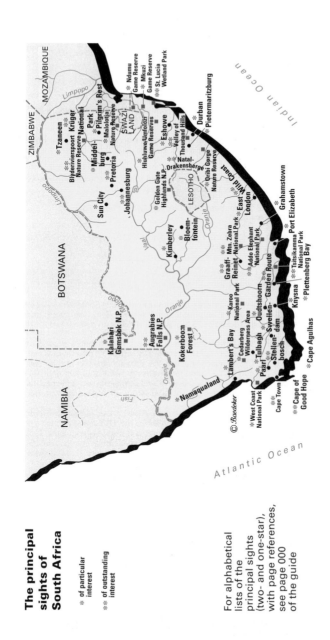

The principal sights of South Africa

* of particular interest

** of outstanding interest

For alphabetical lists of the principal sights (two- and one-star), with page references, see page 000 of the guide

ZIMBABWE

MOZAMBIQUE

BOTSWANA

NAMIBIA

LESOTHO

SWAZI-LAND

Limpopo

Fish

Oranje

Vaal

Oranje

Oranje

Atlantic Ocean

Indian Ocean

© Baedeker

* Tzaneen

* Ndumu Game Reserve

* Mkuzi Game Reserve

** St. Lucia Wetland Park

* Pilgrim's Rest

Kruger National Park

Blyderivierspoort Nature Reserve

* Middelburg

* Malolotja Nature Reserve

* Pretoria

Johannesburg

* Sun City

* Golden Gate Highlands N.P.

Eshowe

Valley of a Thousand Hills

Natal-Drakensberge

Oribi Gorge Nature Reserve

Hluhluwe/Umfolozi Game Reserves

Durban

Pietermaritzburg

Kimberley

Bloemfontein

Wild Coast

East London

Grahamstown

Port Elizabeth

Kalahari Gemsbok N.P.

Augrabies Falls N.P.

* Karoo National Park

* Mtn. Zebra National Park

Graaff-Reinet

Addo Elephant National Park

Kokerboom Forest

Cedarberg Wilderness Area

Oudtshoorn

Garden Route

Knysna

Tsitsikamma National Park

** Plettenberg Bay

Lambert's Bay

Tulbagh

Paarl

Stellenbosch

Swellendam

West Coast National Park

Cape Town

** Cape of Good Hope

* Cape Agulhas

Namaqualand

437

Language

Nelspruit	Tourist Information Shop No. 5, Promenade Centre, Louis Trichardt Street, Nelspruit 1200. Tel. 01311/55 19 88
Pietersburg	Corner of Vorster and Landdros Maré Streets, Pietersburg 0700 Tel. 01521/95 30 25
Port Elizabeth	Satour House, 21–23 Donkin Street, Port Elizabeth 6000 Tel. 041/52 13 15
Potchefstroom	Royal Hotel Building (1st floor), Lombard Street, Potchefstroom 2520 Tel. 0148/2 93 16 11
Pretoria	Tourist Rendezvous, Travel Centre, Sammy Marks Complex, corner of Prinsloo and Vermeulen Streets, Pretoria 0001 Tel. 012/3 13 36 94
	In most towns there is a local tourist information centre or publicity association, identified by the letter "i" on a green ground.
Swaziland	Swaziland Tourist Board, PO Box 451, Swazi Plaza, Mbabane Tel. 09268/4 25 31
Lesotho	Lesotho Tourist Board, Victoria Building, 209 Kingsway, Box 1378, Maseru 100. Tel. 09266/31 28 96

Language

Since the new constitution came into force in 1994 South Africa has eleven national and official languages: nine different Bantu languages together with English (spoken by 35% of whites and 73% of Asians) and Afrikaans.

Afrikaans

Afrikaans, which from 1925 to 1994 was the country's second official language alongside English, is spoken by some 90% of coloureds and 54% of whites. The Afrikaans-speakers are strongly attached to their *taal* (language), and in 1975 erected the imposing Taal Monument on a hill near Paarl, where Arnoldus Pannevis, a local schoolmaster, published the first newspaper in Afrikaans (1876) and wrote an Afrikaans grammar and dictionary.

Afrikaans originally developed out of the various dialects (western Brabant, Zeeland, South Holland) spoken by the 17th century Dutch settlers. New words were taken in from Bantu and Khoisan languages, German, English, French, Portuguese and Malay, while others changed their meaning; and pronunciation, spelling and grammar were likewise altered by contacts with these other languages.

Pronunciation
of Afrikaans

a: like u in cup
aa, ae: ah (long)
aai: like y in why
au: like ow in cow
c: k
ch k; sometimes like ch in loch
e: like e in hen
ee: like ee in beer
eeu: like ew in dew
ei: like ay in day
eu: like ee in beer with lips pouted
g: like ch in loch
gh: like g in gay
i: like e in anger
ie: ee (long)
j: like y in you

o, oo: oo (short) followed by a rapidly spoken w
oe: oo (short)
ou: like oa in coat
r: rolled (strongly in initial position, lightly in final)
s: s
sch: sk (initial or medial), s (final)
sj: sh
tj: ch
u: as in French "deux" (short); sometimes as in "du"
ui: like ay in day but longer and with lips pouted
v: f
w: v
y: like ay in day

In diphthongs each vowel is pronounced separately, with the same sound as when standing by itself.

a, e, i and o are frequently nasalised before ng, n and m, usually when followed by an f, g, h, l, r, s, v, w or z.

Useful Expressions in Afrikaans

English	Afrikaans
Good morning	Goeie more
Good day, good afternoon	Goeie middag, dag
Good evening	Goeie naand
Goodbye	Tot siens
Yes, no	Ja, nee
Thank you	Dankie
Please	Asseblief
I beg your pardon	Ekskuus (tog)
Excuse me	Verskoon my
Not at all	Plesier
Mr, Mrs (also used as forms of address)	Meneer, Mevrou
When is/are . . . open?	Wanneer is . . . oop?
When do(es) . . . close?	Wanneer word . . . gesluit?
How do I get to . . .?	Hoe kom ek na . . .?
How long will it take?	Hoe lank sal dit neem?
How far is it to . . .?	Hoe ver is dit na . . .?
Where can I get . . .?	Waar kan ek . . . kry?
Where is . . .?	Waar is . . .?
Please give me . . .	Gee my asseblief . . .
Is there . . . here?	Is daar . . .?
I need . . .	Ek het . . . nodig
I should like . . .	Ek wil graag . . .
Have you . . .?	Het u . . .?
What does it cost?	Wat kos dit?
I like that	Ek hou daarvan
I don't like that	Ek hou nie daarvan nie
That is too dear	Dit is te duur
Have you anything cheaper/better?	Het u nie iets goerkopers/beters nie?
Can you change money?	Kan u geld wissel?
What is that in English/Afrikaans?	Wat noem 'n mens dit in Engels/Afrikaans?
I speak no . . .	En praat geen . . . nie
I do not understand	Ek verstaan u nie
Please speak more slowly	Sal u asseblief 'n bietjie stadiger praat
Please write it	Skryf dit asseblief neer
What time is it?	Hoe laat is dit?

Literature

Days of week	Sunday	Sondag
	Monday	Maandag
	Tuesday	Dinsdag
	Wednesday	Woensdag
	Thursday	Donderdag
	Friday	Vrydag
	Saturday	Saterdag

Numbers

0	nul	19	negetien
1	een	20	twintig
2	twee	21	een(-)en(-)twintig
3	drie	22	twee-en-twintig
4	vier	30	dertig
5	vyf	40	veertig
6	ses	50	vyftig
7	sewe	60	sestig
8	ag, agt	70	sewentig
9	nege	80	tag(gen)tig
10	tien	90	negentig
11	elf	100	(een) honderd
12	twaalf	200	twee honderd
13	dertien	330	drie honderd en dertig
14	veertien	1000	duisend
15	vyftien	100,000	honderd duisend
16	sestien	1 million	een miljoen
17	sewentien	1 billion	een miljard
18	agtien, agttien		

"Teach Yourself Afrikaans"

For those who want to know more of the language "Teach Yourself Afrikaans", by Helena van Schalkwyk (Teach Yourself Books, London, 1988), is recommended.

Zulu

Zulu is spoken in South Africa by some 9 million Zulus, more tha 8 million of them living in KwaZulu/Natal. A characteristic feature of the Zulu language is its click sounds. There is a rich orally transmitted literature (myths, legends, riddles, proverbs and dance and ceremonial songs).

Some Zulu expressions

Good day	Soubona
Thank you	Jabonga
How are you?	Sapila?
I am well	Japila
What is . . . called?	Ubani ikhama lakho . . .?

Literature

Newspaper

The weekly "SA Times", published in London, gives up-to-date news on South Africa and South African life. Publishers' address:
"SA Times", 102 Hatton Square, 16/16A Baldwin's Gardens, London EC1N 7RJ, tel. 0044171/405 6148.

Bookshop

A South African bookshop with a wide range of literature on South Africa in German and English is Ulrich Naumann, 17 Burg Street, Cape Town 8001, tel. 021/23 78 32. Books can be ordered by post.

Some suggestions for further reading:

Leonard Thompson, "A History of South Africa" (revised edition), Yale University Press, 1995
Thomas Pakenham, "The Struggle for Africa", Abacus, 1991
Anthony Trollope, "Travels in South Africa" (1877), republished by Alan Sutton, 1987

Nelson Mandela, "Long Walk to Freedom", Abacus 1995
Laurens Van der Post, "The Lost World of the Kalahari", Penguin, 1962

T. V. Bulpin, "Discovering Southern Africa", T. V. Bulpin Publications, 1992
Chris and Tilde Stuart, "Field Guide to the National Parks and Nature
    Reserves of Southern Africa", Struik, Cape Town, 1993
Chris and Tilde Stuart, "Field Guide to the Mammals of South Africa", New
    Holland, 1992
Kenneth Newman, "Birds of Southern Africa"
Eve Palmer, "Field Guide to the Trees of Southern Africa", Collins, 1977
D. Hughes, P. Hands and J. Kench, "South African Wine", Struik, Cape
    Town, 1992
Penny Miller, "Myths and Legends of Southern Africa", T. V. Bulpin Publi-
    cations, 1979

Olive Schreiner, "The Story of an African Farm" (1883), Penguin, 1981
Sir Percy Fitzpatrick, "Jock of the Bushveld", 1909
Alan Paton, "Cry the Beloved Country", Scribner, 1948
Alex La Guma, "A Walk in the Night", Heinemann, 1967
André Brink, "A Dry White Season", W. H. Allen, 1969
Nadine Gordimer, "The Lying Days", Penguin, 1980
J. M. Coetzee, "Waiting for the Barbarians", Penguin, 1988
Steve Biko, "I Write What I Like", Penguin, 1988
Breyten Breytenbach, "All One Horse", Faber and Faber, 1990
Rian Malan, "My Traitor's Heart", Bodley Head, 1990
Dan Jacobson, "The Electronic Elephant: A Southern African Journey",
    Hamish Hamilton, 1994

Medical Aid

Medical care in South Africa, both in general and consultant practice and in
hospital, is in line with European and American standards.
   Doctors are listed in the telephone book under "Medical practitioners".

Since South Africa has no national health service, visitors must pay for all
medical treatment. It is essential, therefore, to take out short-term health
insurance before leaving home.

Motoring in South Africa

In South Africa traffic goes on the left, with overtaking on the right.
   Seat belts must be worn.
   Driving under the influence of alcohol is a serious offence, and traffic
laws are strictly enforced.
   Speed limits: 60km/37 miles an hour in urban areas, 100km/62 miles an
hour on rural roads and 120km/75 miles an hour on freeways unless
otherwise indicated.
   A valid national driver's licence, provided it has the driver's photograph
and is printed in English, is accepted. If your licence does not meet these
requirements you should obtain an international driving permit.
   All cars must have third party insurance. It is, of course, advisable to take
out comprehensive insurance cover.
   An excellent road network links the largest metropolitan areas with the
smallest villages. Most major roads are asphalted, but even unsurfaced
roads can usually be negotiated without difficulty. There are tolls on some
freeways. Care is required when driving in the country, since grazing land is
not fenced and animals may stray on to the road.

Cars are not the only users of the roads in South Africa!

Survival in the wilderness: eat or be eaten

Filling stations are conveniently situated along main and country roads. Most are open 24 hours a day.

Automobile Association of South Africa

The Automobile Association of South Africa (AA) provides an excellent service for motorists. It will help members of foreign motoring organisations free of charge on production of their membership card.

Some addresses:

Martinhammeschlag Way, tel. 021/21 15 50	Cape Town
33 St George Street, tel. 031/30 10 34	Durban
27 Fleet Street, tel. 0431/2 12 71	East London
66 De Corte Street, Braamfontein, tel. 011/4 07 10 00	Johannesburg
13 New Main Street, tel. 0531/2 52 07	Kimberley
Library Garden (1st floor), tel. 01521/7 51 45	Pietersburg
2 Granville Road, Greenacres 6001, tel. 041/34 13 19	Port Elizabeth
370 Vorhoekkers Road, Gezina 0084, tel. 012/70 42 87	Pretoria
Skukuza Camp in Kruger National Park, tel. 01311/6 51 64	Skukuza

National Parks

South Africa has an extraordinarily rich and varied flora and fauna, on both land and water. With only 4% of the African land mass and just under 0.8% of the world's total land area, it has almost 10% of all higher plants (22,600 out of a world total of 250,000 species), 8% of all species of birds (718 out of 9000), 5.8% of mammals (227 out of 3927, including 43 species of marine mammals) and 4.6% of all reptiles (286 out of 6214 species). Compared with this the United States, which is seven times the size of South Africa, has only around 15,000 species of plants, and Australia, six times its size, has only 656 species of birds and 224 species of mammals. While Europe has only one species of kingfisher, South Africa has ten. There are two types of heath in the northern hemisphere; in South Africa there are around 500. South Africa has the world's largest land mammal, the elephant; its second largest, the white rhinoceros; its tallest, the giraffe; its fastest, the cheetah; its smallest, the pygmy shrew; the largest bird in the world, the ostrich; the largest flying bird, the Kori bustard; and the world's largest reptile, the leatherback turtle. Off the coasts of South Africa, far out to sea, cruises the largest mammal in the world, the blue whale. South Africa has many endemic species of animals and plants (i.e. species found nowhere else) – 15% of the mammals and 6% of the birds. The flora of South Africa is so different from that of other parts of the world that it has been classed as one of the world's six plant kingdoms.

The great variety of species in South Africa – which did not suffer from the ice ages which destroyed almost all plant and animal life in Europe – reflects the variety of habitats it offers (see Facts and Figures, Topography).

A proper conservation policy is essential to protect South Africa's great wealth of plant and animal life. There has been much thoughtless destruction by man in the past. The last bluebuck (a species of antelope) was killed in 1880, and soon afterwards the same fate befell the quagga, a relative of the zebra. In spite of intensive efforts by the South African government for the protection of nature the list of animals and plants (mostly endemic species) threatened with extinction is a long one. Among the most endangered animals are the river rabbit, the roan antelope and the wild dog; and 1500 species of plants are on the "red list".

A recent poll of non-African visitors to South Africa revealed that nine out of ten came mainly for the country's wild life and natural beauty.

Protection of wild life

The protection of wild life in South Africa has a long history. The first regulations controlling hunting were introduced by Jan van Riebeeck in 1656. The first game reserve, the Kruger National Park, was established in 1898, and there are now another 16 National Parks, a National Lake Area and several hundred regional and private game parks, the most important of which are shown on the map on p. 445. Altogether there are over 580 reserves with a total area of more than 72,000sq.km/28,000sq. miles – though this is no more than 5.8% of the total area of South Africa.

Increasing numbers of reserves have been established in recent years: a necessary development, because many of the existing reserves are threatened with closure. Small reserves in remote areas do not attract enough visitors to finance their maintenance; and even the Kruger National Park faces enormous problems, since it is threatened with the drying up of most of the rivers which provide water for its game. New reserves are also required to provide at least temporary homes for migrating animals and to ensure that they are not confined to one particular place.

In some reserves shooting is permitted (on payment of an appropriate charge), but in most of them visitors are allowed only to observe the game.

All the National Parks have simple but comfortable accommodation for visitors in straw-roofed huts (rondavels) or bungalows. Accommodation in the private game reserves ranges from comfortable to luxurious. It is essential to book accommodation in plenty of time.

Visitors are usually able to explore the reserves in their own car; frequently they can join a conducted tour. Increasingly available, too, are hikes through the wilderness led by experienced rangers (advance booking necessary). There are also, particularly in private game reserves, conducted tours of small parties in open jeeps.

Information

Satour (see Information) publishes a brochure on the South African game reserves and leaflets on the animals and plants of South Africa, accommodation available in reserves, etc.

When to visit

Between May and August – the South African winter – the bush grass is shorter and offers less concealment for game, which can thus be more readily observed by visitors. During the dry months (August to October) the animals stay close to the waterholes, which offer good opportunities for observation. The best time for observing birds is from September to March or April, when they can be seen in large numbers.

The big five

The "big five" are the elephant, the lion, the rhinoceros, the leopard and the buffalo.

Elephants are commonest in the Transvaal, in the north of KwaZulu/Natal and in the Northern and Eastern Cape.

The African lion lives in the Northern and Eastern Transvaal, in the north and east of KwaZulu/Natal and in the Northern Cape.

The black and white rhinos live in the Eastern Transvaal, the North-West Province, the north and east of KwaZulu/Natal, the Orange Free State and the Northern Cape. The African leopard is found in the Northern and Eastern Transvaal, the north and east of KwaZulu/Natal and the mountain regions of the Cape.

The African buffalo roams through the Northern and Eastern Transvaal, KwaZulu/Natal and the Addo Elephant Park.

Warning

Visitors should remember at all times that in the wilderness the laws of nature prevail. When driving through a game reserve never get out of your

National Parks, Game and Nature Reserve

1 Kruger National Park
2 Ndumu Game Reserve
3 Itala Game Reserve
4 Mkuzi Game Reserve
5 Hluhluwe Game Reserve
6 Umfolozi Game Reserve
7 St Lucia Game Reserve
8 Giant's Castle Game Reserve
9 Royal Natal National Park
10 Golden Gate Highlands National Park
11 Vaalbos National Park
12 Mountain Zebra National Park
13 Zuurberg National Park
14 Addo Elephant National Park
15 Tsitsikamma National Park
16 Wilderness National Park
17 Bontebok National Park
18 Karoo National Park
19 West Coast National Park
20 Tankwa Karoo National Park
21 Augrabies Falls National Park
22 Kalahari Gemsbok National Park
23 Richtersveld National Park

car, and do not open the car door for the sake of getting a better photograph: a passing lion may look lethargic, but it can attack suddenly at lightning speed.

Bird-watching

The Kruger National Park and Kalahari Gemsbok National Park are among the last strongholds of many species of vulture and eagle. Ndumu, Mkuzi, Lake Sibay and St Lucia in KwaZulu/Natal are the breeding areas of huge flocks of pelicans and flamingos. Innumerable sunbirds live in the fynbos regions of the Western Cape, and the Langebaan Lagoon is populated in summer by 50,000 birds, mostly dunlins. In the Orange Free State there are huge numbers of birds to be seen in the depressions in the goldfields and the Seekoeivlei Nature Reserve.

Some South African National Parks

Kruger National Park

Location: Eastern Transvaal, 400km/250 miles north of Johannesburg. Area: 20,000sq.km/7700sq. miles. There are eight entrances.
   Steppe and savanna; all South African species of animals, including the "big five" (lion, leopard, buffalo, elephant, rhinoceros); more than 130 species of mammals, some 500 species of birds, more than 100 different reptiles and up to 1880 species of plants (including 350 trees and shrubs).

Hiking trails and tours by car, with or without guides.

Elephants in the Kruger National Park

National Parks Board	Reservations: National Parks Board, PO Box 787, Pretoria 0001, tel. 012/ 3 43 20 07, fax 3 43 20 06.

To the west of the Kruger National Park is an area of cultivated savanna in which there are many private game and nature reserves, with game lodges ranging from the comfortable to the luxurious, including the Timbavati Game Reserve (75,000 hectares/185,000 acres, with an abundance of animals and birds; birthplace of the white lion) and Sabi Sand Nature Reserve (privately owned; 65,000 hectares/160,000 acres; rich wild life).

Ndumu Game Reserve

Location: north-eastern corner of KwaZulu/Natal, on the Mozambique border, 470km/290 miles north of Durban. Area: 10,117 hectares/24,989 acres.

Tropical and subtropical country, dense forests, a paradise for birds; situated on the flood plain of the Pongola River; hippopotamuses, crocodiles, nyalas, bushbucks, black and white rhinos.

KwaZulu/Natal Parks Board

Reservations: KwaZulu/Natal Parks Board, Private Bag X9024, Pietermaritzburg 3200, tel. 0331/94 66 96, fax 42 19 48.

Itala Game Reserve

Location: north-western corner of KwaZulu/Natal, north of Louwsburg on the Eastern Transvaal border, 70km/43 miles south-west of Pongola. Area: 30,000 hectares/75,000 acres.

Mostly open bush; deeply indented valleys with interesting riverbank vegetation. Black and white rhinos, giraffes, baboons, cheetahs, antelope species; ober 300 species of birds. Between March and October hiking trips and tours by car.

Reservations: KwaZulu/Natal Parks Board (for address, see above).

Mkuzi Game Reserve

Location: KwaZulu/Natal, 335km/208 miles north of Durban on the coast road. Area: 34,644 hectares/85,571 acres.

Low-growing thorny scrub alternating with open park-like country with many species of trees. Klipspringers, elands, mountain reedbucks, water-

bucks, impalas, giraffes, black and white rhinos, leopards, hippopotamuses, crocodiles and 413 species of birds.

Hiking trails, including the 3km/2 mile long Fig Forest Walk; tours by car.

Reservations: KwaZulu/Natal Parks Board (for address, see above).

Location: north-eastern KwaZulu/Natal, 270km/168 miles north of Durban.
Area (both reserves): 96,000 hectares/237,000 acres.

**Hluhluwe and
Umfolozi
Game Reserves**

The two reserves are separated by a strip of land 8km/5 miles wide.

The main part of the reserves lies in a wedge-shaped watershed area
between the White and Black Umfolozi Rivers; small trees and woody
scrub. Both species of rhinoceros – amounting to roughly a quarter of the
total African rhinoceros population – live here, 320 black and 1750 white
rhinos. China is the main market for smuggled rhinoceros horn, which is
processed to produce a febrifuge and is also sought after throughout Asia
as a specific for increasing male potency. Red and grey duikers, elephants,
steenboks, klipspringers, mountain reedbucks, impalas, nyalas, water-
bucks, zebras, blue wildebeests, buffaloes, giraffes, warthogs, lions,
leopards, cheetahs, spotted hyenas, black-backed jackals, crocodiles,
baboons and over 300 species of birds.

Hiking trails and car tours.

Reservations: KwaZulu/Natal Parks Board (for address, see above).

Location: KwaZulu/Natal, extending 58km/36 miles north from the mouth
of the St Lucia River along the Zululand coast.

St Lucia region

There are three separate reserves:

St Lucia Marine Reserve (44,480 hectares/109,865 acres), extending
3km/2 miles out to sea (turtles).

Cape Vidal State Forest (113,313 hectares/279,883 acres), 32km/20 miles
north of the St Lucia estuary: an area of wooded coastal dunes with an
astonishing abundance of tropical plants and animals; many hiking trails.

St Lucia Park, a 1km/½ mile wide strip of land almost completely encircling a lake (12,545 hectares/30,985 acres); subtropical coastal forest; four
rivers flowing into the lake. Hippopotamuses, crocodiles, Goliath herons
and other fish-eating birds, pelicans and flamingos.

Hiking trails; boat trips. Holiday complex, with good fishing.

Reservations: KwaZulu/Natal Parks Board (for address, see above).

Location: KwaZulu/Natal, 69km/43 miles south-west of Estcourt. Area:
34,638 hectares/85,555 acres.

**Giant's Castle
Game Reserve**

Situated in the foothills of the KwaZulu/Natal Drakensberg. Grassland,
woodland, bush and scrub; the Bushman's and Little Tugela Rivers flow
through the reserve. 12 species of antelope and 140 species of birds,
including the mighty bearded vulture.

Some 50km/30 miles of hiking and riding trails; fishing; Bushman
Museum.

Reservations: KwaZulu/Natal Parks Board (for address, see above).

Location: KwaZulu/Natal, 98km/61 miles west of Ladysmith, bordering the
Rugged Glen Nature Reserve. Area: 8094 hectares/19,992 acres.

**Royal Natal
National Park**

On the slopes of the Drakensberg, with one of the sources of the Tugela
River. Grassland, woodland, proteas, evergreen montane forest, bush,
fynbos, heathland.

Black wildebeests, mountain reedbucks, rheboks, blesboks, klipspringers; many birds, including black eagles, bearded vultures, Cape vultures
and jackal buzzards.

31 hiking and riding trails ranging in length between 3km/2 miles and
45km/28 miles.

Reservations: KwaZulu/Natal Parks Board (for address, see above).

Location: KwaZulu/Natal, on the scenic Highlands Route, at the foot of the
Maluti Mountains, near the Lesotho border. Area: 11,630 hectares/28,725
acres.

**Golden Gate
Highlands
National Park**

Bizarre rock formations; montane grassland, with many different shrubs
and tuberose plants. Luxuriant show of flowers from spring to autumn.

Rheboks, oribis, springboks, black wildebeests, blesboks, elands, steppe zebras, Cape otters, baboons and 140 species of birds, including bearded vultures and Verreaux's eagles.

Hiking trails.

Reservations: National Parks Board (for address, see above).

Vaalbos National Park

Location: Northern Cape, near Kimberley. White and black rhinos, buffaloes, giraffes, zebras, wildebeests, oryxes and elands.

No accommodation for visitors.

Mountain Zebra National Park

Location: Eastern Cape, 27km/17 miles west of Cradock. Area: 6536 hectares/16,144 acres.

Mainly dry grassland with dwarf shrubs, larger shrubs and dense woodland. In addition to mountain zebras there are large herds of elands, springboks, blesboks, black wildebeests, kudus, duikers, steenboks, elands and mountain reedbucks; more than 200 species of birds, including a breeding colony of Verreaux's eagles.

Hiking trails.

Reservations: National Parks Board (for address, see above).

Zuurberg National Park

Location: Eastern Cape, 70km/43 miles from Port Elizabeth and 16km/10 miles north of Addo Elephant Park.

Antelopes, mountain zebras, hippopotamuses, caracals, leopards, jackals and many species of birds.

Reservations: Port Elizabeth Publicity Association, tel. 041/52 13 15.

Addo Elephant National Park

Location: Eastern Cape, 72km/45 miles north of Port Elizabeth, near the Zuurberg range. Area: 14,754 hectares/36,442 acres.

The Addo bush country consists of a scrub of creeping plants, shrubs and small trees.

More than 120 elephants; black rhinos, buffaloes, antelope species; after dark, bush pigs, porcupines and anteaters; 180 species of birds, including hawks, finches, moorhens, francolins and little grebes.

Reservations: National Parks Board (for address, see above).

Tsitsikamma National Park

Location: Eastern Cape, between the mouth of the Groot River (near Humansdorp) and Plettenberg Bay. Area: 2840 hectares/7015 acres.

The National Park is 80km/50 miles long and extends up to 5km/3 miles out to sea. The slopes of the hills are covered with evergreen forest, with fynbos vegetation on the crests of the hills and the plateaux. Yellowwood trees stand amid heath and proteas, with ferns, wild orchids and many species of lilies. The fauna includes rock rabbits, bushbucks, grysboks, blue duikers, baboons, vervet monkeys and 210 species of birds, including 35 different seabirds.

Hiking trails, including the 41km/25 mile long Otter Trail (prior booking required).

Reservations: National Parks Board (for address, see above).

Wilderness National Park

Location: Western Cape, between Knysna and George, extending from the Goukamma Nature Reserve in the east to the Touw River in the west. Area: 10,600 hectares/26,200 acres.

The National Park takes in the estuary of the Touw River (known as the Wilderness Lagoon), a series of swamp areas (Serpentine, Eilandvlei, Langvlei, Rondevlei, Swartvlei) and the Knysna Lagoon.

Cape otters, many species of bat, antelopes and seabirds and birds living on the coast and in woodland. It has one of the widest ranges of water birds of any bird reserve in South Africa.

Good fishing in Swartvlei.

Reservations: National Parks Board (for address, see above).

Bontebok National Park

Location: Western Cape, 7km/4½ miles south-east of Swellendam. Area: 3236 hectares/7993 acres.

Surrounded by a rich variety of plant life. In spring the countryside is carpeted with flowers.

Holiday cottages in the Addo Elephant Park

Over 300 bonteboks, rheboks, grysboks, mountain zebras, steenboks, grey duikers and almost 200 species of birds.

Fishing is permitted in the Breede River. Two short hiking trails.

Reservations: National Parks Board (for address, see above).

Karoo National Park

Location: Western and Northern Cape, north of Beaufort West. Area: 32,792 hectares/80,997 acres.

Low hills and open fields with many different trees, perennial grasses, bush and undergrowth. 50 different species of mammals large and small, including mountain zebras, oryxes, elands, black wildebeests and springboks. Hiking trails and car tours.

Reservations: National Parks Board (for address, see above).

West Coast National Park

Location: Western Cape; Langebaan, 100km/60 miles north of Cape Town. Area: 32,494 hectares/80,260 acres. Beach almost 30km/19 miles long.

The Langebaan Lagoon, to the south of Saldanha Bay, is one of the world's great wetland biotopes. In spring there is a profusion of daisies, gazanias and mesembryanthemums. The park is one of the most important bird reserves in the world: thousands of cormorants, seagulls, curlew sandpipers and flamingos live round the lagoon, and in summer there may be anything up to 55,000 birds, two-thirds of them curlew sandpipers. Large numbers of migrant birds from the Arctic also call in here.

Water sports are permitted in part of the park; another part may be visited only by boat; and the rest of the park is closed to the public.

Boat trips, canoeing routes, hiking trails. Information in Geelbek education centre.

Reservations: National Parks Board (for address, see above)

Tankwa Karoo National Park

Location: Northern Cape, 95km/59 miles south of Calvinia. Area: 27,064 hectares/66,848 acres.

Karoo vegetation. No tourist facilities.

Augrabies Falls National Park	Location: Northern Cape, on the Orange River 120km/75 miles west of Upington. Area: 88,000 hectares/217,500 acres. The main attractions of this National Park are its impressive waterfalls. Rich flora, including the kokerboom ("quiver tree"). The fauna includes black rhinos, elands, baboons and the smaller antelopes, particularly klipspringers. Hiking trails. Reservations: National Parks Board (for address, see above).
Kalahari Gemsbok National Park	Location: Northern Cape; in the north-west of South Africa, on the borders of Botswana and Namibia. Area: 959,103 hectares/2,368,984 acres. Semi-desert. The characteristic features of the area between the dried-up beds of the Nossob and Auob Rivers are the grass-covered Kalahari dunes. Most of the game lives in the dried-up river-beds – large herds of blue wildebeests, oryxes and elands, with smaller groups of red hartebeests, steenboks and duikers; Kalahari lions, cheetahs, leopards, wild dogs, spotted and brown hyenas, numerous smaller mammals and 215 species of birds. Reservations: National Parks Board (for address, see above).
Richtersveld National Park	Location: Northern Cape. Area: 162,445 hectares/401,239 acres. Highland desert; hills, gorges. Succulents and endemic plants. Numerous species of birds; otherwise relatively little fauna. In order to preserve the delicate eco-system, tourists are not encouraged; no accommodation or food available.

All the National Parks listed here are described in the A to Z section of the guide and can be found by consulting the Index.

Newspapers and Periodicals

More than 5000 newspapers and periodicals are published in South Africa. Newspapers are sold at street corners in the morning and afternoon as well as in newsagents' shops. European and American papers are usually only to be found in the larger branches of the CNA bookselling chain.

Night Life

In all the larger towns there are discos, jazz bars, cabarets, night clubs and sometimes casinos. For what is available in Johannesburg and Cape Town see Music, Theatre, Dance in the introductory section of this guide. For the most part, however, the "night life" of South Africans is confined to an evening meal in a restaurant. At night, except in the bars of hotels, practically nothing happens.

A wider range of entertainment is offered by Sun City/Lost City, the huge holiday complex 2½ hours' drive from Johannesburg which was built in the then nominally independent homeland of Bophuthatswana to avoid South Africa's stricter moral attitudes, ban on gambling and liquor licensing laws. Among its amenities are a casino, a variety theatre and a large concert hall.
See also Theatre, Concerts, Opera

Opening Times

See Business Hours

Photography

Films are dearer in South Africa than in Europe or America, but prices for developing them are lower. Shopping centres usually have a one-hour development service.

For photographs of animals, particularly with a telephoto lens, it is advisable to use films of 24 DIN or higher.

Postal Services and Telephones

Stamps can be bought only in post offices. The postage on a letter to Europe (airmail) is R 1.15, to North America R1.40; postcards are 90 cents. Mail may take about a week to reach its destination. — Postage

Most post offices are open Mon.–Fri. 8am–4.30pm, Sat. 8am–noon. Except in the head post offices of the larger towns there is a lunch break between 1 and 2pm. — Post offices

Mailboxes, painted red, are mostly of the traditional British pillar type. — Mailboxes

Except in remote country areas the telephone system is fully automatic, with direct dialling to most parts of the world. International calls are best made from a post office, where you pay after the call; they can also be made from blue payphones, but for this you will need plenty of coins. — Telephone

South Africa to Britain: 0944
South Africa to USA or Canada: 091
Britain to South Africa: 0027
USA or Canada to South Africa: 01127
— International dialling codes

When telephoning to Britain or South Africa the zero of the local dialling code should be omitted.

A 3-minute local call costs 24 cents. An international call from a payphone costs R6 per minute; for a call from a post office the minimum charge is for 3 minutes; and hotels commonly charge two or three times the official rate for an international call.

Dial 1023 for South Africa
Dial 0903 for International
— Information

Emergency calls throughout South Africa: tel. 1 01 11 — Emergency calls

Faxes can be sent from hotels but not from post offices. — Fax

To Lesotho: 00266
To Swaziland: 00268
— Dialling codes for Lesotho and Swaziland

Public Holidays

Under new arrangements approved by Parliament in 1994 South Africa has 12 public holidays:

January 1st	New Year's Day
March 21st	Human Rights Day (commemorating the Sharpeville massacre in 1960)
March/April	Good Friday
March/April	Family Day (Easter Monday)

April 27th	Constitution Day Freedom Day (commemorating the coming into force of the transitional constitution and the first free election in 1994)
May 1st	Workers' Day
June 16th	Youth Day (commemorating the schoolchildren's uprising in Soweto in 1976)
August 9th	National Women's Day
September 24th	Heritage Day (previously the Zulus' Shaka Day)
December 16th	Day of Reconciliation (previously Day of the Vow, commemorating the vow taken by the voortrekkers before the battle of Blood River in 1838; date of foundation of Umkhonto we Sizwe, the militant wing of the ANC, in 1961)
December 25th	Christmas Day
December 26th	Day of Goodwill

When a holiday falls on a Sunday it is moved to the following Monday. Jews and Asians have their own holidays.

Public Transport

See Bus Services; Railways; Taxis

Radio and Television

Radio and television services are provided by the South African Broadcasting Corporation (SABC), established in 1936, with headquarters in Johannesburg.

Radio

At present there are 23 radio programmes in the eleven national languages, including English and Afrikaans.

Television

Television came to South Africa in 1976. The SABC now transmits programmes in nine languages: on TV1 in English and Afrikaans, on CCV-TV in Zulu, Xhosa, South and North Sotho, Tswana, Hindi, Tamil, English and Afrikaans. The independent channel TSS transmits mainly cultural and educational programmes. In 1991 TV1 had around 5 million viewers daily and CCC-TV just over 6 million. Some 8% of transmission time on all channels is taken up by advertising.

M-Net is a subscription television service established in 1985 by a consortium of newspaper publishers. Its programmes are sent in coded form, for which subscribers have a decoder, but it also has two hours daily of uncoded programmes for all viewers. It has at present around 750,000 subscribers. It has channels for Indian viewers (East-Net) and Portuguese viewers (Canal Portugues), special children's programmes (K-TV) and an international channel (M-Net International, MNI), which also transmits BBC news bulletins. M-Net can be received round all the large towns and, via satellite, in some country areas. It is the third largest pay TV channel outside the United States.

The Christian Television Service (CTV) transmits on TV1 and TV4 (CCV).

Railways

The main South African towns are linked by an efficient railway system. The distances to be covered, however, are considerable and the trains not particularly fast, so that for a long journey it is preferable to travel overnight (the ordinary fare covers the cost of a sleeper). A seat reservation ticket is required (preferably bought in advance but also available from the ticket collector).

First class coaches have compartments for 2 to 4 passengers, second class coaches for 3 to 6. All long-distance trains have a restaurant car.

Children under 6 accompanying an adult travel free; children between 6 and 12 pay half fare; students pay half fare; passengers over 60 pay 60% of the full fare; and foreign visitors staying less than 3 months in South Africa are entitled to a reduction of 25% on the first class fare.

Concession fares

South African Railways, PO Box 1111, Johannesburg 2000, tel. 011/7 74 45 04

Information on services and fares

Suburban trains, particularly in Johannesburg, should be avoided because of the high incidence of violent crime.

Warning

Steam Trains in South Africa

The legendary Blue Train, a luxury train which first ran in 1901, travels three times weekly (Mon., Wed. and Fri.) during the main holiday season between Cape Town, Johannesburg and Pretoria. The journey of 1500km/930 miles takes about 25 hours. Fares vary according to class (of which there are five), ranging between R1575 (single compartment with wash-basin) and R6300 (luxury suite with living and sleeping compartments, bath and WC for two people), including meals (which are of high quality). (Fares subject to change.)

Blue Train
(map, p. 415)

The Blue Train now also runs between Pretoria and Nelspruit and between Pretoria and the Victoria Falls in Zimbabwe.

Blue Train Reservations, Private Bag X47, Johannesburg 2000, tel. 011/7 74 44 69. In view of the great demand bookings should be made at least 6 months in advance.

Reservations

The Outeniqua Choo-Tjoe on its run from George to Knysna

Restaurants

Rovos Rail

A trip on Rovos Rail, the South African equivalent of the Orient Express, is a very special experience. This steam train, consisting of eight coaches dating from the 1920s drawn by three old locomotives of 1893, 1926 and 1938, offers every comfort (including first-rate cuisine) on a journey (including excursions and safaris) which takes passengers back to the days of the pioneers, gold-diggers and big game hunters. The train carries a maximum of 40 passengers, who are looked after by a staff of 14.

Rovos Rail runs between:
Pretoria and Cape Town (3 days; fares between R2500 and R3400)
Pretoria and the Kruger National Park (22 hours; fares between R2000 and R2500)
Cape Town and Dar-es-Salaam (10 days; fares on application, for whole journey only)
Fares include meals, drinks and insurance.

Reservations

PO Box 2837, Pretoria 0001, tel. 012/3 23 60 52. In view of the great demand bookings should be made at least 6 months in advance.

Magaliesberg Express

This steam train runs between Johannesburg and the Magaliesberg Mountains, north-west of the city. Dep. Johannesburg Sun. 8.45am, arr. 10.30am; return (after barbecue lunch) dep. 4pm, arr. 7.45pm. Fare R40; children half price.

Reservations

Preservation Group, PO Box 1419, Roosevelt Park 2129, tel. 011/8 88 11 54

Banana Express

The Banana Express runs between Port Shepstone and Itzosha, passing through extensive banana plantations. Dep. Port Shepstone Thur. 10am, Sun. 11am. The journey takes 2½ hours; fare R20.

Reservations

Banana Express Office, PO Box 115, Umtentwini 4235, tel. 0391/7 64 43

Apple Express

This narrow-gauge line formerly transported apples from the fruit-growing area to Port Elizabeth. It now runs between Port Elizabeth and Thornhill on Saturdays and Mondays from December 8th to January 5th. Dep. Port Elizabeth 10am, arr. Thornhill noon; dep. Thornhill 2pm, arr. Port Elizabeth 4pm. Fare R46.

Reservations

Apple Express, Port Elizabeth station, tel. 041/5 07 23 33

Outeniqua Choo-Tjoe

The Outenique Choo-Tjoe is not a luxury train like the Blue Train but an ordinary suburban train. Between George and Knysna it follows the beautiful Garden Route for some 100km/60 miles. It runs daily, except Sundays and public holidays. Dep. George 8am, arr. Knysna 10.22am; dep. Knysna 10.35am, arr. George 1.15pm. Fare R25 single, R35 return.

Reservations

Outeniqua Choo-Tjoe, George station, tel. 0441/73 82 02.

Restaurants (a selection)

Amanzimtoti

Razzmatazz (South African cuisine)
21 Beach Road, tel. 031/9 03 41 31

Bloemfontein

Beef Baron (steakhouse)
22 Second Avenue, tel. 051/47 42 90

Camelot (international cuisine)
94A Voortrekker Street, tel. 051/47 77 27

Carousel (South African cuisine)
C. R. Swart Building, Elizabeth Street, tel. 051/48 02 51

New York (international cuisine)
Sanlam Arcade, tel. 051/47 72 79

Boschendal Estate (South African cuisine)
Pniel Road, Groot Drakenstein, tel. 02211/4 12 52

Buitenverwachting (French cuisine)
Buitenverwachting Estate, Klein Constantia
Road, Constantia, tel. 021/7 94 35 22

Champers (French cuisine)
Deer Park Shopping Centre, Deer Park Drive,
Highlands Estate, tel. 021/45 43 35

Floris Smit Huis (French cuisine)
Corner of Loop and Church Streets,
tel. 021/23 34 14

Bay Restaurant (international cuisine)
Bay Hotel, Victoria Road, Camps Bay,
tel. 021/4 38 44 44

Choices (French cuisine)
34 Loop Street, tel. 021/4 19 69 50

Chez Simone (French cuisine)
Thibault Square, tel. 021/21 77 36

Fisherman's Cottage (fish dishes)
3 Gray Road, Plumstead, tel. 021/7 97 63 41

John Jackson (international cuisine)
Peninsula Hotel, 313 Beach Road, Sea Point,
tel. 021/4 39 83 02

Leinster Hall (international cuisine)
7 Weltevreden Street, Gardens,
tel. 021/24 18 36

Peer (international cuisine)
Pierhead, Waterfront, tel. 021/21 71 13

A tempting assortment of seafood

Tastevin (international cuisine)
Cape Sun Hotel, Strand Street, tel. 021/23 88 44

Grill Room (international cuisine)
Mount Nelson Hotel, Orange Street, tel. 021/23 10 00

Truffles (international cuisine)
161 Main Road, Heathfield, tel. 021/72 61 61

Anatoli (Turkish cuisine)
24 Napier Street, tel. 021/4 19 25 01

Black Marlin (fish dishes)
Main Road, Miller's Point, Simonstown, tel. 021/7 86 16 21

Blake's (French cuisine)
Nico Malan Opera House, tel. 021/21 74 78

Blues (international cuisine)
Promenade, Victoria Road, Camps Bay, tel. 021/4 38 20 40

Brass Bell (fish dishes)
Waterfront, Kalk Bay Harbour, tel. 021/7 88 54 56

Restaurants

Café Paradiso (international cuisine)
110 Kloof Street, Gardens, tel. 021/23 86 53

Gaylords (Indian cuisine)
65 Main Road, Muizenberg, tel. 021/7 88 54 70

La Med (Mediterranean cuisine)
Glen Country Club, Victoria Road, Clifton, tel. 021/4 38 56 00

La Vita (Italian cuisine)
Dean Street Arcade, Newlands, tel. 021/6 85 20 51

Mariner's Wharf (fish dishes)
Harbour Road, Hout Bay Harbour, tel. 021/7 90 11 00

Napier Street (French cuisine)
34 Napier Street, tel. 021/25 15 57

Old Colonial (international cuisine)
39 Barnet Street, Gardens, tel. 021/45 49 09

On the Rocks (South African cuisine)
45 Stadler Road, Bloubergstrand, tel. 021/56 19 88

Ons Huisie (fish dishes)
Stadler Road, Bloubergstrand, tel. 021/56 15 53

Rozenhof (French cuisine)
18 Kloof Street, Gardens, tel. 021/24 19 68

San Marco (Mediterranean cuisine)
92 Main Road, Sea Point, tel. 021/4 39 27 58

Shrimpton's (international cuisine)
19 Alexander Road, Muizenberg, tel. 021/88 52 25

Beachcomber (fish dishes)
41 Victoria Road, Camps Bay, tel. 021/4 38 12 13

Durban
Top-class
restaurants

Michael's (French cuisine)
15 Waterfall Centre, tel. 031/7 63 34 29

Royal Grill (French cuisine)
Royal Hotel, 267 Smith Street, tel. 031/3 04 03 31

Sukihama (Japanese cuisine)
Hotel Elangeni, Snell Parade, tel. 031/37 13 21

St Geran (French cuisine)
31 Aliwal Road, tel. 031/3 04 75 09

Gourmet
restaurants

Chatters (French cuisine)
32 Hermitage Street, tel. 031/3 06 18 96

La Dolce Vita (Italian cuisine)
Durdoc Centre, 460 Smith Street, tel. 031/3 01 33 47

Landaus (French cuisine)
Avonmore Centre, 9th Avenue, tel. 031/23 91 35

Le Troquet (French cuisine)
860 Old Man Road, Cowies Hill, tel. 031/86 53 88

Punchinello's (fish dishes)
Hotel Elangeni, Snell Parade, tel. 031/37 13 21

The Colony (international cuisine)
The Oceanic, Sol Harris Crescent, tel. 031/3 68 27 89

The Grapevine (international cuisine)
Edward Hotel, Marine Parade, tel. 031/37 36 81

Wolfgang's (international cuisine)
136 Flonda Road, tel. 031/23 28 61

Mermaid (Indian cuisine)   Traditional
Teachers Centre, 113 Albert Street, tel. 031/3 09 30 46   restaurants

British Middle East Sporting and Dining Club Restaurant (Indian cuisine)
16 Stamford Hill Road, tel. 031/3 09 40 17

Ulundi (Indian cuisine)
Royal Hotel, 267 Smith Street, tel. 031/3 04 03 31

Le Petit (French cuisine)   **East London**
54 Beach Road, Nahoon, tel. 0431/35 36 85

Mövenpick (international cuisine)
Orient Beach, Esplanade, tel. 0431/2 18 40

Swiss Inn (international cuisine)
Central Square, Gladstone Street, tel. 0431/43 52 26

That Italian Place (Italian cuisine)
83A Old Transkei Road, Nahoon, tel. 0431/35 16 54

La Petite Ferme (South African cuisine)   **Franschhoek**
Franschhoek Pass (near Huguenot Monument), tel. 02212/30 16

Le Quartier Français (French cuisine)
Main Road, tel. 02212/21 51

Carousel (international cuisine)   **George**
38 Courtenay Street, tel. 0441/73 43 24

Italian Pizzeria (Italian cuisine)
Courtenay Street, tel. 0441/73 29 18

Montagu Restaurant (French cuisine)
Fancourt Hotel Blanco, tel. 0441/70 82 82

The Copper Pot (French cuisine)
Multi Centre, Meade Street, tel. 0441/74 31 91

The Old Town House (South African cuisine)
Market Street, tel. 0441/74 36 63

The Toothpick (steakhouse)
79 Davidson Road, tel. 0441/73 37 14

Burgundy (French cuisine)   **Hermanus**
Market Square, tel. 0283/2 28 00

Chapters (French cuisine)   **Johannesburg**
Sandton Sun Hotel, Sandton, tel. 011/7 83 87 01   Top-class
                                                                restaurants

Herbert Baker (international cuisine)
Dysart House, 5 Winchester Road, Parktown, tel. 011/7 26 62 19

Restaurants

Les Marquis (French cuisine)
12 Feldman Drive, Sandton, tel. 011/7 83 89 47

Le Canard (international cuisine)
163 Rivonia Road, Morningside, Sandton, tel. 011/8 84 45 97

Linger Longer (South African cuisine)
94 Juta Street, Braamfontein, tel. 011/3 39 78 14

Ma Cuisine (French cuisine)
Corner of 7th and 3rd Avenues, Parktown North, tel. 011/8 80 19 46

St James (French cuisine)
Johannesburg Sun, corner of Jeppe and Smal Streets, tel. 011/29 70 11

The Three Ships (French cuisine)
Carlton Hotel, Commissioner Street, tel. 011/3 31 89 11

Zoo Lake (international cuisine)
Zoo Lake Gardens, Parkview, tel. 01/6 46 88 07

Gourmet restaurants

Daruma (Japanese cuisine)
Corner of Corlett Drive and Athol Oaklands Avenue, Melrose North, tel. 011/4 47 22 60

Grayston (international cuisine)
Sandton Holiday Inn, Sandton, tel. 011/7 83 52 62

Harridans (international cuisine)
Market Theatre, Bree Street, Newtown, tel. 011/8 38 69 60

The Homestead (international cuisine)
Horwood's Farm, Homestead Road, Edenvale, tel. 011/4 53 81 02

Traditional cuisine

Anton van Wouw Restaurant (South African cuisine)
111 Sivewright Street, Doornfontein, tel. 011/4 02 79 16

Chaplin's (fish dishes)
85 4th Avenue, Melville, tel. 011/7 26 54 11

Fisherman's Grotto (fish dishes)
14A Plein Street, tel. 011/8 34 62 11

Gramadoelas Africana (South African cuisine)
31 Bok Street, Joubert Park, tel. 011/7 25 17 95

Horatio's (fish dishes)
Corner of 3rd Avenue and 7th Street, Melville, tel. 011/7 26 28 90

Leipoldt's (South African cuisine)
94 Juta Street, Braamfontein, tel. 011/3 39 18 57

Tastevin (international cuisine)
Sunnyside Park Hotel, 2 York Road, Parktown, tel. 011/6 43 72 26

T'Rien (fish dishes)
79 3rd Avenue, Melville, tel. 011/4 82 23 66

Kimberley

Mario's
Pick'n'Pay Centre, tel. 0531/81 17 38

Shillings (international cuisine)
Kimberley Sun Hotel, Du Toitspan Road, tel. 0531/3 17 51

Umberto's (Italian cuisine)
Jones Street, tel. 0531/2 57 41

The Tapas (international cuisine)   **Knysna**
Thesen's Jetty, tel. 0445/1 19 27

O'Pescador (fish dishes)
Brenton–Belvidere road, tel. 0445/87 10 64

The Anchorage (fish dishes)
Garden Route, Centre Main Street, tel. 0445/2 22 30

The Islander (fish dishes)
Harkerville National Road (between Knysna and Plettenberg Bay), tel.
0445/77 76

Selati (South African cuisine)   **Kruger Park/**
Skukuza Camp, tel. 01311/6 56 11   **Skukuza Camp**

Camelot (steakhouse)   **Mossel Bay**
10 Market Street, tel. 0444/91 10 00

The Gannet (fish dishes)
Bartolomeu Diaz Museum Complex, Market Street, tel. 0444/91 18 85

Pavilion (international cuisine)
Beachfront, tel. 0444/45 67

Café Mozart (German cuisine)   **Nelspruit**
Promenade Centre, tel. 01311/2 26 37

Costa do Sol (international cuisine)
Brown Street, tel. 01311/2 63 82

Wins Restaurant (international cuisine)
Tarentaal Trading Post, tel. 01311/4 45 02

Rawdon's Hotel Restaurant (international cuisine)   **Nottingham Road**
Old Main Road, Nottingham Road, tel. 0333/3 60 44

Laborie Wine House (South African cuisine)   **Paarl**
Taillefer Street, Suider Paarl, tel. 02211/63 20 34

Rhebokskloof (international cuisine)
Rhebokskloof Wine Estate, tel. 02211/63 86 06

Da Vinci (Italian cuisine)   **Pietermaritzburg**
117 Commercial Road, tel. 0331/5 66 32

Els Amics (French cuisine)
380 Longmarket Street, tel. 0331/5 65 24

Lien Wah (Chinese cuisine)
Hilton Hotel, Hilton Road, tel. 0331/3 33 11

Spotted Dog (international cuisine)
262 Burger Street, tel. 0331/94 55 81

White Mischief (international cuisine)
180 Loop Street, tel. 0331/42 45 79

Die Klause (South African cuisine)   **Pietersburg**
53A Hans van Rensburg Street, tel. 01521/7 38 91

The Armoury (international cuisine)
Ranch Hotel, Great North Road, tel. 01521/7 53 77

Restaurants

Villa Italia (Italian cuisine)
Kirk Centre, Schoeman Street, tel. 01521/91 42 00

Pilgrim's Rest   Mount Sheba Hotel (international cuisine)
Tel. 01315/8 12 41

Plettenberg Bay   Le Rendezvous (French cuisine)
Main Street, tel. 04457/3 13 90

Seven Cellars (French cuisine)
Formosa Inn, tel. 04457/3 20 60

The Med Seafood Bistro (French cuisine)
Village Square, Main Street, tel. 04457/3 31 02

Port Alfred   Wahoo Restaurants (European cuisine)
Fish River Sun Hotel, tel. 0403/61 21 01

Port Edward   Kontiki Grill (Greek cuisine)
Wild Coast Sun Hotel, tel. 0471/5 91 11

Commodore (fish dishes)
Wild Coast Sun Hotel, tel. 0471/5 91 11

Port Elizabeth   Coachman (steakhouse)
10 Lawrence Street, tel. 041/52 25 11

Kreg and Fox (South African cuisine)
31 Clyde Street, tel. 041/55 45 47

La Fontaine (French cuisine)
Park Towers, Rink Street, tel. 041/55 90 29

Mamma Leone's (fish dishes)
67 Parliament Street, tel. 041/55 11 25

Nelson's Arms (fish dishes)
3 Trinder Square, tel. 041/55 90 49

Old Austria (German cuisine)
42 Uitenhage Road, Sydenham, tel. 041/54 12 04

Royal Delhi (international cuisine)
10 Burges Street, tel. 041/33 82 16

Sir Rufane Donkin Rooms (international cuisine)
5 George Street, tel. 041/55 55 34

The Bell (international cuisine)
Beach Hotel, Beach Road, Summerstrand, tel. 041/53 21 61

The Bengal Tiger (international cuisine)
29 Webber Street, South End, tel. 041/51 10 20

Pretoria   Ambassadeur (international cuisine)
Burgerspark Hotel, Van der Walt Street, Burgerspark, tel. 012/3 22 75 00

Caraffe (Italian cuisine)
46 Selati Street, Alphen Park, tel. 012/3 46 33 44

Chez Patrice (French cuisine)
Corner of Soutpansberg and Wells Streets, Riviera, tel. 012/3 29 40 28

Cynthia's (international cuisine)
Maroelana Centre, Maroelana Street, Maroelana, tel. 012/46 32 29

Diep in die Berg (international cuisine)
Hans Strydom Drive, The Willows, tel. 012/8 07 01 11

Gerard Moerdyk (South African cuisine)
752 Park Street, Arcadia, tel. 012/3 44 48 56

La Cantina (Italian cuisine)
895 Pretorius Street, tel. 012/3 22 42 11

La Madeleine (international cuisine)
258 Esselen Street, Sunnyside, tel. 012/44 60 76

La Perla (Swiss cuisine)
Didacta Building, 211 Skinner Street, tel. 012/3 22 27 59

Lombardy (French cuisine)
Tweefontein Farm, Lynwood, tel. 012/8 07 00 81

Scarabaeus (international cuisine)
Lynnwood Road, tel. 012/87 11 51

Stadt Hamburg (German cuisine)
Brae Street, Willow Bree, The Willows, tel. 012/83 32 73

Toulouse (French cuisine)
Fountains Valley, Groenkloof, tel. 012/3 41 75 11

Crayfish Inn (fish dishes)   **Ramsgate**
Marine Drive, tel. 03931/44 10

Doornbusch (South African cuisine)   **Stellenbosch**
Old Strand Road, tel. 02231/61 63

Decameron (Italian cuisine)
50 Plein Street, tel. 02231/83 33 31

De Volkskombuis (South African cuisine)
Old Strand Road, tel. 02231/7 21 21

Ralph's (international cuisine)
13 Andringa Street, tel. 02231/83 35 32

Crytal Court (Californian cuisine)   **Sun City**
Palace Hotel, tel. 01465/7 30 00

Silver Forest (international cuisine)
Main Hotel, tel. 01465/2 10 00

Peninsula (international cuisine)
Cascades Hotel, tel. 01465/2 10 00

Villa del Palazzo (Italian cuisine)
Palace Hotel, tel. 01465/7 30 00

Paddagang Wine House (South African cuisine)   **Tulbagh**
23 Church Street, tel. 0236/30 02 42

Iron Crown (South African cuisine)   **Tzaneen**
Haenertsburg, tel. 01 52 72

Villa Italia (Italian cuisine)
Danie Joubert Street, tel. 0152/3 07 13 00

Le Musk (South African cuisine)   **Upington**
11 Schroder Street, tel. 054/2 49 71

Le Raisin (international cuisine)
11 Fick Street, tel. 054/2 33 51

White River   Bag-Dad Café (bistro)
Hazyview Road, tel. 01311/3 28 28

Jatinga (international cuisine)
Plaston Road, tel. 01311/3 19 32

Restaurants in Lesotho

Maseru   Auberge, Kingsway, tel. 09266/31 27 75
Boccaccio, Orpen Road, tel. 09266/32 58 53
China Garden, Orpen Road, tel. 09266/31 39 15

Restaurants in Swaziland

Ezulwini   Calabash, beyond Timbali camping site, tel. 09268/6 11 87
First Horse, on Mbabane–Manzini road, at Yen Saan Hotel, tel. 09268/
6 11 37
Forrester's (international cuisine), Ezulwini Sun Hotel, tel. 09268/6 12 01
Gigi's (international cuisine), Royal Swazi Sun Hotel, tel. 09268/6 10 01

Manzini   Las Cabanas, 6km/4 miles west, tel. 52221/8 41 30

Mbabane   La Casserole, The Mall, tel. 42221/4 64 26
Marco's Trattoria, Allister Miller Street, tel. 42221/4 50 29
First Horse (international cuisine), Yen Saan Mews, Main Road, tel. 09268/
6 11 37

Piggs Peak   Egumeni (international cuisine), Protea Piggs Peak Hotel and Casino, tel.
09268/7 11 04

Riding

South Africa's varied landscape and warm climate provide ideal conditions
for riding. In various parts of the country there are riding trails, and in many
National Parks there are organised pony treks through magnificent
scenery.
Lesotho, the "Roof of Africa", with its mountains rising to
3000m/10,000ft, offers attractive pony treks in hilly country on its small but
tough Basotho horses.

Shopping and Souvenirs

Warning   Visitors should be cautious about buying animal products (including skins,
etc.) in view of the regulations for the protection of endangered species.
Under the Washington Agreement of 1975 the import and export of many
endangered species of animals and plants, or products of such animals and
plants, are either completely banned or permitted only with a special
certificate or permit. On the banned list are all spotted felines, all rhinoceroses, various species of tortoise and all species of turtle, several species of
crocodile, large snakes, elephants (including ivory), two of the three South
African species of zebra, the bontebok and the sable antelope; among the
plants on the banned list are certain species of orchid and aloe, palm ferns
and tree ferns.
There are heavy fines for contravention of the regulations.

Native arts and crafts – hand-woven carpets, pottery, basketwork, wood-carving and much else besides – make very popular souvenirs of a trip to South Africa. Since the various Bantu peoples have developed their own art forms and styles there is a wide range of choice. Tempting displays can be seen in the "curio shops" in towns and in the weekly markets.

Craft products

The Ndebele are famed for their brilliantly painted house fronts, but they also produce fine beadwork (e.g. in the form of loincloths) and copper and brass armlets. Large (3 feet high) dolls wearing garments elaborately ornamented with beadwork are symbols of female fertility and male potency.

The Zulus are also skilled in the craft of beadwork. They make small cloth dolls decorated with bead embroidery and vessels made from gourds (calabashes), which are also decorated with beadwork. Other items in their repertoire are carved figures of animals and beer strainers and corn baskets woven from reeds or grass.

Typical Xhosa products are inxhilis (a traditional type of bag, coloured white and orange and ornamented with beads and buttons), elaborately worked table covers, isibinquos (three-quarter-length embroidered skirts with matching waistcoats) and inquawes (long pipes decorated with beads).

The Venda make attractive brightly coloured clay pots, while the Tsonga make knotted mats of dyed sisal.

In buying skin or leather goods you should check where they come from: imported articles are considerably dearer than in Europe or North America, while local products are up to 40% cheaper: for example Swakara reversible coats (Persian lamb on one side, napa leather on the other) and articles made from impala skins and ostrich or buffalo leather. There is a wide choice of handbags, wallets, suitcases and shoes.

Clothing

Bush and safari clothing is relatively cheap in the shops in National Parks and in curio shops in town.

Cloth dolls with beadwork decoration and carved wooden animals

Shopping and Souvenirs

Gold and precious stones

For many visitors South Africa is the land of gold and diamonds. On diamonds see the entry under that heading. On the Krugerrand see Famous People, Paul Kruger, and the entry on Currency, above.

Antiques

The antiques trade is booming in South Africa: both Sotheby's and Christie's have branches on the Cape. Most antiques (furniture, silver, etc.) were brought in by immigrants; the oldest date from around 1820. Antique jewellery in particular is very reasonably priced. The main centres of the antiques trade are Cape Town and Johannesburg.

Opening times

See Business Hours

Markets

There are more than 200 weekly or monthly markets in South Africa, among the best known of which are the market outside the Market Theatre in Johannesburg and the one in Greenmarket Square in Cape Town. In Durban's Indian Market haggling over the price is expected: the dealers' prices for their wares (exotic jewellery, woodcarving, clothing, Indian spices, etc.) have a built-in allowance for reductions.

Cafés

A South African café is not a café in the normal European or American sense but a shop or corner kiosk selling newspapers, foodstuffs, cigarettes, sweets, soft drinks, etc. They usually open at 6am and close at midnight.

Bottle stores

Alcoholic beverages are normally sold only in "bottle stores". In these shops you can buy drinks to accompany your meal in an unlicensed restaurant.

Cape Town

Antique dealers

Ashbey's Galleries, 43 Church Street
Atkinson'a Antiques, 213 Long Street
Elizabeth Power (antique jewellery), 113 Loop Street
Kay's Antiques, Shop G37, Cavendish Square, Claremont
Myra's Antiques, 78 Church Street
Peter Visser Antiques, 117 Long Street

Art galleries

The Art Scene, 74 Regent Road, Sea Point
Ashbey's Galleries, 43 Church Street
The Cape Gallery, 60 Church Street
Die Kunskamer, Saambou Building, 14 Burg Street
The Yellow Door, 79 Hatfield Street

Bookshops

Clarke's Bookshop, 211 Long Street
Cranfords, 259 Long Street
Juta and Co., 1 Bree Street
Ulrich Naumann, 17 Burg Street
Florian Thieme (with modern secondhand), 167 Kloof Street

Camping equipment

Camp and Climb, 6 Pepper Street
Cape Union Mart Group, Mostert and Corporation Streets

Golfing equipment

The Pro Shop, 19 Loop Street

Jewellery

Kohler, Master Goldsmith and Jeweller, 64 St George's Street
Murdocks Jewellers, 100 Adderley Street
Newmans Jewellers, Shop 33, Stuttaford Town Square
Peter Gilder Jewellers, Shop 33, Constantia Village, Constantia
Pinns the Jewellers, 30 St George's Mall
Tanur Jewellery Co., Shop 47, Golden Acre Shopping Centre
Urry Diamonds, NBS Waldorf, 80 St George's Street
Uwe Koetter Jewellers, 101 St George's Street

Kottler's Gifts and Curios, 23 Adderley Street   Leather goods
Rooikrans Leather, Shop 18, Tygervalley Centre, Bellville
Tusk 2, St George's Mall, St George's Street

African Market, Pearl House, 19 Heerengracht   Souvenir shops
African Souvenir and Assegaai Curios, Greenmarket Square
Kottler's Gifts and Curios, 23 Adderley Street
Kwazulu Curios, 15 Castle Street
Pezulu, George House, 70 St George's Mall
Tusk 2, St George's Mall, St George's Street
Zimbabwe Curios, NBS Waldorf, 80 St George's Street

Duty-free shop at D. F. Malan Airport: leather goods, books, videos, souvenirs, jewellery and accessories, gifts, flowers (proteas), liqueurs, spirits, wine, coins

Durban

Reid and Moore, Workshop Shopping Centre (ground floor), 99 Aliwal   Antiques
   Street
Home Decor, Workshop Shopping Centre (upper level), 99 Aliwal Street
Grassroots Gallery, 119A Jan Hofmeyer Road, Westville

Adams Booksellers and Stationers, 341 West Street   Bookshops
Central News Agency, 369 Smith Street

Sad Sacks, 95 Moore Road   Camping
Maverick Outdoor Gear, The Outdoor Inn, 8 Aliwal Street   equipment
The Quartermaster, Shop 60, Workshop Shopping Centre, 99 Aliwal Street

The Pro Shop, 405 Smith Street   Golfing
Durban Golf Shop, Boland Bank House, 221 West Street   equipment

Randles Jewellers, 412 West Street   Jewellers
Cameys Jewellers, 331 West Street
Durban Diamond Cutting Works, Shop 4, Boland Bank Building, 223 West
   Street

Leather World, 311 West Street   Leather goods
The Coachman, Shop 21, Workshop Shopping Centre, 99 Aliwal Street

Afrique African Curios, 8 West Street   Souvenirs
Indian Market, 155 Victoria Street (spices, clothing, jewellery and accessories, semi-precious stones)
The Workshop, 99 Aliwal Street (jewellery and accessories, literature, art, clothing, souvenirs, carpets, sports equipment)
The Beachfront (stalls with leather goods, jewellery, clothing)
Antiques and Bygones, The Old Church, 50 Aliwal Street
African Art Centre, 8 Guild Hall Arcade, 35 Gardiner Street

Johannesburg

Old Magic, Carlton Shopping Centre, 151 Commissioner Street   Antiques
Alternatives, Rosebank Mall, 50 Bath Avenue, Rosebank
No. 13, Village Walk, Maude and Rivonia Roads, Sandton

Great Graphics, Carlton Shopping Centre, 151 Commissioner Street   Art galleries
Art and Frame, East Gate Shopping Centre, 43 Bradford Road, Bedfordview
Natalie Knight Gallery/Goodman Gallery, Hyde Park Shopping Centre, Jan
   Smuts Avenue, Sandton
Pars Gallery and Ultimate Frames, Village Walk, Maude and Rivonia Roads,
   Sandton

Shopping and Souvenirs

Bookshops	Book and Gift Corner and C.N.A., Carlton Shopping Centre, 151 Commissioner Street
	Sheldons the Bookshop and C.N.A., East Gate Shopping Centre, 43 Bradford Road, Bedfordview
	Exclusive Books, Hyde Park Shopping Centre, Jan Smuts Avenue, Sandton
	Jeffrey Sharpe Rare Books, Rosebank Mall, 50 Bath Avenue, Rosebank
	The Bookworm and C.N.A., Sandton City Shopping Centre, Rivonia Road, Sandton
	Exclusive Books, corner of Maude and Rivonia Roads, Sandton
	Estoril Books, Hillbrow
	Lohmiller, Shop 25, Centrepoint, Hill Street Mall, Randburg
Camping equipment	Carlton Sports, Carlton Shopping Centre, 151 Commissioner Street
	Cape Union Mart and Caves, East Gate Shopping Centre, 43 Bradford Road, Bedfordview
	Trappers Trading, Rosebank Mall, 50 Bath Avenue, Rosebank
Souvenir shops	Art Afrikana, Bushman Shop, Ivy's Curios, Springbok Curios and Tiger's Eye, Carlton Shopping Centre, 151 Commissioner Street
	Tiger's Eye, East Gate Shopping Centre, 43 Bradford Road, Bedfordview
	Helen De Leeuw and Iteking, Hyde Park Shopping Centre, Jan Smuts Avenue, Sandton
	Bushwillow, Rosebank Mall, 50 Bath Avenue, Rosebank
	Indaba Curios, Pula Pula and Tiger's Eye, Sandton City Shopping Centre, Rivonia Road, Sandton
Shopping centres	Market Theatre flea market, Bree and Wolhard Streets (jewellery, clothing)
	Carlton Centre, 249 Commissioner Street (jewellery and accessories, literature, art, clothing, souvenirs, sports equipment, carpets)
	Sandton City Shopping Centre, Rivonia Road, Sandton (jewellery and accessories, literature, art, clothing, souvenirs, sports equipment, carpets)
	Diagonal Street (various muti shops selling traditional medicines)
	Gold Reef City, Northern Parkway (jewellery and accessories, art, clothing, souvenirs)
	Eastgate, 43 Bradford Road, Bedfordview (jewellery and accessories, literature, art, clothing, souvenirs, sports equipment, carpets)
	Oriental Plaza, near Bree and Main Streets, Fordsburg (spices, traditional medicines, Indian fabrics and jewellery)

KwaZulu/Natal · Zululand

There are stalls selling fruit and vegetables, basketwork and pottery along the whole length of N 2.

Shakaland and Kwabetitunga	14km/8½ miles from Eshowe on R 68 (the Melmoth–Vryheid road), on the left of the road, is a souvenir shop selling Zulu beadwork.
	Stewart's Farm
	3km/2 miles from Shakaland, on the right of R 68, is a souvenir shop selling Zulu shields, spears, drums and skins.

Garden Route

Knysna	Several shops selling yellowwood and stinkwood carving and furniture
Oudtshoorn	Ostrich products, eggs, feather-dusters, ash trays, leather accessories
Stellenbosch	Oom Samie se Winkel, Dorpstraat: a typical general store and junk shop selling wine, books, glass, cool boxes, fruit, vegetables, bakeries, etc.

Swaziland

African Market (fruit, vegetables, basketwork)   Mbabane

Ezulwini
Matenga Crafts, outside the town on the road to Manzini (weaving, pottery;
candle factory, which visitors can see round)

Along the banks of the river are numerous traditional markets.   Nkomati River

Sport

See Canoeing; Diving; Fishing; Flying; Golf; Riding; Surfing; Walking

Surfing

South Africa has some of the best and least crowded surfing beaches in the
world. Surfing conditions along its 3000km/1865 miles of coast are fantastic. There is something for every taste: gentle swells for beginners (Algoa
Bay and Silvic Bay, Port Elizabeth), breakers up to 3m/10ft high for experts
who like to practise jumping (St Francis Bay, Jeffrey's Bay, round the
mouth of the Swartkop River, Nordhoek, near Cape Town on the west
coast). Surfers who go in for speed will enjoy the glass-smooth waters of
Langebaan Bay, 100km/60 miles north of Cape Town on the west coast.
    Water temperatures on the South African coast differ considerably. The
Atlantic, round Cape Town, has temperatures up to 18°C/64°F, while on the

A surfer at Bloubergstrand, near Cape Town

Indian Ocean, round Durban (a popular surfing centre), the water reaches a
pleasant 24°C/75°F.

The best wind conditions, resulting from an area of high pressure, are
between October and April, with winds around 6 on the Beaufort scale.
Between April and August there is usually a depression over South Africa,
with less good winds but waves over 2m/6ft high.

Surfing is not yet widely popular in South Africa, and as a result it is not
always possible to hire surfboards. The best plan is to enquire about the
cost of transport by air and take your own equipment. (Car rental firms may
not be happy about their cars being used to transport surfboards, and it
may then be necessary to buy a roof-rack.)

Taxis

Taxi fares vary from town to town. There is usually a basic charge of 3 rands
plus 3 rands per kilometre and waiting time at 10 rands per hour. Taxis must
be picked up from taxi ranks or ordered by phone: they cannot be hailed in
the street. For longer journeys it is advisable to agree on the fare before
setting out.

Tennis

Tennis is a very popular sport in South Africa. There are tennis courts
throughout the country, and many hotels have their own courts (see
Hotels).

Information   South African Tennis Union, PO Box 2211, Johannesburg 2000, tel. 011/
4 02 35 80

Theatre, Concerts, Opera

There is no lack of cultural life in South Africa. For western tastes there are
opera, ballet and classical music (fully up to international standards), and
for those interested in African culture there are dancing, music and drama.
The following are the leading South African theatres.

Bloemfontein   Sand du Plessis Theatre, Markgraaf and St Andrew Streets, PO Box 1292,
Bloemfontein, tel. 051/47 77 71

Cape Town   Baxter Concert Hall, Main Road, Rondebosch 7700, tel. 021/6 85 78 80
Dock Road Theatre, Waterfront, Cape Town 8001, tel. 021/4 19 77 22
Nico Theatre, Foreshore, tel. 021/21 54 70
Theatre on the Bay, Link Street, tel. 021/4 38 33 01

Durban   Durban Playhouse Theatre Complex, 231 Smith Street, Durban 4001, tel.
031/3 04 36 31
Elizabeth Sneddon Theatre, University of Natal, King George V Avenue, tel.
031/2 60 31 33

Johannesburg   Alexander Theatre, 36 Stiemens Street, Braamfontein 2001, tel. 011/
7 20 70 94
Market Theatre, corner of Bree Street and Wolhuter Street, Newtown 2001,
tel. 011/83 21 46 41
New Black Sun, corner of Rockey and Raymond Streets, Yeoville 2198, tel.
011/6 48 97 09
Windybrow, 161 Nugget Street, Hillbrow 2001, tel. 011/7 20 70 09
Wits Theatre, Jorissen Street, Braamfontein 2001, tel. 011/7 16 51 40

Musion Theatre and Aula Theatre, both in University of Pretoria, Pretoria 0002, tel. 012/4 20 23 15
Piet van der Walt Theatre, Pretoria Showgrounds, tel. 012/21 65 01
State Theatre, corner of Church Street and Prinsloo Street, tel. 012/3 22 16 65

Pretoria

The simplest and most time-saving way of buying tickets for the theatre, opera, cinema or concerts is through the Computicket central booking system, which has offices in shopping centres in all large South African towns.

Buying tickets

Cape Town: tel. 021/21 47 15
Durban: tel. 031/3 04 27 53
Johannesburg: tel. 011/3 31 99 91

Information on ticket offices

Time

South Africa is two hours ahead of Greenwich Mean Time and seven hours ahead of Eastern Standard Time in the United States. There is no daylight saving (Summer Time).

Tipping

It is usual to give a tip of 10% of the bill, even in restaurants which include a 10% service charge.
   Taxi-drivers expect a tip of 10% of the fare. A porter gets 1 rand per item of luggage, a chambermaid 1 rand per day.

Walking

South Africa is a marvellous country for walkers, with a variety of scenery offering endless choice – mountains, plateaux, forests, bush country, grassland steppe, coastal areas, etc. There are hiking trails of varying length, from a few hours to several days, and in all grades of difficulty from easy to extreme, with or without guides – past waterfalls and crystal-clear streams and lakes, through game reserves with the prospect of seeing the game at close quarters, up 3000m/10,000ft mountains, along the coast on sun-bleached sand, spending the night in tents or caves or rebuilt gold-diggers' cottages.

Overnight accommodation on the longer walks must be booked well in advance (on some of the walks there is a year's waiting list).

Clive Walker Trails and Safaris, PO Box 645, Bedfordview 2008, tel. 011/4 53 76 45
Drifters Adventure Tours, PO Box 48434, Roosevelt Park 2129, tel. 011/8 88 11 60
National Parks Board, PO Box 787, Pretoria 0001, tel. 012/3 43 97 70
KwaZulu/Natal Parks Board, PO Box 662, Pietermaritzburg 3200, tel. 0331/47 19 81
Wilderness Leadership School, PO Box 53058, Yellowwood Park 4011, tel. 031/42 86 42
Wilderness Safaris, PO Box 651171, Benmore 2010, tel. 011/8 84 14 58

Information

Weights and Measures

South Africa is on the metric system, with kilometres instead of miles, metres instead of feet and yards, kilograms instead of pounds, and so on.

When to Go

You can have a holiday in South Africa at any time of year, but the main holiday season is from October to March, the South African summer. The high point of the season is December. Most South Africans take their summer holidays between Christmas and the middle of January, when many holiday areas are overcrowded. During this period holiday accommodation must be booked well in advance.

The hottest months in the year are January and February, the coldest is July. March, April, May and September are also good months to travel in. In winter (June to August) it is dry, and these are the best months to visit game parks, since the grass is not so high and the animals can be seen better. At this time of year there is a great deal of rain in Cape Town, but is dry in the interior of the country, where the rain falls in the summer (October to March), usually in the form of thunder showers in the evening.

See also Facts and Figures, Climate

Wine

South Africa claims to have some of the most beautiful wine-growing country in the world. Natural conditions on the Cape and the hills immediately inland are ideal for vines. Thanks to the prevailing west winds the climate in this region is cooler and moister than farther north and east beyond the hills, where irrigation is necessary and the main products are fortified wines and spirits. The soil on the Cape is so fertile that only a tenth as much fertiliser is required as in the old wine-growing regions in Europe. There is a growing period of eight months, there is never any frost or hail, there is no rain in autumn and there is little trouble with the diseases that affect other vineyards. Cool nights after hot days are the rule, reducing night-time respiration for the vine leaves. The vines are unable to consume the sugars accumulated during the day and thus store more of them.

From the earliest days of wine-growing in South Africa there was a lack of demand for fine table wines. The most celebrated South African wine was the legendary dessert Muscat of Constantia, which was preferred by European courts in the early 19th century to Yquem, Tokay and Madeira. Britain, the most important export market, was always more interested in the sherry than in the red wines of the Cape, while the South Africans themselves were the world's thirstiest brandy drinkers. It was only gradually that changing conditions led to a marked improvement in the quality of the wine, and since the mid 1970s South Africa has been recognised as one of the world's leading wine-producing nations.

Wines of origin

In 1973 a new system of quality control, comparable to the French system of *appellations contrôlées*, was introduced, providing for the classification of wines as "wines of origin". Under this system there are 14 recognised areas of origin, and strict requirements are laid down for indicating a wine's area of origin, vineyard, grape type, year and quality, certified by a government seal on the bottle. Some 40 wineries are entitled to use the term "estate"; and the word "superior" on the wine label guarantees that the wine is made exclusively from a particular type of grape. These regulations fostered the development of new, small wineries using oak casks for the maturing of their wine, whose success in the 1980s encouraged others to

Wine on the Cape

During Napoleon's exile on St Helena the British governor of the island frequently complained of the high cost of meeting his prisoner's wishes, for Napoleon was inordinately fond of the Muscat wine of the Cape with which he solaced his years of exile. He was by no means the only monarch of the 18th and 19th centuries who was fond of South African wines. Frederick the Great of Prussia rated the wines of the Cape above all others; even the austere Bismarck liked them; and the 18th century German poet Klopstock wrote an ode in praise of them.

The surprising thing is that it is only in quite recent years that the South Africans themselves have taken a liking to their own wines – and this in spite of the fact that wine has been made on the Cape for over 300 years. In 1652, acting on behalf of the Dutch East India Company, Jan van Riebeeck established the first permanent white settlement on the Cape and founded Cape Town, and soon afterwards sent for vine cuttings from Europe, which arrived in 1654. The Company had packed the cuttings, which came from the Rhine, in damp sailcloth; but the sailcloth must have been too wet, for the cuttings had already taken root. A further consignment of vines from German, French, Spanish and Bohemian vineyards which arrived in the following year had better luck, and in 1659 the first South African wine was produced – 15 litres (26 pints), made from French muscatel grapes. On February 2nd 1659 van Riebeeck wrote in his diary: "Today for the first time, the Lord be praised, wine was made from Cape grapes." Probably the wine was fairly sour, for none of the first settlers had any experience of wine-making.

Professional wine-making on the Cape began only after Simon van der Stel, the new commandant of the settlement and a future governor of the East India Company, founded the second oldest Dutch settlement in South Africa, named Stellenbosch after him, in a sunny and fertile valley to the east of Cape Town (1679). He planted 10,000 vines on his property of Groot Constantia, under Table Mountain – the oldest wine estate in South Africa.

The Stellenbosch area still has more wine estates and wine-producers than any other part of the country. A great boost was given to wine production in South Africa by the arrival of Huguenot refugees from France, who settled round Franschhoek ("French Corner"), to the east of Paarl and Stellenbosch, between 1688 and 1690 and developed what is still an important wine-growing region. At the end of the 19th century South Africa's vineyards were ravaged by phylloxera, but by importing phylloxera-resistant vines from America South African wine-growers managed to reach their previous production level by 1918. That year also saw the foundation of the wine-producers' cooperative organisation, the Kooperatieve Wijnbouwers Vereeniging van Zuid-Afrika (KWV), with headquarters in Paarl, which still controls the prices, quantities and quality of South African wines; it now has some 6000 members.

buy oak casks in France. More care is now given to the picking of the grapes
and to the care of wine in the cellar. Around 1975 the wine estates had
begun to supplement their established Cabernet Sauvignon vines with
plantations of the more demanding Chardonnay, Sauvignon Blanc and
Pinot Noir grapes. In 1992 the much criticised power of the KWV organisation to control the country's wine production by the allotment of quo-
tas was abandoned and wine-producers were left free to develop their
vineyards as they saw fit.

Statistics

South Africa is now the tenth largest wine-producer in the world, contributing 2.5% of total world production from its 100,000 hectares/250,000
acres of vineyards. Annual output is more than 9 million hectolitres (198
million gallons), 70% of which is exported. There are something like 3000
different South African wines, more than 90% of them white. Domestic
consumption is an annual 9.72 litres (2.14 gallons) per head, compared
with 8.4 litres (1.85 gallons) per head in the United States. In addition to still
wines (including fine wines of Trockenbeerenauslese standard) there are
sparkling wines (with traditional fermentation in bottle), port-style fortified
wines and spirits (brandy). There are 70 wine cooperatives, which account
for 75% of total production. The remaining 25% comes from 5000 individual wine-makers and wineries, from wine-producers who are also wine
merchants and from KWV.

**Types of grape
Red wine**

The best and most richly flavoured of South African red wines have been
made since 1982 from the Cabernet Sauvignon grape (originally from
Bordeaux), which at present accounts for 2.6% of grapes in cultivation.

A specifically South African grape is the Pinotage (2%), created in 1925
by crossing Pinot Noir (from Burgundy) with Cinsaut (originally from the
south of France; formerly known in South Africa as Hermitage). It com-
bines the qualities of both parents, the fruitiness of the Pinot grape and the
sweetness of the Hermitage.

In the Clos Cabrière cellars, Franschhoek

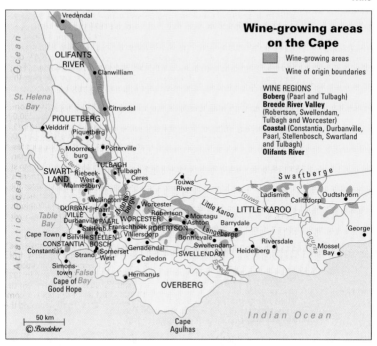

Wine-growing areas on the Cape

Wine-growing areas

— Wine of origin boundaries

WINE REGIONS
Boberg (Paarl and Tulbagh)
Breede River Valley
(Robertson, Swellendam,
Tulbagh and Worcester)
Coastal (Constantia, Durbanville,
Paarl, Stellenbosch, Swartland
and Tulbagh)
Olifants River

Other types of grape used in the production of red wine are Cabernet Franc (0.15%), Pinot Noir (0.37%), Cinsaut (7.0%; this grape produces fresh table wines), Shiraz (0.9%), Pontac (very little) and Merlot Noir (0.93%).

White wine production is dominated by Chenin Blanc (31.9%), a grape which originally came from the Loire and is usually known in South Africa as Steen. With its naturally high acidity it produces fresh and lively wines even after a very hot summer. Its great advantage, however, is its versatility: it is used in the making of sweet and dry table wines, sparkling wine and sherry.

White wine

The Sémillon or Green Grape (1.5%) and the Cape Riesling (producing a fruity wine which has no resemblance to European riesling; 3.8%) have long been grown, with varying success, as have Palomino (9.7%; for sherry) and Colombard (6.2%; producing a full-bodied and well balanced wine). Other traditional white varieties produce wine of lower standard.

The Rhein-Riesling grape is a recent introduction (0.14%). Chardonnay (1.5%) and Sauvignon Blanc (3.6%) were banned for many years by government regulation (reflecting the protectionist and conservative attitudes of KWV) and are still little grown. In the inland regions the Muscat of Alexandria grape (known in South Africa as Hanepoot; 5.7%) is grown for the making of sweet wines.

The main wine-growing region is round Stellenbosch and Paarl. The principal centre of production is Stellenbosch, with more wine estates and wine-producers than in other parts of the country (23 wine estates, 15 private wineries and 5 small cooperatives). It is also the headquarters of the largest wine firm in South Africa, the Stellenbosch Farmers' Winery. Paarl

Wine estates (wineries)

473

is the main centre of the sherry and dessert wine industries and the head-quarters of KWV.

Wine-growing
areas and
wine routes

There are 13 "wine routes" through the wine-growing areas, established from 1971 onwards on the model of similar routes in France and Germany. The chief places on the routes are Constantia (with a famous estate, now state-owned, specialising in red wines), Stellenbosch, Paarl and Fransch-hoek. Here visitors, after extensive wine tastings, can stock up with South African wines.

Information on wine routes can be obtained from local tourist offices.

Farther north, on the coast, are the wine-growing areas of Malmesbury and Piquetberg. With no hills to halt the rain clouds, this is not an ideal area for wine-growing; nevertheless it produces port-like red wines and dry white wines. Farther north, on the Olifants River, it is even drier, and without irrigation the growing of vines would not be possible. The produc-tion of table wine in this area is relatively new; the traditional products are spirits and grape juice.

Conditions are more favourable in the Tulbagh hills, and some of South Africa's best white wines are produced here, as well as light wines made from the Steen and Riesling grapes and strong wines for sherry. Tulbagh, like Paarl, is entitled to use the *appellation contrôlée* of Boberg for its port- and sherry-style wines.

Worcester, Robertson, Swellendam and the Little Karoo specialise in the production of dessert wines and spirits, though table wines are also in-creasingly being produced.

Further
information

For further information on South African wines the following books are recommended:

Hugh Johnson's "Wine Companion", London, 1987,
Dave Hughes, Phyllis Hands and John Kench, "South African Wines", Struik Publishers, Cape Town, 1992.

Youth Hostels

South Africa has 37 affiliated HI youth hostels, but a similar purpose is served by its numerous YMCAs and YWCAs.

Some addresses:

Cape Town

Abe Bailey Youth Hostel, 2 Maynard Road, Muizenberg 7951, tel. 021/
7 88 23 01
YMCA, 60 Queen Victoria Street, Gardens 8001, tel. 021/24 12 47
YWCA, 20 Bellevue Street, Gardens 8001, tel. 021/23 37 11

Durban

Durban Beach Youth Hostel, 19 Smith Street, tel. 031/32 49 45

East London

East London Backpackers', 128 Moore Street, East London 5021, tel. 0431/
2 34 23

Johannesburg

Fairview Youth Hostel, 4 College Street, Johannesburg, PO Box 33774, Jeepstown 2043, tel. 011/6 18 20 48
YMCA, 104 Rissik Street, Braamfontein, PO Box 23222, Joubert Park 2044, tel. 011/4 03 34 26
YWCA, 311 Dunwell Road, Braamfontein 2001, tel. 011/4 03 38 30

Kimberley

Kimberley Youth Hostel, Bloemfontein Road, Kimberley 8300, tel. 0531/
2 85 77

Index

Index

Index

Principal Sights at a Glance

Map showing principal sights in Practical Information, page 437

Note: The places listed above are merely a selection of the principal sights – places of interest in themselves or for attractions in the surrounding area. There are of course innumerable other sights in South Africa, to which attention is drawn by one or two stars.

Imprint

206 illustrations, 12 general maps, 10 town plans, 8 drawings, 3 special plans, 1 cross-section, 1 large map of South Africa

Original German text: Birgit Borowski and Anja Schliebitz (Nature, Culture, History in part; Sights from A to Z; Practical Information in part), with contributions from Achim Bourmer (Famous People, Specials, Practical Information in part), Carmen Galenschovski (Sights from A to Z in part), Prof. Wolfgang Hassenpflug (Climate), Robert von Lucius (Art and Culture in part, Special "Miracle on the Cape"), Dr Reinhard Paesler (Facts and Figures in part)

Editorial work: Baedeker-Redaktion (Anja Schliebitz, Birgit Borowski)

Cartography: Christoph Gallus, Hohberg; Istituto Geografico De Agostini, Novara

Source of illustrations: Archiv für Kunst und Geschichte, Berlin (3); Associated Press (1); Bildagentur Schuster (6); Bildarchiv Steffens (1); Bohnacker (15); Borowski/Schliebitz (89); dpa (4); Fotoagentur Helga Lade (7); Foto-agentur Schapowalow (2); HB Verlags- und Vertriebs-Gesellschaft mbH (2); IFA-Bilderteam (8); Istituto Geografico De Agostini (16); Kierig (2); von Lucius (3); Pansegrau (35); Satour (5); Ullstein Bilderdienst (5); ZEFA (1)

General direction: Dr Peter Baumgarten, Baedeker Stuttgart

English translation: James Hogarth

1st English edition 1996

© Baedeker Stuttgart
Original German edition 1996

© 1996 Jarrold and Sons Limited
English language edition worldwide

© 1996 The Automobile Association
United Kingdom and Ireland

Published in the United States by:
Macmillan Travel
A Simon & Schuster Macmillan Company
1633 Broadway
New York, NY 10019–6785

Macmillan is a registered trademark of Macmillan, Inc.

Distributed in the United Kingdom by the Publishing Division of the Automobile Association, Fanum House, Basingstoke, Hampshire RG21 2EA

A CIP catalogue record of this book is available from the British Library

Licensed user:
Mairs Geographischer Verlag GmbH & Co.,
Ostfildern-Kemnat bei Stuttgart

Printed in Italy by G. Canale & C.S.p.A – Borgaro T.se –Turin

ISBN 0–02–861355–4 USA and Canada
    0 7495 1420 5 UK